## Praise for
### *No Nonsense: Time Management*

"Karen Leland and Keith Bailey have written a practical book that can transform the way you and your team think about time management. The shift from productivity as a function of time to productivity based on completion and energy management can be a game changer for the overwhelmed executive."

—ASHA SAXENA, CEO, Coaching International
and adjunct professor, Columbia University

"The principles in *No Nonsense: Time Management* turned my world upside down and helped me realize what time management really is versus what it really isn't! So helpful!"

—BEN DECKER, CEO, Decker Communications

"Time is one of our most valuable assets and successful leaders use theirs wisely and with clarity. This book provides practical insights for leaders and their staffs to improve their effectiveness and put proven best practices to work immediately."

—VIVEK BAPAT, senior vice president, marketing, SAP

# NO NONSENSE

## TIME
# Management

# NO NONSENSE

## TIME

## Management

50 Tips to Hack Your Time and
Get Everything Done

**Karen Tiber Leland & Keith Bailey**

CAREER
PRESS

This edition first published in 2020 by Career Press, an imprint of
Red Wheel/Weiser, LLC
With offices at:
65 Parker Street, Suite 7
Newburyport, MA 01950
*www.careerpress.com*
*www.redwheelweiser.com*

ISBN: 978-1-63265-177-8
Library of Congress Cataloging-in-Publication Data available upon request.

Cover design by Kathryn Sky-Peck
Interior by Steve Amarillo / Urban Design LLC
Typeset in Adobe Dapifer and Minion Pro

Printed in the United States of America
IBI
10  9  8  7  6  5  4  3  2  1

*For Deborah, until the end of time.*

—Keith Bailey

*To my mother and father, Norman and Barbara Tiber, who gave me the gift of critical thinking combined with heart.*

—Karen Tiber Leland

*This book is dedicated to the memory of John Garner, our mentor and friend, who told us many years ago that you can't manage time, you can only manage your energy.*

# Contents

# Introduction

In the late 1980s, the phrase "work-life balance" began to appear around office water coolers and cubicles everywhere. Today, it's a staple of business books, consulting gurus, and television talk shows. Work-life balance describes the relationship between career achievement (getting ahead, being productive, professional accomplishment) and personal fulfillment (family, friends, hobbies, contribution). But despite all the hype, the last two decades have seen an increase in the average work week from 43.6 hours to 47.1 hours. In addition, a 2019 study from Rescue Time on work-life balance reported that:

- 21% of working hours are spent on entertainment, news, and social media.

- 28% of workers start their day before 8:30 AM (and 5% start before 7:00 AM).

- 40% of people use their computers after 10:00 PM.

- 26% of work is done outside normal working hours.

For many people, the problem is a catch-22: If you spend more time on your personal life, your work falls behind. But if you spend too much time at the office, your family life and sense of well-being can suffer. Although we don't believe there is a single solution, we do believe that learning to manage time and energy makes a substantial difference in achieving a healthy work-life balance.

The smart solutions, powerful habits, and proven time hacks given in this book come from time-management workshops we have led for corporations over the past thirty years, tens of thousands of employee-attitude surveys we have conducted, a review of the most recent research by some of the leading behavioral scientists in the field, and up-close observations of our clients as they learn to be more productive while balancing their careers and personal lives.

But before jumping in, we think it's essential to acknowledge the great debt we owe to the giants of time management who have come before us. We can all learn how to make the most of our day from these masters.

# Learn from the Masters

Throughout history, great philosophers, business masterminds, and even presidents have pondered the question: How can I best use my time? Their answers underlie many of the ways we think about time today. Here are just a few.

## *The Psychologist*

In 1943, Abraham Maslow wrote his famous paper *A Theory of Human Motivation*. Maslow's idea was that people are most able to cope with the larger issues of their lives (i.e., achievement, creativity, problem-solving) when their fundamental needs (food, warmth, shelter, safety) are taken care of. This hierarchical view of human needs inspired the POSEC method.

- *P*rioritize your time according to the goals that you want to accomplish in life. If you start by knowing where you want to go, it's easier to get there.

- *O*rganize yourself by creating structures that allow you to meet your basic need to feel stable and secure in both your finances and your family. This may mean setting up a regular Friday-night dinner with your family or having a certain percentage of your paycheck automatically deposited to a savings account.

- *S*treamline the things that you have to do, but don't necessarily like to do (like chores), by simplifying them or making them more efficient. For example, do all your routine errands (bank deposit, post office, grocery store) in one outing, rather than in separate trips.

- *E*conomize by reducing the amount of time and energy you invest in things that are not urgent and that you view as a low priority. For example, you may want to clean out your desk, but don't need to spend a whole day doing it.

- *C*ontribute by giving your time and energy back to the community through a charity or a good cause. Many people find that, when they have prioritized, organized, streamlined, and economized, they have a natural inclination to contribute to a larger purpose.

## The Business Guru

Stephen Covey, in his best-selling book *First Things First* (Free Press), tells a story that illustrates the importance of making your most important tasks your highest priority. In the book, Covey describes a time-management teacher filling a mason jar with large rocks and asking his students if the jar is full. When they respond "yes," he proved them wrong by adding gravel to fill in the spaces between the rocks. Asked if the jar is now full, the students were not so sure. He then added sand and water to fill in the remaining spaces. When the teacher asked what the point of the demonstration was, the students replied that, if you look hard enough, you can always fit more into your life. No, the teacher explained. The point is that, if you don't put the big rocks in first, they will never fit. Do you tend to make time in your day for the gravel, sand, and water, but never find time for the big rocks?

## The President

Dwight D. Eisenhower was quoted as saying: "What is important is seldom urgent and what is urgent is seldom important." This philosophy is the basis for the Eisenhower method of prioritizing, which sorts tasks by the following criteria:

- Tasks that are unimportant and not urgent should be done later, deleted, or delegated.

- Tasks that are important and urgent should be done now and not delegated.

- Tasks that are unimportant and urgent should be done now and, whenever possible, delegated.

- Tasks that are important and not urgent should be given a high priority, scheduled, and not delegated.

## The Consultant

In 2001, David Allen wrote his best-selling book *Getting Things Done* and instantly became the first celebrity productivity consultant. His method was based on the idea that productivity is achieved by moving planned tasks and projects out of the mind and onto an external source (paper, tablet, etc.), then sorting them into actionable work items. There are five pillars to Allen's method:

- Capture everything.
- Clarify what you have to do.
- Organize by category and priority.
- Reflect on your to-do list.
- Engage and get to work.

Allen was almost single-handedly responsible for a whole generation of workers learning to prioritize.

## The Economist

Vilfredo Pareto, an Italian economist in the early 20th century, is credited with the discovery of the 80/20 principle. Way back in 1897 (before the Internet), Pareto observed that 80 percent of the wealth was owned by 20 percent of the population. Much has changed since then, but Pareto's theory of disproportion is still widely applied to almost every aspect of business, from quality control to time management. Here are some of the ways that the 80/20 rule may be impacting you—and what you can do about it:

- 80% of your goals are achieved by working on 20% of your tasks. Identify which of your to-do's will move you the farthest toward accomplishing your important goals and make those a top priority.

- 20% of your efforts produce 80% of your results. Learn to recognize which of your labors make the most effective use of your time.

- 80% of the value you receive from business reading comes from 20% of the material. Determine which business publications—magazines, blogs, books—consistently produce the most value and drop the rest.

- 20% of your co-workers give you 80% of the support you need. Identify who has your back at work, and return the favor in kind. Make a priority of maintaining your relationship with these people and acknowledge them for the ways in which they make your work life easier.

- 80% of the value your client receives relates to 20% of what your company does. Make the effort to determine the most important measures by which your customer judges you and invest your time in making those top-notch.

- 20% of your time-management habits cause 80% of your productivity problems. If you really look, most of your time issues can be boiled down to one or two bad habits, like lack of prioritization, multitasking, or procrastination. Identify your worst habits and work on improving them.

## *The Disruptor*

According to his website, *New York Times* best-selling author Tim Ferriss says he "teaches you how to escape the 9 to 5, live anywhere, and join the new rich." That was the premise and promise of Ferriss's book *The Four-Hour Work Week.* A smash hit with millennials looking to avoid the corporate drudgery of their parent's generation, this book has given voice to the work-from-anywhere during-the-hours-you-choose crowd.

Now that you know some of the legacy of the great names in the world of time management, there is one thing left to do before jumping in to improve your productivity skills—and that's to assess where you are now.

# PART 1

# Assess Your Current Relationship with Time

Getting a beat on where you stand today in terms of time-management competency can help you determine where you need to go and how to get there. It can also help you assess how far you've come once you take the journey to shore up your skills. Here are four important techniques you can use to take the pulse of your time-management skills.

# Determine Your Current Level of Time Literacy

To get an idea of your current level of time literacy, answer the questions below using the following guide:

1 = Almost never

2 = Once in a while

3 = Frequently

4 = All the time

1. I create a daily to-do list and then prioritize it.                  _____

2. Whenever possible, I do my most important tasks early in the day.     _____

3. The state of my desktop inspires me to get work done.                 _____

4. I have specific, written goals for my business and personal life.     _____

5.  I arrive at meetings on time and prepared. _____

6.  I delegate whatever I can. _____

7.  My inbox is under control, and
    I process the work in it regularly. _____

8.  I close my office door or take other
    measures to prevent interruptions
    when I need to focus. _____

9.  I know when and how to say "no"
    to other people's requests. _____

10. I meet my project deadlines. _____

11. I can find any information I need
    within five minutes. _____

12. I spend less than 30% of my day
    putting out fires. _____

13. I keep my email inbox organized
    and up to date. _____

14. My office files are neat, organized,
    and up to date. _____

15. I tackle difficult or unpleasant tasks
    without delay. _____

Total score: _____

- Score of 50–60: Congratulations! You are a time-management superstar. You obviously understand the core principles of time management and have been able to translate them into everyday actions. To move to the next level, choose an area that you would like to enhance, and use the information in this book or take a class to help you further develop that skill.

- Score of 35–49: You have a good grasp on your time but are losing energy and focus because of a few bad time habits. Review the questions and focus your attention on the areas where you scored a 2 or lower. Consider reaching out to someone you work with (and trust) to help you identify when you are caught in non-productive time behaviors. Find the specific techniques in this book that address the areas you need to improve.

- Score of 15–34: Your time literacy could use some education. You may be experiencing procrastination or burnout due to poor time management or just be overwhelmed by your task load. Pick one item from the list and, using the principles, practices, and exercises in this book, work on it until your score in that area has increased by a point.

## Top Eleven Cyber Time Crimes

- Not closing the loop
- Not following up
- Not returning communications
- Pretending time doesn't matter
- Not respecting schedules

- Not honoring deadlines

- Treating other people as commodities

- Not respecting others' feelings

- Not saying "thank you"

- Not giving credit where credit is due

- Not recognizing the difference between an emergency task and an important one

# Time-Management Crimes in an Online World

With all its upsides and promises of improved communication and connection, the Internet has come with some significant downsides as well. In fact, it has created an environment in which what we call the time-management crimes of the online world thrive. If you are really serious about improving your productivity, while at the same time being a better human being, avoid these like the plague.

## *Don't Be Careless and Thoughtless about Closing the Loop*

You know the drill. You spend several hours (if not days) crafting a top-notch proposal in response to a prospect's request. The client's promise? To get back to you by a given date with a "yes" or "no." The due date comes and goes, with no response. You email—no reply. You call—nada. Two weeks go by, you email again—still no response. At this point, you couldn't care less about getting the business, you just want some closure. Other examples of how people can be careless and thoughtless about not closing the loop include:

- Saying they will do something by a certain date, failing to do it, and not communicating that they won't make the timeline

- Promising to follow up on something and then not doing it

- Beginning an important conversation, being interrupted (or stopping in the middle), and then not getting back to it

- Failing to return phone calls or emails that they have an obligation to answer

Does any of this sound familiar? If you're like most business people today, you have been on both sides of this coin—both perpetrating and being at the mercy of these incompletions. We know you're busy, we know you're overwhelmed, and we know that sometimes you just don't want to have a confrontation or say "no." But for the sake of time saved and feelings spared, make a commitment to be a person who closes the loop and gets back to people when you say you will.

## *Don't Pretend That Time Doesn't Matter*

You know the meeting starts at 1:00 PM, but you don't arrive until 1:30 and mumble an unconvincing "sorry" as you slide into your seat. Around the office, you have garnered a reputation for being unreliable. We often underestimate the impact that our failure to take time seriously has on other people, as well as on our own reputations. Other examples of pretending that time does not matter include:

- Continually breaking your promise about when you will do something

- Constantly being late for meetings and appointments and making others wait for you

- Forgetting meetings and appointments

- Regularly rescheduling meeting and appointments

- Not returning phone calls, emails, and texts in a timely manner

- Not doing what you say you will do, by the time you said you would do it

- Failing to acknowledge and apologize for missing a deadline

- Not communicating that you will be late on a promised deadline or for an appointment

If you've ever been on the receiving end of this type of behavior (and who hasn't?), you know how horrible it feels and how much resentment and mistrust it breeds toward the other person. The bottom line is that better relationships lead to a more efficient and satisfying use of time. Decide to treat other people's time with the respect it deserves. Ironically, it will free up your own time.

## *Don't Treat Other People Like Commodities*

In our swipe-right, swipe-left world, it has become easy to think of other people as disposable—as cogs in the wheel of our goals and objectives. If a person doesn't come up with the answer you need instantly, you move on rather than wasting your time. The problem with this way of thinking is that, while it seems efficient, just below the surface, a simmering cauldron of hurt feelings, misunderstandings, and resentments is brewing, all of which take up time and energy. Some of the most common ways in which we treat other people like commodities in business today include:

- Failing to acknowledge their feelings about a specific project, goal, or issue

- Not saying "thank you" or showing appreciation when they do something—even if it's their job

- Refusing or forgetting to give credit for their ideas or contributions to a project, goal, or situation, regardless of size

- Moving on to someone else when we hit the first speed bump in the road of a project, goal, or situation

- Ghosting people when we decide it's too uncomfortable to have a difficult conversation with them

All the research shows that the best working relationships come from having the tenacity to work through the hard things. Make a decision to invest in your working relationships with others for the long-term gains, not the short-term impact.

# #2.

# Understand Your
# Relationship with Time

Philosophers and scientists have been trying to understand time since—well, since time began. Just defining it is tricky enough. Some definitions are as simple as "a series of passing moments"; others are more complex, like the one found on *spacetodayonline*, which describes time as

*A human perception defined as the length of an interval separating two points on a non-spatial continuum in which events occur in apparently irreversible succession from the past through the present to the future.*

The problem with time doesn't end at our attempt to define it, however. All the things you tell yourself and believe about time further encumber your relationship with it. For example, have you ever said or thought that there just wasn't enough time in the day?

## *Exercise*

In the space below, write down the definitions, thoughts, and ideas you have about time.

_____

_____

_____

_____

_____

_____

_____

_____

_____

Does what you wrote reflect a "use it or lose it" attitude? Does it conjure up a sense of cosmic mystery or a down-to-earth move-ment of hands around a clock? Does what you wrote reflect a positive or negative relationship with time? Regardless, all of this is what you are trying to manage when you talk about time man-agement. Ask yourself: "Is this possible?" "Am I crazy?" When you try to manage time, you are trying to manage something that nobody fully understands, that no one can define, and about which nobody even agrees.

If you step back and take a rational look at time, however, a minute is always a minute, an hour is always an hour, and a day is always a day. Admittedly, if you're organized and focused, time does seem to zip by enjoyably and productively. If you're disorganized and distracted, it tends to creep by slowly, painfully, and often unproductively. But in reality, the actual amount of time remains unchanged.

For example, imagine you have a proposal to prepare for a key client within the next hour. The client's emails and attached files are easily accessible on your desktop, you have turned off your incoming email alarm, and you've let your co-workers know that you are not to be disturbed. All these actions help you to focus and, even though it's an intense hour of work, you get the report done with a sigh of satisfaction.

Now take this same scenario and imagine that you can't easily find the client's emails because they were forwarded from someone else and you can't remember who, you keep getting interrupted by emails, and, at least three times, your co-workers pop their heads into your cube to ask a question or share a doughnut. At the end of the hour, the proposal is only half-finished and you are irritated and frustrated, and now need to stay late.

Same hour, different results. So, although it appears that you can't really manage time, you can manage your experience with it—your energy, your efficiency, and your effectiveness. Have you ever noticed how some people you work with always seem to make the most of their time while others fritter it away? Time is the common denominator here. It's the way in which they manage themselves that is different. Which person would you rather be?

# #3.

# Get Out of Time Denial

Every April 15, millions of Americans tear their hair out trying to meet the midnight deadline for filing tax returns. The reasons for this last-minute rush? Procrastination and denial—specifically, denial about how long it will really take to locate and sort receipts, pull together paperwork, and crunch the numbers so that the forms can finally be filled out and sent on their merry way.

How long does it take you to prepare and fill out your tax return? According to government estimates, it takes taxpayers 28.5 hours to complete an average tax return with itemized deductions and income reported from interest, dividends, and capital gains.

The tendency to underestimate the amount of time something will take is not limited to serious matters like taxes, however. It can also be seen in something as mundane as showing up on time for appointments.

The underlying culprit in all these scenarios is time denial—an inaccurate accounting of the amount of time it will *really* take to get from point A to point B. To get out of time denial and make a more accurate assessment of the time needed to get somewhere or do something, try the following techniques.

## Work Backward

Begin with the end in mind so that you can figure out, in reverse, what it will take to meet your deadline. Work backward to calculate steps that need to be taken and the time they will take; this helps clarify exactly what needs to get done by when.

For example, say your annual business dinner with the big boss is scheduled for 7:30 PM at the hot new restaurant, Café du Posh. Operating in time denial, you plan on leaving the office at 7:00 PM. This allows a cutting-it-close fifteen minutes of driving time and a fifteen-minute window for getting ready. However, working in reverse, a more realistic time plan may be:

## Goal: Dinner Reservation at 7:30

| | |
|---|---|
| Arriving 5 minutes early | 7:25 (5 minutes) |
| Parking | 7:15 (10 minutes) |
| Driving, assuming heavy traffic | 6:55 (20 minutes) |
| Getting from your office to your car | 6:50 (5 minutes) |
| Completing work, loose ends, etc. | 6:40 (10 minutes) |

Without time denial, a realistic departure time becomes 6:40 instead of 7:00. That's a whole twenty minutes that was not accounted for in the first assessment!

## Consider the Worst-Case Scenario

Time denial can soften and blur the realities of what it will take to get from point A to point B. Always add a 10 percent time factor for emergencies, changes, and delays. For example, traffic may be heavier than you imagined, you may have to do an unexpected last-minute task, or parking may prove difficult.

## Don't Underestimate the Little Things

A lot of lateness occurs because insufficient attention was paid to the little things, especially those that connect one activity to the next. For example, as you are getting ready to leave, you must gather together your wallet, phone, purse, and keys, and then add your destination into the GPS. All these things add time that needs to be accounted for.

# #4.
# Keep an Activity Log

"There are not enough hours in the day." "I don't have enough time to get it all done." "I have more on my plate than I can handle." These are just a few of the popular phrases in the litany of time complaints business people proffer on a daily basis.

Despite the very real fact that, in many cases, you do have too much to do with too little time, a recent survey by America Online and *Salary.com* revealed that the average employee admits to wasting more than two hours every work day. Which activities are eating away at American workers' precious productivity? According to the survey, the top time-wasters include:

| | |
|---|---|
| Surfing the web | 44.7% |
| Chatting with co-workers | 23.4% |
| Doing personal business | 6.8% |
| Spacing out | 3.9% |
| Running errands | 3.1% |
| Personal phone calls | 2.3% |
| Applying for other jobs | 1.3% |
| Planning personal events | 1.0% |

"But I hardly do any of the above," you loudly protest. "I never waste time at work!" The truth is that most people (even you overachieving overachievers) have some bad time habits that eat into their efficiency and effectiveness.

One way of discovering how you really spend your time—including where your bad habits may lie—is to keep a detailed daily activity log for an entire week. Here's how it works.

## Step 1: Write Down All Your Activities

Each day, from the moment you get to work to the moment you leave, write down everything you do (business or personal) and how much time you spend on each item. Pretend you are an impartial auditor sent to create a detailed and accurate overview of how you use your time.

For example, if your first fifteen minutes in the office are taken up with chatting about last night's Yankees game over a cup of coffee in the break room, log it. If you then spend the next twenty minutes checking email, log it. And so on. By the end of your day, your log may look like this.

| Start | Finish | Activity | Time Invested | Return | Cost |
|-------|--------|----------|---------------|--------|------|
| 8:30 | 8:45 | Chatted with Fred, got coffee | 00:15 | | |
| 8:45 | 9:05 | Checked email | 00:20 | | |
| 9:05 | 9:35 | Web "research" on vacation packages to Aruba | 00:30 | | |
| 9:35 | 9:45 | Prepared for Operations meeting | 00:10 | | |

| | | | | | |
|---|---|---|---|---|---|
| 9:45 | 9:55 | Checked email | 00:10 | | |
| 9:55 | 11:30 | Weekly Operations meeting | 1:35 | | |
| 11:30 | 12:00 | Informal debrief with Jim from Operations | 00:30 | | |
| 12:00 | 12:45 | Lunch | 00:45 | | |
| 12:45 | 1:05 | Chatted about meeting fallout | 00:20 | | |
| 1:05 | 1:15 | Phone call with Aruba vacation specialist | 00:10 | | |
| 1:15 | 2:10 | Listened and responded to voicemails | 1:05 | | |
| 2:10 | 2:35 | Looked for last quarter's budget numbers!! | 00:15 | | |
| 2:35 | 2:45 | Waited for Budget meeting to begin | 00:10 | | |
| 2:45 | 4:15 | Budget meeting | 1:30 | | |
| 4:15 | 4:30 | Evaluated today's activity log | 00:15 | | |
| | | C totals: | | | |

## Step 2: Assign Each Item a Return Value

At the end of each day, review your log and assign a return value of A, B, or C to each line item. Use the following as a guide.

- A = I received a high return on this item toward an important objective.

- B = I received a medium return on this item toward an important objective.

- C = I received a low return on this item toward an important objective.

## *Step 3: Determine the Cost of C Items*

In order to figure out the cost of each item, start by determining your hourly wage. If you are a consultant, accountant, or attorney, and already get paid by the hour, this is no problem. If, however, you are paid a yearly salary, use the following formula, which assumes a forty-hour work week and a salary of $70,000, to make an educated guess about what your hourly rate is.

$70,000 ÷ 2000 (approximate number of hours in a year)
= $35 an hour

Once you have determined your hourly wage, figure the cost for each C item you have listed by multiplying the actual amount of time invested in that item by your hourly wage. For example, assuming an hourly wage of $35, a fifteen-minute C item has a total cost of about nine dollars. Enter this amount in the cost column. The focus is on C items here because these items usually offer little or no return, and are relatively unproductive.

## *Step 4: Analyze Your Daily Activity Log*

To see how much time during a particular day was spent on low-priority items, add the time invested in your C items and place the total at the bottom of the log. Now do the same for your C-item costs. Based on a wage of $35 per hour, your completed activity log now looks like this:

| Start | Finish | Activity | Time Invested | Return | Cost |
|-------|--------|----------|---------------|--------|------|
| 8:30 | 8:45 | Chatted with Fred, got coffee | 0:15 | C | $10 |
| 8:45 | 9:05 | Checked email | 00:20 | B | |
| 9:05 | 9:35 | Web "research" on vacation packages to Aruba | 00:30 | C | $20 |
| 9:35 | 9:45 | Prepared for Operations meeting | 00:10 | B | |
| 9:45 | 9:55 | Checked email | 00:10 | B | |
| 9:55 | 11:30 | Weekly Operations meeting | 1:35 | A | |
| 11:30 | 12:00 | Informal debrief with Jim from Operations | 00:30 | B | |
| 12:00 | 12:45 | Lunch | 00:45 | B | |
| 12:45 | 1:05 | Chatted about meeting fallout | 00:20 | C | $13 |
| 1:05 | 1:15 | Phone call with Aruba vacation specialist | 00:10 | C | $7 |
| 1:15 | 2:10 | Listened and responded to voicemails | 1:05 | B | |
| 2:10 | 2:35 | Looked for last quarters budget numbers!! | 00:15 | C | $10 |
| 2:35 | 2:45 | Waited for Budget meeting to begin | 00:10 | C | $7 |
| 2:45 | 4:15 | Budget meeting | 1:30 | B | |
| 4:15 | 4:30 | Evaluated today's activity log | 00:15 | B | |
| | | C totals: | 1:55 | | $66 |

This chart shows that almost two hours, and sixty-six dollars, were spent on C items during this day. In other words, two hours of your time went into activities that produced very little return for your efforts.

## *Exercise*

To find out more about your time effectiveness, complete an activity log for each day of the work week. You may be surprised by the amount of time you spend chatting with co-workers, reading mail, dealing with interruptions, and other C-value work. Use a review of this log to become aware of where your time is actually being spent, any bad habits you have fallen into (like surfing the web for airline deals thirty minutes a day), and any adjustments you may want to make in how you currently invest your time.

Make five copies of this blank activity log and, for one week, keep track of how you spend your time.

| Start | Finish | Activity | Time Invested | Return | Cost |
|-------|--------|----------|---------------|--------|------|
|       |        |          |               |        |      |
|       |        |          |               |        |      |
|       |        |          |               |        |      |
|       |        |          |               |        |      |
|       |        |          |               |        |      |
|       |        |          |               |        |      |
|       |        |          |               |        |      |
|       |        |          |               |        |      |
|       |        |          |               |        |      |
|       |        |          |               |        |      |
|       |        |          |               |        |      |
|       |        |          |               |        |      |
|       |        |          |               |        |      |
|       |        |          |               |        |      |
|       |        |          |               |        |      |
|       |        | C totals: |              |        |      |

# PART 2

# Set, Design, and
# Achieve Your Goals

Under the day-to-day pressures of business obligations and family life, it can be easy to develop tunnel vision when setting goals and to focus only on those that are work-related. However, having goals in all areas of life leads to a better work-life balance, a sense of time being richly spent, and a greater sense of accomplishment. Try stepping back and thinking about your goals in terms of your broader life. Consider setting goals in these important areas of your life:

- Financial
- Career and business
- Free and leisure time
- Health and well-being
- Relationships
- Personal growth
- Making a difference

Use the following exercise to stimulate your thinking and open up new areas and opportunities in your life.

## *Exercise*

Write down whatever comes to mind as you think about your personal goals. Be sure to let your imagination wander. It's important not to edit yourself, since you may be surprised at some of the things you come up with. After you're done, you can go back through and cross out the goals that are just pipe dreams!

# GOALS EXERCISE Part 1

**CAREER**       Promotion, new skills, sales targets,
                 entrepreneurial ideas, development plans, etc.

One Month: _____

Six Months: _____

One Year: _____

**FINANCE**       Budgeting, investments, savings, retirement,
                  taxes, charitable donations, etc.

One Month: _____

Six Months: _____

One Year: _____

**PERSONAL**        Self-awareness, sprituality, education, etc.

**DEVELOPMENT**

One Month: _____

Six Months: _____

One Year: _____

**CREATIVITY**       Writing, art, photography, cooking, etc.

One Month: _____

Six Months: _____

One Year: _____

# GOALS EXERCISE Part 2

**HEALTH**    Exercise, weight management, diet, medical support, allergies, etc.

One Month: _____

Six Months: _____

One Year: _____

**HOME**    Buying, selling, remodeling, decorating, landscaping, etc.

One Month: _____

Six Months: _____

One Year: _____

**RELATIONSHIPS** Family, friends, dating, partners, coworkers, children, pets, etc.

One Month: _____

Six Months: _____

One Year: _____

**RECREATION**    Hiking, golfing, running, sports, vacations, sailing, skiing, etc.

One Month: _____

Six Months: _____

One Year: _____

# State Your Goals in the Positive

There are two ways to articulate a goal—as something you are moving toward and as something you are moving away from. Stating a goal in the positive (I want to weigh 125 pounds) is a way of building a bridge to your future. On the other hand, stating a goal in the negative (I want to lose twenty pounds) is more like burning that bridge behind you. Think of one goal you have been talking about in the negative and turn it around to a positive statement of accomplishment. How does this change the way you feel about the goal?

# #5.

# Make Your Goals Specific

Now that you have identified a variety of goals you want to achieve, let's take a look at some of the challenges and best practices for achieving them.

In the famous children's book *Alice and Wonderland*, Alice asks the Cheshire Cat:

........................................................................

*"Would you tell me, please, which way I ought to go from here?"*

*"That depends a good deal on where you want to get to," said the Cat.*

........................................................................

Goals, as both the cat and any savvy business professional know, provide clear guidelines for choosing how you are going to invest the time and energy you have available in any given minute, hour, day, or lifetime.

Yet, despite what seems like common sense and top-notch advice from some of the world's best thinkers, most business people still don't take the art of goal-setting seriously enough.

Thinking about or telling a colleague what you'd like to have happen in the future is a worthy start, but it won't necessarily pay off at the finish line. For example, ask almost any group of 100 people to raise their hands if they have a *goal* to have more money, and 90 percent of them will enthusiastically wave their paws high in the air. But when you point out that finding a quarter on the ground could easily fulfill this goal, those same people will shake their heads and say: "But that's not what I meant!"

In order to increase your chances of meeting your goals, try making them as specific as possible (including setting a time frame). Being precise in the goals you articulate helps you know how much progress you have made and exactly when you have arrived. Consider this general goal statement:

*I want to improve my presentation skills.*

But how will you know when you have achieved that? What specific metrics tell you that you are, in fact, a better speaker? A better-defined goal might be:

*Within the next six months, I want to improve my presentation skills by feeling more comfortable using eye contact, weaving in stories, and integrating PowerPoint into my speeches. These efforts will result in my evaluation scores going from 6 to 8 out of 10.*

If the thought of creating goals that are this detailed and precise brings up the dread of being locked into a direction or timeline that you can't change, relax. You create your goals, and you can change them at any time. Just because you generate a goal does not mean that it's carved in stone. If circumstances change and the aim is no longer appropriate, you are free to adjust or even abandon it.

## Write Down Your Goals

Writing down your goals helps you realize them for two reasons:

- When you store your goal in a place where you can review it regularly, you remember it better and it appears more real.

- When you write down your goal, you access what neuroscientists call the "generation effect," which means you remember things you have created better than things you have only read. By writing down goals and making them solid and specific, you help sear them into your brain by increasing the cognitive processing taking place.

# #6.

# Achieve Your Goals Every Day

Now that you've set goals in all areas of your life, wouldn't it be wonderful if all you had to do was kick back and wait for the universe to deliver them to you? While you will occasionally be graced with this effortless miracle of instant achievement, more often than not, your goals require self-effort to make them happen. Too often, the pull of urgent matters at work forces you to focus on items that need your immediate attention, and your less pressing (but still important) goals sit ignored. These four steps can help you consistently and regularly invest time toward achieving your goals and making them a reality.

## *Step One: Identify a Goal*

Start by identifying one goal that you want to achieve, but have not found the time to work on. For example:

- Goal: Write an article for the company blog on "How to make your presentations more dynamic and engaging."

## Step Two: Schedule Some Time

Look at your calendar and physically block out a specific time when you plan to work on this particular goal. In general, try to schedule a period of no less than fifteen minutes and no more than an hour.

It's a good idea to turn your phone off (or at least set it to silent) and close your email (just for a short while) so that you are as distraction-free as possible. A noise-cancelling headset can also help in a noisy environment.

## Step Three: Create a To-Do List

Now that you have a time period blocked out, create a to-do list of actions you can get done within that time frame that will help you achieve the goal. Items on your to-do list may include:

- Research statistics and studies about presentation dynamics.

- Contact Susan in marketing to find out how she prepares her presentations and makes them so much fun.

- Lay out the three topics I want to cover in the blog.

- Start a first draft—with no judgment!

Warning! Stay focused on the goal you have chosen and avoid getting seduced into your social-media apps.

## *Step Four: Be Consistent*

Do this every day, week, or month for—well, the rest of your life! Regularly reviewing and setting aside time to work on your most important goals will transport you out of a hope that they will become a reality and into a high probability that they will.

In the early stages of achieving a goal—particularly a large, lifetime goal—you may find reading, attending classes, or pursuing other educational activities useful. In this stage, your way of working on the goal is likely to include researching and preparing to dive in.

# #7.

# Create Structure and Support for Your Goals

Day-Timers, Inc. released a study of over 1,000 adults that showed that people achieve their goals when there is a powerful combination of internal motivation and external support. Here are the top motivators and support cited by respondents who were successful at reaching their objectives:

- 86% noted determination to make it, even when it got hard.

- 76% made a commitment for the long haul.

- 76% accepted setbacks and got back on track.

- 71% found that visualization was an aid to success.

- 59% rewarded themselves for success.

- 57% told other people.

- 44% set up reminders.

- 40% created a step-by-step plan.

- 39% asked for help and didn't do it alone.

Joseph Grenny, author of *Influencer: The Power to Change Anything*, agrees and adds that his research has shown that people who used at least four of the following six strategies were four times more likely to change their behavior and achieve their goals.

## Deliberately Practice

It's not enough just to have a goal to write a novel, be named salesperson of year, or climb Mount Everest. Reaching any goal, regardless of size, involves action and practice, as well as intention and clarity. Identifying what specific behaviors and habits you need to develop and/or change and making a point to practice each one on a regular basis will help you gain the new skills you need to achieve your objectives.

## Create Cues

Many of the goals you want to achieve require new attitudes and practices. Posting prompts about the behaviors you want to change in highly visible places will remind you to keep these new habits front and center in your mind.

## Give Yourself Incentives

Too many people wait until they have reached the finish line before they reward themselves. Instead, celebrate the small wins all along the way and reward yourself for achieving milestone accomplishments in the overall goal you are pursuing.

## Find Encouragement

As Ralph Waldo Emerson said: "Our chief want in life is somebody who shall make us do what we can." When it comes to achieving your goals, success is usually not a solo effort. Having a buddy, team, or support group who can celebrate your successes, help you maintain perspective when things are not going exactly as planned, and prop you up during the rough times are invaluable parts of reaching any goal.

## Get Coaching

Coaching is a more formal approach to getting support that is distinct from joining a group or finding a buddy. Many people find it useful to pay a professional coach (someone who has experience in or knowledge about the area they are working on) to help them navigate their way through the learning curve of achieving their objectives. Others find a mentor, someone who wants to contribute their time, experience, and knowledge as a way of giving back.

Either way, the coach you choose should be someone you trust to give you feedback on what you are doing right and specific suggestions for how you can improve.

## Embody Your Values

Make sure the goals you choose are anchored in something that is of core importance to you. Goals that consist of other people's good ideas or goals that you feel you *should* have are the ones most likely to fail. By setting your sights on goals that are a reflection of your most important values in life, you will have an authentic desire to achieve them.

# Beware the "Not-Goal"

Whenever you set your sights on a goal (regardless of its size or scope), you also create the possibility for its polar opposite—the "not goal." A not-goal is anything that looks as if it could get in the way of you achieving your objective. It usually involves feelings of fear, confusion, and worry, of discomfort and doubt, of being overwhelmed. A not-goal is always in relative proportion to the size of the aim you have set, so a small goal usually sparks a relatively small not-goal and a large goal often dredges up a large one.

For example, let's say you've set a relatively small goal of cleaning out your file drawer. You open up your long-forgotten folders and confront the ugly truth about all the papers you have been unceremoniously stuffing into them for years. Reports you printed out to read later, but didn't. Receipts, old tax information and returns. As you move deeper into the drawer, you become overwhelmed, you yawn, and then you start to panic. Your brain clamors for air and silently screams: "Abandon ship! This was not a good idea!"

Sitting there, surrounded by a mess of paperwork and your own dark thoughts, you are smack dab in the middle of a not-goal.

A strong desire takes hold to shove everything back in, slam the drawer, and walk away.

Whenever you are faced with the *inevitable* not-goal, you have an option about where to put your attention. If you focus on the not-goal—and in this case, walk away—your time will have been wasted. If, however, you recognize the not-goal and make a conscious choice to focus on your objective instead, the outcome will be a clean file drawer.

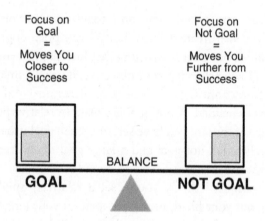

Focus on
Goal
=
Moves You
Closer to
Success

Focus on
Not Goal
=
Moves You
Further from
Success

BALANCE

**GOAL**

**NOT GOAL**

As your goals get bigger and bolder, the not-goals also grow. For example, you set a significant goal to form a task team to develop and implement a company-wide quality-improvement strategy. After inviting a highly considered group of players to join the team, you receive a few rabid responses saying: "I don't think we need this sort of thing company-wide. Let departments handle it themselves." Several other people write notes saying they are just too busy to participate. The person you had hoped would head up the committee briskly informs you that she is spread way to thin already. She would love to help but can't! Despite your best intentions, here you are face to face with a sizable not-goal.

The optimistic enthusiasm you started with has now mutated into skepticism. "Fine," you think, "if no one else cares, why should I?" You may even begin to wonder if you should actually be doing this job, in this company.

Once again, you have a choice about where you focus. If you zero in on the not-goal, you may decide that your goal was just too much to take on and quit the project. On the other hand, if you keep your eyes on the prize, you can use the power of your commitment and your skill at negotiation to find ways to work around the roadblocks presented.

Too many people fail to realize that a not-goal is a natural part of any worthwhile endeavor and consequently give up too often and too soon. Learn to see not-goals as a sign that you're on the right track and ask yourself what actions you can take to work through these obstacles. Then consider the people you know who could offer helpful advice or assistance.

# Break Bad Habits That
# Hold You Back

Bad time-management habits don't suddenly appear overnight; they develop slowly over time as certain habitual behaviors begin to overlay the way you work. And nothing is more detrimental to the achievement of your goals than the bad time-management habits that hold you back. The good news is that, with awareness and effort, you can break your bad habits (it takes about twenty-one days) and turn time-wasters on their head. These five steps can help you get those habits under control.

## *Step One: Name Your Bad Habits*

Take a look at the following list of common bad time-management habits and check off any that apply to you. Feel free to add your own at the bottom.

- Procrastinating to the point of lost productivity and opportunity

- Disorganized files, emails, desk, or work space

- Chaotic email and filing system

- Messy piles of paperwork
- Operating in crisis mode
- Over-promising and under-delivering
- Not meeting deadlines to which you agreed
- Not keeping your promises about time
- Continually being late for meetings and appointments
- Constantly interrupting yourself by checking your phone, tablet, and other devices
- Arriving at meetings unprepared
- Not keeping a daily to-do list
- Lack of prioritization
- Failure to delegate
- Multitasking to the point of distraction

## Step Two: Identify the Negative Impact

Take a look at the items you checked and choose one that you are willing to put some effort into changing. What negative impact has this bad habit had in your business (and perhaps personal) life? For example, let's say you checked "Arriving at meetings unprepared." The negative impact on yourself and others may include:

- You feel unable to make a decision in the meeting.
- You can't fully contribute to the conversation.
- The progress of the group is hindered.
- You lose credibility with your co-workers.

My bad time habit is:

_____

_____

_____

_____

_____

_____

_____

_____

_____

_____

The negative impact it has on me and those around me includes:

_____

_____

_____

_____

_____

_____

_____

_____

_____

_____

## *Step Three: Brainstorm Positive Results*

Next, think about the positive results that could come about if you changed this habit. How would turning this habit around impact you? How about your co-workers, family, friends? For example:

......................................................................................

*If I arrived for meetings prepared, it would reduce my stress level. I would feel more knowledgeable about the issues and be able to make faster decisions. Others would see me as a responsible team player.*

......................................................................................

The positive results that could come out of my changing this habit are:

_____

_____

_____

_____

_____

_____

_____

_____

_____

_____

## Step Four: Break the Habit Down into Specific Steps

If you look closely, all negative habits are made up of a series of steps and the thoughts that go along with them. For example, when informed about an upcoming meeting:

- You add it to your calendar, and tell yourself that you will prepare for it later.

- As the meeting gets closer, you start to get stressed and notice that you don't have the time you need to prepare for it adequately.

- You tell yourself that you are not prepared because you had other things to do that couldn't wait.

Your negative time habits also consist of a string of actions and thoughts that go along with them. Write them below.

The specific steps of my bad habit are:

_____

_____

_____

_____

_____

_____

_____

_____

_____

_____

## *Step Five: Create Alternative Actions*

Now get creative and think of some alternate ways you could act and consider actions you can take to turn your bad habits into good ones. For example:

- At the same time as entering the meeting in your calendar, add at least one reminder alert.

- Carve out a thirty-minute block of preparation time.

- Consider this appointment with yourself as a high-priority and don't let it be crowded out by other urgent items.

- Schedule an alert to notify you thirty minutes before the start of the meeting so that you have time to look over the meeting agenda and your notes before you arrive.

My alternative actions include:

_____

_____

_____

_____

_____

_____

_____

_____

_____

# PART 3

# Avoid Interruptions, Distractions, and Multitasking

How often do you think that you get interrupted at work by external sources like other people, phone calls, and emails? How about the self-interruptions caused by your own multitasking or surfing the web? In both cases, probably more often than you realize.

One study by Gloria Mark, a professor at the University of California Irvine, found that workers spend on average only 10.5 minutes on a task before being interrupted, and that it takes an average of 23.25 minutes for them to return to the original task. The study also showed that 56 percent of that time, the distraction is caused by an external force, and 44 percent of the time by self-interruption.

In another study from the Institute of Psychiatry at the University of London, it was reported that, when workers are constantly juggling emails, phone calls, and text messages, their IQ falls ten points.

The bottom line? In today's high-pressure workplace, learning to overcome distractions, to deal with interruptions, and to manage multitasking are all key to successful time management. Here are a few proven ways that disruption-weary workers can fight distraction and find their focus.

# #10.

# Keep an Interruption Log

You're hard at work on that top-priority proposal when your co-worker in the next cubicle bursts in and asks if you've got a moment to help him fix the printer. Reluctantly, you stop what you are doing to rescue your colleague. Twenty minutes later, you're back at work on your proposal, but your former focus has fizzled. As a starting point, let's find out how often you *really* get interrupted at work (and by what).

## *Exercise*

Schedule a forty-five minute window to focus specifically on a project or task that you can do in your office, ideally at your desk. Using a clock, stopwatch, or timer, keep track of every interruption (external or self-generated) that occurs and log it. For example, let's say your forty-five-minute work window began at 1:00 PM.

# Sample Interruption Log

| Interruption | Self/ Other | Time Began | Time Ended | Total Time |
|---|---|---|---|---|
| Call home | Self | 1:05 | 1:06 | 1 minute |
| Phone rings | Other | 1:10 | 1:20 | 10 minutes |
| Get coffee | Self | 1:30 | 1:35 | 5 minutes |
| Co-worker question | Other | 1:40 | 1:44 | 4 minutes |
| Email ding | Other | 1:43 | 1:45 | 2 minutes |
| **Total** | | | | **22 minutes** |

Analysis of this log shows that, of the forty-five minutes of focused time scheduled, twenty-two minutes, or 48 percent, were taken up by interruptions. Use the following blank Interruption Log to keep tabs on yourself for one forty-five-minute period. Then analyze your interruption patterns and ask yourself these questions:

- How often do I *really* get interrupted when I try to focus?

- Are my interruptions more external or self-generated?

- What kinds of things interrupt me most frequently?

- What am I doing (or not doing) that contributes to my being interrupted?

- How are these interruptions affecting my focus and productivity?

# Interruption Log

| Interruption | Self/Other | Time Began | Time Ended | Total Time |
|---|---|---|---|---|
| | | | | |
| | | | | |
| | | | | |
| | | | | |
| | | | | |
| | | | | |
| | | | | |
| | | | | |
| | | | | |
| | | | | |
| | | | | |
| | | | | |
| | | | | |
| | | | | |
| | | | | |
| | | | | |
| | | | | |
| | | | | |
| **Total** | | | | |

Now that you have a sense of how often you are being interrupted and by what, here are a few simple, straightforward ways to stay on track.

# #11.

# Avoid Interruptions from Others

Do you have a second? Can you take a few minutes to look at this? Are you able to meet right now? Common questions. But if you say "yes" too often, your focus and productivity can suffer. Try these tips to keep others from hijacking your day.

## *Propose a Later Time*

The next time someone strolls into your office asking if you have a few minutes to talk, say: "I'd be happy to, but not right now." Instead of assuming you need to drop everything you're doing and respond on the spot, make an appointment with that person for later in the day or in the week.

## *Set a Time Limit*

If the matter is urgent, ask how much time the person needs and negotiate to give them that much (or less) and no more at the moment. If future discussions are needed, you can schedule another meeting. This can help you keep interruptions to a minimum and educate everyone around you to be more efficient in how they use your time.

## Bypass the Story

To limit the impact of an interruption, encourage people to bypass the story and get straight to the point. Ask them to summarize in a few sentences what they need from you, the solution they propose, and the specific time by which they need it.

## Change Locations

One way to prevent interruptions is to make it harder for people to find you. If you have a particular project that requires a great deal of concentration, consider commandeering an empty office or conference room and working from there.

## Schedule Open-Door Hours

Instead of a default open-door policy that encourages people to interrupt you whenever they feel like it, try posting and promoting open-door hours on specific days. With a little encouragement, most people will wait until the posted times to talk to you about non-urgent matters.

## Store Supplies Elsewhere

Does everyone come into your office to access the printer, office supplies, marketing materials, or the coffee machine? If so, try moving these distractors to a location where you are not continually disturbed by their retrieval or use.

## Don't Be Unavailable

The point of limiting interruptions, especially during times when you need to focus, is to improve your productivity and effectiveness. It is not, however, to avoid talking to anyone in your organization ever again. Always keep in mind the bigger picture of what benefits your co-workers, department, and company.

### Executive Strategies

A study of 247 senior-level executives conducted by the Center for Creative Leadership asked interviewees what strategies they use to promote better concentration.

- 29% close their doors, including posting *Do Not Disturb* signs.

- 18% prioritize their calendars by scheduling specific times for work appointments and open time.

- 14% use their executive assistants to screen calls and people, only letting the most important through.

- 13% turn off their cell phones and office phones, and only take urgent calls.

- 12% telecommute from home or work off-site, including planning what specific work they will do on an airplane or in an airport.

- 6% limit email by setting specific times to check it, turning off the alert, and using their assistants to pre-screen emails.

- 4% arrive early, stay late, or work on weekends so they can get work done when no one else is around.

# #12.

# Stop Self-Interruptions

Self-interruption involves stopping a task before it's finished by switching your focus to a different task. Some of the most common self-interruptions include:

- Writing down an idea, thought, or to-do item you just thought of

- Stopping to do something you forgot needed doing

- Looking up one thing on the Internet, but then following a random series of links

- Pursuing social media when you get a ping

According to the study by Gloria Marks, 40 percent of the time, when workers are interrupted, they don't return to their original tasks at all, but instead wander off in a new direction.

For example, imagine you are working at your desk when the phone rings (interruption #1). It's a co-worker asking you to check to see if her last expense invoice was paid. You oblige. You're just about to end the conversation and get back to your reading when she asks if you can resend a copy of the new expense policy (interruption #2). You oblige again. Now you are two interruptions away from your original task. Unchecked, this can grow to three, four, or even more interruptions.

So how can you keep from interrupting yourself? Try these five simple strategies.

## Block Out Time

Try blocking out a defined window of time on your planner to focus on a particular project. Blocks of between twenty and forty-five minutes are optimal, since they are long enough to achieve something, but short enough to allow you to handle other items that may come up.

## Time Yourself

Timer apps can help you focus on one thing at a time. They are structured to give you short bursts of work time, with alternating breaks. Most track your overall progress on specific tasks. By the way, if your ability to focus has diminished in direct proportion to your use of social media and the web, these timing apps can help strengthen your attention-span skills.

## Keep Pen and Paper Handy

In the predictable event that a random thought, forgotten to-do, or prize-winning idea pops into your head, don't stop to think about it. Instead, quickly jot it down on a piece of paper as a way to capture it in the moment. Why paper? Writing it down the old fashioned way helps you steer clear of electronic interruptions.

## Do Your Hardest Task Later in the Day

While popular time-management wisdom often suggests doing your more difficult tasks earlier in the day when your attention is fresh, one study by Victor Gonzalez from Instituto Tecnologico Autonomo in Mexico suggests that the opposite is true. Gonzalez did an analysis of 889 hours of observed task-switching behavior with individuals across three high-technology information work organizations. "Informants interrupted themselves more often the earlier it was in the day and less often as the day progressed," says Gonzalez.

# #13.

# Overcome Multitasking Madness

On an average day, you probably email a memo to co-workers, surf the web for the latest greatest cat video, fill out sales reports, and sit in on several video calls—usually all at the same time! One study by Rubinstein, Meyer, and Evans found that, when people switch back and forth between tasks, there is a substantial loss of efficiency and accuracy, in some cases up to as much as 50 percent.

In today's non-stop work environment—courtesy of smartphones, email, and texting—the five projects people used to manage in a day have tripled to fifteen. Too much input and too little control have left modern workers struggling with far more than they can handle productively. To overcome multitasking madness, try these simple techniques.

## *Turn Off Your Technology*

The ding of an email, the ping of a text. These seemingly harmless inputs can tempt you to stray from the job at hand and multitask. Try putting your phone in airplane mode, or using a piece of software that keeps you from surfing the web for short periods of time.

## Create Designated Task Times

By setting aside a selected time period to do all your phone calls, emails, or errands at once, you can reduce the amount of time you spend going back and forth between them.

## Make the Most of Your Morning

In her book *Never Check Email in the Morning*, author Julie Morgenstern recommends that people avoid checking email for the first hour each day and instead spend the time working on an important task or project that requires focus.

## Capture All Incoming To-Do's in Writing

Instead of feeling pressure to do an item "now" lest you forget, write down your to-do's so your brain can relax, secure in the knowledge that you have the item identified and stored. Any "notes" feature on your smartphone can help you capture an idea and do a brain dump instantly.

## Maintain a Desktop Inbox

Don't just rely on your email inbox or filing system. By putting a physical inbox on your desk, you can temporarily place items that need your attention in a location where you can easily find them.

## Plan Some Open Space

Instead of booking every minute of every workday, leave some open time when you can catch up on anything new that comes in, or process old items that have been hanging around.

# Don't Multitask, Multipurpose

If all this talk about concentration and singular focus makes you break out in a sweat, relax and check out the cousin of multitasking—multipurposing. By doing two things at once (combining tasks), you can save time and effort. For example, listen to business books while driving, catch up on reading memos and reports while on the treadmill, have a working business breakfast, or plow through paperwork on the plane or in the doctor's office.

# #14.

# Give Yourself a Procrastination Inoculation

A study by Dr. Piers Steel, a professor at the University of Calgary, concluded that procrastination is on the rise. According to Steel's research, in 1978, about 15 percent of the population were considered moderate procrastinators. Today, that number is up to 60 percent, a four-fold increase.

Another significant finding was that up to 95 percent of North Americans claim they procrastinate around work issues, costing businesses billions in lost revenue and productivity. While procrastination is, to some degree, a natural phenomenon and can't be completely eradicated, utilizing the following strategies can help beat it down.

## *Take the Pulse of Your Procrastination*

According to a study by Timothy Pychyl at the University of Ottawa, up to 70 percent of North Americans have a problem with procrastination. Are you one of them? Take the quiz below to determine your current level of procrastination.

Thinking about your day-to-day work life, choose the most accurate value for the following statements. Tally your score to see how big a role procrastination plays in your work life.

1 = Almost never

2 = Once in a while

3 = Frequently

4 = All the time

1. I regularly put off starting tasks, projects, and activities I don't enjoy doing. _____

2. Even when I have a specific deadline, I wait until the last minute to take action. _____

3. When I have to make a tough decision, I put it off as long as possible. _____

4. Even though I feel badly when I don't get started on an important task, this rarely motivates me to get going. _____

5. I am regularly late for meetings and appointments. _____

6. I find myself needing to ask for time extensions on work due. _____

7. I regularly say to myself: "I will do it tomorrow." _____

8. I have lost business or damaged relationships by putting things off. _____

9. Even when I am excited about starting
   a new project, I have trouble initiating it. _____

10. I can easily lose my focus and
    become distracted by trivial matters. _____

Total score: _____

- Score of 10–15: Congratulations! Other than the normal procrastination here and there, you are not a chronic or problem procrastinator. To improve your get-it-done muscle even more, determine several high-priority goals and schedule a specific day and period of time to work on them.

- Score of 16–25: You are not a serious procrastinator, but you could benefit from using a priority system to make you more effective and efficient. Resist the lure of the trivial by using a priority system based on achievement and importance, not crisis and time sensitivity.

- Score of 26–32: Procrastination is having a negative impact on your work life and career. One reason may be that you feel overwhelmed with all the things you have on your plate. Try breaking your bigger projects into smaller tasks. This will help you take action more quickly and easily.

- Score of 33–40: You have a serious case of procrastination. Evaluate the impact this is having on your professional accomplishments and relationships.

Many serious procrastinators are distracted by technology. Email, voicemail, instant messaging, and the Internet are all wonderful tools, but when they cause constant interruption, they make it almost impossible to focus at work. Draw a line by creating some technology-free times.

## Take Advantage of Your Power Hours

Are you an early riser who tackles your morning to-do list with all the gusto of a bear eating honey? Perhaps you're a night-owl and crank through your most pressing projects at 11:00 PM?

Either way, knowing and taking advantage of your natural energy patterns will help you steer clear of procrastination by using your power times to tackle the projects you find most challenging.

## Use the Clout of Your Calendar

Do you have a task that has been lingering on your to-do list for days, weeks, or even (gulp) months? If so, use the clout of your calendar to move from inertia to action. Open your planner, smartphone, or tablet and schedule a specific date and time when you promise yourself that you will work on that item—and that item only.

## Decide on the Next Action

One reason people procrastinate is that they feel intimidated by the task as it is currently stated and can't figure out what to do next. To avoid being overwhelmed, figure out the next smallest, easiest, and most comfortable action you can take to move forward. By breaking down the bigger less-defined items into smaller more specific chunks, you tell your mind: "I can do this."

## Give Yourself Credit All Along the Way

The moment you take any action (no matter how small), give yourself credit. Don't wait until the entire to-do list is complete before experiencing at least some degree of satisfaction and accomplishment. This type of recognition has been shown to build a positive momentum that encourages action and beats back inertia.

## Be Decisive

Deciding what to do with that piece of paper won't be any easier tomorrow than it is today. Train yourself to categorize every item that comes across your desk as something to do now, something to delegate or dump, or something to defer. By the way, deferring something does not mean placing it back in the pile and pretending it does not exist. That is the pathway to procrastination. It means putting it in a dated tickler file (electronic or otherwise), scheduling a time to do it, or moving it to a "maybe-someday" to-do list where the guilt and stress of procrastination don't apply.

# Manage Outgoing and Incoming Calls

Email and texting have outpaced talking on the phone as the favored means of communication. And while you may have a good deal of control over the calls you make, the emails you send, and the texts you type, you have decidedly less over those you receive. Your phone rings and messages ping whether it's a convenient time for you or not.

Managing your incoming and outgoing calls is a significant step toward taking back control of your time. It's amazing how simple this is to do if you just follow these few basic time-savers.

## Incoming Calls

### *Don't Answer*

Just because your phone rings doesn't mean you need to pick it up. We often act like those rats you read about in psychological experiments. Our automatic response to the stimulus of the phone ringing is to answer it. If you are in the middle of a meeting, working on an important to-do item, or even just in a hyper-focused mode, leave it alone and let the caller leave a message.

## Schedule a Call-back

If the caller is someone important with whom you need to speak, but it's still not a good time for you to talk, avoid the brusk "I can't talk right now." Instead, schedule a call-back. By setting up a phone appointment there and then, you avoid the endless telephone tag that can suck up so much of your day. Alternatively, if you think the topic can be handled by email, suggest moving the conversation online.

## Bottom-Line It

If you have ever been stuck on the phone with someone who drones on and on while you are on deadline, you know the pain of the long-winded call. Instead of sitting there politely while your time is being wasted, cut to the chase by prompting the person along. Try this short and to the point phrase: "I only have X minutes, but tell me how I can help you today (what I can do for you, etc.). I will do what I can in the time I have."

## Bring the Call to a Close

Once you have gotten to the point in the call where you need to get off, or you have handled the business, it's time to wrap it up. Gently restate what has been accomplished or agreed to, then say "thanks for the call" or "good talking to you" to signal that you are at the end.

# Outgoing Calls

## Schedule Call Time

One way to stop interrupting your work flow or compromising your concentration is to schedule your calls for a dedicated block of time. Try keeping a separate list of the calls you need to make and plan a time to make them in your calendar.

## Create a Call Plan

Unless you are just calling someone to catch up, creating a specific agenda can be a great time-saver. You may even consider emailing recipients the topics you want to discuss so they can prepare for the call. A call plan keeps everyone on track so you can avoid roaming into irrelevant territory.

## Ask If It's a Good Time to Talk

One way to insure that you are not wasting someone's time is simply to ask if it is a good time for the other person to talk at the outset. If the answer is "no," schedule a call-back time that works. If the answer is "yes," the very fact that you asked will garner you more of the person's attention.

## Cut to the Chase When Leaving Messages

Long-winded messages that try to cover the content of an entire phone call will be deleted after a few seconds. Instead, leave a short and to-the-point message with your name, the purpose of your call, a call-back number, and some good times to reach you.

Follow up with an email to insure the person has what they need to get back to you.

## Texting

Texting can be as big an interruption as phone calls—even more so in some cases. Many texts don't need an immediate response, so answering them when you have a free moment is better than dropping whatever you are doing and getting distracted. A few other things to keep in mind:

- When sending a text, keep it brief and save time for both you and your recipients.

- If you receive a long, involved text, consider calling the person or having them call you.

- Take the extra nanosecond to reread your texts to insure Autospell didn't get *crested* (creative).

# PART 4

# Learn to Delegate

How do you manage your time when there don't seem to be enough hours in the day to get everything done? Delegation. It's an essential tool for time management. While every manager knows what delegation is, however, few really understand how to make the most of it. When done well, delegation is a win-win scenario for both parties, saving time on the assigner's part and building the abilities of the assignee. Thinking of delegation as a development opportunity for your team members, rather than as a burdensome undertaking, makes it a productive habit for every manager. Not to mention that probably the only way you can deal with your workload is to share it with others!

# #16.

# Size Up Your Delegation Skills

Assuming that you're sold on the necessity of being a demon delegator, a good place to start is by evaluating your current delegation attitude and skill set.

## *Exercise*

Read through the following statements and enter the number that best reflects your current assessment of yourself. Use the following as a guideline:

1 = Never

2 = Sometimes

3 = Much of the time

4 = Almost always

1. The jobs I delegate usually get done the way I want them to be done.   _____

2. I take the time to delegate the right task to the right person.   _____

3. When I give clear instructions and they are not followed, I see it as an opportunity *both* to improve how I communicate and to train my staff. _____

4. Work I delegate gets done as well as if I had done it myself. _____

5. I consider my staff's current workload before delegating. _____

6. When I delegate work, I almost never have to do it over. _____

7. When I delegate, I explain the parameters of how a job should be done. _____

8. I delegate both routine and non-routine tasks to my staff. _____

9. I believe that delegation saves me time. _____

10. In many cases, my staff can do the work I delegate to them better than I can. _____

Total score: _____

- Score of 32–40: Congratulations! You are a skilled delegator and see assigning tasks and projects to your staff as a way to save you time and develop their abilities. To improve even further, try your hand at delegating something more strategic or of higher priority to a trusted member of your staff. If the item you delegate requires you to coach and mentor your staff member closely, all the better. Teaching a subordinate a new skill is satisfying and will free you up to work on other projects.

- Score of 21–31: You are doing a decent job at delegation and, with a little more effort, can reap big time-saving rewards. Use an activity log to determine what specific tasks you can delegate to your staff on a daily basis and begin to do so. Consider taking a class on delegation or asking another manager in the company who excels at this skill to coach or mentor you.

- Score of 10–20: Delegation is not your strongest suit and this is probably hindering your time-management efforts. Start by reviewing the statements and see if you can find a trend. Are you a poor delegator because you don't take the time to pass things on properly? Do you distrust other people to do the job as well as you would do it? Try to identify the main underlying reason why you don't delegate (or do it poorly) and check out the other delegation techniques in this book to help you improve.

No matter what your skill level, here are some keys to making delegation an opportunity for everyone.

# #17.

# Determine the Tasks to Assign

To determine what potential actions you can assign, check out the five task types below.

## *Routine Tasks*

These are the everyday tasks that you do to maintain your working environment. They are the routine, mundane actions that keep your office humming—errands, expense reports, paperwork, low-priority emails, etc. Consider assigning these to new employees to check out their work habits and abilities. These can also be doled out to staff that may be between projects or find themselves with a bit of free time on their hands (as if!).

## *Tasks You Don't Have Time to Do*

This is a group of items that are not necessarily routine but of only moderate priority. If more urgent or important matters are occupying your attention, pass these on to a capable subordinate you know can handle the additional work.

## Tasks That Involve Problem-Solving

There are some tasks before you that require a particular knowledge or skill to move forward. If one or more of your subordinates has the expertise or experience to tackle a particular problem, consider assigning it to them.

## Tasks That Build an Individual's Capabilities

When properly managed, delegation can become a tool for training and developing your staff. Determine which tasks you now do that you could hand over to staff members that will provide a significant opportunity for their growth and development.

## Tasks That Represent a Change in Job Emphasis

Over time, you may find that the emphasis of your job has changed, and you now have new responsibilities that require you to take on additional activities. As a matter of practicality, you can delegate "old" activities associated with your previous job emphasis to make time and room for the new ones you need to take on.

## Exercise

Review each of the five task types above and determine one *real* item you are willing and able to delegate.

1.    A routine task I could delegate is:

_____

_____

2.  A task I don't have time to do and could delegate is:

_____

_____

3.  A task I could delegate that involves problem-solving is:

_____

_____

4.  A task I could delegate that will build someone's capability is:

_____

_____

5.  A task I could delegate that represents a change in job emphasis is:

_____

_____

# Questions to Ask Yourself Before Delegating

- Is it crucial that I be the one to do this task or is there someone else who has the expertise, experience, skill, or savvy needed to do it?

- Is there someone else I work with who would grow and develop as a result of my assigning this task?

- Is this an ongoing task that will become routine in the future?

- Am I willing to take (and/or do I have) the time (and/or energy) necessary to delegate this task effectively?

# #18.

# Create a Delegation Plan

Delegation is not a data dump of your entire unwanted, hard-to-do, not-so-interesting tasks onto the head of another person. Rather, it is a carefully crafted process of defining what you want done, identifying the specific end results you expect, and articulating the process by which the other person can win at delivering it. To insure that the time you invest in delegating is well spent, use the following five-step process.

## *Step One: Define the End Results*

One of the most obvious mistakes that managers make when delegating is failing to provide clarity about the end results they expect. Before you have a sit-down with one of your staff members, clarify in your own mind the dimensions of the assignment to be carried out. Ask yourself what the specific conditions are that, if met, will satisfy you. It's a common mistake to assume that these conditions are implicit and that you don't need to make them explicit. You do. For example, if you are delegating a report to a subordinate:

- Do you want your subordinate to do the research for the report and present you with the initial findings verbally or in writing before creating the report? Or . . .

- Do you want the person to do the research for the report, write up a first draft, and show it to you? Or . . .

- Do you want the person to do the research, write the report, and then oversee production and distribution of the report, just checking in with you from time to time to make sure everything is on the right track?

## Step Two: Clarify the Parameters

Depending on the importance of the item delegated and the willingness and ability of the person to whom you are delegating, the degree of control and influence you exercise will vary. There are three basic types of delegation, each allowing the team member a varying degree of autonomy. Decide ahead of time which type best fits the task you are turning over.

- Assignment: You tell the staff member what is to be done and how to do it.

- Involvement: You tell the staff member what is to be done and determine together how to do it.

- Empowerment: You tell the staff member the result to be accomplished and let him or her decide how to do it.

## Step Three: Come to a Mutual Agreement

Once an item has been delegated, it's important to give the other person an opportunity to obtain some ownership over it. People usually have one of four responses to a delegated item:

- They accept the assignment as is.

- They refuse the assignment flat out (rare, but it does happen).

- They accept the assignment, but want to negotiate the details of its delivery.

- They accept the assignment, but with certain conditions attached.

Don't automatically assume a delegated item has been accepted as is. Instead, come to a mutual agreement on who will do what by when and negotiate the details of delivery at the start. Having this degree of clarity on the front end can save scads of time and frustration on the back end.

## Step Four: Follow Through and Provide Support

Delegate, don't abdicate. When you transfer an item to a staff member, the responsibility for its completion still rests with you. To chart your staff's progress:

- Ask them how things are going.

- Set milestone meetings to review and discuss progress.

- Check in on quality control from time to time.

- Ask staff members to account for their progress and problems occasionally.

- Be available to answer questions and provide feedback.

- Inform other people within the company of the staff member's responsibility.

- Periodically ask the staff member what support is needed from you.

- Provide the staff person with any ongoing information or necessary updates.

## *Step Five: Evaluate the Success of the Delegation*

It's de-motivating to put time and effort into an assignment and then not receive any response (let alone appreciation or acknowledgment) for what has been accomplished. The last step in delegating like a pro is to recognize the results of the delegation and determine areas for improvement. These include:

- Identifying the learning, growth, and development that occurred

- Rewarding and/or thanking staff for their efforts and the results produced

- Highlighting aspects of the job that could be improved in the future

- Determining areas where your delegation skills could be improved in the future

By taking this last step, you not only give your staff the feeling of a job well done, you also increase their willingness to take on delegated items in the future.

# #19.

# Decide to Whom You Will Delegate

Once you have gone through the process of picking and choosing which tasks on your massive to-do list can be passed on, the next step is to decide to whom they should be delegated. Remember that, while you may be ready and raring to download, not all staff members are willing or able to honor your requests. Part of your job is to pave the way for delegation by building up your staff's abilities and increasing their willingness to take on tasks.

To increase willingness:

- Delegate items that are associated with things you know that staff members like to do.

- Include staff members in the process of setting the goals and then delegating items associated with these goals.

- Explain the importance of the delegated item and clarify how your staff's participation will make a difference in its accomplishment.

- Explain how doing the delegated item will benefit staff members directly.


To increase ability:

- Delegate items that will challenge your staff's current capabilities but are still within their existing skill set.

- Provide formal training that will help staff take on the delegated item.

- Offer to coach staff members, or get them a coach who can help them deliver on the job delegated.

- Have staff work with you on a similar project, so they can develop the skills necessary to take on future delegated items.

To prepare yourself for successful delegation, choose one item that you want to delegate. Evaluate your existing staff and fill in their names in the appropriate boxes below.

*Choose an item that you want to delegate. Consider your existing team and fill in their names in the appropriate boxes below.*

**ITEM** _____

**WILLINGNESS** (vertical axis)

**Not Able - Not Willing**

_____
_____
_____
_____
_____
_____
_____

Needs motivation and training

**Able - Not Willing**

_____
_____
_____
_____
_____
_____
_____

Needs motivation

**Willing - Not Able**

_____
_____
_____
_____
_____
_____
_____

Needs training

**Able - Willing**

_____
_____
_____
_____
_____
_____
_____

Needs challenges

**ABILITY**

## Exercise

Here are three different delegation responses to the same scenario that can help you polish up your delegation delivery. Rate the effectiveness of the delegation after each response.

An upset customer calls the service center of an online retailer and informs Greg, the agent, that he has been charged a restocking fee because he returned his purchase without its original box. Greg, who has only been on the job for a few weeks, puts the customer on hold and explains the situation to his supervisor, Mavis.

........................................................................

*I have a customer who is upset because he is being charged a restocking fee. He says it was impossible to get his product out of the box without destroying the original packing, so therefore we should waive the charge. He's also a frequent shopper with us. What should I do?*

........................................................................

How would you rate the delegation effectiveness (good, fair, or poor) of the following responses from Mavis?

- Response #1: Don't worry about it. Send the call over to me and I'll handle it.

    I rate this delegation as:  ○ Good  ○ Fair  ○ Poor

    Why? _____

    _____

    _____

    _____

- Response #2: No worries, this happens all the time. Just tell him you spoke with your supervisor and she said our restocking policy is clearly visible on our site and we can't make an exception. If he gives you any problem, transfer him over to me.

  I rate this delegation as:   ○ Good   ○ Fair   ○ Poor

  Why? _____

  _____

  _____

  _____

- Response #3: Greg, you have enough experience and smarts to handle this. What do you think is the best way to resolve this situation? You know our policy, but as you said, this is a regular customer. Use your own good judgment and I will stand by any decision you make. Just keep in mind that the goal here is to do what's right by both the customer and the company.

  I rate this delegation as:   ○ Good   ○ Fair   ○ Poor

  Why? _____

  _____

  _____

  _____

And the answer is. . .

- Response #1 is a poor example of delegation. By telling Greg that she will handle the situation, Mavis misses a major opportunity to train Greg to deal with this type of occurrence in the future. She also encourages him to bring all difficult problems to her, rather than learning to handle them himself.

    > Do: Take a long-term view of things and, whenever possible, make the time now to train people in the ongoing skills they will need to get their jobs done over time.

    > Don't: Jump in and do it all yourself because it seems easier at the moment to do so. This type of short-term thinking leads to a time-management nightmare in which you (and only you) can make things work.

- Response #2 is a fair example of delegation. By explaining the policy, Mavis educates Greg and trains him how to handle these situations. She also allows him to communicate the decision to the customer, which will help him to deal with customer disagreements in the future. What Mavis has not done, however, is empower Greg to look beyond the policy and use his good judgment.

    > Do: Educate staff on the rules, regulations, policies, and procedures that apply to the item you are delegating, so that they can make appropriate decisions.

Don't: Minimize the creative power of your staff by limiting the discussion to the rules only. Real delegation is only possible with people who understand the reasons for the policies and the circumstances in which they can be altered.

- Response #3 is a good example of delegation. Mavis expresses her confidence in Greg and, even more to the point, proves her trust by letting him make the call. She highlights the two most important points for him to consider (the customer is a regular and company policy), and empowers Greg to weigh these two factors against the ultimate goal.

Do: Give staff the biggest picture possible when you delegate an item. Having a big perspective helps them to make the best decisions and take the most appropriate actions toward the desired end.

Don't: Be afraid to delegate something that is a little over someone's head or presents a challenge. As long as you are there to support the person and back up the decision, a little stretch goes a long way.

# Delegation Do's and Don'ts

- *Do* take a long-term view of things.

- *Don't* jump in and do it all yourself.

- *Do* educate staff on the rules, regulations, policies, and procedures.

- *Don't* minimize the creative power of your staff by limiting the discussion to the rules only.

- *Do* give staff the biggest picture possible.

- *Don't* be afraid to delegate something that is a little over someone's head.

# PART 5

# Manage Your Online
# and Off-Line Meetings

The results on meeting management are in—and it's not pretty.

A 2019 report by the online scheduling service Doodle presented results from a study of 19 million meetings involving more than 6,500 workers in the US, the UK, and Germany.

According to this report, the cost of poorly organized meetings is $399 billion in the US alone. Some of the specific consequences of mismanaged meetings included:

- Not having enough time to finish the rest of the work on an employee's plate (44%)

- Leaving the meeting confused by unclear action items (43%)

- Irrelevant attendees holding up the progress of the meeting (31%)

We have all sat through meetings where we question the sanity of spending so much time talking about nothing, when we could actually have been doing something valuable with our day.

But what exactly makes these meetings time-wasters? Usually, it's a combination of poor planning, poor execution, and poor follow-up. To make the meetings you run a shining example of time well spent and avoid the pitfalls outlined in Doodle's report, try some of the following strategies.

# #20.

# Give Every Meeting (Big or Small) Structure

If you want to make an immediate improvement in your meeting time management, use the PAL (Purpose, Agenda, and Limits) method prior to any meeting you run. This simple and straightforward technique ensures a basic level of meeting mindfulness that prevents wasted time and effort. Even regular meetings will benefit when you apply the following PAL principles.

## **P** *Determine the Purpose of the Meeting*

In his book *The Seven Habits of Highly Effective People*, author Stephen Covey tells us to "begin with the end in mind." Before convening any meeting, take some time to write down a few sentences that articulate your overall objective. A good place to start is to think about what you hope will have happened by the *end* of the session. For example:

- The task team will agree on the location and theme of this year's holiday office party.

- The sales group will be able to discuss our latest product with customers easily.

- The finance department will arrive at a decision about which vendor to hire to help with the office makeover.

The more specific and concrete you make your meeting's purpose, the more focused your gathering will be and the greater your ability to evaluate your overall success.

##  Set a Specific Agenda

Think of a stated agenda as the roadmap that will guide you through the meeting, keep you from veering off course, and help you avoid getting distracted by extraneous events. A well-defined agenda lets all participants know what to expect from the meeting *and* what will be expected of them. In some cases, you may want to develop the agenda in collaboration with other members of your company. In general, a well-rounded agenda includes:

- The intended purpose of the meeting

- The date, start time, and finish time

- The location

- Specific objectives to be achieved

- Topics to be discussed (in order)

- Any background information the participants need to know

- Any other relevant information like dress code, prep work, etc.

Here's an example of an effective memo calling for a meeting:

*To:*      *Sales Team*

*From:*    *Bruce Buttermilk*

*Subject:*  *Baseball Team Uniform Meeting*

*Date:*     *January 27*

*Location:* *International House of Pancakes*

*Times:*    *7:30 AM – 9:00 AM*

*Purpose:*  *To agree on the baseball team uniform design for this year's softball tournament.*

*Agenda:*   *Coffee, pancake breakfast, and socializing*

            *Introduction of new team members*

            *Review of last year's color-scheme suggestions*

            *Presentation by the art department of sample team-uniform drawings*

            *Discussion of pros and cons of various uniform designs*

            *Vote on uniform design*

# L Stick to a Time Limit

Meetings that start late and run over wreak havoc with everyone's schedule and test both patience and goodwill. Every meeting you set up should have stated start and finish times—that you stick to. If you discipline yourself and your co-workers to take your time limits seriously, your meetings will be more productive.

# #21.

# Develop Good Meeting-Management Habits

The Microsoft Office Personal Productivity Challenge studied over 38,000 people in 200 countries. It found that, in the United States, workers spend 5.5 hours a week in meetings, with 71 percent proclaiming that these meetings are unproductive.

One way to beat back unproductive meeting time is to integrate some key habits into the planning and running of your meetings. These strategies can help.

## *Assign Prep Work*

If you want to raise the stakes for those attending, give them something to think about or prepare prior to arrival. Among other things, you can ask members to read background information, come prepared with a suggested solution to a given problem, or show up ready to share a good story that illustrates the topic of the meeting. At a minimum, make sure everyone invited receives the agenda at least twenty-four hours before the meeting, as this will at least get them mentally prepared to participate.

## Invite the Right People

Deciding whom to invite and whom to leave out of a particular meeting may seem like an obvious step, but how often has a decision been put off or a conclusion delayed because the right people (decision makers, stake holders, informed parties, experts, etc.) were not in the room? In reviewing your purpose and agenda for the meeting, make an initial list of those you think should be invited and then ask a colleague or two for their two cents before you finalize the invites.

## Don't Delay

Right off the bat, you can set the mood for the meeting by starting on time. This honors those who showed up promptly and lets the tardy know you mean what you say when it comes to timelines.

## Conduct Check-Ins

If you have a meeting that lasts more than a few hours, check in every now and then to ensure that you're on track. Go around the room and ask each participant to give you feedback on how the meeting is progressing. Try to avoid generalizations like "Fine," "Good," Okay," or "Not great" by asking people to provide specific evaluations. For example:

- "We seem to be covering a lot of ground" is more descriptive than "Fine."

- "We don't seem to be sticking to our timeline very well" is more helpful than "Okay."

The more unambiguous the responses, the better the chance of adjusting your course when necessary. Be sure to check in with the more senior people in the group last. This prevents the other participants from having to offer an opinion counter to that of their bosses, or their bosses' boss.

## *Assign Action Items All Along the Way*

A meeting without action items is like matzo-ball soup without the matzo balls. Don't move on from a significant discussion point within a meeting without flagging potential action items (no matter how small) and assigning them to group members. Doling out tasks that make their way to the surface of the conversation during the meeting prevents delay in getting things done down the road.

## *Avoid a Rush to Judgment*

Beware of letting end-of-meeting madness push everyone into a "Let's just make a decision already, end the suffering, be done with this meeting, and get back to our real jobs" mentality. This can lead to both poor decisions that everyone buys into and to good decisions that no one supports. It's far better to schedule a follow-up meeting to conclude the matter completely.

## *Ponder Your Process*

It's always a good idea to spend a few minutes at the end of every meeting reviewing the success of the process itself. Asking the group to describe what worked well about the meeting and what actions could be taken next time to improve sets the stage for future enhancements.

## Close with Closure

Just as you started on time, end on time. Always leave a few minutes to review the actions assigned during the meeting and to verify the next meeting time. Minutes, including agreed-upon to-do's, should be sent out within a few days.

## Mind Your Meeting Minutes

Don't underestimate the importance of being able to go back and look up minutes from old meetings. They can provide useful information for verifying agreements made, affirming decisions rendered, and determining actions committed to. To keep the facts at your fingertips easily and quickly, file all meeting minutes by date.

# #22.

# Promote Participation in Meetings

Nothing can slow down the momentum of a meeting and waste time like unengaged, uncooperative, or uninterested participants. The problem of engagement is made even more difficult when meeting attendees are distracted by cell phones. Knowing how to deal with these difficult-to-please participants will greatly increase your meeting's effectiveness.

## *Bored and Showing It*

Participants who are bored can bring down the mood of a meeting like a lead balloon. Their refusal to participate leaves you doing all the work. Instead of wading through the molasses of their disinterest, save time and energy by doing a fun exercise that shakes the group out of its doldrums.

Pose a question that relates to the agenda and ask everyone to write down their answer. Then go around the room and have everyone share what they came up with.

Create a five-question quiz that is relevant to the agenda that tests everyone's knowledge of the subject at hand. Have individuals write down their answers on a piece of paper, then go through correct answers and discuss.

## Meeting Hogs

These are the people who know the answer to everything and take issue with anything anyone else says. Left unchecked, they can turn a lively group of participants into a quiet crowd of suppressed attendees. To rein them in, make it clear that you are interested in hearing from everyone in the group by saying:

*"I appreciate you sharing your opinion about this, and now I'd like to hear what other people have to say."*

Break out into discussion groups so participants can share their ideas and opinions in a smaller, "safer" environment. Have a member from each group report on what happened. This technique is also good for dealing with shy people who feel uncomfortable speaking in front of the whole group.

## Angry and Upset

Occasionally, a few individuals (or even your whole group) will be up in arms about a particularly hot agenda item. To keep the session from turning into a time-wasting complain-a-thon, express empathy for the emotion, but suggest that the time in the meeting would best be spent focusing on solutions. Try saying:

> *"I understand that this is upsetting and I can see why you are angry, but I want us to spend our time figuring out how we are going to solve this problem, not just complaining about it."*

## Shy and Timid

It is not unusual for people with great ideas to feel uncomfortable sharing them in a big group. Rather than miss out on their valuable input, encourage quieter members to participate by saying:

> *"I haven't heard much from you this afternoon. Is there anything you'd like to add?"*

## Turn Off Your Screens

It's not unusual in meetings to have attendees who look at their phones reading emails, texts, and the like. While this is often an indication of total boredom, it's also a bad habit that is now considered normal. To maintain focus and participation in your meetings, try something radical. Ask everyone (politely) to put their screens away so that you can move through the meeting quickly and end early. What a concept!

# #23.

# Strengthen Your
# Meeting-Facilitation Skills

According to a 2005 study on meetings published in the *Journal of Applied Psychology,* goal-oriented staff report that their job satisfaction goes down as the number of meetings they attend goes up! Don't just sit back and play the passive part of monitor for the meetings you chair. Instead, take on the proactive role of facilitator using some of the following techniques.

## *Direct the Discussion*

Rather than allowing the meeting to veer off in a variety of different directions based in individual agendas and random streams of consciousness, keep the group focused and on track by gently guiding them toward the stated purpose and agenda of the meeting. If the discussion wanders, try saying one of the following:

- "We have gotten a bit off the topic, let's go back to the main point."

- "I think we should stay focused on . . ."

- "That's a good point, but one that should probably be discussed in a separate meeting."

## *Model Good Listening*

As the facilitator, you set the tone for the meetings you lead. Avoid distracted behaviors like answering your cell phone, text messaging, checking your email, etc. Instead, listen carefully to what is being said and show interest by taking notes, paraphrasing, and nodding. This creates a mood of respect and attention that everyone can emulate. Remember, the more focus people bring to a meeting, the faster it goes.

## *Encourage Participation*

If people feel that they have made a valuable contribution to a meeting, they are less likely to think that their time was wasted. Below are some ways you can encourage participation and give everyone a chance to have his or her say:

- Graciously suggest that a long-winded speaker who is dominating the group discussion get to the heart of the point so that others have time to express their opinions as well.

- Set a two-minute time limit per person for the sharing of ideas and feedback.

- Ask the group a question and go around the room requesting a response from each person.

- Offer to answer excessive and/or off-point questions that are taking up the group's time after the meeting.

## Recap Results

To reaffirm the value of the meeting (and the time invested), summarize the next steps, decisions, and accomplishments that came out of the session before adjourning.

## Establish Ground Rules

Ground rules set out a common code of conduct and help keep unproductive meeting behavior to a minimum. While different ground rules are appropriate for different groups and situations, some of the more common include:

- Don't interrupt when someone else is talking.

- Critique the idea, not the person.

- Be back from breaks on time.

- Don't answer cell phones when in the session.

- Mute your devices.

# Create Connection When Video Conferencing

Anyone who has ever sat in an airport terminal for three or four hours waiting for the weather to clear so a flight can take off knows that travel has become increasingly difficult—not to mention expensive. As a result, video conferencing has become a popular way to bring groups of individuals in various geographic locations together virtually.

According to one study of IT decision-makers and professionals by Forrester Consulting, 74 percent of respondents said that video-conference calls have increased over the past two years. The ability to communicate across the globe and to meet remotely has resulted in more than a 200-fold increase in daily users of video technologies. But bringing meaning to these meetings is another story. To ensure that your video-conference calls are both popular and productive, integrate the following best practices.

## *Test Before Talking*

One of the biggest video-conferencing time-management issues is failing to test connections prior to the start of a session. Keeping ten people waiting while you sort out your technical issues is a sure way to waste the time of those involved. The key is to ensure that the connections are working at least ten minutes prior to the scheduled call.

## Make Mute Your Default

Dogs barking in the background, talking from the adjacent office, the sound of air conditioning whoshing away. Even the smallest sounds can distract participants and steal focus. As a general best practice, ask all participants to mute their microphones at the top of the call.

## Have Someone Lead the Video Conference

In the same way that you would put someone in charge of a face-to-face meeting, put a dedicated facilitator in charge of each video conference to ensure that everyone's time is well spent. A few techniques this leader can use that lend themselves to video conferencing include:

- Use the PAL method described earlier to create a purpose, an agenda, and limits for the call.

- Give participants each two minutes to give an update on their area of responsibility and then facilitate a discussion and/or questions after each person speaks.

- Divide the call into topic sections and ask participants involved in each section to provide their input one at a time. Then facilitate an open discussion with the rest of the group.

## *Try Taking the Video out of Video Conferencing*

Although it may seem counter-intuitive, recent research has highlighted the intense emotional focus required to pay attention on video calls. The continuous staring required on these calls can be more fatiguing than the attention required in face-to-face meetings, where we naturally glance out the window or look at others in the room. Before making video a mandatory part of any meeting, consider if you really need it. Factors such as how well the attendees know each other, how many people are attending the meeting, and how casual or important the topic of the call can help guide your choice about whether to use video—or not.

# Make the Most of an Off-Site

If you or your team needs some concentrated time to sort out a strategy, solve a big problem, or step back and innovate, an off-site meeting may be just what the doctor ordered. Getting away from the office and the usual interruptions can revive your enthusiasm for a business or project and rev up your focus. Use these strategies to make the most of your meeting time away from the office.

## *Have a Sleep-Over*

If possible, stay for longer than a day. Even though you save money by eliminating overnight accommodations, you miss out on the opportunity to socialize and informally discuss work-related issues in the evening.

## *Go Easy on the PowerPoint*

While certain data is no doubt important to communicate, back-to-back PowerPoint presentations and endless ramblings in a half-lit room invite drowsiness—especially after lunch! Instead, create an agenda that incorporates group exercises, discussion, role-plays, hands-on working sessions, demonstrations, and interesting outside speakers.

## *Leave Some Breathing Room*

A tightly packed schedule with no downtime leads to information overload and off-site burn-out. Don't jam each day so chock full of activities that attendees never get a chance to catch their breath and reflect on what's being discussed.

## *Build in Flexibility*

Don't be so tied to an agenda or timeline that a hot, heavy, and important discussion gets shelved just so that you can stay on schedule. The point of the retreat is to draw people in and get them to think, act, and participate in new ways.

## *Play*

While you want your off-site to be productive, you don't want it to be a grind. Setting up activities for play is an important part of the package. These may include a golf outing, dinner at a popular restaurant, a visit to a museum, theater tickets, spa time, etc.

## *Off-Site Checklist*

Here are a few things to consider that can make your off-site a success before you even arrive:

- What is the purpose/theme of the off-site?

- Given the purpose, who should be invited?

- Who will select the site, make the arrangements, and coordinate with the site management?

- What kind of "welcome" packet do you want attendees to receive on arrival?

- Do you need audiovisual equipment? If so, who will be responsible for it?

- Who is your contact person at the site? Is this the person to whom any deliveries should be addressed?

- Will you have any presentations during lunch or dinner? If so, is the catering department aware of your plans?

- Do you want organized entertainment in the evenings? What will it be and who will organize it?

- What time is staff expected to arrive? Do they need driving directions? Is a meal being served upon arrival? Are you offering vegetarian food to those who need it?

- Once at the site, who will be responsible for overseeing arrivals, room allocation, and registration?

- How do you want to begin and end the off-site?

# #26.

# Use Meetings to Step Back and Solve Problems

Contrary to the belief (popular among high achievers and productivity superstars) that it's better to fire first and aim second, taking just a small amount of time on the front end to reflect on a problem can save frustration and effort on the back end. Short, to-the-point meetings can provide a great opportunity to get things done the right way—the first time. The following guidelines will help you structure a meeting specifically designed for problem-solving.

## *Find the Real Cause of the Problem*

Is the problem you have identified the real one or just a sign of a deeper issue? Coming up with solutions that address the symptoms of a problem may be a good interim step, but if you don't get to the heart of what's not working, more effort will be required down the road. A good way to get at the cause of the perceived problem is to ask yourself and your co-workers: Why does this problem really exist? Keep asking that question until you get to what you consider to be the essential cause.

For example, if the initial problem was stated as "The quality of our responses to incoming phone calls has deteriorated," reflection and discussion may reveal that your staff needs training on the new telephone system. Even further inquiry may make it clear that the underlying reason is that you can't take staff off the phones long enough to put them through the training program!

## Brainstorm Possible Solutions

The whole idea behind brainstorming is to encourage as many ideas as possible to come forth. Sometimes, an idea that seems crazy and far-fetched can become the initiative and inspiration that leads to a stellar solution. For example, if the cause of the problem is that you can't take staff off the phones long enough to get them trained, some possible solutions may include:

- Design a shorter phone training that fits into your shift schedule.

- Take the current four-hour training and break it down into four, one-hour modules.

- Pay staff to come in on their off-time to attend the training.

- Turn the live training into an online program with home-study manuals.

## Choose a Viable Solution

After listing a few possible solutions, it will become obvious which ones are the most practical. Before leaping head-first into a solution, however, be sure to consider:

- The short-term impact of the solution

- The long-term impact of the solution

- The relative cost of implementing the solution

- The availability of resources needed to implement the solution

- The commitment and support of management needed to implement the solution

- The chances that the solution will create a new problem(s)

## *Implement Force Field Analysis*

If you're thinking about implementing a change (personal or business, big or small), you can avoid the wasted time of a less-than-viable solution by applying Force Field Analysis—a four-step process that helps you objectively assess the barriers to and drivers toward a successful solution. In order for any change to take hold, the driving forces (those pushing for the change) must be greater than the hindering forces (those pushing against it).

- Write down the specific proposed change/solution on a worksheet divided into two columns.

- In the left-hand column, list all the forces that are hindering or pushing *against* the proposed change/solution.

- In the right-hand column, list all the forces that are supporting or pushing *for* the proposed change/solution.

- Using a scale of 1 to 10 (1 = weak, 10 = strong), score the relative strength of each of the forces. Do this for both columns.

Here's an example. Imagine you are considering hiring a full-time web-marketing expert to do a search-engine-optimization campaign for your small business. Your worksheet might look like this:

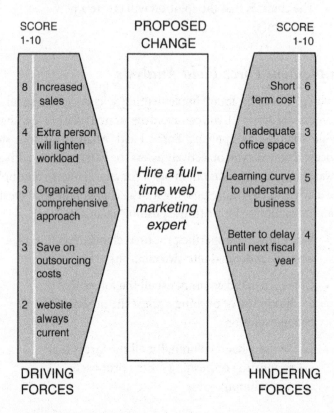

## FORCE FIELD ANALYSIS EXAMPLE

| SCORE 1-10 | DRIVING FORCES | PROPOSED CHANGE | HINDERING FORCES | SCORE 1-10 |
|---|---|---|---|---|
| 8 | Increased sales | | Short term cost | 6 |
| 4 | Extra person will lighten workload | *Hire a full-time web marketing expert* | Inadequate office space | 3 |
| 3 | Organized and comprehensive approach | | Learning curve to understand business | 5 |
| 3 | Save on outsourcing costs | | Better to delay until next fiscal year | 4 |
| 2 | website always current | | | |

# FORCE FIELD ANALYSIS WORKSHEET

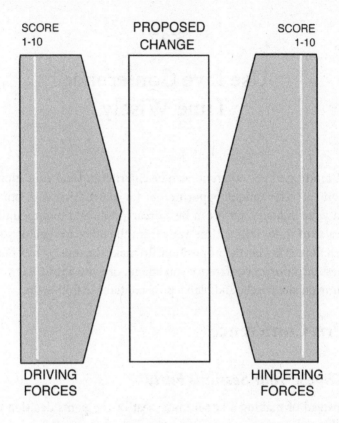

SCORE
1-10

PROPOSED
CHANGE

SCORE
1-10

DRIVING
FORCES

HINDERING
FORCES

Looking at the worksheet, this decision will more than likely be successful because the driving forces outweigh the hindering forces by two points. If the opposite were true and the hindering forces were greater than the driving forces, the chances of success would be reduced.

# #27.

# Use Live Conference
# Time Wisely

Attending a live conference can be entertaining and educational and can offer unique opportunities for networking with others in your industry. Or it can be a dreary, dull, and disappointing waste of time. Taking time away from the office for you or your employees is a costly proposition. To make the most of any business or industry conference you attend, prepare ahead, use your time on site wisely, and plan a post-conference follow-up.

## Pre-Conference

### *Choose Your Sessions Early*

Instead of making a last-minute, seat-of-the-pants decision on what sessions to attend over coffee and croissants the morning of the conference, take the time to review the conference agenda and sessions well in advance. This gives you time to check out the websites of various presenters, research best recommendations from colleagues, and put together a more well-rounded agenda.

To get the most bang for your buck when choosing tracks, give strong consideration to sessions that:

- Offer a practical application of the topic being discussed

- Expand your current knowledge and skill set

- Fall outside your comfort zone and stretch you to learn something new and/or challenging

- Are presented by someone you admire or have wanted to hear speak for a long time

## *Set Up Appointments in Advance*

Do some research on which vendors, colleagues, and potential customers may be attending the same conference and set up appointments now to meet with them later. Many people wait and hope to contact people casually at conferences. While this type of spontaneous get-together does occur and can be helpful, some opportunities should not be left to chance.

## *Prepare an Elevator Speech*

You will be asked this one question dozens (if not hundreds) of times as you stand in line for the breakfast buffet, settle into your seat for a session, and sip coffee on a break: What do you do?

Having a pithy and punchy description of your work (project, goal, or dream) will make networking and standing around in line more productive. The key is to develop a snappy and interesting thirty-second description (elevator speech) of what you do.

## *Plan to Stay at the Conference Hotel*

Even super-duper large conference hotels sometimes book up in advance. As soon as you know you want to attend a conference, book a room at the hosting hotel or one as close as possible to the location where the events will be held. Staying at the conference hotel will save you time in the morning, since your commute will be in an elevator, not on a congested roadway. Likewise, taking breaks, making phone calls, and checking emails is more comfortable and convenient in the privacy of your own room, just a few floors above.

# At the Conference

## *Have a Back-Up Plan*

If, fifteen minutes into your carefully chosen session, your eyes start to roll up into the back of your head, have a back-up plan in mind.

## *Map Out Where You Are Going*

Study the event map and figure out at the beginning of each day the route you will follow to get to each session. This will save you having to sprint through corridors, run over roads, and dash down tunnels in order to be on time. Remember to leave extra time for slow elevators and side conversations.

# Manage Your Energy

Really listening hour after hour and day after day takes more energy than you realize. To make sure you have the stamina to focus on what you are learning, get enough sleep and be mindful of your alcohol intake at the evening events. A hangover will most certainly not improve your concentration. In addition, conferences are notorious for testing the intestinal fortitude of even the strongest among us. To avoid falling asleep a few minutes into your first afternoon session, forego the chocolate decadence cheese cake fudge brownie à la mode at lunch.

## *Maximize Networking*

Set a goal to meet at least one new person each day of the conference. The more you participate in the sessions and activities offered, the more value you will take away. Whenever practical, attend the conference with a colleague or co-worker. By attending different sessions, you can swap what you learned and, in effect, each have attended two sessions at the same time. Now that's time management in an instant!

# Post-Conference

## *Schedule a Post-Conference Follow-Up*

The business cards you gathered at the conference are so exciting when you first get them that they seem to burn a hole in your pocket! But back at the office, those same cards, amidst all the things you now have to catch up on, can seem like a rock weighing you down. Within a few days of the conference (or on the plane ride home), make a to-do list of the people you need to follow up with and the actions you want to take. Transfer all relative information from the brochures and business cards to the list, open up your calendar, and commit to a specific date and time within the next week to process the items on the list.

# PART 6

# Maximize Your To-Do Lists and Calendars

If you're like most people, the first thing that pops into your mind when you think of time management is a daily to-do list. Hardly a novel idea. Time-management gurus and business big shots alike have been touting their use for an eternity. There is just something so satisfying about writing down an item and then checking it off.

But beyond the feel-good factor, daily to-do lists help you allocate your time, prioritize your efforts, and focus your energies. Survey after survey for the past eighty years have concluded the same immutable fact: Even when you are overwhelmed with tasks, the most important thing you can do is make a plan on how to get them done, starting with a to-do list. Writing down tasks makes you more effective.

# #28.

# Create an Effective
# Daily To-Do List

Here are some pointers on how to construct an effective to-do list:

- List items that *have* to get done, as well as items you *want* to do.

- Create a roadmap of what you think you can realistically achieve in a day, not a fantasy of what you wish you could do. An overly ambitious to-do list will leave you feeling disheartened and de-motivated at the end of the day.

- Plan items that can be completed in one or two action steps that day.

- Build in flexibility so you are able to adjust as emergencies and interruptions arise.

- Save time by grouping similar activities like phone calls, errands, and emails together so they can be done all at once.

- Choose several items with different priorities, including a few that are not urgent but are still important to get done.

- At the end of each day, transfer items that did not get done to the next day's to-do list or to another date in the future.

- Review the list periodically during the day to keep the tasks front and center in your mind.

Despite its ease of use and obvious benefit, many people still don't avail themselves of this essential time-management tool.

# Don't Be Short-Sighted

While a daily to-do list helps you administer short-term action items, there are three additional categories of to-do lists that can help you capture and manage longer-term tasks, goals, dreams, commitments, and projects—both business and personal.

## Eyes on the Prize

Three techniques that can keep you from being short-sighted and help you look forward are:

- Monthly to-do lists
- Project lists
- Someday to-do lists

## Monthly To-Do Lists

A monthly to-do list is the perfect place to write down objectives that are not urgent, but are still important and contain multiple steps. For example, let's say it's February and you want to update your finances. While not a specific action item itself, there are lots of related one-step tasks that can help you accomplish this goal that you could put in your weekly or daily schedule, including:

- Make an appointment with the attorney to revise your will.

- Call your stockbroker and review all your current positions.

- Complete the retirement-planner questionnaire your accountant sent you.

- Apply for house refinance at current lower rates.

- Balance your checkbook.

## Project Lists

A project list is a perfect holding place for items that take a longer period of time to come to fruition (months and years instead of days and weeks). Give each project an overall project title and an associated list of major milestones. For example, if your project is to remodel your office, the major milestones may include:

- Develop an overall budget.

- Select an architect to oversee the job.

- Survey staff to determine the most desired and needed changes.

- Come up with initial renderings.

Each of these milestones will then generate a list of specific tasks connected with it, which you can place on your monthly, weekly, and daily to-do lists.

## Someday To-Do Lists

Everyone has one—the "someday when I retire, make more money, have more time, get around to it" wish list. These are the good ideas you want to get done someday. Even if they seem as if they are an eternity away, write them down. You may or may not ever get around to them, but, by capturing them on paper, you won't spend your cerebral energy trying to hold them in your mind.

# #29.

# Retool Your Priority System

In his book, *CEO Logic: How to Think and Act Like a Chief Executive*, Ray Johnson writes,

> *Prioritizing is the answer to time-management problems —not computers, efficiency experts, or matrix scheduling. You do not need to do work faster or to eliminate gaps in productivity to make better use of your time. You need to spend more time on the right things ...*

While many people prioritize their tasks, most use a system that is based on emergency and crisis. They assign items an A, B, C (or 1, 2, 3) value based on which fire needs to be put out first! The problem with this method is that it only addresses the actions that impact you now and not the ones (like your goals and projects) that affect you in the future. To retool your priority system, start by distinguishing between tasks that are urgent and those that are important.

- Urgent tasks are those that require immediate action and attention.

- Important tasks are those that move you closer to an important goal.

## *Urgent Tasks Unrelated to Your Goals*

While everyone has urgent tasks that must get done, these tasks are often not important. In other words, they may produce the lowest return (for the time and energy you invest) toward your most important business and personal goals. A priority system that gives these urgent-but-not-goal-related items a value of A or 1 keeps you stuck in resolving emergencies or maintaining the status quo. Unfortunately, it also prevents you from paying sufficient attention to the items that move you toward your goals and objectives. To retool your priority system, assign items that are urgent but unimportant (i.e., not goal-related) a priority value of C.

## *Goal-Related Tasks That Are Urgent*

Some items on your to-do list are both urgent *and* related to your goals. In other words, the return you get for the time and energy you invest in these items is high. To retool your priority system, assign items that are urgent and important (i.e., goal-related) a priority value of A.

## *Goal-Related Tasks That Are Not Urgent*

Think of one thing that, if done on a regular basis, would improve the quality of your life. Chances are this item—whatever it is—is important but not urgent. Too often, the actions that have a very high return for the time and energy invested sit by the wayside because they are not nagging at you to get done. To retool your priority system, assign items that are goal-related but not urgent a priority value of B.

Let's say that some of your most important business and personal goals include:

- Redesign sales onboarding process.

- Increase sales by 10% this quarter.

- Learn to water ski.

- Plan a family trip to Hawaii next summer.

Using the above criteria to prioritize, your to-do list may look something like this:

| Task | A/B/C |
|------|-------|
| Make bank deposit (urgent, but not goal-related) | C |
| Research Hawaii hotels (goal-related, but not urgent) | B |
| Increase sales-team headcount | A |
| Collect feedback about current onboarding pros and cons | B |
| Return call to unhappy customer (urgent and important) | A |
| Research water ski schools on the web | B |

## *Exercise*

Write down in the chart below several to-do items you got done yesterday. Using the above priority system, assign each one an A, B, or C priority.

| Task | A/B/C |
|---|---|
|  |  |
|  |  |
|  |  |
|  |  |
|  |  |
|  |  |

# #30.

# Utilize the Four D's

The daily to-do list. It's both the bane of freewheeling, spontaneous entrepreneurs and the savior of compulsive, high-powered players everywhere. Whichever side you fall on psychologically, the list remains one of the best time-management tools around. Writing down all your intended achievements for the day is only part of the story, however. Deciding on what to do with each task is the other. To maximize your effectiveness, efficiency, and energy for every item on your list, decide which of these four D's applies to it.

## *Do*

Some items on your daily to do-list excite and inspire you to seize the day and make them happen—now. Others just have to get done by a certain deadline. In either case, for tasks that must find their way to the finish line today—as the Nike commercial says—"Just Do It."

The key questions to ask here are:

- Is this an item that can easily and quickly be done now?

- Is this an item I have set aside a specific period of time to do?

- Is this an item that will take less than five minutes to complete?

## *Dump*

Some actions make their way through your calendar, transferred from day to day or week to week. If you find yourself continually putting off an item, it's usually due to three things.

- The task is too big and needs to be broken down into bite-size chunks.

- The task is not clearly defined enough for you to take action on it.

- The task is something you don't really want, need, or intend to do.

If this last reason fits, there is no shame in saying "no" to an action—especially if it's one you thought up. If, however, the item came from your boss, while it may be tempting to dump it, that's probably not a good idea.

The key questions to ask here are:

- Do I really need or want to do this?

- Is this something I am committed to or just a good idea?

- Do I have this item on my list out of desire or guilt?

## Delegate

Just because you thought up the task does not mean you have to be the one to execute it. One of the best strategies for instantly creating time is to transfer an item to someone else's inbox. Consideration, of course, needs to be given to the other person's availability, ability, and willingness. Still, you can always consider the option of passing on a piece of the work to someone else.

The key questions to ask here are:

- Do I really need to be the one to do this item?

- Is there someone else equally or more competent whom I could pay to do this or to whom I could pass on the task?

## Defer

Many items on your daily to-do list are there just as place-holders for ideas or tasks that could be accomplished within a greater time frame. By reflecting on your priorities, goals, and commitments, you can more easily determine which bits and pieces don't require action today but can be put off until tomorrow. The key here is to write down the item immediately on another date when you plan to get it done.

The key questions to ask here are:

- Is it essential or important that this be done today, or can it wait?

- Will there be any serious negative consequences if I delay doing this item?

# The Four D's in Action

One way to invoke the four D's actively every day is to mark them on your to-do list. By taking a decisive action on each task, you complete it for that day.

In the example below, every to-do item on the list has been categorized as:

√     Done

→     Deferred

D     Delegated

X     Dumped

| Task | Priority | √ |
|------|:--------:|:-:|
| Complete expense report for Thailand trip | B | → |
| Email boss re next week's sales kickoff | A | √ |
| Call district manager to discuss problem on Adams account | A | √ |
| Upgrade laptop system software | C | → |
| Schedule video conference with team for product launch | A | D |
| Add Carol to database for newsletter distribution | B | √ |
| Get noise-cancelling headphones for upcoming trip | C | X |

## Exercise

Take a look at your to-do list from yesterday and today. Which items got done? Check them off now. Are there any items you have decided you should abandon? Cross them off or put an X next to them now. What items can you delegate and to whom? Put a D next to them now. Which items need to be deferred to another day, week, month, or even year? Move them and then put an arrow next to them now. How do you feel? Relieved? Energized? More complete? Making a firm decision about your next action on an item is one of the keys to energy management.

# #31.

# Choose Paper or Digital

We spend a lot of our lives plugged into the digital world, so using our smartphones, tablets, or laptops to manage our tasks seems like a no-brainer. While most of us enjoy having our calendars readily available on our digital devices, having your to-do's on the same device as your news, social media, phone, messages, flight itinerary, GPS, house alarm, weather report, stock ticker, and browser can lead to confusion, distraction, and—if things don't sync correctly—frustration and the dreaded deletion!

So which path should you choose? Here's a checklist to inform your choice:

- Use a high-tech, digital solution if:

    You find it works well and you love accessing your lists from different devices.

    You share your tasks with others in your network.

    You don't have that many to-do's each day.

    Your job would make a paper planner inconvenient to carry (sky diver, lion tamer, scuba diver, etc.).

Your to-do's get deferred or deleted as a normal part of your day.

- A low-tech, paper solution may work better if:

   You like the feeling of pen on paper.

   You are following our to-do list system and the columns are easier to add on paper.

   You like to make notes quickly without having to find an app.

   You get frustrated/distracted by online solutions.

   Syncing continues to be one of the great mysteries of the universe.

   You find it easy and satisfying to navigate a planner or notebook.

   You're a Luddite. Period.

# Putting Together a Paper Planner

Paper planners come with a plethora of pages, some of which, while nifty at first glance, don't really do much for you in the way of productivity. And they can be heavy as a brick. What you need are the following basics that allow you to manage your day, week, and month sanely.

## *To-Do List*

These are the daily pages where you list your tasks for the day and add any relevant notes/memos. Often, the columns of pre-printed pages aren't enough, so feel free to draw in your own. If you're not the type who writes your to-do's down more than a week ahead, then carry only seven daily pages at a time. At the end of one week, take out the old pages (you may want to archive them) and add the next seven days of fresh pages. Be sure to transfer any items that were not finished from last week.

## Notes

Always have blank paper on hand in your planner so that you can capture any notes that don't fit into your appointment calendar or to-do list. This also allows you to take careful notes at big meetings to help you stay focused.

## Projects

For easy access, it's a good idea to give each project you are working on its own separate page(s). As you plan for a certain task associated with the project to be completed on a specific day, move that task to your daily to-do list.

# #32.

# Generate Energy with Your To-Do List

Whenever you complete something (big or small), an eruption of energy bursts forth and livens up your day with a sense of accomplishment. For example, think of the thrill you get when you put a check mark next to an item on your to-do list, finally finish up that six-month project, or even clean out your pencil cup.

Although time can't really be managed (an hour, after all, is an hour), your energy can be. One of the underlying principles of time management is that closure creates energy. Anytime you finish something (regardless of its size), you increase the amount of liveliness you experience. This can manifest in many ways, including feeling relieved, uplifted, inspired, renewed, energized, delighted, thrilled, and proud.

Continually creating closure can help you stay motivated. And one of the best sources for producing ongoing energy is your average, everyday to-do list.

Assume that you have a daily to-do list that looks something like this:

| Task | Priority |
|------|:--------:|
| Complete expense report for Thailand trip | B |
| Email boss re next week's sales kickoff | A |
| Call district manager to discuss problem on Adams account | A |
| Upgrade laptop system software | C |
| Schedule video conference with team for product launch | A |
| Add Carol to database for newsletter distribution | B |
| Get noise-cancelling headphones for upcoming trip | C |

Standard operating procedure for many people is to work their way (between interruptions) through the list and, at the end of the day, to realize their gains and give a mental nod to their efforts. The tasks that fell by the wayside are often transferred to the next day's to-do list.

The problem with this system is that it overlooks the ongoing opportunity to generate energy all day long by recognizing what got done—*on the spot*. The key is to acknowledge the completion of an item (regardless of size or priority) as soon as it's finished by:

- Putting a checkmark next to the item
- Crossing it off the list
- Highlighting the item

Assume that you have already been at work for a few hours and have completed several of the items on your to-do list. Your updated list might look like this:

| Task | Priority | √ |
|---|---|---|
| Complete expense report for Thailand trip | B | |
| Email boss re next week's sales kickoff | A | √ |
| Call district manager to discuss problem on Adams account | A | √ |
| Upgrade laptop system software | C | |
| Schedule video conference with team for product launch | A | |
| Add Carol to database for newsletter distribution | B | √ |
| Get noise-cancelling headphones for upcoming trip | C | |

By taking a few seconds to acknowledge that an item has been completed, you charge up your closure battery throughout the day, instead of just at the end of it. Try it and see. Open up today's to-do list. Are there any items on it that you have finished but not recognized by checking them off? If so, do it now! How did that make you feel?

# Add Your Interruptions

If you find yourself fielding a lot of interruptions resulting in new to-do items during the day, add them to your list and check them off when completed. By recognizing these new entries as complete, you can turn them from time-stealers into energy-creators.

# PART 7

# Minimize Unfinished Business

Everyone has, at one time or another, experienced both the energetic lift of getting things done and the down-and-out doldrums of unfinished business. Anything that lacks closure (no matter how small) has the potential to drain your liveliness and steal your focus. This can manifest by feeling worried, stressed, depressed, overwhelmed, grumpy, guilty, frustrated, and tired. Here's a typical example of how you can start off in the morning with lots of energy and good intentions, yet end up with your spirit sapped and your energy drained because the little things around you have been left incomplete.

## A Day in the Life of Small and Seemingly Insignificant Incompletions

To begin with, you wake up refreshed and raring to go. There are a lot of exciting things happening at work these days, and your job puts you right in the middle of the action. Driving into work, you stare out at the traffic, tossing over in your mind the proposal that you promised to send yesterday but didn't.

Arriving at work, you walk into your office and notice the broken printer (which you have been meaning to take to the recycling center for the past few months) still shoved in the corner. As you open up your email, your eye catches the blinking yellow light on the postage machine which has been flashing its "low postage" warning for the past few days.

Turning your attention to your desk, a stack of folders that needs to be sorted and filed catches your eye. Holding them down is a makeshift paperweight—your half-filled mug of cold coffee, just where you put it last night before you left. You turn on your computer and attempt to locate the proposal you should have done yesterday, that you must get done today. Unfortunately, your desktop is covered with files and it's difficult to locate the proposal.

Frustrated at not being able to find the proposal, you check your email. Several messages from yesterday need to be answered and, overnight, a few new urgent ones came in. You need to attend to them, but you are suddenly feeling *so* tired that you swoop up your mug and head straight for the coffee machine. What happened to all that vim and vigor you started with just a few hours ago? Drained away by the droves of unfinished business.

Why is it that such seemingly little things can have such a big impact? Think of your brain as a computer with a limited (a very large but still limited) amount of memory. The fuller it becomes, the less capacity it has to process new information efficiently. Regardless of whether your incomplete items are at home or at work, they all contribute to how much focus you can bring to bear on the tasks at hand.

## *Exercise*

To clear away the mental clutter and create more space, make a list of those tasks that lack closure and then make a plan to get them done—or at least decide that you are never going to get them done and declare them complete. Use the following list to help you identify a few general areas where unfinished business often lurks. Circle each item as either:

A – In good shape

B – Needs work

C – Needs serious attention

- My closets and drawers are organized and uncluttered.

  A   B   C

  If not, what needs to be done?

  _____

- My home repairs are up-to-date.

  A   B   C

  If not, what needs to be done?

  _____

- My finances are in order

  A   B   C

  If not, what needs to be done?

  _____

- My office space is neat and organized.

  A   B   C

  If not, what needs to be done?

  _____

- My computer files are organized and easy to find.

  A   B   C

  If not, what needs to be done?

  _____

- I am up-to-date with my phone calls and emails.

  A   B   C

  If not, what needs to be done?

  _____

- I am up-to-date on my commitments with clients.

  A   B   C

  If not, what needs to be done?

  _____

- I am up-to-date on my commitments with co-workers.

  A   B   C

  If not, what needs to be done?

  _____

- I have no conversations that I am putting off.

  A   B   C

  If not, what needs to be done?

  _____

Take a few minutes and look over your B and C items. Choose two that you find yourself thinking about often and commit to taking some action on them within the next week. Actually sit down and schedule some time to get them done. Continue this process every week until all your B and C items have moved into the A column.

Now that you have gotten an overview of where your current level of completion stands, it's time to take on the specifics of creating closure. Despite living in an online world, it's still essential to start with your actual stuff.

# #33.

# Sort Your Stuff

Stuff. It's everywhere. Pencil cups overflowing, online files to the max, and, the digital world aside, paperwork piled a mile high. Everyone needs their business bits and pieces, but taken to an extreme, out-of-control stuff becomes clutter. And clutter saps your energy and slows you down. If your clutter-clearing efforts have fallen short, don't despair. Below is an easy process to sort out your physical stuff and reclaim your space—one drawer at a time.

## *Choose a Limited Area to Work On*

Assuming you don't have an entire day to dedicate to the decluttering of your office, choose a single "stuff-sorting" area to work on. Be sure to allot an adequate amount of time so that you can finish what you start. For example, if your whole desk needs cleaning out, but you only have thirty minutes, start with your two top drawers.

# Do a "T" Scan

Moving in a logical direction (right to left, top to bottom, front to back), scan the stuff in front of you and, as you come across each item, assign it a category—trash, treasure, transfer, or temptation. Then act accordingly.

- Trash: An item that no longer works, you no longer need, or you no longer like. It has outlived its usefulness and is ready to make the journey from your office to the wastebasket.

    Action: Throw this out now! If the item is still in good working shape, put it in a box to give to charity.

- Treasure: An item you need, you like, and/or you use. It belongs exactly where it is.

    Action: Don't do a thing. Leave it as it and be glad you found it.

- Transfer: An item that you want to keep, but that does not belong in the location where you found it.

    Action: Put it in a box for transfer to its proper place when the sorting session is over.

- Temptation: An item over which you feel conflicted. Part of you wants to keep it and part of you is not sure you will ever use it. To help decide, ask yourself:

    Do I have more than one of these?

    How useful will this *really* be in the future?

When was the last time I used this?

Is this something I need to keep for legal reasons?

What is the worst thing that could happen if I get rid of this?

Make a decision now. For better or worse, choose a course of action on this item and bring it to closure.

## *Organize Your Stuff*

This is the part of the sorting session where you begin to think of plastic as the most magical substance every invented. Using a variety of drawer, desk, and cabinet organizers, rearrange your "treasures" so you can easily see and access them.

Now, step back, breathe deeply, and declare this area a clutter-free zone!

# #34.

# Tame Your Paper Tiger

Long, long ago in a galaxy far, far away, we all used paper to keep track of our various and sundry appointments, to-do's, potential clients, and other business activities. Today, our calendars are mostly kept on our phones, our client information lives online, and our to-do lists float out there in the cloud.

And yet . . . one glance around our homes and offices reveals towering piles of paper stuffed into overflowing inboxes. Despite our appetite for electronic organizing, paper still seems to be a big part of the time-management scene.

The first step in taming your paper tiger is to go through your desktop inbox regularly, one piece of paper at a time. Start from the top of the pile and make a decision about what your next action is going to be for each item. Decide how you want to handle each item according to the following categories.

## *Now Paperwork*

These are things that require your immediate attention. For example, items for signature, urgent memos, time-limited to-do's, etc. When you come across an item like this in your inbox, if you can deal with it in two to five minutes, do it on the spot. You'll get a warm and tingly feeling when you only have to handle that piece of paper once. On the other hand, if the item requires more time to process (ten minutes or longer), schedule a specific time and day when you can do it, within the next two days. This prevents you from forgetting and suffering the consequences of not handling a time-sensitive item.

## Later Paperwork

These are the items on which you intend to take action but that don't require the immediate attention of those in the Now category. They may include invoices, bills, inquiries, brochures, etc. This group also includes items about which you need more information in order to process. To avoid a plethora of Later papers turning your inbox into the leaning tower of Pisa, place these items in a second inbox or file folder marked "In process" and review them once a week, moving as many as possible to the Now pile.

## Reference Paperwork

While you don't need to take any specific action on these items, you may want to reference the material down the road. For example, at tax time, you will need all your receipts from the year readily available. For items that fall into this category, place them, clearly labeled, in your filing system.

# Windows of Time

You can spend two minutes, two hours, or two days processing the items in your inbox. In order to be most efficient, decide ahead of time how much time you will spend in a particular session.

- The two-minute window: Pick one item that requires only one quick step to process and finish it.

- The good five minutes: Some items can't be done in a nanosecond, but are only a few steps away from completion—for example mailing a brochure. The next time you find yourself with a spare five minutes (it could happen), pick one of these items and do it.

- The hour purge: If you have several hefty items in your box that will take multiple steps to complete and require research, plan on this longer window of time to get them done.

- The dedicated day: If you have spring cleaning fever and your inbox is a total disaster, consider setting aside a day (even a Saturday) to just plow through and process it all.

# #35.

# Clean Out Your Physical File Drawers

Now that you've gained some ground on your desktop paperwork, it's time to look under the rock, so to speak, and take on your paper filing system. Unfortunately, before you can create a new super-organized filing system, you must tackle the dreaded task of cleaning out the old one.

While it may feel daunting to plod through the dusty memos of yesteryear, it can be uplifting to find forgotten (but important) bits and pieces, and energizing to throw away all that unnecessary paper. Working from front to back, start with one file and, as you examine the contents, ask yourself these questions.

## *What Actions Do I Need to Take on This?*

If seeing the contents of the file sparks any actions you need to take, make a note of them on your to-do list and/or schedule a time to get them done. For example, a memo from a senior executive in your company requesting ideas on a new product launch, or information on a potential new customer account, or a brochure for an upcoming conference. If you need to keep the data in the file until you complete the action item, either put it in a file or in your inbox. If not, throw it out and use the to-do list as your ticker to get it done.

## *Do I Need This for Tax or Legal Purposes?*

While the item may be taking up space in your system, if you need to keep it for legal or tax purposes, label it clearly for easy retrieval down the road and then re-file. This category can include papers you may need for an audit, old contracts that apply to current vendor relationships, invoices, expense records, and other items not duplicated elsewhere. If you are not sure, keep it until you are *certain* that it is safe to discard.

## *Is This Recent Reference Material?*

Out-of-date journals, old brochures from distant conventions, and invitations to networking events long-since over have no place in your current filling system. Dump them immediately! Keep other reference items like articles, brochures, course notes, and seminar workbooks that are still of use now or in the near future.

## *Will I Really Ever Need This Again?*

Don't fall into the trap of saving something just because there is a small chance that someday, in some way, somehow, you may need it. Instead, ask yourself if you can think of a specific (and realistic) situation in which this document could be useful or needed. If not, send it to the big wastepaper basket in the sky.

When all else fails, ask yourself: "What is the worst possible thing that could happen if I threw this away?" If you can live with the answer, toss it.

## Scan It

The proliferation of small, multi-sheet scanners (including phone apps) makes it easier than ever to scan multipage documents that you still want to keep, but not as a hard copy in your files.

# #36.

# Review and Renew
# Your Paper Files

From the outside, all file drawers look neat and organized. But when you open them, the ugly truth is revealed. If your system is a muddled mess, you are probably in need of some R&R—relabeling and reorganizing. Before you begin, gather together the following supplies:

- Hanging file folders (legal or letter with plastic attachable tabs)

- Manila files (legal or letter, 3 or 5 cut)

- Adhesive labels (white or clear)

- Black marking pen

- Label maker (optional)

Supplies in hand, start by making a list of the broad categories you will need. These categories form the core structure of your system and will be used to label your hanging folders. Examples of common categories include:

- Clients
- Conferences
- Contracts
- Finances
- Insurance
- Legal
- Office equipment
- Projects
- Research
- Travel

Once you have a complete list, make a hanging-file label for each category and insert it in the plastic holder. When attached to the folder, these sit above the tops of all other files and can be seen and accessed easily. Place the labeled hanging folders in your filing system. Depending on your preference, you can either arrange them alphabetically or place those more frequently used toward the front.

Next, sort each of your main categories into sub-categories to be used in labeling your manila file folders. For example, the Clients hanging folder may be broken down into one file for each individual account; the Finances hanging folder may contain a folder for expense reports, one for invoices, and one for 401 K; the Office Equipment hanging folder may require a separate manila folder for individual items like your computer, printer, phone, and copier.

Now the exciting part. Once you have the sub-category list complete, label each manila folder and place it behind the appropriate broad-category hanging file. Sort the manila folders in each category alphabetically to make finding them as easy as possible.

## Choose Your Words Carefully

When creating a filing system, be sure to choose words that have the most meaning to you. For example, are you more likely to look for the file that says:

- Finances or Money?
- Car or Automobile?
- Clients or Accounts?
- Travel or Trips?
- Research or Reference?

The point of a filing system is to help you retrieve items you need quickly and easily, not just stockpile paperwork. Labeling items in a way that is the most natural to how you think and talk will make this easier.

# #37.

# Capture Your Open Items

Open items are those tasks, to-do's, projects, goals, ideas, and actions (business or personal) that you need or want to do but have not yet done. They may tug at you to get them done today or be as far off in the future as retirement. The trick is to gather them together by *writing them down* so that you don't have to waste valuable mental real estate trying to keep track of them.

Think of your brain as a computer hard drive that can only hold so much data. When a hard drive reaches its capacity, it starts to slow down and wonky things happen. By capturing your open items on a list, your brain is freed up to focus on what's in front of you right now. The ideas and to-do items that comprise these lists come from a variety of sources, including:

- Conversations with family, friends, and business associates

- Something you read (books, magazines, business briefs, research papers)

- Items you receive in the mail (brochures, invitations, pamphlets)

- Emails

- Classes you take

- Conferences you attend

- Voicemail

- Professional groups you have joined

- Meetings you attend

- Your inbox

- Your desktop

- Your file drawers

- Your closets, cupboards, and cabinets

If you only do one activity from this book, make it this one. Just taking the time to capture all the open items in your life and write them down can dramatically improve your ability to focus and get things done. You can do this all in one sitting (in which case you will need at least a day) or in short spurts. To drain your brain, try the following techniques.

## Go Through All Your Physical Spaces

At work and at home, look through your desk drawers, desktop, inbox, closets, cupboards, shelves, and file drawers and make a master to-do list of anything that needs to be done based on what you see. For example, when you look in your file drawer, you may need to clean out last year's financial file and store the receipts, make file-folder labels for the most recently added documents, or follow up with a potential client whose business card you found stuck in one of the folders.

## Go Through Your Electronic Spaces

Look through your email inbox and voicemails and add any action items to the existing master to-do list that you are not going to handle immediately and that are not recorded elsewhere. For example, an email from a colleague requesting that you make a few changes to a report you wrote, a voice message from your brother about possible dates for a family reunion, an email from the professional association of crawfish-catchers announcing their annual crab-feed fund-raiser.

## Go Through Your Own Brain

Look through your own mind and, using the source list above, write down any relevant to-do items. Once you have done this final emptying out, you can keep your system squeaky clean by adding to your master to-do list anything that pops into your head.

# #38.

# Break Down Your Big To-Do's into Bite-Size Pieces

Urban legend and Internet lore has it that on June 20, 1995, Dick Miller completed eating the last chunk of a 2,800-pound automobile. He started with two lug nuts and finished, five years later, by devouring the last of the clutch housing. So the next time you get stopped dead in your tracks by a colossal, gargantuan, oversized, almost-impossible-to-surmount project, remember to do what the mysterious Mr. Miller did, and break your endeavor down into digestible, doable, bite-size pieces.

BIG CHUNK SIZE

SMALL CHUNK SIZE

Thankfully, in the world of work, breaking down tasks doesn't require eating a car (although some of your tasks may be just as difficult to swallow). Instead, it means looking at your projects, goals, and more daunting tasks from a new perspective.

Breaking tasks down is about determining the actions you can quickly and easily take, without getting overwhelmed.

Traditional project management involves breaking a large project down into logical milestones. For example, if you have a goal to implement a company-wide training on diversity in the workplace, your main objectives may include:

1. Form a task team to determine key learning objectives for the training and set up a weekly video-conference call.

2. Create a request for proposal (RFP) for potential vendors.

3. Select a vendor.

4. Create a master class schedule.

5. Conduct post-training assessments online.

Although these steps represent a logical progression, all these actions are fairly substantial and could seem overwhelming to implement—which, in turn, can lead to procrastination. Upon closer examination, each of these milestones is composed of a string of mini-tasks. For example, selecting a vendor can be broken down into the following series of smaller to-do's:

1. Develop a list of accredited vendors to receive the RFP.

2. Send the RFP out to the potential vendor list via email.

3. Convene a task-team video conference to review all proposals sent in by potential vendors.

4. Create a short list of three or four potential vendors.

5. Call references for vendors on the short list.

6. Invite vendors on the short list to make a presentation to the team.

7. Schedule vendor presentations to the task team.

8. Determine the vendor of choice and negotiate contract details.

9. Send a thank-you to all vendors who submitted proposals.

Even the above mini-tasks could be further broken down into smaller chunks. For example, developing a list of accredited vendors to receive the RFP may include:

1. Conduct web research about appropriate vendors.

2. Get a suggested list of vendors from the HR department.

3. Ask colleagues in another company who have implemented a similar training for potential vendors.

The trick to breaking down tasks is to learn how to distill the action you want to take into as many smaller steps as you need to in order to be able to confront getting them done—mentally, emotionally, and physically.

## Exercise

Think of a project, goal, or task that you want to get done but that has become stalled or stuck in the mud. Describe it below.

_____

_____

_____

_____

_____

_____

_____

Now, break that task down into as many mini-tasks as you can think of that seem doable. If the mini-task you have listed seems overwhelming, break it down into even smaller action items. When done, you should have a to-do list of actions you can take that will move you forward on your project but seem relatively easy to do. You know you have reached the right task size when you breathe a sigh a relief.

**Mini-task #1:**

_____

_____

**Mini-task #2:**

_____

_____

**Mini-task #3:**

_____

_____

**Mini-task #4:**

_____

_____

**Mini-task #5:**

_____

_____

**Mini-task #6:**

_____

_____

**Mini-task #7:**

_____

_____

**Mini-task #8:**

_____

_____

# Break Tasks Down When . . .

- You feel overwhelmed by the task

- You have been procrastinating about getting the item done

- You have transferred the item five times in your calendar

- The thought of doing the task makes you want to cry

# #39.

# Broaden Your
# Definition of Finished

Here is the cold, hard reality: Nobody, not even the most efficiently awesome time gurus on the planet, get everything that they planned done in one day—except sometimes. It's the nature of work that, despite all preparation and the best intentions, some items scheduled for today must be put off until tomorrow.

For example, imagine you have an A-priority item on your to-do list to call back a customer regarding a recent bill. You have tried to reach him several times with no luck. He returned your call, but you were out at a business lunch. A round of telephone tag ensues and you are about to leave for a meeting that will last the rest of the day. After one more valiant, but unsuccessful, attempt, you give up and move the call to tomorrow's to-do list.

At this point, you have two choices. You can feel bad about the item being left unfinished, get dragged down by a nagging sense of incompletion, call yourself names, and delve into the depths of shame at having to transfer the task to tomorrow. Or you can broaden your definition of what "finished" means.

When you look up the word "finished" in the dictionary, you will find synonyms that include "over," "ended," "done," and "complete." This traditional definition implies that you have moved successfully from point A to point B. Mission accomplished. Done. Finito.

Such a narrow and limited definition can be expanded, however, to include synonyms for the word "complete," like "whole," "inclusive," "broad," and "wide-ranging." These secondary synonyms allow you to create a sense of closure on all your day's to-do items, even the ones you don't get done.

Sound like a contradiction in terms? *Au contraire*. While you may not be able to *finish* every item on your to-do list, you can *complete* every item by knowing where you stand with each one. Where you stand with an item is based on making a clear decision about the next action you are going to take. Are you going to do it now? Okay. It's done and complete. Are you going to assign it to someone else? Great. Pass it along and it's complete. Are you going to abandon it? Fair enough. Cross it off your list and be done with it. Are you going to transfer it? Excellent. Move it to another day, week, or month and rest easy knowing that you have it planned for the future.

Items that are delegated or transferred usually require follow up at some point and won't be finished until they are done or abandoned. However, for that day, they can be complete because you know your next step in their achievement. The only option that won't give you a sense of completion is ignoring the task and not making a firm decision about its next step.

# PART 8

# Embrace Personal Productivity Habits

Searching online for "time-management tools" will bring up 98,000,000 different articles, most of them dealing with goal-setting, prioritizing, organizing, and delegating. No problem. These are all important aspects of good time management. But it's also a good idea to focus on some of the less obvious ways we can better manage our time and our stress levels.

Here are six (often overlooked) tips that can help save your day.

# #40.

# Cultivate Time-Efficient Conversations

Everyday conversations—a salesperson talking on the phone with a potential client, a service rep solving a customer's problem, a team leader brainstorming solutions with a team—are, to a business, what an engine is to an automobile. Without them, nothing moves. Yet many conversations at work seem to go nowhere fast and don't produce the desired results. Knowing what kinds of conversations create action and which create inertia is a crucial skill for making the most of your day.

## *Action Conversations*

Conversations that contain a request usually fall into this category. Depending on the other person's working style, you may express that request more or less strongly and specifically. For example:

- More specific: Kim, I need you to get in by 7:30 tomorrow morning so that we can finish the inventory by noon. Can you do that?

- Less specific: Rana, I don't think I can get that inventory done by tomorrow. Would you be able to help me out?

The more specific, clear, and strong a request is, the more time-efficient it becomes, since it leaves nothing to chance and makes the possibility of the task getting done on time and to spec that much greater. To insure that your requests are as time-friendly as possible, make sure they include the following:

- Specific outcomes: A request that is stated in terms that are too general carries with it the potential to waste time, energy, and money. For example:

  > *Kim, I am speaking at a conference next week, and I need all the information you can get me from R&D.*

- Not knowing what is really wanted, Kim may work overtime to create a 100-page document that takes time away from another higher-priority project. Or she could email a few quick notes. In either case, you may not get what you really wanted and needed. Most of your co-workers are not certified mind-readers and, while they may be able to guess correctly about some of what you want some of the time, it pays to be clear up front. For example:

  > *Rana, I am speaking at a conference tomorrow and I need a two-page overview on our latest product from R&D.*

- Time frame: A specific time frame, agreed on by you and the other person, helps guarantee that you will get what you want when you want it. For example:

  *Kim, I need the final Q3 sales numbers as soon as possible.*

- This request could be interpreted many different ways, because "as soon as possible" could mean next week to one person or "as soon as I'm done with everything else on my plate" to another. A more time-efficient time frame would be:

  *Rana, I need the final Q3 sales numbers by noon tomorrow.*

- Background information: When making a request, don't assume that the other person knows as much about the background details as you do. For example, Jill sends an email to her co-worker Mike in accounting saying:

  *I need my expense invoice reimbursed by the end of the week.*

- Mike, having no background information from Jill, has to look up the details, which results in a one-week delay of the check getting cut. Here is the same request with the background information added:

  *Mike, my expense invoice, #3421 for $651.23, was submitted on 3/15/20. Due to an internal*

*accounting error it was not paid on time. Would it*
*be possible to get it paid by the end of this week?*

## Inertial Conversations

A far cry from action conversations, these conversations are one of the biggest time-wasters in the workplace, because they are often centered on personal opinions with no commitment to resolution. They most often rear their ugly heads in four specific forms. Beware—they will lead you down the path of lost productivity.

- Wishing conversations: These pie-in-the-sky discussions focus on desires but don't move anything forward. For example:

    *Every quarter we have to do the inventory and every quarter I am hard pressed to get it done on time. I wish they'd make the process easier!*

- Judging conversations: These accomplish venting and nothing more. While everyone has a tendency to make negative judgments, these conversations never transform into anything productive. For example:

    *The last company I worked for had a very good inventory process. They really knew what they were doing. Not like this place.*

- Whining conversations: Different from complaining (which, if done responsibly, can lead to action), whining is rarely directed at anyone who can do anything about the situation. For example:

> *I hate this inventory process. It never seems to get any easier. I can't stand the software we have to use. The whole process needs to be upgraded. I dread this time of year.*

- Status quo conversations: If you have ever sat in a meeting where there was a lot of discussion but nothing seemed to happen, then you left wondering what all the hot air was about, you understand this fruitless and frustrating form of inertial conversation. Unlike brainstorming, which is a discussion that eventually leads to action, discussion for discussion's sake maintains the status quo and is ultimately frustrating.

# #41.

# Don't Get Caught in the "Yes" Trap

You're standing around the water cooler minding your own business when your co-worker from the next cubicle starts pleading with you to organize the Dunk the Clown booth at next month's company picnic. You quickly connect the dots and realize that, between your upcoming town hall presentation and your aunt's annual visit, the answer must be "no." You open your mouth to say: "I'm sorry. I wish I could, but I can't." But instead, you do a 180-degree turn and blurt out: "Okay, I can do that."

"No." This small, two-letter word doesn't have to be so difficult to say if you learn to say "yes" to the right things and "no" to the wrong ones. This is easier to do if you understand these three "yes" traps and their solutions.

## Trap 1: Good Candy

Remember, when you were young, there was always one house on the street that handed out really good Halloween candy? Your plans always included a visit to that address! Even as an adult, no one wants to feel as if they are missing out, so you say "yes" for fear that, if you decline, you could be passing up an opportunity.

Smart Solution: When you want to participate, but the timing or scope is wrong, offer an option or ask for a rain check:

- "I'd love to be asked at another time."

- "Can I have a rain-check on that?"

- "Maybe next week, month, year."

## Trap 2: Bad Guy

Saying "no" is not just a problem for the willy-nilly and weak-kneed. Feeling an internal pressure to say "yes" has nothing to do with education, success, or smarts. The fear is that, if you say "no," you may be perceived as unfriendly, uncooperative, or not a team player.

Smart Solution: Let the other person know you understand his or her situation or feelings:

- "I know how important this is, and I feel bad, but I'm not in a position to say 'yes.'"

- "I feel bad, but I'm not able to help right now."

## Trap 3: You Like Me!

Wow! They want you to be in charge of the company softball team. Of course, you are flattered. Who wouldn't be? Everyone wants to be liked. The opportunity to be part of a group is rewarding, but even things that are fun can become a burden if you're overextended.

Smart Solution: In this 24/7 can-do culture, the pressure to say "yes" to everything can be overwhelming. Create a boundary that lets other people know when you have reached your time, energy, and attention limits:

- "I have too many other things on my plate right now."
- "I have competing priorities."
- "I really don't have the time."

## Exercise

How often are you caught in the "yes" trap? You may surprised. The more of these questions you answer with "true," the more you need to recover your ability to just say "no"!

Circle true or false:

| | | |
|---|---|---|
| 1. I often say "yes" for fear of missing out on something. | True | False |
| 2. I frequently worry that, if I say "no," I may hurt someone's feelings. | True | False |
| 3. I often think that, if I say "no," I may be viewed as uncooperative or not a team player. | True | False |
| 4. I frequently feel guilty when I say "no," especially if I can see what is needed. | True | False |
| 5. I want people to like me, so I often say "yes," even when I don't really have the time or energy. | True | False |
| 6. In general, it makes me feel uncomfortable to say "no." | True | False |

# #42.

# Move Your Body

If you are one of the millions who work at a desk, talk on the phone, or type at a keyboard, you know the pain of a cramped wrist, crimped neck, and tight shoulders. Sitting in the same position hour after hour can be bad for your health and is a drain on your energy and concentration. Try these simple exercises to give your body a break and your focus a boost. Of course, none of these are a substitute for medical care and all stretches should be done slowly and gently. They should cause no pain! If you have any doubt about whether you can (or should) do these, check with your doctor before moving a muscle.

## Upper Back and Shoulders

Place your hands on your shoulders. With your elbows down, push your shoulders back. Hold for twenty seconds. Repeat four times.

## Lower Back

Stand up and exhale while you slowly drop your head toward your knees. Allow your hands to drop to your ankles. Hold for five seconds. Inhale while you slowly unwind and return upright. Repeat four times.

## Neck

Gently turn your head to the left, looking over your left shoulder and hold for ten seconds. Next, gently turn your head to the right, looking over your right shoulder and hold for ten seconds. Repeat four times.

## Wrists

Place your palms together at chest height. Push your palms together while slightly lifting your elbows. Hold for five seconds. While still holding your palms together, rotate your hands down so your fingertips point to the floor. Hold for five seconds and release. Repeat four times.

## Back and Hips

Place your palms on your lower back. Gently move your chest forward and stretch your upper torso backward. Hold for five seconds. Repeat four times.

## Legs

Sit in your chair and, holding in your abs, extend your left leg in front of you until it is level with your hip. Hold for two seconds. Next, holding in your abs, extend your right leg until it is level with your hip. Hold for two seconds. Repeat two times.

# Boost Your Productivity with Exercise

In a study of 200 office workers by the Leeds Metropolitan University in the UK, six out of ten people surveyed reported that their time-management skills, mental performance, and ability to meet deadlines improved on days when they exercised. The overall performance boost was about 15 percent, according to Jim McKenna, professor of physical activity and health at the university.

# #43.

# Get a Good Night's Sleep

If you're having a bad day at work, the problem may not be your overbearing boss or cranky co-worker. It may be a lack of sleep. Consider the findings of these studies.

The National Sleep Foundation's 2018 poll reported that 65 percent of respondents believe they are more effective at getting things done when they've had a good night's sleep. The same study shows that, despite this, good sleeping habits are low on our list of priorities.

A comprehensive review of published scientific data concluded that, for most adults, seven to nine hours a night is the required amount of sleep. Forty percent of Americans are sleeping fewer than seven hours a night during the workweek and 75 percent of those surveyed reported problems sleeping a few nights a week, which often resulted in missed workdays and errors on the job.

According to the Better Sleep Council, over 65 percent of Americans lose sleep because of stress. The Anxiety and Depression Association of America suggests one way to reduce anxiety and sleep soundly:

> *Prioritize your to-do list. Spend your time and energy on the tasks that are truly important, and break up large projects into smaller, more easily managed tasks. Delegate when you can.*

To improve your snooze and awaken to a better work life, try these techniques.

## Sleep on Schedule

Establish a pattern of sleep by going to bed and getting up at roughly the same time each day. This helps your body set an automatic clock that tells it when to go to bed! There are numerous smartphone apps that can help you manage this.

## Block the Light

The darker your room is, the better you'll sleep. Wear an eye mask, cover the electronics, turn off the nightlight, and close the door to prevent light from creeping in.

If you are in a hotel room with a bright digital clock, cover it up with a towel. If the TV power button is glowing red, stick a couple of post-it notes over it. Travel with good ear plugs to block out the noise from the party animals down the hall.

## Avoid Stimulation

Watching television, working, or even exercising within an hour of going to bed can cause delays in getting to sleep due to over-stimulation. Instead, plan a few pre-bedtime rituals like soaking in a warm tub, listening to white noise or a relaxation CD, or doing some light reading. These can all help prepare your mind and body for rest.

## Watch What You Eat and Drink

Drinking caffeinated coffee, tea, or soft drinks late in the day can interfere with your slumber. In addition, while eating sugary foods or drinking alcohol may put you to sleep fast, these will often wake you up in the middle of the night. Skip the sugar and try foods that are high in the amino acid tryptophan—foods like turkey, low-fat dairy products, bananas, and hummus.

## Wear a Pair of Socks

One way the body readies itself for sleep is to widen the blood vessels in the hands and feet to help radiate heat. Research shows that people with cold feet often have trouble falling asleep. So, instead of counting sheep, put on a pair of socks.

## Experiment with White Noise

For many, white noise enables a better night's sleep by shutting out those pesky sounds that keep you from dozing off—dogs barking, traffic rumbling and, when you're in a hotel, noise from the neighboring room. Technically, white noise is a sound that remains consistent across all audible frequencies. If you're a sensitive sleeper, it's worth a try. There are plenty of white-noise apps to choose from on your smartphone.

# #44.

# Take a Real Vacation

Have you ever noticed that stories about life in the very far-off future often present a vision where leisure and vacations are the rule and hard work the exception? In reality, however, for all the talk about technology and its impact on time off, most people don't really know how to get away and leave it all behind.

A survey by the recruiting firm Hudson found that more than half of American workers fail to take all their vacation days. Thirty percent say they use less than half their allotted time and 20 percent take only a few days instead of a week or two. Another survey by OfficeTeam found that 76 percent of executives attend to office duties several times while on vacation and 33 percent conduct business every day. One reason so many people find it difficult to disconnect is a lack of planning before leaving. Here are some tips to help you make the most of your vacation.

## *Spread the Word*

Notify clients, co-workers, and vendors of the dates you will be gone and designate a point person they can contact in your absence. Be sure to leave this information on your voicemail and email as well.

## Delegate Decisions

Authorize a co-worker in whom you have confidence to make decisions on your behalf while you're gone. Make sure to leave any important information your colleagues may need readily available and easily accessible on your desk.

## Limit Contact

If you have to check in with your office, schedule specific days and times when you are going to make contact and stick to it. If your co-workers know that you are not *on-call*, the chances of them interrupting you with office issues are greatly reduced.

## Plan Ahead

If practical, schedule your vacation during a slower period at work and let your manager know as soon as possible so he or she can plan for your absence.

## Unplug

Consider leaving your computer at home. If you need access to email or the Internet, use the hotel's business center.

## Create Closure

Get ready to go a few weeks before you leave by closing any open items that could come back to haunt you while you are away. This includes paying bills, updating reports, sending off proposals and invoices, and cleaning off your desk so it's neat and tidy when you return.

## *Prepare for Your Return*

To put your mind at ease about all the work you will have to do upon returning, create a to-do list before you go of items you will need to handle within your first few days back (See #45).

# #45.

# Stay Sane After Returning from Vacation

For most people, the excitement of going on vacation is equaled only by the stress they feel a few days before getting back to work. Returning to the office can often wipe out (within hours) all the relaxation built up over a week on Waikiki. Worry not. With a little bit of organizing, you can avoid the "back-from-vacation blues" and ensure that the benefits of your vacation are felt long after your plane touches down.

## *Catch Up First*

Before the raging river of your to-do list carries you away, begin by catching up with your co-workers. Penelope Trunk, author of *Brazen Careerist*, says that burying your head in paperwork the minute you hit your office and griping to everyone about how overwhelmed you are makes you look too inefficient to even take a vacation. Instead, Trunk says the best strategy is take a walk around the office.

> *Share about your vacation and ask people how they are doing and what's been going on. This gives them a chance to let you know about something they may have wanted to talk with you about, but didn't feel comfortable hitting you with your first day back.*

## Don't Clutter Up Your Calendar

David Allen, author of *Ready For Anything*, says business people misjudge the amount of time it takes to get caught up. "It takes an hour a day on average for the typical professional to gather, process, and organize all their inputs," says Allen. "Think about how many days you will be away and then assign an hour for each day. If you're gone for two weeks, that's two days at least." Allen suggests keeping a relatively clear calendar on those first few days back.

## Remember the 80/20 Rule

While you were away, tons of to-do's (electronic and otherwise) will have made their way into your inbox. But not all of these warrant immediate action. "Most people want to come running in and start going through all their emails," says Dr. Pamela Dodd, author of *The 25 Best Time Management Tools and Techniques*. Instead, she suggests that people determine the most important 20 percent of the open items to get done, which will produce 80 percent of the results in terms of getting back to work smoothly.

## Make Changes

Vacations not only give you a much needed break from the stresses of work, they also provide an opportunity to step back and get some perspective on your life. "Vacations give you thinking space," says Trunk, "but you can't leverage that if you go back to your desk and do exactly the same thing." She says people need to think about how they are going to change to accommodate what they discovered while away.

For example, if your vacation sparked a yearning to spend more time on your photography, when you get back, try to stop booking meetings on Fridays after 3:00 PM. Doing so could allow you to leave a bit early and spend the later part of the afternoon pursuing your hobby.

# PART 9

# Right-Size Your Social Media and Email

So far, we've shown you how to gain some ground on your physical files and paperwork, your goals and priorities, and even your sleep patterns. But no self-respecting book on time management would be complete without a strong dose of advice on how to tackle your online life—from a time-management point of view, at least.

In today's world, online time management involves sifting, sorting, organizing, and controlling a wide variety of items, including email, social media, and online files.

According to one study from Microsoft, US workers spend an average of seven hours a day on their computers, while another survey from Accountemps found that workers spend an average of six weeks a year looking for things.

While these two statistics may seem unrelated, they are not. Think about this. One of the places we undoubtedly look for things is on our computers. How much time did you spend this past week searching for a file you stashed somewhere on your laptop?

Some of our recent experiences of hunting and pecking for a client contract on our own computers led us to the conclusion that, just as we give our closets a good cleaning from time to time, an occasional computer decluttering is needed as well. Here are some proven ways you can make your online life more manageable and free-up more time in the process.

# #46.

# Give Your Laptop a New Lease on Life

Since computer memory has increased exponentially over the years, storage is not, in general, a big issue. However, the bad habit of indiscriminately dumping information onto our computers is. Here are a few ways to keep your hard drive clear of clutter.

- Delete any old working drafts of documents that have since been updated or are no longer useful.

- Dump files that are so old that the information in them is outdated and never used.

- Empty files that you created but never did anything with or that have no content.

- Eliminate files that have different names but contain duplicate materials.

- Delete all those hundreds (or thousands) of unusable digital photos from your last trip.

With the old crap cleaned out, your next step is to set up a logical filing system.

Try to mirror your paper filing system on your computer. The more your main folders resemble the names and categories you use to file paper, the easier it will be for you to find and to file various documents.

In addition, create a Working File or Pending folder that lives on your desktop and can hold anything you are currently working on and need to access quickly and easily. While much of your computer may be used for the archiving of information, this folder can hold the most current information and projects.

Finally, organize and update the bookmarks on your browser. Just as you may have random files floating around your hard drive, you more than likely have a ton of bookmarks that are not organized in any particular way. Use your browser's features to make folders with logical names that you can group and then fill with your various bookmarks.

# #47.

# Get Control of Your Email

For most of us, our email inboxes have become the dumping ground for all our unhandled to-do's. To begin the process of email clean-up, start by going through your mailbox and deleting all old messages that you no longer need. Then be sure to delete the messages from the trash file.

Because most people have enough room on their computer to keep old email, they often skip this step. However, it has been my experience that, the more current and up-to-date your email is, the less time you will spend searching for what you really need.

Next, establish an email filing system. One method is to set up your email folders the same way you classify your work. For example, if you generally reference your work by client, then set up folders by client name. If you generally reference by product, then set up by product name.

Finally, don't fall into the trap of just ignoring the items on your computer. In the same way that a junk drawer, closet, or even room can become a black hole that drains your energy, random files floating around in an unorganized fashion can become the clutter that clogs up your computer.

# #48.

# Sort Out Your Electronic Inbox

If you've ever tried to find something specific in a cluttered cupboard, you know how time-consuming and frustrating it can be. Plowing through old boxes of junk and piles of paper and bric-a-brac saved from Auntie Mildred's wedding can eat up your time and test your patience. A messy email inbox can create a similar level of dysfunction-inducing clutter and drive you crazy. A few minutes spent organizing your online life now will pay off tenfold in time saved later.

There are two aspects to sorting out your inbox. One involves cleaning out and categorizing the email you already have; the second involves managing new emails as they arrive.

To begin with, do a house-cleaning of your mailbox and delete old messages (including spam) hanging around that you no longer need. If you are like most people, you have enough memory in your computer to store the entire Library of Congress collection, so it's temping just to keep old email and skip this step. But remember, the tidier your email is, the less time you will spend searching for what you need.

Next, establish an email filing system that makes it relatively easy to find past messages. One method is to set up your email folders to mirror the way you organize your work files. For example, if you generally reference your work by account name, then set up your email folders by account name. If you generally reference by date, then set up your folders by date.

How many times have you given your attention to the same email (looked at it, opened it, re-read it) and then moved to another task without taking any action? Once you have an orderly inbox, keep new arrivals from muddling your new-found neatness by not letting emails linger in hopes that they will read and answer themselves. Alan Lakein, in his famous book *How To Manage Your Time and Life,* encouraged people to handle every piece of paper only once. The same principle applies to emails. The simple solution is to deal with every message that comes in quickly by taking one of the following actions.

## *Reply*

If the message sparks an action that you can do within a reasonable amount of time (five minutes or less) handle it now. If an instant response is not practical, flag it for action later or move the item to an established Pending folder, so that it doesn't get ignored or lost down the road. If the item will require a chunk of time to handle (fifteen minutes or longer), you can also open your date book and schedule a specific time to get it done. Be careful not to create too large a backlog of future to-do items. A twice-weekly review of these items, with corresponding action, should keep your Pending file from overflowing.

## File

If the appropriate file folder does not already exist, create whatever folders you need so that you can collect emails from the same source, subject, client, or project together.

## Delete

In the same way that throwing out a pile of old magazines that has been hanging around your house for six months can be so satisfying, so is deciding *not* to take action on a nonessential email. If the thought of dumping something you may need in the future makes you shudder in fear, here are a few questions you can ask yourself to determine if the item is a keeper or not.

- Does the message contain important information I can use now or in the future?

- Does the message relate to an important project, goal, or task I am currently working on?

- Does the message contain information that it's necessary for me to keep for legal, tax, or policy reasons?

## Forward

If the item in the email is one that can or should be delegated to someone else, send it on its way ASAP. If you need to take action, but also want to include someone else in the message, forward it to them now, not later.

Finally, don't use the default "ignore" as a way to deal with incoming messages. Anything you just let sit for too long can become lost in the crowd, a drain on your mental energy and just more mailbox clutter.

# #49.

# Streamline Your Outgoing Email

Knowing how to write emails that produce the results you want *and* save time for yourself and others enhances your online productivity. The following practices can help you streamline your emails.

## *Prune Your Prose*

According to a recent survey by ClickZ, 60 percent of people at work often read less than half of each email message they receive. To keep your emails from ending up in the "dumped-due-to-lack-of-interest" pile, trim the fat by removing extraneous fluff and getting right to the heart of the matter. For example, consider the following message, prior to pruning:

> *I was very surprised and encouraged by the meeting we had two days ago regarding the new systems that we plan to introduce in the spring of next year. I feel that everyone who attended the meeting was well-prepared and organized, and understood the specific issues of the*

*integration process. As we discussed at the meeting, it is only with all of us collaborating together that we will be able to foresee possible problems and deal with them efficiently as they arise. I look forward to our next meeting, which is on Friday the 27th at 9:30 AM.*

Here is the same message after pruning:

*Thank you for being so prepared for the systems meeting two days ago. I look forward to working together toward an efficient implementation. Our next meeting is on Friday the 27th at 9:30 AM.*

## Prioritize Your Paragraphs

While the general rule "shorter is better" applies to most emails, some messages are, by nature, meatier than others and take up more space. In that case, the key is to identify your most important piece of information and place it in the first paragraph of your message. This ensures that your A-priority information gets read, even if the rest of the email doesn't. For example, in the following message, the fourth paragraph contains the main point, but is the last piece of information offered.

*Dear Ms. Goodlight:*

*Thank you for your order. The answers to your questions are as follows:*

*We have over 200 different lamp designs in stock and can order non-stocked items to arrive within one week. All of our lamps are made of the highest quality materials and are guaranteed for two years. Custom designs are available upon request.*

*For wholesale customers, we do offer a 30-days-net payment policy. You can apply for this by contacting Mr. Barney Smith at bsmith@loveourlamps.com. He will send you the proper paperwork to fill out. It usually takes up to two weeks to process an application.*

*The lamp you have ordered is available in chrome or nickel. Once we know which finish you require, we will ship it to you immediately.*

*If you have any other questions, please do not hesitate to contact me.*

To make this email more productive and efficient, the paragraphs should be re-ordered as follows so that the information is offered in order of descending importance:

*Dear Ms. Goodlight:*

*Thank you for your order. The lamp you have ordered is available in chrome or nickel. Once we know which finish you require, we will ship it to you immediately.*

*The answers to your questions are as follows:*

*For wholesale customers, we do offer a 30-days-net payment policy. You can apply for this by contacting Mr. Barney Smith at bsmith@loveourlamps.com. He will send you the proper paperwork to fill out. It usually takes up to two weeks to process an application.*

*We have over 200 different lamp designs in stock and can order non-stocked items to arrive within one week. All of our lamps are made of the highest quality materials and are guaranteed for two years. Custom designs are available upon request.*

*If you have any other questions, please do not hesitate to contact me.*

# #50.

# Use Social Media Wisely

According to one study by Statista, people spend 2.5 hours a day on social media. And regardless of whether you spend those hours posting or perusing, they can turn into a huge time-sink if not well managed. If you struggle with your social-media time management, you are not alone. Use the following tips to help you keep your online communications in check.

## *Begin with the End in Mind*

Before you leap into a social media posting frenzy, it's a good idea to determine your main objective. Targeted social campaigns ultimately take up less time and produce a better result, so consider carefully what you actually want to achieve. For example, are you looking to increase the number of potential customers in your sales funnel? Do you want to raise your visibility and brand equity? Are you trying to build up a social following in preparation for selling a book? Knowing what you want before you start posting is a more productive way to go.

## Narrow Your Focus

Not all social media sites are created equal. More specifically, not all social media sites cater to all audiences. Consider the sites where your ideal clients spend their time. Where do they consume information? For example, LinkedIn is a more business-to-business site, while Facebook caters to the business-to-consumer crowd. By narrowing your focus and posting mainly on sites where you know your customers (or potential customers) are more likely to be saves wasted effort and time.

## Create an Editorial Calendar

Posting three to five times a week can become a burden when you have to figure out from scratch what to write about every time. One way to shortcut this process and save yourself tons of time is to create an editorial calendar. Simply put, an editorial calendar is a month-by-month plan for the topics about which you are going to post.

Most editorial calendars include the SEO (search engine optimization) words and phrases for your business, as well as relevant topics for each month—posts about gratitude at Thanksgiving, about setting goals in January, and calling for spring cleaning your office in April. The bottom line is that planning what you want to post about ahead of time makes you more productive and effective.

## Schedule Your Posts

Tools like Hootsuite allow you to write and place your tweets and Facebook updates in a queue for posting prior to the day/

week you want them to load. By putting up a week's worth of posts at one time, you save time by not having to go in and out of the site.

## *Plan and Limit Your Social-Media Surfing*

If you have ever gone down the rabbit hole of a social-media surf fest, you know what a huge time-waster it can be. Constantly interrupting your work (and focus) to see what the latest and greatest is among your friends can take you away from your more important priorities and goals. One simple solution is to schedule your social-media time and give it a time limit. For example, allot fifteen minutes to Facebook in the morning or twenty minutes to Twitter at the end of the day.

# Conclusion

When all is said and done, the art of time management is really the art of decision-making. It's the courage to choose what actions you are going to take and when you are going to take them, and deciding how you will get them done. It's about choosing your most important life goals and prioritizing accordingly.

In the day-to-day world of business, these choices happen as part of managing your workflow. Entire books, systems, and programs have been created on the topic, though, in essence, the idea is elegantly simple:

- Information enters your world from your voicemail, email, snail mail, other people, and your own brain.

- You capture that information in a variety of places, including your to-do lists, your inbox, your email, and your paper files.

- You decide what you are going to do about each of these inputs. Are you going to address it now? Do it later? Delegate it? Dump it?

- You take the actions necessary to move items through the process until they are done, finished, complete.

Sounds simple, doesn't it? In a way, it is. But the discipline and skills necessary to do this require the tools, techniques, and tips offered in this book and others like it. You can become a master at working your workflow. All it takes is practice and commitment—and just a bit of time.

# About the Authors

## *Karen Tiber Leland*

Karen Tiber Leland is the founder of Sterling Marketing Group, a branding, marketing, and color-strategy firm that works with companies and individuals to build stronger personal, team, and business brands. Her clients have included Twitter, LinkedIn, Apple, American Express, and Google. She is the best-selling author of nine books, which have sold more than 400,000 copies. Her latest is *The Brand Mapping Strategy: Design, Build and Accelerate Your Brand.* Karen writes regularly for Inc.com and has been interviewed by the *Today Show,* CNN, Fox News, and *Oprah.* She has spoken at Harvard, Yale, and TEDx, among other venues.

Karen lives in New York City, where, for fun, she acts, takes photographs, and sees as much Broadway theater as is humanly possible.

## *Keith Bailey*

Keith Bailey is an executive communications coach who works with companies like Google, Fidelity Investments, Bank of America, World Vision, United Health Group, Netflix, Marriott Hotels, Lufthansa German Airlines, and the British government.

His expertise and business insights have been featured in numerous newspapers and magazines, and on TV. This is his eighth business book.

Keith has a BA in photography and loves to cook, take photographs, and throw pots. He lives in Santa Fe, New Mexico, with his wife, Deborah, and miniature poodle, Curry.

## DATE DUE

| SEP 2 7 2002 | |
| --- | --- |
| 9-17-02 | |
| | |
| SEP 1 8 REC'D | |
| | |
| | |
| | |
| | |
| | |
| | |
| | |
| | |
| | |
| | |
| | |
| | |
| | |

DEMCO, INC. 38-2931

# NORTH AMERICA
# FROM EARLIEST DISCOVERY
# TO FIRST SETTLEMENTS

*The Norse Voyages to 1612*

*the text of this book is printed
on 100% recycled paper*

*The*

*New American Nation Series*

EDITED BY

# HENRY STEELE COMMAGER

AND

# RICHARD B. MORRIS

# NORTH AMERICA FROM EARLIEST DISCOVERY TO FIRST SETTLEMENTS

## THE NORSE VOYAGES TO 1612

By DAVID B. QUINN

ILLUSTRATED

HARPER COLOPHON BOOKS

Harper & Row, Publishers
New York, Hagerstown, San Francisco, London

NORTH AMERICA FROM EARLIEST DISCOVERY TO FIRST SETTLEMENTS: THE NORSE VOYAGES TO 1612. Copyright © 1977 by David B. Quinn. All rights reserved. Printed in the United States of America. No part of this book may be used or reproduced in any manner whatsoever without written permission except in the case of brief quotations embodied in critical articles and reviews. For information address Harper & Row, Publishers, Inc., 10 East 53d Street, New York, N.Y. 10022. Published simultaneously in Canada by Fitzhenry & Whiteside Limited, Toronto.

First HARPER COLOPHON edition published 1978

ISBN: 0-06-090603-0

78 79 80 81 82 10 9 8 7 6 5 4 3 2 1

To the Quinns
Alison, Nick, Rory and Brigid
and the Children
of the Next Generation

# Contents

# Illustrations

# Maps and Drawings

# Preface

THE object in this volume has been to provide a reasonably balanced view of the activities of those European peoples who discovered, explored and attempted to settle North America down to the time when the first colonies—Spanish, English and French—had taken root. On such a large canvas it will be clear that the choice of topics has had to be fairly selective. Generally, I have tried to provide a basic narrative, with such analysis as appeared necessary to explain what was happening without impeding the story too drastically. Some more systematic treatment has been given to three topics which could not be covered inside a chronological framework: the Amerindian society encountered by the Europeans, European technology, ideology and institutions and the economic exploitation of North America.

The discovery, early exploration, economic exploitation and settlement of North America is a field in which much work has been done in recent years and more is in progress. What follows is very much a report on existing knowledge, extended at some points by my own investigations. It is an area in which there are many topics on which we have no, or only very imperfect, information. Some of the missing information may well be forthcoming in fragmentary disclosures as archives are combed more closely; some will emerge as field archeology is more fully employed to investigate the earliest physical traces of European contact with North America; some is gone for ever. It is clear that we now make mistakes or construct

inadequate hypotheses because the materials are too few or too imperfect to allow accurate interpretations, so that the element of guesswork—and informed guesswork often produces good results when not pushed too far—remains significant in some areas of interpretation.

An attempt has been made in these pages to convey a concrete impression of what sort of settlements were tried out by different colonizing groups. By keeping an even balance between Spanish, French and English colonizing activities, a basis for comparison and contrast should emerge: each plank and stone and brick laid during this period had some significance for later settlement.

Finally, the most striking thing about this period for Europeans is the gradual emergence on the maps and in the narratives brought eastward across the Atlantic of a whole new continent, and it is hoped that something of the novelty of this disclosure, as well as the stages by which it took place, will be evident in this book. To Americans, on the other hand, this is their prehistory, the phase which made it possible for there to be Americans in a still unrealized future.

There is a certain necessary overlap between this and other volumes in the series, more especially with John E. Pomfret and Floyd M. Shumway, *Founding the American Colonies, 1583–1660,* who look forward to the next stage in growth and development and to the American future. I gained much from talking about this period with Jack Pomfret when I worked at the Henry E. Huntington Library at San Marino some years ago. Wilcomb E. Washburn, *The Indian in America,* covers a whole canvas where I have only had to touch on one segment, and he has also been helpful with advice. W. J. Eccles, in *France in America,* and Charles Gibson in *Spain in America,* also helped to put parts of this book into a wider context. I owe much to two other writers in the series, Wesley Frank Craven and Louis B. Wright.

Many obligations have been incurred in preparing this volume. Alison Quinn worked closely on the documents with me and may well be responsible for nearly as much of it as myself, while she has acted as my assiduous and constructive critic throughout and even made my index: so much loving care is not often found. A great deal is owed to the John Carter Brown Library and its present and past directors, Thomas R. Adams and the late Lawrence C. Wroth; to the

Folger Library, and its former director, Louis B. Wright, as well as to my friends in the College of William and Mary, who together gave me the opportunity to work in American libraries and directed me when I faltered in one way or another. A number of British and continental libraries and archives have also contributed to its completion. My university provided many of the opportunities which made its writing possible. I owe indeed a great deal to my students at Liverpool, not least to Gillian T. Cell, Susan Hillier, Joyce Lorimer and Colin R. Steele, who have themselves done independent work in this field.

Alan Hodgkiss drew the sketchmaps and Philip and Brigid Wainwright the remaining in-text illustrations. Wilcomb E. Washburn acted as an expert adviser in the final stages. Corona Machemer carried the author's typescript through to completion and Ann Adelman was my excellent copy editor. Their help has been greatly appreciated.

DAVID B. QUINN

University of Liverpool, July 1976

# CHAPTER 1

# *The Amerindian Context*

---

THE first discoveries of the Americas, and the exploration and exploitation of their lands and resources, took place in prehistoric times. They were made by human communities, which crossed from Asia for this purpose. By far the greater part of the human history of the Americas springs from these distant events, but it can be told only imperfectly on the basis of archeological and other non-literary materials. Comparatively speaking, the later interventions from Europe occupy only a tiny period of American history as a whole. Yet Europeans, from the first, left some literary traces of their presence and so enabled a historical story to be told both of their experiences and of the aboriginal populations they encountered. Furthermore, as soon as they appeared, they began to alter drastically the deep-rooted characteristics of native society, and rapidly proceeded to replace and destroy much of what had existed for long periods of time. It is this which makes it important to stress that European intervention in North America, as in other parts of the Americas, did not take place in a vacuum. Rather, from the first appearance of Europeans, an interaction took place between them and the Indian society (or Amerindian, as anthropologists prefer at present to say) in which they found themselves. And this is why it is essential to give some brief general picture of Indian society in the eastern part of the continent at the start of any study of European intervention in North America.[1]

1. General works of exceptional value are Harold E. Driver, *Indians of North America*, 2nd edition (Chicago, 1969), with an important bibliography; H. E. Driver and

1

The precise character of human diffusion in North America after the first crossing of a land bridge from Asia perhaps as long ago as 40,000 B.C. is a complex story—one which is only slowly being worked out from archeological and anthropological indications and which it may never be possible to tell in detail. If the original diffusion areas were in the Far West, and if it is likely that many movements subsequently took place from north to south, this certainly does not explain the major movements of the past two millennia or so. Pressures of climate, subsistence and population have worked in diverse ways to distribute and redistribute populations over the very large and varied territories of the continent. Students of the California Indians, for example, are very much aware that the peculiar diversities and unities of the Central Valley complex of early historic times was the product of pressures and movements from both north and south, which produced an exceptional amalgam of languages and local varieties of custom and dress superimposed on a basically similar pattern of subsistence.[2] It would therefore be unwise to attempt any historical survey which compressed the very complicated story of Amerindian culture, so far as it is known, into too brief a compass.

The preoccupation of academic writers in this field with culture in climax and decline can usefully spotlight for us those areas which were of exceptional interest at the opening of the sixteenth century.[3] These were the Northwest culture of the coastal lands from northern California to southern Alaska, with its rich fish- and fur-based economy, its social stratification and its elaborate houses and ceremonial monuments; the California Central Valley culture, which, being based largely on acorn-eating, was marked by variety and color in its cultural pursuits rather than by agricultural or hunt-

William C. Massey, "Comparative Studies of North American Indians," *American Philosophical Society, Transactions,* LXVII (1957), 165–456; Gordon R. Willey, *An Introduction to American Archaeology,* I, *North and Middle America* (Englewood Cliffs, N.J., 1966).

2. See Robert F. Heizer and M. A. Whipple, *The California Indians,* 2nd edition (Berkeley and Los Angeles, 1971), pp. 3–46, 73–83.

3. Alfred L. Kroeber, *Cultural and Natural Areas of Native North America,* University of California Publications in American Archaeology and Ethnology, XXVIII, 1939, is the basic study; Driver, *Indians,* pp. 17–24, indicates the later approach to the subject of culture areas.

ing activity;[4] the Pueblo culture, residual from earlier irrigation-based cultures widespread in the southwest, and exhibiting very well integrated small communities, with communal dwellings and a high level of ceremonial activity, based on weaving and the exploitation of flood plain agriculture in a single river valley, that of the Río Grande; and finally the Lower Mississippi culture, which was centered in the lower and middle parts of the valley but had some influence between the Lower Great Lakes and the Gulf of Mexico. This last culture was based on corn-growing; its burial mounds and other ceremonial centers bear witness to a rich institutional life which expressed itself in powerful tribal units that extended their range of contacts through frequent warfare well into the southeast from modern Florida to South Carolina.[5]

The rest of North America was covered by tribal groupings which were less distinctive in their cultural pattern, though showing much variety in detail; the uniformity of their hunting, fishing, at least partially mobile societies, with some agriculture south of approximately 45° N., is striking. The typical Amerindian was not drawn from one of the so-called climax cultures, but from one of these other groupings, distinguished rather by the requirements of climatic zones and by the accidents of such characteristics as language distribution rather than by distinctions in basic culture. Compared with the high culture areas of the Valley of Mexico, the Yucatán peninsula and the Andean coastal belt, the level of cultural achievement in North America was modest. All Amerindians within it were at a neolithic level of development. Though copper was used in places for ornament, so far as we know metal tools were not current at the opening of the sixteenth century. The area within which weaving was practiced was extremely limited and was clearly an extension from the Mexican high culture area. Political units remained very small: from the tribelets of northern California,

4. The fullest account is A. L. Kroeber, *Handbook of the Indians of California,* Smithsonian Institution, Bureau of American Ethnology, Bulletin no. 78, 1925; also Heizer and Whipple, *California Indians.* See also R. F. Heizer, *Francis Drake and the California Indians* (Berkeley, 1947).

5. My own information on the eastern Indians stems as much from conversation as from reading. William C. Sturtevant, J. C. Harrington, Neil M. Judd, Frank G. Speck, William N. Fenton, Wendell S. Hadlock, Jacques Rousseau, Gordon M. Day, Wilcomb E. Washburn, and Frederick Johnson are amongst those who helped to form my opinions; but, living or dead, they are not responsible for them.

through the tiny pueblo republics of the southwest, to the hunter-warrior tribes of the Iroquois and the larger settled tribal complexes of the Creek Indians, there was nothing in the way of political organization which approached the form of a state. It is clear, too, that cultural change was slow; the small tribal units were closely attached to their own specific way of life and were reluctant to respond to external stimulus, even though there was a slow trickle of cultural influence from Mexico both by way of the Gulf of Mexico[6] and by gradual permeation through the southwest, and, too, some southward spread of Eskimo techniques.

The limitations in cyclical culture changes and the failure of Amerindians to develop more complex social units and advanced techniques are not to be explained by any defect in Amerindian intelligence. A partial explanation can be found in their relatively low populations throughout history—though recent research inclines toward higher estimates than previously thought—and the relative generosity of the North American terrain to human communities. Subsistence—whether on acorns, buffalo, fish, corn or caribou—was easy in most areas, so that traditional patterns of life could be repeated with little change over long periods in the small community units which were typical. At the same time it is clear that North American Indian society was not static; change was continuing even if not at any rapid pace. And the swift response of Amerindian communities to white intrusion showed the capacity of many (though not all) for adaptation. Within the period with which we are mainly concerned, from the beginning of the sixteenth century to the early years of the seventeenth, a large number of the Amerindian societies had been touched in some degree by European contact, and many were readjusting their economies and, to some slight degree, their social and religious organization to meet the new challenges. Between the fifteenth and seventeenth centuries, New Stone Age cultures leaped into the Iron Age over an appreciable part of the continent.

What kind of Amerindian society did Europeans come into contact with during this period? It must be stressed that much of the early contact between Europeans and Amerindians was both slight

6. William C. Sturtevant, *The Significance of Ethnological Similarities Between Southeastern North America and the Antilles,* Yale University Publications in Anthropology, no. 64, 1960.

TRADITIONAL
CULTURE AREAS
AND TRIBAL LOCATIONS
NORTH AMERICA

and impermanent. For example, the Spaniards scarcely came within range of the distinctive Northwest culture province, and their contact with the Central Valley culture in California was also slight. A brief visit by Francis Drake in 1579 provided vignettes of the Coast Miwok culture; other glimpses, happy and not so happy, are provided by Vizcaino's voyage up the California coast in 1602–03. The Indians of the more southerly parts of California appear only fleetingly in Spanish narratives and are scarcely differentiated from those of the northern shores of western Mexico, while the Yuma-Mohave culture of the upper part of the Gulf of California does not appear to have attracted much attention. By contrast, from their first sighting by Fray Marcos in 1538, the Pueblos exercised a peculiar fascination for the Spaniards—both in their semi-mythical form of the Seven Cities of Cíbola and in their reality as a belt of village communities along the middle Río Grande Valley. Consequently they were described in particular detail. They were also, in the last years of the sixteenth century, invaded by the Spaniards, exploited and partially Christianized, so that by 1612 they had been incorporated into the Spanish imperial system. The only culture in the west to be so encapsulated, they nevertheless remained culturally more or less intact thanks to the strength of their community bonds.

The Plains Indians were glimpsed only occasionally during the forays which Coronado and later Oñate made into the wide spaces that lay between the central river valleys and the western mountain ranges. We get but a slight impression of these restless people—their endless hunt for buffalo, their conical tepees, and their characteristic dog travois for transport. By the beginning of the seventeenth century, they were on the verge of a cultural transformation: so far as we know, no European before 1612 ever saw a Plains Indian on a horse; but it is now generally agreed that 1600 marks the approximate date when the horse came in by way of trade with the Hispanicized south, transforming what had been a subsistence society into one of abundance by making the buffalo so much more vulnerable to attack.

The Prairie Indians were met very briefly by Hernando de Soto in the final stages of his journey up the Arkansas River Valley, and created no distinctive impression; but the Lower Mississippi culture more vividly impressed him and his men. From the Natchez to the Choctaw and from the Upper Creeks to the Lower Creeks on the

Atlantic seaboard, the siz...
ing the chiefly class and it...
capacity of the tribes for wa...
oped social order. The invalua...
by the Soto expedition is som...
Upper and Lower Creek society...
1560s. In modern times excavation...
late mound complexes such as that...
has further enhanced the image of t...

The main continuing contacts of the...
populations were with those which live... ...the
Florida peninsula and Labrador. The Sp... ...shed the
Indians of the southern part of the Florida ... from all others: their natural standard of life, gathering ... fishing, was low,
they claimed, and their tribal power and influence sustained only by
Spanish artifacts pillaged from wrecks shortly after 1520 and onwards. However, both the French and Spanish had a considerable
respect, if not always a liking, for the Muskogean tribes a little
farther north—the Timucua, for example—which extended also to
the Upper Creeks. Northward, from Cape Fear all the way to the
southern part of modern Maine, contacts between Europeans and
the coastal Algonkian people had more similarities than differences
because the basic material culture over this entire area varied little
from tribe to tribe. Further north along the coast, the marginal
corn-growing of the Micmac and Beothuk shaded into the simple
mobile hunting and gathering of the Montagnais-Nascapi. Up the
St. Lawrence, the French confronted a more complex grouping of
Iroquois and Huron with which they were forced to define their
relations well before the end of the period. Eskimo bands were
encountered only sparingly in Labrador and, further away, in Baffin
Island and Greenland.

Eastern North America was almost certainly the last major area
in North America to be occupied by man, but archeologists are not
yet agreed on the precise date. What seems certain is that this
occupation took place from the west and that it took the form of a
gradual infiltration, whether overland or by way of river systems, by
successive human groups; the white invasion of the sixteenth century was clearly the first to come from the east. Precise migration
patterns remain to be established, but it is probable that the main

of a slow trickle through the passes in
ns, with occasional more rapid movements
ys, notably those of the St. Lawrence, the Hud-
ware and the Susquehanna. There were also early
ts round the base of the Appalachian mountain system in
utheast. For the most part, settlement of the east proceeded
slowly, uninterrupted either by catastrophic intrusions from outside
or decisive cultural revolutions from within. The one major instance
of relatively rapid change which can be charted was the spread of
cultivation from the south and west; this transformed much of the
east into a wholly or partially agricultural society. Further, there do
not appear to have been any major climatic or economic features in
the east to attract any special concentrations of people, although
within the area of major agricultural activity, the population appears
to have been moderately high compared with most other parts of
the continent. There were, however, minor tribal concentrations in
those districts where conditions for hunting, fishing, crop-raising or
a combination of these were exceptionally favorable.

The east remained subject to continued infiltration at both its
northern and southern extremities. The Polar and sub-Polar Eskimoid cultures adapted early to extreme climatic conditions. This
gave them a freedom to move round the northern fringes of North
America which was not shared by most of the Amerindian culture
groups. Their movement from the farthest limits of Alaska to
Greenland and as far south as the St. Lawrence took place with
considerable rapidity. The limits of their southern penetration
tended to vary with climatic cycles: in warmer centuries these limits
were well to the north and in colder times well to the south—the
more severe the winters, the farther south could their cold-adapted
society exist. Whether advancing or retreating, however, they exercised an appreciable cultural influence on the more northerly Amerindian groups with which they were in contact, so that certain
weapons and tools in New England and the St. Lawrence Valley
bore recognizable Eskimoid traces at the opening of historic times.

At the other, southern limit of the eastern continent the Amerindian peoples were subject to some degree of continual influence,
mainly cultural, from the south. The chief centers of social and
cultural development in the Americas from early times were round
the Caribbean; cultural infiltration of the continent from

Mesoamerica came largely through the Gulf of Mexico and into the Mississippi Valley, whence it slowly seeped throughout the southeast and diffused northward amongst the coastal and riverine peoples of the east. Whether there were also some trans-Caribbean influences by way of Florida is still being debated. What is known is that the domestication of plants and of animals (dogs only) began in the south well before the period of European contact and intervention.

So far, archeology does not record any major changes in the character of Amerindian society in eastern North America between roughly the years A.D. 1000 to 1600. But this does not mean that no movements of population took place during this period. In fact, we have seen that there were several shifts, mainly climatically determined, in the Eskimoid-Amerindian contact zone. Furthermore, through both the St. Lawrence Valley and the mountain passes further south, immigrants continued at times to filter into the east. The mound-building culture, a repository of Mesoamerican influence, had a remarkable flowering in modern Georgia and influenced other Amerindian groups up the east coast and in the interior as far north as the Lower Great Lakes. Religious symbols—anthropomorphic representations of Indian deities, for example—and various cult symbols spread northward along the coast from Florida to the Chesapeake or farther north. The diffusion of house and settlement patterns, decorative styles and cultivated plants, continued down to the time of European contact, mostly from the south. But there were north-to-south influences too: if the round, palm-thatched house spread from the Gulf coast to the limits of the Creek culture in the southeast, the longhouse, apparently of Iroquois origin, spread as far south as the coastal Carolina Algonkians of the Carolina sounds and Outer Banks.[7]

Primarily sedentary cultures, such as those of modern Florida, Georgia and South Carolina, were the exception rather than the rule during this period. The predominant pattern was one of some seasonal movement, justifying at times the description seasonal nomadism. A characteristic pattern was the maintenance of a base village as an agricultural nexus for spring and early summer cultiva-

7. For the area from Florida to Virginia, John R. Swanton, *The Indians of the Southeastern United States,* Bureau of American Ethnology, Bulletin no. 137, Washington, D.C., 1946, is the fullest compendium.

tion, often combined with a summer fishing shift, or division, and, almost invariably, a winter hunting season engaged in mainly by the men. This pattern held true for most of the Algonkian-speaking peoples—those south of modern Maine—and also for the Iroquois. The Hurons were perhaps an exception[8] because they preferred a sedentary life, except when on the warpath, and tended to trade for their furs with other tribes rather than go to seek them. Farther north, near or beyond the limits of grain cultivation, nomadism was more nearly total, though still tending to follow the seasonal patterns dominated by fishing, gathering, and hunting.

Societal units in most of eastern North America were small and did not reach the size of those in the Lower Mississippi culture. There was perhaps a tendency toward more elaborate groupings. We know of cases where a single chief exercised a certain degree of authority over a dozen or more individual tribes, yet it is doubtful whether we can speak of anything as clearly defined as a confederation or "kingdom." Quite possibly it was during the period of early European contact and even under a degree of European influence that the Powhatan confederacy, "despotate" or "centralized monarchy"—whichever it is thought to be—[9] came into existence in the later sixteenth century. Certainly this was a factor with which the English colony at Jamestown had to reckon. Similarly, although the traditional date for the creation of the League of the Iroquois is about 1570, modern research places it later, appreciably after the development of permanent contact with the French and so probably a little after this period.

The Muskogean linguistic grouping, extending from the Timucua to the Coosa tribe after 1500, remained most subject to Mississippian influences and was the most advanced culture in the east, though its several parts exhibited many local variations.[10] The Algonkian-speaking group from modern North Carolina to Maine showed more basic cultural uniformity at a somewhat lower level

8. Bruce G. Trigger, *The Hurons: Farmers of the North* (New York, 1969).

9. Washburn, *Indian in America*, p. 46; P. L. Barbour, *Pocochontas and Her World* (Boston, 1970), p. 4.

10. Regina Flannery, *An Analysis of Coastal Algonquian Culture*, Catholic University of American Anthropological Series, no. 7, 1939, is a useful summary. Frederick Johnson (ed.), *Man in Northeastern North America*, Papers of the Robert S. Peabody Foundation for Archeology no. 3, 1946, is a guide to northern Algonkian and Eskimo activity. On the Eskimo, see also Edward M. Weyer, *The Eskimos* (1932).

than in the southeast.[11] The formidable Iroquois tribes—and the Huron and Tobacco Indians also—exhibited at once a combination of more northerly and more southerly cultural characteristics.[12] On the one hand they lived in strong, carefully constructed village units, engaged vigorously in agriculture, and had powerful chiefs; on the other, they were closely involved in hunting—expending much time and trouble on this—and, uniquely it would seem in the east, in trading successfully what they hunted. The more northerly Algonkian group, ranging from the partly settled Algonquins and Ottawa to the wholly nomadic Montagnais-Nascapi, were essentially hunters and gatherers. Many of them had little in the way of territorial roots, though they acknowledged broadly defined territorial hunting limits; they lived in small bands, oscillating between the extremes of gluttony and starvation, although sharing in their artifacts and clothing—as well as in their linguistic bases—some of the characteristics of the more prosperous and developed Algonkian cultures farther south.[13]

There was only a limited amount of interpenetration between these groupings. Montagnais went to the St. Lawrence in summer to barter furs with Micmac who came to fish; there they might meet St. Lawrence Iroquois (or Hurons, perhaps the same thing) who had come far from the interior to fish and to barter skins and some Lake Superior copper. The Iroquois penetrated inland from modern New York State to interior North Carolina chiefly as traders; the Susquehanna, in particular, played this role. Through the Iroquois, Lake Superior copper came down the Piedmont almost as far as the

11. The John White drawings of coastal Carolina Algonkian Indians, made in 1584–87, provide generally reliable evidence on dress and ornament for the more southerly part of the Algonkian area. They are best reproduced in Paul Hulton and D. B. Quinn, *The American Drawings of John White*, 2 vols. (London and Chapel Hill, N.C., 1964). The drawings of Timucua and adjoining tribes by Jacques le Moyne de Morgues (in Theodor de Bry, *America*, part ii [Frankfurt am Main, 1591]) are also valuable but are contaminated to a much greater degree by European influences. See Paul Hulton, *The Work of Jacques le Moyne de Morgues* (London, 1977).

12. Elizabeth Tooker (ed.), *Iroquois Culture History and Prehistory* (Albany, N.Y., 1967).

13. Charles C. Willoughby, *Antiquities of the New England Indians* (Cambridge, Mass., 1935) is still of some value; see also Gordon M. Day, "English-Indian Contacts in New England," *Ethnohistory*, IX (1962), 24–40; Alfred G. Bailey, *The Conflict of European and Eastern Algonkian Cultures, 1534–1700*, 2nd edition (Toronto, 1969). Francis Jennings *The Invasion of America* (Chapel Hill, N.C., 1975), offers new insights on the results of early contacts.

lesser supplies gleaned from the southern ranges of the Appalachians came north. We have indications of fairly far-reaching trade from the salt deposits of the Tennessee River Valley to the south and also across the Appalachians to the Atlantic coast, and there are signs of some trade in stone from the mountainous area to the almost stoneless coastal plain in modern North Carolina. Soapstone too, for pipes, moved fairly widely from its origins.

But apart from a scant knowledge of Iroquois trade, we have little idea of the mechanism of interchange between these different tribes and cultural groupings. Hernando de Soto's experience might suggest that there was a trading *lingua franca* which enabled his interpreter, Juan Ortiz, to make himself understood well beyond the confines of a single linguistic group. Cabeza de Vaca's experience might also demonstrate that a medicine man could travel and make a living by ranging over wide areas and through a series of only distantly related cultures. In the absence of adequate European records and of decisive archeological evidence alike, however, speculation on such matters cannot be taken very far.

Wars over hunting and fishing territories for plunder, sport, and for the perpetuation of hostile traditions helped to keep the population down in many areas. The comparatively favorable conditions along Chesapeake Bay and in the Lower Hudson Valley encouraged higher population densities in certain areas. So did regions of high-fertility soil where agriculture was practiced with some intensity, though it must be remembered that there was little or no soil fertilization or rotation and that cultivation areas had to be shifted fairly frequently to newly cleared land. Tribal economies were normally self-sufficient except for such marginal commodities as have been mentioned as articles of trade. How far the basic commodities—furs, skins, dried fish, dried meat and corn—were exchanged between tribes is almost unknown, aside from what little is heard of such exchanges along the St. Lawrence Valley in summer. In most cases, however, it did not take Europeans long to establish an exchange basis with the tribes they encountered, and as they developed more regular contacts, to build up a commodity purchase and distribution system from it. It may be that trading was more prevalent in indigenous society than we have evidence for.

If there were tendencies toward tribal consolidation in the sixteenth century, and possibly earlier, there were also indications of

disruptive elements at work. The mound-building culture of central Georgia, with its fine copper ornaments and its elaborate stone and pottery figures, was breaking up, probably as a result of the failure of its associated irrigation system, which had no other parallel in the east. It can scarcely be overemphasized that the tribal units encountered by Europeans throughout the east were mainly small; they were therefore exceptionally vulnerable to pressure and saturation by the overpowering effects of European culture.

Amerindian water-transport was by canoe, single-trunk dugouts in the south, birchbark within the effective growth limits of the paper birch, with some intermingling along a marginal zone, and with Eskimo bone or timber framed kayaks and umiaks, skin covered, in the north. Movement by water, mainly by river and lake rather than by sea (except for the Eskimo), gave the Indians of the north, especially, though all tribes in the east to some extent, a considerable degree of mobility. Using canoes, they went to hunt, to fight and to fish. The birchbark canoe in particular was an exceptionally flexible artifact. It could be made in the wilds by an Indian when needed, repaired from material obtainable by anyone with a cutting instrument, and carried over rapids, bars, and watersheds. It was most typically used by tribes with both a fixed base and an extended hunting area—invaluable in the St. Lawrence Valley and the Great Lakes area, though also used extensively in other parts wherever birch grew. Long hunting and fishing trips were characteristic of the more northerly Algonkian and certain Iroquois groups. The birchbark canoe was thus a vital means by which Indians living at a distance from European trading posts could make contact with them; and at a later stage it was equally vital to the Europeans in extending their contacts among the Indians, bringing goods for exchange to them and taking furs in return.

For the Indian, at least in the St. Lawrence area, canoe travel meant the possibility of distant culture contacts. The same could scarcely be said of the southern areas served by the single trunk dugout canoe, serviceable though it could be. It was heavier to move and impossible to portage, and so was used within a much narrower range by most of the tribes that employed it. It is possible that in the Mississippi Valley itself dugout canoes were used at times for longer excursions, as they would later be used by European explorers, but there appears to be no record of this.

The mobility of the northern Indians meant that extensive contacts with Europeans could take place quite rapidly and that Europeans themselves could move expeditiously through various Amerindian areas. Farther south—south of modern Maine—tribes had to be approached in smaller units, and were themselves less surely in contact with their more distant neighbors. Their knowledge of what lay beyond their immediate tribal grouping was often hazy and imprecise, whereas farther north it was often both extensive and accurate. All Indians knew their own hunting grounds, however extensive, very accurately; but beyond that their knowledge varied greatly. Many Indians could sketch maps on sand; could describe in their own terminology the routes they traveled; and could also follow hunting trails with great accuracy. But many of them displayed little curiosity about distant parts and had little idea of distance or ability to describe routes or make maps or diagrams of any sort, although they might go through the motions of so doing in order to placate impatient Europeans. None of the peoples living to the east of the Alleghenies and Appalachians, except the Susquehanna and perhaps some other Iroquois groups, seem to have had any idea of what lay beyond the great mountain chains or even approximately where the mountains were located. Dwellers in the coastal plain might occasionally venture into the Piedmont, but rarely, if ever, into the highlands. Most of the easterners who lived on the shores of the Atlantic Ocean had, then, little knowledge of or command of their macroscopic environment. Those to the north, and especially those in the St. Lawrence Valley, had a much more wide-ranging view, and—it is clear—a much deeper interest in the interrelationships, both physical and human, of the wider territories with which they were in contact.

The offensive and defensive equipment of the Amerindians was limited to weapons of wood, sinew, bone and stone. Bows and arrows, light throwing darts, clubs, axes and hammers covered practically the whole range of their armament. The Eskimo added the refinement of the harpoon, which they had passed to some of the Amerindian groups to the south of them; they also had specialized bird-darts. It appears that some wicker armor was used before white influence was possible, but in certain areas this was adopted in imitation of European armor. The Indian weapons sufficed for hunting and for intertribal conflict; they were of little use against

substantial numbers of Europeans armed with metal weapons or, more particularly, against firearms—inefficient as those of the sixteenth century frequently were. This does not mean that the Indians were not serious foes when they decided to be so. They had a long tradition of ambush and of surprise attack, and had learned to use fire as a weapon against hostile villages which could also be turned against European settlements. They were brave and constant in fighting under their own leaders, ruthless in conflict; this made them more formidable in the face of less determined or unprofessional Europeans than their equipment might otherwise have done. But their concept of war was episodic—short seasonal campaigns followed by long "off" seasons.

The typical form of Amerindian housing in the south was mud-walled, generally round though sometimes rectangular, with palmetto-leaf thatch. Over wide areas of territory, both Algonkian and Iroquois, the longhouse predominated. This had a pole frame, bent to take an arched roof, and was covered with bark or mats or even skins. It was large, sometimes acting as a multi-family unit; equipped with sleeping benches and racks for holding gear and stores, it held little else (though the Iroquois houses had storage lofts). In New England a domed wigwam of bark or mats over posts was usual, sometimes found alongside the longhouse. There was also a conical wigwam, more general farther north still but widely used as a temporary dwelling in hunting or fishing trips. The Eskimo summer houses, which were generally rectangular, roofed with skins over wood or whalebone supports, contrasted with the circular plan of their domed winter ice-block igloos.

In general, the Amerindian villages were small: a hundred households would constitute a large settlement in most areas. Some villages were open, with the houses scattered through the partly cleared woodland; others were compact, enclosed within a palisade. This was often a not very formidable fence, though we hear of stoutly defended villages among the Upper Creeks, and the Iroquois had elaborate high wooden defenses, with an inner gallery and watch towers. Within the villages and small towns in the south there were storage barns, mainly for the maize harvest and for seed, though dried food of other sorts was also deposited there. Farther north most storage appears to have been within the longhouses. The chief's house was normally distinguished by its size, and

amongst the Creeks we hear of chiefs' houses with balconies. Villages inside the Lower Mississippi culture normally contained a mound which had some ceremonial significance. Elsewhere there were other types of ceremonial centers in villages—circles of posts; perpetual fires; ossuaries. In compact villages the central space was normally left open (the Spaniards refer to villages having *plazas* in the south), sometimes with a communal fire in the center. Temple mounds dominated many settlements. Effigy mounds in the shape of a bird, bear or snake were probably maintained as monuments of the early Temple Mound period on an intertribal basis.

Around all these villages, from Florida to Maine, were evidences of agricultural and horticultural activity, varying in precise content from place to place, the cultivated ground being richer and more extensive in the south. Maize and beans, frequently intercropped, were the staples; squashes and gourds were also universal. Sunflowers and passion fruit (maypops) were common in the southeast; tobacco patches appear in most villages, even toward the north, where corn-growing became peripheral rather than basic. Nut trees do not appear to have been deliberately cultivated but they grew round the villages of those who consumed them. In places where the extent of soil which could be cleared round a village was limited there was no alternative, once it had become impoverished, but to move the site; where there was adequate choice of cultivable land nearby, new patches were brought into use as the old became used up. The cleared areas round the villages thus tended to grow, though the older ones were covered fairly rapidly with second growth timber.

Dogs were the only domestic animals. From time to time, they were eaten—on ceremonial occasions, or simply when food was short. Copper was widely used for ornament, though usually in small quantities. Along the St. Lawrence and south from the Great Lakes it was traded from the copper beds of Lake Superior, though precisely how far south has not yet been determined. It was apparently obtained also where it appeared naturally in the Connecticut Valley, on southern slopes in the Alleghenies, on the Roanoke River, and near the southern extremity of the Appalachian range. Copper was being used extensively for sheet copper ornament in the late Temple Mound area in northern Georgia and may have been annealed within the limits of the Lower Mississippi culture.

Elsewhere it was not worked in ways which made it suitable for tools or weapons. Small nuggets of silver were sometimes collected and used for ornament. No use of native gold has so far been verified, but in the extreme southeast quantities of Spanish silver and gold, obtained from shipwrecked vessels, circulated fairly widely after about 1530. Pearls (from both oyster and mussel) were collected extensively and used as ornaments in the south. Farther north, shell beads took their place: wampum belts made from certain beads were symbols of respect and prestige presents; so too in some areas were feather ornaments or skins decorated with porcupine quills.

No cotton was grown or used anywhere in the east, nor was there any weaving, though coverings were made of fur-strip weft on vegetable fiber warp, a development of the highly developed mat- and net-making activity of all the more settled tribes. Dyes were extracted from vegetable sources—black from sumach, red from puccoon—and appear to have been traded at times. The farther north one went, the greater the dependence on furs and skins for mantles, leggings, and moccasins. In the south the emphasis was largely on finely dressed and ornamented deerskin mantles and hangings; even the simple apron skirts adopted by many women were fringed and decorated with pearls. But clothing in the warmer areas was limited to breechclout or skirts in the summer. Only in the Eskimoid zones were there tailored garments, jackets and trousers, with hoods, skin boots and stockings as an effective defense against Arctic conditions. Yet the war and ceremonial attire was often elaborate, employing heads and tails of beasts and birds as well as skins and feathers.

The more prosperous the tribe, the more complex its social gradations tended to be. We have evidence of chiefs who controlled a substantial number of villages—Spanish sources indicate that the Upper Creek chieftain might have as many as forty. In such cases the chief lived in some state and was treated with considerable reverence, carried on a litter, fanned with feather wands. Lesser mortals lived in lesser state, though most chiefs were polygamous by virtue of their office even where monogamy was normal for their subjects, and almost all were treated with considerable deference unless they failed in war. In the richer areas, too, the chief took a substantial part of the tribe's total produce for himself; Powhatan had a string of storehouses for his perquisites of office. Elders

enjoyed much prestige and some power: councils usually preceded any major turn of tribal policy. Cult-leaders—whether priests, medicine men, or shamans combining the functions of healers and interceders with the gods—were widely represented and had some appreciable status, especially in the interpretation of natural phenomena and in setting times and places when it would be propitious to make war. They served a wide range of animistic and personified natural forces. Ceremonial of a religious character, especially in dance displays, helped to bind the society together.

There appears to have been little attempt at differentiation of labor, except between the sexes. Men were expected universally to play a full part in hunting, fishing and war; they also contributed the basic structural work on the village. Women bore all or much the greater share in agriculture and pottery-making as well as in running the households and making materials for both clothes and houses. In large parts of the south succession was matrilineal, and descent through the eldest child of the eldest sister of the chief led to a number of women becoming chiefs, gaining, it appears, as much respect as men. Men who reacted against their sexual and social role formally changed their sexual status so that transsexuality was general from Florida westward to the Mississippi in the south. Such persons, a few in each village, had specialized tasks in dealing with the sick and dead, but otherwise dressed, spoke, and worked like women. The parallel change of role by women has not been observed in the east.

The Amerindian society was well adapted to the woods, rivers and shores, and rich agricultural land which distinguished much of eastern North America. In the north, climatic conditions might be harsh and comforts few; in other areas, war might continue beyond the limits of rational competition. Yet in general, for most of the time, Indian life was satisfying without demanding too great an individual or collective effort. The patterns of living were well adapted to the environment. Occasionally natural catastrophes might destroy or scatter a tribe, but most of these people in their aboriginal state showed a striking capacity to survive, and many managed to carry this capacity over into the contact period. The social coherence of many tribes (though not all) was somewhat limited; their physical resources for resisting external aggression, when this took the shape of European power, were not substantial.

Yet the Amerindians in the east, although they were ultimately swamped by the Europeans, did not prove incapable of adaptation. During the sixteenth century many of them learned something of how to maintain themselves while developing closer contacts with the newcomers and increasingly acquiring the habit of trade. What they did not experience before 1612 was sustained, large-scale white settlement, which was in the end to destroy most of them. They lacked, too, immunity against the European diseases—colds, influenza, measles, smallpox, fevers—which would prove finally more deadly than swords, guns, or alcohol.

Discovery must be seen as a reciprocal process. The Amerindian discovery of Europe through the occasional visits over the century of favored individuals (who did not always survive the experience) brought some understanding of the European homelands to a limited number of Indians.[14] This went step by step with the discovery, on a more extensive scale, of Amerindians by Europeans. But with continuous European settlement, cultural submersion was soon to take the place of reciprocity.

14. Carolyn Foreman, *Indians Abroad, 1493–1938* (Norman, Okla., 1943), is a preliminary sketch of the subject.

# CHAPTER 2

## *The Norse Threshold*

A S early as the sixteenth century, Europeans interested in New
World discovery began to discuss the origin of the Amerindian
and Eskimo populations found there; this discussion continued in
the seventeenth and eighteenth centuries to produce a voluminous
but somewhat repetitive literature. If there were people in the
Americas, they must have found their way to the New World after
Noah's Flood, since the Biblical stories were implicitly accepted.
Consequently, America must have been known to the ancients.
There were hints of distant lands in the Bible, in Greek and Latin
classical literature, in early Christian legend and medieval secular
tales; from them arose the possibility of Atlantic crossings by Jews,
Phoenicians, Carthaginians, Greeks, Romans, Irish saints, Iberian
refugees from Muslim invasion, Norwegians, even Welsh prince-
adventurers. These found themselves incorporated in a body of
doctrine which maintained that, since America must have been inhabited long before its discovery, the tales or constructs on earlier
Old World contacts from the east were in theory acceptable to those
who did not think Acosta's intelligent conclusion that America was
inhabited from Asia sufficient to explain the whole range of human
enterprise and society found in the New World from the Arctic to
Patagonia.[1]

1. Joseph de Acosta, *Historia natural y moral de las Indias* (Seville, 1590); see Lee E.
Huddleston, *Origins of the American Indian. European Concepts,* 1492–1729. (Austin, Tex., 1967), and Jacques Lafaye, *Quetzalcoatl et Guadalupe* (Paris, 1974), pp.
51–77.

The tales of the occupation of the Americas, which had been developed for the illustration of Biblical history, gradually gave way in the eighteenth and nineteenth centuries to a more scientific skepticism, which swept them all under the carpet, accepting instead only the attested voyages from the fifteenth century onwards. An element of attachment to the old stories lingered, however, and after about 1870 sprouted many new variations of the old myths. Apart from the eccentricities of individual writers—of which early American history has had many—there were two main reasons for their growth and survival. The first was that the representatives of the successive national groups that poured into North America liked to cultivate any tales which seemed to show that their ancestors had a share in American discovery and so enhanced their national pride in the adopted country. The second was that Americans desired—and still desire—to extend the range of their cultural history. The Amerindian past has seemed too foreign and too limited; a longer heritage of cultural contact with Europe appears more fitting to a powerful state which has, nevertheless, rather shallow historical roots in its present territories. Consequently, the cultivation of alleged discoveries of artifacts and of documentary evidence to sustain the older myths or to permit the erection of new ones has gradually grown into an extensive industry. Though wholly outside the territory of accepted historical scholarship, this mythic history seems liable to invade, by repetition and invention, the field of scholarly research and interpretation. The Kensington Stone, Dighton Rock and other manufactures or misinterpretations won considerable acceptance before being discredited by reputable scholarship; the highly sophisticated Vinland Map won even more.[2] Of those legends which had appeared among the older myths, only one has secured its place among the realities of history: that which asserted that the Norsemen played a part in American discovery in the eleventh century and possibly maintained some slight contact with American shores until the mid-fourteenth century. Even here the definition of what is and is not acceptable has allowed the mythmakers to win some gains at the expense of critical scholarship,

2. See Erik Wahlgren, *The Kensington Stone* (Madison, Wis., 1958); Helen Wallis (and others), "The Strange Case of the Vinland Map," *Geographical Journal*, CXL (1974), 183–214. The discussion and bibliography in Wilcomb E. Washburn (ed.), *The Vinland Map Conference* (Chicago, 1971), set out the many issues raised by the map before scientific tests had established that it was almost certainly spurious.

although they have not so far managed to consolidate them. It must be emphasized that before the late fifteenth century, aside from very limited Norse contacts, no Europeans are known to have crossed the Atlantic to North America; nor can it even be argued that it is likely they did so. The whole elaborate structure of the pseudo-historians who believe otherwise is no more than a series of mental constructs, composed of wish-fulfillment and invention, not historical evidence. At the same time, the story of Norse activity in the Americas is gradually becoming a little more clearly defined, though there are still substantial areas where conjecture and knowledge jostle uneasily together.

Greenland was the first landmass in the west in longitudes close to those of America to be visited by Europeans. The occupation of parts of modern Greenland by the Norsemen was a continuation of the island-hopping which had brought their ancestors from the mainland of Europe to far northern—and western—Iceland. To that extent the Greenland colony was a projection of Europe. The conversion of the settlers to Christianity, the visits of clergy from Europe, the knitting of the Greenland settlements by trade to Iceland and Norway, and the sovereignty of the king of Norway in those far distant parts, like the ecclesiastical authority of the Pope, extended and consolidated the European links. It is possible to incorporate the history of the Greenland colony integrally into a history of northern Europe: it is possible also virtually to exclude it from a history of America.[3] Yet Greenland was an Atlantic land that faced both ways, as the Azores were to do and later still Newfoundland at various times. The Greenland settlements faced west; they were in the same climatic zone as the American Arctic; and they were separated by only a few hundred miles of navigable sea from Baffin Island and Labrador. Thus their inhabitants lived a life in no way distinct from that which they would have led, in similar latitudes, on the great western continent itself. Finally, they were in contact with America—tentatively and intermittently, it is true, but as an extension of their way of life in Greenland, not as something different or separate from it.

3. Finn Gad, *A History of Greenland*, I, *To 1700* (London, 1970), and Fridtjof Nansen, *In Northern Mists*, 2 vols. (London, 1911), give an extensive view of the Greenland setting.

Modern continental and national allegiances cannot remove the reality that the Greenland colony was in a sense an "American" experience for Europeans. Had the colony survived into the new era of discovery, this would have been obvious; the fact that it faded away before the discoveries took place has enabled this "American" aspect to be minimized. But it should not be overemphasized either. Unless spectacular archeological discoveries are made which completely upset what has so far been established, we must conclude that the character of the Greenland settlements continued to be molded by Europe and by very local conditions, and that the influence of the discovery of Helluland, Markland and Vinland—the American lands found and, to some very limited extent, exploited by the settlers—were only marginal in their influence on the Greenland colony and its people.

In no other area of American studies is it so necessary to state what the evidence consists of before attempting to make a narrative out of it. The first datable references to a Norse discovery of lands to the west of Greenland appear in the manuscript of Adam of Bremen's "History of the Archbishops of Hamburg-Bremen," written circa 1270–76, in which he reported[4] that he had heard from Swein Estridsson, king of the Danes, of an island "which is called Wineland, because vines grow there and give the noblest wine," while there was also evidence that unsown corn grew there. Ari Thorgilsson, writing his "Book of the Icelanders" *(Islendinga-bok)*[5] before 1134, mentions "Skraelings" whom the Greenlanders found occupying "Vinland," but gives no connected detail. An Icelandic geography, begun before 1159 (though finished later) says[6] that Helluland is south of Greenland; next to it is Markland, and then it is not far to Vinland the Good. Only after these data have been recorded can the versions of the two sagas or tales which give us our connected stories of the Norse discovery be dated; but it is probable that behind each of them lay a long oral tradition and, almost certainly, versions written earlier than those to which we now have access.

4. Adam of Bremen, *History of the Archbishops of Bremen,* translated by Francis T. Tschan (New York, 1959), pp. 215–20; see D. B. Quinn, *North American Discovery, Circa 1000–1612* (New York, 1971), pp. 22–23.

5. "The Book of the Icelanders," edited and translated by Halldór Hermannsson, *Icelandica,* XX (1930), 64.

6. H. Hermannsson, "The Problem of Wineland," *Icelandica,* XIXV (1936), 64.

The Greenlanders' saga *(Groenlandinga saga)* is now considered to have been written about 1200, that is, less than two hundred years after the events it records; Eirik the Red's saga *(Eiríks saga rauda)* is considered to belong to the second half of the thirteenth century, probably not before 1270. The opinion of the authorities who regard the Greenlanders' saga as the earlier now regard it also as the more authoritative, with Eirik's being a later, more narrowly based compilation.[7] Precisely the opposite view was expressed in 1936 by Hermannsson.[8] Almost all serious scholars regard both as reliable, historical sources only within narrow limits. A Danish writer[9] says that, since the sagas were "written on the basis of the ancient partly oral tradition many years later," they cannot without further proof be used as a reliable historical source, "even though their authors regarded their work as a sort of historical account." In Greenland an appreciable amount of the information they convey has been established by archeology, and if this is so, it seems likely that "their accounts of the course of events . . . must be accepted in broad outline." For North America there is so far only one archeological site which is almost certainly Norse. In view of the conflicts and discrepancies between the two sagas, it is difficult to determine what was the outline of events with any approach to precision, even though the time scale within which they took place—the decade 1000–10, with perhaps some extension beyond the later date—can be cross-checked against Icelandic and Greenland data and is reasonably well established.[10]

Eirik the Red was exiled from Iceland in 981 or 982 and went to explore a land earlier sighted to the west of Iceland.[11] Working his way along the hostile East Greenland coast, he rounded Cape Farewell and found in West Greenland good harbors and green, reasonably level pastures. He returned to Iceland to sing the praises of his

7. Gwyn Jones, *The North Atlantic Saga* (London, 1965), pp. 225–228, and his introduction to the reprint of Geoffrey M. Gathorne-Hardy, *The Norse Discoverers of America* (London, 1970), p. xviii.

8. Hermannsson, "The Problem of Wineland," 6–47.

9. Knud J. Krogh, *Viking Greenland* (Copenhagen, 1967), p. 14.

10. For the data obtained from the sagas Jones, *North Atlantic Saga*, gives the translations used below; Magnus Magnusson and Hermann Pálsson, *The Vinland Sagas* (Harmondsworth, Middx., and Baltimore, 1965), provide another valuable translation. The original texts were authoritatively edited by Halldór Hermannsson, *The Vinland Sagas* (Ithaca, N.Y., 1944).

11. Jones, *North Atlantic Saga*, pp. 143–144.

THE NORSE ROUTE
FROM GREENLAND
TO NORTH AMERICA
(After H. Ingstad)

Green Land, and in 985 or 986 led fourteen ships to found what came to be known as the Eastern Settlement on Julianehåb. He himself went on northward to establish his own Western Settlement on Godthåb Fjord, and to build up his household there at Brattahlid. He had a family of three sons, Leif, Thorvald and Thorstein, and a daughter, Freydis.

Bjarni Herjolfsson, another Icelander, had been in Norway, and when he returned found that his father had followed Eirik to Greenland. In turn, Bjarni followed his father.[12] His ship was soon lost on the western waters, but he eventually made a landfall where "the land was not mountainous and was covered with forest and low hills," and then sailed on again. Next, he saw a land "high mountainous and glaciered," though he was not yet convinced that it was Greenland; but on his final attempt he found himself on the Greenland coast at his father's farm at Herjolfnes. Later, he went to visit Eirik at Brattahlid, told him of his discoveries, and raised the question of exploring the new lands.

So much for the Greenlanders' saga account of the discovery of the western lands. But Eirik's saga says[13] it was Leif Eiriksson who made the first discovery. In 999 Leif visited Norway, was converted to Christianity, and undertook to introduce it into Greenland. On his way homeward in 1000 he was blown off course and "lighted on those lands whose existence he had not so much as dreamt of before" (Bjarni now being ignored); here were "wheatfields wild there and vines too"; maple trees were seen. Some timbers for house-building as well as samples of other things were brought to Brattahlid. Then Thorstein, his brother, took up the discovery, setting out to explore the new lands; but his voyage was abortive, his ships being carried away (it was said to Iceland) before he could succeed in returning to Greenland.

The other story, in the Greenlanders' saga,[14] is that Bjarni, having made his first visit to Greenland, returned to Norway and then after some time set out again for Greenland, where he had discussions with Eirik about the lands he had discovered. This would seem to have been in 1000. Eirik was not fit to go; Leif, his eldest son, took Bjarni's ship and went back on Bjarni's old track. He found the land

12. *Ibid.*, pp. 146–148.
13. *Ibid.*, pp. 172–173.
14. *Ibid.*, pp. 148–151.

with the glaciers—"great glaciers, and right up to the glaciers from the sea as it were a single slab of rock"—and decided to call it Helluland (Flatstone Land). Then Leif and his men sailed on further to sight the second land, which they reconnoitered, finding the country "flat and covered with forest, with extensive white sand wherever they went, and shelving gently to the sea," so that they called it Markland (Timberland). They set sail and were two days out at sea before they sighted the third land. First of all there was a grassy, dew-covered offshore island; then a mainland cape pointing north. They worked westward to the sound between island and cape. The ship grounded, but they got her off and into a river and eventually to a lake through which the river flowed. They liked the site, camped there, and decided to build a homestead and winter there.

In a famous passage, the saga continues: "There was no lack of salmon there in river or lake, and salmon larger than they had ever seen before. The nature of the land was so choice, it seemed to them that none of the cattle would require fodder for the winter"—they had intended to settle if they brought their livestock with them and so grassy land was one objective. "Day and night were of more equal length there than in Greenland or Iceland." Parties were sent out to explore, and one man, a German, Tyrkir, found "grapes and vines." They loaded a boat with the vines and grapes and cut timber for the ship's cargo, while "Leif gave the land a name in accordance with the good things they found in it, calling it Vinland." In the spring they brought their cargo, grapes and all, to Brattahlid, where Eirik is said to have died later in the year—though it may have been in 1007, not 1001, that he died.

According to the same saga,[15] Thorvald was the next of the brothers to take up western voyaging, using Leif's ship, sailing to Vinland, and wintering in Leif's homestead, Leifsbudir, where they lived on fish that they managed to catch. In the spring they went exploring westward, continuing through the summer and returning to Leifsbudir in the autumn. They reported that they had seen "a beautiful and well-wooded land, the woods scarcely any distance from the sea, with white sands, and a great many islands and shallows." Apart from one wooden "grain-holder," they found no signs of human

15. *Ibid.*, pp. 152–153.

occupation. Another winter at Leifsbudir followed, and this time in the spring they explored to the north. In heavy weather their ship ran aground, ripping off the keel; they rebuilt it on the nearby cape, which they called Kjalarnes (Keelhead). Then, sailing eastward, they entered a fjord and moored the ship near "a headland jutting out there which was entirely covered with forest." Here they found their first trace of human habitation: three skin boats with nine men in them. They killed eight of them and took two of the boats, the ninth escaping in his boat. Threatened later by a whole fleet of boats, they managed to defend themselves and drive the natives off, but Thorvald was wounded and died of his wound. They buried him at the headland, which they named Krossanes since he was a Christian. The rest returned to Leifsbudir, wintered again, "gathered grapes and vines for the ship," and then went back to Greenland to report to Leif.

Thorstein determined to find his brother's grave and bring his body back to Greenland. With his wife Gudrid, he re-equipped the same ship and set out, but was able to make no headway and so put back to Lysufjord. There disease struck his crew and eventually himself; he died, and Gudrid brought his body and his ship back to Brattahlid.

This would seem to have covered the years 1002 to 1005 or 1006. We now have a story in two versions. The Greenlanders' saga[16] says that a man from Norway, Thorfinn Karlsefni, wintered with Leif at Brattahlid, and after the new year married the widow Gudrid. With his new wife, sixty men and five women, and much livestock, he set out to occupy Leif's old homestead, to which Leif had agreed. They arrived safely and settled in, helped by finding the meat of a stranded whale. They enjoyed hunting, fishing and, of course, grapes, while timber was cut and dressed. They wintered safely and the next summer the native Skraelings came with packs of sables and other furs to trade. They wanted arms but Thorfinn gave them only milk. Thorfinn stockaded the homestead in case they came back during the second winter. They did so and were again treated in the same way, but when one attempted to steal arms he was killed. The Skraelings then appeared in force and there was a battle in the forest, in which the natives were defeated. A further winter passed;

16. *Ibid.*, pp. 156–158.

then Karlsefni decided to return to Greenland. This they did, bearing "many valuable commodities in the shape of vines, grapes and furs." This would cover the years 1005–09 or 1006–10.

The Eirik's saga version differs.[17] Karlsefni and Snorri Thordandsson, in one ship, and Bjarni Gunolfson and Thorhall Gumlasson in another, reached Brattahlid on a trading and colonizing expedition. They stayed over the winter and Karlsefni married Gudrid. They then got Leif's permission to go to Vinland. With both ships, 160 men in all and some women, they sailed north to Bjarneyjar (apparently Bjarni's Isle, discovered by him, and not just Bear Island). Two days sailing further on they found a land with "a great forest and many wild animals" and an island with a polar bear on it (they called it Bjarney—Bear—Island), and the nearby land Markland. Still two further days sailing and they reached a headland which marked the beginning of "an open harborless coast there, with long beaches and sands." Finding the keel of a ship at the place they called Kjalarnes, they named the beaches Furdustrander (Marvelstrand) because "it was such a long business sailing along them." After that they encountered a coast in which were many bays. Two Irish ("Scots") with them were sent to reconnoiter, and they returned with grapes and selfsown wheat: Karlsefni congratulated them on finding "a choice productive land." They reached a fjord running in from the sea at whose mouth was an island they named Straumsey (with many seabirds' nests); then, sailing up the fjord— they named it Straumsfjord—they settled within sight of mountains on land which had good grass. The winter was hard since they had insufficient food, though their cattle did well. Thorhall the Hunter became touched in the head and wandered off. A dead whale came ashore and provided meat which sickened them, but after they recovered they caught plenty of fish. They went further up the fjord in spring, hunting, fishing and collecting birds' eggs.

Their exploration plan was for one party to go north: Thorhall Gumlasson took nine men for this expedition since he believed Vinland to lie to the north of Furdustrander and Kjalarnes. Meanwhile Karlsefni took the main party south. But Thorhall was driven out to sea, made for Ireland where his party was enslaved, and there died. Karlsefni sailed "for a long time" until he reached "a river

17. *Ibid.*, pp. 176–187.

which flowed down from the land into a lake and so to the sea," the estuary being barred and the ship able to enter only at full tide. They named it Hop and found there fields of selfsown wheat where the land was low, "and vines wherever it was hilly." They trapped halibut, their cattle did well and there was good hunting. A fleet of skin boats with "small, ill favoured men . . . ugly hair on their heads . . . big eyes . . . broad in the cheeks," came to inspect them but rowed away again. So they settled for the winter, some in houses near the lake, others further into the mainland: "no snow fell, and their entire stock found its food grazing in the open."

In spring, the Skraeling boats came to trade furs for cloth (they would not give them weapons). Although frightened away once by Karlsefni's bull, they returned to attack. Karlsefni's men held them back for a time, then retreated to the shelter of some rocks. Gudrid rallied them and they were driven off with the loss of two men. Now Karlsefni decided to leave the land, since "there would always be fear and strife dogging them there on account of those who already inhabited it." Sailing north, they found some Skraelings asleep and killed them; they also found a cape where there were many animals. Karlsefni returned to Straumsfjord. Bjarni and Gudrid continued to the north to look for Thorhall, past Kjalarnes—westward from which was "a wilderness of forest-land"—encountering a one-legged creature which shot arrows at them, and then came south again.

And so they spent a third winter at Straumsfjord, though now there were divisions and quarrels amongst the settlers. In the spring they set out for home, reached Markland, and captured some Skrae-lings from whom they managed to extract information—as they thought—about their country. They returned to winter with Eirik the Red (who may well have been dead by then) while Karlsefni eventually went back to Iceland. It does not seem possible to recon-cile in detail the two versions of Karlsefni's expedition: the topo-graphical indications appear to be quite distinct. Such divergences should act as a warning against any attempt to use the sagas alone as evidence of where the Norse explorers went.

The Greenlanders' saga adds a further voyage.[18] Freydis, Eirik's daughter, entered into a partnership with two recently arrived Ice-

18. *Ibid.*, pp. 158–162.

landers, Helgi and Finnbolgi, and their followers to go to Vinland.
Leif once again said they could use Leifsbudir. The two ships arrived there, but Freydis took the homestead for her own followers
and excluded her partners, who built their hall "further away from
the sea by the lakeside." There appears to have been bad feeling
between them throughout the settling period. During the winter,
Freydis came to covet her partners' ship. She tricked her husband
into believing that Helgi and Finnbolgi had physically maltreated
her and so incited him to attack and kill them and their men, while
she herself polished off the five women. She took both ships and all
their possessions as well as her own back to Greenland, trying to
cover up what had happened, though it came out in the end. When
Karlsefni eventually went to Norway, a man from Bremen bought
from him the figurehead of his ship, carved from maple wood from
Vinland, the first import specifically said to have come from North
America to Europe.

These tales—however agreeable or otherwise they may appear to
the modern historian—establish little more than that for a period
of some ten years, in the opening decade of the eleventh century,
a number of expeditions went from Greenland to the western
lands.[19] There does not seem to be much difficulty in identifying
Helluland with some part or other of the long coastline of Baffin
Island, or Markland with the coast of Labrador further south
(though the tree line may have been rather farther north in the
eleventh century than at present), even if the whole coast southward
from where trees began could give the name some justification. But
Vinland has proved wholly elusive: how do Leifsbudir, Straumsfjord, and Hop relate to each other? Was the Leifsbudir of one saga
the Straumsfjord of the other? Or were Hop, Leifsbudir, and
Straumsfjord somewhere else? Gwyn Jones has pointed out that the
Vinland of the Greenlanders' saga is static: it centers on Leifsbudir.
The Vinland of Eirik the Red's saga is more mobile, and the implication is that it covers a wide area, with at least two centers.

19. The best brief study of these is in Jones, *North Atlantic Saga*, pp. 77–97, with
some added points in his introduction to the reprint of Gathorne-Hardy, *The Norse
Discoverers of America*, which is itself of interest. Einar Haugen, *Voyages to Vinland* (New
York, 1942), is valuable. The discoveries of Helge Ingstad (pp. 36–39 below) mean
that many of the older narrative discussions have been outdated. The controversial
literature on the location of Vinland is almost unlimited.

The vines and grapes of Vinland are still a locus for scholarly controversy which has never been resolved. Are they real grapes growing perhaps rather farther north, in the milder climate of the time, than the 44° N. latitude of modern times which is their limit? If so, why did they appear to have been available in the spring? Or was there an early misinterpretation of an archaic word *vin, vinber*, "grass," for meadowland, which soon corrupted the tales? Or were the "grapes" merely some other berries from which wines could be made? Or indeed, at the limits of skepticism, is the inclusion of grapes just another indication that much of the saga story, in either version, is fiction; and if the grapes, how much else? The problem is to avoid credulity at one extreme and virtually complete skepticism, such as Nansen's,[20] at the other. Most Canadians tend to accept that all the Vinland voyages took place within their territory; most Americans hope that it can be proved that Vinland was within the present territory of the United States. But such modern preferences have little to do with the study of the Vinland voyages themselves.

It may be that we can see certain patterns emerging. Eirik the Red set himself up as lord of a self-contained territory in Greenland, from which his men ranged in their hunting expeditions well beyond the Arctic Circle. Later men were to go certainly to beyond 72°N., possibly much further north. The Vinland expeditions can be seen as attempts to create a further extension of this lordship by him and his sons farther to the west. Leifsbudir can be seen as a second Brattahlid, the central homestead of a lordship, which he intended as a focus for a territory for his son Leif. That Leif regarded it as such is indicated, perhaps, in the sagas by his reported refusal to relinquish it to any other member of his family except on a temporary basis. Moreover, it can be seen as a designated location for further groups arriving from Iceland. Brattahlid could support only so many people under a single lordship. Newcomers were diverted westwards. Thus we find that Karlsefni and his companions were sent on western colonizing expeditions; so were the ill-fated part-

20. Fridtjof Nansen, *In Northern Mists,* in 1911 accepted the fact of the Norse voyages, but regarded the sagas as wholly unreliable in their topography and as mere tales based on distant memories of voyages. Matti E. Kapps, "Shifting Vinlands," *Terrae Incognitae,* III (1971), 97–106, indicates how widely estimates can vary from one another (his own require some revision).

ners of Freydis. There we might think of them as being exploited by Eirik the Red's sons and daughter. Karlsefni, even though he had been accepted into the family, quit after his three years were up since he could not find a life which was both quiet and profitable in Vinland; Helgi and Finnbolgi were not so fortunate. The western lands were attractive as providing timber that was stouter and less rotten than the driftwood most extensively used in Greenland, but permanent settlement was not necessary to exploit this. The hunting that we hear about was presumably largely of moose and caribou; the polar bears, the whales, the salmon, the halibut could all be acquired directly from Greenland itself, and the summer expeditions along the shores of the western lands to acquire supplementary supplies may have continued. Grazing was somewhat different: grassland had special attractions, as no doubt had the climate which permitted it to exist. But grasslands, to be fully exploited, did require permanent settlement. The grasslands in northern Newfoundland may well have been better than those in Greenland; those on coasts farther south were very far from the Greenland bases and settlers would have tended to be isolated there. Agricultural settlement would have involved the wholesale colonizing of a new area —the creation, as it were, of the Further Western Settlement to add to the Eastern Settlement and Western Settlement in Greenland. The small numbers of those who went on the voyages; the strains between the settlers which emerge in the saga stories; the impact of aboriginal hostility balanced against the small gains in fur trading; the probable capital loss to Eirik's family group of a decade's experimentation—all these factors (or at least such of them as may prove relevant) add up to good reasons for abandoning any attempt to maintain a settlement or even a major exploring program for the western lands.

The Greenland settlements had a long and not unprosperous history after the ending of the series of so-called Vinland voyages.[21] From 985 to 1261 the Greenlanders were independent, though they kept close contacts with Iceland and less close ones with Norway. Around 1260, both Iceland and the Greenlanders were under pressure from the king of Norway to accept his authority: the Greenland-

21. Krogh, *Viking Greenland,* and Gad, *History of Greenland,* I, contain full accounts of the Greenland settlements; for its broader context, Gwyn Jones, *A History of the Vikings* (London, 1968) is valuable.

ers did so in 1261, the Icelanders in 1262. The inducement in the case of Iceland was the promise of annual subsidies of food; the case of Greenland was apparently similar since an annual trading ship thereafter made her way from Norway to the Eastern Settlement. The settlements had between them at their peak some three to four hundred homesteads and some eighteen or nineteen ecclesiastical establishments. Estimates of population vary widely: 2,000 is an absolute minimum; 4,000 appears a reasonable estimate and 6,000 just possible. From 985 to 1200, the climate was mild; from 1200 to 1300, it was becoming colder, and thereafter remained static for a while. It was during this period that the Western Settlement declined. The climate may have made the keeping of livestock increasingly difficult, and the marginal changes in distribution of marine and land animals may have led to a decline in hunting and fishing. Certainly Thule Eskimo were coming down from the north in some numbers. Although decisive evidence of severe conflict between them and the settlers is lacking, their competition for declining food resources may have been more important than their mutual hostility.

In all this Vinland plays, in the surviving records, almost no part. In 1121 we are told that Eirik, the Greenlanders' bishop (a missionary bishop, not a territorial one at this time, apparently) either "set out for Vinland" or "went to look for" it. But whether he wished to convert the aborigines, or to revive exploration, and whether he succeeded in his expedition is unknown. Then, 226 years later, a small vessel from Greenland, with seventeen or eighteen men on board, limped into the harbor of Snaefelsnes in Iceland, having been blown off course on her way from Markland, and thus providing evidence of a continued trade in timber from the western lands.[22] By this time the Western Settlement was dying: by 1350 it had, apparently, come to an end. The lordship founded by Eirik the Red had had a life of some 365 years, compared with the mere decade that Vinland had lasted. The Eastern Settlement declined much more slowly, though decline it did. The period of the union of Norway and Sweden with Denmark in 1361 roughly coincided with the decline and ending of the visit of the annual trading ship

22. Translated by Gwyn Jones, *North Atlantic Saga*, p. 96, from Gustav Storm, *Islandske Annaler indtil 1578* (Christiana, 1888), pp. 112, 320; Quinn, *North American Discovery*, pp. 19–20.

(1369); thereafter, trading contacts with Norway and Iceland seem to have become very intermittent. Gardar had still an active Greenland community at the opening of the fifteenth century since a wedding was celebrated there in 1408 at which some Icelanders, who returned in 1410, were present. That is the last datable contact with the Greenlanders. The latest occupants of the Eastern Settlement are not now understood to have suffered severely from malnutrition, though they may have been plagued by epidemic diseases.[23]

The earliest Christians in the Western Settlement, as excavated, appear to have been buried with minimal grave goods; those of the later Eastern Settlement were buried in their clothes, many of which have survived, and this might suggest they were not in a state of severe economic distress. The clothes were those of the peasants and poorer townspeople of northern Europe, which did not change significantly between 1150 and 1400. The most recent view is that only two rather more elaborate women's dresses, and, most significantly, a buttoned man's dress of a type which appears in Norway about 1400, record anything which may point to contacts around or shortly after 1400. By that time the climate was getting milder again. But it was then that all evidence for the continuation of the settlement disappears, though the Roman authorities continued to assume until the end of the fifteenth century that a Christian community, cut off, survived in Greenland. It may have gone by 1425, or by 1450; the chance that any individuals survived to overlap with the new discoverers of the western lands—the Englishmen, Portuguese, Italians in the Spanish and English service—is minimal. Scandinavians like to think that they did survive since this would give Denmark, the heir to medieval Greenland, a claim to have had a continuous hold on transatlantic land all the way from 985 to 1500 or later. Few people now seriously consider there are likely to have been survi-

23. An optimistic view of the survival of the colonists is taken in Gad, *History of Greenland*, I, 152–57; and a somewhat more pessimistic one by Krogh, *Viking Greenland*, pp. 72–73 (whose views on the dating of clothing have modified those of Gad). Björn Thorsteinsson, *Enska Öldin* (Reykjavik, 1970), considers that English ships were trading with the colony in the fifteenth century, but has no authoritative evidence. Tryggvi J. Oleson, *Early Voyages and Northern Approaches, 1000–1632* (Toronto, 1963), pp. 44–90, developed an extravagant theory of the dispersal of the colonists and their assimilation with the Eskimo. Discoveries of early sites in the Ungava peninsula and elsewhere in northern Quebec have produced so far insoluble problems of interpretation (see *Saga-Book*, XVIII [1970–71], 216–219).

vors after 1500.[24] It cannot, however, be stressed too strongly that Greenland gives transatlantic history a continuity which it otherwise could not have had, and that the first European colony across the ocean was in many respects the pioneer of those which followed 1492, even if the Vinland voyages occupied only a tiny part of its history.

There is a modern appendix which must be added to the Vinland story. Near the entrance to the Strait of Belle Isle, at the eastern end and on the Newfoundland side, not far from the dominating bulk of Belle Isle, the archeologist Helge Ingstad, following as it happened in the footsteps of Jorgen Meldgård, in 1960 found a site which he considered, from surface indications, likely to be one of those used by the Norse voyagers.[25] From 1961 to 1968 he and his wife, Anne Stine Ingstad, identified and excavated fifteen occupation sites, the majority of them former houses, on the edge of a stream and surrounded on two sides by meadowy expanses at L'Anse aux Meadows. The most prominent feature was a large building, very similar in outline and character to those "halls" identified in Greenland as the nuclei of the major homesteads. The "hall"—and it would appear to have been such—had an ember pit similar to those used in Greenland and other Scandinavian countries, and also a substantial number of rooms. The smaller houses varied from fairly substantial house enclosures to small booths. There were boatsheds (or what seemed to be such) and a smithy. In the latter were substantial residues of slag and bog iron, indicating that the iron had been forged on the spot—and there is indeed bog iron readily available. The buildings were defined by collapsed turf walls, a number showing a substantial number of layers, but there were no traces of roof timbers: stones were used to define

24. *Norse Atlantic Saga*, pp. 89–94; *History of the Vikings*, pp. 306–311. H. G. Bandi, *Eskimo Prehistory* (London, 1969), p. 171, thought they may have been "wiped out some time around 1500, but we do not know exactly how."

25. Helge Ingstad, *Land Under the Pole Star* (London, 1966) and *Westward to Vinland* (London, 1969), gives an account of the background to the discovery of the L'Anse aux Meadows site and of the early stages in its excavation. Anne Stine Ingstad, "The Norse Settlement at L'Anse aux Meadows. A Preliminary Report from the Excavations, 1961–1968," *Acta Archaeologica*, XLI (Copenhagen, 1970), 109–154, is the most authoritative account (see *Geographical Journal*, CXL [1974], 202, 205). A full discussion of all the implications of the discovery must await the final report on the excavations.

footings in some cases. Scraps of iron and copper were found but no large deposit of artifacts. A spindle whorl of soapstone was identical with a number found in Greenland; a ring-headed bronze pin had close Norse analogies; and there was a stone lamp of a type used in Greenland. The acid soil, moving ice or scavenging Eskimo (some Eskimo artifacts were found) may account for the lack of more specific evidence of Norse occupation. Radio carbon analysis of suitable materials gave readings acceptably close to A.D. 1000. The published data appear to be sufficient to establish L'Anse aux Meadows with little doubt as a site occupied by the Greenlanders in the eleventh century. The complete absence of any artifacts which can be linked specifically with a later period would appear to rule out the theory that it was a Basque whaling station.

This discovery revolutionizes the study of the Vinland saga tales. A homestead has at last been discovered which compares in scale with Brattahlid, though somewhat smaller and simpler in its layout. The paucity of artifacts and the absence of burials makes it most unlikely that it was occupied for any protracted period; on the other hand, it is substantial enough to have been occupied intermittently over a decade or so. It would seem, in theory, to fit the requirements of a Leifsbudir, a Straumsfjord (or a combined Leifsbudir-Straumsfjord), or even a Hop. It would, of course, be wishful thinking, not historical deduction, to say that it has been identified with any of them. In the circumstances of their transmission, it is unlikely that the sagas would hand down correctly topographical details which would fit in with all the requirements of a single site, since alterations in the original details of the stories must have taken place. At the same time, it is now possible to begin the task of relating the sagas to one real place, whether or not they fit it, and to discover whether the attendant details of other possible locations can be related to the present site or not. Clearly there are no grapes, and it is most unlikely that climatic differences between the eleventh and twentieth centuries could have led to vines fruiting effectively in the 5 to 6 degrees north of their present limit which would be required. The whale, salmon, halibut and polar bears brought south by icebergs could all be found within reach of L'Anse aux Meadows—but, of course, at many other places as well. Hunting would have had to be confined to sea mammals or the smaller land mammals, but across the Strait of Belle Isle, Labrador could provide moose and

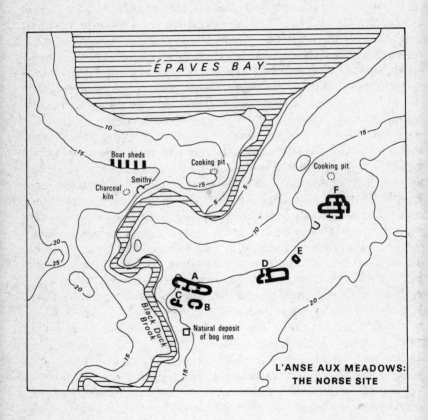

ÉPAVES BAY

Boat sheds

Cooking pit

Smithy

Charcoal
kiln

Cooking pit

F

D

E

A

C

B

Black Duck Brook

Natural deposit
of bog iron

L'ANSE AUX MEADOWS:
THE NORSE SITE

caribou. By virtue of its rugged northern coast in particular, the Strait could reasonably be described as a fjord.

The site of the newly discovered settlement was located, as the saga-described sites were, on a stream; this runs from a pond but is unlikely ever to have been a lake into which a ship could run as in Eirik's saga. The coastline has probably changed its profile since A.D. 1000 as the shore is rising, but present calculations do not suggest a very radical change in the topography, though this is still debatable. But such clues are not specific enough. There is grass and grazing round the site, and apparently this makes it the first accessible site on the route from Greenland where there would have been any possibility of feeding cattle. This indication is rather more promising if, in the milder climate of the eleventh century, there was more or better grass than now, which seems not improbable. On the other hand, good grass is now available only for a short season in summer and early fall, though perhaps the grazing season was longer then. Certainly, stock could not now be left in the open, as the sagas indicate, over winter, and it does not seem very likely that this could have been done in the eleventh century. For northern Newfoundland to have no winter snow would be remarkable in the present century. All we can say is that, if we exclude grapes, most of the other specific indications of the sagas about Leif's homestead could be met, making allowances for changes in the stories during transmission, or assuming they were accurate when first told.

Both Gwyn Jones and Helge Ingstad have concluded that for voyagers from Greenland, northern Newfoundland is relatively easy of access and is a reasonable place for the Greenlanders to have settled, especially as they did not remain there for any very extended periods. They also examine the saga stories of what the voyagers say about their journey on their way to the site where they made the homestead. After Markland had been identified, we have their extensive white strands, Wonderstrands, which can plausibly be seen as the 40-mile beaches of Labrador, south of the prominent keel-shaped headland, Cape Porcupine. Then there was a two-day sail until the third land was sighted, which had its offshore island (Belle Isle?) and its northward pointing cape (Cape Bauld?), while, rounding the island, was the site which has now been found. This sequence can be paralleled in the story of both Eirik's and Karl-sefni's voyages (unless they are the same voyage in two differing

stories). The settlement at L'Anse aux Meadows is in sight of mountains, as in the saga; the fjord could have been explored westward in late spring as the ice clears early and may have gone earlier then. Then, as now, the settlers could have wintered fairly easily as the Basque whalers sometimes did on these coasts in the sixteenth century, and then have hunted, fished and taken birds' eggs in the spring. A Leifsbudir-Straumsfjord could have been the L'Anse aux Meadows site.

All this adds up to a plausible association of Leifsbudir-Straumsfjord with the Newfoundland location, but it is not an identification. We are inevitably still left guessing, if not in such a total vacuum as before 1961. The sagas indicate that explorations extended well to the south of Leifsbudir-Straumsfjord, and Hop was evidently one place associated with these explorations. This makes it plausible, again, to suggest that a site was occupied for at least a brief time inside the region where grapes ripened. There would thus be Vinland I, which would equal the Strait of Belle Isle and its adjacent shores; and Vinland II, farther south, south of Cape Breton Island perhaps, just conceivably as far as Cape Cod. This is pure hypothesis, not as yet buttressed with any archeological indications whatsoever. If the grapes were real grapes, however, we may think of them as being found in some brief reconnaissance to the south and, being status symbols amongst northern peoples (implying wealth, luxury and a warm place from which they came), transferred in story to the more northern sites and associated generally with the Vinland voyages in the tales which lay behind the written sagas. This would bring the various designations of Vinland together into one general location, even though the grapes came from a part which was visited more briefly outside the area and was not Leifsbudir (or Straumsfjord). Such a suggestion has no more authority than many others that have been made, but some such "translation" of names and places is not improbable in the circumstances under which the evidence was handed down. Though the new site takes us from myth toward history, we cannot yet expect any consensus in interpreting either the location of Vinland or the precise course of the Vinland voyages.

# CHAPTER 3

# *The Atlantic Setting*

W HAT led Europeans out into the ocean to the west?[1] Certainly, there was a plentiful supply of legends about the ocean sea. There were Old Irish Sea Tales of Bran and of the Utopian "Land of Youth" which lay beyond the ocean.[2] There was, somewhat more realistically, the legend and history of St. Brendan,[3] which, though supposedly associated with the events of the sixth century, may be thought to have been influenced by some concrete details from the Norse occupation of Iceland in the ninth century, which modified the surviving written versions. There were stories in Portugal about the refugees from the Moorish invasions of the eighth century, who had gone to sea under a bishop and founded seven cities in some far western Island of the Seven Cities which re-emerged in the fifteenth century in a refurbished guise. And no doubt there were others. What is not clear is whether such fanciful tales had any direct influence at all in starting men thinking about the possibilities of what lay beyond the great fringe of western

1. William H. Babcock, *Legendary Islands in the Atlantic* (New York, 1922), and Richard Hennig, *Terrae Incognitae,* 2nd edition, 4 vols. (Amsterdam, 1944–56), are storehouses of often uncritical information and legend on the Atlantic. This is not a matter to which definitive answers can be given since too many factors remain unknown.

2. Thomas J. Westropp, "Brasil and the Legendary Islands of the North Atlantic," *Proceedings of the Royal Irish Academy,* XXX (1912), sect. C, no. 8, 225–226.

3. The standard edition is *Navigatio Sancti Brandani,* edited by Carl Selmer (Notre Dame, Ind., 1959), the introduction to which is valuable. There are translations of the "Life" and the "Navigation" in Denis O'Donaghue, *Brendaniana* (Dublin, 1893).

waters, along which European craft crept gingerly all the way from Norway to Gibraltar in the short stretches that comprised the normal medieval coasting voyage. An impression conveyed by these stories is that legend was legend only, and had little influence until it was called in to reinforce the actual material objectives of the search to the west in the late fourteenth and fifteenth centuries.

A number of factors were bringing Europeans more boldly into the ocean in the fourteenth century. The Norwegian crown had lost contact with Greenland in any systematic way not long after the middle of the fourteenth century, but had continued to maintain reasonably close links with Iceland itself. In that century both German vessels, from the Hanseatic base at Bergen, and English, from east coast ports, were making their way on trading voyages and probably also, in the case of the English, on fishing trips to Iceland. This opened up to the English a substantial area of northern waters, well beyond northwestern Europe, which had hitherto been the preserve only of the Norwegians and Danes. European fisheries elsewhere were expanding their range. Fishing vessels from France and the Iberian peninsula, operating off the southwestern and west coasts of Ireland, were probably working farther out to sea toward the limits of the continental shelf, which gave many of them experience of oceanic conditions under which fish could still be caught. The whale fishers of western Europe, the Basques, were operating with increasing vigor off the shores of Galicia and in the Bay of Biscay, and were perhaps making forays well out into deeper waters of the ocean. It may well be that the Black Death, by so greatly depleting the capacity of men to exploit the land, turned them more decisively toward the sea in an attempt to obtain the fish and fats which they had fewer resources to accumulate on land. Undoubtedly the reservoir of experience which seamen on the western border of Europe had shared for so long was now being enlarged.

The trading nucleus of Europe was still the Mediterranean.[4] In the thirteenth century, the Italians developed carracks which could sail and galleys which could be rowed as well as sailed outwards from the southern sea along the oceanic shores to the Low Countries and to England. And well before the end of the thirteenth century, the Italian colonists in Portugal and in some Spanish ports

4. See Alwyn A. Ruddock, *The Mediterranean Trade of Southampton* (Southampton, 1951).

were looking southward along the African coast for possible new routes which could be commercially exploited. Whether, before 1300, they were consciously concerned with circumnavigating Africa is still debatable, but they were most probably inflamed by knowledge of the gold which reached the shores of the Atlantic by way of trans-Saharan caravans and wished to find its source. The galleys were not suitable for deep sea work, but the carracks could be developed to undertake it. In the fourteenth century, the Mediterranean-northern European trade routes from Venice and Genoa to England and the Low Countries ran a chain of commerce round the western ocean fringes of Europe. The increase in trade from the thirteenth century onward meant that demands for all European products which could be exploited and exchanged went up. Fish could provide food for non-agricultural populations at a lower rate of occupational investment than agriculture itself. Along with this went an increased demand for the fish and whale oil that were needed for lubrication and light so as to maintain commercial growth. More cloth was available, which meant more use of olive oil for soap, and the necessary substitution of cruder oils from the sea to be added to tallow for other purposes.

There were no very strong academic opinions current in the thirteenth and early fourteenth centuries on the western ocean. It was considered to mark the western rim of the landmass and to be therefore a rather irrelevant subject for speculation. True, Aristotle's speculations about finding that India was not far beyond the Strait of Gibraltar were not unknown, nor indeed were Arabic views that the western ocean was the Sea of Darkness, the Green Sea, and the Circumambient Ocean, and as such impassable.[5] These views were not universal. Roger Bacon (ca. 1214–ca. 1294) had revived the views of Aristotle, Seneca and Pliny that India might be accessible by traveling westward. In his *Opus majus,* he expressed the view that more than half the circumference of the earth was land: experience and a steady compilation of the latitude and longitude of known places might reveal how much land around the earth there was.[6] There was a gradual increase in the circulation of such ideas

5. Charles Jourdain, *De l'influence d'Aristote et des interprèts sur la découverte du Nouveau-Monde* (Paris, 1861).

6. Roger Bacon, *Opus Majus,* translated by R. B. Burke, 2 vols. (Philadelphia, 1928), I, 310–320; George Sarton, *Introduction to the History of Science,* 3 vols. (Washington, D.C., 1927–47), III, 44.

but little real development for a century after Bacon's death.

Like most people who saw them, the scholars—while prepared to demonstrate that the world was round and therefore theoretically capable of being circumnavigated—were content to accept the typical medieval world maps, which had changed little from the eleventh to the fourteenth century. These showed a more or less circular disk, Jerusalem-centered and surrounded by a watery fringe, as being all that need concern men. Since the landmass, poised in a single hemisphere, was apparently entire, there was little value to be anticipated from the watery wastes of the second hemisphere.

The development of quite a different kind of map, the marine chart—built up from sailing directions (portolans) and observations made as vessels followed specific coastlines and set down names and outlines of coasts which were precise guides to coastal navigators—gradually created in the late thirteenth century and early fourteenth century an accurate chart of the coasts of the Mediterranean. In the hands of the Aragonese, who were in contact with Arab as well as Christian learning, the portolan chart became the basis for a more comprehensive cartography. The Catalan world atlas of 1375 used medieval data on a world scale, but applied it especially to the Atlantic fringes of Spain and Portugal and began the process, so far as we can tell, of placing islands increasingly associated with older legends in the waters beyond (if not very far beyond) the continental shelf. Once this process took hold and became customary, and when the marine chart came to cover the carrack and galley route up the Atlantic coasts as far as the Low Countries, Europeans had a well-defined and accurate base on which to project outward into the Atlantic their speculations and expectations of land beyond European limits. There is no doubt that Castilian and Portuguese navigators had found their way to the Canary Islands well before 1400, and had discovered and lost sight of other islands out to sea. Thus some knowledge of land to the west, even if imperfect, was being gained to add to the island-studded marine charts where legend and knowledge were inextricably intertwined.

When, after the capture of Ceuta in 1415, the Portuguese turned to the problems of exploring southward along the western coast of Atlantic Africa, their attention was bound to be turned also to island discoveries at some distance from land whose position could be fixed and which could possibly be exploited economically. Portugal

The Earth on a Polar Projection

was looking not only for the gold of the African desert and its hinterland but for fishing and sealing grounds, as well as for fertile land that might be used to extend the somewhat exiguous limits behind which, once her rivalry with Castile had been resolved, she had been confined. The discovery of Atlantic islands—first Madeira and its attendant islets, and then somewhat later the Azores—was not accidental, but arose from a logical extension of previously developed needs and expectations.

If we see the academic thinkers of the thirteenth and most of the fourteenth centuries as being rather slow to take up the question of the cosmographical implications of the earth's sphericity, the same cannot be said of those of the turn of the fourteenth century and of the early fifteenth century. There is no doubt that the translation from the Greek of a recently acquired Byzantine manuscript of Claudius Ptolemy's second-century "Geography" in the early years of the fifteenth century was as much effect as cause of an outbreak of cosmographical and macro-geographic speculation. The translation[7] would not have been made, nor would it have had such rapid influence, had it not apparently answered with specific text and maps questions which were being asked and which it seemed to resolve. Pierre d'Ailly's "Ymago mundi," which attempted to survey the earth in its setting and in its surface relations on a more modern basis than that of Ptolemy, was completed between 1410 and 1415.[8] D'Ailly saw that the Ptolemaic formula for presenting a spherical surface on a two-dimensional plane (his famous simple conic projection), and Ptolemy's emphasis on the dual guide to location provided by latitude and longitude, enabled men to grasp simple relationships in space which had previously been difficult to understand and even more difficult to set down on paper. Ptolemy had stated that land comprised about half the surface of the globe from east to west and so extended to little more than 180 out of 360 degrees. However, this still left the world map which accompanied his text with unterminated land on the farthest east; thus, speculation that there might be land to the west arose from this depiction of the earth's surface. We have no guarantee that the maps which accom-

7. Claudius Ptolemy, *The Geography,* translated by Edward L. Stevenson (New York, 1932); Carlos Sanz, *La geographia de Ptolemeo ampliado* (Madrid, 1959).

8. Pierre d'Ailly, *Ymago Mundi,* edited and translated by Edmond Buron, 3 vols. (Paris, 1930).

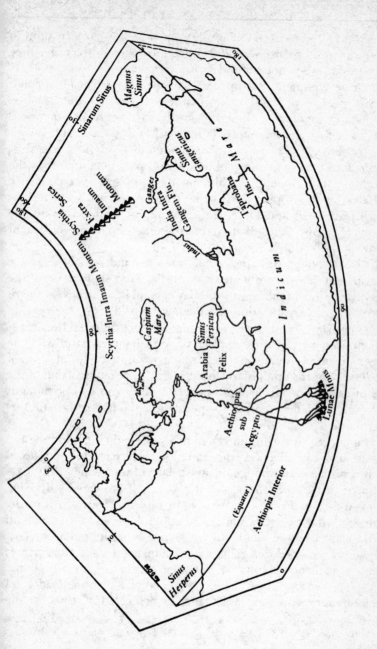

The Ptolemaic World Map

panied the Greek text to western Europe bore any close relation to those compiled before A.D. 200. But in the fifteenth century they were taken to be contemporary with the text.

Such developments might have remained largely academic and uninfluential in practical affairs had it not been for the fact that many of the merchants of the Italian city states were also the intellectuals of their communities. The revival of interest in and knowledge of classical antiquity was shared not only by clerics and aristocrats but also by men engaged in practical pursuits, notably in the development of commerce. This helped to lead to the pre-eminence of Italians in developing the marine chart and the maps which combined traditional and Ptolemaic cartographic traditions with the results of empirical observation. It also influenced the development alike of navigational techniques and of ship construction, and helped to produce the experimentally minded individuals who were to lead, and indeed to dominate, so much of the exploration of the western ocean and the lands which lay beyond it.[9] The development of the map in synthesizing the medieval world view, the revived Ptolemaic view and the marine chart which incorporated the practical applications of cartography, thus went hand in hand with the development of trading and exploring expeditions. The addition of modern maps to copies of the Ptolemaic atlas began with that of the northwestern European lands in the late 1420s and may be thought to have provided a stimulus to speculation about what lay still further west.

This process was continued and in a sense culminated in the Fra Mauro map, compiled in Venice in 1458–9, which not only put down all the available knowledge of the surface of the globe on a single surface, but also began the major revision of Ptolemy by deriving from Arab sources an authoritative picture of Africa which finally contradicted the closed Indian ocean of Ptolemy and replaced it on world maps by an open one. It was, too, a Florentine doctor, Toscanelli, who carried this geographical thinking a stage still further, culminating in his program for obtaining access from the west to the farther east in the 1470s. The emergence of Italians as leaders of Atlantic enterprises—from Cadamosto before 1460, through the

9. Carlo M. Cipolla, *Guns and Sails in the Early Phase of European Expansion, 1400–1700* (London, 1965); Charles Verlinden, *The Beginnings of Modern Colonization* (Ithaca, N.Y., 1970).

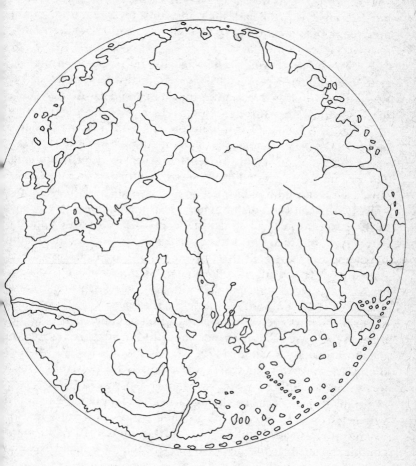

The Fra Mauro World Map, 1459
(Original in the Biblioteca Marciana, Venice)

Columbus brothers and the Cabots, father and son, in the late fifteenth and the opening of the sixteenth century, to Verrazzano and others as late as the 1520s—follows from this line of development, even if we still find some difficulty in accounting for the precise range and extent of Italian influence on the western European countries.

The expanding activities of the small though dynamic Portuguese state in the fifteenth century are most dramatically centered on the slow but eventful progress down the almost endless African shore to the eventual breakthrough, toward the end of the fifteenth century, into the Indian Ocean. The parallel and closely associated movement of the Portuguese out into the Atlantic was a less spectacular process. Yet, had the prize of the discovery of continental America not been wrested from them by Columbus and the Castilians, their acquisition of knowledge of the ocean and their occupation of the Atlantic islands[10] might have seemed a more integral part of the process which led to that discovery than otherwise appears. The finding of the Madeira group before 1420 was followed by the beginnings of settlement there about 1425, soon to bring rich rewards in wines and sugar to Portuguese settlers and their backers. Madeira was developed parallel with the first discoveries of the Azores in 1427, and with the subsequent expansion of that discovery over the next twelve years, along with the beginnings of settlement in the more easterly islands about 1440 and its completion in the most westerly by about 1475. What is still unknown is whether the first discovery of the Azores was a rediscovery of islands known for a time a century before, or whether it resulted from vessels returning from the Canaries being carried too far out to sea, or even whether it was the product of a deliberate policy of probing for fishing grounds and land far beyond the limits of the European continental shelf. In all the circumstances the most likely explanation seems to have been the last.

Italians in Portugal who were in touch with advanced Italian ideas on the subject, and Portuguese who were under their influence, are likely to have been behind the plans for exploiting the possibilities of westward voyages as early as the 1430s—perhaps appreciably

10. On the Atlantic islands, see T. Bentley Duncan, *Atlantic Islands* (Chicago, 1972), chapter 2; S. E. Morison, *Portuguese Voyages to America in the Fifteenth Century* (Cambridge, Mass., 1940).

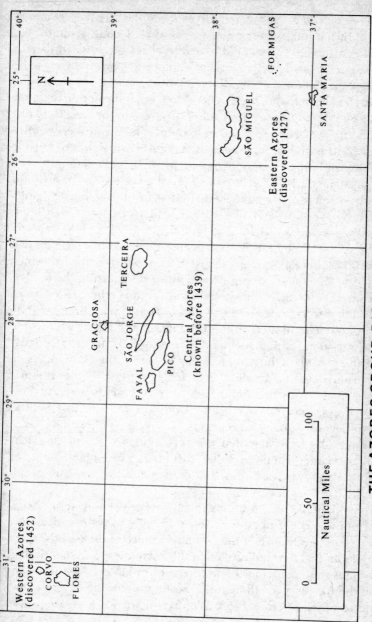

THE AZORES GROUP, DISCOVERED 1427 – 1452

earlier. To Portuguese fishing interests and the thrusting commercialism of the military Order of Christ alike, fishing grounds and land for sugar and vines would have offered adequate incentives for some appreciable degree of oceanic exploration and are likely to be the explanation for the first discovery of the Azores. But once the islands had been found, there is little doubt that the notion that they might be stepping stones for further progress to the west is almost certain to have been projected onto them. The mapmakers made a major contribution here. On a map of the Atlantic shores of Europe made by an Italian, Zuane Pizzigano, in 1424, there first appeared two substantial islands well to the west of all other real or mythical islands. Satanazes was a medium-sized island to the north; Antilia (which was soon to assimilate the legendary Island of the Seven Cities) was a substantial, long rectangular block of land in the ocean a little to the south of it. Both appeared due west from the Iberian peninsula. Thereafter, many maps of the western seaboard, which tended to show more ocean extending westward from the land as the century went on, in one way or another copied these two islands. And so they were added to the islands of Brasil, Saint Brendan (one or both often duplicated on the same map), and others which went some way, along with Madeira and the Azores as they were discovered and placed on the map, to filling in part of the empty space in the western ocean. Armando Cortesão has argued[11] that the first representation of Antilia and Satanazes represents a recent Portuguese discovery of Caribbean islands (in 1424 or just before) which they were unable to repeat in later years. Others have taken the more skeptical view that the rectangular space occupied by Antilia was intended in an earlier, lost map to be a blank frame for a caption and was transformed into an island by Pizzigano or another.

The weight of the indications so far are against a western discovery from which Portuguese vessels were able to return. Whatever the precise significance of the first appearance of the islands, there is no doubt that they indicated that the Portuguese and their Italian associates were conscious of an interest in islands to the west, beyond the Azores, even though the exploration of the latter did not come to an end before 1453. We may, if we wish, associate this

11. Armando Cortesão, *The Nautical Chart of 1424* (Coimbra, 1954).

interest in western islands with the advocates of oceanic exploration who were linked in one way or another with Prince Henry the Navigator. After his death in 1460 there was a pause in West African exploration, which had already produced tangible economic results, and a slackening off too, it would seem, in activity and speculation about possible westward approaches to Asia. Speculation continued through the 1460s; but the spectacular advances down the African coast in the 1470s and 1480s, and the final turning of the southern tip of the continent in 1488, continued to distract the Portuguese from their western concerns, even though the colonization of the Azores went on apace and a profitable exploitation of the islands (through such products as wine and woad) was developed—admittedly partly by Flemish settlers rather than the Portuguese themselves.

The pattern of Portuguese trade was not limited to expansion to the south and west. As Portugal's commercial resources grew, her trade with England also expanded. A new and important link arose out of the participation of the western English port of Bristol in the Iceland trade and fishery. After the 1420s Bristol ships were bringing cod from Iceland, either traded from the Icelanders or caught by English vessels. This was transhipped from England to Portugal, often in Portuguese ships, sometimes it might appear by exchanges made at the Irish port of Galway.[12]

From the English, the Portuguese could learn something of the problems and perils (and the means of surmounting them) in the seas far to the northwest; and from the Portuguese, the English could glean a little about the Portuguese movement down the African coast and into the Atlantic, and could confirm it during the course of their busy trade with Lisbon and the Algarve. Moreover, both nations were equipping themselves with larger and more seaworthy vessels. For use in harsher waters, the northern trading vessel was now taking on and modifying some of the characteristics of the Mediterranean carrack. The Portuguese vessels were learning to exploit the Mediterranean lateen sail, both alone and in combination with the square sail, and adding a second (later a third) course to provide greater driving power and more flexible steering capacity, while at the same time modifying the hull form to make each

12. D. B. Quinn, *England and the Discovery of America* (New York, 1974), pp. 51–55.

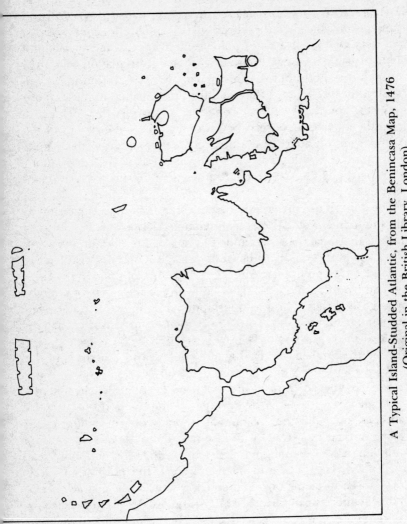

A Typical Island-Studded Atlantic, from the Benincasa Map, 1476
(Original in the British Library, London)

vessel more speedy and seaworthy. Clearly, both nations were becoming increasingly equipped for longer oceanic voyages. As to the effects of these developments in the larger trading craft on the form of the smaller vessels—especially those of the fishermen who were making progressively longer voyages out into the Atlantic, from England to the waters of northwest Iceland, from Portugal to the farther Azores—we have virtually no information. But here again it is certain that the round ship, broad and short, which had been typical of earlier centuries, gave place to a longer, narrower and more seaworthy vessel.[13]

The Fra Mauro world map[14] which had been brought to Portugal before 1460, when translated from its pictorial form into a more realistic setting, gave Portugal a picture of a landmass extending round the North Pole in either direction and illustrating clearly the possibilities of sailing westward to reach land in Asia. But realistically displayed, this was scarcely encouraging, since it could be argued that, in view of the general acceptance of a figure of some 22,000 to 24,000 miles for the circumference of the earth at the equator, Asia might lie anywhere between 10,000 and 12,000 miles from Europe. True, on the basis of Fra Mauro's view of the world, it might be possible to creep to Asia round the more northerly rim of the earth's surface; it also appeared possible, on the basis of his information on Africa, to work all the way down its west coast, round its most southern tip, and so commence the long haul up the east coast until at least Arabia and India were reached. But such coastal approaches were rather less attractive than the impossibly long direct ocean voyage westward over the ocean from Europe to Asia, especially as Fra Mauro in his map was careful to stress the harsh cold and the savage inhabitants of the northern climes along which such a voyage round the northern rim of the landmass would be made. If possession of this map gave the Portuguese a world view which was comprehensive of the whole globe, it was a view that favored expansion by way of Africa

13. R. Morton Nance, *The Ship of the Renaissance*, Society for Nautical Research, Maritime Miscellany Series 10 (London, 1955).

14. Reproduced and edited by T. Gasparrini-Leporace, *Il mappomondo di Fra Mauro* (Venice, 1956). The surviving version in Venice is believed to be a replica, though not necessarily an exact one, of the lost map sent to Portugal before Fra Mauro's death in 1459.

The Florence *Mappemonde*, 1457
(Original in the Biblioteca Nazionale, Florence)

rather than by the northwest route to Asia, or directly to Asia by sea by sailing west.

It was Paulo Pozzi Toscanelli who, in 1474, produced a world map (now lost) and a descriptive letter which provided a possibly more attractive western projection. Toscanelli had been impressed both by the alleged discovery of Antilia and by reading in Marco Polo that Cipango (Japan) lay 1,000 or 1,500 miles to the east of southern China, and in similar latitudes, as he understood (or misunderstood) Polo. Moreover, Polo had indicated that the eastward land extension of Asia was greater than that accepted, though not dogmatically insisted on, by Ptolemy. Ptolemy's "Terra Incognita," which was the name given on some versions of his world map for the unterminated land that lay farthest east, could well be Polo's Cathay. Therefore, the sea route from Europe to Asia might plausibly be shorter than had hitherto been envisaged, while both Antilia and Cipango could act as stepping stones on the way. If, in addition, it could be argued that 24,000 miles or thereabouts for the circumference of the earth was much too great (the classical Greek estimates were now known to differ rather widely and the unit of measurement was uncertain), then a voyage to Asia across the Atlantic became feasible.

Toscanelli[15] finally settled on a figure for the gap between Europe and Asia of some 6,000 to 6,500 miles. He reckoned that a ship might be able to sail continuously through the ocean for some 2,500 miles, when she could put in to refit at Antilia which he evidently regarded as a civilized country. She would then make a further 2,500 miles to Japan, and again refit, and so be able to travel the final 1,500 miles at the most to Polo's Quinsay (Hang-chow), from which all other parts of Asia would be accessible to her. This controlled and documented fantasy had a strong appeal to the Portuguese and was soon to appeal equally to an Italian guest of theirs, Christopher Columbus.

The Portuguese had not indeed allowed the Atlantic to go unsearched after the farthest Azores were reached.[16] As early as 1452,

15. For the text, see S. E. Morison (ed.), *Journals and Other Documents on the Life and Voyages of Christopher Columbus* (New York, 1963), pp. 11–15; Quinn, *North American Discovery* (1971), pp. 27–28. See the discussion in S. E. Morison, *Christopher Columbus, Admiral of the Ocean Sea* 1 vol. ed. (New York, 1942), pp. 33–34, 63–65.

16. Morison, *Portuguese Voyages to America in the Fifteenth Century,* has summarized the material in English. Fuller accounts will be found in Damião Peres, *Historia dos*

Diogo de Tieve was sailing westward from the Azores in search of further islands. He appears to have been caught on his course by the westerlies and carried back on the Gulf Stream so that he ended up by rediscovering not America but Ireland. Even in the doldrums period after 1460, royal grants continued to be given to men who either believed they had located further islands or thought they were capable of doing so. João Vogado, who set out in 1462 to find two of the islands he had seen located on a marine chart, Lovo and Capraria, was no more successful than he would have been if he had chosen any others of the stock of imagined places on the oceanic maps. The land which Fernandes de Tavira found in 1462, also somewhere out to sea, northwestward between the Canaries and Madeira, did not show itself again when searched for. Ruis Gonsalves de Camera in 1473 got a wider license still when he went to look for "an island which he or his ships may be able to discover," though he did not prove able to do so.[17] We could, of course, do with much more information on what impelled these men to make such voyages and the Portuguese crown to charter them; but it does not seem that they are an important series of links in the chain which led to the discovery of America, though they may well have provided some further information on oceanic sailing conditions in the west.

A circumstantial chain of evidence has been produced to build up a claim that a joint Portuguese-Danish expedition made a successful voyage to North America in 1472 or an adjacent date.[18] Based on certain diplomatic connections between Portugal and Denmark in the fifteenth century, the claim, without documentary authority, is made that João Vas Corte Real of Terceira in the Azores visited Denmark about 1470. A late Azorean Portuguese source, Gaspar Fructuoso (d. 1591), claimed that Corte Real made an undated voyage under the orders of Afonso V, discovered Newfoundland,

---

descobrimentos Portugueses, 2nd edition (Coimbra, 1960), and Jaime Cortesão, Os descobrimentos portugueses, 2 vols. (Lisbon, 1959–60), I.

17. The texts of these and other charters are in J. Ramos-Coelho (ed.), Alguns documentos da Torre do Tombo (Lisbon, 1891).

18. Sofus Larsen, The Discovery of America Twenty Years Before Columbus (Copenhagen, 1925), built up the argument. It is rejected in Morison, Portuguese Voyages and European Discovery of America, I, 89–94, 108–109, and also in Quinn, England and the Discovery of America, pp. 43–55; it is accepted by R. Hennig, Terrae Incognitae, IV (1956), 247–282, and by Tryggvi J. Oleson, Early Voyages and Northern Approaches, 1000–1632 (Montreal, 1963), pp. 118–120.

and then was rewarded with the captaincy of Angra in Terceira in 1474; but as most of the other things he says about this period are wrong, this is scarcely good evidence in itself. Then we have a globe published about 1537 (the Frisius-Mercator globe) which displays a Northwest Passage round North America with an inscription saying that it is the Strait of the Three Brothers (the Corte Real brothers of the next generation, in their voyages of 1500–03) and that Johannes Scolvus the Dane came in 1476 to make contact with certain people there. Nothing whatever is known of Scolvus.

A final item is a letter to Christian IV of Denmark from Carsten Grip, burgomaster of Kiel, written in 1551 and saying that a map has been offered for sale in Paris—it has not been identified—with an inscription claiming that "the two captains Pyning and Pothorst, who by your majesty's royal grandfather, King Christian I, were sent forth with several ships in order to search for new islands in the north," had set up a beacon on a rock off Greenland. Dedrick Pining and Hans Pothorst were Germans in the Danish service in Iceland who were active between about 1473 and 1494 at sea to the west of Iceland and in conflict with East Greenland Eskimo, Pining serving for a time as the Danish king's representative in Iceland. Sofus Larsen, and those who have followed him, have built up a narrative which makes Afonso V obtain the support of Christian I for an expedition led, in 1472, by João Vas Corte Real in association with Pining and Pothorst, and with John Scolvus as pilot, which discovered some part of northeastern North America. But the evidence is all late; it does not hang together, except with the use of much pure speculation, and is in fact highly unlikely. If João Vas Corte Real sighted America before Columbus, as is not impossible, it was almost certainly not in 1472 or thereabouts but much later, in the late 1480s. Either way the vital evidence is lacking.

On the other hand the grant to Fernão Telles in 1474[19] to proceed from the Azores on a westward search was, it appears, a significant move. In November 1475 this charter was supplemented by another, which might seem to have been inspired by the assumption of Toscanelli in his letter that Antilia had been found and was already in the possession of the Portuguese. King Afonso explained that the earlier charter had dealt with islands in general but had not

19. Extracts from the Telles charter are given in Quinn, *North American Discovery* (1971), pp. 30–31.

specified whether they were to be uninhabited ones only or inhabited ones as well. Telles was now to be free to occupy inhabited islands provided they were not off the coast of Guinea. This explanation was thought necessary since "it might happen that, in sending out to seek them, his ships or people might find the Seven Cities or some other inhabited islands which at the present time have not been navigated to or discovered or traded with by my subjects." This appears to make clear that, whatever the maps showing Antilia indicated, the Portuguese crown was not aware that Antilia (in its guise of the Island of the Seven Cities) had been reached by any Portuguese. So Cortesão's theory is destroyed, but on the other hand the association with the Toscanelli letter is reinforced, since it now appeared to Afonso V important that Telles should find Antilia, perhaps in order that it might be used for just such an experiment as Toscanelli had suggested for a voyage westward to seek Cathay. Telles is not known to have been more successful in making western discoveries than his precursors, but he opened the way for a more ambitious promoter, Christopher Columbus.

It seems likely that the English were the first to take advantage of the expansion of knowledge of the Atlantic to make an effective foray into the western Atlantic.[20] The Bristol men had specialized in fishing for cod in the rough and distant waters of western Iceland, but were finding their work increasingly harassed by Hanseatic vessels—at that time favored by the king of Denmark as his commercial instruments for the exploitation of the Iceland trade. The English were driven to look elsewhere, probably in the deeper waters off Ireland on the edge of the continental shelf. By 1480, they were also learning a good deal about the Portuguese discovery of Atlantic islands and were setting their hopes on the discovery of the Isle of Brasil farther afield. It was thought to lie westward of County Kerry in southwest Ireland, some maps suggesting it to be quite near the land, some much further to the west. Like St. Brendan's Isle, with which it was sometimes conflated, it appeared in duplicate on some marine charts of the Atlantic. Whether there were any Portuguese involved in the ventures which took the Bristol men westward in

20. The texts of the English documents on the earliest English ventures appear in James A. Williamson, *The Cabot Voyages* (Cambridge, Eng., Hakluyt Society, 1962), pp. 187–189, 211–214; E. M. Carus-Wilson, *Overseas Trade of Bristol in the Late Middle Ages* (Bristol, 1937), p. 157.

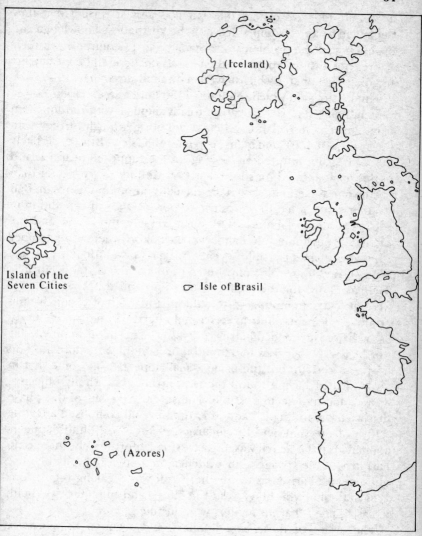

(Iceland)

Island of the
Seven Cities

▷ Isle of Brasil

(Azores)

The Westward Perspective of the Paris Map, *circa* 1490
(Original in the Bibliothèque Nationale, Paris)

1480 and 1481 we cannot tell, but it is almost certain that they depended to some extent at least on the Portuguese knowledge and experience of the problems of oceanic sailing acquired from their Azores possessions and from the various unsuccessful experiments in going farther still which have been mentioned.

The Bristol ship which set out in 1480 under an experienced sea captain named Lloyd, probably already familiar with the long run from Portugal to Iceland and back, did not get much further than the west coast of Ireland in his search for the Isle of Brasil. It is likely that Lloyd concentrated on looking for the supposed nearer island of this name located on some charts off County Kerry, rather than for the one sometimes shown on the maps far out in the ocean. Bad weather contributed to the return to port. A second expedition in 1481 was more elaborate. Two small vessels, the *George* and the *Trinity*, set out about July 7 and were back shortly before September 24, giving them a possible seventy-five days or a little more at sea. They carried some salt, contributed by one of the customs officials, Thomas Croft, for the exploring mission, and this suggests they were at least attempting to test the possibilities of a new fishing ground. Their mission was described after their return as one to "search for and find the Isle of Brasil." The implication of this wording—whether they had found it or had only attempted to find it—is not certain; but the balance may appear to lie somewhat in favor of their having found the island, though a wholly objective answer does not seem possible. The several versions of this phase that we have, in English and in Latin, were all composed after the return of the ship, and the inclusion of the word "find" appears anomalous if the search was unsuccessful. Unfortunately, there is no narrative of the voyage. Our evidence on it emerged only because questions had arisen as to whether Croft was breaking regulations against trading whilst he was still an official and an inquiry was held; it was decided that his actions were justified.

The origin of these expeditions would seem to be a licence granted in 1480 to a group of Bristol merchants, all active in the Iceland and Portuguese trades, and with them Croft, to send out small vessels over the next three years freed from certain usual restrictions and customs duties. If expeditions were sent during the remaining currency of the licence in 1482, no record of them has so far appeared. It can be suggested that these expeditions were

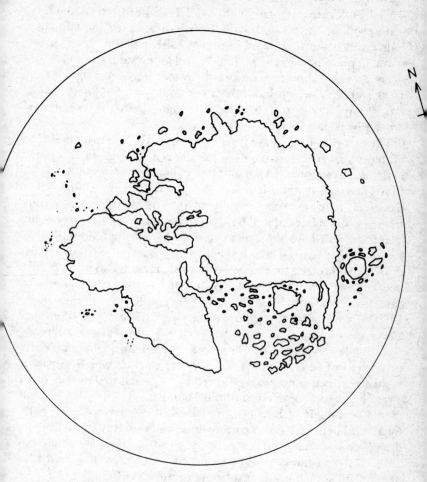

The *Mappemonde* on the Paris Map, *circa* 1490

primarily to establish a new fishery to replace the Iceland fishery. Such an island—part of Newfoundland, it might appear—is likely to have been located as a landmark for a fishing ground. While there is no proof of this, John Day in 1497 indicated to Columbus that John Cabot's Newfoundland (found in 1497) was the island already found in times past by the men of Bristol as, he said, Columbus was aware. We also know that westward voyages were taking place from 1490 and 1491 which look like a continuation of pioneer fishing expeditions across the Atlantic, although again they cannot be proved to be so.

The evidence in this case is partly firm, partly circumstantial. The evidence that John Day believed there was a voyage which resulted in the discovery of an island and that Columbus believed this to be so is good, but it stems from some time—an unknown time—after the event. A voyage was certainly made in 1481 which, on circumstantial grounds, could well have been the discovery voyage; but the proof that a discovery was made cannot be considered conclusive. We know that voyages which seem to have been voyages of discovery were authorized for four years in 1480, and that an unsuccessful one was made in that year. The fact that no voyages are known to have been made in 1482, 1483 or 1484, while the permission of 1480 lasted, can be interpreted in two ways: either no further voyages of exploration were made because a discovery had already been made; or no further attempts seemed justifiable since the expedition of 1481, like that of 1480, had not succeeded. Again, is clear that Pedro de Ayala believed in 1498 that two to four ships a year had been going out into the Atlantic from 1490 or 1491—in search of the Isle of Brasil or the Island of the Seven Cities, as he (or Cabot) believed. One possible interpretation is that the English discovery was made in the period 1490–95; another is that the voyages were fishing voyages to a bank marked by an island (the "Isle of Brasil," equivalent to some part of Newfoundland) found some time before. The individual bricks are reasonably sound but the structure that they make is not invulnerable. They add up to a highly circumstantial, yet not precisely established case for an English discovery before Columbus.[21]

21. This case is argued in full in Quinn, *England and the Discovery of America.* J. A. Williamson, *The Cabot Voyages* (Cambridge, Eng. 1962), pp. 19–32, accepted that there was a pre-Columbian discovery but thought it most likely to have taken place

There is no clear evidence of Portuguese expeditions after 1476 until 1486. In that year Fernão Dulmo (Ferdinand van Olmos), a Flemish settler in the Azores, received a licence[22] "to discover a great island, or islands, or mainland nearby the coast which is supposed to be the island of the Seven Cities." Moreover, in 1487, he made arrangements for his initial voyage to be followed by a second expedition even though he had apparently not yet set out on his first. From his licence, it might appear that further discussion and speculation had produced a theory about landmasses to the west which was more specific than the earlier ones, although there is no clear evidence that new discoveries had been made in the meantime by the Portuguese. Certainly, several maps contained an island, evidently the Isle of the Seven Cities (alias Antilia), which was located in the west; only this was not located in the usual place, opposite or in a somewhat lower latitude than Portugal, but rather, westward from or appreciably more northerly than the Azores. One such map, known as the Milan-Catalan map, derives from pre-1493 information on the Atlantic even if it was drawn at a later date; another is the Paris map of about 1490–93. Indeed, the latter declared in an inscription that the Island of the Seven Cities had been already colonized by the Portuguese. If this was so, we know nothing specific about it although this is documentary evidence that could possibly be correct. João Vas Corte Real, the Azorean sailor, was the father of the Corte Real brothers whose discoveries of 1500 to 1503 were to be of such great importance and could have made earlier voyages to the west. His son Gaspar is mentioned in a licence

"in the early 1490's" (p. 31). Alwyn A. Ruddock, "John Day of Bristol and the English Voyages Across the Atlantic Before 1497," *Geographical Journal*, CXXXII (1966), 229, 231–232, took the view that the early discovery was "entirely accidental" and had been almost forgotten by the 1480s. S. E. Morison, *European Discovery of America*, I (1971), 208, maintains the view that no such discovery can have taken place and that the John Day letter merely represented Bristol gossip in 1497–8. For the statement in John Day letter see pp. 119–120 below. Contributions to the London *Times* on April 15 and 30, May 1 and 6, 1976 drew attention to the arrival of exceptional cargoes of fish at Bristol, allegedly from Ireland, between 1479 and 1504. The suggestion was made by Mr. Forbes Taylor that the fish was being brought secretly from Newfoundland. This seems just possible, though the cargoes may more probably have represented a clandestine trade with Iceland, disguised so as to avoid the Hanseatic embargo.

22. An extract from the charter is given in Quinn, *North American Discovery*, pp. 31–32; the evidence is discussed in Verlinden, *The Beginnings of Modern Colonization*, pp. 181–195.

of 1500 as having already made voyages, and these—his father's and his own—could perhaps have stretched back into the 1480s. However, we still cannot make a firm claim that any Portuguese ship had crossed the Atlantic before 1500.

Just as the English voyages of 1480 and 1481 (and perhaps later ones) probably owed something to the Portuguese, so too the greatest of the Atlantic planners and voyagers of the period, Christopher Columbus, owed a great deal to the country he adopted as his own, about or a little after the time that the Toscanelli letter reached Portugal.[23] It was probably on a Portuguese ship that Columbus visited Galway and perhaps also Bristol in 1476–77, and it must have been on a Bristol vessel that he went to Iceland. This was certainly one turning point in the development of his ambition to cross the Atlantic, since he learned of a savage couple who had been cast away from some far country on the Irish coast and this stirred his imagination. He began to collect information about strange pieces of timber that came from the west and were picked up on European shores. Whether he obtained any evidence about earlier Norse voyages is very doubtful, but he is likely to have been involved then and later in discussions with the Bristol men on what was or was not to be found by voyaging westward from the latitude of the British Isles. His later residence in Madeira and his trading voyage or voyages to Guinea gave him practical nautical experience in the Atlantic. It seems that by 1485, or perhaps a little earlier, he had copied the Toscanelli letter, studied Pierre d'Ailly's great work, and steeped himself both in the current cosmographical theories and in the maps which were being produced of the western European shores and the ocean that lay off them.

His basic theory rested on that of Toscanelli but was further refined. Columbus seems to have claimed that he would find Antilia some 1,500 miles westward from the Canaries on the 28th parallel, and Cipango 1,000 miles further on, with Cathay only one further 1,000 miles beyond, so making a mere 4,500 miles from Spain to

23. We depend for nearly all we know of Columbus in this period on his son's biography, whatever problems exist about the corruption of its text. The best edition in English is *The Life of the Admiral Christopher Columbus by His Son Ferdinand,* translated by Benjamin Keen (New Brunswick, N.J., 1959), (pp. 3–44 deal with his life before 1492). For the problems presented by the text, see A. Cioranescu, "Christophe Colomb: sources de sa biographie," M. Ballesteros-Gaibrois (and others), *La découverte de l'Amérique* (Paris, 1971), pp. 39–50.

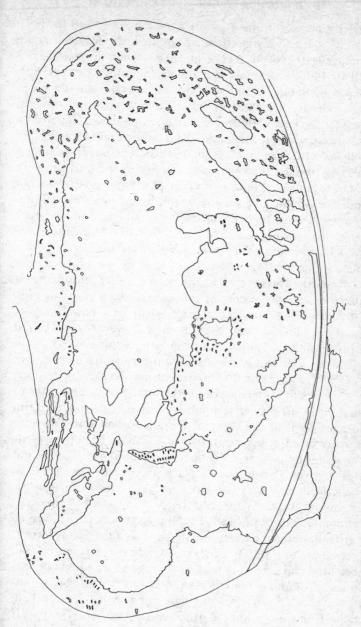

The Henricus Martellus Map, *circa* 1490
(Original in the Beinecke Library, Yale University)

Asia. His arguments on these points were easily resisted by those whom King John II consulted, since on an orthodox view some 10,000 miles lay between Europe and Asia. After his rejection in Portugal in 1486, Columbus and his cartographer brother Bartholomew worked out a variation of this plan to take to other European monarchs. It appears highly unlikely that this matched the plan presented to the king of Portugal, since it would have involved a long southward voyage from either England or France into waters from which Portuguese and Castilians alike were busily excluding foreigners by the 1480s. But it did clearly involve a convenient halfway house between England or France and Cipango that was not the traditional Antilia, and this could have been found in the island we have already mentioned, the *northerly* located Island of the Seven Cities, perhaps now being differentiated from the first Antilia, despite the fact that the two were the same in origin.

No plan of this sort exists, although some vestiges of its content may survive in the Paris map. The map could either reflect current Portuguese views independent of Columbus, which he partly took over, or it could be a reflection in a Portuguese-based map of some of the brothers' ideas. Bartholomew however was rejected by Henry VII after an inquiry, and later also by the advisers of the young Charles VIII in France. As he appears to have spent five years, 1488–93, away from his brother, he may have made not one but several visits to both countries with varying plans and maps to back them up. Christopher Columbus himself had gone to Spain to repeat his pleas at the court of Ferdinand and Isabella, since Castile, recognized as sovereign over the Canary Islands in 1481, had now some status as an Atlantic power and had also opted out of competing with Portugal for a place on the southern route to the Indies. Columbus was back in Portugal to meet Bartolomeu Dias on his return from the decisive voyage which turned the southern limit of Africa in 1488. Then he went back to Spain to be again rejected, but made a last-minute appeal to the Spanish court at the opening of 1492 when Isabella, after a further refusal, finally relented and agreed to back his voyage to Asia on very generous terms. Columbus himself related later (how reliably it cannot be ascertained) that after this agreement had been reached, news came from his brother Bartholomew that both Henry VII and Charles VIII had changed their minds too and were ready to

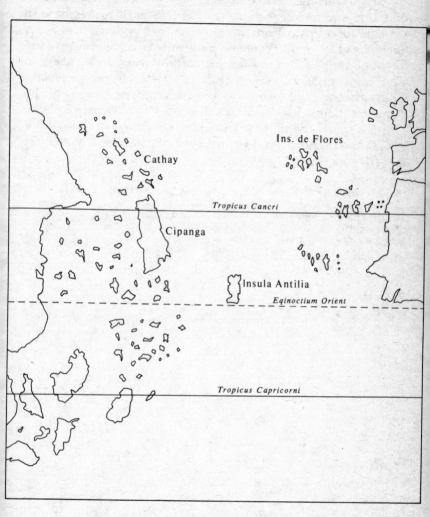

Martin Behaim's Westward Perspective, 1492
(The Behaim Globe is at Nürnberg)

back him, although now too late.[24]

Until 1492, most of the searches in the Atlantic had been for islands that might have an economic value in themselves. The view of geographers and cartographers which Toscanelli expressed in an extreme form, that islands were not an end in themselves but a means by which contact could be made with Asia, was growing. And it was given formal expression by Martin Behaim at Nürnberg in 1492, while Columbus was at sea, when he published his famous globe showing Antilia, Cipango and Cathay where Toscanelli and Columbus hoped to find them.[25] But it was Columbus who gave practical expression to these views and transformed the search for islands into the discovery, as he believed, of the coast of Asia across the Atlantic.

24. S. E. Morison, *Admiral of the Ocean Sea. A Life of Christopher Columbus,* 2 vols. (Boston, 1942), is still the standard life: his views have remained almost static, as is seen from *The European Discovery of America,* II, 3–271. Some modifications to these views, for the early period, are proposed in Quinn, *England and the Discovery of America,* pp. 68–84, 103–111. See also Marianne Mahn-Lot, "Colomb, Bristol et l'Atlantique Nord," *Annales,* XIX (1964), 528–530.

25. E. G. Ravenstein, *Martin Behaim, His Life and His Globe* (London, 1907).

# CHAPTER 4

# *European Technology, Ideology and Institutions: Their Impact on North America* [1]

A T the point where westward voyaging again became possible in the later fifteenth century it seems desirable to describe briefly the equipment, both physical and ideological, which the Europeans had at their disposal when they launched themselves toward the still undiscovered America. Their ships and guns and navigating techniques are clearly important, but so too are their opinions on the physical setting, on man and on God. Clearly, there are many areas of human consciousness and preconception where it is impossible to be either comprehensive or dogmatic, yet it would be equally risky to ignore such areas entirely. The story of how these first Europeans crossed the ocean and invaded North America in itself reveals the nature of their approach, as well as throwing light on the adequacy of their physical equipment and their way of looking at the world. It is important to stress that the transplanting of European mores outside the countries of their origin and across the ocean was something more extensive than what inevitably took place when colonists were sent to live in North America. The whole spectrum of their interactions with the new physical environment and with the aboriginal society (already sketched in outline) is relevant to the question of what they were, what they were attempting to do, and how they did it, and helps to explain the

1. This chapter incorporates part of the first chapter of William P. Cumming, Raleigh A. Skelton and David B. Quinn, *The Discovery of North America* (London,1971), pp. 13–28, by kind permission of the late Paul Elek and Elek Books Ltd.

nature of their failures and their successes alike.

First, it must be stressed that the discovery of America was not an isolated or self-contained event. Rather, it was made and exploited for purposes that were relevant to the European society from which the discoverers sprang. The exploration and exploitation which followed discovery were directly conditioned by the equipment and the mentality of the men who went across the ocean to involve themselves in one way or another with America; the trade in which they engaged and the settlements which they subsequently fostered were projections of Europe in a new environment. Most of the discoverers in the earliest stages of contact with North America— explorers, fishermen, merchants, searchers for minerals or medicinal plants, and such like—were wholly absorbed in what they were doing. They believed that when they were figuring out the lie of the land, getting a clear idea of the course of the rivers, trying to understand the main constituents of the vegetation, looking for cultivable lands, or setting down those features of American Indian life which were novel or interesting, they were concerned with the thing-in-itself, with the objective situation in which they themselves acted as detached observers. Yet all of them had built into them the intention, conscious or otherwise, of involving North America with their European homeland. And all were conditioned by the outlook and the needs of Renaissance Europe.

The white searchers of the ocean who found and explored North America in the late fifteenth century were themselves at a point of transition in their technology, their ideology, and the character of their social organization. Above all, they had developed the instruments of war, so that they not only had at their disposal the full accessories of the iron age—armor, swords, and spears—but had also passed into the phase of rapid advance in projectile and percussive weapons. The perfected longbow and the mechanized crossbow were giving place to the handgun (though still clumsy) and the cannon (now ship-portable), which placed them beyond the military resources of Amerindian society. The horse also—in some ways their most effective military instrument—provided both mobility and shock effect. Armor too was a significant strength in warfare but it proved burdensome and hence was liable to be discarded in hot climates. The Spaniards, significantly, would come to prefer the arrow-proof padded jacket of the Aztecs, the *escupile*, in summer

campaigns, although metal headpieces were thought essential. In static warfare they were immensely at an advantage, though this was balanced to some extent by their vulnerability to surprise and ambush and to insufficient mobility in the less open field.[2]

It may seem a little surprising to put land weapons before ships in discussing the instruments with which Europeans began the exploration and conquest of America. But while marine technology and navigational know-how brought Europeans to America and enabled them to carry out a long, discontinuous sequence of exploration, the fact remains that if the European arms had not been so overwhelmingly superior to those of the indigenous peoples, the European impact on North America—indeed, on any part of the Americas—would have been marginal only, as was the case in the sixteenth century in European relations with China.

The Atlantic Ocean in the fifteenth century constituted a formidable barrier to European ships and sailors. Admittedly, it could be crossed in the northwest by vessels moving from island to island, as the Norsemen had done much earlier; and many English and later Hanseatic ships were to continue to follow the old Norse routes as far as western Iceland. But economic incentives, until the Northwest Passage concept developed, were insufficient to attract ships farther west. Much later, when the Canaries current and the Northeast Trades were discovered late in the fifteenth century, the Atlantic could be crossed also in subtropical and tropical latitudes. But before the discovery of the Trades, any attempt to sail far out into the ocean was beset by problems. There were no known landfalls, although a number of Atlantic islands had been found before the end of the century which would provide a few small specific objectives. Soundings were impossible beyond the limits of the continental shelf until some signs of hitherto undiscovered land were seen. The great ocean swell and strong, often violent winds were intimidating, and indeed dangerous to the small vessels of the time. The major difficulty was that until well on into the fifteenth century few ships were equipped to sail in any direction except with the wind behind them. For most months in the year the prevailing westerlies, between a little north of 30° and beyond 60°, offered a complete barrier to effective progress directly to the west. Only brave experiment and

2. See especially Carlo M. Cipolla, *Guns and Sails in the Early Phase of European Expansion, 1480–1700* (1965).

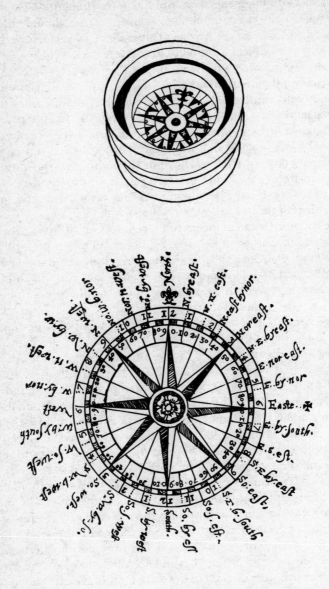

Calculating Direction: Compass (top) and Compass Rose

careful observation could teach seamen from Portugal, northern Spain, France and England that there were spells of east and northerly winds which might, in spring and early summer, reverse the normal wind direction and make westward oceanic sailing possible and, with good fortune, even easy.

In developing a mastery of oceanic sailing, the seaman had to depend first of all on his senses—those of sight, sound and smell—and on his cumulative interpretation, based on experience, of winds, currents, phases of the moon, tides, the color of the water, and indications of changing weather once he was outside sight of land. Visual observation of the Pole Star and of certain other stars could give him some elementary guides to direction, but he could easily lose his way in the ocean wastes. Once he began to bring equipment to his aid in navigation, he depended first of all on his compass and on an effective rudder that would enable him to steer a steady course.[3] Sounding with the lead was an older skill, but it was only useful in relatively shallow water, although regular attempts to find bottom were helpful exercises when a landfall might for any reason be expected. The expert seaman could often estimate speed with some degree of accuracy by visual observation alone; he was aided from early in the sixteenth century by the use of a log line (chip log) and half-hour glass which could produce, in skilled hands, a reasonably accurate result. From the thirteenth century, the marine chart had been developed in the Mediterranean. This applied the lists of described features and named places (compiled in the portolans or lists of sailing directions carried by successive masters of vessels sailing on regular courses) to the outlines of the coasts. Such charts were extended to the western European coasts along the routes of Italian trading vessels and, already in the fourteenth century, were given an Atlantic dimension. Islands, whether imagined or real, were shown well away from land and began to

3. On navigation, the best studies in English are Eva G. R. Taylor, *The Haven-finding Art* (London, 1956), and David W. Waters, *The Art of Navigation in England in Tudor and Stuart Times* (London, 1958). Romola and R. C. Anderson, *The Sailing-Ship* (New York, 1963), give a very clear outline of development; R. Morton Nance, "The Ship of the Renaissance," *The Mariner's Mirror*, XLI (1955), 180–192, 281–298, provides a concise account of basic changes in hull form and sail plan—see pp. 83, 86. Michel Mollat (ed.), *Le navire et l'économie maritime du Nord de l'Europe du Moyen-Age au XVIII<sup>e</sup> siècle* (Paris, 1960), has valuable specialized information. Smaller vessels are admirably illustrated in Lionel Willis and Basil Greenhill, *The Coastal Trade* (London, 1975).

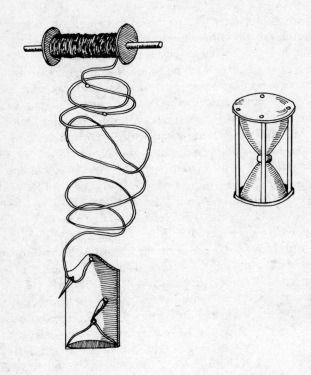

Calculating Speed: The Log Line (left) and the Half-Hour Glass

remove the impression of the ocean as being empty of land, even though so many of the islands shown had never been and never would be seen. Between the end of the fourteenth century and the 1460s, the islands discovered comprised the Canaries, Madeiras, Azores and Cape Verdes; their discovery meant that there might well prove to be others which ships could reach. Moreover, rhumb lines—straight lines drawn outwards from windroses—on the oceanic surface of the charts provided some indication of courses that might be followed by the use of rudder and compass.

The art of dead reckoning was developed by plotting direction run and distance traveled on a blank chart with dividers, later aided by parallel rulers, and so making up a picture of the course made good. For much of the fifteenth century this remained a specialized procedure, used only on a limited number of exploring voyages; it was rendered more helpful when a simple mathematical procedure for averaging out directions traveled (set out on a traverse table) was developed and applied. This was especially useful when frequent changes of course proved necessary for one reason or another. Throughout the later Middle Ages the astrolabe had been used on land to obtain angular elevations of heavenly bodies, for astronomical and astrological purposes. In a simplified way, this instrument could also be used at sea to take observations of the height of the sun at noon, even if a ship was rarely still enough for much accuracy. It did provide a means of establishing approximate latitude, though only toward the very end of the century were tables available to turn angular readings easily into degrees of latitude.

The quadrant, which gave an angular reading from a pendulum swinging across an engraved metal plate, proved another helpful device. Here too readings were difficult to obtain in rough weather, but it was easier to average out a series of individual observations. The cross staff provided a simple and sturdy instrument which was often preferred, despite an Atlantic sky as often overcast as not. If a series of sights could be obtained, it became possible to establish a course along a selected line of latitude; the practice of "running down the latitude," which was to continue for many generations in ocean sailing, was already in use during the later fifteenth century.

The instruments in use all involved direct optical observation of the sun, so that improvements in accuracy were unlikely. If an oceanic explorer did not envisage a specific objective across the ocean,

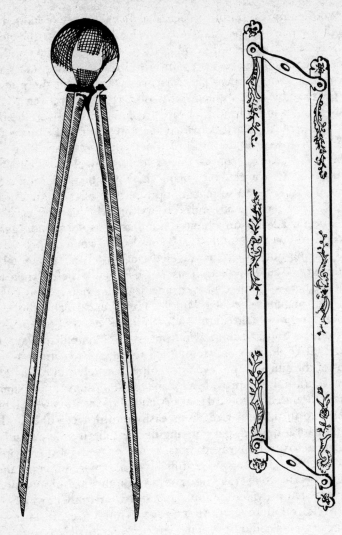

Charting: Dividers (left) and Parallel Rulers

such procedures had little firm purpose, although Columbus in 1492 expected to run down the latitude of 28°—sailing due west from the Canaries—until he reached Antilia—the large imaginary island that had appeared on many charts. The Pole Star could be observed by instrument as well as by eye more frequently than the sun, and close observation and the use of written rules—known as the "Regiment" of Polaris—gradually refined all observations so that compass bearings could be checked and latitudes taken from the Pole Star verified. Variation of the compass was noted and recorded by Cabot off Newfoundland in 1497 even though it was not understood. The Guards, which moved, or appeared to move, round Polaris, were used to obtain the time, which could then be read off after observation from a simple diagram. This was important in order to time noon sights. Cumulatively, these various methods of observation, employing some instrumentation at least, could provide a means of following a course with a certain degree of consistency across oceanic distances. However, few seamen were able or willing to use such instruments to any extent—Columbus is known to have used his astrolabe only.

Latitudes at sea could be estimated with good fortune to within half a degree, even if they might also be out by as much as 2 degrees. Estimates of longitude at sea could only be worked out roughly by dead reckoning where the margin of error was normally very wide. There were strong incentives to establish the latitude of known destinations as accurately as possible, but in making for a continental rather than an island destination defective estimates did not greatly matter. Once land became accessible, observations on shore with the astrolabe could usually provide reasonably accurate corrections. No quick method of establishing longitude on land existed, though a steady series of astronomical observations and estimates of distances travelled on the ground could pin down the longitude of a particular place if anyone was there long enough to make them. The inability to estimate longitude with any degree of accuracy at sea could cause serious hardship or even disaster; vessels sailing into the ocean with no precise idea of where they could expect to make a landfall could run out of provisions and fresh water without ever sighting land. This was the main difficulty in getting crews to attempt oceanic sailing in the fifteenth century. The guesses of the geographers could give little assurance that land would be found

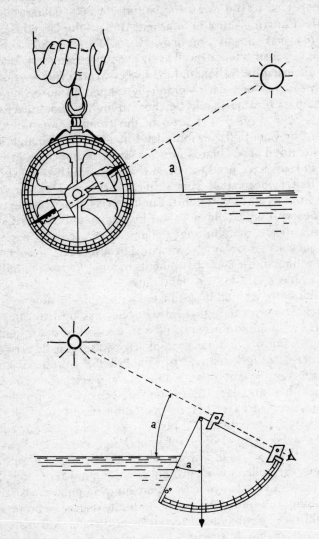

Latitude-Finding by Sun Sights: Astrolabe (top) and Quadrant

within the limits of the range of the vessels searching for it.

Oceanic voyages had to be carefully planned and provisioned, and the men taking part in them required above all experience, endurance and courage. If the seaman had all these qualities, but not the patience or skill to use instruments other than his compass, he could yet often make his way successfully across the ocean once pioneer courses had been sailed by others. Thousands of masters of fishing vessels were to take their craft successfully to the Newfoundland Banks and Island from shortly after 1500 while displaying little interest or skill in instrumental navigation. Of course, if he was skilled in using instruments and had a body of practical skills as well, the seaman was better equipped for making the longer and more novel voyages. Coastal sailing, once the ocean had been passed and continental land reached, was within the skill of most experienced seamen. Many ships disappeared on ocean voyages, but it must be remembered that they were also frequently lost in routine coastal voyages along well-known European coasts and that this continued to be the case throughout the age of sail.

The best seaman could do little unless he had a sound and efficient ship. The shipbuilder's craft was one where traditional local skills in adapting vessels to the purposes for which they were to be employed were strong, but the craftsmen were also open to novel ideas about construction and utilization if they understood that these had a substantial advantage over older types. Most shipbuilders expected to build vessels which were both durable and maneuverable; but once ships began to sail farther and under novel conditions, new designs and new scales of construction were forced on shipbuilders in the areas where skills and accessible materials, primarily timber, were readily available. A sufficient degree of innovation over most of western Europe took place in the fifteenth century to provide adequate oceangoing ships, and innovation continued into the sixteenth century so as to make them fully effective for ocean sailing.[4]

Most of the vessels used along the western European coastlines at the opening of the fifteenth century were short and broad in the beam. They varied very much in size, though the average was very small by subsequent standards: vessels of 15 to 100 tons comprised

4. See pp. 83, 86, 87, 89, 91, 92.

Latitude-Finding by Sun Sights: Cross Staff (top)
and Davis Staff or Back-Staff

The Development of European Ships, 1400–1600: Hull Evolution. (1) through (7) are increasingly complex carracks; (8) is the first galleon; (9) is an intermediate form between carrack and galleon and (10) is a later galleon. (From R. Morton Nance, *The Ship of the Renaissance* [1955]).

most of the merchant fleets of European states. Many of them were little more than capacious, decked, broad-bottomed boats, with scant accommodation for crew or equipment, and space only for a basic cargo to be carried a relatively short distance. These were adequate for coastal sailing but were neither safe nor reliable on the ocean. They were almost universally powered by a single large mainsail which could be an effective means of propulsion with the wind behind it. When the winds were contrary, a harbor or anchorage had to be found for such a ship; obviously this type of vessel was not suitable in most cases for sailing off the European shores into the ocean.

From the Mediterranean the use of the triangular lateen sail spread early in the century to southern Spain and Portugal, and later to northern Spain and France. This allowed the vessel to sail with winds coming in from either side, though not of course directly into the wind. The vessels to which they were fitted were also made relatively longer and narrower. These ships were known as caravels, and took somewhat different forms in Andalusia and in Portugal. They proved excellent for the pioneering voyages which the Portuguese made down the west coast of Africa and some distance out into the western ocean in the first half of the fifteenth century. The early single-masted, lateen-rigged vessels were small, but they were soon followed by larger and longer ones, with two lateen-rigged masts and even three. These continued to be employed by Portugal down to the end of the century. The main function of the lateen sail was, however, destined to be as an auxiliary. The combination of the standard northern mainmast, with its squaresail, and the lateen-rigged mizzenmast was first developed in Andalusia. It was soon taken up by the Portuguese and spread more gradually to northern Spain, France and eventually England. By 1500 two masts, foremast and mainmast, carrying square sails, and a mizzen with a lateen become the pattern for most oceangoing ships of the crucial decades of the discoveries between the 1480s and 1500s. The Portuguese, once they had combined driving power with maneuverability, built larger vessels of this type—the *caravela redonda*—with which they proved able to sail to India and back. By that time the sail pattern on main- and foremast was becoming complex. A second, and soon a third, course was added, and the combination of sails of varying sizes in predominantly square-rigged ships provided much

more effective and more maneuverable vessels than any hitherto developed. The lateen was retained on one, and later, two masts (as mizzen and bonaventure mizzen). Such vessels had a wide range of maneuver in varying winds, and they had the power to make long voyages at relatively high speeds in comparison with the earlier ships.

While these vital changes in sail plan were taking place, ships were becoming more complex in their construction and generally larger. As they grew longer and narrower, they were also built higher in the water, with single decks giving way gradually to multiple decks, and stern- and forecastles being incorporated into their design (adapted from the clumsy defensive and offensive platforms of earlier war vessels). The ship thus became capable of stowing a larger and more varied cargo, of offering quarters for officers and seamen necessary for their good health on long voyages, of providing additional space for working on charts, keeping logs and such like, and of improving observation facilities for the watch.

The main bulk carriers in northern waters in the late fifteenth and early sixteenth centuries were the carracks. These had adopted the newer sail plans and some of the more sophisticated decking of the Iberian vessels, but they remained rather broad-beamed and clumsy compared with the *caravela redonda*. The newer, medium-sized vessels of 60 to 100 tons from almost anywhere along the western seaboard were capable of making oceanic voyages by about 1500, though there continued to be many local variations in ship construction and in sailing skills. The smaller vessels in France and England often remained somewhat broad and clumsy, with quite primitive equipment.

The precise nature of the commercial and technical drives that improved the sailing qualities and cargo-carrying capacity of western European vessels are difficult to pin down. Periods of prosperity and depression followed each other several times during the century, but certainly maritime commerce improved rapidly in the last quarter of the fifteenth century. The decline of the Italian city galley fleets, plying from Italy to northern Europe, offered incentives to vessels from the Atlantic littoral to make longer voyages to take their place. The bulk of trade between the Netherlands and England to Spain and Portugal was undoubtedly increasing. Gradually, the improvements made in Iberian shipping were taken up farther

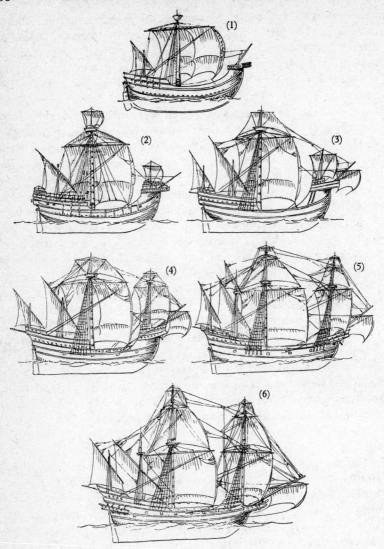

The Development of European Ships, 1400–1600: The Evolution of Sail Plan. (1) *c.* 1430; (2) *c.* 1450; (3) *c.* 1500; (4) *c.* 1530; (5) *c.* 1560; (6)*c.* 1600. (From *The Ship of the Renaissance*)

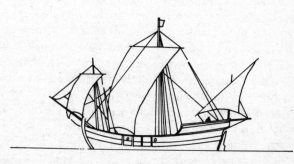

Spanish Ships of the Sixteenth Century: Fragata (top), Barcolongo (middle), and Caravela (After Albert Manucy, *Florida's Menéndez* [1962])

north, while northern innovations were also incorporated into vessels built farther south, as more northern vessels used Iberian ports and vice versa. The pattern of development in each area differed appreciably, but the general effect of improved technical efficiency was almost universal.

Within a single decade from 1492, Columbus, Cabot, the Corte Real brothers, and others had proved capable of taking vessels safely across the Atlantic and home again, even though there were also frequent losses on record. Columbus, by exploiting the Canaries Current and the Northeast Trades outward and the Gulf Stream and the Westerlies homeward, gave the Spaniards the great initial advantage of a relatively safe and easy (though extended) passage across the ocean each way. This enabled them to begin the swift exploitation of their island and mainland discoveries in the Caribbean so as to develop there the first transatlantic empire. The route too was suitable for square-rigged vessels, and these, often rather broadly built like the northern carracks, continued to dominate the Spanish transatlantic merchant marine.

There was no such standard route for crossing the ocean in more northerly latitudes. The Corte Reals had learned how to get from the Azores to America by sailing first north and then west, not northwest. The English and French, if the westerlies were dominant, continued to find it difficult to make effective progress into the Atlantic even with a flexible sail plan. They tended to sail well to the southwest into mid-Atlantic before making their way north again. If they went too far south they were liable to find themselves becalmed in the region of light airs, the doldrums, north of the belt of the Northeast Trades. Some were to prefer to reach southeastern North America until well into the seventeenth century by making the long haul down to the Canaries and then following the Spanish route first westward and then northward. Mostly, the French and English tended to await a period when winds were in an easterly direction and sail westward in their own latitudes or only a relatively short distance to the south before making their northing. They could not rely on such winds carrying them all the way across. Such passages could be very rapid, taking as little as two or three weeks only; equally, if the ships ran into westerly winds, they might take up to three months. The return voyage from North America could also be rapid—as little as two weeks and, more usually, a month or there-

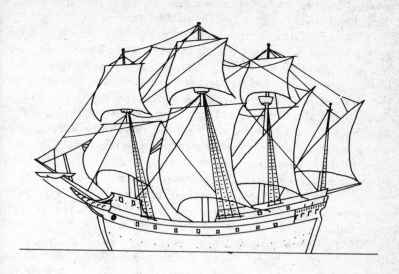

Spanish Ships of the Sixteenth Century: Navio (top) and Galéon
(After Albert Manucy)

abouts—but heavy winds and high seas made the easterly passage often highly dangerous, especially in the fall.

The Newfoundland fishermen soon managed to make their way, year after year, across the Atlantic in ships as small as 20 tons and rarely, for the first half of the sixteenth century, of more than about 80 tons. From Newfoundland access to the Gulf of St. Lawrence by the Strait of Belle Isle was easy enough. Cape Breton became a favorite landfall and they could then progress down the coast of the Maritimes. But for reasons which do not seem to be fully understood, reaching southern New England from Newfoundland did not prove so easy. Access from France or England to latitudes in North America between 26° and 35° N. was seldom achieved by a direct voyage before the early seventeenth century; it was obtained either by a slow voyage down the coast from Newfoundland, or, more commonly, by the long expedition by way of the Canaries and the Caribbean. Thus a curious anomaly developed. The Caribbean and Central America rapidly became accessible to Spain, and Newfoundland to a wide range of European fishermen: the zone in between was harder to reach or to exploit.

The sixteenth-century ship developed on the basis of the improvements of the latter part of the fifteenth century. The sail plan became steadily more complex, giving at the same time greater driving power and more flexibility in adjusting to various types of weather and wind direction. Four masts became common for the larger vessels, two of them being lateen-rigged; up to four courses were employed on the foremast and mainmast. The hull form also became more sophisticated. Additional decks provided for a new variety of cargo and stores, as well as for cannon, and for more specialized accommodation for both crew and passengers. Most ships engaged in oceanic crossings were armed, as attempted interception by open or covert enemies was frequent. The construction of the stern became more elaborate, gun ports at several levels being allowed for, and the great cabin used by the officers became part of a complex of sleeping and other apartments, rounded off late in the century by a stern gallery which was valuable for observation. There was a tendency to build up both sterncastle and forecastle too high for real stability in the first half of the century, but this was usually confined to naval vessels. The forecastle provided somewhat more habitable quarters for the crew; gradually it was built less high

Sixteenth-Century French Ships
(After Guillame de Testu)

English Ships of the Sixteenth Century

in the water and the bow extended forward. The galleon, after mid-century, developed a beaklike projection on the bow which could be used as a forward gallery.

The increasing care to make hull forms more streamlined for both grace and speed led to the emergence of the galleon. Originally a small speedy vessel, she had become by mid-century, in the hands of the French, a highly effective ship with excellent sailing qualities. The type was improved by the English later, when they studied the shapes of fishes and attempted to make hull forms conform to their lines. The English galleon as a war vessel could be a large ship, up to 1,000 tons, but more usually about 500. Her form influenced the design of the more far-ranging merchant vessels, especially as these had to be increasingly capable of fighting off hostile ships. She was perhaps twice as fast and infinitely more maneuverable than the comparably sized square-rigged Spanish merchantship; the Spanish war galleons were on the average larger than the English galleons and more heavily armed, but they were broad and sluggish in the water and consequently vulnerable when attacked by a number of small English galleons at sea. This helped to explain the victory of the English naval craft and armed merchantmen over the Armada in 1588, and their considerable success at sea when attacking or being attacked by Spanish ships, whether on the ocean routes or in the Caribbean.

Spain brought more colonists to North America than the English and French did in the later sixteenth century, and for the vital decade in Florida history, 1565–74, many of the vessels taking part came direct from Spain. The total amount of French and English shipping involved in trade and colonization of North America in this period (outside the codfishing and whaling fleets) was small, and almost all the ships took part in fighting at sea or were prepared to do so. Spanish vessels going directly to the Caribbean and returning from there were normally in convoy, and did not need to be so well armed. But as the sea war went on, increasing numbers were equipped with at least some means of defending themselves. Generally the rather slow, heavily laden Spanish vessels were an easy prey for French and English privateers, if they could be separated from their powerful escort galleons. At the same time, Spain does not appear to have lost many ships going directly to North America or near its shores. Most interceptions were off the Azores or nearer

Spain on the return voyages, and the tradition of arming merchant-men involved in trade with North America survived the conclusion of peace in 1604.

In the later sixteenth and early seventeenth centuries, it became usual for oceanic navigation to be done largely by the book, with the aid of a more varied range of instruments. Printed navigation manuals were early used by the Portuguese and Spaniards and were translated and adapted to the French, English and later Dutch needs. Early on, astronomical navigation for use in ocean voyaging had been systematically studied by pilots in Spain and Portugal; only late in the sixteenth century was such formal training begun in England and France. Improvements to the older instruments and the development of new ones—notably the back (or Davis) staff, which obviated direct observation of the sun by eye—made for more effective observations. The taking of noon sights of the sun became more precise, and tables for converting angular distances into latitudes were almost universally employed; a set of rules for using the Pole Star produced a number of refinements in observation too. Much serious attention was given to dip, to variation, and to longitude, though with little result in the last case as no reliable timepiece could yet be constructed and this was vital for easy observation.

America—South, Central and North—began to appear recognizably on the marine charts of the period,[5] so that the eastern coasts at least could be identified with an increasing degree of accuracy, even though much detail remained obscure and the west coast continued to be poorly drawn. Sailing directions giving indications of how to reach out across the ocean began to be written down and coasts described. The Mercator world map of 1569 was the first plane chart from which the seamen could get true direction. In 1599, Edward Wright put in print a practical method of constructing such a chart and gave an example in a world map of the same year, while Thomas Harriot had for some time been working on and explaining the use of instruments and the mathematical niceties of the solution of the spherical triangle to seamen. While longitude at sea could still not be established except by dead reckoning (which was becoming somewhat less defective as systematic skills were developed in oper-

5. Gerald R. Crone, *Maps and Their Makers* (London, 1953), and Norman Thrower, *Maps and Man* (Englewood Cliffs, N.J., 1972), are good general introductions. Raleigh A. Skelton, *Explorers' Maps* (London, 1958), indicates how explorers used them.

ating it), the gradual pinning down of the longitude of particular places in North America provided a growing number of reference points which could be valuable to seamen planning their courses. Atlases of sea charts (waggoners, as they were to be called) appeared before 1600; if they did not offer much guidance in American waters, these did render the return voyages to European ports less hazardous, and they also provided models on which comparable maps of North American waters might be constructed.

In the early seventeenth century it was not an exceptionally risky procedure for an experienced master to take a vessel across the North Atlantic. There were, however, appreciable and continuing risks, granted the nature of the weather encountered and the comparative fragility of the sailing vessels. There was, too, the fact that ships had little in the way of facilities for carrying passengers and that intending colonists had very much to bear at sea. Nonetheless, during the first 120 years of Atlantic trafficking a reasonable measure of skill, experience and confidence had been accumulated so that large-scale settlement in North America was now possible.

One further point about shipping has some significance. Once their Caribbean and Central American colonies had been established, the Spaniards had a great advantage in the exploration of North America in that they could use many small vessels built in the West Indies which might not easily have made the Atlantic passage. By contrast, the other western European powers during this period had to build almost all their ships and boats in Europe and sail or carry them across the ocean. Otherwise there was little to choose between the French, English and Portuguese ability to sail across the Atlantic.

More specifically, the western European peoples varied in the degree to which they exploited various techniques of exploration in North America; nor did they always depend on their own nationals in doing so. Significantly, the Italians, who had taught so much to the Iberian nations, continued to appear prominently in the American field. Giovanni Caboto, Sebastiano Caboto and Giovanni da Verrazzano—better known perhaps as John Cabot, Sebastian Cabot and, in France, Jean de Vérrazane—are only the leading names in a fairly numerous brood. If the Portuguese made many of the early sea charts of Newfoundland, Labrador and the Maritimes, it was largely the Italians who worked them up into intelligible maps of the

new continent, though they gradually gave place in this skill to the Dutch in the latter part of the sixteenth century and were almost submerged by them in the seventeenth. The Spanish expeditions—for example, those of Gomes, Cabrilho and of Vicente Gonzales to Chesapeake Bay in 1588—often used Portuguese pilots. To the end of the sixteenth century English explorers liked to have a Portuguese pilot with them—Drake rarely sailed without one—and a number of foreigners also appeared as pilots in the later French expeditions, even though the standard of French navigation was very high indeed by the later sixteenth century. For both Spaniards and Portuguese it was normal to carry a painter on board an expedition,[6] whose function was primarily to draw (or paint) maps from the crude charts compiled by the navigators and masters. He might perhaps also sketch animals, plants or native peoples and decorate his finished maps with a few land curiosities—and his sea with whales and monsters. The systematic use of a painter to record the natural products and peoples of North America began with the French in 1564, when Jacques le Moyne de Morgues was sent to make a graphic survey of Florida; a selection of his drawings appeared in the form of engravings in 1591. The Spaniards had been less dependent on the brush before the great Mexican survey of Francisco Hernandez in the 1570s.

The English were the first to exploit the technique of the Spanish "geographical report" *(relación geográfica)*—a questionnaire with answers—in combination with large numbers of naturalistic drawings of Amerindians, fish, plants, birds and animals so as to build up a detailed survey in words and pictures of the new land in which settlements were intended and which it was proposed to exploit systematically. The work of Thomas Harriot and John White in the year 1585–6 in what was then Virginia (now North Carolina and southern Virginia) was of great value to subsequent English expeditions and inquirers. Thomas Harriot's *A briefe and true report of the new found land of Virginia,* published in 1588 and reprinted with engravings of many of White's drawings in 1590, did more to open up North America to European knowledge (along with the parallel publication of Le Moyne) than any number of voyages themselves.

6. Paul H. Hulton and David B. Quinn, *The American Drawings of John White,* 2 vols. (London and Chapel Hill, N.C., 1964), deals in vol. I with many of the aspects of illustrating newly discovered lands and peoples.

Publicity by narrative was also significant.[7] Although Europeans, with their command of print, could wield considerable weapons of publicity, it was not until the appearance of Ramusio's *Viaggi et navigationi* in the 1550s that a significant body of material on North America was circulated. The narratives of the Verrazzano and Cartier voyages were largely known, in the original Italian or in translations, from Ramusio. France did not publicize her North American exploits very systematically, but late in the sixteenth century, between 1582 and 1600, Richard Hakluyt put in print not only a great deal of material on English activities—almost every scrap he could find—but much on French explorations as well. On the continent his work was used and developed by Theodor de Bry in his famous series of illustrated volumes. Samuel Purchas continued the work of Richard Hakluyt in England between 1613 and 1625, while in France after 1603 a stream of narrative emerged from the expeditions of Champlain and Lescarbot.

This verbal recording derived in the main from participants in voyages at the time of their performance rather than from vague reminiscences of their exploits after some time had elapsed. Many of them were based on the ship's log, with its column for "Occurrences"; and this was built into detailed narrative journals of what took place. We lack journals for some of the major voyages and have inadequate ones for others, but in general we can follow the major explorations and early attempts at settlement at first hand in the words of the men actually concerned. By the late sixteenth century, a basic problem of communication had been solved: accounts of North American voyages were being written in simple vernacular language, accessible to all who could read, and were not confined to educated men who knew Latin, so that a popular bridge by means of printed words was erected across the Atlantic. Champlain's simple honest prose was paralleled by the even more rugged and accessible narrative style of Captain John Smith. The rise of a popular audience for writings relating to North America was an essential stage in making its potential as an area of settlement as well as trade known to the literate middle classes of western Europe, more especially in the early seventeenth century to the English, but also to the French and Dutch.

7. Chapter 22 provides further indications of written and published records of voyages and explorations.

Of the ideological equipment with which Europeans left their own societies,[8] religion was the most important. It was the sense of being involved in and sustained by the Church which, more than color or national feeling, made Europeans feel distinct from and superior to those peoples they met outside. To be non-Christian placed Amerindian peoples outside some sort of pale. Anti-Muslim feeling had bitten so deeply into the Spaniards that they wore their religion like a sword not only against the Arabs and Turks but against all who were not, or who did not rapidly become, Christians. The famous, or infamous, *Requerimiento* of 1514 ordered all Indians who encountered a Spanish expedition to agree on the spot to become Christians or else suffer death or enslavement. As this was often read in Spanish, it was a manifesto to the explorers rather than to the Amerindians that forceable conversion of the native peoples was the first duty of a Spaniard in America. In practice they had frequently other priorities, while Spanish government policy in particular cases was not wholly consistent with its manifesto, but its existence indicates clearly where Spain stood in this matter. The Portuguese attitude was to some extent similar, but not so decided.

The feeling existed amongst French and English too in more attenuated forms. And the Reformation merely complicated these attitudes—Spaniards extended their desire to kill all non-Christians to those who had rebelled against the true Church. The Protestants, whether French or English, could be almost as uncompromising as the Spaniards, although having emerged from societies that were themselves divided, the possibility of a degree of toleration of non-Christian beliefs was not so far removed. Basically, most Europeans tended to despise Amerindians because they were not Christians. The urge to convert them was partly expediency: the alternative of kill or convert was intermittently present in both the Spanish and the English mind. Those who believed that Christianity offered a better life and that such a life ought to be offered to non-Christians were always few, but they grew more numerous in reaction against

8. On the background that conditioned them, see Louis Gottschalk, L. C. Mackinney and E. H. Pritchard, *The Foundations of the Modern World, 1300–1775* Unesco, History of Mankind, IV, 2 parts (New York and London, 1969). A broad conspectus of European ideological interactions with America will be found in Fredi Chiapelli (ed.), *First Images of America*, 2 vols. (Berkeley and Los Angeles, 1976).

the intolerable inhumanity of the merely righteous. In the sixteenth century the contacts of European Christians with North America, apart from Mexico, were slight and transient. Little sustained brutality against non-Christians took place, although the Spaniards several times showed their capacity for it; but missionary activity there, either for expediency's sake or for principle, was spasmodic and almost wholly ineffective (though after 1600 it made some headway in Florida). The Christian ideology at this stage was probably more effective in determining attitudes than action.

There was a secular trend too amongst the explorers which was often significant and sometimes dominant. Medieval theology had been more all-embracing in its theoretical ascendancy over men's minds than its practice. Latin and Greek literature, even if admitted to a quasi-Christian status, had kept open a less committed intellectual view of the world. The revived interest in and knowledge of the classical past—in literature at least—and its popularization by the circulation of printed works, left its mark on most educated men. Roman, and sometimes Greek, precedent was regarded as a guide to action in the present.[9] If Europeans, when they went to America, at times employed archaic stereotypes drawn from the classics, they also used these mentors to point their curiosity and to stir them to objective comment on empirical relationships with the indigenous peoples. It is hard to say, of course, just how far a classical education was really the father of a lay, agnostic and to some extent scientific attitude. Perhaps in a society where the hold of the Church was gradually slipping and where doctrinal certainties were being challenged, it acted more as a vehicle for secularism than as its creator. The Spaniards were not all insulated from Renaissance secularism, and some of their greatest observers, Oviedo, for example, were products of the Italian Renaissance. There is no doubt that the Italians who played such a part in American exploration—Vespucci if not Columbus, Verrazzano if not John Cabot—were more secular than Christian-oriented in their reactions to the new life of the American west. The Frenchmen, too, were throughout essentially secular-minded and objective in their reactions to Amerindian society. So too were a few Englishmen, notably Thomas Harriot. The Portuguese observer of Soto's expedition, the Gentleman of Elvas,

9. See D. B. Quinn, "Renaissance Influences on English Colonization," *Transactions of the Royal Historical Society*, XXVI (1976), 73–93.

was less a victim of European myopia than most Spaniards. Spaniards could be objective about Indians insofar as they studied them in order to exploit them or convert them; but, in North America at least, they did not seriously attempt to understand them, or collaborate with them, on either detached or approximately level terms. This may have been due not only to Christian aloofness but also to the fact that Spaniards by the time they met North American Indians in any numbers had many indigenous dependents in other parts of the Americas and so adopted preconceived attitudes of familiar contempt toward them.

Although in the longer run Europeans were to develop a distinctive colonial outlook in each of the settlements in which they established themselves firmly in any considerable number, those who took part in the early exploration of North America and those who settled in the earliest colonies remained fully European in their outlook. They judged almost everything they saw on the basis of European preconceptions; their minds were formed by their growth and education in a European community; and many of their activities in the New World were the direct consequence of habits of thought and action acquired in Europe. This must be stressed if we are to gain any real insight into what Europeans did in or thought about North America in this initial period. The carryover from Europe was not, except in the case of very transient visitors, absolute and complete; yet the effect of conditions in North America on either the activities or the outlook of the Europeans who went there was minimal.

European society was hierarchical—the hierarchy of birth and of status (or order) informed every expedition from Europe to America. Men of gentle and noble birth took natural command over sailors, soldiers, and settlers alike. In a settlement they expected and were accorded priority in war, in civil authority and in comfort: their views of Amerindian life tended to prevail, at least in action. Spain had a superfluity of persons of noble birth—in the Americas more individuals claimed the privileges of nobility than were qualified to receive them. Spain was feudal but in America particularly it was a feudalism open to talents, so that almost everyone of any personality or education aspired to hold land and to rule men. The Frenchman had a certain qualified respect for birth, and Frenchmen of quality expected to be singled out in American expeditions and

settlements; the same was true of Englishmen, if they were perhaps stiffer in holding out for the privileges of gentility. All the Europeans consequently paid some attention to Amerindian hierarchy. The existence of chiefs and elders, and of some degree of formality and ceremonial in their contacts, made it appear that these peoples were not wholly without signs of civilization in their social structure. The Spaniards were most inclined to treat Indian chiefs as non-commissioned officers (*cacique* virtually equaled sergeant), whose status was to be respected only by being kept subordinate to Spanish wishes and needs.

It was the French who were most willing to take Indian status at its own valuation, to listen to interminable harangues in incomprehensible languages, to participate in formal festivals, to make alliances and involve themselves in native wars. The rapport between Laudonnière and the Timucuan chief Saturiwa—even if they often disagreed—is not paralleled in any other known relationship in sixteenth-century North America. Similarly, Champlain from 1603 onward showed an immense capacity for making friends with many Indian chiefs and producing a continuing atmosphere of mutual trust. Once again the English occupied an intermediate position: impressed by the claims of Indian "kings," they were at times prepared to grant them feudal status (Manteo in 1587 on Roanoke Island) or even recognition as subordinate kings (Powhatan in 1608). But in closer intercourse, Englishmen easily came to despise Indian socio-political arrangements and, as they saw them, pretensions, and tended to equip themselves, as the French rarely did, with a built-in attitude of superiority. But whenever they came ashore, and wherever they established a settlement, whether temporary or permanent, European hierarchies in some measure were established on American soil. These contained in themselves elements of conflict with those of the indigenous population whose lands they took (in most cases) without permission, and in which they began, in some degree, to recreate a European social order. It need hardly be stressed that inside nearly every expedition, and in every colonial settlement almost without exception, the internal struggle for position in the hierarchy was continuous and often disruptive.

European society was acquisitive and mercantile.[10] At every stage

10. John H. Parry, *The Age of Reconnaissance* (London and New York, 1963), is the best general introduction to the early stages of European overseas expansion in its

of European activity in North America, the profitable exchange of goods and the exploitation of natural resources were primary motives that impelled men across the oceans and made their contact with the land and its inhabitants continuous and systematic. The exploitation of natural resources did not inevitably disturb the native society. Hundreds of European vessels could resort to the Grand Banks for fishing every season without affecting the Amerindian peoples in any way—so long as they confined themselves to the Banks fishery and brought their fish home green-salted to Europe. But as soon as they had developed an inshore fishery, and built stages and flakes and store- and boathouses to dry the fish, to render the oil and shelter their boats, then an exploitation nexus was established with the native people of Newfoundland. It was not one-sided. Beothuk Indians could steal or seize European lines, nets, tools, weapons and even boats (risking death if they were caught), and they could balance such loss of inshore fishing as they had suffered by the exchange of pelts for European commodities. But here as elsewhere, when the less highly organized Indian groups had to deal with strongly individualistic fishermen, contact soon led to the retreat of the natives into the interior and the less accessible bays; in the longer run, of course, it meant their gradual extinction.

Where the Indians were more numerous and more firmly organized, contacts over fishing and fur trading might involve occasional skirmishing but no drastic changes in Indian life. The Micmac, longest of all in contact with Europeans in this period, retained their indigenous system almost intact. It was often possible, before European settlement began, to assimilate European and Indian demands into a reasonably equitable system of exchange. The French proved realistic and successful in developing a seasonal relationship of this nature along the shores of the Gulf and later the river of the St. Lawrence, and on the coast of the Maritimes from Cape Breton down to Maine. But whenever Europeans established trading contacts of a regular character, they tended to assume exclusive rights of access—Basques contested with Normans, Bretons with Englishmen. Moreover, even before settling they often adopted a pro-

---

economic and technological aspects. Michel Mollat and Paul Adam (eds.), *Les aspects internationaux de la découverte océanique aux xv<sup>e</sup> et xvi<sup>e</sup> siècles* (Paris, 1966), contains studies throwing much light on the economic and other problems of Europeans crossing the oceans for the first time.

prietorial attitude toward the Indian territories. Chauvin did not ask permission (we think) to settle a year-round post at Tadoussac in 1600–1, nor Champlain at Ste Croix in 1604 or at Port Royal in 1605. The attitude of the English was even more cavalier in waiving the land rights of the indigenous peoples. Sir Humphrey Gilbert carved out (on paper) estates of millions of acres in the vicinity of Narragansett Bay which he had never seen and which, in all probability, had never been sighted by any Englishman. The first Virginia of 1585 and the second Virginia of 1607 were appropriated on equally flimsy pretexts, even though an element of "purchase" was being introduced about this time into a relationship in which the two parties had a very different approach to property rights.[11]

Since the primary purpose of European contact was exploitation, colonies were settled almost wholly for their economic value.[12] Trade with the native peoples was one objective and it remained the chief one in French Canada long after our period. In most cases where the English were engaged in settlement, Indian trade was secondary to the direct use of the land. This might be by extraction —as in the case of the allegedly auriferous minerals of Baffin Island in 1577–8, or the many "mines" found or alleged to be found elsewhere by almost every visiting party. Or it might mean the cutting of timber for sale in Europe or to set in motion the manufacture in the colony of iron, potash, glass, or some other industrial product. But it was most often the land itself that was wanted for occupation and cultivation. Indians were rarely asked if they wished to surrender some or all of their territories; even when dispossessed of part of their land, they were often expected to produce a surplus of agricultural produce to help feed the newcomers and were sometimes roughly treated when they did not do so. When they interfered in any way with settlers or settlement, they were regarded as enemies and often cleared from the areas nearby. By and large they did not respond satisfactorily to impressment as labor by the newcomers. A few were made servants, but most refused to work under instructions. In Spanish Florida there was an attempt to employ

11. See Francis Jennings, "Virgin Land and Savage People," *American Quarterly*, XXIII (1971), 519–541, and his extended treatment in *The Invasion of America* (Chapel Hill, N.C. 1975).

12. The introduction to Quinn, *North American Discovery* (1971), pp. xx–xli, discusses the commercial prospects of North America in this period.

them for construction and agricultural purposes—once, for a short time, even formally enslaving them. The Spaniards who made the most spectacular expeditions into the interior in the early period also exploited the Indians for porterage as well as food supplies. Hernando de Soto's wanderings are a long record of food levies and of the use of relays of impressed Indian porters who made it possible for his unwieldy company to proceed. As the licensed conqueror (adelantado) of Florida, Pedro Menéndez de Avilés was allocated the revenues of Florida—almost all of them to be levied from the Indian inhabitants—as his salary, so that food-tributes became the symbol of permanent Spanish occupation when direct labor services failed to prove effective.

The Spanish settlers envisaged agricultural exploitation of the land (using, if they could, Indian penal labor) as an inevitable implication of European settlement; when Spanish settlers were driven from Santa Elena to Cuba in 1576, they even took some of their Indian dependents with them. It could be argued (and was in the past) that Indian settlement was thin in the east—though recent estimates have extended the earlier ones considerably. This was true overall, though an economy largely dependent on hunting required an extensive range of territory. But the parts which the Europeans wished first to occupy were almost invariably districts that were fairly thickly settled already, so that the impact of even a few hundred white settlers on the native economy could have serious consequences. Further, the European attempts to exploit the land and achieve both self-sufficiency and a surplus proved inadequate to support the settling population, even for the experienced Spaniards in Florida. When supplies were delayed or the domestic resources behind a particular settlement gave out, the Europeans became economically dependent to a great degree on the local Indians. They might rely on their good will in the initial stages, but once this was exhausted they had either to exploit the Indians more effectively for food or labor or else be placed in the position of fighting for their lives against a foe who had acquired an important additional weapon—starvation.

Europeans had grown up within a bureaucratic framework at home and they brought it with them to North America. Fishermen and fur traders might leave ports from Lisbon and Viana north to Bristol and Galway with little ceremony, and conduct their affairs of

the shores of North America without state intervention, until or unless they clashed too violently there with men of other states. But most expeditions of exploration and all expeditions for settlement operated inside a framework of permissions derived from the nature and structure of the European nation state. Indeed, as North America was not regarded as occupied by peoples with any stable political structure or with any inalienable rights of possession, exploration was normally taken in hand under the auspices of one or other of the western littorine states, which gradually asserted its claims and ultimately its sovereignty to such American land as it could effectively profess to occupy and exploit. Spain claimed exclusive privileges over, and sovereignty in, the whole of North America by virtue of a papal donation and a treaty with Portugal made before any Spaniard or Portuguese had set foot on any part of North America or even knew it existed. And she was prepared to attempt to establish that claim by force well into the seventeenth century. The duke of Lerma in 1607 was still confidently telling the English ambassador that the bulls of Pope Alexander VI in 1493 finally and effectively barred the English from Virginia or any other part of North America. Portugal laid claim to a considerable extent of coastline on the basis of false conclusions about longitude drawn from the 1494 treaty with Spain, as well as from explorations made in and after 1500. France asserted at one time or another—from the initial annexations made during Verrazzano's voyage in 1524 down to the time of Champlain—that New France extended from Florida to Hudson Bay. The English claims were usually based on the Cabot voyages, but sometimes on even earlier alleged discoveries.

The establishment of the simplest post required royal instructions or charters, which often set out in great detail the bureaucratic structure of the administration to be maintained there. The simplest trading post sported a governor, a cape merchant, and a captain of soldiers at the least. Institutional buildings, a headquarters building for military, civil and commercial administration, for example, were amongst the earliest in all colonial settlements. A settlement of about one hundred men on Roanoke Island in 1585 had a governor (who doubled the role with that of colonel of the military arm of the colony), an admiral, a number of army captains, a council, a cape merchant, a surveyor, an artist and a metallurgist, so that between administrators and specialists there was only a small rank and file.

The Spanish administration in Florida was even more top-heavy. The *adelantado*, or governor-conqueror, when absent, was represented by a deputy governor; there was also a treasurer, an accountant, a factor (sometimes assistants to each of these as well), and a series of military officers in descending rank from the governor. Sometimes the superfluity of officers and of ranks could be an embarrassment to decisive action, but usually they had little effective power. Their significance was rather that the nation state which had despatched them, and which expected to continue to supervise them—directly in the case of Spain; indirectly, through companies, in the case of France and England—considered these officials as in some sort representatives of its own sovereignty and the forerunners of a fully developed territorial administration. So, if a settlement could survive, whether with direct state aid or not, it automatically became a growing point for a territorial and institutional projection of the national state, and was expected to carry forward with it the institutions of the state as it grew and developed, modified only in such minor ways as might be required by local conditions in America. Europeans therefore went to America encapsulated in an administrative cocoon from which a network of organization would in the long run be spun.

The involvement of the majority of the Europeans concerned with North America in this elementary stage of discovering and exploiting the country was not very great. Most of the explorers were absorbed in what they were doing, whether it was fishing, trading, looking for cultivable lands or prospecting for minerals—or even just figuring out the lie of the land, its topography, its vegetation, its human population in the most provisional way. Yet almost all of them had in their background, whether conscious of it or not, the intention to involve North America in the longer run with their European homeland. The type of society from which they sprang is thus entirely relevant to the story of exploration which must inevitably take up a major part of a book on the sixteenth century, even if it is less easy to categorize Europeans than Amerindians in ethnographic terms.

The Europeans had a number of advantages in the realm of social anthropology over their Amerindian opposite numbers. They were more versatile artifact users. They had a religion with a firm institutional structure which claimed to be ecumenical, and which gave

them almost complete confidence in the rectitude of whatever they did. They had at their disposal (even those who were illiterate) a body of knowledge of human history and concepts which gave them a long historical perspective and enabled them to envisage their historical role as, they believed, the representatives of the superior civilization of the world. They had enough scientific knowledge and curiosity to master the physical problems of transport and maintenance in a new environment, even if they did not master them very rapidly. They had confidence that they could carry their institutional and bureaucratic structures into a completely different environment. They had a highly specialized acquisitiveness in the form of trading and exploitative objectives and techniques. They were, however, in some degree the prisoners of their European environment even when they were settling in North America. They found it hard to digest and harder to enjoy food of a different kind from that they were accustomed to. They proved unskillful in the essential arts of hunting and sometimes (surprisingly) of fishing. Their science was often quite insufficient to guide them through divides of climate, diet, and disease. They expected America to be too much like Europe too soon—they retained too long their cultural umbilical cord.

For these reasons, the process of assimilation and settlement proved to be a slow, painful business of cultural adaptation, which was by no means satisfactorily achieved. In remaining subjectively European for so long, these men indicated some of the weaknesses which civilizations can impose; by persisting in their occupations and developing permanent settlements, in the end they enabled the strengths of their different cultural level to assert themselves. The white men studied the Indians, as well as berating, attacking and missionizing them; and the wiser observers, like Harriot and Champlain, understood something of the rationale of their social practices. But most Europeans, whether guided by the Amerindians or imitating them, were slow to become adjusted to American limitations. Although in the end they did acclimatize both themselves and their cultural imperatives in the new land, the way that they did so (we must reflect) helped to make inevitable the liquidation of the indigenous cultures.

# CHAPTER 5

## The Rediscovery of America, 1492–1510

THE basic fact about the rediscovery of America was that Christopher Columbus opened up the Americas effectively to European exploitation and discovery,[1] so that the crucial voyage is the one he made in 1492. It was his insistence that there was gold to be had, and that the islands he discovered lay on the fringes of a spice-rich Asia, which produced the capital and the diplomatic effort that within a few years had made the new discoveries a major issue for the European community, insofar as it is possible to speak of such an entity at this time. But discovery comes a very close second to this exploitation. The progressive disclosure of major islands that followed the first voyage, the assertion of a Castilian monopoly and the establishment of a Castilian colony on Española, enabled the later islands to be found—Cuba when fully delimited, Puerto Rico, Jamaica and the rest—and to be knit into a European-dominated sphere even before the existence of the mainland was effectively established. Dramatic as was Columbus's voyage of 1498, when he first saw an appreciable extent of continental land, and the last voyage, when he careered precariously down part of the coast of Central America, the comprehension of the nature of the discover-

1. The basic lives of Columbus are those by Samuel Eliot Morison, *Admiral of the Ocean Sea. A Life of Christopher Columbus*, 2 vols. (1942), and Antonio Ballesteros y Berreta, *Cristóbal Cólon y el descubrimiento de America*, 2 vols. (Madrid, 1945). S. E. Morison (ed.), *Journals and Other Documents on the Life and Voyages of Christopher Columbus* (1963), is a useful collection of materials in translation.

ies lay with others—with Ojeda and his 1499 voyage; with Bastidas and those who ranged the corner round which South America turned to the north; and with Vespucci, who fully grasped in 1501 the great continental character of South America. Columbus's adhesion to the view that the New World was Asia in some strange disguise thus became outmoded. The concept of a New World was already in existence if not fully realized before Martin Waldseemüller daringly showed a new pair of continents in 1507 and gave the southern one the name America, which by transference was soon applied to its northern counterpart also.

When on Friday, August 3, 1492, Columbus left Spain in the *Santa Maria*—together with the *Pinto* and *Niña*—he was bound for India, or more specifically for Cathay, by way of Antilia and Cipango. Making his way south to the Canaries, he estimated his northing and then ran along the 28th parallel en route to Antilia, the Island of the Seven Cities, having finally convinced himself that this was the parallel on which lay one of the major islands mapped so vigorously on earlier charts. On September 19 he was ready to find the island, but no island appeared: "The admiral did not wish to be delayed by beating to windward in order to make sure whether there was land in that direction, but he was certain that to the north and to the south there were some islands, as in truth there were, and he went through the midst of them, because his wish was to press onward towards the Indies."[2] The island had turned into a group of islands; they were there, it seemed, for him—though no one has seen them since. He then turned for some unknown reason from his true west course to a course west-southwest, on his way to Cipango. Land was sighted on the evening of Thursday, October 11, and on Friday, October 12, he solemnly took possession for the Catholic kings of the Island of Guanahaní (named San Salvador by him), and later turned southward to the Caribbean and his discoveries there.

Columbus's apparently casual change of course had a substantial consequence for North America. Had he held to the latitude of 28°, he would have made land on the mainland in the vicinity of Cape Cañaveral. The continental character of the new land might much sooner have become apparent, and North America, not the Caribbean, would probably have become the focus, or at least one

2. *The Journal of Christopher Columbus,* translated by Cecil Jane and edited by L. A. Vigneras (London, 1960), p. 12.

focus, for Spanish activity in the west. As it was, the history of the discovery of North America was to be detached from the main Spanish enterprises for some crucial years. It was left instead to the English and the Portuguese to delineate parts of the continent on the map, which were integrated only slowly with the Spanish area as the implications of Waldseemüller's hypothesis were gradually realized in theory and confirmed in practice. Before Ponce de León, so far as we know, the existence of a contiguous major landmass to the north of the Caribbean remained unknown to Spain, though within a few years from that point it had been fully grasped and accepted.

The question of who had priority in rediscovering North America is largely a matter of intellectual rather than practical interest. It did not greatly matter whether men from Bristol or men from Terceira first saw land in the west, so long as they did not align their sovereigns behind them in attempts to obtain exclusive rights and thus manipulate discovery and control exploitation in these areas. Once the discovery by Columbus of gold- and spice-bearing islands in the west had been established, however, priorities become a matter of some importance. Portugal made her pre-emptive bid when she criticized the papal division of spheres of influence between Spain and Portugal in the two bulls *Inter caetera* in 1493. The line was to be drawn along the meridian running north and south from a point 100 leagues west of the Azores: after hard bargaining, the Portuguese were able to get this altered in the Treaty of Tordesillas in 1494 to a point 360 leagues west of the Cape Verde Islands. When more discoveries had been made, it was found that this brought a substantial part of South America within Portugal's sphere—giving rise to intermittent scholarly speculation ever since that Portugal knew more of the southern Atlantic than she admitted publicly at the time. It was also believed for a long time, since longitude determination at sea remained wildly inaccurate, that the islands and mainland discovered within the next decade lying in the latitudes between roughly 45° to 55°N. were inside the Portuguese sphere as laid down in 1494.[3]

3. Jaime Cortesão, *Os descobrimentos portugueses*, 2 vols. (1959–60), maintained that Portugal had previous knowledge of America; Duarte Leite, *História dos descobrimentos*, 2 vols. (Lisbon, 1958), I, 688, denied the possibility. See Fernando Castel-Branco, "O tratado de Tordesillas e o Brasil," Demetrio Ramos (ed.), *El tratado de Tordesillas y su proyección*, 2 vols. (Valladolid, 1973–74), I, 323–325.

The position of England in this situation was a difficult one. If a discovery of a fishing bank, backed by some island land, had been made in or about 1481 and not precisely charted, then there could be little hope of using this as a card to play against either Castile or Portugal in view of the papal sanctions which had been given to their division of the extra-European world. Had it not been made, then certainly the men of Bristol were out in the Atlantic looking for land again in 1490 or 1491, well before Columbus set sail. And if they had found land earlier, they were clearly at this time renewing and developing their contacts with it, though still perhaps only as a background to and a landmark for a fishery. What was known in England of Columbus's discovery in the year or so after it was made is wholly a matter of speculation. The contents of his "Letter," published in Barcelona and Rome in 1493, may have taken a little time to filter to England. But the bulls and the conferences between Portugal and Castile were neither hidden nor impenetrable, and it is most probable that in 1494, very shortly after the completion of the Treaty of Tordesillas, it was known what the modifications of the proposed papal division amounted to in theory, even if they could not yet be established in practice. It is perhaps significant (though it may have been accidental only) that Elizabethan England preferred a date of 1494 for the English discovery of America.[4] This would have allowed England priority in gaining effective contact with land which was by then known not to be within the 1494 Tordesillas limits. But there is little doubt that whatever had gone on before 1494, in that year the English had to start again and formulate both action and policy in regard to Atlantic voyaging, now probably for the first time under some degree of royal patronage. One question which cannot be resolved so far is why overt royal patronage was reserved until 1496; and why, when it came, it was given to an Italian rather than to one or more of the Bristol men who had initiated the Atlantic enterprises.

Then, too, what about France? As her sovereign had, like Henry VII, been approached by Bartholomew Columbus before Christopher Columbus sailed, it would be reasonable to expect that she too would be concerned to assert some French interest in the new discoveries. Even if we have no evidence that French sailors had

4. James A. Williamson (ed.), *The Cabot Voyages* (1962), pp. 27–29, 201–202.

been active as far afield in the west as the Portuguese and English fishermen, they had certainly penetrated down to Guinea in the wake of the Portuguese and so were active in the Atlantic. But there does not appear to be any evidence of French reactions in 1492, except the statement by Las Casas[5] that Charles VIII was rapidly apprised of Columbus's discovery and that this sent Bartholomew hurrying to Spain in 1493 to catch his brother before he set out on his second voyage. We can only assume that the decision to invade Italy and the launching of French forces on this campaign on September 2, 1494, diverted France for some years from any active concern with western waters. And even when such concern did appear, it was independent action by French fishermen, anxious to get a share in the new grounds off Newfoundland, rather than government sponsorship or action, which brought France slowly into the western field.

Portugal is scarcely likely to have been wholly inactive in the west, though most of her interest was directed toward the breakthrough to the east which Bartolomeu Dias's voyage in 1488 had made possible. But it may be that in 1494, before the death of John II, a patent had been given to Pedro de Barcelos and João Fernandes, *labrador* (small landholder) of Terceira, to renew searches in the western ocean, though no charter to them is now extant.[6] It may also have been about this time (more probably a few years later, even after news of Cabot's discoveries in 1497 came through), that Gaspar Corte Real was authorized to attempt discoveries in the Atlantic, though likewise there is no charter to this effect. It seems most unlikely that Portugal would have made no attempt to delimit her western limits under the treaty of 1494 within the next few years, and also improbable that any fresh discoveries were made by her subjects before 1500; however, the possibility of discoveries for which we have no documentary evidence during this period, 1494–1500, cannot be wholly ruled out.

So far, we have no clear picture of the circumstances in which John Cabot (Giovanni Caboto) came to England. Born in Genoa, he had obtained Venetian nationality and had penetrated into Muslim Arabia before coming to Portugal and then to Spain. Like Columbus, he was trying to sell the idea of the possibilities of a voyage

5. Bartolomé de Las Casas, *Obras escogidas*, 5 vols. (Madrid, 1957–58), I, 281.
6. H. P. Biggar, *Precursors of Jacques Cartier* (Ottawa, 1911), pp. 98–99, 31.

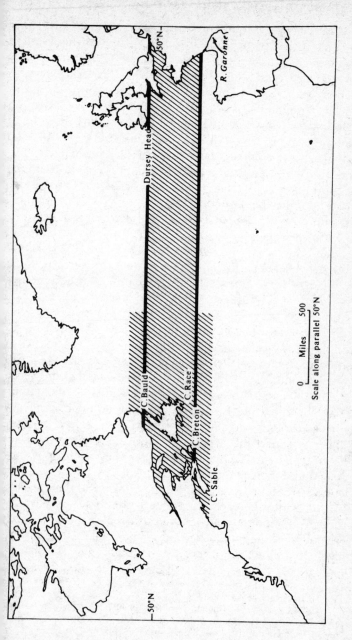

The North and South Limits of John Cabot's Voyage, 1497

westward to Asia. We do not know what were his individual variations on this theme or how his advocacy to the Portuguese and Spanish sovereigns related to that of Columbus. He had clearly been wholly unsuccessful in obtaining any royal patronage, and as Juan Caboto Montecalunya, he was designing harbor works at Valencia in the Aragonese part of the Spanish kingdom in 1491 and 1492. He was evidently still in Spain when Columbus returned in 1493 with news of his discoveries. At some point between 1493 and 1495 Cabot came to England, settled in Bristol, and began to experiment in Atlantic voyages and to make preliminary contacts with the English court in order to obtain the backing he had failed to receive in the courts of the Iberian monarchs.[7]

Cabot's purpose was simple. He knew enough about the convergence of the meridians to realize that the distance by sea from England to Cathay would be appreciably shorter at 50° N. than at 28°, though he believed that the land of the Great Khan lay at comparable distances to the west from England to those Columbus had postulated in 1492. Precisely when he arrived in Bristol and how he grafted his project onto earlier Bristol voyaging traditions —whether or not they had involved the discovery of islands near a fishery in the west—is not yet clear. If the Spanish representative in England, Ayala, is correct, then anything up to four ships a year had been going out into the Atlantic to look for the Island of the Seven Cities from 1490 or 1491 onwards.[8] This is a quite incredible number to have been leaving Bristol on anything so uneconomically productive as exploration. These vessels, it is suggested by some protagonists of a surviving Greenland colony, may have been trading with the residual Greenland colonists. They could, possibly, have been going fishing at the western edge of the continental shelf off Ireland where there were good fishing banks, and then making casting voyages into the ocean for new islands. It seems least unlikely, though it cannot be stated more positively at this point, that they were going fishing on the Newfoundland Banks and occasionally going on to look at and for those fog-shrouded shores which lay

7. Williamson, *Cabot Voyages*, pp. 33–44, 190–199. Fresh information for background is promised in a forthcoming book, by Alwyn A. Ruddock, "Columbus, Cabot and the English Discovery of America."

8. Despatch of July 25, 1498, Biggar, *Precursors*, pp. 27–29; Williamson, *Cabot Voyages*, pp. 228–229; and see Quinn, *England and the Discovery of America*, pp. 9–10 for a modification of the translation in Biggar and Williamson.

to the north of the Banks in modern Newfoundland.[9] To these fishermen-explorers Cabot now attached himself.

Cabot made an unsuccessful voyage before he achieved a successful one. This may have been in 1495 since until he had made some attempt to get to sea he would not be a good candidate for royal recognition. He obtained a patent from the crown on March 3, 1496, which authorized him to annex to the English crown such lands as he, and his sons, Lewis, Sebastian and Sancius (Ludovico, Sebastiano, and Sancio), should find, to possess and govern under the crown. Henry, in making this grant, was deliberately ignoring the papal division and the Treaty of Tordesillas, though insofar as the Pope's moral authority existed he was to some extent bound by the former, but he was free of any restraint by the latter to which he had not been a party. If Cabot reached a rich part of Asia, he felt he was in a position to challenge, in these northern waters, any threat Spain or Portugal might offer. Cabot, some think, only made his unsuccessful voyage, when he was driven back by bad weather in the summer of 1496, after getting his charter.[10] So far, consideration of when he went is wholly a matter of opinion, and does not appear to matter greatly. But on his departure in May 1597, about May 22, Cabot in the *Matthew*, after passing the Irish coast, sailed westward for a little over a month and on June 24 sighted land, annexed the land to the crown of England, and, it may be thought, took his position by an observation of the sun.[11] On the evidence

9. Biggar, *Precursors*, pp. 62, 68, 86–87; Williamson, *Cabot Voyages*, pp. 23–24. For the alternative suggestion of a continuing clandestine trade with Iceland see p. 65 above.

10. L. A. Vigneras, "The Cape Breton Landfall, 1494 or 1497?", *Canadian Historical Review*, XXXVII (1957), 225; Williamson, *Cabot Voyages*, p. 54, and see Quinn, *England and the Discovery of America*, p. 93.

11. The evidence for the name of the *Matthew* is very slight (D. B. Quinn, "John Cabot's *Matthew*," *Times Literary Supplement*, June 8, 1967, p. 517). The letter from John Day to the "Almirante Mayor" (Christopher Columbus), was written either in December 1497 or January 1498, and gives the best account of the voyage (though it raises many problems). First published by L. A. Vigneras, "New Light on the 1497 Voyage," *Hispanic-American Historical Review*, XXXVI (1956), 503–509, there are convenient translations in Williamson, *Cabot Voyages*, pp. 211–214; Quinn, *North American Discovery* (1971), pp. 43–45; Morison, *European Discovery of America*, I, 206–209. The sketch map, without scale it seems certain, which he enclosed is likely to have formed, in a vastly enlarged version, "the sea discovered by the English" (*Mar descubierta por ingleses*), and a coast marked by English flags on the map begun by Juan de la Cosa in 1500 (L. Campeau, "Jean Cabot et la découverte de l'Amérique du Nord," *Revue d'Histoire de Amérique Française*, XIX [1965], 398–408; Quinn, *England and the Discovery*

we have—the letter sent by John Day to Columbus at the end of 1497 (or the beginning of 1498) already referred to—it might seem that his course was something to the south of west, as he can be argued to have sailed from about 51° 20′ N. (the mid-latitude of the mouth of the Bristol Channel) to somewhere like Cape Canso on Nova Scotia, or Cape Breton on Cape Breton Island. It could have brought him further north, to Cape Race perhaps, or further south, possibly to Cape Sable or beyond, since latitude observations were so inaccurate at the time even if made on land. At sea, an error of up to 2 degrees (or about 140 land miles) would be possible; on land, accuracy within appreciably less than 1 degree should have been possible.

Cape Breton, or an approximation to it, seems the least unlikely landfall, in spite of many other attempts to track down Cabot's course in detail to other parts of North America. Then, again according to John Day, he sailed a little way south and turned eastward once more, presumably sailing up the east coast of Newfoundland and taking off for home at "the Cape nearest Ireland," most plausibly identified as Cape Bauld at the opening of the Strait of Belle Isle, though again with appreciable doubt. In this reading, "the sea discovered by the English" (on the 1500 map of Juan de la Cosa) would be the waters between the Maritimes and Newfoundland, and the islands seen on the return, two of the many islands off northeast Newfoundland.

S. E. Morison has argued for a wholly Newfoundland coasting, making Cabot's landfall Cape Bauld, his course a coastal traverse first south along the Newfoundland coast, and then a return course northward to pick up his original landfall at Cape Bauld, from which he returned. Cape Bauld makes a good choice for the cape west of Ireland since it is almost exactly in the latitude of Dursey Head in County Kerry where Day appears to say it was. But it does not fit very well as a point of both arrival and departure, since, after saying that the *Matthew* coasted a little to the south before turning north again, Day notes that "most of the land was discovered after turning back." We must not conclude that this theory is necessarily wrong, however, since too literal an adhesion to such texts as we have is

*of America*, pp. 97–101). Also L. A. Vigneras, *Discovery of South America and the Andalusian Voyages* (1976), pp. 7–12.

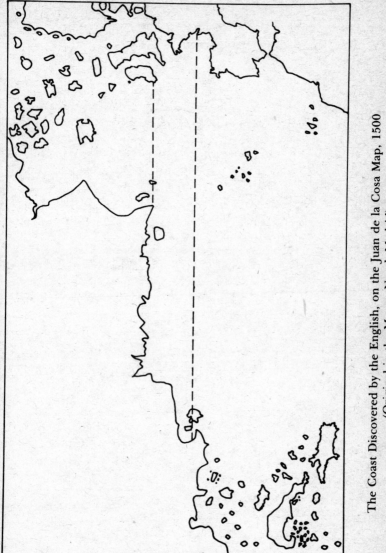

The Coast Discovered by the English, on the Juan de la Cosa Map, 1500
(Original in the Museo Naval, Madrid)

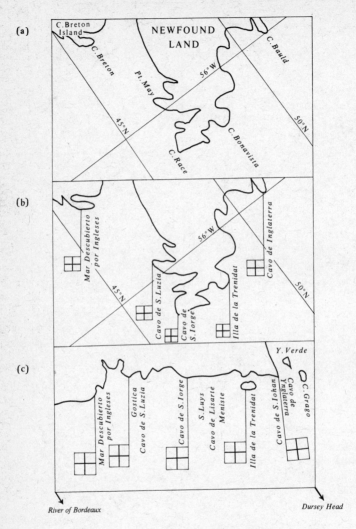

(a) Modern chart, with the probable location of the flagged points

(b) Modern chart, with the names and flags from the Cosa map

(c) THE ENGLISH COASTS on the map of Juan de la Cosa, 1500

JOHN CABOT'S VOYAGE 1497:

the evidence of the John Day letter and the Juan de la Cosa map

risky. The case is argued well; yet it appears somewhat less likely than the other simple explanation already given.[12] Additional solutions which bring Cabot round Newfoundland or which attempt to give a minute account of where he went from Cape Breton onwards to Cape Bauld, are less likely, either because they involve more exploration than he is likely to have undertaken on a first reconnaissance, or because they attempt to supply too much detail in circumstances where even the outlines are less than certain and where detail must involve too high a degree of conjecture.[13]

The fish at sea off the land were so numerous that they were the most noteworthy specific discovery (if they were not already known to Bristol fishermen). The coniferous forests were impressive. Fleeting forms seen on land suggested the presence of inhabitants, and the sailors discovered snares, a netting needle (a stick pierced at both ends, either painted red or in a red wood), and a fire site, which appeared to confirm human occupation. The *Matthew* had an outward run of about twenty-five days and, with a following wind, sighted Brittany after about fifteen days on the run homeward, on about August 8. The final run to Bristol must have been a rapid one, since Cabot had somehow got to London by August 10 or 11.

He talked freely of his experiences in London to Italians from Venice and Milan after having received his reward from the king, £10 followed by a pension of £20 a year. He had, he believed, found the more northerly shores of the land of the Great Khan. Others, like John Day, were rather more skeptical. They refused to identify where he had been, except to characterize the first landfall as the southern part of the Island of the Seven Cities and the northern point of departure as from a "mainland"—a term that could be used of a large island referring to the whole or the greater part of his

12. Morison, *European Discovery of America*, I, 157–211, especially 170–186.

13. The two more important of these are Melvin Jackson, "The Labrador Landfall of John Cabot, 1497," *Canadian Historical Review*, XLIV (1963), 122–141 (bringing Cabot to Labrador, through the Strait of Belle Isle, western Newfoundland, Cabot Strait and halfway up the east coast of Newfoundland), and John T. Juricek, "John Cabot's First Voyage," *Smithsonian Journal of History*, II (1967–68), 1–22 (who postulates a landfall at the northern tip of Cape Breton Island, coasting off Cape Breton Island, then exploration of southern Newfoundland, doubling back on his course, returning to the southeast for close inshore exploration all the way north to Cape Bauld). Both are too elaborate for the evidence we have, Jackson's too long, Juricek's too intricate, but each contains useful insights on maritime knowledge and experience in the period.

coasting.[14] He made a sketch with some names given to outstanding coastal features but without scale or orientation, which Day sent to Columbus and which is likely to have been the basis for the representation of the English coasts on the map begun by Juan de la Cosa in 1500. Later Cabot made a mappemonde, a version of at least part of which came into Spanish hands though it has not survived, and a globe which fitted his discoveries into his world picture. We can assume that these were rather like the profile of eastern Asia on the Behaim map, or that they incorporated the English coasts on the Cosa map, and that his own territories, as he would now consider them, lay somewhere to the south of the great Horn of Asia which traditionally continued the landmass some way eastward.[15] The Spanish representative, Ayala, considered that they clearly infringed the area claimed by Spain, though it seems this was challenged in court circles.[16] Of course no one really knew; but from August 1497, England had some stake in the Atlantic discoveries. It remained to see what she would make of them.

Henry VII, cautious and parsimonious as he was, proposed to attempt to exploit the supposed new route to Asia. He encouraged London merchants to take a share in a new expedition and himself provided money toward equipping a ship specially for the next voyage. Bristol was expected at first to put up no less than five more. Trade with civilized Asiatics was envisaged, possibly after passing southward along a coast whose inhabitants were fairly primitive. John Day was cautious when he reported in December 1497 (or early January 1498) what was going on, avoiding any considerable degree of speculation. Cabot was more ambitious—he was going to be a great ruler. He would bring Italians to occupy positions of power in state and Church as well as Englishmen. Henry had now a stake in the Christianizing of the benighted natives of the newly discovered land, since the papal banners had been planted alongside the English ones as a sign that Christians had come to Asia to

14. Day writes of "the mainland and islands," "the Island of the Seven Cities," "the Island of Brasil . . . the mainland that the men from Bristol found" (Quinn, *North American Discovery*, pp. 43–45).

15. Cabot was reported in England to have claimed to have "discovered mainland 700 leagues away, which is the country of the Grand Khan, and that he coasted it for 300 leagues. . . . And on his way back he saw two islands" (Williamson, *Cabot Voyages*, p. 208). On the map evidence, see R. A. Skelton, in *ibid.*, pp. 297–307.

16. Williamson, *Cabot Voyages*, pp. 228–229.

proselytize—and perhaps also as a diplomatic counter to the exclusive claim of Spain and Portugal to have papal sponsorship overseas, and so an attempt to get the rigor of the bulls of 1493 modified. At the same time, there is no evidence that Henry was willing to challenge the papacy; certainly he would have been forced to meet a Spanish challenge had the next voyage been a successful one.

Cabot's gamble on making a profitable voyage to Asia did not in the end attract any substantial investment from either the king (who donated only £113 8s.), the London merchants (trade goods) or the city of Bristol (which gave only four ships instead of at least five). It was, however, a venture which had the modest backing of the state and the merchants of two major trading cities. The squadron set out from Bristol, apparently in May, to meet disaster. One vessel put back to Ireland badly damaged, according to news received in July. John Cabot was drowned at sea, and all of his ships, except possibly one, appear to have vanished. The failure to follow up the voyage may well have been due to a further discovery which made it unlikely that the land found was Asia—though this would imply that at least one vessel returned. Several men involved in the voyage are also known to have returned, though they could have come back in the damaged ship.[17] The older story of the voyage—that it proceeded into Arctic latitudes, and then coasted down the North American coast a long way—[18] is now transferred by most writers, with very high probability, to a voyage made by John Cabot's son, Sebastian (who must have been a survivor if he was sent on the 1498 expedition), in 1508–9. John Cabot's pension was paid for a year, then he disappears finally from view when it was realized that he was indeed lost. Henry VII and the London merchants retreated altogether from any participation in westward ventures for some years.

At the time when John Cabot first set out, Portugal was almost ready to stake her own claim to western lands. It seems likely that the Pedro Barcelos-João Fernandes partnership and Gaspar Corte Real were already attempting to get westward from the Azores, and

17. *Ibid.*, pp. 217–225, 228. On the survival of Thomas Bradley and Lancelot Thirkill, see Quinn, *England and the Discovery of America*, p. 102.
18. For this approach, see Williamson, *Voyages of the Cabots* (1929), pp. 176–197; and H. P. Biggar, "The First Explorers of the North American Coast," in A. P. Newton (ed.), *The Great Age of Discovery* (London, 1932), pp. 134–136.

there is a slight chance that one or other had already sighted some land there. But we have no formal claim that land had been located to the west within the Portuguese sphere, as it was supposed. Certainly the grant to Gaspar Corte Real on May 12, 1500, of any lands he might find was given to him in connection with one or more voyages he had made in the past (os dias pasados) to find such lands; but the implications were clearly that he had not yet found them. An earlier grant, on October 29, 1499, had permitted João Fernandes to search for and discover certain islands of which he should have the governorship if he succeeded. Here too the implication is very imprecise.[19] It could be taken, most obviously, to mean he had as yet made no discovery; or it could mean that he had made a discovery but had failed to report it and was attempting to get royal authority to rule the place before making his discovery known. This would fit in with a later claim that Barcelos and he had voyaged for over three years. It is probable, however, that before doing anything further, Gaspar Corte Real had obtained his grant and set out on his 1500 voyage. On this occasion, he pursued a northerly course, and thus avoided running into the westerlies which normally barred direct access for ships of that time from the Azores to the American mainland.[20] He sighted Cape Farewell and the mountainous land behind it in Greenland, then turned westward, perhaps not yet making an American landfall, and returned to claim he had found new lands for the king.

The consequences for João Fernandes were significant, although they must be based on conjecture only. Fernandes disappears from view from October 1499 until 1501, when he reappears in Bristol in association, along with other Azorean Portuguese, with Bristol merchants. The most likely solution is that before 1500 (or even in 1500) he had made an overseas discovery he was not yet prepared to publicize, but that when Corte Real returned with his claim to have found land, Fernandes either was forced to back down on his own claims or else thought discretion better than conflict, since the Corte Real family was dominant in Terceira by this time. He thus set off to Bristol to share his knowledge, whatever it amounted to, with the Englishmen who already had some experience of both successful and unsuccessful Atlantic voyaging. This reconstruction

19. Biggar, *Precursors*, pp. 31–37.
20. Morison, *Portuguese Voyages to America in the Fifteenth Century*, pp. 23–29.

is feasible, but not so far supported by any clear evidence.[21]

Early in 1501, Gaspar Corte Real was ready to make a second voyage, for which he received support in Portugal from the king, so that he was able to take two ships from there. They returned to the Greenland landmark he had located and then turned westward. They may have reached the northern tip of Labrador and even have recorded the turning of the land westward at Cape Chidley, or they may have touched Labrador somewhat further south. There is no doubt that they coasted a part of Labrador, Newfoundland, and some considerable part of the mainland. They found no remarkable products except the massive conifers from which masts could be made. They landed at least once and on one such occasion were met by a large number of Indians; this is likely to have taken place south of Cape Breton, where the Indians would have come to the shore for the summer fishing and gathering. Probably they were Micmac, though just possibly from a more southerly Algonkian tribe. Corte Real was clearly well aware that West Africa had been above all a source of slaves for Portugal since its discovery and was anxious to exploit a second source of servile labor in the west. Some fifty Indians were therefore caught, shipped to Lisbon, and put up for sale. The men who brought the vessel back were able to give an account of a long continental shore which did not sound in the least like Asia. However, this was not Corte Real's own ship; he did not himself appear and was soon given up for lost.

In the spring of 1502, his brother Miguel received a grant of half the lands found by him and set out, again with two ships, and supplies on board granted to them by the king. It is probable that Miguel attempted to traverse the route followed by his brother, though perhaps only from the point where he was last seen. Once again some unknown disaster struck the expedition. A ship came home, but not Miguel's: he too was lost in western waters. The Portuguese discoveries which had developed so favorably were, within two years after Gaspar Corte Real's initial discovery, to suffer a very similar fate to those of John Cabot—crippling losses and then

21. Quinn, *England and the Discovery of America*, pp. 112–114. Morison, *European Discovery of America*, I, 210–213, 218–219, 242–244, gives not only his own views but a selection of the many possible solutions to the Fernandes problem propounded by others.

failure of royal backing and a descent into obscurity for some time.[22]

A world map sent to Italy before the end of 1502, the Cantino map, contains much information, some of it confusing, on the new discoveries. On the eastern side of the line of demarcation a peninsular Greenland is shown with an inscription marking the 1500 discovery. Again to the east of the line the discoveries of 1501 are shown as an island, covered with enormous trees. Then, well to the west, and clearly in the Spanish zone, is a continental coastline, with one cape jutting out at the north in the latitude of the island previously noted, and another facing Cuba and the other Caribbean islands. This is clearly intended to be Asia but an extensive nomenclature on it does not fit that of other maps purporting to show eastern Asia.[23] It might be thought to represent coastal sailing on a second stage in the 1501 voyage by Miguel Corte Real's ships in 1502, possibly even as far south as Florida, though in the absence of further information, this must remain conjectural only. The assumption that the coast was recognized as a continental one, distinct from Asia, must be rejected.

Bristol was again sending out expeditions from 1501 onward. The genesis of the series of voyages which took place in the new century remains obscure. It is not unlikely that moves were on foot to try at least to exploit the fisheries on either a new or a revived basis by the Bristol fishing interests shortly after 1498, but that a new drive was given to this enterprise by the arrival of João Fernandez, Francisco Fernandes and João Gonsalves from Terceira late in 1500 or very early in 1501 and their association in a western project with the Bristol men on the strength of having made a discovery of their own in western waters. We cannot say what this discovery was, but it is possible that it was the same as that of Gaspar Corte Real in 1500–01, namely, of Cape Farewell, as a marker to a westward route along a southward-running mainland shore. If Gaspar Corte Real coasted Labrador in 1501, it is not unlikely that Fernandes did the same earlier, though it is possible that his discoveries were made not north of Newfoundland

22. The documentary evidence here is sparse (Bigger, *Precursors*, pp. 32–37, 59–70).

23. Henry Harrisse, *Découverte et évolution cartographique de Terre-Neuve* (Paris and London, 1900), pp. 8–11, 31–33 (and plate III), 43–47; Skelton in Williamson, *Cabot Voyages*, pp. 307, 309–310. The Cantino map contains an inscription concerning Gaspar Corte Real's voyage of 1500 and was compiled by September 1502 (Quinn, *England and the Discovery of America*, p. 117).

but on the mainland southwestward from it.

King Henry VII on March 19, 1501, granted a patent to the three Azoreans in association with Richard Warde, Thomas Asshehurst and John Thomas of Bristol. This gave them extensive rights of exploration and settlement, with the right to bring in one ship's lading a year duty free. They were to have a monopoly for ten years of such lands as they might discover which were "unknown to all Christians." We cannot tell who were their backers at court or, apart from the men named in the charter, in Bristol. Their patent did not set aside John Cabot's patent of 1496, of which Sebastian Cabot was a surviving grantee, which continued to be valid in so far as it covered lands discovered in 1497 (or conceivably in 1498 also). A voyage was made under the new grant in 1501, but we hear nothing of its nature and results, except that a Bristol man was given a reward at the opening of 1502 for his part in discovering an island.[24] It might appear, from absence of reference to him in all subsequent documents, that João Fernandes was lost on this voyage.

At the opening of 1502, it would appear that the Cabot syndicate was revived. Hugh Elyot, Robert Thorne, the elder, William his brother, and Thomas, William's son who were, almost certainly, the principal surviving partners of John Cabot, renewed the Cabot ventures. Sebastian was apparently still a minor and his name does not appear in this year or the next. Elyot and the Thornes bought a French ship, which they renamed the *Gabriel,* receiving in January 1502 a royal bounty of £20 for their import of a ship rated at over 100 tons. They sent the *Gabriel* on a fishing expedition under Thomas Amayne whom Dr. Ruddock—who found the reference—says was a family connection of the Thornes. The *Gabriel* of Bristol brought back to that port 18 lasts of salt fish worth £180, belonging to Hugh Elyot. He was granted freedom from subsidy of £9, the normal rate of tax, apparently on the grounds that the fish was brought under the charter of 1496 to John Cabot. Though the document recording this makes no specific mention of Newfoundland,[25] it seems that this is the first record of a cargo of fish from

24. Williamson, *Cabot Voyages*, pp. 235–247, 215.

25. Alwyn A. Ruddock, "The Reputation of Sebastian Cabot," *Bulletin of the Institute of Historical Research*, XLVII (1974), 98 (from Public Record Office, London. E368/276, m. 11d.); see Williamson, *Cabot Voyages*, pp. 247–248; Quinn, *England and the Discovery of America*, p. 122.

American waters, and marks the opening of the great Newfoundland fishery, in which it is clear the English have the priority. Amongst a number of references to rewards to explorers in the royal records for 1502 the payment of £20 to "the merchantes of bristoll that have been in the new founde isle" probably reflects the fact that some members of the Elyot, Thorne, Cabot partnership themselves voyaged in the *Gabriel* to Newfoundland, and it is likely that amongst them was the young Sebastian Cabot.

It would appear that the members of the 1501 syndicate put two vessels to sea in 1502 also, since on September 26, the considerable reward of a £10 annual pension each was made to Francisco Fernandes and João Gonsalves for their services "as capitaignes into the new founde lande." Where the *Gabriel* went fishing, the other two vessels went exploring. Rewards were given to sailors who brought hawks and an eagle from the new island to the king. Moreover, three men were brought to the king's court, described as being dressed in skins and eating their meat raw (or perhaps half raw). They were seen there a year later dressed as Englishmen, but were not heard to speak.[26] Clearly mercantile activity was taking place in this year, with the first recorded contacts between English and Amerindians. The captives appear to have been Indians rather than Eskimo, and they are likely to have been Micmac or other mainland Algonkians (like those sent back by Miguel Corte Real in the same year), so that an extending range of activity on American shores is evident.

When all three ships were safely back in England it became clear that rivalry between the two groups was unnecessary and that a fusion of their interests was desirable. An approach was made to Henry VII for a new charter and this was granted on December 8, 1502.[27] Hugh Elyot, representing what we may call the Cabot partnership, was named first, then Thomas Asshehurst, one of the Bristol partners of the 1501 group, and finally João Gonsalves and Francisco Fernandes. It is clear from what we know of the association later on that Elyot and the Cabot group were dominant in it. The association was known by a company title which was something

26. Williamson, *Cabot Voyages*, pp. 215–216, 220–223, 247–249, and see Quinn, *England and the Discovery of America*, pp. 117–118; Morison, *European Discovery of America*, I, 219.

27. Williamson, *Cabot Voyages*, pp. 250–261.

like the Company of Adventurers into the Newfound Islands, and it was to remain in operation from 1503 to 1505 or 1506.

The 1502 patent carefully reserved the rights already granted and so did not set aside the charters of 1496 and 1501 in so far as lands discovered and possibly already in the possession of the grantees might be concerned. Its chief novelty was that it forbade the grantees to enter lands discovered by the Portuguese or by the subjects of any other friendly princes "and in possession of which these same princes now find themselves." This enunciated the doctrine of effective possession. Its appearance would suggest that the Portuguese, and possibly the Spaniards as well, had put forward the claim that the lands into which the English were penetrating were within the spheres covered by the Treaty of Tordesillas in 1494, though no diplomatic documents to this effect appear to have survived. The charter gave a negative answer to any such claims unless they were backed by effective occupation and possession, and was the English answer to the claim of a Portuguese-Castilian overseas monopoly.

We have little or no evidence that the Portuguese were following up the discoveries made by the ill-fated Corte Real brothers by any attempt to establish effective possession. Another brother may or may not have gone to look for Gaspar and Miguel in 1503 with two ships supplied by King Manoel,[28] and he may have survived to have given further details of the transatlantic lands. If he went at all he is likely to have been the head of the family, Vasco Annes (or Eanes) Corte Real, captain of Angra in Terceira, the eldest son of João Vas Corte Real, to whom the Corte Real patent was regranted in 1506. Fishing expeditions, possibly both from Portugal and the Azores, were apparently being made to Newfoundland, since by 1506 customs duties were being levied in Portugal on fish from Newfoundland (Terra Nova), indicating the existence of an established fishery. The Corte Real family retained some proprietory interest in the lands to the west as the Barcelos family were to do also, and may have exercised, through their representatives, some supervision over the fishery, or taken some toll from its proceeds. The line of demarcation, shown on the Cantino map of 1502, gave the Portuguese a foothold in the new land, if a rather tenuous one, while it would appear that both Spain and Portugal—for a time at least—

28. Damião de Goes (or Góis), *Chronica do Rei Dom Emanuel* (Lisbon, 1566), part i, chapter 66 (fol. 65*v*.).

accepted that Terra Nova was Portuguese.

There is little evidence of English transatlantic activity in 1503. What there is—a bow and arrows and a hawk as presents for the king —suggests that contacts and possibly commerce with the Amerindians were continuing. In 1504, also, a priest is noted as going to the new island and this would also suggest continuing exploration and contact, though it is scarcely necessary to assume that missionary work was also being attempted. The other side of the enterprise, the fishery, is much better represented. Henry VII lent Hugh Elyot £50 for one year, which was probably used for the fishing venture. The guarantor was Sir Bartholomew Rede, a prominent goldsmith and ex-Lord Mayor of London, and the money was duly repaid in 1505.[29] Continued royal support is significant of Henry's hope that something was still to be gained from western venturing, though the smallness of the sum indicates he had still little confidence that much would come of it, while Rede's association hints that the London merchant bankers were also keeping a watch on the situation. Dr. Ruddock has produced clear evidence that two vessels, the *Gabriel* once more and the *Jesus,* were at Newfoundland fishing and returned after the end of September with a substantial cargo of fish.[30] The shipmasters were named as Philip Ketymer and Richard Savery, and the shippers as Hugh Elyot, Robert and William Thorne, John Thomas (whose name was omitted from the 1502 patent), Thomas Assheford (for Asshehurst) and certain alien merchants as the factors of the shippers. The salt fish amounted to 20 lasts (240 barrels) and there were also 7 tuns, 1 pipe of fish livers (cod livers to make train oil) for which exemption from duty was successfully claimed. These items demonstrate that the Bristol fishery at Newfoundland was now well under way and the repayment of Elyot's £50 in the spring of 1505 indicates that profits were probably being made.

The 1505 record includes some data on the equipping of a ship for a western voyage. William Clerk, a London merchant, who also had apparently Bristol connections, laid out £144 18s 6d on fitting out the ship *Michell (Michael?)* for Hugh Elyot for a transatlantic

29. See Williamson, *Cabot Voyages,* pp. 216, 250–261; Quinn, *England and the Discovery of America,* pp. 121–123, plates following p. 294.

30. Ruddock, "Reputation of Sebastian Cabot," pp. 97–98 (from P.R.O. E 368/278, m. 2; C 1/406/5; E 356/24, m. 2).

voyage. Much of the equipment and victualling—ropes, sails, flour and beer—were standard items for any voyage, but the barreling in the form of tuns, pipes and hogsheads, once again indicates that fishing was intended and that the objectives were barreled salt fish and cod livers. The rewards given in mid-August to certain Portuguese—João Gonsalves and Francisco Fernandes we would assume—imply a voyage by another vessel to the mainland. They brought "popyngais" (parrots), and "Cattes of the mountaigne" (bobcats), with other stuff, for the king. These are evidence of trade or trapping on the North American mainland. The parrots can only have been specimens of the Carolina parakeet, which ranged some way up the New England coast from its southern home, though some specimens might have been brought from the south by Indians and traded with the Englishmen rather farther to the north. The bobcats (Lynx rufus) might have been obtained over a much wider area. It seems probable, however, that one or more of the ships of the syndicate was ranging well to the south along the mainland coast, past what are now the shores of the United States.[31]

The most valuable piece of evidence about this group to have emerged is that Sebastian Cabot was an active member of the syndicate of 1502–05. We do not know his precise age, but it has been plausibly conjectured that he was about thirteen or fourteen when John Cabot sailed in 1497.[32] This would make him about twenty years of age in 1502, sufficiently grown up to take a personal share in rebuilding the hopes shattered when his father was lost. A royal grant of a pension to him on April 3, 1505, had been known since 1922; but Dr. Ruddock has found that this copy is defective and omits a crucial phrase which she has been able to restore from another copy. This establishes that the pension was granted to him "in consideracion of the diligent service and attendance . . . doon unto us in and about the fyndinge of the newe founde landes."[33] The most obvious interpretation of this (though clearly it will excite other glosses) is that Cabot had been involved in the western enterprises at least since 1502 and that the explanation attempted above

31. Williamson, *Cabot Voyages*, pp. 216, 262–264; Quinn, *England and the Discovery of America*, pp. 123–126, plate following p. 294.

32. The evidence is reviewed by Williamson, *Cabot Voyages*, pp. 35–37, 50; see also Quinn, *England and the Discovery of America*, p. 133.

33. Printed for the first time in Ruddock, "Reputation of Sebastian Cabot," pp. 98–99 (from P.R.O. E 368/279).

of the reshuffle of 1502 may be correct. It is worth noticing that we have "newe found landes" as a plural and not any more a single newly found island, so that we can suggest that part of his contribution was to further exploration during the years 1502–1505. Why Sebastian should have been singled out for reward on account of services to the king is less clear. This may be only a formula, but it could well represent some contributions to the cartography of the new lands or some interpretation of their significance for further English voyages. It may be suggested that this involved the establishment of the continental character of North America ahead of the Waldseemüller hypothesis, since the next time we hear of Sebastian he is trying to get round North America, rather than sail directly to it on the assumption that it was itself Asia.

The ventures of 1505 were the last of the series. It would appear that commerce, at least, was proving wholly unprofitable, though we cannot say this about the fishery. Hugh Elyot was in financial difficulty not long after he had repaid the king his loan and was unable to pay William Clerk's bills for fitting out the *Michell.* Elyot claimed that Francisco Fernandes owed him money; Fernandes claimed that Elyot owed him money. The Company of Adventurers dissolved in a series of lawsuits of which we do not know the outcome,[34] and the voyages across the Atlantic for commerce and exploration were interrupted, though it is unlikely that those for the codfishery ceased.

The picture of English activity we now have divides into several phases. The first is an ambitious one when John Cabot, after exploring the Newfoundland coast, expects to open up direct contact between England and Asia but dies in the attempt, which is not resumed. Then the Azorean Portuguese direct some of the Bristol men to parts of the North American mainland, where trading contacts with coastal Indians continue from 1501 or 1502 until 1505 but then break down, presumably because an adequate basis for profitable exchange had not been established. We cannot indicate where this may have taken place—whether at a few adjacent localities or ranged along the coast from Labrador to New England. There is some slight evidence that it reached as far south as New England and even conceivably a little further. On the other hand, there was

34. Williamson, *Cabot Voyages,* pp. 263–264; Quinn, *England and the Discovery of America,* pp. 127–130; Morison, *European Discovery of America,* I, 220.

a fishery in operation. This is now established, thanks to Dr. Ruddock's discoveries, from 1502 onwards. But if one ship has been traced in 1502, two in 1504, and one in 1505, this is all the evidence we have so far about the initiation of the exploitation of one of North America's major resources. It does, however, take us that much further. If commerce languished, there is no need to consider that the fishery did so as well. Most probably it continued steadily each season, though not necessarily growing substantially in scale.

We have no comparable materials on the Portuguese activity after 1503. It is probable, from the extent to which Portuguese nomenclature is to be found on maps of what became Labrador, Newfoundland, Cape Breton and Nova Scotia, that many Portuguese vessels were coming to the area. Some no doubt were only fishing vessels and confined themselves almost wholly to the Banks; but others ranged the coasts. The Corte Real family would have been likely to have attempted to retain some of their supremacy in the fishery and on the Portuguese-frequented coasts. Vasco Annes Corte Real—the eldest son of João Vas—had survived while his brothers were lost in the western ocean. He took over the rights of his brothers in 1506 and had them confirmed to him again in 1510, but just how active he and the vessels set out by him were is apparently quite unknown. Similarly, we know that Pedro de Barcelos remained until his death in 1507 actively interested in the New Lands and that his heirs continued to assert rights there.[35]

France now enters the picture as the third partner in the Newfoundland fisheries. The year 1504 sees the first datable voyage from Normandy. Probably the Bretons began their activity within a very short time afterwards, though how long it was before they were followed by the French Basques is not yet known.[36] Thomas Aubert of Rouen was the leading pioneer: in 1509, he succeeded in bringing seven male Indians back with him across the Atlantic to Normandy.[37] These are unlikely to have been Beothuk; more probably Micmac. In any case, they caused a good deal of interest in France and are the first North Americans to be described in some detail.

35. Biggar, *Precursors*, pp. 92–96, 98–102, 143–145; L. A. Vigneras, "The Voyages of Diogo and Manoel de Barcelos to Canada in the Sixteenth Century," *Terrae Incognitae*, V (1973), 61–64.

36. C. A. Julien, *Les voyages de découverte et les premier établissements* (Paris, 1948), p. 25.

37. Harrisse, *Découverte et évolution cartographique de Terre-Neuve*, pp. 162–163.

It is by no means certain that they were detained in France, since later the French made a habit of bringing people from the Americas to Europe with the promise of returning them to their friends, which they usually tried to keep. If these men returned, they may well have been the first Amerindians to bring back direct information from Europe to North America, and to initiate a reciprocal culture contact. By 1509 it is clear that the English and Portuguese on the Banks and on the shores of Newfoundland and the adjacent mainland had been joined by the French. Basques on the French side of the border were active from 1512 at least and the Spanish Basques were probably not far behind. North American waters, where fish were quite exceptionally plentiful, were thus attracting a truly international fishery, which appears to have been untrammeled by the various individual and national claims that accompanied the activities of the explorers. In this way an economic nexus was established between Europe and North America; and what had been an incredibly risky venture only a short time before became a route for several hundred fishermen at least each spring and summer.

In 1507 Martin Waldseemüller changed the world, or at least the appearance of it on the map, by placing his pair of continents between Europe and Asia.[38] In 1508, it appears, Sebastian Cabot set out to sail round the northern rim of the more northerly of the new continents and to get to Asia by a passage lying well to the north of the now increasingly well-known fishing grounds off Newfoundland. We cannot yet tell whether these two events were cause and effect, or whether they took place independently. It can be argued that the English voyages had provided substantial arguments for treating North America as a separate continental landmass well before Waldseemüller's theoretical construct of the new continents appeared. Moreover, details of Gaspar Corte Real's voyage of 1501 may have been available in Bristol well before 1508 which indicated that he had reached well beyond 50° N. on the Labrador coast and had possibly some indication that the land opened suddenly into a westward-lying strait at Cape Chidley. Certainly, several maps exist (dating from the period 1504–12, and perhaps from the earlier part of this range) showing a substantial northwesterly trend between what we can recognize as Labrador and Greenland toward a point

38. Josef Fischer and Franz von Weiser, *Die älteste Karte mit dem Namen Amerika aus dem Jahre 1507* (Innsbruck, 1903; Amsterdam, 1968).

where there seems to be a passage to the west. These may well indicate that other Portuguese voyages had followed in Gaspar Corte Real's track. Nevertheless, Sebastian Cabot's determination to search for a Northwest Passage may indeed have arisen entirely from his own calculations and opinions.

It has for a long time been widely, though not universally, accepted that Cabot set out in 1508 on his voyage with two ships, though the evidence for it has been late and somewhat indirect. Unpublished contemporary evidence now indicates that Cabot was out of England at the end of the reign of Henry VII and returned at the opening of the reign of Henry VIII, as had previously been thought. He failed to collect the three installments of his pension due to him at Michaelmas 1507 and at Easter and Michaelmas 1508 and signed a receipt for them only on May 7, 1509.[39] Whether he was out of England for the whole period from October 1507 to the beginning of May 1509, which this might suggest, is not clear. The other evidence we have would suggest that he did not leave on his voyage until the summer of 1508, but the date of his receipt would strongly indicate that he returned only after Henry VIII succeeded to the throne on April 22, 1509.

Much of the early evidence on this expedition was formerly assigned to the 1498 voyage made by his father. While this leaves the 1498 voyage almost undocumented (as has been shown), it may prove necessary to reconsider whether some part of it may have to be reassigned to an earlier voyage, made before 1505, by Sebastian Cabot himself. He told several incompatible stories about his experiences, and it must now be asked whether he was talking at one time about his own voyage made some time between 1502 and 1504 and at another time about the voyage of 1508–09, though no firm answer can so far be given. We must still attempt to conflate the most likely parts of his stories and apply them provisionally to 1508–09.

Cabot had two ships, but whether they were supplied by the king —as indicated in one place—or were his own is not known. They are also said to have had on board as many as three hundred men. This number seems most unlikely unless it was clearly intended to estab-

39. P.R.O., Enrolled Customs, E356/24, m.3v.; Memoranda Roll, Lord Treasurer's Remembrances, Status and Visus, and Proceedings, Hilary term, 1 Henry VIII, E368/283.

lish a way-station along the supposed route from Europe to Cathay. We have, so far, no information that Henry VII contributed anything whatever toward the voyage or lent or hired any royal ships to him. He sailed in late May or early June, since by early July he was in northern latitudes, where there were icebergs and almost continuous daylight, though the land was free on account of the melting of the ice. This would apply along a wide range of latitudes at this time of year. One account says that he established his latitude with a quadrant at 55° N., on the coast of Labrador above Hamilton Inlet, while the rapid and congested movement of the icebergs might appear to indicate a location rather farther north, near Cape Chidley at the opening of Hudson Strait at about 60° N. where the icebergs converge.

In a letter he himself wrote later in his life he claimed to have been by June 11 as far north as 67° 30′ N., inside the Arctic Circle. This would place him well up the coast of Baffin Island where the sea may not have been open at this early date. Either he is romancing in this story, or he is referring to two distinct voyages, the lower latitude in the voyage made by him between 1502 and 1504 and the higher one in 1508–09. It is not possible to say which interpretation is correct. He claimed that his men were severely affected by the cold —as they might well have been in close contact with a stream of icebergs—and refused to continue the voyage. This appears not unlikely. The fact that Cabot maintained for the rest of his life that he knew there was a passage round America indicates with some likelihood that he had gone far enough north to observe the opening of Hudson Strait. Less likely is his sighting of open water to the east of Baffin Island.

Cabot then came south—how far is conjectural. Some people who knew him thought as far as about 36° N., that is to Chesapeake Bay or a little further south; others said to Florida, but to Spaniards or Portuguese this could mean almost anywhere along the coast between 25° and 40° N. We can suggest that he made some tentative exploration of entries which might indicate a more southerly passage through North America, as he remarked on the intelligence of the Indians he encountered on his way. He may well be thought to have sailed home on the Gulf Stream current, having wintered in American waters. Cabot—as we saw—arrived after the new king, Henry VIII, had come to the throne. Henry VIII employed him in

his Gascon campaign in 1511. Then, at the request of Ferdinand of Aragon to Henry VIII, he passed into the service of Spain on account of his knowledge of cartography and of the "Baccalaos," which could mean Newfoundland (also Tierra Nueva) to Spaniards, or just of North America in general.[40]

The English had been the pioneers in the exploration of northeastern North America and had both disclosed and initially exploited the codfishery. This is true at whatever of the alternative dates we place their first discoveries. Though the first series of voyages ended in disaster for John Cabot, they were revived in 1501, to last until 1505 with an increasing degree of organization. Eventually they went bankrupt, so that the fishery was left to individual rather than corporate enterprise and was soon shared in increasing numbers by Portuguese, French and Spaniards. The Portuguese had gone through a similar cycle: great discoveries, high hopes and then disaster, followed by more cautious and again private rather than corporate fishing enterprises. France made no ambitious voyages, but the individual enterprise of her fishermen carved out a share for her in the fishery. The Spaniards came last, again probably with a few individual enterprises and subsequently in 1511 an attempted corporate enterprise which came to nothing. The English broke through once more in 1508–9 with an ambitious attempt to open up a passage round America to Asia. Their failure to achieve this aim meant that they too retired from exploring enterprises. By 1512, knowledge of northeastern North America had grown as much by the failure of the major exploring enterprises as by their successes. The beneficiaries were not governments or states but the entrepreneurs who fitted out fishing vessels, and the masters and crews who sailed them and fished in American waters to return each year before winter set in.

By about 1512 we can say that North America was well established on the maps, though some still considered it an outcrop of Asia rather than an independent continent. Such notions were to give

40. Williamson, *Voyages of the Cabots* (1929), pp. 70–83, and *Cabot Voyages*, p. 281; Quinn, *England and the Discovery of America*, pp. 139–143. Morison, *European Discovery of America*, I, 220–221, remained somewhat skeptical about the evidence for the 1508–9 voyage; Ruddock, "Reputation of Sebastian Cabot," p. 98, speaks of it as being "disastrous," but gives no details of why she does so.

way before the more advanced concept quite soon—probably the turning point when Waldseemüller's theory became orthodoxy was the 1513 edition of Ptolemy's "Geography," which showed a credible pair of Americas. Most of what knowledge there was was confined to the northeast and centered on Newfoundland, though it extended a considerable way to the northwest and some way also to the south (there is still considerable obscurity about the intensity and extent of the southern explorations). North American waters were known to the subjects of all four western European nations. No monopoly of access had been established and exploitation had begun virtually free from national controls. A little was known in three countries—Spain being the exception—about the peoples of North America, if contacts with them had hitherto been slight and somewhat unpromising. What characterizes the period for the historian down to this date is the sparcity and poor quality of the evidence we have. Much of what is written must be based on uncertain or insufficient evidence and any attempt to tell a coherent story is liable to lead to the use of too great a proportion of guesswork. Students of this period should take any reconstruction as provisional and tentative only, liable to be altered not only by changes in the historian's reaction to such data as there is but also, more drastically, by the appearance of even small pieces of additional evidence which may force the revision of quite basic areas of the reconstructed narrative.

From the point of view of the sources on which it is founded, the history of North America emerges from its dark ages some time in the second decade of the sixteenth century. Even if thereafter it continues to have problems of defective or contradictory evidence, they are less fundamental than they had been between 1000 and 1510.

# CHAPTER 6

## *The First Spanish Expeditions to the Southeast, 1513–1526*

I F we ask where the southernmost part of North America begins, we may find it difficult to give an answer that is wholly satisfactory historically, particularly in terms of the expanding Spanish régime in the Americas in the sixteenth century. In physical terms, it is difficult to find any natural boundary further north than the narrow waist of north-central Central America just above the Yucatan peninsula.[1] The boundaries to which we are accustomed and those which determine the framework of this volume were largely set in the middle of the nineteenth century only. Columbus's failure to make his first landfall on the Florida peninsula in 1492 meant that the early nuclei of Spanish power were all well to the south of what is now known as North America. The 1849 Mexico-United States boundary on the west coast is wholly arbitrary; and that in the east, along the Rio Grande, only marginally less so. The viceroyalty of New Spain from 1550 extended as far to the north as the viceroys wished or cared to attempt to assert any Spanish authority. Nor was this attitude modified until the eighteenth century.

The early concentration of Spanish activity in the major Caribbean islands, particularly Hispaniola, meant that exploring activity was extended radially from there. The primary expansion was directed to the south, which does not concern us, and to the west,

[1] Woodbury Lowery, *The Spanish Settlements Within the Present Limits of the United States, 1513–1561* (New York, 1901), is still the standard secondary work on the topics covered in this chapter.

which does. Until at the earliest 1507, and at the latest 1513, the land to the west of the islands was thought to be, or at least thought likely to be, Asiatic. Balboa's discovery of the Pacific in 1513, combined with the attempts by Pedrarias from 1514 to lay some foundations for Spanish authority on the mainland—first on the Caribbean side, and then, after 1519, on the Pacific—are necessary preludes to the Spanish penetration of North America. When, in 1516, the restless and unsatisfied conquerors of Cuba began prospecting north of the coastal zone where Pedrarias was preoccupied, the process was taken a vital stage further. The successive expeditions of Francisco Hernández de Córdoba in 1517 and of Juan de Grijalva in 1518 laid down firm outlines for the Mexican coast and the Gulf of Mexico round to Florida, which Alonso Alvarez de Pineda further defined in 1519. The gradual approach to Aztec Mexico was completed in the same year when Hernando Cortés, with his small force, invaded the first highly organized society so far discovered in the Americas, finding it rich both in precious metals and in agricultural resources and techniques, and possessing an ecclesiastical system as elaborate and pervasive as that of the medieval Catholic Church at its height.

At the same time a southern limit of the northern continent began to appear and the possibilities of finding fresh Mexicos there emerged. It was inevitable that Spain should at least turn to the lands north of the Gulf of Mexico and lying along the Atlantic shore. She needed some opportunities for those of her restless settlers who could not be admitted to the exclusive colonial despotate which Cortés had created in the years 1519 to 1522 and which was only very gradually opened up to freer Spanish penetration. Once installed in Mexico also, the Spaniards, even after Cortés's exclusive control had given way before 1530, had no conception of limiting the possible northern expansion of Spanish enterprise either on the east or the west. Until the 1550s the Spaniards did not even contemplate, for practical reasons, the establishment of a fixed frontier to the north. If, indeed, they halted their expansion in the third quarter of the sixteenth century, they revived it with only rather nominal restraints in the fourth. But the initial assumption remained intact: that Spain's imperial title to the north was undoubted, however it might remain undefined or even undefinable. Consequently, all other European intervention in the north was irrelevant as well as

illegitimate. Indeed, the papal donation of 1493, reinforced by the treaty of 1494 with Portugal, was only a second line of defense in the assertion of Spain's rights in North America. Her basic assumption was that it was her imperial right, as a great conquering monarchy, to assert her claim to vast unlimited and unoccupied territories, which she might or might not wish at some future date to bring under her control. This option on the north lies behind most of Spain's thinking on North America in our period.

It would appear that the Florida peninsula was known by, at the latest, 1500. We do not know who first sighted it. A projection in the direction of Cuba in the Juan de la Cosa map, begun in 1500, balanced a more northerly projection (the old Horn of Asia) in the landmass shown bordering the North Atlantic. A similar pair of projections can be seen in the Cantino map of 1502,[2] and in later versions Labrador and Florida are named as the two complementary projections. The fact that the first known circumnavigation of Cuba did not take place until 1508 has naturally led to some skepticism about the dates of the La Cosa and Cantino maps. But if there is doubt about when the La Cosa map was completed, there is none about the Cantino; on present evidence, the appearance of a completed Cuba and the Florida peninsula would seem to stem from a voyage of 1499 or thereabouts, well known in its own time, but not now recorded in the documents. The earliest Florida was, of course, regarded as part of Asia, but it is probable that before 1512 the land to the north of the Caribbean was recognized by the Spaniards as being part of a separate continent. By that time too, it is most probable that the Florida Strait, with its northward-flowing current, was well known to Spanish navigators making their way back to Europe from the Caribbean.

Juan Ponce de León, a veteran of the second Columbus voyage of 1493, had emulated the example of the conquerors of Cuba by launching out on the conquest of Puerto Rico after 1508, when Hispaniola had become saturated with men and depleted of resources.[3] But he was soon satiated in Puerto Rico also and, as the

2. Appropriate sections of both the Cosa and Cantino maps will be found reproduced in (for example), H. Harrisse, *Découverte et évolution cartographique de Terre-Neuve* (1900), J. A. Williamson, *The Cabot Voyages* (1962); and L. C. Wroth, *The Voyages of Giovanni da Verrazzano* (1970).

3. The only biography is in Spanish, Vicente Murga Sans, *Juan Ponce de León* (San Juan, P.R., 1959). The chronicle evidence for his North American ventures in 1512

*conquistadores* of Cuba were to do a few years later, began to look about him for lands where he could make his next pre-emptive bid for a great fortune. He found a goal from the tales of a Fountain of Youth, or at least of some attractive territory in Bimini north or northeast of Puerto Rico. In 1513 Ponce de León set out from his Puerto Rican base to look for Bimini. His ships made land on the eastern side of the Florida peninsula on Whit Sunday (Pasqua Florida) and this gave the new land its name at his hands. There is no firm evidence where he landed to inspect the country and find it fertile, but it was probably between Matanzas and the St. Johns River. His attempts to work his way out into the Florida Strait and so southward were hampered by the current, and in recording this he was putting down the first notice we have of the existence of the Gulf Stream. He managed to work his way down the peninsular coast, skirting the keys, and then up the west coast, concluding (probably from a brief impression of the deep indentation of what was either Charlotte Harbor or Tampa Bay) that what he had discovered was an island comparable in scale with Cuba. Going ashore on the west coast, he was opposed by the local Indians possibly of the Calusa tribe, but did not come into serious conflict with them and was able to withdraw without loss to Havana.

Ponce de León's objective thereafter was to occupy "the islands of Bimini and Florida"—the latter being now formally attached to the "new island." King Ferdinand granted these territories to him to conquer in 1514. He did not exercise his option for seven years, for reasons which are not yet wholly explained. By the time he was ready to colonize Florida, the whole perspective in which it would be considered had changed.

The gradual discovery that Central America was a long, narrow, curving piece of land which wrapped the Caribbean Islands round the greater part of a circle, with Florida at the extreme end of a mainland to the north, was a piecemeal process. The crucial stage in the history of Florida was the expedition of Hernández de Córdoba in 1517. He had worked around the Yucatán peninsula and encountered most promising traces of a rich native culture when he was defeated by the Maya at the battle of Champotón. This trau-

---

and 1521 is conveniently translated in J. F. Davis, "History of Juan Ponce de León's Voyages to Florida," *Florida Historical Quarterly*, XIV (1935), no. 1.

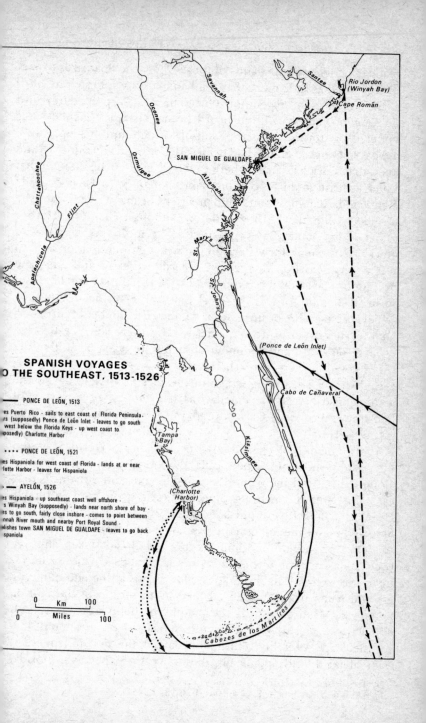

SPANISH VOYAGES
TO THE SOUTHEAST, 1513-1526

—— PONCE DE LEÓN, 1513

...es Puerto Rico - sails to east coast of Florida Peninsula -
...rs (supposedly) Ponce de León Inlet - leaves to go south
...west below the Florida Keys - up west coast to
...posedly) Charlotte Harbor

•••• PONCE DE LEÓN, 1521

...es Hispaniola for west coast of Florida - lands at or near
...lotte Harbor - leaves for Hispaniola

• AYELÓN, 1526

...es Hispaniola - up southeast coast well offshore -
...s Winyah Bay (supposedly) - lands near north shore of bay -
...es to go south, fairly close inshore - comes to point between
...nnah River mouth and nearby Port Royal Sound -
...ablishes town SAN MIGUEL DE GUALDAPE - leaves to go back
...spaniola

0    Km    100

0    Miles    100

Chattahoochee

Apalachicola

Flint

Oconee

Ocmulgee

Savannah

Altamaha

St. Marys

St. Johns

SAN MIGUEL DE GUALDAPE

Santee

Rio Jordon
(Winyah Bay)

Cape Román

(Ponce de León Inlet)

Cabo de Cañaveral

(Tampa
Bay)

Kissimmee

(Charlotte
Harbor)

Cabezes de los Martires

matic experience at the hands of those whom the Spaniards probably regarded as little more than wild animals was a desperate blow to the morale of the expedition. One of the vessels, piloted by Pedro de Alaminos and having on board Bernal Díaz del Castillo,[4] was buffeted by storms across the Gulf of Mexico until her men were almost starving. Alaminos had been with Ponce de León in 1513 and knew that Florida lay somewhere to the east. There he thought that water at least could be obtained and a passage to Havana easily completed. Alaminos found land precisely, he maintained, where he had been with the 1513 expedition, although Charlotte Harbor rather than Tampa Bay is favored as its location. Sailors were quickly sent ashore for water and the sick men were put on land to rest and, it was hoped, recover. Guards were set and adequate precautions taken (as it was thought) to protect the shore party from surprise. In spite of this the local Calusa Indians again attacked, achieving a measure of surprise, and inflicted a number of casualties on the already dispirited Spaniards. However, some water was brought on board and a number of men were taken off so that the vessel could in the end reach Havana.

In 1519 came the final stage in the placing of Florida on the map. Alonso Alvarez de Pineda was sent out by the governor of Jamaica, Francisco de Garay, to approach Mexico by a new route and so forestall Cortés, who had now embarked on his decisive mission. Pineda sailed northward from Cuba to Florida, coasted the western shore of the peninsula, then worked his way westward along the coast of the Gulf of Mexico. He noted the rivers as they came in sight, commenting especially on a great river, probably Mobile Bay and River, and later made what is thought to be the first sighting of the Mississippi. He sailed all the way from Florida to Vera Cruz, where he found Cortés had already taken effective precautions against intrusion by rivals. Pineda's major achievement was to have established that Florida was at the end of a long arc which ran from Yucatán all the way to the tip of the Florida peninsula. Henceforward the southern boundary of central and eastern North America could appear as a continuous line on the map. After his return, Pineda put the first independent map of the Florida peninsula to survive on paper as: "Florida,

4. Bernal Diaz del Castillo, *The True History of the Conquest of New Spain*, 5 vols., edited and translated by A. P. Maudsley, I (1908), 26–31.

or Bimini, found by Juan Ponce."[5]

Ponce de León was ready for his *entrada* by February 1521. He set out from Havana with two hundred colonists and fifty horses, together with cattle, mares, pigs, sheep and goats to enable stockraising to be begun rapidly. The colonists were also equipped with seeds and tools. It is clear that he hoped to exploit the rich land and good climate he had earlier observed. He landed in Florida at the Bay of Carlos (Charlotte Harbor?), which has been variously located by modern writers. All that can be said is that it was well up the peninsula; the balance of opinion is that it was on the west coast, where he had been before, though it could have been on the east. He landed his men and women and settled them and their belongings in temporary accommodation. At that point a large force of Indians descended on them. The Indians fought strongly but they were no match for Spanish arms and horses; they were driven off and the Spaniards added up their losses and injuries. Unfortunately for the settlement, its leader, Ponce de León, had been badly wounded by an arrow.

The episode and the condition of Ponce de León together acted to discourage the settlers. They decided to re-embark and return to Cuba, and the soldiers managed to evacuate almost all the settlers without further loss. By the time the ships returned to Havana, Ponce de León was dying. Many of the soldiers and settlers also fell ill, it was thought from disease contracted in Florida, and again a number died. Florida thus destroyed the first Spanish colony and gained a bad reputation for its savage Indians and its supposed unhealthiness. Yet Ponce de León had called attention to Florida as a possible location for a Spanish settlement.

While Ponce de León was carrying out his last fatal expedition, steps were already being taken which were to lead to a fresh Spanish attempt at colonization in the southeast.[6] Lucas Vásquez de Ayllón, a legal official in Hispaniola, had acquired a large interest in the

5. It is in the Archivo de Indias, Seville, and is reproduced in Wroth, *Voyages of Verrazzano*, plate 16 (and see pp. 294, 316).

6. On the Ayllón expedition, besides Lowery, *Spanish Settlements*, Paul Quattebaum, *The Land Called Chicora* (Gainesville, Fla., 1956) is useful for detail if somewhat amateurish. It must be supplemented by the chronicle evidence, in chronological order, of Peter Martyr, *Decades*, translated by F. A. MacNutt, I (1912), 254–268; Gonzalo Fernández de Oviedo, *Historia general y natural de las Indias*, IV (1959), 325–330; Francisco López de Gómera, *Historia general de las Indias*, I (1932), 89–93; and Antonio de Herrera y Tordesillas, *Historia de los hechos de los castellanos*, II (1934), 26–28.

sugar industry and, like other entrepreneurs, was suffering from a shortage of labor as the indigenes and imported Arawak and Carib slave labor were rapidly dying off. At the end of 1520, he sent a vessel northward under Francisco Gordillo to prospect the Bahamas and perhaps also the mainland, for sources of additional manpower. Another official with similar objectives, Juan Ortiz de Matienzos, had sent a vessel to the Bahamas under Pedro de Quexos to seize slaves. Neither vessel appears to have had any success in prospecting or slave-taking until they joined forces in June 1521. Then, sailing northward, they encountered the mainland at a river mouth they named Rio de San Juan Bautista. There they were well received by the Indians, a number of whom were invited on board and given presents. Members of the expedition went inland to explore, and were made much of in the villages they visited.

After their return to the vessels they again invited Indians on board, but this time seized both men and women and kept them prisoner. On their way back to Hispaniola, one ship was lost (it was Matienzos' but Quexos was evidently at that time on board Ayllón's vessel). Some seventy captives were brought to Santo Domingo. By that time it had become impolitic for Ayllón to involve himself in slave-catching, since attempts were being made to enforce the Laws of Burgos of 1512, which forbade the capture of Indians for slave labor. Instead, he denounced Matienzos and got the slaves released.[7] However, since no arrangements were made to send them home, most of them apparently died of starvation in the end. One was christened and taught Spanish. Named Francisco de Chicora, he inspired Ayllón with the desire to acquire a solid title to the land where nominal royal possession had been taken on June 30, 1521; so Ayllón took the Indian with him to Spain, where his imagination worked full-time to circulate improbable stories about his homeland. There Ayllón obtained a grant, dated June 12, 1523,[8] authorizing him to colonize and Christianize part of the mainland, between 35 and 37°N., at his own expense within three years. The names of nineteen provinces in it have not proved meaningful and

7. Gómera, *Historia*, I, 29, maintains that Ayllón was looking for slaves from the beginning, while modern commentators prefer to believe his vessels went to explore the mainland and linked up only fortuitously with the slaving vessel.

8. The patent is in M. Fernández de Navarrete, *Obras*, II (Madrid, 1964), 51–53, 102–107. It is translated in Quattlebaum, *Land Called Chicora*, pp. 135–144.

all remain unknown except that of Chicora, said to be the location from which the Indians captured in 1521 came.

In 1525 Ayllón was able to send Quexos, who had now entered his service, on a mission of reconnaissance up the coast. A few of the enslaved Indians may have survived to be repatriated but this is not certain. The voyage is supposed to have covered some 250 leagues, or 650 miles, which would have brought him from the tip of Florida to some little way south of Cape Fear. The Indians are said to have been friendly and to have supplied a few potential interpreters to go back with him. This paved the way for the attempt to establish a colony.

In July 1526, Ayllón left Hispaniola with six vessels containing some five hundred men and women for the colony, together with horses, farm animals and negro slaves. He sailed direct to the place where the slaves had been taken (or so we are led to imply), Francisco's Chicora. Three Dominican friars accompanied the party as missionaries. They entered a river, and there the flagship was lost with many stores, though her complement was saved. Exploration of the hinterland produced little evidence of good land—and certainly none of a strait trending toward the Pacific which all explorers looked for at that time. Francisco de Chicora gave Ayllón the slip, and it might seem that the Indians boycotted his men since there is no reference to their reactions. Exploring parties, using a craft constructed when the flagship broke up, reported better land some 50 leagues (130 miles) away. To this site Ayllón successfully removed his colonists and landed them. A secondary voyage was then begun toward the west, from which we can assume that this was down the coast.

The colonists now entered a large bay, moved up a substantial river, and built themselves near its banks the town of San Miguel de Gualdape—the first Spanish municipality to be established in North America as defined in this volume—under an *alcalde* apparently named Malaves. We have no details except that houses, not mere temporary dwellings, were erected. The land proved salt and marshy, characteristic of much of the South Carolina coast. It is probable that stores were depleted and that no large supplies of corn were obtained from the Indians—though relations with them seem to have been good at first—but fever and other illnesses gradually submerged the colony. Amongst those attacked was Ayllón

himself, who died on October 18, 1526. His lieutenant, Francisco Gomez, was unable to maintain effective control over the colonists. A military party, under Ginez Donçel, turned on Gomez and the civilian administration and took control, antagonizing the Indians by vigorous corn-collecting policies which led to fighting with them. Donçel was in turn overthrown, and Gomez re-established control.

Finally the decision was made to abandon the settlement as untenable. Only one vessel, *La Santa Catalina,* reached Hispaniola with some 150 survivors. How far disease was responsible for the disaster is not known. The logistics of settlement in outlying areas where there were no immediately realizable capital assets, such as gold, or a population engaged in intensive agriculture, were still not understood. Ayllón's expedition gave Spain a further name which could be applied to a territory on the North American mainland—La Tierra de Ayllón—which appears on Ribeiro's world map of 1529 occupying all the space between La Tierra de Estaban Gomez (with its southern terminus just south of Cape Cod) and Ponce de León's peninsular Florida.

There are considerable difficulties in assigning locations for Ayllón's two landings in 1526, which cannot be considered to have been solved satisfactorily. It seems clear that the expedition did not even touch the lowest latitude (35°) prescribed in the 1523 grant. The limit assigned to the exploration in 1525, 250 leagues, would bring the vessels to somewhere between Winyah Bay at 33° 20′ and the Cape Fear River at 33° 50′; and if this is correct, Chicora would lie in this region. Oviedo put the Rio de Jordan—the name given to the place where he first landed—at 33° 40′, that is, between the two entries already indicated, though estimation of latitude within a limit of half a degree is about as near accuracy as could be attained by most observers, so that it could meet the requirements of either. Oviedo then takes the distance from there to the second landing place as being 40 to 45 leagues, giving a range roughly between 100 and 120 miles. If the first landing was at Winyah Bay, then a range of this order down the coast would put the location of San Miguel de Gualdape somewhere between modern St. Helena Sound to the north and the mouth of the Savannah River (Tybee Roads) to the south. Winyah Bay is taken as a likely place for the first landing, rather than the Cape Fear River, because the evidence of the Her-

nando de Soto expedition fits in with a location for the second within the limits indicated. At Cofitachequi, on the Savannah River, in 1540 were found "a dirk and beads, that had belonged to Christians, who, the Indians said, had many years before been in the port, distant two days' journey. He that had been there was the governor Licentiate Ayllon," says the Gentleman of Elvas, while Biedma reported that the Indians had told him the site was 30 leagues away.[9] None of the three entries mentioned are as near as this, but they are within the range of 100 to 120 miles.

On ethnographic and linguistic grounds the Savannah River has been favored, while the Spaniards themselves came to believe that the site was on Port Royal Sound or nearby. La Punta de Santa Elena, later identified with the modern Hilton Head, was said to have been the landmark found in 1521 which was employed again in 1526. Herrera, writing in the 1590s, put the location of the colony at "Orizta," the coastal territory of the Cusabo tribe, Oristan, which comprised the area around and a little to the north of Port Royal Sound and included St. Helena Sound.[10] Until fresh evidence is found, this appears to be as much as can usefully be said on the location of the first Spanish town on the coast.

The Spaniards had already turned their attention to the Gulf coast. Francisco de Garay, governor of Jamaica, attempted to capitalize on Pineda's discoveries in 1519 by obtaining a grant in 1521 to conquer the province of Amichel, between the western part of the Florida peninsula (to which Ponce de León had prior rights) round the Gulf all the way to wherever Cortés's northern coastal limits might lie. Before the grant had been finalized, Diego de Carmago had gone ahead to define the western limits of his proposed territory, which he managed to place at Pánuco where the Rio Grande reached the sea. Garay himself set out only in 1523, when, making

9. Frederick W. Hodge and Thomas H. Lewis, *Spanish Explorers in the Southern United States, 1528–1543* (New York, 1907), p. 174; Edward G. Bourne, *Narratives of Hernando de Soto,* II (1904), 13.

10. Lowery, *Spanish Settlements,* I, 447–452, discusses most of the source material. He is inclined to make the first landing at the Cape Fear River and the second on the Pee Dee (behind Winyah Bay) (pp. 165–167), though in his discussion of sources he stresses the weight of Biedma's and Oviedo's evidence; Quattlebaum, *Land Called Chicora,* pp. 20–31, favors Cape Fear River and Winyah Bay (specifically Waccamaw Neck), respectively. J. R. Swanton, *Indians of the Southeastern United States* (1946), pp. 36–37, 66–67, accepts the Savannah River as the site of the second landing and the colony.

for Pánuco, he fell into the hands of Cortés and shortly afterwards died.[11]

Garay's abortive voyage was a prelude to the venture which was to be the last of the early series of coasting expeditions and the first of those which penetrated the interior. This was that under Pánfilo de Narváez, who had been, like Cortés, one of the minor instruments of Velasquez in the conquest of Cuba, and who had tried ineffectively to compete with Cortés for the honor of conquering Mexico. He had been outgeneraled and Cortés had enlisted the whole of his force on his side. Narváez remained in obscurity for some time after his disgrace, then emerged as a would-be successor to Garay and Ponce de León. His charter of December 11, 1526, authorized him to conquer and occupy from the Cape of Florida to the Rio de las Palmas, a little to the west of Pánuco. The expedition he mounted in Spain in 1527 was larger than Ayllón's of the previous year; it amounted to some six hundred men, together with a few women and negroes, and included a number of friars who were to convert the Indians. Setting out on June 17, his fleet was scattered and he was not able to reassemble all his ships at Cuba. He finally set out again in the spring of 1528, reaching the west coast of Florida on April 14.[12] He appears to have landed near the entrance to Tampa Bay with the four hundred men still left to him. While his men plundered the villages round the bay, Narváez read the formal *Requerimiento*, which required the Indians to submit to the Spanish crown and accept Christianity, and threatened that if they did not comply, they would be treated as enemies.

Gradually Narváez put his force in order and dismissed his ships, arranging for them to return with supplies and to coast the Gulf

11. Navarrete, _Obras_, II, 48–51, 98–102.

12. Álvar Núñez Cabeza de Vaca's *Relación* (Zamora, 1542), is the basic text. The standard translation is in Hodge and Lewis, *Spanish Explorers in the Southern United States*, pp. 1–126. *The Narrative of Alvar Nuñez Cabeza de Vaca*, with an introduction by F. Bannon (Barre, Mass., 1972), reprints Fanny Bandelier's translation of the *Relación* with a new translation by G. Theisen of the official report from Oviedo. A racy popular edition is *Cabeza de Vaca's Adventures in the Unknown Interior of America*, edited and translated by Cyclone Covey (New York, 1961). There are brief accounts in Oviedo, *Historia general*, IV (1959), 285–320, and A. de Herrera, *Historia*, III (1934), 214–220. The modern accounts in Lowery, *Spanish Settlements*, Morris Bishop, *The Odyssey of Cabeza de Vaca* (1933), Cleve Hallenback, *Journey and Route of Cabeza de Vaca* (1940), and John Upton Terrell, *Journey into Darkness* (1962), produce a variety of approaches. J. R. Swanton, *Indians of the Southeastern United States*, pp. 37–39, has some useful indications of Indian contacts.

shores westward from Florida until he made contact with them at a suitable harbor. He himself was determined to march north as soon as possible, but his supplies were low and his company moved slowly up the peninsula, plundering any Indian villages they encountered. They took an Indian as a guide, who gave them to understand that they could get supplies of food in a district called Apalachee. They had to bridge several rivers as they moved on, one of them the Suwannee. Then they worked through wooded country until they came to the large Apalachee Indian town called Ibitachuco, not far from modern Tallahassee, on June 25. There they drove the Indians away from their own recently ripened early corn crop and collected and ground it for themselves. On July 20 they set out southeastward toward the Gulf.

The expedition had been suffering since it reached the Apalachee territory from repeated harrying attacks by the Indians, and this process of attrition was to continue as they advanced. On July 29, they reached and occupied an Indian town called Aute, apparently not very far from the mouth of the Apalachicola River.[13] The second in command, Álvar Núñez Cabeza de Vaca, was sent to reconnoiter. He found a complex system of inlets which led toward the sea and eventually located an arm of Apalachicola Bay which appeared suitable as a coastal base. At Aute, Narváez had been able to find fresh supplies but was continually attacked by Indians, while he himself along with a number of his men fell ill. The removal of the force to the coastal site did not prove easy. Discipline was poor and there was a movement to abandon the sick, including Narváez, to the Indians. From his own narrative, Cabeza de Vaca would make it appear that he rallied the men and completed the evacuation. At this point the expedition was in a state of crisis, with insufficient resources (it was thought) to enable it to establish a permanent base. The chances of the ship which was to patrol the coast making contact with them now seemed slight—indeed it failed totally to do so. Eventually, the only solution appeared to be to attempt to pull out and transport the survivors back along the Gulf coast to Mexico. This could be done only by means of boats which they proceeded to construct. By using the plentiful timber of the area, with palmetto and resin for caulking, palmetto for ropes, and such cloth as they

13. Hodge and Lewis, *Spanish Explorers in the Southern United States*, p. 33, identify it as St. Mark's Bay, at the head of Apalachee Bay.

could assemble for sails, four vessels, each some 45 feet long, had been constructed by September 20. But Indian attacks continued to decimate them, as did deaths from disease, so that on embarkation there were only some two hundred survivors, and the horses had been gradually killed off for food.

They left Apalachicola Bay—giving it the name of Bahía de Caballos—on September 22. Working their way slowly and uncertainly along the coast for more than a month, their supplies of food and especially water were at last used up. At or near Pensacola Bay they decided to put in to land to attempt to get more supplies. There were many Indians there from whom fish and maize were obtained and they collected water in quantity. Then, at night, the Indians attacked, wounding and killing a number of men (Narváez was wounded in the face). A rearguard enabled the rest to reach the boats, where an attempted attack by Indians in canoes led to some thirty canoes being destroyed. They were then able to set out once more.

Morale was understandably low. Contacts with Choctaw Indians along the coast were not friendly. They passed the mouth of a great river, the Mississippi. Putting out to sea to shorten their journey, the boats were separated; as food got scarcer, control over the vessels lessened. Eventually, on November 6, two of the boats were driven ashore on Galveston Island. Cabeza de Vaca gives a vivid account of the wretched conditions under which they now had to live: the bands of Karankawa Indians who lived there were miserably poor fishermen who survived on roots in the winter. Narváez was behind the two wrecked vessels and managed to pick up some survivors from a fourth boat when it sank. He himself then put out to sea and disappeared. The expedition had lost all coherence. Individuals or tiny groups of men looked after their own needs as best they could; most of them died. Gradually a few got to the mainland and attempted to walk back to Mexico. Only four succeeded in doing so.[14] The supply ship is said to have patrolled the coasts for a year and saw no sign of the lost explorers.

Narváez, so far as the authorities in Mexico, Santo Domingo and Spain were concerned, had vanished into a North American wilderness. The destruction of his expedition was the result of poor plan-

14. The adventures of Cabeza de Vaca and his companions, 1528–36, occupy the greater part of his *Relación:* they are briefly dealt with on pp. 192–194 below.

ning and bad luck: Narváez showed little capacity for leadership and seemed to have no very clear idea of his objectives. He was vaguely concerned to seek precious metals and pearls but had no serious plans for doing so. He might have tried to establish a group of small fortified villages, under which some agriculture could have been practiced; instead, he and his men showed the military virtues of endurance only. Cabeza de Vaca proved himself to have been more steadfast and ingenious, but did not pretend that he could have done better as the overall leader of the expedition. If the Ayllón expedition had shown that the logistics of colonization were faulty, that of Narváez demonstrated that knowledge of how to conduct a military expedition—for this is what his venture became after his landing at Tampa Bay—in North American circumstances was also inadequate.

Nonetheless, by the end of 1528 Spain had done her best to deploy her spare adventurers along the coasts running all the way from a little to the south of Cape Fear round to the Rio Grande at Pánuco. As a result, she had built up a body of information on the area which was of some appreciable value, although vague in certain essential geographical data and lacking any coherent structure. Apart from the Florida peninsula, however, the configuration of North America still remained amorphous, its mysteries and resources almost wholly unplumbed.

# CHAPTER 7

## *The Disclosure of the Eastern Coastline, 1523–1530*

ON September 7, 1522, Sebastian Elcano brought the *Victoria* into San Lucar, having completed the first voyage round the world. This notable achievement set in motion a whole new wave of expeditions which brought about a much fuller and clearer knowledge of the eastern shores of North America. Within five years it had led to the compilation and circulation in cartographic form of profiles of the coast which were to influence much of the subsequent mapping and exploration of the area down at least to the end of the sixteenth century. The geographical factor in the achievement of the Magellan-Elcano voyage which received most attention from those who were interested in commerce was the discovery of a water passage through the southern part of South America to the Pacific. This provided direct access from Europe, by western voyaging, to the Spice Islands, without penetrating the eastern zone which the Portuguese not only claimed as their own but had effectively opened up with their fleets by way of the Cape of Good Hope True, Spain claimed for herself the land and the water routes beyond the line agreed between her and Portugal in 1494; but with France and England facing the western ocean, untied by any obligation to respect the Spanish claim where it was not backed by effective occupation, and already having fishing interests in western waters, competition from them in attempting to open up direct contacts with the Far East was to be expected. The Southwest Passage through the Straits of Magellan was far away and, it was soon

learned, difficult as well; yet if there was one passage through the Americas there might be others, and, if so, they might be found in the northern as well as in the southern hemisphere.

Sebastian Cabot, in Spanish service since 1512 and chief pilot since 1518, had traversed the northern seas himself while in the English service. He was convinced that there was a Northwest Passage, though on his visit to London in 1521 he had failed to persuade the London merchants that it was worth investing money in a further attempt to find it. The *Victoria*'s return changed European attitudes about western passages. North America was seen more definitely as a barrier, but possibly a penetrable one, between Europe and the Far East.

Spain was determined to retain her lead. Five ships were already under construction in Bilbao in March 1523, for an expedition whereby García Jofre de Loaysa was to attempt to consolidate the Spanish position in the spice trade. Then, on March 27, 1523, arrangements were made for Estevão Gomes—a Portuguese pilot in the service of the Casa de Contratación (House of Trade), under Sebastian Cabot—to take a vessel on reconnaissance to search for a shorter passage to the Far East by exploring the estuaries and channels between Florida and the fishery off Newfoundland. But Loaysa did not leave until 1525, and Gomes's new ship was not ready for the sea until the autumn of 1524.[1] The consequence was that Spain lost the initiative in searching for a new passage to the Far East by way of North America.

France managed to be first in the field. By 1520, the French stake in the Newfoundland fishery was substantial, and by 1522 she had entered the profitable business of plundering Spanish ships coming from the West Indies. Jean Ango of Le Havre, amongst other entrepreneurs, had ideas of carrying French ships into open competition with the Iberian powers, even though there was a war in progress with England at the time. Then, too, Antonio Pigafetta, the Venetian who had accompanied Elcano on his circumnavigation, brought

1. The main authorities on the Spanish preparations and the Gomes voyage are J. T. Medina, *El portugues, Esteban Gómez en el servicio de España* (Santiago, Chile, 1908), and three papers by L. A. Vigneras, "El viaje de Estaban Gómez a Norte America," *Revista de Indias*, XVII (1957), 189–208; "The Voyage of Esteban Gómez from Florida to the Baccalaos," *Terrae Incognitae*, II (1970), 25–28; and "The Cartographer Diogo Ribeiro," *Imago Mundi*, XVI (1962), 77–83. There is a vigorous narrative in Morison, *European Discovery of America*, vol. I (1972), *The Northern Voyages*, pp. 326–334.

word of his experiences within a few months to the Queen Mother of France, Louise of Savoy; and when he returned to Italy, he left an account of the journey behind him. What other contacts Pigafetta made in France are not known, but as early as March 1523 plans were being drawn up for a voyage "to the place called the Indies in Cathay." The contract was signed on March 23 but was subsequently enlarged by the addition of an association of merchants, mainly Italian, who were concerned with the Lyons silk industry and hoped to tap China as a source for raw silk, and of Norman merchants whose mercantile interests were much wider. The key figure in the original contract and in command of the expedition which emerged from it was the Florentine Giovanni da Verrazzano (Jean de Vérrazane), for some time a French resident, who evidently also received a commission from Francis I authorizing him to make the voyage.[2]

Verrazzano was ready in the summer of 1523. With four ships he sailed out into the Atlantic, where he almost met with total disaster. Two ships were lost, two put back to Brittany. The probability is that his voyage was begun too late to follow safely the route used by the Newfoundland fishing fleet and so encountered adverse westerly gales. When Verrazzano had regrouped his resources, he set out again in a single caravel of perhaps 100 tons, La Dauphine, on a more southerly track. On January 17, 1524, the Madeiras were briefly sighted. He ran down the latitude of 32° N., evidently expecting to reach the shores of Florida already explored by Spain at this latitude; but La Dauphine was put off her course by a storm in late February and sighted land on March 20, being somewhat unsure of

2. The contract of March 23, 1523, was first printed by Michel Mollat, "Choix de documents relatifs à la Normandie pour servir à l'histoire du commerce maritime (xve–xvie siècles)", Mélanges de la Société de l' Histoire de Normandie, 6th series (Rouen-Paris, 1958), 153–159. The authoritative text of Verrazzano's narrative letter to Francis I (the manuscript of which is now in the Pierpont Morgan Library, New York) first appeared in A. Bacchiani, "Giovanni da Verrazzano e le sue scoperte nell' America settentrionale (1524) secondo l'inedito codice sincrono Cellàre di Roma," Bolletino della Reale Società Geografica Italiana, XLVI (1909), 1274–1323. It was edited in English by E. H. Hall, "The Voyage of Giovanni da Verrazzano 1424," in 15th Annual Report, 1910, of the American Scenic and Historic Preservation Society, Appendix A (Albany, N.Y., 1910), and in French by C. A. Julien, Les Français en Amérique pendant la première moitié du XVIe siècle (Paris, 1948). A new translation, with facsimile and transcription, is in Lawrence C. Wroth, The Voyages of Giovanni da Verrazzano, 1524–1528 (New Haven and London, 1970). This also contains the authoritative account of the voyage and its consequences. Unless new evidence appears, it is definitive.

her position. Verrazzano claimed that the latitude was 34°—we can take it that this was not far from Cape Fear but some little way to the south. Verrazzano wished to get back to the latitude of his original course and worked his way southward some 160 miles in order to do so. Then the somewhat featureless coast and the fear of intruding on territory which the Spaniards might already hold made him turn northward again. He made some contact with the Cusabo Indians and showed signs of his intelligent and humane approach to the Amerindian population in his comments on them; he also showed some appreciation of the natural features of the American landscape in praising its beauty, its fine vegetation, and, in this instance, its good climate.

The first major discovery was made when he was between 35 and 36 degrees on March 25. As he noted afterwards, "we . . . found there an isthmus one mile wide and about two hundred miles long, in which we could see the eastern sea from the ship, half way between west and north. This is, doubtless, the one which goes round the tip of India, China and Cathay."[3] This illusion of a new and narrower Panama-type isthmus was conveyed to him by the barrier-island chain of the Carolina Outer Banks, extending from 50 miles north of Cape Fear almost to the modern Virginia state line, with Pamlico Sound, Roanoke Sound, Albemarle Sound and Currituck Inlet making up, in his mind, a picture of the Pacific Ocean within sight from masthead in the Atlantic. This grand assumption was to remain from his own time until late in the century a geographic theory which substantially influenced not only Italian, French and English cartography but also the pattern of subsequent exploration. It must be said of Verrazzano that his coastal survey cannot have been a very thorough one—shoals would have prevented him from making it so—since there were a number of inlets through the Outer Banks through which he could himself have tested his discovery.

Other contacts with the Indians on the coast—in one of which a young Indian boy was seized as a trophy to be brought back to France—marked successive visits to the shore as *La Dauphine* made her way northward. Trees, grapevines and other vegetation were remarked on in the lands which he named Arcadia and Lorraine from about midway up the Virginia eastern shore to New Jersey,

3. Wroth, *Voyages of Verrazzano*, p. 136.

though he made no extended reconnaissance of any inlets until he came almost to 40°. There he made his second major discovery, that of the Narrows. The mouth of the Hudson was to evade subsequent explorers until 1609, but Verrazzano found it before it was lost sight of once more. He spoke of Manhattan Island (as it was to become) as "a very agreeable place between two small but prominent hills; between them a very wide river, deep at its mouth, flowed out into the sea."[4] Penetrating the river in his shallop, he found friendly Indians in many canoes and an excellent harbor. He called the region Angoulême. He did not, apparently, regard the Hudson as a possible route through North America.

Then, passing along the shore of Long Island, he noted Block Island, which he named Aloysia after Queen Louise, and worked his way along the southern shore of New England, finding and entering Narragansett Bay. By this time his ship needed some attention and his men some rest; he is likely to have found an appropriate place for this in sheltered Newport Harbor. The shore nearby and the waters round the ship were soon visited by large numbers of Indians, who proved most friendly and accommodating. Presumably Wampanoag (though perhaps with some Narragansett among them), at this point in the spring they were coming down to the shore for their summer fishing and collecting. They proved willing to give the Europeans some maize (though they must have been near the end of their winter reserves) and other food, likely to have consisted chiefly of deerflesh and some seafood, taking little in exchange except blue and red bells and other trinkets. Verrazzano paid a good deal of attention to the Indians, noting their copper ornaments as possible clues to mineral wealth inland; and his educated observations, brief as they are, are basic in the ethnography of sixteenth-century North America. Relations with them remained wholly friendly. The wide expanse of the bay led him to explore it thoroughly, noting five islands within it and its value as a fleet anchorage, but finding, too, that it did not offer a water passage into the interior. His Refuge (Refugio), as he called it, remained a goal for later navigators which would not be rediscovered for nearly a century.

After fifteen days *La Dauphine* was ready to set sail. Verrazzano

4. *Ibid.,* p. 137.

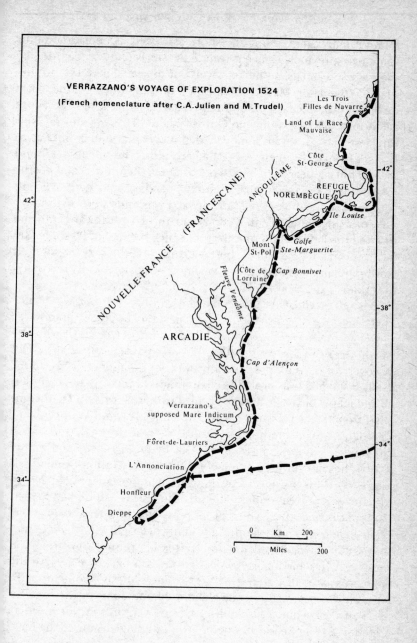

**VERRAZZANO'S VOYAGE OF EXPLORATION 1524**

(French nomenclature after C.A. Julien and M. Trudel)

Les Trois
Filles de Navarre

Land of La Race
Mauvaise

Côte
St-George

REFUGE

NOREMBÈGUE

Ile Louise

NOUVELLE-FRANCE (FRANCESCANE)

ANGOULÊME

Mont
St-Pol

Golfe
Ste-Marguerite

Côte de
Lorraine

Cap Bonnivet

*Fleuve Vendôme*

ARCADIE

Cap d'Alençon

Verrazzano's
supposed Mare Indicum

Fôret-de-Lauriers

L'Annonciation

Honfleur

Dieppe

42°

38°

34°

42°

38°

34°

0      Km      200

0      Miles      200

found it impossible to hug the shore as closely as he had done for some time previously since it trended easterly and was guarded by shallows and shoals, so he kept well out to sea. When, beyond the islands (the later Martha's Vineyard and Nantucket), the coast turned north, similar conditions prevailed. He reached the shore again only after crossing the Gulf of Maine. How far up the New England coast this was cannot be definitely ascertained, but Casco Bay has been favored on reasonable grounds. The Indians he found thereabouts appeared to him to be savage in their habits and hostile in attitude (perhaps Abenaki hunting bands?), and he moved off again as soon as possible. Many attractive islands were sighted off the coast of Maine. Then Verrazzano turned northward until he reached the latitude of Cape Breton, which he put at 50°, some 200 miles too far to the north; here he turned eastward and sighted Newfoundland. Finally, his stores almost gone, he rapidly recrossed the Atlantic to reach Dieppe on July 8, 1524.

This quick, efficient, and significant reconnaissance gave France a certain lead in the race for a western passage. But the famous letter which Verrazzano sent to Francis I when he arrived dealt with the North American shore rather than possible passages through it. The discovery of the supposed isthmus was not mentioned in the letter itself, although it was probably communicated verbally and included on the map which Verrazzano or his brother Gerolamo soon compiled from the coastal surveys and which is likely to have been kept confidential for some time, in France at least. In the letter he did not hold out hopes of reaching Asia by any easy, certain route. Rather, he concentrated on elaborating the conclusion—one which was to give his voyage some long-term importance—that North America was a great, independent continent, which he had named La Francescane (the Nova Francia of his brother's map, New France), and which was important in its own right. "He alleges and shows it," said a friend not long after his return, "greater than Europe, Africa and a part of Asia . . . and this exclusive of what the Spaniards have discovered."[5] Verrazzano's thesis about the isthmus, which we may suspect he elaborated only some little time after his return, gave him a case for urging new ventures in North America, but it is clear he was not tied to this one single route to the East.

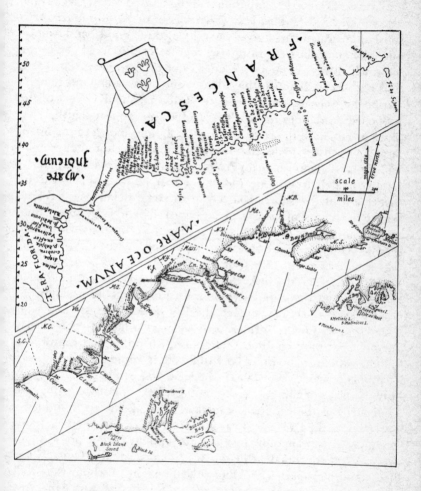

The French Profile of Eastern North America: Vesconte de Maggiolo's Map of Verrazzano's route in 1527, and a modern map of the coast traversed, arranged for comparison. (After W. F. Ganong, *Crucial Maps in the Early Cartography of Canada, III,* Transactions of the Royal Society of Canada, 3d ser., sec. II, XXV [1931]. Reprinted by permission of the University of Toronto Press.

The Verrazzano voyage had been rapidly prepared and swiftly executed; the Gomes voyage was begun in a more leisurely fashion. His ship, commissioned in 1523, did not come from the Bilbao yards until the following year and then had to be fitted out in La Coruña. *Nuestra Señora de la Anunciada* was a vessel of 75 tons, carrying a substantial armament, a good quantity of trade goods, and twenty-nine men, including a Portuguese interpreter who had been to the Moluccas. Estevão Gomes set out in her on September 24, 1524, took her efficiently across the Atlantic, and then, sailing through the Caribbean, set off from Santiago de Cuba for the discovery of the supposed passage to the Pacific.[6] It does not appear that he paid much attention to the coast of Florida, already known to the Spaniards, or even to the disappointingly continuous shore between 30 and about 40 degrees north. From the southern New England coast (approximately from Point Judith onward), he made a very careful inspection of the shore, charting it in some detail. We have no narrative account of his voyage and must depend largely on somewhat conflicting map evidence. It is clear that, once past Cape Cod —which Gomes was the first to locate and put on the map—contact was established with the Indians. Trinkets in the form of bells, combs, scissors and a little cloth were dispensed to them either in trade or as gifts and, possibly, in return for some information.

At a great river, first named the Rio de Santa Maria and later Gomes River (in the form Rio de Gamas), which can be clearly identified as the Penobscot, he enticed on board and captured a number of Indians to bring back to Spain. It would appear that, like Champlain many years later, when Gomes penetrated the great estuary of the Penobscot he thought that here at last was a possible equivalent of the Strait of Magellan. Instead, the river suddenly narrowed at the Fall Line, near modern Bangor, to become a moderately sized stream only. Just as, at this point, Champlain was met with a great concourse of Penobscot Indians, so must Gomes have been; and he took back a shipload, fifty-eight of whom were still alive when he returned to Spain. We are told in one source that this occurred at 42°, but the maps put the Penobscot at approximately

6. The view that Gomes sailed from north to south (retained by Morison, *Northern Voyages*, pp. 326–334), appears to be now superseded by Vigneras's papers, which argue, almost conclusively, that the voyage was from south to north, a view adopted here.

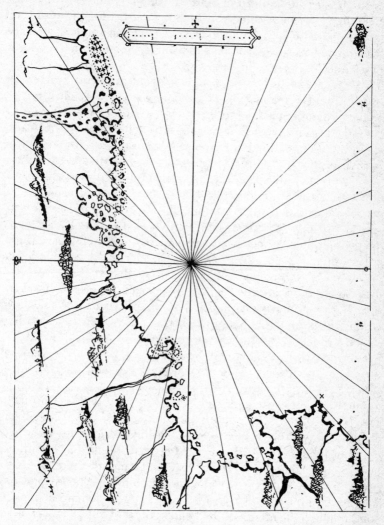

The Discovery of New England by Estevão Gomes, 1525.
(After Alonso de Santa Cruz, *Islario*)

its correct latitude of some 44° 30′ N. Gomes in seizing the Indians was repeating the pattern of Gaspar Corte Real in 1501. He may thereafter have penetrated the Bay of Fundy, though he did not record its termination as an inlet. Then, sailing some way up the coast of modern Nova Scotia, he took off for Spain from Cape Race, arriving at La Coruña on August 21, 1525.

Just as Verrazzano had brought valuable information on the North American mainland and a theory about an isthmus, but no report of a direct passage to the Pacific, so too Gomes could offer no hope of such a passage to Spain. At best, he may have been able to suggest the possibility of a portage from the headwaters of the Penobscot. From the Spanish point of view, North America had a negative value only; it appeared to be simply a barrier which shut off western Europe, in this case France and England, from hope of direct contact with further Asia, and this was something of an advantage to Spain. The Indians brought back by Gomes may have opened up the prospect to some Spaniards of a useful slave trade, but opinion in Spain was turning against such gross exploitation of Amerindians (though not of negroes), so that the captives, first distributed to private speculators, were taken into royal guardianship. Baptized, they were parceled out to guardians who may have treated them somewhat better as Christian servants than as heathen slaves. Three were trained as interpreters in case Spain wished to resume activity in what is now New England, but nothing came of this. The chief legacy of the expedition was a new map of North America.

The Portuguese cartographer Diego Ribeiro was at La Coruña to meet Gomes in 1525 and triumphantly carried off copies of his charts. These Ribeiro incorporated on his world map[7] as a new coastline for eastern North America between 30° and 45° N., with the inscription: "Land discovered by Estevan Gómez this year, 1525, by order of his Majesty." A new northward-pointing cape (Cape Cod) was placed between 38 and 40 degrees north, somewhat too far south; though the mouth of the Penobscot, at about 44°, was not far wrong. Subsequent cartographers tended to pull the cape southward, and did not allow sufficiently for the long, east-west trend in

7. Vigneras, "The Cartographer Diogo Ribeiro," pp. 77–82. The map is reproduced in H. Harrisse, *Découverte et évolution cartographique de Terre-Neuve* (1900), plate X.

the coast from the mouth of the Hudson to southern Massachusetts, so that it became confused with Cape Henry, placed rather too far north, as the Spaniards came to explore the coast in the vicinity of Chesapeake Bay. In this way it was assimilated into the *padron real,* the official Spanish sailing directions and set of maps, and so helped to make up the characteristic Spanish profile of eastern North America. Alonso de Santa Cruz compiled his *Islario* from such official records about 1540 and included in it detailed charts from Gomes's discovery, giving much information on the coast from Cape Cod to Nova Scotia, of excellent quality for their time.[8] In his inscriptions, "The land which the pilot Estevan Gomez discovered" is centered on the Penobscot (later vulgarized to the River of Gamas), while modern Massachusetts is assimilated with the "Land discovered by the pilot Ayllón," which in fact did not extend much beyond the limits of modern South Carolina, that is, south of 34°.

Spain turned instead to further exploration of the South American coast, and the great expedition which Sebastian Cabot led, so unsuccessfully, to the Plate in 1526 submerged further concern with passages through or round North America. In France, too, the Verrazzano voyage had less impact than might have been expected. During 1524 Francis I was deeply involved with Italy and is unlikely to have taken a great interest in the long letter which Verrazzano had sent him after his return. Moreover, Francis himself was taken prisoner after his disastrous defeat at Pavia on February 26, 1525, at the hands of the forces of the emperor Charles V. The explorer was left to his own resources. He appears to have made contact with Henry VIII and may have visited the English court, though he cannot have received much encouragement. He did leave a map in England, possibly one drawn by his brother Gerolamo, which the king retained and which, though it has not survived, clearly showed his isthmus.[9] He was also in communication with Portugal. The publication in 1525 in Paris of Pigafetta's *Le voyage et nauigation faict par les Espaignols es Isles de Mollucques*[10] revived mercantile interest in France in voyages to Asia, but this time toward the Spice Islands

8. Alonso de Santa Cruz, *Islario de todas las islas del mundo circa 1540,* edited by Antonio Blásquez (Madrid, 1922), figs. 5 and 106–108.

9. See Wroth, *Voyages of Verrazzano,* pp. 162–163, 166–168.

10. Reproduced in facsimile with a translation by Paula Spurlin Paige as *The Voyage of Magellan. The Journal of Antonio Pigafetta* (Englewood Cliffs, N.J., 1969).

rather than China. At length, under the patronage of the admiral of France, Philippe Chabot, a syndicate was formed in April 1526 by which Giovanni da Verrazzano and his brother Gerolamo agreed to take three vessels on a voyage to the Moluccas. There is no clear account of this voyage. It appears that the brothers each tried to pass the Cape of Good Hope but were unable to do so. The third ship under an unnamed commander did reach the East Indies but suffered disaster in the end. The Verrazzanos turned back to search the coast of Brazil, and returned to France in 1527.[11]

By that time the English were also in the field. Apparently the visit of Giovanni da Verrazzano, if it took place, and the map left with the king, at length helped to lead to an English venture to follow up the earlier searches for a western passage.[12] The objective was to renew the search for a Northwest Passage which had been attempted in 1508–9 and projected in 1521. Joined to this aim was a subsidiary one. If the Passage did not exist or was impracticable, then the coastline to the south should be investigated with the aid of the Verrazzano map and his isthmus perhaps also sought for. We have very little direct evidence on the background of the expedition but it seems clear that it was largely organized and financed under the king's auspices, though merchant capital may also have been employed in it. Its commander, John Rut, was a captain in the king's service who normally commanded the royal wine ship, the *Mary Guildford*, when she made her annual voyage to Bordeaux late each year to fetch wine for the court. During the summer she usually lay in the Thames in charge of shipkeepers; but in 1527 she was put in Rut's charge, with another ship, the *Samson*, for an expedition to North America.

Leaving the Thames on May 20 and Plymouth on June 10, the two vessels apparently followed the fishermen's track to Newfoundland, but turned northward along the Labrador coast on entering American waters. They parted company in a storm on July 1 and the *Samson* disappeared. Nothing is known of her fate. The sources are somewhat corrupt, so that it is not clear how far north the *Mary Guildford* was when she met icebergs on July 3. Unless she was by chance hemmed in by floating ice, it is difficult to accept the later

11. Wroth, *Voyages of Verrazzano*, pp. 219–235; with a more detailed account in Jean Habert, *La vie et les voyages de Jean de Verrazane* (Ottawa, 1964).

12. Quinn, *England and the Discovery of America*, pp. 171–182.

report that men died on board from cold. The figure of 53° for her northing could be a miswriting for 58°; a figure of 64° is also given. At 58° N. she would be in the vicinity of Cape Chidley, not far from the opening of Hudson Strait, roughly where Cabot is likely to have reached in 1508; at 64° she would have been well up the coast of Baffin Island in Davis Strait. In any case she turned south, and on his way Rut explored some of the Labrador harbors, putting in at an inlet near Cape de Bas in 52°. This might appear to be the harbor, St. Lewis Inlet, and the cape, Cape St. Charles or Cape St. Lewis, but little reliance can be placed on these identifications. After waiting ten days in case the *Samson* came in view, the *Mary Guildford* made her way to St. John's Harbour. Here Rut and others found means to send letters home by one of the French ships fishing there and so leave some documentary evidence on the voyage.

The vessel then began her long voyage down the east coast, following in reverse Verrazzano's route. How thorough and successful the search was for Verrazzano's Refugio, his great river in Angoulême, and the isthmus he had named Verrazanio, we cannot tell as the information is sparse. Her pilot, an Italian from Piedmont, was killed by Indians when he went ashore at one point. The ship eventually passed through the Florida Strait and reached the Mona Channel, meeting a Spanish ship at Mona on November 19.

Whether the visit to the Spanish West Indies was accidental or deliberate we do not know. So far as we can tell, the *Mary Guildford* was the first English vessel to have penetrated there. The English proved willing to talk freely to the crew of the Spanish vessel at Mona. Their task had been to reach the country of the Great Khan —in whose existence as a reigning monarch the English apparently still believed—and they had been sent out on this long voyage by King Henry. They gave some indications of their struggle with the ice in northern latitudes—at one point the sea was said to have boiled, but we can perhaps put this down to difficulties in translation. The ship later tried to enter the harbor of Santo Domingo to trade with woolen cloth, linen and pewter, intended it would seem to have been sold in Cathay in return for victuals of which they were short. As they made to enter the inner harbor, however, a warning shot turned the *Mary Guildford* away. She then put in at Ocoa and took some food by force, going on to barter peacefully at the isolated settlement of San German in southwest Puerto Rico before

embarking on her return voyage. This was evidently made safely and speedily, since she was able to set out again in the autumn of 1528 for Bordeaux on her wine-lading voyage under her usual commander, John Rut.

We have no knowledge of what information she brought home apart from the fragments already noted. No trace of surveys has been found, nor are there any indications of novel discoveries along the great stretch of coast she had traversed. With her return, however, the English were fully apprised of the great latitudinal extent of eastern North America and were now in a position, if they wished, to make a more detailed inspection of the coast. Yet the voyage does not appear to have been followed up. It rounds off the sequence of three voyages within three years under the auspices of France, Spain and England, respectively, which provided confirmation that North America was a continuous landmass extending from the 60s of north latitude down to the Caribbean without any obvious major break in the coastline.

Meanwhile, having failed to enter the Indian Ocean and reach the Moluccas by the route normally followed by the Portuguese, the Verrazzano brothers turned in 1528 to the west. They set out to examine the coast of Central America for the same purpose. We have few details of this voyage, but, after a survey of the Florida peninsula (probably the eastern side only), the vessels made their way through the Bahamas apparently to Trinidad and then along the north coast of South America and round past Darien. At some point Giovanni da Verrazzano was killed by Indians and the expedition broke up.[13] Gerolamo came home and the ship, *La Flamengue*, brought in a cargo of brazilwood, apparently picked up in the West Indies. It was Gerolamo who played the principal part in disseminating the geographical ideas and discoveries of his brother through his maps. Probably one of Gerolamo's maps lay behind the important world map of Vesconte de Maggiolo (1527) where the Verrazzanian profile of eastern North America is shown. His own major map (1529) is at least equally important. Giovanni da Verrazzano's letter on the voyage of 1524 appeared in 1556.[14] Many other cartographers, especially those of the Norman school in the 1540s, came under the

13. Wroth, *Voyages of Verrazzano*, pp. 236–262; also Habert, *Vie et voyages de Jean de Verrazane*.

14. G. B. Ramusio, *Viaggi et navigationi*, III (1556), fols. 420–422.

Verrazzanian influence,[15] which continued to have considerable impact down to the opening years of the seventeenth century.

These three great coasting voyages destroyed many illusions about the insubstantial character of the new continent which faced western Europe across the ocean. It could no longer be seen as a limited, perhaps multi-insular, landmass: its magnitude and its apparent unity had been clearly demonstrated, though the voyages did not, of course, end the search for passages through North America or round it. Even when we narrow our perspective to the eastern shoreline, the voyages enabled European monarchs, entrepreneurs and geographers to form some general impressions of the nature of the new lands and threw some light on their possibilities for economic exploitation.

Verrazzano certainly brought vividly to France a picture of a varied, lovely and richly endowed land, which stretched far beyond the limits he had previously imagined and whose variety offered many possibilities for exploitation—even if it was not the silk-producing Cathay for which he had initially sought—so that henceforth to Francis I and others who saw Verrazzano's letter to the king this New France overseas appeared to offer immense potentialities. Throughout the twenty years after Verrazzano's return the French king believed this to be true, though in the end he was disillusioned by the result of the enterprises of 1534–43. Then too, after 1556, Verrazzano's letter was in print in Italian and could be read by all who might have an interest in the western ocean and the lands which lay beyond it.

We have no similar report of Gomes to his Spanish masters, but it is clear from the emphasis which Spanish historians placed on his voyage that his picture of North America as another Spain across the ocean was well received. Its grapes and, he thought, its olives, its deer and fish of all sorts made up an attractive picture. Most interesting was his revelation of its human potential. The slaves he brought back proved something of an embarrassment, but they indicated that there might well be an indigenous labor force available in the area we know as New England for Spanish *conquistadores*

15. R. A. Skelton, "The Influence of Verrazzano on 16th Century Cartography," *Giornate Commemorative de Giovanni da Verrazzano* (Florence, 1970), pp. 58–59, 65–66; Wroth, *Voyages of Verrazzano*, pp. 165–216.

if they were to venture there. At the same time, the reports of Gomes do not seem to have offset the cumulative effects of the Ponce de León, Ayllón and Narváez disasters (1521–28), which brought Spain to the point of writing off the southeastern shores of North America, at least, as wholly inhospitable to white men and their native inhabitants as wholly inimical. We do not know how much or how little they picked up about Verrazzano's reports. Their attitude did not begin to change again until after the reappearance of Cabeza de Vaca in 1536.

The English explorers, who had made the longest run of all down the coast, have left us no surviving reports. But there was no doubt in the minds of the Spaniards with whom they spoke in the Caribbean that they had experienced exciting events, a great variety of climatic conditions, and had learned a great deal of what North America was like—they were naturally more reticent in speaking of what they thought of the land's economic potentialities. The English, too, learned rapidly of the French achievement, but no record of any attempt to exploit the information gathered on the John Rut voyage has yet come to light.

What of Portugal? We do not know whether Gomes conveyed to his native country any of the information on North America he had gathered for Spain, but the Rio de Gamas (Gomes River)—the Penobscot—which soon began to appear on the maps indicated that a Portuguese had been there. Not long before his voyage, Portugal had been engaged in obscure colonizing attempts in the vicinity of Cape Breton; after their failure, there is no evidence of further Portuguese initiatives in North America in the short term.

England, Spain and Portugal were all inclined to accept the new information about North America so far as they were separately aware of it, but to take no action as a result. The joint exploitation of the codfishery and its gradual extension into whale fishing and fur trading could go on without either official or corporate ventures. France alone had been fired by a genuine desire to investigate further, to make sure that what Verrazzano and other informants about North America reported had substance, and to establish whether or not a New France needed to be, or could be, created in the west.

# CHAPTER 8

## *The Inland Voyages—Cartier and Roberval*

THE Verrazzano voyage of 1524 had given France a considerable advantage over the other western states in the relatively clear and full picture it had provided of the eastern North American coastline—though we cannot be certain how far this knowledge was disseminated outside court and Norman mercantile circles. The vigor and versatility of the regional French fishing communities in exploiting the Newfoundland codfisheries on the Newfoundland Banks, on the inshore fishery along the east and south coasts of the island, and in the Cape Breton region had also accumulated an especially full picture of local conditions there, even if the fishermen were probably reticent about the precise areas in which they caught most fish and were generally not inclined to speculate extensively on the geographical setting of their activities. France too had been active in voyaging to Brazil from 1504 onward, and it is clear that by 1530 she had gained much information on trading with the Indians there. She was well placed, therefore, for further explorations in the North Atlantic. We may perhaps think of the Cartier voyages as being one expression of the rivalry of Brittany and Normandy for the gains of the overseas world. Verrazzano's had been primarily a Norman effort; Cartier's was to be primarily a Breton one. But each had the backing of Francis I, and each represented more than mere provincial economic interests.

There is nothing which associates Jacques Cartier definitively with the Verrazzano voyage, even if it would appear that he was

familiar with its results. Yet Cartier himself clearly demonstrated—by his confidence in his first and subsequent navigations across the Atlantic—previous on the spot acquaintance with the Newfoundland fisheries. He was also well informed about Brazil, most probably through personal contact with the Brazilian Indians, or by close contact with other Frenchmen who had been there. It would seem that his curiosity (or possibly that of other Frenchmen who had been on the Newfoundland coast) had been aroused by the opening of the Strait of Belle Isle, and that one major objective of his 1534 voyage was to ascertain whether this was the opening through the western landmass that Verrazzano had failed to disclose but which nonetheless might exist. The somewhat mysterious "Discorso d'un gran capitano," first published in 1556, would appear to represent French knowledge of the eastern end of the Strait about 1529 or 1530. It recorded that in the Strait was the Bay of Castles (*Golfo de Castelli*), where there was "a large wooden enclosure" (*una gran serradura di legno*).[1] The character of the enclosure remains wholly mysterious. Cartier's voyage was from the beginning intended to explore the Strait. A document of March 19, 1534, describes him as having been commissioned by the king "to voyage and go to the New Lands and to pass the Strait of the Bay of Castles" (*allez aux Terres Neuffves, passez le destroict de la baye des Chasteaulx*), where, according to another document of the same month, he would go "to discover certain islands and lands where it is said he should find great quantities of gold and other rich things."[2] The expedition of 1534 was then intended to disclose a passage to Asia, but also to reveal lands rich in gold and other things along the way.

Francis I, in the intervals of his conflict with Spain in Europe, turned from time to time to plans for challenging the Spanish monopoly in the west and that of the Portuguese in the east. The objectives behind his support of the Verrazzano and Cartier ventures alike were to supplant Spanish domination of the western lands by a balancing French domination of the slowly unfolding

1. Giovanni Battista Ramusio, *Viaggi et navigationi*, 3 vols. (Venice 1550–59), III (1556). Reprinted and discussed in Bernard G. Hoffman, "Account of a Voyage Conducted in 1529 to the New World, Africa, Madagascar, and Sumatra," translated from the Italian, with Notes and Comments, in *Ethnohistory*, X (1963), 1–79, especially 14, 34, 53–54.

2. H. P. Biggar (ed.), *Collection of Documents Concerning Cartier and Roberval* (Ottawa, 1940), pp. 42–43.

North American continent and also to use it as a stepping stone, if not a water passage, to Asia. Jacques Cartier, an experienced seaman, was apparently introduced to the king by Jean le Veneur, bishop of Lisieux, grand almoner to the king, as a person who could be relied on to conduct an effective western expedition. Le Veneur had accompanied Francis I when, at an interview at Marseilles in October 1533, Pope Clement VII gave it as his opinion that the bull *Inter caetera* upon which Spanish claims to a monopoly of the New World were largely based applied only to lands already known in 1493, and "not to lands subsequently discovered by other monarchs."[3] While this did not abrogate the bull of 1493, it gave Francis I at least a pretext for his forward policy in the west which could be used to oppose the official Spanish view in Europe. Cartier was given royal authority to take with him three ships of 60 tons each, victualed for fifteen months, and to impress seamen at St. Malo if he needed them.[4] The length of time for which they were victualed indicates that it was hoped they would get to Asia and return safely again.

Cartier left St. Malo with two 60-ton vessels on April 20 and returned on September 5 following. He showed his mastery of Atlantic sailing by a twenty-day voyage, at the end of which he made a landfall at Bonavista in eastern Newfoundland.[5] A visit to Funk Island brought an addition to their stores: a quantity of salted seabirds, mainly great auks. On May 27 they tried to enter the Bay of Castles, that is the Strait of Belle Isle, but their progress was blocked by icebergs and they were not able to enter it until June. Cartier worked his way carefully from bay to bay along the northern shore, investigated the inlets which were soon to afford shelter to the whalers from the Basque coasts, but found the shore itself repellent

3. Baron de La Chapelle, "Jean Le Veneur et le Canada," *Nova Francia*, VI (Paris, 1931), 341–343; C. A. Julien, *Les voyages de découverte et les premiers établissements* (1948), p. 116; Bernard G. Hoffman, *Cabot to Cartier* (Toronto, 1961), pp. 112–113.

4. Biggar, *Collection* (1930), pp. 44–45.

5. The best edition of the texts in French and English is H. P. Biggar, *The Voyages of Jacques Cartier* (Ottawa, 1924), though the French edition in C. A. Julien, *Les Français en Amérique pendant le premier moitier du XVIe siècle* (Paris, 1946), represents in its notes more recent scholarship. Biggar, *Voyages* (1924), pp. 3–81, covers the first voyage. Though written in the third person, the narrative is likely to be Cartier's own, revised for the king's use after his return. This is rejected by a number of authorities by whom Jean Poulet is preferred as the author (see Julien, *Les Français en Amérique*, p. 21; Biggar, *Voyages*, p. 93).

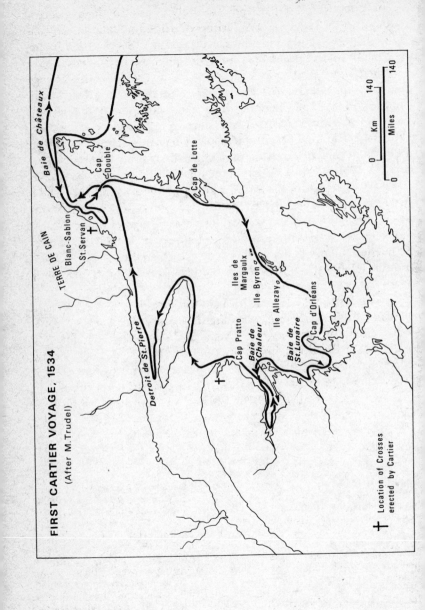

**FIRST CARTIER VOYAGE, 1534**
(After M. Trudel)

Baie de Châteaux

Cap Double

TERRE DE CAIN

Blanc-Sablon
St.Servan

Cap de Lotte

Detroit de St.Pierre

Iles de Margaulx

Ile Byron

Ile Allezay

Cap d'Orléans

Cap Pratto

Baie de Chaleur

Baie de St.Lunaire

✝ Location of Crosses
erected by Cartier

0    Km    140

0    Miles    140

and useless, "the land that God gave to Cain"—an epithet which has endured. At what is now Sketatica Bay they found a codfishing vessel from La Rochelle, which indicates that Cartier was by no means the first to investigate the Strait. On June 15 they turned southward across the Strait and worked their way down the west coast of Newfoundland, the first known exploration of that shore, finding large cod offshore near Bear Head, and taking off westward on June 24. Bird Rocks, Brion and the Magdalen Islands led the ships past haunts of numerous seabirds and walrus until, on July 1, mainland was sighted (as they thought) to the west. This was Prince Edward Island, along the northern shore of which he coasted for some way and then, without discovering that it was an island, turned northward to reach the authentic mainland at Miramichi Bay on July 2. The supposed mainland looked green and fertile—an impression that continued after July 2. On July 3, Cartier began the systematic and detailed inspection of the large opening at which he found himself, Chaleur Bay. He examined the shores of the bay until July 12, when he finally decided that it did not, in fact, lead into the interior. The water and air were warm, the soil was level, wooded, and producing grass and fruit, so that the outlook was very favorable. For the next ten days they worked their way up the coast of the Gaspé peninsula, noticing as they went the fine fields and meadows near the shore. They set up a cross to mark the entrance to Gaspé Harbour, then set out northward from it, on what proved to be the first lap of their homeward journey, on July 25.

Cartier had encountered Indians in birchbark canoes off the Labrador coast, apparently Montagnais who had come up from the southwest to take seal; but he had no close contact with Amerindians until he entered Chaleur Bay. This contained a large number of Micmac in their canoes, who had come to the coast for the summer fishing. On July 6 a gathering of Indians invited his men to come on shore, "holding up to us some furs on sticks." Cartier was exploring in his longboat and was afraid to do so; indeed, to get away from the canoes which were closing in on him, he fired several shots and frightened them off. The following day relations were established, the Indians "making signs to us that they had come to barter with us; and held up some furs of small value." Two Frenchmen went ashore, offering them knives and other goods, "and the two parties traded together."

This was the beginning of the North American fur trade so far as we have any record, but it may well be that the willingness to trade, if Cartier reported correctly, arose from earlier contacts with Europeans of which we have no record. Otherwise we must conclude that in the Chaleur-Gaspé area, Indians of various tribes came in summer to trade with each other, for furs among other things, since a ceremonial receiving and giving of gifts, as opposed to direct exchange for commercial purposes, would not have taken place so rapidly or informally. Once confidence was established, the French bartered freely with some three hundred Indians, who danced around them as they discarded their fur clothing in exchange for French trinkets and weapons. When they moved on to Gaspé, they encountered a further large group of Indians—again estimated at about three hundred—who came to fish. These people were very different from the Micmac. They had come from a distance, had no furs to trade and little clothing. Their fishing nets, the maize and dried plums they had with them for food, and their willingness to dance and celebrate the gifts of knives, beads, combs and suchlike which Cartier gave them, as also their capacity for stealing from the visitors, were all recorded. Their chief came in a canoe to harangue the Frenchmen about the cross they had set up after a ceremony as a sign of French possession; they seized him and his canoe, and arranged to take two young Indians, whom they thought to be his sons, to France. This he accepted and gifts were exchanged. Cartier later learned from his captives that the chief who was taken and released was Donnaconna, from far upstream; the other two being the chief's son Dom Agaya and another young man, Taignoagny. It occurred to him that if they could be taught to speak French, a linguistic bridge might well disclose significant information on their homeland.

Cartier's course on July 25 took him northeastward to the south coast of Anticosti, so that he missed the entrance to the St. Lawrence River. He followed the island to its eastern extremity and, rounding Cape East, worked along its north shore until it became clear that a strait lay between the island and the mainland, which he called St. Peter's Strait. He then crossed to the mainland shore, following it eastward to Natashkwan Point, where he left the land and sailed due east until he picked up first the Newfoundland coast and then the western end of the Strait of Belle Isle. He anchored

1.   The First Delineation of North America as a Separate Continent, in Martin Waldseemüller's *Universalis Cosmographia*, 1567.

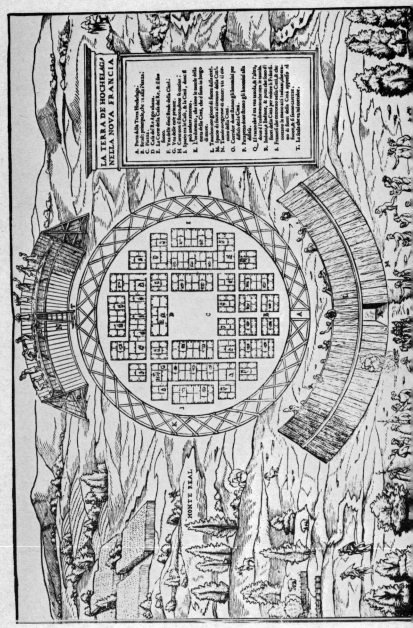

2. Iroquois Indian Settlement at Hochelaga. After Cartier's description in 1535. Ramusio, *Navigationi et viaggi*, III, 1556, fol. 446v.-447.)

...ing the French Post of Charlesfort on Liboure Island between the mainland and Parris
... Santa Elena (Port Royal) Sound, 1562. (T. de Bry, *America,* part ii, 1591, plate 9.
... said to represent the building of La Caroline in 1564, this drawing fits best with the
...struction. La Caroline, as the next illustrations show, was not on an island.)

...ing La Caroline (Fort Caroline), the French fort erected on the south bank of the St.
...ver (the River of May) in 1564 and destroyed by the Spaniards in 1565. (T. de Bry,
...II, 1591, pl. 10, after a drawing by Jacques Le Moyne.)

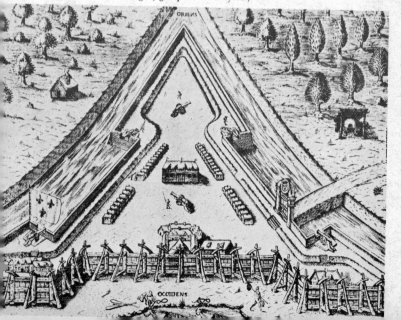

SOVRSE DE LA
RIVIÈRE DE MAY

BRAS DE MER

John Carter Brown
Library

LE PORT DE L'ENTRÉE

5. La Caroline. (*Coppie d'une lettre venant de la Floride*, 1565.)

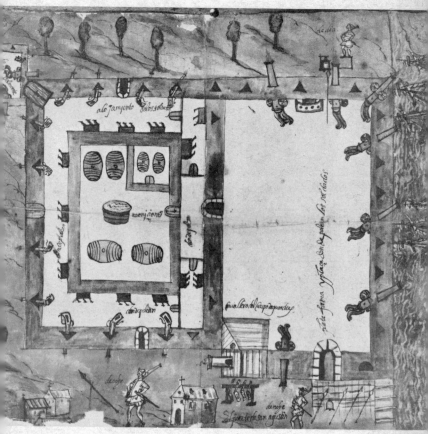

The following labels appear within the plan:

*a le jamyento de los soldados*

*cerij nones*

*caxa de plan*

*cerij nones*

*candeplan*

*guia clero de clacapo dagoardas*

*pla la forma ygnfaca con de pasa por los de santes*

*de nobe*

*de nobe*

*S Guerterde san agustin*

The presidio of San Agustín, 1577. (A.G.I., Mapas y Planos, México 44. This has usually dated 1595, but L. A. Vigneras, in "Fortificiones de la Florida," *Anuario de Estudios Amer-*, XVI, 1958, 4, argued that this is an earlier plan included by mistake among the 1595 ials. (Reprinted by permission of the Archivo General de Indias, Sevilla.)

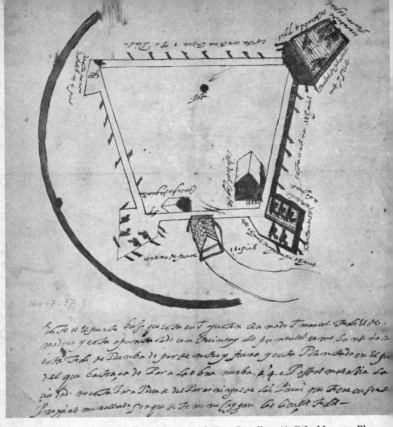

7. San Mateo Fort, on the site of the French Fort Caroline. (A.G.I., Mapas y Planos México 45.)

8. The presidio of San Agustín, 1580. (A.G.I., Patronato Real 257.4.6.)

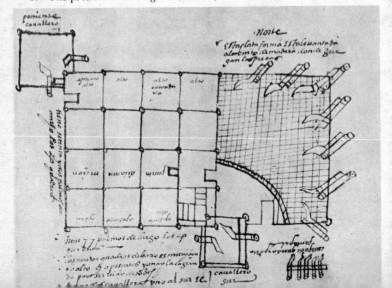

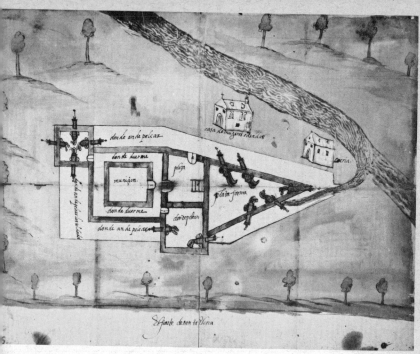

Santa Elena Fort, Parris Island, Port Royal Sound. (A.G.I., Mapas y Planos, México 46. Printed by permission of the Archivo General de Indias, Sevilla.)

Santa Elena Fort, Rebuilt on Parris Island, 1583. (A.G.I., Indiferente General, 1887.)

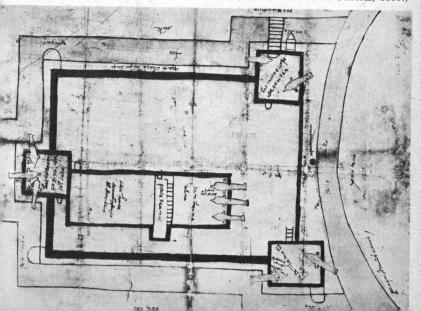

11. The arrival of the English at Roanoke Island, 1584. (T. de Bry, *America*, part i, 1590, plate 2.)

12. Pomeioc Village, 1585, by John White. (British Museum, I partment of Prints and Drawings.)

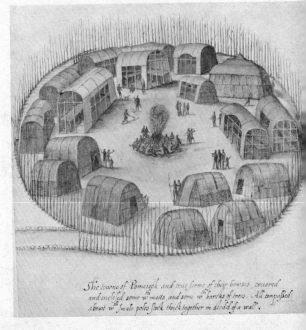

The towne of Pomeiock and true forme of their howses, covered and inclosed some wth matts and some wth barcks of trees. All compassed abowt wth smale poles stuck thick together in steed of a wall.

Their ripe corne

Their greene corne.

Corne newly sprong.

Their sitting at meate

The place of solemne prayer

e house wherin the Tombe of their Herounds standeth.

SECOTON.

A Ceremony in their prayers w
strange gestures and songs dansing
about posts carued on the topps
lyke mens faces.

Secotan Village, 1585, by John White. (British Museum, Department of Prints
d Drawings.)

14.   Fort Perimeter on Roanoke Island, 1585. As excavated by J. C. Harrington, 1947-1950.

15.   Fort Perimeter on Roanoke Island, 1585, as rebuilt by J. C. Harrington, 1950. (Courtesy of National Parks Service.)

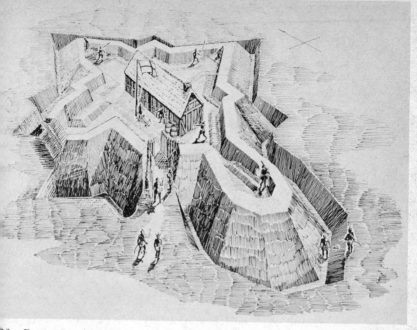

16. Fort on Roanoke Island. A modern artist's conception. (Courtesy of National Parks Service.)

7. The Saguenay *Habitacion* of Chauvin, 1600-1601, at the mouth of the Saguenay River. (Samuel Champlain, *Les voyages*, 1613.)

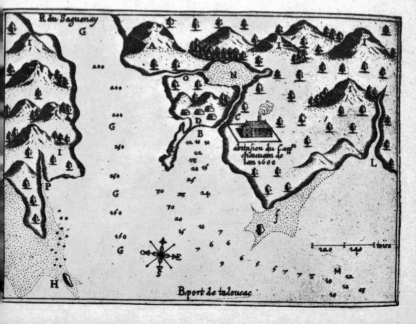

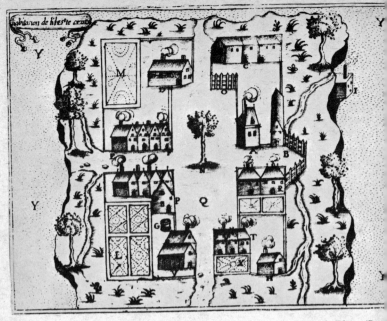

18. The Ste. Croix Settlement, 1604, on Dochet Island in the St. Croix River. (San
Champlain, *Les voyages*, 1613.)

19. Port Royal *Habitacion*, 1605, at Annapolis Basin, Nova Scotia. (Samuel Champ
*Les voyages*, 1613.)

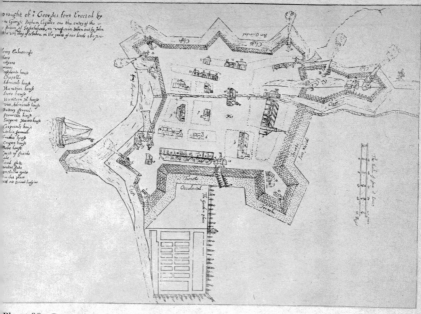

Plan of St. George's Fort, on the Sagadahoc (Kennebec) River, 1607-1608. (A. G. Simancas, ... o Inglaterra 2586, fol. 147.)

21. Québec *Habitacion*, 1608. (Samuel Champlain, *Les voyages*, 1613.)

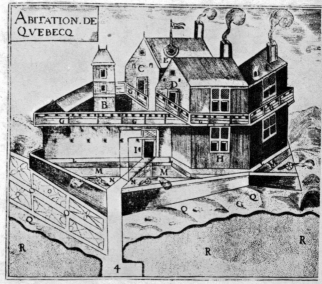

22. Glasshouse, Jamestown, 1608. These are the only surviving remains of the first James settlement, excavated in 1941 by J. C. Harrington. (Courtesy of J. C. Harrington.)

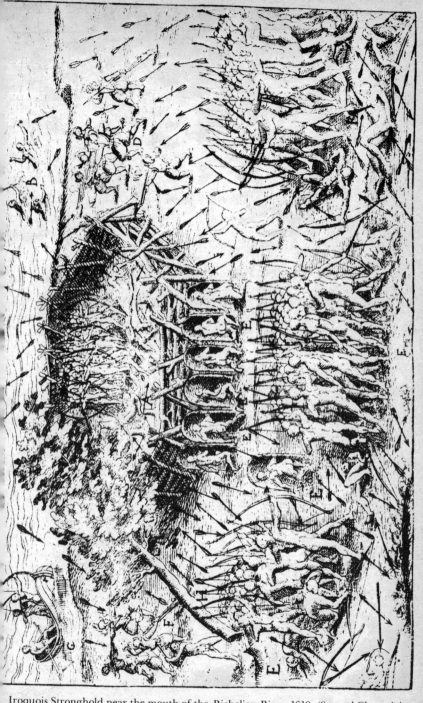

Iroquois Stronghold near the mouth of the Richelieu River, 1610. (Samuel Champlain, *Voyages*, 1613.)

24. Aerial view of Cupers Cove (now Cupids Cove) settlement site, 1611. (Courtesy of Dr. R. A. Barakat.)

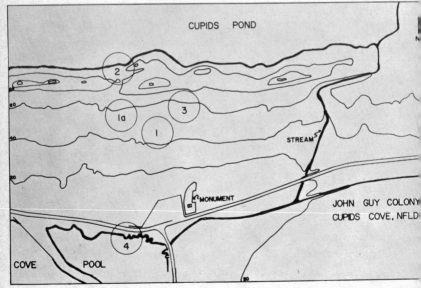

CUPIDS POND

2

1a  3

1

STREAM

MONUMENT

JOHN GUY COLONY
CUPIDS COVE, NFLD

4

COVE  POOL

25. Sketchplan of the settlement site at Cupids Cove, Newfoundland. Excavated 1973-1974. (Sketchplan by Dr. R. A. Barakat.)

at Blanc Sablon on August 9 and set out for France on August 15, reaching port at St. Malo with characteristic efficiency on September 5.

The speed, competence and certainty with which this voyage was made set a new standard in North American discovery and one which was to be rarely surpassed. Cartier had discovered and charted an inland sea—for so the Gulf of St. Lawrence seemed to him. He suspected that if he had followed the west coast of Newfoundland further to the south he would have reached an opening to the east (Cabot Strait was to be discovered on the next voyage); while at the northwestern end there was a dual channel, north and south of Anticosti, leading to the west. This was the route, he was sure, to further discoveries, quite probably to a channel through the mainland which his Indian hostages, when they could be made to speak, would unlock for him. In the meantime he had brought substantial evidence about climate and anchorages, good and bad terrain, details of seabirds (great auks and gannets in particular), of seal and walrus, cod and salmon, and of the fine timber for masts and other purposes to be had on the mainland. The Indians gave promise of at least some trade and of substantial assistance in the further exploration of the interior. On the other hand, there were no signs of gold or of civilized man. The early summer in the Strait of Belle Isle was as harsh as later summer on Chaleur Bay and at Gaspé was encouragingly hot. A vivid sense of place informs the narrative. Like Verrazzano's letter earlier, it brought back a sharp impression of the continent to add to the advantages which the French already enjoyed in their appreciation of North American prospects.

The two Indians duly learned enough French to convince Cartier's backers as well as himself that the great opening to the west of Gaspé led far into the country, while Taignoagny and Dom Agaya gave information of a sort also about the great "kingdom of Saguenay" which lay far inland from their own Canada. Even if there was much lack of definition in what was pieced together, there was enough to indicate that a major breakthrough into the interior of North America was possible. This could in turn lead to the disclosure of a route leading to Asia and so justify an immediate following up of the first expedition. A prompt and decisive action by Philippe

Chabot as admiral of Brittany, on October 30, set a new expedition under way. Cartier was authorized to take three ships, again victualed for fifteen months but this time to winter in the country, to the land "beyond the New Lands" which he had discovered. The fitting out of the expedition was put in hand at once and three ships—the *Grande Hermine,* the *Petite Hermine* and the *Émerillon,* the last a small bark for exploration work—were equipped over the winter in hope of an early start. But plague in Brittany delayed the voyage. A list of seventy-three men to serve under Cartier was made on March 3, 1535; he did not in fact get under way until May 19, when he left St. Malo with the two French-speaking Indians as interpreters and guides.[6]

The crossing was much slower than in 1534[7] but the *Grande Hermine* reached Funk Island on July 7, killed and loaded some seabirds there, and then made her rendezvous at Blanc Sablon on July 11, though she had to wait for a further eleven days for her two consorts. They set out westward along the Labrador coast on July 29, carefully recording the coastline in case they missed any channel leading from the north. This time, they worked their way through the Strait of St. Peter into the mouth of the St. Lawrence River on August 15, and so established that the earlier reconnaissance and the information gained from the Indians tallied exactly. Wishing to define the entrance closely, Cartier coasted the western end of Anticosti to pick up the mainland to the south, at Cape Magdalen, and then made an extended loop round to the north again so as to pick up once more the entrance to St. Peter's Strait and relate the two entrances to the river to one another. He then turned westward upstream, keeping to the north shore for a time but being later attracted by the greener and pleasanter southern bank.

Cartier held this course until on September 1 a deep river valley was observed on the north bank. This was the Saguenay River which the Indians had told them of, where began, they said, "the kingdom of Saguenay." They sailed across to the mouth, where they found four canoes fishing for seal; the Indians identified these as having come from their own Canada, and so for the first time renewed

6. Biggar, *Collection* (1930), pp. 44–56, covers the period October 1534 to May 1535.

7. Biggar, *Voyages,* pp. 85–246, provides an excellent edition. The author is again not named, but he is not, this time, Cartier, and most probably Jean Poulet, purser of the expedition (see *ibid.,* p. 85; Julien, *Les Français en Amérique,* p. 21).

contact with their tribe. On September 7 Cartier left Grosse Island and, according to the Indians, entered their own territory of Canada. As they worked their way up to the Island of Orleans, many more Indians were encountered. This led the chief, Donnaconna, to come down to welcome Dom Agaya and Taignoagny back and greet Cartier with gifts and ceremonies. He returned to make a long harangue on the following day, while the vessels worked along to the end of the island and entered "a forking of the waters . . . where there is a small river and a harbour with a bar." This was at the junction of the St. Charles River with the St. Lawrence, where, under the name of Sainte Croix, Cartier was to decide within the next ten days to make his headquarters and to bring his ships. In the meantime he explored the Isle of Orleans (which he called Bacchus Island, from the grapes found on it), and having left his two Indians to return to their tribe, located their village, Stadacona. He found that their hostages had now changed in attitude and become suspicious of their captors, though they continued to assure them they would later on lead them upstream to a mysterious "Kingdom of Hochelega" of which they apparently had already given Cartier's men high hopes.

The pleasantly wooded and fertile shores of the river had so far raised high hopes of its western reaches. The rich woods, the groves of nut trees on the islands, whale—the *beluga,* not like any whale they knew—and the eels and other fish had all been noted as they progressed. Cartier was anxious to get settled for the winter but was not willing to do so until he had carried his exploration up to Hochelaga. In the midst of frequent and friendly contacts with Donnaconna, who had presented him with two small children to take back to France, he made no progress in getting his former hostages to set a date to accompany him. Finally, they refused. We cannot say precisely why; it may be that their medicine men convinced them it would be unlucky, or they may have been afraid to face the unknown or virtually unknown Indians of the Upper St. Lawrence Valley. A practical and specific reason, which is likely to have weighed with Donnaconna, is that if they went upstream and made contact with richer and more sophisticated Indians, they would in turn desert Canada and their precious iron, brass and copper, as well as minor objects like beads and toys, be transferred to the hands of other more favored tribes.

In the end Cartier gave up trying to persuade them after they had

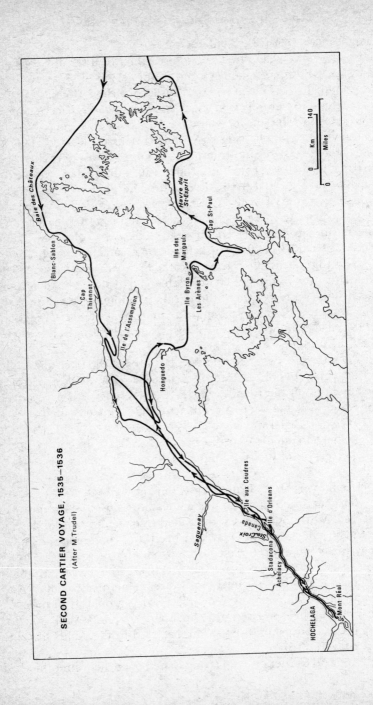

SECOND CARTIER VOYAGE, 1535—1536
(After M.Trudel)

Baie des Châteaux

Blanc-Sablon

Cap Thiennot

Ile de l'Assomption

Honguedo

Iles des Margaulx

Ile Byron

Les Arènes

Havre du St-Esprit

Cap St-Paul

Saguenay

Ile aux Coudres

Sta-Croix

Ile d'Orleans

Stadacona

Achelacy

Canada

Mont Réal

HOCHELAGA

0    Km    140

0    Miles

tried to play a trick on him by sending downstream a canoe with three Indians in it dressed up as devils, who they said, brought bad tidings from their God, Cugouagny, that Cartier would be overwhelmed by ice and snow if he went to Hochelaga. When this was not received seriously by the French, Donnaconna and the rest reconciled themselves to seeing Cartier go, though without guides. On September 19 Cartier took the *Émerillon* and two ships' boats to make the journey. Some 30 miles upstream at Achelacy he met with Indians who evidently spoke a similar language to those at Stadacona and warned him by signs of the difficulties of the Richelieu Rapids he was about to enter. But the rich woods, the loaded grapevines and the abundance of bird life beckoned him on. He made his way with some difficulty through Lake St. Peter, then decided it was risky to bring *Émerillon* any further, so he left her and her men at the head of the lake to await his return.

From September 29 to October 2, his party made their way forward until they came within sight of the Island of Montreal near the north bank. Cartier had encountered increasing numbers of Indians on the river as he advanced and had given them some small gifts. He had little difficulty in realizing that he must have reached Hochelaga when he found an assembly of what was reckoned to be more than 1,000 men, women and children turned out to greet him. Cartier went ashore and was greeted as a friend, neither he nor the Indians showing any fear of each other, the women coming to have him touch their babies. Fish and corn were showered on the French, and knives and beads handed out by them in return.

On October 3, a Sunday, Cartier led twenty-four of his men to the principal village on a hill several miles away, leaving eight sailors to guard the boats. A leading chief came from the village to meet them and there was the usual exchange of unintelligible speeches, after which Cartier was led through the cornfields to "the village of Hochelaga, near and adjacent to a mountain, the slopes of which are fertile and cultivated, and from the top of which one can see a long distance."[8] The "mountain" (800 feet high), they called "Mont Royal." The village was encircled by a triple palisade, some 30 feet in height, inside which galleries were placed from which stones

8. James F. Pendergast and Bruce G. Trigger, *Cartier's Hochelaga and the Dawson Site* (Montreal, 1972), is an exhaustive and authoritative study of the people of Hochelaga and of the site and character of their village.

could be hurled at attacking enemies. There was a single defended gate, but within were some fifty longhouses, each over 100 feet long by 30 to 40 feet wide, with partitions and lofts, and a firespace in the middle. This was a formidable settlement, with 1,000 or more inhabitants, and one like it would not be seen again on the St. Lawrence by Europeans for a long time. Cartier's men took notes of what was eaten and how it was cooked, how the Indians slept and dressed, and how they specially prized the white wampum beads. Their reception in the village was warm, the chieftain in his porcupine headdress being carried in state (he was apparently paralyzed). The French proffered rings and tin brooches and were offered food in return.

The village was on the slope of the "Mountain" and they were now brought to the top. Cartier gathered from the Indians that the St. Lawrence was barred by falls but that above them it could be followed for a three months' journey. The Ottawa was shown to him —thought by the Indians to be the river which flowed to the "kingdom of Saguenay" (the precise geography of which was to remain a puzzle). Copper was understood to come from far up the Ottawa. This visit was the highlight of Cartier's expedition so far. He returned to his boats on October 5, and made speed back to St. Peter's Lake, where the *Émerillon* was found waiting. They all returned to Ste Croix on October 11.

Although myth and reality often became confused in Indian tales (even if they usually had a realistic foundation), and although linguistic misinterpretations were liable to lead to serious misconceptions, some sense can probably be made of the tales of the "kingdom of Saguenay" which came to play such a large part in the literature of the Cartier voyages. The Huron tribesmen, whose homeland was on Georgian Bay in Lake Huron (the third of the five Great Lakes), were the great traders of the Great Lakes Basin, and in the early seventeenth century were to be one of the mainstays of the French fur trade. Their western trading contacts extended to Lake Superior, and they were thence one of the main purveyors of Lake Superior copper to the eastern Indians of the Canadian Shield and St. Lawrence Basin. It might appear that one route by which they dispersed their copper, and possibly other trade goods as well, was from Mattawa River to the Ottawa River. The route from Georgian Bay to there was up the French River to Lake Nipissing and

then down the Mattawa River to the Ottawa. Some of the copper from there was apparently traded by river, lake and portage for nearly 350 miles to Lake St. John, and thence down to the mouth of the Saguenay River, where it was dispersed among the tribes of the St. Lawrence Valley.

The Indians of the St. Lawrence Valley considered this copper to have come from a distant tribe which lived far away to the north and to the west up the Saguenay River; hence the "kingdom of Saguenay." Moreover, the same nomadic Indians who brought the copper as far as Lake St. John were also ranging far enough north to be aware of or even in contact with the Eskimo of Hudson Bay. From this came the tales of the white men with clothes like those worn by the Frenchmen, namely, pale Eskimo wearing tailored fur clothing, of whom Cartier and Champlain after him were to hear. This theory cannot be proved by documentary materials but it appears likely, even probable. Where the differentiation of metals with gold and copper came in (since to most Amerindians in the north and east copper was the only metal with which they were familiar and for which they had a name) and also the mention of precious stones and spices, is not clear, though quite possibly it stemmed from the linguistic weaknesses of Cartier and his men, as well as from the inventions of the Indians, Dom Agaya and later Donnaconna, who were brought to France and pleased their hosts by telling them what they wished to hear. How the "kingdom of Saguenay" could be both far to the north and still farther to the west remained to Cartier and his successors an enduring mystery.

In the meantime a fort had been built on shore on the St. Charles River, by the harbor, "enclosed on all sides with large wooden logs, planted upright, with artillery pointing every way, and in a good state to defend us against the whole countryside." This was the first French settlement in North America and the first St. Lawrence settlement, so far as we are aware, to be occupied since that at L'Anse aux Meadows more than five hundred years before. Cartier now strengthened it with deep, wide ditches outside, and a gate and drawbridge, so that it could be easily defended. From mid-November 1535 to April 13, 1536, for full five months, Cartier and his men were frozen in and snowed up in a hard Canadian winter. This meant great physical hardship for them—much greater than they can have anticipated. The fuel and certainly their food supplies

proved inadequate. By mid-December disease was noted amongst the Indians, with whom, eventually, contact was broken off as they were thought likely to be contagious. The Indians disappeared for a time in their mid-winter hunting season. Then disease attacked the French and many died. Of 110 survivors in mid-February, only 10 remained in good health.

A little later the Indians came back, among them Dom Agaya, who had been ill but had recovered. He brought Cartier the branches of a tree and showed him how to grind up the bark and leaves, boil the mixture, drink the juice and put the dregs on the swollen limbs. With its aid, Cartier claimed, those who were ill made a quick recovery. This tree, *Annedda*, as they called it, was probably the Eastern White Cedar, and the curative agent Vitamin C (though some would have been destroyed in the heating).[9] The disease was, of course, scurvy but in a form so severe that Cartier did not recognize it. Donnaconna then left on a further two months' hunting trip, but other Indians came to barter fresh meat and fish for goods so that the Frenchmen's health was maintained. Throughout the winter Cartier feared that Donnaconna would finally attack them, but in April, when the snow suddenly disappeared, he reappeared accompanied by many strange Indians. Cartier now decided he would return to France without attempting further exploration. First, however, he planned to kidnap Donnaconna, whose tales of the interior, highly colored as they were, had intrigued him. Donnaconna was duly enticed into the fort and captured, along with Taignoagny, Dom Agaya and others. When brought on shipboard and assured that he would be given a good time in France and returned, he apparently decided to make the best of it. Presents were exchanged: wampum for brass kettles and hatchets. The two vessels (the third had been broken up) set sail on May 6, after setting up a cross and taking formal possession for France. At Saguenay other Indians of his tribe said farewell to Donnaconna with gifts of bundles of beaver and seal skins; strangely enough, these are all the furs we hear of on the second voyage. The river was in spate and the weather in the Gulf was bad. Cartier decided to test the presumed existence of a

9. The precise identification of the coniferous tree whose leaves and bark supplied Vitamin C to the sufferers from scurvy has been debated. Jacques Rousseau, "L'Annedda et l'Arbre de Vie," *Revue d'Histoire de l'Amérique Français* (VIII, 1954), 171–213, decided that it was most probably the Eastern White Cedar, *Thuja occidentalis*.

outheast exit from the Gulf, and passed through it (Cabot Strait)
afely into the Atlantic at the beginning of June. Later they entered
enews Harbour to take in fuel and water. Then they sailed for
ome, reaching St. Malo on July 16 after an absence of fourteen
months.

Cartier's reports this time were ambiguous. He had been success-
l in pushing 1,000 miles into the interior, and yet had not found
route to the South Sea. He had learned that it was possible to make
s way by rivers and lakes something like as far westward again (for
he is likely to have interpreted the three moons' journey the
ochelaga Indians described to him). The metal of which they had
oken might appear to have been copper, but could be gold or
ver. Cartier had a goldsmith with him and the few quills of metal-
: dust he brought back may indeed have been gold. Donnaconna
d told him even stranger tales, based he claimed on far journey-
gs. In "the land of the Saguenay," wherever it was, there were
mmense quantities of gold, rubies and other rich things, and that
e men there are white as in France and go clothed in woolens."
had wilder stories still of people who drank but did not eat, of
gmies and one-legged men, "and other marvels too long to re-
e." It seems likely that Dom Agaya and Taignoagny had filled him
with fables in the tradition of Sir John Mandeville's "Travels"
led in France which he now in turn relayed to Cartier. How much
d how little these affected Cartier's reputation in France cannot
told. But Donnaconna did not survive the good living in France
long and was never to see Canada again. Certainly Cartier's
orts this time did not stress the urgency for fresh expeditions.
ancis I could take time to digest the new reports before acting on
m. This he did. It was to be four years and three months before
rtier was recommissioned to return to Canada.

rancis I can be shown to have to have been genuinely interested
Canada and its prospects. He was not, however, sure in his own
nd what should be done about it. Between 1533 and 1536 it
med worth using North American exploration as a stick to beat
arles V into admitting France to some claim to prospect parts of
erica unoccupied and unexplored by Spain. After 1536 he wav-
d between conciliating Charles and outmaneuvering him—by
ting himself up as the bringer of Catholic Christianity to North

American Indians so as to get the support of the Church (even though Paul III refused to commit the papacy to any revision of the earlier bulls) and by sending Cartier out on a rather ambiguous mission, to prospect for gold and a passage to Asia once again.[10] When finally he made up his mind in 1541, it was for an occupation of Canada as a forward base for French American imperialism, under the command of a Protestant, who was a symbol of hostility to the papacy as well as to Charles V. In the course of this decision, Francis I taunted the Spanish ambassador in Paris in 1540 that he had just as much right to intervene in new lands as Spain. The ambassador reported: "as to what I told him that permission to navigate these parts was conceded to your Majesty's predecessors by the Pope, and applied to them [the lands to which Cartier was to go], he answered that the Popes hold spiritual jurisdiction, but that it does not lie with them to distribute lands among kings, and that the Kings of France, and other Christians, were not summoned when the partition took place."[11]

Cartier had proposed to go out in 1538 with 274 men to settle a strong post in Canada, the ostensible purpose of which was missionary activity, but which would have been in fact a forward base for the search for the "kingdom of Saguenay" which had become in some French minds a kind of Eldorado in the west. Francis I in 1539 saw it in Donnaconna's terms as "a large city called Sagana where there are many mines of gold and silver in great abundance, and men and women dress and wear shoes like we do; and that there is abundance of clove, nutmeg and pepper."[12] The commission eventually issued to Cartier on October 17, 1540, was very general in content.[13] Cartier was to search for lands which would link up with Asia and also to engage in missionary endeavor; to aid him he was to have convicts assigned to do the hard work of establishing posts in Canada and Hochelaga. But on January 17, 1541, the king changed his mind. The commander of the expedition was to be the Protestant, Jean François de la Roque, seigneur de Roberval, who was to go out as the king's lieutenant and settle the western lands

10. The twists and turns of policy are admirably followed in Julien, *Voyages de découverte*, pp. 131–150.

11. Biggar, *Collection* (1930), p. 170.

12. *Ibid.*, p. 77.

13. *Ibid.*, pp. 128–132.

as part of a French empire.[14] Cartier was to be the executive arm of the expedition only. Cartier's own preparations were already well advanced; he was now to go ahead under Roberval's authority. Large numbers of convicts were to be enabled to go, as well as volunteers who hoped to settle. But the core of the expedition was to be a military garrison, for which Roberval would be responsible. Naturally it was not possible to raise arms and equipment for such a force very rapidly, and when it became clear that there would be delays it was decided that Cartier should go ahead and Roberval would follow, since the king insisted that an expedition should get to sea as early as possible.

Cartier duly left St. Malo with five ships on May 23, 1541.[15] He had a difficult crossing and his ships delayed some time at Newfoundland to recuperate and await Roberval's arrival. They eventually went ahead and reached Ste Croix only on August 23, having been three months on a journey which Cartier had previously made in two months. We do not know how many men Cartier had except that there were several hundred. He had no Indians with him, since Donnaconna and all his adult companions had died in the meantime. Stadacona was found to have a chief, Agona, who was not unduly discouraged when it was made clear to him that Donnaconna was dead, since he was now assured of his own position in the tribe. The old site was unsuitable for so many men or ships, so Cartier brought his ships some 9 miles beyond his previous site and installed them on the north bank of the river, at a tributary, the Cape Rouge River, under the high mass of Cape Rouge. At a lower level he established a settlement and then cut a way to the top of Cape Rouge, where he "made a fort to keepe the nether Fort and the ships, and all things that might passe as well by the great as by this small river."[16]

Two ships were sent back to France. Leaving the Sieur de Beaupré to complete the settlement, which had been named Charlesbourg Royal, and to have turnips and other vegetables sown, Cartier himself made his way upstream so that he could plan

14. *Ibid.*, pp. 178–185.
15. The only surviving account is incomplete. It was preserved in English by Richard Hakluyt, *Principal navigations*, III (London, 1600), 232–237. (ed. Glasgow, 1903–04 12 vols., VII, 263–272); Biggar, *Voyages* (1924), pp. 249–260.
16. *Ibid.*, 254.

his proposed expedition to Saguenay the following spring. His old contact, the chief of Achelay, renewed relations with him, and he moved on to Hochelaga, arriving at the first rapid (St. Mary's) on September 11. His boats would not pass it, but Cartier found a path which led up past the second rapid (the Lachine). Through communication with Indian guides and a visit to a village, the visitors learned that the Ottawa River was not navigable and that the third rapid was not far away. There seems to be some ambiguity whether this rapid was the Long Sault (with the Carillon) on the Ottawa or the Lachine on the St. Lawrence. The Indians made up diagrams to show him the layout of the rapids, calculating that 6 leagues (some 18 miles) travel by land would bring them to the head of the rapids. Apparently also they indicated that the Ottawa was the route to rich Saguenay.

This was as far as Cartier was to get in his search for the mythical kingdom of Saguenay. The Indians turned out in force (some four hundred of them) to greet Cartier as he left—he returned to the settlement to find that they had been behaving with some degree of hostility and had ceased to trade fish with the settlers. The breaking off of the surviving narrative at this point leaves us with no knowledge of how the winter passed, except that thereafter Cartier decided he could not "with his small company withstand the Savages, which went about dayly to annoy him."[17] The good relations which had subsisted, on the whole, from 1534 to 1536 had given way to friction and some hostility. Cartier had another reason for thinking it was time to come home: near Charlesbourg Royal he had found "good store of stones, which we esteemed to be Diaments," an iron "mine" (or outcrop),[18] and "certaine leaves of fine gold as thicke as a mans nail."[19] None of these were what he thought they were, though the "gold" was later tried in a furnace and found to be good. He and his men gathered what they could, then set off in May for France, putting in at Newfoundland in June, probably at St. John's Harbour, on their way to France which they reached before September 7.

17. *Ibid.*, 264.
18. See *ibid.*, 255, 264, 457, 459, 461. Biggar, *Collection* (1930), p. 451.
19. Again only an incomplete account in English was preserved in Richard Hakluyt *Principal navigations*, III (1600), 240–242 (ed. 1903–04, VIII, 283–287); Biggar, *Voyages* (1924), pp. 263–270.

Roberval had not been able to get his equipment or men together in time to sail in 1541. But by April 1542 he was ready. He had with him two hundred settlers, including women (for the first time in an American settlement venture mounted in France). His three ships had a difficult passage from La Rochelle to Newfoundland between April 16 and June 7. Staying there to recuperate, they were surprised to see Cartier's ships come in on their way to France. Roberval ordered Cartier to return but he refused, because, as the narrator of the Roberval expedition put it, he "would have all the glory of the discoveries of those parts," and slipped away. In fact, on his return to France the ore and stones were discredited: "Canada diamonds" were long a name for spurious gems as a result. Roberval evidently knew of the location of Cartier's fort and brought his own expedition there safely at the end of July. However, the rebuilding or extension of the forts, now renamed Francy Roy, took time. It seems probable that he greatly extended the upper-level occupation on Cape Rouge, as we hear there of "a great Towre, and another of fortie or fiftie feete long: where in there were divers Chambers, an Hall, a Kitchine, houses of office, Sellers high and lowe, and near unto it were an Oven and Milles, and a well before the house."[20] Below, near the water, was another "great Towre of two stories high," and also "two courtes of good buylding" for stores and servants' quarters. The settlement was therefore an elaborate and potentially permanent one.

Two ships were sent home and the colonists, the first true colony France had sent, settled down for the winter. Severe rules, stringently enforced, were imposed; rations were assigned to make sure that stores would last through the winter. For a time, the Indians brought them quantities of shad. But in the end scurvy overcame them; almost all must have sickened, and at least fifty died of it before the ice began to break in April. By June 5, 1543, Roberval had only one hundred men left. With seventy he worked his way upstream in eight boats, leaving thirty at the settlement, who were given a time to await Roberval's return. If he did not come, they were to go back to France in the two barks left to them. A party arrived back to inform those left behind that eight men had been lost when a boat overturned, and on June 19 another boat came

20. *Ibid.*, p. 266; Biggar, *Collection* (1930), p. 447.

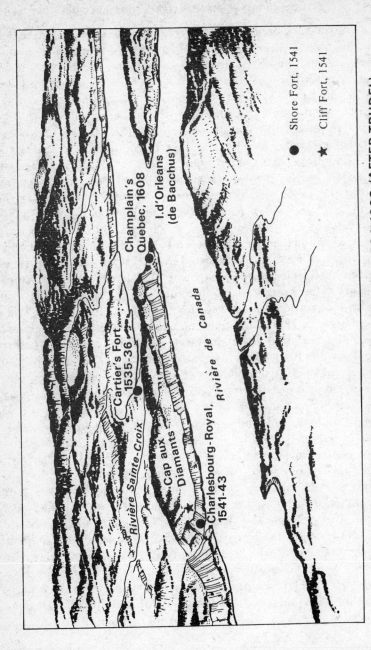

FRENCH SETTLEMENTS IN THE QUEBEC AREA, 1534-1608 (AFTER TRUDEL)

Champlain's
Quebec, 1608

I. d'Orleans
(de Bacchus)

Cartier's Fort,
1535-36

Rivière Sainte-Croix

Cap aux
Diamants

Rivière de Canada

Charlesbourg-Royal,
1541-43

● Shore Fort, 1541

★ Cliff Fort, 1541

back to say that the garrison should wait until July 22. This is all we know definitely about Roberval's expedition toward Saguenay. He got back to the fort by the end of June. Two ships, the *Anne* and the *Gallion,* were sent out in the spring to bring supplies; in them Roberval and his men returned by September 11, defeated colonists.[21]

We may never know precisely why they admitted defeat—most probably it was due to inability to come to grips with the elusive Saguenay and fear of another winter's scurvy. Cartier, though his treasure proved false, was soon forgiven; Roberval for a time was in disgrace and had lost much of his capital. The interior of North America had indeed been deeply pierced by the expeditions of 1534–43, and the maps were permanently altered by these enterprises. But the continent had proved intractable, very difficult to live in—though parties of Frenchmen had done so on three separate winters—and its riches either defective, elusive or, it must have seemed after 1543, nonexistent. The cost of the ventures had come almost wholly from the royal treasury; Francis I wrote off New France as a bad debt.

The Cartier-Roberval expeditions were in many respects the most significant penetrations of North America yet to be made. They were genuine pioneering attempts to establish Europeans well inside the interior of North America. The efforts in 1535–36 and 1541–43 to create French colonial establishments (however humble that of 1535–36 may seem) on the St. Lawrence are of great interest —the temporary camps of Soto and Coronado, 1539–1543, were of a different sort. The challenge which a Canadian winter offered to European settlers had, however, proved a major one. The Cartier-Roberval expeditions tend to be somewhat overshadowed in modern eyes by the great Spanish expeditions across the greater part of the continent. The French series, strung out over nine years, had a considerable degree of continuity whose failure was unfortunate but which also left behind it a residue of experience and of knowledge. This was to survive through the narratives of the first two voyages which Ramusio made available in print in Italian in 1556 (the *Brief recit* on the second voyage had already appeared in French in 1545), thus receiving more publicity for some years than the Spanish expeditions. The maps too were not allowed to remain in

21. *Ibid.*, pp. 471–472, 475.

the obscurity of manuscript: the published map of 1544 with which the name of Sebastian Cabot is associated, was the first to record something of the St. Lawrence discoveries. Thereafter the area discovered by the French was elaborated on successive printed maps to give authentic substance to the interior of part of North America. The constructions of the cartographers which extended westward and northward from the 1000 mile range from the Strait of Belle Isle to Montreal had no substance in reality.

Richard Eden introduced the French achievement to the English in 1555 when in his *Decades of the New World or West India* he spoke of "the great and large countreys named Canada, Ochelaga, and Sangunnai . . . well inhabited and pleasaunt countreys, and named by hym [Cartier] Nova Francia." He made Cartier say: "Oh what doo the Christian Princes meane that in such landes discovered they do not assigne certeine colonies to inhabite the same to bringe those people . . . to better civilitie and to embrace owre religion."

The lasting significance of the French expeditions of 1534–45 was that they created a tradition that not only the coastline sketched out by Verrazzano but also the great interior valley explored by Cartier constituted a New France which could still, at will, be occupied by France. As such, these expeditions represented a standing challenge to the Spanish claim to a monopoly of rights to North America as a whole. This challenge would not be relinquished by the French during the next generation, and would eventually be taken up actively once again.

# CHAPTER 9

# *The Inland Voyages—Coronado and Soto*

---

## I

AT some stage it was almost inevitable that Spain would attempt to explore the interior of North America. The conquest of Mexico from 1519 forward and the conquest of Peru in the 1530s had produced so much novelty and wealth that probing expeditions outward from both centers in search of still further aboriginal empires and bullion-rich territories were begun shortly after the initial successes. We may indeed see the Ponce de León, Ayllón and Narváez ventures as being tentative attempts to discover whether any riches existed on the shores of the Gulf of Mexico, of the Florida peninsula and of the coast beyond. But by 1530 all these had proved complete disappointments. They had ended in tragedy, disillusionment or, in the case of Narváez and his men, disappearance. Only in the interior, it might be thought, could riches lie. Later in the 1530s it seemed indeed as if luxury and variety in native life and riches in jewels (and perhaps in gold) might be found there. Consequently, the last years of the decade found major expeditions being planned and mounted,[1] which were intended finally to penetrate the inland territories, to solve the mysteries, and perhaps uncover new riches for those who participated in them.

1. The most useful account of all the expeditions taken together is still Woodbury Lowery, *The Spanish Settlements Within the Present Limits of the United States, 1513–1561* (1901), 191–350.

It was the appearance of Álvar Núñez Cabeza de Vaca, with three companions, in Mexico in 1536 which gave the exploration of the west a major impetus.[2] All hope of survivors of Narváez's expedition had long been given up, so that the arrival of a small group of them in western America when Narváez had been lost in the east was sensational. After Cabeza de Vaca had been thrown ashore in 1528 off the Texas coast (whether on Galveston Island or what is now the Velasco peninsula cannot be ascertained since the offshore islands have undergone many changes), he entered into a long apprenticeship with the coastal Indians who were his captors. His companions died or were scattered after a few of them had, like Cabeza de Vaca, been initiated as medicine men by the Indians. Later, when he was moved to the mainland, Cabeza de Vaca became a prisoner on parole who managed to acquire the skills of peddler and huckster. After a long period of harsh servitude, he finally enjoyed a measure of freedom in which he encountered three other toughened survivors, who had also been, in their day, medicine men on the Texas coast. These were the black Estevánico, Andrés Dorantes de Carranca and Alonzo del Castillo Maldonado. Eventually the four men found an opportunity to make off together in what they reckoned was September 1534. They knew enough of the barren coastlands and their fierce nomadic Indians to discard any idea of working south, the short way, to Pánuco. Instead, heartened by the luxury of prickly pears to eat and evidence of buffalo, they set off northward and then gradually turned to the northwest and west. The eighteen months' walk which brought them to Mexico can only be charted in outline since their topography was necessarily vague, though Cabeza de Vaca's objective observations of Indian customs and food enable their route to be followed in broad outline. They hoped in the end to reach the Pacific or get some indications which would lead them down to central Mexico.

2. The standard Spanish text of Cabeza de Vaca's "Relation" is *Relación de los naufragios y comentarios de Alvar Núñez Cabeza de Vaca*, with an introduction by Manuel Serrano y Sanz, 2 vols. (Madrid, 1906); the most convenient translation is in F. W Hodge and T. H. Lewis, *Spanish Explorers in the United States, 1528–1543* (1907), pp 1–126. *The Narrative of Alvar Núñez Cabeza de Vaca*, with an introduction by J. F Bannon (Barre, Mass., 1972), has additional material. Cleve Hallenbeck, *The Journey and Route of Cabeza de Vaca* (1940), is valuable. Morris Bishop, *The Odyssey of Cabeza de Vaca* (1933), and John U. Terrel, *Journey into Darkness* (1962), are readable popular accounts.

They set themselves up as a traveling team of medicine men. With a combination of traditional Indian techniques and the use of Christian prayers (to which was added a considerable gift for showmanship), they established a reputation as healers and holy men whose fame went ahead of them and usually ensured that they were respected, feasted and given employment—indeed, they seem to have done appreciably better than the local shamans.

Reaching the Texan Colorado River, they were able to turn westward along its valley. Thereafter they worked their way northwestward and then west from one tribe to the next picking up a retinue of Indians from various tribes who followed them, as men possessed of magical powers. Vague rumors of what might be Mexico to the south came to them; first they reached the Pecos River and later still the Rio Grande, both of which they crossed, keeping on in a generally westward direction. They were following a track to the southward of the Pueblo culture until near the Rio Grande Valley they came upon permanent villages and cultivation. There they began to hear of "populous towns and very large houses" in the north and eventually on the Sonora were to obtain specimens of blankets, deerskins, turquoise and other stones which came from the Pueblo Indians. There was difficult country to cross before they reached the Sonora Valley. But by the time they came to the large Indian settlement which they named Pueblo de los Corazones, they were able to learn something of the sea—the Gulf of California—which lay not far away. They had, they realized, crossed the continent. It now remained to turn south to Mexico, keeping to the west of the great mountain chain of the Sierra Madre.

This was in part a harsh and troubled country, with increasing rumors of Spanish activity in the shape of slave-raiding parties. Later, near the Rio Sinaloa, they made contact with one such party and—their Indian retinue dispersing in dismay—were brought down to Culiacán in April. Thence, after an uncomfortable course of readjustment to European ways, they came to the city of Mexico on July 24, where they were made much of by both the viceroy, Antonio de Mendoza, and by Cortés himself. Cabeza de Vaca made a full report and his companions were questioned. Much of the topography of their remarkable journey remained misty since neither maps nor journals could provide a clear framework for their travels. Cabeza de Vaca's own report, which he repeated in Spain

when he arrived there in August 1537, was published at Zamora in 1542. It was full and reasonably specific, and did not exaggerate what he had seen on his journeys. It did, however, inflame interest in Mexico in the north, and also helped to focus renewed attention in Spain herself on what lay beyond the Gulf of Mexico as well as to the east of the Gulf of California. It was the most powerful single impulse behind the inland voyages which followed.

## II

The viceroy was anxious to follow up the Cabeza de Vaca reports, particularly those about large towns, rich in cotton and bullion, in the north. He chose Francisco Vásquez de Coronado (to whom we should correctly refer as Vásquez de Coronado rather than Coronado) to do so in 1537, hoping to get Dorantes to lead a preliminary expedition, a further reconnaissance, which might be a prelude to a conquering expedition. Dorantes would not take part and this left only the black, Estevánico, who was not considered suitable to go alone, but was joined by two experienced Franciscan friars, Marcos de Niza (Marcus de Nice) and Onorato.[3]

In March 1539 the party was sent out with a number of Indians, some of whom came from well to the north near the coast. Unfortunately, Fray Onorato was taken ill and had to return. Their technique was for Estevánico to go ahead, dressed in his medicine man regalia, and pick up as guides and associates any Indians who were interested. Fray Marcos kept a slower pace, collecting information as he went and being refreshed from time to time by reports from the forward party. After they entered Sinaloa, Marcos began to pick up tales of the Pueblo region and invented the name "the Seven Cities of Cíbola" which was to cling to them for many years (it was even to be linked with the tales of the "Seven Cities of Antilia" that had been current in the fifteenth century). These "cities" were said to be many-storied and richly decorated with turquoise. As he worked his way northward toward Corazones on the Sonora River, where Cabeza de Vaca had been, the tales became more specific; Marcos was able to see turquoise, blankets (*mantas*) and buffalo

3. Texts in George P. Hammond and Agapito Rey (eds.), *Narratives of the Coronado Expedition, 1540–1542* (Albuquerque, N.M., 1940), pp. 58–82; the fullest edition is Cleve Hallenbeck (ed.), *The Journey of Fray Marcos de Niza* (Glendale, Calif., 1949).

hides which came, it was said, from Cíbola, while there had been earlier reports that the people there had many gold ornaments. Estevánico was now ahead with some three hundred Indians who had gone with him out of curiosity across the long desert route northeast of Corazones, having arranged to send back messages to Fray Marcos from time to time.

The precise route of the long trail which led to Zuñi is not known, but can be roughly traced from later evidence. Receiving increasingly urgent messages from Estevánico indicating that he was getting near to Cíbola, Marcos hurried on, only to be met with fugitives from the Indian retinue who informed him that disaster had overtaken the black. He had indeed reached Cíbola, and going forward to the town had tried to impress the chief with his medicine routine. The Zuñi, refusing to accept him as a friendly visitor, had captured and killed him, along with some of his Indians, the rest fleeing when it was seen that Estevánico's medicine was not powerful enough to save him. Fray Marcos hurriedly distributed his goods amongst the Indians who were with him and the refugees to placate them for their loss. He went ahead, he claimed, with two guides until he saw Cíbola himself,[4] "which is situated on a plain at the skirt of a round hill. It has the appearance of a very beautiful town, the best that I have seen in these parts. The houses are of the sort that the Indians had described to me, all of stone, with their stories and terraces, as it appeared from a hill where I was able to view it. The city is bigger than the city of Mexico." With this view (if indeed he saw the pueblo of Hawíkuh) he turned back on his long road and successfully reached Culiacán and Compostela, where he reported to Coronado in June, made his formal depositions in July, and was with Mendoza by August 1539. His reports, even if they prove fallible in modern critical hands, were powerful evidence at the time of a rich and civilized group of settlements in the north, and the claim that one of them was "bigger than Mexico" was a claim indeed.

It has been pointed out that the northern ventures of the post-1536 period were not solely inspired by Cabeza de Vaca's story. They represented also the continuing rivalry between Mendoza as viceroy and Hernando Cortés as Marqués de Valle as to which of them could impress the emperor Charles V most with his zeal to

4. Hallenbeck, *Journey*, pp. 33–34.

expand Mexico, though Cortés eventually gave up the struggle and left to continue his campaign in Spain in September 1539. Nor was it only Fray Marcos's reports of the supposed wealth of "The Seven Cities of Cíbola" that made Francisco Vásquez de Coronado an enthusiast for northern exploration, which was now put in hand on a large scale with himself as the designated leader of a major expedition. Rumors of gold, silver, and precious stones far to the north and in great quantity had been reaching the frontier districts of Mexico—where minerals such as these had already been known for some years—and appeared to give substance to the narratives of both Cabeza de Vaca and Fray Marcos. Moreover, a successful expedition to the north could not only make the discoverers rich but, if there were fertile lands and rich settlements as well, would open up yet another Mexico which offered much more attractive living than the rough northern ones into which the Spaniards had been spreading as they had moved out from the valley.

Preparations for a major expedition were pushed on with considerable speed.[5] Coronado was commissioned on January 6, 1540, to take command, while Mendoza inspected the expedition at the capital of New Galicia, Compostela, on February 22. The roll call was an impressive one.[6] There were 287 Spanish soldiers (250 on horseback), between 6 and 10 priests and friars (including Fray Marcos), perhaps some 100 other Spaniards, some 1,000 Indian "allies," and possibly 300 servants and slaves—a total of 400 Spaniards in all and some 1,300 others, with baggage horses, mules, cattle and sheep for food on the hoof, about as many animals as men. The expedition as a whole was incredibly slow and unwieldly but, as it proved, well thought out and effectively organized as a

5. The best account of the expedition is by Pedro de Castañeda de Majeram, first published, in Spanish and English, in G. P. Winship, "The Coronado Expedition, 1540–1542," Smithsonian Institution, Bureau of American Ethnology, Bulletin no. 14 (1896), 329–637; he published a slightly revised translation, *The Journey of Coronado, 1540–1542* (1904), which is reprinted in Hodge and Lewis, *Spanish Explorers.* The best collection of documents on the expedition as a whole (including Castañeda) is Hammond and Rey, *Narratives.* Herbert E. Bolton, *Coronado on the Turquoise Trail* (Albuquerqe, N.M., 1940), also as *Coronado, Knight of Pueblos and Plains* (New York, 1940; Albuquerque, N.M., 1964), and A. Grove Day, *Coronado's Quest* (Berkeley, 1940) are the standard biographical accounts.

6. Hammond and Rey, *Narratives,* pp. 7–14, 87–108; Bolton, *Coronado,* pp. 66–74. The precise numbers of those who reached the Pueblo area are probably impossible to calculate.

military exercise. Hernando de Alarcón was to go up the coast and transmit additional stores to Coronado from as far north as he could.[7] Fray Marcos had been told when he set out that it was thought the continent narrowed as one went north, so that a sharp coastal trend toward the east was evidently anticipated, one that would bring the vessels near to the "Seven Cities" at their expected latitude—though, of course, this speculation proved to be totally unjustified.

The expedition made its way slowly and somewhat painfully to the frontier town of Culiacán, then launched northward into the wilderness. The plan was for Coronado to take two hundred men, with some Indians and food on the hoof, with Fray Marcos as guide, to act as a reconnaissance party, while Tristán de Arellano followed with the main body more slowly behind. So long as they were in the rolling country of northern Mexico they could make reasonable progress from one river valley to the next, from the Mayo to the Yaquí to the Sonora, the going getting more difficult across the counterscarp as they went but compensated for by wider and more fertile valleys. Coronado was well received by the Lower Pima Indians, who had helped both Cabeza de Vaca and Fray Marcos. They reached Corazones on May 26, which represented an effective average of 12 miles a day. As it was still early summer, the Indians had little corn to spare but there was some. They were now in a region where they could see some irrigation practiced in the valley bottoms. Then, striking over the watershed, Coronado reached the San Pedro, where the people were poor and spare food nonexistent. At a place the Indians called Chichilticalli they were near the Gila River. From there they entered a barren and depopulated area, where Fray Marcos had previously experienced considerable hardship. For 150 miles Coronado and his men suffered, men and animals dying and even he himself becoming disheartened as they reached the White Mountain region in the territory of the roving Apaches (modern north Arizona). Coronado was now far from the Gulf of California and out of reach of any help from Alarcón. As they entered the Little Colorado (Red River) Valley, Fray Marcos was sure they were not far from Cíbola: and he was right.

On the edge of the Pueblo country, the Zuñi were indeed on the

7. Hammond and Rey, *Narratives*, p. 160.

watch and four of their envoys made contact with the expedition. Interpretation of what they said proved difficult but it was understood that they offered the expedition supplies of corn. Their probable qualification that this was contingent on the Spanish turning away was not appreciated. At the pueblo of Hawíkuh, the Zuñi prepared to fight. Meanwhile, as they made their way up the Zuñi River, Coronado and his men at last saw the three-story mass of Hawíkuh before them. They had reached Cíbola and this was the first of its "Seven Cities" (though in fact there were only six and the name applied to the group, not to the first one seen).

Castañeda's narrative reflects the bitter disappointment of the Spanish members of the expedition:[8]

When they got within sight of the first pueblo, which was Cíbola, the curses that some hurled at Fray Marcos were such that God forbid they may befall him. It is a small rocky pueblo, all crumpled up, there being many farm settlements in New Spain that look better from afar. It is a pueblo of three or four stories and has some 200 warriors. The houses are small, have little space and no patios, for one patio serves a whole section.

Coronado was rather more expansive in his letter to Mendoza of August 3, if no less critical of Fray Marcos;[9] indeed, he sees some analogies with Spanish towns:

Not to be too verbose, I can assure you that he [Fray Marcos] has not told the truth in a single thing that he said, but everything is the opposite of what he related, except the name of the cities and the large stone houses. For, though they are not decorated with turquoises, nor made of lime or good bricks, nevertheless they are very good houses, three and four and five stories high, where there are very good homes and good rooms with corridors, and some quite good rooms underground and paved, which are built for winter and which were something like estufas [or sweatbaths; they were kivas].[10]

The Seven Cities are seven little villages, all having the kind of houses I have described. They are all within a radius of four leagues. All together they are called the kingdom of Cíbola. Each has its own name, and no single one is called Cíbola, but all together they are called Cíbola. This one which I have called a city I have named Granada, both because it has some

8. Ibid., p. 208.
9. Ibid., pp. 162–178, especially p. 170.
10. Harold E. Driver, Indians of North America, 2nd edition (Chicago, 1969), pp. 131, 351 (on the ceremonial role of the kiva in Pueblo society).

similarity to it and in honor of your Lordship. In this one where I am now lodged there are perhaps 200 houses, all surrounded by a wall, and it seems to me that, together with the others which are not surrounded [that is dwellings outside the enclosed pueblo], there might be in all 500 hearths.

There is another town near by, which is one of the seven, but somewhat larger than this, and another of the same size as this; the other four are somewhat smaller.

This report of Coronado's was made after the first clashes with the Zuñi. The tribesmen had come out to resist the intruders. Coronado then read them the *Requerimiento,* and even had some passages of it translated, requiring them to submit to Spain and to the Christian religion; naturally they refused. A preliminary skirmish scattered the tribal forces, who then proceeded to evacuate their turquoises and non-combatants from Hawíkuh[11] and vigorously defended it against a Spanish assault. Coronado was injured by stones thrown at him, but fatal injuries were few. When the pueblo was stormed the surviving occupants retreated in good order, leaving quantities of corn for the hungry Spaniards. After the battle, a peace of sorts was arranged with the Zuñi, who philosophically accepted the parasitic Spanish force since they could do nothing else, and thereafter supplied it with the necessities of life.

Coronado, taking the broader perspective, told Mendoza that he thought that the "North Sea," the Atlantic Ocean, was not too far away (it was in fact some 2,000 miles off) and that the western ocean, the Pacific, was no more than 150 leagues, under 400 miles (when it was over 600). He had at least made a notable salient into western America.

The logistics of the enterprise from this point became complex. Coronado, with his advance guard, was strong enough to maintain his position, but could do little more than make extended reconnaissances unless his main body came up. He sent messengers across the desert to Arellano to get him to make contact now that Cíbola had been reached. A forward base had been established at Corazones, now named San Gerónimo de los Corazones, so that an advance from the Sonora Valley by the army was now possible. In the meantime, Alarcón had probed the Gulf of California to its termination in the estuary of the Colorado River. He had entered

11. See Frederick W. Hodge, *History of Hawíkuh* (Los Angeles, 1937).

the river on August 26 and went up as far as the confluence of the Gila River with it. There he could make no contact with Coronado since he did not know in which direction to strike and there were no welcoming parties. He had picked up rumors of a white invasion of the interior, but these were quite unlocalized. After sixteen days, he returned to the head of the Gulf and brought his stores back to Mexico, indicating that Coronado had failed to carry out his end of the arrangement. A reconnaissance party from Corazones eventually reached the coast and was directed by the Yuma Indians to the point where Alarcón had left messages, which were duly found, but this was months afterwards and the party got back to Corazones only on January 18, 1541.

The reconnaissances which Coronado sent out gradually brought him a fairly complete picture of the Pueblo country so that, from their reports, he could visualize what lay to the west and north and east. Pedro de Továr reached Tusáyan, the center of the Hopi tribe. They, like the Zuñi, defied the Spaniards to begin with, but after having been scattered by a cavalry charge, submitted and were interrogated. Apparently they had more turquoise but nothing in the way of gold and silver; however, they gave news of a river to the west which they thought the Spaniards ought to see. On Továr's return to Granada with this news, López de Cárdenas was despatched with a party to find it. His search revealed the valley of the Colorado River, and the wonders of the Grand Canyon. One of his men reported[12] that "it was utterly impossible to find a way down, either for horses or foot. . . . The canyon is so lined with rock that one could hardly see the river. . . . From the top it looked like an arroyo." Another said[13] that "from the edge . . . it looked as if the opposite side must have been three or four leagues by air." They could not cross: there was nothing material to be gained in the region that they could see, and so they returned to report on their exciting but barren discovery.

A party was now sent out to locate the Pecos (Cicuye) tribal area, after some gifts had come from there.[14] Hernando de Alvarado, their leader, on his way found Acoma, a large pueblo on a high, flat rock. His party was small enough to be received peaceably and with

12. Hammond and Rey, *Narratives*, p. 287.
13. *Ibid.*, p. 215.
14. *Ibid.*, p. 19.

gifts. From Acoma, Alvarado reached the main group of Pueblo tribes in the Upper Rio Grande Valley. Here the cultivable area was wide and the land near the river fertile. The numerous villages of the Tiguex district (the name of the principal pueblo as well) proved very attractive and the people well disposed.[15] From there he reached Pecos at the eastern edge of the Pueblo area. At Pecos he encountered the maverick Indian who was to become notorious as "the Turk" when he attached himself to the Spaniards; he was full of tales of a gold-rich area to the northeast. The party worked their way beyond the Pueblo territory and reached the Canadian River, where they briefly had a view of the Great Plains and of the buffalo herds on them. This was to prove the crucial reconnaissance. When Alvarado made his report after he returned to Hawíkuh, Coronado instructed Cárdenas to move to Tiguex,· occupy the principal pueblo and prepare it as a headquarters for himself as he intended to move there.

At this point, in November 1540, Arellano came up with the main body after a difficult journey through the desert. Coronado now had to dispose of nearly 2,000 persons among the pueblos, a major imposition on their resources even though Arellano brought a considerable quantity of equipment and some stores; he decided to move with his combined force into Tiguex and disperse his men among the Rio Grande pueblos.[16] Meanwhile, the Turk's tales were becoming more specific: the country of Quivira had a large river and great canoes with sails . . . there was gold in various forms, a great

15. Castañeda writes: "Tiguex is a province of twelve pueblos on the banks of a large and mighty river. Some pueblos are on one bank, some on the other. It is a spacious valley two leagues wide. To the east there is a snow-covered sierra [the Sandia range], very high and rough. At its foot, on the other side, there are seven pueblos, four in the plain and three sheltered on the slope of the sierra" (Hammond and Rey, *Narratives,* pp. 253–254).

16. An anonymous account summarizes the layout of the Río Grande pueblos: "Twenty leagues east of this rock [Acoma] we found a well-settled river, flowing from north to south. Along it there must be seventy pueblos altogether. They are of the same type as Cíbola, except that they are almost all of well-built mud walls. Their food is exactly the same. These natives grow cotton—I mean those who live by the river—which the others do not. There was plenty of maize there. . . . These settlements extend more than fifty leagues from north to south along this river, some pueblos being fifteen or twenty leagues apart. This river originates at the limits of the settlement north of the slopes of the sierras" ("Relación del Suceso," Hammond and Rey, *Narratives,* p. 288). The standard account of the area is Adolph F. Bandelier and Edgar L. Hewitt, *Indians of the Rio Grande Valley* (Albuquerque, N.M., 1937).

golden eagle, dishes, bowls and also wrought silver. A troublemaker from the beginning, the Turk accused various pueblo chiefs of concealing a gold bracelet from Quivira from the Spaniards, who thereupon tortured them in vain to get them to reveal it, incidentally revealing just how harsh they could be.

The winter proved a severe test. Settled in and around the pueblos, the Spaniards found themselves inadequately equipped against the cold. They tore the blankets and even the clothing from the Indians and treated them with increasing cruelty. The end result, not surprisingly, was revolt. The Spanish horses were driven off and impounded at Arenal, and the Indians came out to fight. Arenal pueblo was taken by storm. Cárdenas burned many of his prisoners at the stake, yet even this did not prevent the Mohì from resisting. Their pueblo fortifications amazingly withstood a siege of fifty days, but in the end they were broken and many killed. By March all had been terrorized into submission.

On April 23, 1541, Coronado was ready with a large mobile force for a march to Quivira. He set out through the mountain pass to the northeast, leaving the pueblo area at Pecos with which he was still on friendly terms. He was soon out on the Great Plains, where he met only nomadic hunting Indians—Querechos and Teyas—and many buffalo. The trackless plains seemed limitless as well as featureless; he decided to go ahead with a small reconnaissance party of thirty horse and a few foot. Ironically, if he had turned southeast he might well have reached the Gulf of Mexico. Arellano was sent back with the main force, up the Pecos River, and was in Tiguex in July. The great stone houses Coronado was promised by the Turk obstinately refused to appear. At length the Great Plains gave place to the Prairies and to Indians who cultivated the soil as well as hunting buffalo. After forty days they reached the Wichita tribe, which did in fact have the straw houses the Turk had mentioned among his less startling forecasts.

The party was in what is now central Kansas, on the Arkansas River,[17] which in the end flowed into the Mississippi and thence into the Gulf of Mexico. But Coronado was more interested in the lack of metals in Indian hands than the significance of transcontinental

17. Bolton, *Coronado* (1964), pp. 292–295, places his estimated eastward limit as in the vicinity of Lindsborg, Kansas, on the Kansas River, but it must remain somewhat debatable.

drainage systems. The Turk was seized and admitted that though they had reached Quivira, there were no riches there. His admissions under torture that he had been the instrument of a plot to draw Coronado away from the Pueblo area to his death in the northeast cannot be verified, because he was shortly executed. The expedition had reached its furthest eastward limit, and the riches Coronado sought had receded into myth. It was time to return.

On the way back, Coronado followed a more direct route to Pecos, by way of the Canadian River, and, reaching Pecos, linked up with a force sent by Arellano to return to the Rio Grande and his pueblo base at Tiguex. His long march ended in September with the whole army reunited at Tiguex.

Winter set in again before any decision on future explorations had been made. The atmosphere was sober, even pessimistic. This time more care was taken to balance Spanish necessities against Indian resources. The pueblos agreed to give food and blankets, but not in such quantities that their own people were harshly deprived. The arrangement worked, in that the Spaniards avoided any collective excesses against the Indians though there was still oppression. Cárdenas was sent to convoy the wounded and incapacitated back to the base camp at Corazones. When he got there he found that it had been destroyed by fire, the garrison dispersed and its commander Diego de Alcaráz dead. He sent his men on to Mexico, equipped himself as best he could, and returned to Coronado to report what had happened since these events could affect his future plans.

Meantime, Coronado had been wounded in the head by a horse's hoofs, and was more or less out of commission until the spring. As he recovered and was again able to take decisions, he convinced his companions that, whatever still remained to be discovered, they had not now the resources to make further extended reconnaissances. He felt fairly certain that beyond the mountain rim of the Upper Rio Grande there was little but open country, apart from a central mountain range, and no news of or even hope of wealth in human hands, whatever might lie under the soil—many of his men were even more anxious than he to abandon the exploration.

In April all was ready for the return. Everyone except three friars and a handful of laymen left Tiguex. Fray Juan de Padilla, we know, marched off in the end to Quivira and was killed there. A Por-

# EXPLORATION IN THE SOUTHWEST
## 1529 - 1542

GRAND CANYON

Arkansas

Colorado

Little Colorado

Tiguex

Cicuye

Cibola

Acoma

Canadian

Gila

Red

Brazos

Daycao

Rio Grande

Pecos

Colorado

Sonora

Santa
Barbara

Rio Grande

Sinaloa

Culiacan

PACIFIC OCEAN

San Blas

Compostela

Mexico City

**Cabeza de Vaca 1529–1536**

— — — Principal route

· · · · · alternative to part of route

**Francisco Vazquez de Coronado 1540–1542**

——— Principal route

—x—x— with Melchior Diaz to
the mouth of the Colorado river

—o—o— and Tovar to Grand Canyon

| 0 | Km | 400 |
| 0 | Miles | 400 |

tuguese, Andres do Campo, and two Indian novices somehow reached Pánuco in about 1547, having made the first European crossing of the continent from west to east.[18] Those left behind in the Pueblo country simply disappeared. The journey back was rapid, as all impeding chattels were left behind and the way was now well known. There was no need to stay in ruined Corazones since Cárdenas's convoy had gone on to Mexico. Coronado, once the way was clear, took a hundred men and pushed ahead to report his return. He reached Culiacán, left most of his men there, and on June 24 set out for Compostela, and thence for the city of Mexico.

He had much to report, even though the interest and range of his exploration was for some time overshadowed by his failure to find riches and his return empty-handed. He lost his own large investment (some 50,000 ducats) and much of his reputation as well. He was charged with inadequate conduct of the expedition, with mistreatment of the Indians and with other things, but it became clear that as a military commander his conduct had been extremely effective and that he had brought his men safely home with very light casualties. His treatment of the Indians was not considered culpable although Cárdenas was subsequently convicted of cruelty.[19]

Within a few years, the magnitude of Coronado's explorations gradually came to be appreciated and his reputation recovered. Certainly, his was the most successful military expedition conducted by the Spaniards into North America in the sixteenth century—with the possible exception of that of Pedro Menéndez de Avilés in Florida in 1565. He had shown that, with good organization and close attention to the logistics of moving considerable numbers of men and animals, great distances could be traversed, although he was fortunate in that for very long periods he suffered no sustained attacks and, indeed, in most respects came to depend very greatly either on Indian kindness or forbearance. He had nothing to give them and much to take away. It was this negative aspect of his explorations which convinced the viceroy and his successors that there was nothing to be gained by expeditions into the far north and west. And so, for nearly forty years, the history of relations between Spaniards and the North American Indians north of Mexico is a

18. *Ibid.*, pp. 334–342, 358–361, 400–401.
19. The legal proceedings are given in Hammond and Rey, *Narratives*, pp. 313–397.

blank. The Seven Cities of Cíbola and Quivira alike had sunk back into the realm of legend and myth.

### III

Florida had earned a bad name for itself; yet it still appeared as a major question mark—one of the possible areas into which Spanish power might be intruded profitably. One man who believed so was Hernando de Soto, a newly rich *conquistador* who had had fifteen years' service in Central America and Peru and had returned with a great fortune as his share of Pizarro's plunder.[20] Soto was willing to gamble his money for power and somehow hit upon Florida as the area in which he might be able to obtain it. His ambitions were considerable: he asked for leave to conquer all the territory between the Mexican border and the farthest north the Spaniards knew of— Florida and Tierra Nueva—on the east coast. He appears from the start to have centered his hopes on the interior rather than the shores of the area. This was understandable on the analogy of both Mexico and Peru; where the coasts had offered little, the interior had produced a great deal. Charles V was willing to employ Soto on his own terms: he would make the conquest at his own cost and that of any adventurers he could attract to him. He would be permitted to create a great estate for himself and to retain the benefit of a number of the expected revenues from his conquests (though the crown required a half and half division of all bullion and jewels instead of the *quinta* or fifth which was the standard royal share). Otherwise, all lands would go to the crown, though of course the adventurers would get their share also. Soto would be *adelantado*, governor-conqueror, with the right to hand on the title and its powers inside his family on certain conditions.

The grant was made to him on April 20, 1537, and his preparations were well under way when Cabeza de Vaca returned to Spain in early summer of that year. He told Soto something about his experiences and was, in turn, offered a place in the expedition. He refused, and indeed adopted an attitude of secrecy about some of the things he had seen which made them appear potentially valu-

20. Lowery, *Spanish Settlements, 1513–1561*, pp. 213–252, is helpful. The biographies by R. B. Cunninghame Graham, *Hernando de Soto* (London, 1903), and Theodore Maynard, *De Soto and the Conquistadores* (New York, 1930), are now somewhat dated.

able, though his own views about the southeast were by this time scarcely printable. Soto easily mobilized about seven hundred followers in Spain, including some women and slaves. Cuba, of which he was made governor also, was to be his base in the Caribbean from which the expedition could be launched and supplied. He sailed from Spain on April 7, 1538, with ten vessels, all of which reached Havana safely between September and December. There his final preparations were made; slaves and servants were acquired, and horses and livestock for the march inland. When they sailed in May 1539 from Havana, he had six hundred soldiers (with more than one hundred servants), two hundred horses and at least three hundred pigs which accompanied him throughout the march (he had a personal herd of seven hundred when he died). They landed on the western side of the Florida peninsula on May 25, 1539.

It had taken two years to get the expedition to America from the first royal grant, and this cumbersome procedure was to be typical of the whole episode. Soto wished to do things in an elaborate and grandiose way, but had little ability to concentrate on essentials and move ahead effectively. Coronado had been decisive and efficient, not unwilling to apply force when he needed it but selective in its use, realistic in knowing what was and what was not possible for him and his men. Soto, if physically as brave as Coronado, was also fanatically proud, unwilling to admit defeat however realistic it might be to do so, greedy as if nothing less than a new Peru would satisfy him. Overtly ruthless in his dealings with his men and with the Amerindians he encountered, he was not, on the whole, an efficient organizer, though he had a strong sense of self-preservation in adverse circumstances which made his improvisations often seem inspired.

He sailed into Tampa Bay (Bahía de Espíritu Santo)[21] from the south and landed on the southeast side, taking possession of it for

21. Fidalgo de Elvas, *Relaçam verdadeira* (Evora, 1557) was the earliest full narrative to be published. The Gentleman of Elvas was translated by Richard Hakluyt as *Virginia richly valued* (London, 1609). The best modern edition is James A. Robertson (ed.), *True Relation of the Hardships Suffered by Governor Fernando de Soto*, 2 vols. (Deland, Fla., 1933); the most accessible that in Hodge and Lewis, *Spanish Explorers* pp. 127–272. Translation of reports by his secretary, Ranjel, appear in Edward G. Bourne (ed.), *Narratives of Hernando de Soto*, 2 vols. (New York, 1904) II, 41–149, and by Luis Hernández de Biedma, the royal official sent to watch Soto's activities, II, 3–39. Garcilaso de la Vega, *The Florida of the Inca*, translated by John G. and Jeanette J. Varner (Austin, Texas, 1951), is valuable, but it is difficult to separate authentic information from imaginative reconstruction.

the crown on June 3, 1539. On June 4, one of his earliest contacts with the local Indians (of the Timucua group) brought him a valuable prize, a Spaniard—Juan Ortiz—who had been in Florida or thereabouts since Narváez's day and knew much about the country and many of its languages. Ortiz had served with Narváez and had survived, having remained in various degrees of servitude in Indian hands. The unwieldy expedition was slow to move on. Soto knew what his tactics with the inhabitants would be; he would seize the local chief and ransom him back for corn and bearers—with some women for his men—to carry him to the next tribal center, when the chief and most of the bearers would be released (if not all the women) after the process had begun again. Only in this way was progress possible, but the burden it imposed on the Indians was always substantial and sometimes intolerable.

The first stage of the enterprise lasted from June 3, 1539, to October 6, 1539, and was marked by a march to the north,[22] though it is not possible to say that this direction was planned very far in advance; perhaps it was almost entirely circumstance which led Soto in this direction. It took him until August 1 to get his force ready to move. Some ships had been sent back to Cuba; a small garrison was left where he landed. To begin with, Soto was unable to obtain bearers so his progress was very slow indeed. Ortiz led him north toward what he knew to be the corn-rich Apalachee area. Having at last seized a chief and impressed him into providing male bearers and women, Soto had to meet a fierce Indian attack. The Timucua tribe was to prove indomitable in later encounters, and they gave a good account of themselves at Napituca, the so-called Battle of the Lakes, on September 15. However, they were eventually routed and some two hundred taken prisoner, most of whom were retained as slaves. Bridges had to be constructed in order to pass over several rivers before Soto's men reached their first Apalachee village (Ibitachuco) on October 3; on October 6 they came to Anhiaca, the chief town (on or near the site of modern Tallahassee). All round there were wide cornfields. These Soto seized, in spite of Indian resistance, taking corn, pumpkins, beans and dried plums in quantity.

22. The best authority on the route, though often tentative in its conclusions, is United States De Soto Commission, *Final Report* (Washington, D.C., 1939): it is summarized in John R. Swanton, *Indians of the Southeastern United States* (Smithsonian Institution, Bureau of American Ethnology, Bulletin no. 137, 1946), pp. 39–59.

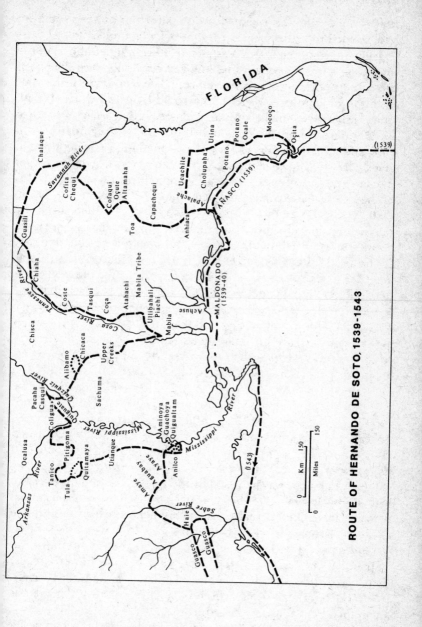

ROUTE OF HERNANDO DE SOTO, 1539-1543

Much of the spoil was retained as stores for the winter since Soto had decided to settle there for the next five months.

The pattern of the march was already becoming established: the long trailing expeditionary force moved slowly forward, living off the country, beating down resistance, taking food and manpower from the Indians as it wished. Soto could treat Indian chiefs with some respect but only when they did precisely what he told them to do; otherwise he could be quite ruthless. He regarded armed opposition as almost inevitable but as something to be suppressed quickly and without compromise, though he was quick to forget Indian resistance if they afterward complied with his orders. This strange parasitic existence seemed almost adequate as an end in itself. Yet Soto was always on the watch for stories of riches to be gained ahead of his line of march, even if in the first stage riches meant winter corn rather than gold or other enduring commodities.

The second stage, from October 6, 1539, to March 3, 1540, was one of inaction for the main body. Preparations for the next stage were put rapidly in hand. Juan de Añasco was entrusted with a major mission: he was to make his way to the coast—the Gulf coast northwest of the Florida peninsula—and there find a suitable port which he was to make sure he could identify in future and indicate precisely to others. He was then to proceed to the landing place and instruct the garrison to evacuate it and march northward to rejoin the main body. Finally, he was to order Francisco Maldonado to take the shipping remaining at the base back to Cuba and to return with supplies in the spring of 1540 to the port Añasco had located and indicated to him (presumably on a chart). Añasco duly performed his mission. The harbor he chose was Achuse, 60 leagues (about 150 miles) from Anhiaca, the modern Pensacola Harbor.

Meanwhile Soto was harassed by the Apalachee Indians over the winter. On December 28 they contrived to burn down a substantial part of Anhiaca and thereafter he and his men were less comfortable in their quarters. He was urged by his men to move on as soon as possible. A captured Indian told Juan Ortiz that to the north, in Yupaha (a Timucua name for the territory of the Lower Creeks) there was a tribe ruled by a woman that had gold and other riches. He now determined to make this his objective, so the next stage was a continuation of his northward march.

Soto still had considerable supplies of maize in hand when he set

out on March 3 on the short stage, the third, of his journey, which would last only until May 13. The going was difficult, since many of the Indian slaves had died over the winter and the Apalachee had evaded conscription as bearers; moreover, it appears that he met no Indians for another 150 miles as he crossed northwestern Georgia (no contemporary name describes it). There were no villages on his route and what Indians there were kept successfully out of his way. He crossed the Flint River only with difficulty, but just when he had used up most of his supplies he entered an area of grain-rich villages (in the province called Capachequi). These were usually evacuated on his approach but his men plundered them for corn and mortars on which to grind the grain—incursions which were normally followed by Indian cut-and-run attacks in revenge. After struggling through wet ground and recrossing the Flint farther up, they came to the Ocute-Altamaha region and there entered into rather more friendly relations with the Indians, since they had corn enough with them not to be too demanding. The Indians, too, were diplomatic enough to offer substantial gifts and so avoid being plundered. From Ichisi (on April 1) and Ocute (on April 10), they made their way northeastward until, just above the Fall Line, they ran out of supplies once more. Finally, at the end of the month they reached the Savannah River, near modern Augusta, and made contact through Ortiz with the woman ruler of a Lower Creek tribe of Cofitachequi.

"The Lady of Cofitachequi," as she appears in the narratives, was an able and attractive woman, well primed with information about Soto's way of proceeding. She was brought to his presence in a litter with a good deal of ceremony, after crossing the river, and flattered him with the gift of a necklace of pearls—the first valuable product of North America (even if they were mussel not oyster pearls) he had seen. The expedition then crossed to the north bank and received many presents of skins and decorated skin mantles, dried deermeat, corn bread (dry wafers to them), and salt brought from across the mountains to the west. These Indians were well clothed in skins, clean, well disciplined, and they turned over half of their substantial village to the Spaniards. The chieftainness removed herself from the town to avoid contact with the men, who wandered around the district helping themselves to corn from the granaries, seeing some notable structures (temples), and collecting, apparently with Indian

good will, several hundred pounds' weight of pearls from ossuaries. Amongst other finds were some Spanish artifacts—beads, rosaries, iron axes—that were evidently relics of the Ayllón colony and evidence of its location on or near the coast further down the Savannah River.[23] Some of the soldiers wished to stay to found a colony, hoping to use the mouth of the river for access by sea to the Caribbean; but Soto was not interested. There was, after all, no gold, and the pearls found were finite in quantity and could not rapidly be increased.

By May the Indians were restive and so was Soto. He was made to understand he might do better toward the northwest. He took with him as a hostage a woman he thought was the "Lady" but who was in fact her niece, with her attendants and a quota of bearers, and set off up the north bank of the Savannah into the high ground between the Savannah and Saluda Rivers toward a vaguely indicated Chiaha where, of course, gold was again said to be found. This stage was to last from May 13 to mid-August; during its course the northward march was to be ended and a southern one begun. In a week they came to Xuala, from which the ground sloped sharply upward to the higher mountains. This was the chief town of the Cheraw Indians, at the end of a range of hills extending to Chattooga Ridge in modern South Carolina. The Indians here were prosperous and again took the initiative in offering food and bearers. Soto then moved on over the watershed, making a comparatively painless passage over the Appalachian chain by the Winding Star Trail to the Little Tennessee River. The narrative of the Gentleman of Elvas says merely[24] that from Cofitachequi to Xuala there were 250 leagues of "mountainous country" and that from thence to Guasili, that is over the Appalachians, "the way is over very rough and lofty ridges." On the way the "Lady," or rather her substitute, gave Soto the slip, but what angered him most was that she took with her a basket of pearls.

Soto had now turned southwestward and given over his northern wanderings. Chiaha, for which he was bound, was said to be very rich. As he worked his way down toward the Tennessee River itself and then along its valley, his force was strung out into a long proces-

23. Hodge and Lewis, *Spanish Explorations*, p. 174; Bourne, *Narratives*, II, 100; and see pp. 145–147 above.

24. Hodge and Lewis, *Spanish Explorations*, p. 177.

sion. Early in June, Indians who brought them presents and gave them corn in their village conducted them to Chiaha (on modern Burns Island in the Tennessee River). From there they went on to Coste, where for the first time for several months they had to fight for their corn supplies. In neither place were "riches," other than corn, to be found. Their advance became more varied as they had to cross the river several times. At Tali the Indians supplied substantial dugout canoes for this purpose.

Finally, they reached the Coosa River, which they followed to Coosa (Coca)—the principal Upper Creek town that was now their objective. This was certainly a center of some importance, even if it had no more gold than any place else. The high chief was the dominant personality in a considerable grouping of tribal units, and in his territory the Temple Mound (II) culture, with its ceremonial centers and its profusion of personal adornment, and the high status of its chiefs, was very imposing,[25] though still far, in Soto's eyes, from the grandeurs of native Inca society which he had seen in Peru. Coosa was apparently in modern Talladega County, Alabama. There the Spaniards were greeted and stayed in some comfort for a month, almost certainly overstaying their welcome; but by mid-August the expedition was ready to be on the move, once again to the south.

The fourth stage of Soto's progress was to last from August 20, 1540, to January 15, 1541, a phase marked by a sharp decline in his fortunes. Its first episodes took him through the High Culture area of the Mississippian culture, which meant that, increasingly, he saw richer agriculture, larger villages (some of which were considerable towns), important temple mounds and other ceremonial symbols, and Indians who had a strong sense of hierarchy and considerable, if still primitive, resources. He could well have been under the impression that at the next tribal area, or the one beyond that, he would reach something like the Inca homeland, though so far as we know he could not identify even copper objects in Indian hands, let alone any gold. Bearing the Coosa chief and his elders as hostages, he moved in heavy rain to the limit of the Creek territory at Talisi —on a bend of the Alabama River. There they acquired bearers,

25. See Gordon R. Willey, *An Introduction to American Archaeology*, I (Englewood Cliffs, N.J., 1966), 298–308; Driver, *Indians of North America* (1969), pp. 303–304; David H. Corkran, *The Creek Frontier, 1540–1783* (Norman, Okla., 1967), pp. 41–45.

women and supplies of corn. They also received a messenger from Tascalusa, the powerful high chief of the Choctaw (Mobile) Indians, welcoming them to his territory. They passed through Choctaw territory until they came to Atahachi, Tascalusa's chief town. Tall, dressed in a feather mantle with a high headdress, the chief received them ceremonially seated in a balconied building in the central square. Dances were held in Soto's honor. Then Tascalusa was told that he would no longer be the great local lord, but only a hostage of the visitors. He appeared to take this well, providing four hundred bearers and promising a gift of one hundred women as they left his territory.

Soto was conducted to the southern town of Mabila (Mobile), a strongly stockaded settlement, which he entered with an advance guard on October 19. Then Tascalusa gave the signal for his men to attack. Those assigned to kill Soto failed to do so, but he was wounded in making his escape. His main force was driven to abandon their baggage, and when Soto had fought his way back into the town in hand-to-hand fighting the whole place was put to the flames, though the Indians were finally defeated. Most of the slaves they had with them, male and female, were killed and Soto admitted to 18 Spaniards killed and 170 wounded (most of them with three or four arrow wounds each). Almost all the baggage, clothing, stores, deerskin mantles, and the long-cared-for pearls were destroyed, while they lost twelve horses and had seventy injured. Soto claimed to have accounted for 2,500 Indians, though Tascalusa probably escaped.

Whatever the result of the fight, Soto had received a considerable blow. Just when it looked as if Indian society was becoming promisingly rich, that he might be on the threshold of discovering an aboriginal civilization, he found himself stripped of most of the trappings of a European army and reduced to the leader of a dispirited and disillusioned band of men. The blow to his pride was all the worse since he had been making his way discreetly southward, unknown to his men, in order to meet Maldonado's supply ships at Achuse. He now heard through the Indian messengers Juan Ortiz had arranged should meet him that Maldonado was in port awaiting him.

Soto faced his worst dilemma so far. In their present state, he knew that his men would insist on giving up the enterprise and

returning to Cuba in the ships if they learned of them. He himself was empty-handed and had not even token samples of his achievements to send with Maldonado to Cuba to show that something had been accomplished. In the end his insane pride drove him to ignore Maldonado, swear Juan Ortiz to secrecy, and carry on with the expedition, though now in a westerly direction as if no help was forthcoming. Thus he gambled on making discoveries elsewhere: the civilized gold- and silver-using Indian society he sought must lie in the west or northwest, if it was not to be found in the east. Should he fail to find it, his expedition might come to disaster in the end —as indeed it did—but at least he would have done all that was physically possible to explore what prospects were left.

As soon as his men could pull themselves together, Soto decided to march northward. He set out between the Tombigbee and Alabama Rivers through difficult country (over the site of modern Montgomery) into a better populated area, part of the Choctaw country, where he received welcome presents of furs against the forthcoming winter. He then worked his way on to Chicaca (Chickasaw) country to the northwest, eventually crossing the border of modern Mississippi, where he found a site, the exact location of which is unknown, in which he chose to winter. It was in a wooded region, with many walnut (and probably pecan) trees, oaks and live oaks, suitable for the pigs he still had with him. There he settled down fairly peacefully to lick his wounds, though there were occasional affrays with the local Indians.

The fifth stage covers most of 1541 from January to November. All was reasonably quiet until March 4 when a band of Indians infiltrated the village and set it alight, while a large force surrounded it and Soto once more had to fight his way out. He lost only twelve Spaniards and had no great number wounded. The Indians took flight fairly rapidly, but fifty horses and three hundred pigs had been killed, and all the spare clothing and such supplies as they had gathered were lost. They robbed a few villages in the district to get some food and coverings, and withstood a slight attack on March 15. Toward the end of April they were able to march out of the Chickasaw country into that of the Alabama Indians. On their way they destroyed an Indian stockade erected to impede their progress toward the northwest. They managed to continue, now due west, toward the great river, the Mississippi, of which they had heard,

devastating much of the territory of the Quiz Quiz Indians on the way (though afterwards making peace with them). In the middle of May they reached the "great river larger than the Danube," said Ranjel,[26] at what has been identified as probably modern Sunflower Landing, some 450 miles from the river's mouth—a notable landmark in North American exploration. The Mississippi was named the Río de Espíritu Santo.

Soto had now lost any real objective. Once he left the Choctaw territory, it was obvious that the level of Indian culture was declining so that any idea of a progressive cultural development toward the west must have disappeared from his mind by the time he reached the Mississippi. All we can say is that he had determined to go on, since perhaps when he was over the physical barrier of the river, he might pass a cultural barrier as well. The logistics of crossing the river were not easy. On May 21 he set his men to cut timber so as to build four large barges which would enable him to cross with his livestock. It took four weeks to do this, though the results were in the end satisfactory. Some Indians in canoes threatened him while he was actually going over on June 18 but did not attack, and the operation was conducted without loss. The barges were taken some way upstream and then dismantled.

The expedition now plunged into eastern Arkansas: "the worst trail for swamps and water that they had found in all Florida," Ranjel said.[27] Soto found that it was near the river that the Indians had most corn, so he kept his main force close to the main channel. His objective now was to find the Pacific. By means of scouting parties, he tried to capture Indians who might be able to tell him of the way to the South Sea or give any hints of where there might be gold. The scouting parties entered the Prairies and also for the first time encountered Plains Indians, who had infiltrated into the Prairies with their mobile nomadic life in conical tepis. These Indians were reported not to cultivate the land but to live off the wild "cattle"—the buffalo herds of the Plains. He then began to inquire about a route "to the other sea," the Pacific.[28]

The main expedition remained at Pacaha near the Mississippi, not far from the mouth of the St. Francis River, until late July. Then they

26. Bourne, *Narratives*, II, 137.
27. *Ibid.*, II, 138.
28. *Ibid.*, II, 31.

worked southward to a town, Quiguate, on the delta at the junction of the White and Arkansas Rivers. There they heard new rumors of gold which brought them on a march northwestward to Coligua at the Great Rock on the Arkansas River; but none was to be found. Soto at last turned southwest and then west to the Ouachita River. When he moved upstream he had a brush with the warlike Tula Indians (Caddos), who fought with long wooden lances or spears, before finally reaching the Great Plains, which were open, well peopled and clearly well cultivated. He found rabbits and corn in plenty, with good timber, and, in this area, some way to the south he settled at Utiangue for his third (and last) winter. The location was somewhere on the west bank of the Ouachita, south of modern Camden.

From the time that the two major expeditions had been planned and despatched, the possibility had existed that one or other of them might make a transcontinental traverse or that they might meet. But there was no clear idea of the width of the continent. Even after both expeditions had returned and there was plenty of time for re-evaluating their territorial span, Castañeda believed that the continent was no more than 600 leagues, under 1,500 miles, wide. Soto landed too early to have known Coronado's final plans, yet Coronado could well have learned something of Soto's. Soto's representatives in Spain did indeed raise the question of a possible demarcation line between their respective spheres of influence. By the time Soto crossed the Mississippi on June 18, Coronado was well advanced on his southern sweep toward Quivira and may even have turned northeastward by then as the Turk directed. On June 29, when Soto was at Pacaha's village just west of the Mississippi, Coronado reached the Arkansas River at the modern Ford, Kansas, south of Quivira. On July 2 or 3, he "wrote a letter to the governor of Harahey and Quivira, believing he was a Christian from the shipwrecked fleet of Florida"[29] (but a presumed survivor of Narváez's fleet; not anyone connected with Soto).

Castañeda, writing well after the event, considered that Coronado should have continued eastward and southeastward in the direction of Florida instead of turning north toward Quivira. While Coronado was at Quivira north of the Arkansas River and was sending out

29. Hammond and Rey, *Narratives of the Coronado Expedition*, p. 303.

parties to explore from there, Soto was at Coligua much further down the river and sent a party north of the river to explore the Ocalusa area. We cannot tell precisely how near they came to each other, but at the closest they must have been under 300 miles apart. Indeed Soto, after he had gone further down the Arkansas River to Quiguate, looked for "guides and interpreters, still with the intention of coming out, if possible, on the other sea [the Pacific]; for the Indians told us that eleven days' travel thence there was a province where they subsisted on certain cattle, and there we could find interpreters for the whole distance to that sea."[30] The concept of a journey from sea to sea was there, but each of the expeditions was stretched to its utmost limit at the point of greatest distance from their starting point. They might possibly have been able to reach each other if luck or good intelligence had favored them; neither was equipped to make the complete crossing. Castañeda, when he wrote, was very conscious that Coronado had crossed a continental watershed and that the streams he encountered late in his journey certainly ran down to the Gulf of Mexico.[31]

By the time he reached the sixth stage of his journey, from November 1541 to May 21, 1542, Soto's expedition had become in many respects a self-sustaining enterprise. Most of its Spanish equipment was gone, but they still had their herd of pigs, now growing fast in numbers. They were used to simple, home-made accommodation. The 1541 winter camp was planned systematically. It had a well-defended perimeter fence, inside which the men, in groups, were allotted stations along with their Indian women and bearers. All the local Indians were excluded from their own village during the night, and this led to friction, resentment, incidents and repression. But slowly some compromises were reached. They were fortunate in the weather since there was only one month of snow and appreciably low temperatures. The health of most of the men remained reasonably good, though many died from earlier wounds or illnesses. The process of adaptation appeared to be well advanced. There were now under 400 Spaniards, only about 300 of them able-bodied, and with only 40 surviving horses; the total number of supernumeraries is not known but it may well have been

30. Bourne, *Narratives of the Career of Hernando de Soto,* II, 31 (Biedma).
31. On Castañeda's geographical ideas, see Hammond and Rey, *Narratives,* pp. 219, 259–264, 282.

1,000 or more. They were beginning to run into severe deficiencies, notably nails for horseshoes. A major blow during the winter was the death of Juan Ortiz. Though they had long passed outside the Muskhogean language group in whose languages he was proficient, he had somehow developed and maintained some degree of linguistic understanding with the tribes they had so far encountered. True, there were a number of bearers who had been retained for some time and who knew some Spanish, but they were only faltering links with the Indians they knew and of little potential value when others, with novel languages, might be encountered.

Soto was finally willing to accept the necessity of returning to make contact with his countrymen. His pride had given way to a measure of realism since his view of the Prairies had shown him that the further west he went, the less likely it seemed that his civilized, gold-rich Indian society could be encountered. At last he was prepared to admit that it probably did not exist. He proposed to go down the Ouachita to the Mississippi and start to build pinnaces which would carry them to the mouth of the river. There they could establish a base from which contact with Cuba could be made and plans for the exploitation of the area already explored drawn up.

Moving away from Utiangue, he entered the province of Anilco —"a most populous region . . . abounding in maize," said the Gentleman of Elvas.[32] There were indeed quantities of corn, beans, dried persimmons, fish and dogs. Threats, war and compromise diplomacy brought them adequate supplies and enabled them to acquire by force or as presents skins and skin mantles to add to their clothing. As Soto moved downstream, the Indians followed him and attacked in some strength but his counterattack killed many of them. He reached the Mississippi at an unidentified place called Guachoya and appeared ready to begin the next stage in his withdrawal program. It was at that point that his career was brought to an abrupt end by fever. He died on May 21, 1542, after handing over command to Luis de Moscoso.

Whatever we may think of Soto's judgment, he certainly made a quite extraordinary contribution to American exploration. He was a remarkable leader in that he kept his men together under an exceptional variety of adverse circumstances and showed admirable

32. Hodge and Lewis, *Spanish Explorers*, pp. 224, 227.

resilience in meeting difficulties as they arose. He lacked a sense of proportion and his combination of obstinacy, greed, tenacity, pride and sheer endurance makes any assessment of him difficult and controversial. Indeed, he can be judged only by his actions. After the Battle of Mabila there had been a considerable element of the irrational in them, but he had the strength of will and the necessary ruthlessness to induce his men to follow wherever he might lead. Whether his pride could have borne the acknowledgment of defeat had he survived to restore contact with his Cuban base is doubtful. His discovery of the Mississippi Basin was an outstanding achievement, though full exploitation of this knowledge was to be very long delayed. Those who accompanied him recorded vital information on the development of the Lower Mississippi culture, as well as providing valuable insights on many local Indian groups. And they give us, with Coronado, the earliest glimpses of both Prairie and Plains Indians. His achievement was made possible only by ruthless exploitation of the Indians on whom he and his men lived. His bearers were treated as slaves, and for some it was long-term slavery; the women he acquired were taken mainly as prostitutes and discarded at will when they had ceased to be of use; the food he stole must have led to great hardship among those Indian tribes who lived close to the margin of subsistence. Yet, if he was a fearsome visitation to many of them and a portent of later white depredations, he was also a commanding figure, an intruding God who drew upon himself much respectful loyalty and equally violent hostility and hatred.

The post-Soto phase from May 1542 to September 1543 was a series of improvisations by the survivors, who only slowly learned to take decisions for themselves but did in the end manage to do so effectively. Moscoso and his men, for example, took a hasty decision that a westward route to Mexico should be attempted. It is difficult to believe that, had they known in detail Cabeza de Vaca's picture of his experiences in Texas, they would have done so. They set out on June 5 and turned northwestward to cross the Ouachita River, then west to the Red River, then southwest. The Caddo tribes— Naguatex, Amaye, and Hacanac—had good supplies of corn but resisted when required to part with them. A number of men and horses were wounded in the fighting which ensued, but enough food was acquired to keep them on the move. Further to the south-

west, after crossing the Sabine River, they found themselves in poor country with relatively few Indians and cultivation in only a small number of scattered districts. As they traveled southwestward through Texas, crossing the Trinity River on their way, they nearly starved to death. Finally, in the territory they knew as Guasco, they had to make the decision whether to push on and risk almost certain death or to return. They decided to turn back, and did so before they had lost too much of their strength.

The objective now was to return to the Caddo tribal areas and rebuild their stocks, so as to enable them to revert to the earlier plan of making boats and descend the Mississippi. The return began in October and was completed by the end of November after much hardship. Little corn had been grown at Anilco, but in the cold weather of an early winter they found an area, Aminoya, near the river where they obtained enough for their immediate needs. They took over a village as quarters for the winter, though it is not known precisely where this was.

All their efforts were now devoted to constructing boats. Seven little vessels were somehow put together and fitted out to sail, with cordage and mats supplied by the Indians under pressure. In March their quarters were nearly flooded out, but in June the water went down and they were ready at last. On July 2, 1543, they took to the water, abandoning some six hundred of the Indian bearers and women they had accumulated. There were 322 Spaniards still alive, about 100 Indians whom they still needed, and 20 horses, as well as a few surviving pigs. Two Indian dugouts were taken also for additional transport, lashed together, carrying a horse or horses; the local Indians came out in their remaining canoes to harass them for some time as they went downstream.

The expedition made fairly good progress until they reached the delta and the division of the river. On their way through the delta they were attacked again, this time by Indians using the atlatl, or spearthrower, which was a formidable weapon when used on water. At last they reached the Gulf coast and took to sea. The improvised craft slowly made their way, against adverse winds, along the coast from July 18 to September 10. They reached Pánuco on the latter day, wild men, long given up for lost, difficult to accept and reassimilate. The total of those who survived was 311, a surprisingly large figure, together with their 100 Indians whom they hoped to

keep as slaves and as the sole element of profit from a venture which for all of them had proved infinitely costly in effort and resources.

Moscoso remains a rather shadowy figure in the narratives. He worked by discussion and cooperation rather than by the ruthless domination which Soto had exercised. But he must have done extremely well to have extricated so many. The number of Indians killed by Soto and his men does not seem to have been less than 4,000, rather more than 10 for every Spaniard that survived.

## IV

While there was no attempt to parallel the Hernando de Soto expedition by other explorations up the Atlantic coast, the situation in the west was quite different. The expeditions of 1513 to 1528 to the southeast had all been unsatisfactory or disastrous, and, for the time being, the coast was written off as a possible location for a settlement. Nor, prior to Cabeza de Vaca's return, had there been any effective exploration of the west coast north of Mexico. Cortés was concerned at the lack of knowledge of the further coasts, and took advantage of the report of the Cabeza de Vaca journey to arrange with the viceroy for Francisco de Ulloa to make an expedition northward by sea from Acapulco.[33] He set out with three ships —the *Santa Agueda, Trinidad* and *Santo Tomás*—on July 8, 1539, and explored first the Gulf of California, which was named the "Sea of Cortés," and then the outer shore of the peninsula, making formal landings to take possession from time to time. From the Isla de Çedros, just north of 28°, he sent Francisco Preciado back in April 1540 with the *Santa Agueda* to report. Ulloa himself sailed on in the *Trinidad,* but if he returned, which is probable but not certain, he is unlikely to have gone north of 30°. He had, however, done important preliminary work of definition. Preciado can have reached Acapulco only on about April 24 or 25, by which time Hernando de Alarcón, who was to second Coronado's efforts by a voyage up the coast, was almost ready to leave. The *San Pedro* and *Santa Catalina* sailed from Acapulco on May 9, having received a report on the Gulf of California from Ulloa's men[34] which was of considerable assist-

33. H. R. Wagner, *Spanish Voyages to the Northwest Coast of America in the Sixteenth Century* (San Francisco, 1929), pp. 11–50.

34. Hammond and Rey, *Narratives,* p. 125.

ance. Alarcón located the mouth of the Colorado River at the head of the Gulf and spent sixteen days exploring its lower reaches; but he was not joined by part of Coronado's forces as planned and eventually returned, making a close inspection of the coast as he went south, and landing to take formal possession at a number of places. He was back in Mexico by November.[35]

The viceroy, Mendoza, had proposed to follow up the Ulloa expedition with a joint effort between himself and Pedro de Alvarado. Alvarado's fleet from Guatemala was at Colima when Alarcón returned, but Alvarado was killed on a local campaign in Mexico and his fleet then dispersed. Mendoza continued his efforts by sending Francisco de Bolanos north in the San Gabriel (perhaps with some other vessels) in September 1541, though we do not know how much further north along the coast he penetrated.[36]

There is much less mystery about the expedition of Juan Rodríguez Cabrillo—or as he is more correctly known, in the Portuguese form of his name, João Rodrigues Cabrilho—[37] who was given charge of two ships from Alvarado's fleet, the San Salvador and Victoria. They sailed from Puerto de Navidad on June 27, 1542, and reached the Isla de Çedros in August. From there they rapidly covered the remaining shore of Baja California, passing San Diego Bay to be the first recorded European visitors to Alta California. Though they landed frequently and described various natural features, their latitude observations were anything from ¾ to 2 degrees out and this error of up to 140 miles makes identifications debatable. As far as Conception Point (that is, beyond modern Santa Barbara), there is not so much controversy; but the Bahía de Pinos has been identified as anything from Monterey in the south to Drake's Bay in the north, the former being the more likely. To the north Cabrillo's Cabo de Nieve was apparently Cypress Point, the end of the snow mountains or Sierra Nevada. Driven south by storms, he put in at Isla de Posesión, apparently San Miguel Island, near Santa Barbara. There he died, on January 3, 1543, from the effects of a fall he had previously suffered on the same island going north. Bartolomé Ferrelo, in the Trinidad, took up command and returned northward up the coast. He certainly passed the Golden

35. Ibid., pp. 124–125; Bolton, Coronado, pp. 153–168.
36. Wagner, Spanish Voyages, pp. 63–71.
37. Ibid., pp. 72–93.

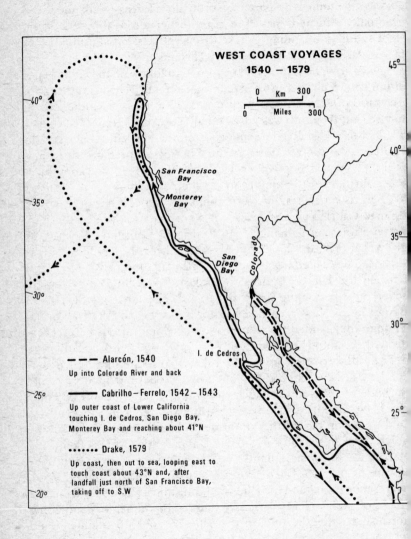

**WEST COAST VOYAGES**
**1540 – 1579**

0   Km   300

0   Miles   300

San Francisco
Bay

Monterey
Bay

San
Diego
Bay

Colorado

I. de Cedros

– – – Alarcón, 1540

Up into Colorado River and back

——— Cabrilho–Ferrelo, 1542–1543

Up outer coast of Lower California
touching I. de Cedros, San Diego Bay,
Monterey Bay and reaching about 41°N

••••• Drake, 1579

Up coast, then out to sea, looping east to
touch coast about 43°N and, after
landfall just north of San Francisco Bay,
taking off to S.W

Gate without recognizing an entrance to San Francisco Bay, and may have reached the coast about the present California-Oregon border at about 41°N., possibly, it has been suggested, the Eel River. There adverse winds forced him again to turn south and back to his point of departure, Puerto de Navidad, on April 14, 1543. By then Coronado had returned unsuccessfully from his search for riches in the north, and interest in further exploration—whether by sea or land—came to an end for more than a generation.

## V

From a modern standpoint, the two great Spanish expeditions can be seen to have been decisive in establishing the extent and character of much of North America. Between them they cut a broad swathe of information through the continent from Atlantic to Pacific. They had exhibited a great variety of American scenery, products and peoples, and also the relatively narrow range of variations which were of economic interest or value to Europeans. The Indians might be suitable subjects for conversion; they might prove useful bearers for an expedition and capable of supplying a certain amount of food for its support. But nowhere was there clear evidence of any appreciable level of civilization or sophistication, nor of mineral or agricultural wealth, though there might still be significant indications that some such features could possibly exist to the north of the areas traversed by the expeditions. We are, however, in a more favored position than contemporaries. The greater part of the information on which we rely was retained in official quarters in Spain, and even the major narratives appeared only slowly and incompletely, a number of them not until the nineteenth century. An overall view of the achievements of the expeditions was not possible for any except a limited circle of officials and survivors. From their point of view, the expeditions had been expensive failures. The greater part of the lands traversed could be written off as of no, or very slight, future interest or value. Coronado's expedition answered the question of what lay to the north of Mexico, but for forty years aroused no further interest in its exploration or development. Hernando de Soto's led the interior of the southeast to be equally written off; when attention was revived, it was in the Gulf coasts, in peninsular Florida and the Atlantic coast north of the peninsula,

rather than the interior. It is, indeed, astonishing how rapidly the scale of the expeditions' wanderings was forgotten and how, even at the end of the century, it could be seriously thought that from, say, Chesapeake Bay to Mexico and New Mexico were distances of only a few hundred miles. The expeditions were not wholly unremembered or entirely uninfluential; but their influence was generally negative and the information they brought back only minimally assimilated into the lore about and knowledge of the northern fringe of the Spanish empire.

For the maps of the generation from 1545 to 1575, however, the expeditions were influential. North America in its southern half took on something of the scale and configuration which related it, more or less adequately, to Mexico and the rest of the Spanish possessions. Comparably in the north, if the Cartier-Roberval expeditions were not wholly forgotten they remained uninfluential, so far as our information goes, for nearly forty years. Their main short term impact, too, was on the maps. The maps of the Norman School, which recorded the discoveries made in and around the St. Lawrence Valley, permanently altered the contours of North America in this region. But a great stretch of the north and an even greater portion of the northwest remained wholly unexplored and therefore still wholly open to the guesses of cartographers and the speculations of would-be projectors and explorers.

The Spaniards had traveled across as well as along the inland waterways to reveal the interior both of the west and the southeast. The French had made a comparable, but much narrower, penetration of the St. Lawrence seaway and gone no further. Marcel Trudel calls the achievement of Hernando de Soto "a spectacular feat that clearly showed up Cartier's and Roberval's timidity."[38] This may be so, but the conditions are scarcely comparable. The Cartier-Roberval ventures were relatively small in scale, with limited financial resources behind them. They took place in an area where, for five months, Europeans were liable to be frozen in under conditions of maximum discomfort. The physical means of movement beyond the Lachine Rapids were not apparent, as none of the expeditions was equipped for exploration by land. The Indians, even if willing, had little in the way of supplies to give the French. The Spanish expedi-

38. Marcel Trudel, *The Beginnings of New France, 1524–1663* (1973), p. 53.

tions, on the other hand, were much larger; they were also backed by the logistics of experience in other parts of the empire and equipped with livestock, as well as major stores for inland travel. They were able, literally, to harness the indigenous peoples into loadcarrying for them. Their horses gave them mobility as well as military power. They passed through territories where they did not suffer undue hardship in wintering and where, in most cases, the Indians had some surplus of foodstuffs to give them or of which they could be deprived.

The qualitative differences between the two sets of inland voyages were very great. Each did as well as could reasonably be expected —Hernando de Soto's rather more so, since Roberval probably had the capacity to reach Lake Ontario and conceivably Lake Erie and to make an extended reconnaissance of the Ottawa River, which he almost certainly did not attempt to do. In general, however, the nature of the terrain and the character of the expeditions was such that each did as much as was possible. Together they left unforgettable traces on the map and on the historical memory.

## VI

There are two further episodes to record. One of them, the attempt of Fray Luis de Cáncer to establish a mission on the west coast of Florida, was an isolated and tragic incident, but one which ties the beginnings of missionary activity in North America with the work of those friars elsewhere who were inspired by the ideals of Bartolomé de las Casas rather than of the time-serving clergy of the major Spanish colonies. The other was a much more elaborate affair. Tristán de Luna aspired to use part of the information brought back by survivors of Hernando de Soto's expedition, not to emulate his endless marches over trackless country, but to exploit his inland route from Florida to the Savannah River and so to establish on the southeast coast, near the site of Ayllón's ill-fated settlement a permanent Spanish base on the Atlantic. This venture was to undergo as many disappointments and to make nearly as many misjudgements as Narváez had done earlier, though it was to avoid total disaster. And when efforts were made, under Villafañe, to recoup its losses and turn failure into success by reverting to the attempt to form a colony near the ill-defined Punta de Santa Elena

these were no more successful and the plans had to be abandoned, though some valuable exploration was done on the coast between Florida and Chesapeake Bay, the latter being explored for the first time by the Spaniards.

The Luna-Villafañe ventures of 1559–61, whatever their lack of success, stand at the junction of three more or less distinct phases of Spanish enterprise in the southeast. Luna assumes some familiarity with the interior of the southeast, which attempts to exploit but not to rival the abandoned wide-ranging efforts of Soto and Coronado. They revive the attempt of Ayllón to create a Spanish colony well up the southeast coast so as to command the Atlantic seaboard at a latitude where the Spain-bound fleets from the Indies would strike out into the open ocean, away from the land, but Villafañe's abortive colony represented the last attempt to do this in isolation from a base farther south, on the Florida peninsula, and so reasonably accessible to Havana and Santo Domingo. The expeditions can thus be seen as preparatory to the final stage which at long last brought about the establishment of a permanent Spanish colony in Florida in 1565.

# VII

The Cáncer mission can be briefly dealt with.[39] Doubts had been raised for a long time by the 1540s about the moral rightness of the Spanish conquest of the Amerindians, and the practice of conquest followed by servitude was being mitigated in certain respects by the imposition of protective codes which culminated in the famous New Laws of the Indies in 1544, which, if they were never fully operative, at least took away the stigma of mindless cruelty from official Spanish policy. The chief objective of the clergy among the reformers had been to create conditions in which Indians might be Christianized under more favorable auspices than hitherto. Mass baptisms in Mexico had, it was realized, meant little to most of those nominally converted. Many friars, Dominicans and Franciscans, had worked hard to pin down Indians along the borders into villages where they

39. The principal source is Fray Gregorio de Beteta's narrative in Buckingham Smith, *Coleccion de varios documentos para la historia de la Florida* (London, 1857), pp. 190–201, while there are narratives in Lowery, *Spanish Settlements, 1513–1561*, pp. 411–427 and V. F. O'Daniel, *The Dominicans in Early Florida* (New York, 1930).

could be gradually turned into Christians. But they found they were followed by officials who proceeded to tax the Indians, by mining and land speculators who wished to exploit their labor, and by soldiers, in turn, to coerce them into becoming submissive subjects of Spain, so that the Christianity they brought was inevitably associated in the minds of those they hoped to convert with political and economic subjugation. A few friars, inspired basically by Las Casas's philosophy that the Indians, in the context of their own society, were inherently good and could be reformed by example only into accepting Christianity, attempted to carry on their missionary task in isolation from all other Spaniards so that Christianity alone, without its secular accompaniments, could be introduced to hitherto uncontaminated Indians.

Luis Cáncer de Barbastro, an idealistic Dominican friar, proposed such a mission in 1548, and he obtained some support and finance for it from the Emperor Charles V in 1549. The plan was to land a small group of missionaries on an inhabited coast and leave them there to make their own way, by force of their ingenuity and, it was hoped, their moral example into the minds and souls of the local Indians, without any armed support or continued protection from Spanish laymen. He left Vera Cruz in the late spring of 1549 in the *Santa Maria de la Encina,* an unarmed vessel, which had Juan de Arana as pilot, to make a landing at some part of western Florida where Spaniards had not hitherto touched and had not yet experienced their exploitative habits. Fray Luis was to go ashore with three other friars, Gregorio de Beteta, Juan Garcia and Diego de Tolosa, a young novice called Fuentes and a Christianized Florida Indian woman, Magdalena, apparently one of the slaves who had survived the Soto expedition, as an interpreter.

The ship coasted western Florida between 28° and 23° 30' N., inshore exploration having to be done by boat as the ship was of too great draft to come near land. An apparently friendly band of Indians was encountered to whom Cáncer spoke and to whom he gave presents. It was arranged with them that a party should accompany the Indians by land to a nearby harbor where the missionaries and their supplies would be established. Cáncer, after going back to the ship for some supplies and presents, returned to find that three of his companions, Diego de Tolosa, Fuentes, and Magdalena, together with a sailor, had disappeared, as had the Indians.

Going back, once more, to the ship, Cáncer got Arana to search for the harbor, apparently Tampa Bay, of which the Indians had told him, though through various mischances it appears to have been sixteen days before they finally entered it. When they eventually landed renewed friendly contact was made with the Indians, among whom Magdalena appeared, saying the Indians were alarmed at the ship's arrival, though she had tried to calm their fears and said that they had not harmed their captives. After returning to the ship, however, Cáncer learnt that a Spaniard, Juan Muñoz, a straggler from Soto's force and long a captive with the Indians, had escaped to the ship and said that the Indians had indeed killed the two religious, though not the soldier. Cáncer felt he should go ashore to confirm this, even though he realised the risks he ran. He was not able to do so for several days owing to bad weather, but on June 15 the boat put in to land. Though Muñoz talked to some Indians from the boat and was very doubtful about their intentions, Cáncer insisted courageously—and perhaps foolhardily—on going ashore alone. He was met in a friendly manner, but was soon set upon and killed, whereupon the Indians began to try to reach the boat, which turned back to the ship leaving the body of the friar in the hands of the Indians. The *Santa Maria,* by this time leaking and with few stores, limped back to Vera Cruz, reaching San Juan de Ulua on July 19 to report the total failure of the mission.

Arana had failed in his task of bringing Cáncer to a place where the Indians had not already suffered at Spanish hands. The Timucua Indians of the Tampa Bay area had already suffered considerable losses and casualties from Soto's army and were therefore liable to resist by force any further Spanish incursions, however peaceful in intention they might be. But had the landing been made elsewhere the result might not have been very different. The Calusa Indians had already shown at Charlotte Harbor their implacable hostility to Spanish intervention; the tribes to the north of the Timucua lands were, like them, alert to any successors to Soto. The policy of the segregated and independent mission with which Cáncer had hoped to experiment, never got a chance to prove its validity. The fault was not with the friars, but with the reputation for violence and exploitation the Spaniards had already won for themselves, throughout much of the southeast. Cáncer's was an isolated event. It was not to be emulated in North America for over twenty years.

# VIII

Tristán de Luna was an elderly and experienced Spaniard who had served long before in the Coronado expedition and who had extensive possessions in Mexico which he was expected to mobilize as his contribution to the expedition.[40] Late in 1558 he was selected by the viceroy of Mexico, Luis de Velasco, as governor and captain general of Florida and Santa Elena. Official Spanish policy had been moving slowly toward a new Florida venture. The primary motive was strategic. French privateers were known to use the coast for obtaining water and fuel and for trading with the Indians. It was feared they would soon go further and establish a shore base in the vicinity of Punta de Santa Elena, a location which remained vague in Spanish minds, though it was thought to lie at or near 33° N. If a Spanish colony could be established there, French attacks on the homeward-bound fleets might be prevented and, in addition, shipwrecked Spaniards and their goods rescued, while there were also ecclesiastical pressures on the crown to renew its missionary activity. Besides a forward base at Santa Elena it was intended that a strong post should be established on the Gulf of Mexico from which Spanish power could be spread eastward and westward along its shores. It was with these objectives in mind that Philip II, in December 1557, had ordered Velasco to put the Florida enterprise into effect.

So many expeditions and ships had come to grief on the southeast coast of North America that there was much reluctance to risk another fiasco such as that of Ayllón in 1526. But the official report of Soto's expedition had stressed the ease with which he had made his way to the territory of the Indian tribe ruled by the Lady of Cofitachequi (whose realms had taken on ever more golden hues since 1540) and from the center of which remains of the Ayllón expedition had been found in the Savannah River basin, giving rise

---

40. The principal sources for the Luna expedition are *The Luna Papers*, edited by Herbert I. Priestley, 2 vols. (Deland, Fla, 1918, reprinted Freeport, N.Y., 1971), and Fray Davilla Padilla, *Historia de la fundacion y discurso de la provincia de Santiago de México, de la orden de predicadores* (Madrid, 1596). Priestley's introduction to the *Luna Papers*, his biography, *Tristán de Luna* (Glendale, Calif., 1936), and Lowery, *Spanish Settlements, 1513–1561*, pp. 351–377, provide adequate accounts, though details of some aspects remain obscure.

to the belief that the sea could be reached in a two days' journey. Moreover, it was believed that from an undefined point on the Gulf it was only some 80 leagues (200 miles) to the Savannah. This innocence was compounded by confusion between the two branches of the Creek Indians, that on the Savannah and that on the Tennessee and Upper Alabama Valleys, in the latter of which Soto had found Coosa and its people agreeably rich in corn. A further influence may have been the publication in 1557, at Evora in Portugal, of the Gentleman of Elvas' *Relaçam verdadeira*, which also mentioned the Ayllón relics, though his geographical indications should have dispelled some of the cartographical and geographical myths which had grown up and which were to lead the Luna expedition astray.

Luna took the oath in the city of Mexico on November 1, 1558, mobilized his forces slowly and finally set out for Florida on June 11, 1559. The military component was roughly similar in scale to that of Coronado and Soto before him, namely, some 500 men. The subsidiary complement was much larger. Soldiers' wives and children, civilian families, a considerable number of Mexican Indian servants and also some slaves amounted to more than a thousand persons. There were some Dominican missionaries among them. The expedition required a fleet of thirteen vessels.

Elaborate and sophisticated instructions were laid for the organization of the territories to be occupied. A formula for the layout of the civilian settlements was provided and arrangements for local administration, on traditional Spanish lines, set out.[41] Luna's privileges and powers were defined in detail, though, as H. I. Priestley says,[42] a firmer definition of his powers as governor in relation to those of his *maestre del campo*, or second in command, Jorge Cerón, and with the royal officials appointed to watch over the interests of the crown might have rendered later disputes less bitter.

On August 14 the expedition entered Ochuse on Pensacola Bay, which was named Bahía de Santa Maria Filipina, and established a headquarters which was intended to be developed into the main shore base of the Gulf coast contingent. On August 19, when disem-

41. Priestley, *Luna Papers*, I, 18–32, 46–52. In accordance with the royal orders Velasco supplied Luna with a description and sketch-map of the town he was to build. The sketch is now lost but the following figure is an attempt to reconstruct it.

42. *Ibid.*, I, xxx.

# PLAN OF TOWN TO BE BUILT AT PUNTA DE SANTA ELENA, 1559

**(CONJECTURAL LAYOUT FOLLOWING A VERBAL DESCRIPTION IN THE *LUNA PAPERS*)**

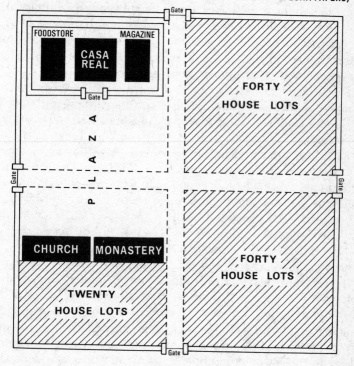

barkation of stores was still incomplete a hurricane struck the fleet at anchor and destroyed all but three of the vessels (a loss which in itself handicapped later supply attempts by Velasco). Reconnaissance parties returned with almost entirely negative reports on Indian occupation and food supplies in the adjoining area to find Luna and his company in an alarming position, with very little in the way of food supplies left to them. A further reconnaissance party brought some corn and beans and welcome news of a somewhat more fertile Indian territory inland on the Alabama River. Santa Maria de Filipina rapidly became untenable and in February 1560 Luna led his whole force northwestward, in search of a new location for his settlement which was found in an abandoned hill-top town of the Mobile Indians. This was reached overland by the main body and was named Santa Cruz de Nanipacana. Such stores as survived, and the remainder of the expedition, went in the surviving ships to Mobile Bay (Bahía Filipina), set up a small post there at Polonza at the mouth of the Alabama River, and made contact upstream with the main body at Nanipacana. At this place, the precise location of which it does not appear possible to ascertain, Luna laid out a compact Spanish town, the first in eastern North America to have a continued existence for over a year. Indian resources in food were finite but the expedition contrived to survive until the fall. Late in September Velasco learned of the expedition's plight. With difficulty he found two ships to bring a lading of food across the Gulf in November for their relief. By February 1561 this supply was exhausted: men, women and children began to die of malnutrition and disease. In the spring little food could be found in Indian hands.

Luna did not neglect his longer-range objectives. He despatched the *sargento mayor*, Mateo del Sauz, with two Dominican friars Domingo de la Anunciación and Domingo de Salazar, with some two hundred soldiers, to reconnoiter the route to the Indian tribe whose territory would point the way to Punta de Santa Elena. This expedition made good progress but it rapidly took a northerly rather than a northeasterly direction. In sixteen days Sauz reached the territory of the Coosa Indians some two hundred miles away in what is now Talledega County, Alabama, and entered the town of Coosa, which he believed to be equivalent to Soto's territory of the Cusabo (or Coosa?) tribe north of the Savannah River a further two hundred miles or so to the east. We do not yet know the details of

the linguistic and topographical confusion which led to this result. Sauz, like Soto before him and Juan Pardo after, was well received by the local Indians. Used to white men, they did not offer their corn stores to the Spaniards but issued them a meager but adequate ration in the quarters they set up some little distance from the village of Coosa itself. Once they were comfortably settled the Spaniards had no desire, it seems, to locate the sea (which was about three hundred miles away to the east) but chose a placid existence, the friars examining the prospects of missionary work, the soldiers eating and sleeping.

At the beginning of August Sauz sent back a party of thirty men under Cristóbal Ramírez to inform Luna of their achievement. Fray Domingo de la Anunciación wrote to Luna to explain how well they had been received. Basic supplies of food were assured and other things could be obtained by barter. But he was not so optimistic about Coosa as a site for a settlement (and seems to have forgotten that the objective for a settlement was the Punta de Santa Elena not Coosa). "As to making a settlement," he said, "it appears to me that the country is not so well suited for it as we thought. It seems very densely forested, and inasmuch as the Indians have a good part of it occupied, if a settlement were to be made it would be imperative to take their land from them. So for this reason and for others it is desirable that you come or send orders as to what is to be done." The Indians had been made aware that the Spaniards were subjects of King Philip and they asked that they should place themselves under his protection, while not renouncing their own tribal leader.

In the meantime further ships sent from Mexico in June failed altogether to reach Mobile Bay, and other plans to assist Luna came to nothing. Luna at Nanipacana had been taking considerable pains and exercising some ingenuity to keep his diminishing force from disintegrating entirely. He was ill and this at times affected his judgment so that he was not a very decisive or consistent leader. In June he was faced with organized protests by various elements in the expedition. The married soldiers made a firm and dignified plea for the abandonment of the plan for a colony as there were clearly insufficient resources in the area to sustain one, and desired Luna to return to Mexico. This protest was followed by one from the Mexican Indians, and, when these had had no effect, one from the principal officers of the expedition, backed up by the royal officials,

supporting the same procedure. Luna at first rejected all such representations but later countered them by proposing a rapid move to the vicinity of Santa Elena as had been intended. Jorge Cerón, his second in command, at length impressed on him the need for a more conservative plan and on June 22 Luna agreed to move back to the coast, first to Mobile Bay, and then a little later to Ochuse on Pensacola Bay. Some men were lost in the moves but supply ships were contacted early in July and vital stores brought ashore. As these were insufficient to feed the whole expedition for long, Luna was induced to allow the women and children, most of the clergy and some of the servants to be sent back to Mexico on one of the ships. The first stage in the abandonment of the original objectives had thus been taken.[43]

Peremptory orders had been sent by Velasco to Luna that he should set out as soon as possible to take possession of the Punta de Santa Elena since it was now believed that the French (in association with some unidentified Scots) were about to descend on this part of the coast and establish a permanent foothold there. Luna had come to doubt the possibility of discovering Soto's precise route and, instead, arranged that the remaining relief vessels should proceed to Santa Elena. Martín Doz, in association with Diego Biedma, took three ships on this mission. They were ill-managed, were scattered in a storm and finally put back in poor shape to Mexico having failed even to round the Florida peninsula,[44] though it was a long time before Luna learnt what had happened to them.

In mid-August Ramírez and his party arrived at Ochuse from Coosa and this seemed at last to offer a feasible objective, even if its relationship to Punta de Santa Elena was wholly undetermined. Luna seized on the letters and reports and urged that all—except a token garrison to be left at Ochuse—should proceed to Coosa. Once again he was met by a total refusal of the senior officers and the royal officials to cooperate. They urged Luna to appeal to Velasco to abandon the enterprise altogether. In the end a paper compromise was reached. The party to be sent to Coosa was to be limited to two hundred men. A very confusing period then followed. Luna issued orders; his officers did their best to delay their execu-

43. *Ibid.*, I, 228–232; Quinn, *North American Discovery*, pp. 93–95.
44. Velasco began from this time onward to doubt whether the objectives of the expedition were attainable (Priestley, *Luna Papers*, I, 188).

tion, the men in some cases resisting mutinously. In the latter instance a few ringleaders were hanged to prevent the rest from getting completely out of order. The royal officials now took the line that Luna had become mentally incapable of continuing in his command on account of illness. The contestants, legalistic to the last, fought their battles mainly by means of paper documents, a major consignment of which reached Velasco in Mexico in October.

In the meantime the officers and royal officials had succeeded in frustrating Luna's plans to send a force to Coosa. Instead, a small party under Juan de Porres was sent inland to bring Sauz and his men from Coosa. With their return, all thought of pushing out a further colonizing party was abandoned. A vessel was found to evacuate a further one hundred unfit men under Pedro de Acuna to Mexico where they were received with some official hostility. For the 400 to 450 persons left at Ochuse a position of stalemate had been reached. Luna was several times publicly humiliated by the friars in his own camp and he was gradually worn down to a point where he offered his resignation from his post to Velasco and desired to be allowed to return to Spain. Velasco, under continued orders to do something about the presumed French threat to the Punta de Santa Elena, had continued to believe in the need for a cross-country march to its vicinity, but he eventually accepted Luna's resignation. He appointed Angel de Villafañe as governor in Luna's place, with an alternative plan of campaign. A small holding party of fifty men was to be left at Ochuse under Diego de Biedma and Antonio Velásquez (with permission to return to Mexico after six months if they received no further orders). The main force was to be carried from the Gulf coast to Santa Elena by sea, and installed in a suitable site. Villafañe, welcomed in Ochuse in April, said farewell to Luna, and carried the expedition to Havana to reorganize. There most of the men found excuses to stay behind. When he set out in May he had only some seventy soldiers dispersed among his four vessels, only one of which, the *San Juan,* was of any considerable size.

With Luna's departure the original expedition had, for most purposes, come to an end. His two-year venture had been distinguished on his part by a certain lack of capacity for dynamic leadership though he himself had shown remarkable tenacity of purpose. He made no attempt to break out of the relatively narrow territory where he was boxed in. It may well be that his reconnaissance

parties found the swamps at the head of the Florida peninsula—interposed between him and Soto's Apalachee (in the vicinity of Tallahassee)—impenetrable. Intelligent persistence in reconnaissance would have revealed possible routes to the Piedmont and so to the route Soto had traveled. He was content to accept Sauz's Coosa as being that located by Soto east of the Appalachians.

Villafañe successfully rounded the tip of Florida and sailed up the coast.[45] His pilot identified to his own satisfaction the Punta de Santa Elena at what was believed to be 33° N. The harbor which the ships entered to the north of it, when possession was formally taken for Spain (as it was to be at other locations along the coast), did not satisfy Villafañe as offering a secure anchorage or an adequate site for a colony. The ships pushed on northward. The promontory at 34° identified as Cabo Román and the Río Grande to the north of it were also declared, after investigation, to be unsatisfactory, as was the Río Jordán when it was explored. The *San Juan* suffered some minor mishaps on shoals so that the smaller vessels were sent ahead to investigate the Río de Canoas at 34° 30' and the Cabo de Trafalgar at 35°, before returning to the flagship. The precise identification of these landfalls and entries cannot be given with confidence as both latitude determination and nomenclature are confused.[46] Near the Río Jordán a hurricane struck the little squadron. Two small vessels were lost and the others damaged. Villafañe with his broken force reached Havana on July 9, 1561. We may indeed ask whether he had seriously intended to comply with his instructions or whether he merely went through the motions of doing so, as he had no confidence in his ability to install an effective colony. The coast of South Carolina then and later proved frustrating to explorers and intending settlers. There was perhaps no more than this to his ill-success.

The year 1561 did produce valuable incidental information about

45. The materials on the Villafañe venture in Priestley, *Luna Papers*, II, 294–301, 307–311, 317–319, and the narrative in Lowery, *Spanish Settlements, 1513–1561*, pp. 374–376, provide an adequate outline, but a detailed inquiry into the expedition is still needed.

46. The latitudes given are clearly both inaccurate (to be expected) and inconsistent, so that little confidence can be placed in identifications: 33° N. Punta de Santa Elena (Hilton Head and Port Royal Sound, 32° 12'–32° 20'); 34° Cabo Román and Río Grande (Cape Romain 33° 01' or Santee Point 33° 07', with Waccamaw River); Río Jordan (Cape Fear River 33° 51'); 34° 30' Río de Canoas (New River Inlet 34° 30'); 35° Cabo de Trafalgar (Cape Lookout 34° 34' or Cape Hatteras 35° 14').

the east coast. Pedro Menéndez de Avilés, the able commander of the guard ships which had convoyed the Indies fleet from Spain, was asked at Havana to take two small vessels on his way back to explore the coast north of the presumed position of the Punta de Santa Elena. He made a close survey of the coast and at 37° entered a great bay, which impressed him so much that he later admitted he thought it extended all the way to the Pacific. This was Chesapeake Bay, named by him Bahía de Madre de Dios (or Bahía de Santa Maria). Contact was made with the local Algonkian Indians at or near the mouth of the James River—they were apparently members of what was later to be known as the Powhatan tribe—and from them obtained by fair means or foul a young Indian who was a son of the ruling chief. This man, later known as Don Luis, was brought to Spain and then sent to Havana to be Christianized. Menéndez's own detailed report of the coastal features has apparently been lost, but it was probably both accurate and complete.[47] It certainly remained in his mind in later years and was to serve him well in the fateful decade after 1564.

For a very long time the Luna expedition was the last of the great Spanish ventures—begun with Narváez a generation before—which attempted to spread Spanish power and population along the Gulf coast. Luna's failure demonstrated how little Spaniards had learned of either the geography or the ecology of southern North America and how easily the most elaborate arrangements to plan and supply such an expedition could break down in practice. Villafañe's experiences on the east coast indicated a similar lack of knowledge and confidence in dealing with the problems of a coast which had been repeatedly investigated since 1513. The joint failures led Philip II on September 23, 1561, to decide at last against any further attempts to garrison or settle Florida. But the era of tentative experiment was almost immediately to give way to more purposive and effective action. The French intervention which followed and the knowledge, personality and ability which Menéndez brought to bear were soon to produce more decisive and more permanent results.

47. Clifford M. Lewis and Albert J. Loomie, *The Spanish Jesuit Mission in Virginia, 1570–1572* (Chapel Hill, N.C., 1953), pp. 14–15, reach somewhat different conclusions on this episode.

# CHAPTER 10

## *The French in Florida, 1562–1565*

AFTER a considerable interval, France again turned her attention to North America, making an attempt to establish advance posts and a colony first in South Carolina (as it later became) and then in Florida.[1] The French concern with North America was in some sort a revival of the former interest aroused by the expeditions of Verrazzano, Cartier and Roberval: French geographers, courtiers, privateering seamen and merchants were all by 1560 interested in the New World, and this created an atmosphere in which it became possible to launch a new North American enterprise. But to some extent, too, it was an outcome of the Hapsburg-Valois struggle in Europe. The activities of French pirates and privateers (they were privateers rather than pirates when there was war between their sovereigns in Europe) in the Caribbean and elsewhere in American waters were part of the long struggle between France and the empire. The peace of Câteau-Cambrésis between these powers in 1559 provided a breathing space only. The occupation of part of North America during that breathing space seemed a wise move for France; the war might be renewed soon and it would then

1. The fullest accounts in English are in Woodbury Lowery, *The Spanish Settlements Within the Present Limits of the United States, 1561–1574* (New York, 1911; reprinted New York, 1964), and Henry Folmer, *Franco-Spanish Rivalry in North America, 1524–1763* (Glendale, Calif., 1953); neither is wholly satisfactory. Those in French, C. A. Julien, *Les Voyages de découverte et les premiers établissements* (Paris, 1948), and Marcel Trudel, *Histoire de la Nouvelle-France*, I *(Les vaines tentatives, 1524–1603)*, (Montreal, 1963), are to be preferred.

be an advantage for Frenchmen to be entrenched in bases close to the Spanish empire.

A further specialized incentive existed for the French Huguenots. They were a minority group in France, and might easily be forced into exile if the tide of Catholicism turned decisively against them at home. America had thus attractions as a place of refuge. In addition, the Huguenots as Protestant heretics were regarded as natural enemies by the Spaniards, and they reciprocated by considering any harm they could do to Spain or any inroads they might make into her empire well worth attempting. There were material incentives also. The French had tried to install themselves in Brazil during the decade 1550–60. This had been primarily a commercial bridgehead, aimed at tapping the rich stores of tropical produce, including especially the valuable dyewoods which Brazil afforded. But Portugal, with a great effort, taking advantage of French involvement in the military and naval struggle with Spain, had rooted out the French settlement there. So the need for a comparable base, in warm latitudes, which might supply some of the economic demands of France was one substantial incentive to explore and exploit the southeastern part of North America, whose climate offered fewer disadvantages than Cartier's Canada.

A parallel economic incentive was piratical. While attacking the Spanish empire during the war was an aspect of French patriotism, and while Huguenots did not need a war to impel them to raid Spanish overseas settlements, the ultimate objective in establishing footholds in North America was to build up bases from which the Spanish empire and the great annual fleets which came through the Florida Strait on the way to Europe could be robbed. By 1560 France had profited from nearly forty years of successful preying on the shipping of the Spanish empire. But the great outgoing and homecoming fleets were increasingly difficult to catch or overpower on the high seas. In the Caribbean and on the Florida coast rich individual prizes, which had fallen out of the convoys, might be picked off and handsome returns for French investors acquired.

Finally, there was the fact that some French vessels had been visiting the shores of what are now the states from Florida northward to Virginia for many years. On plundering cruises to and from the Caribbean they took in wood and water and cleaned their ships. They also traded with the Indians—a French ship of this sort was

trading with the Powhatan Indians in Chesapeake Bay in 1546. Luna and Villafañe had tried unsuccessfully from 1559 to 1561 to establish a settlement on what is now the South Carolina coast in order to deny it to the French.

In 1562 Jean Ribault set out to make his first attempt to establish a French outpost in the southeast. Ribault was an experienced pilot who had been interested in American adventures for more than a decade. His backer was Gaspard de Coligny, admiral of France, but with some assistance or at least approval from the king, Charles IX. Coligny's backing was to continue beyond 1562 into the period of the Laudonnière venture of 1564 and its relief and subsequent destruction in 1565; thus in a real sense, he was the father of the French Florida ventures.

Jean Ribault set sail with two ships and some 150 men on February 8, 1562, from Le Havre. His second in command was René Goulaine de Laudonnière, and the two men designated to remain to found the first French settlement were Captains Albert de la Pierria and Nicolas Barré.[2] After a rapid direct voyage across the Atlantic, Ribault made a landfall on April 29 in Florida at Anastasia Island, the headland of which he named Cap François. His first penetration of the land took place at the mouth of the St. Johns River, where he encountered friendly Indians of the Saturiwa (Timucua) tribe under their chief Saturiwa.[3] Though attracted by this river (which he named the River of May), and erecting a stone column to mark the annexation of Florida to France, Ribault pressed on along the coast. He surveyed and named the successive rivers he touched on until he arrived at St. Helena Sound; there he turned back to the entry to which he had given the name Port Royal (Port Royal Sound), where he had decided to establish his post. Port

2. Jean Ribault, *The whole and true discoverye of Terra Florida* (London, 1563; best edition, ed., Jeannette Thurber Connor [Deland, Fla., 1927, reprinted Gainesville, Fla., 1965]), is the basic authority, supplemented by Laudonnière's "History" (for which see p. 244, n. 5 below). A contribution of substantial importance is W. P. Cumming, "The Parreus Map (1562) of French Florida," *Imago Mundi*, XVII (1963), 27–80.

3. The basic reference material on the Florida Indians is in John R. Swanton, *The Indians of the Southeastern United States* (1946) and *The Indian Tribes of North America* (1953) (Smithsonian Institution, Bureau of American Ethnology, *Bulletin* nos. 137 and 145); John M. Goggin, *Space and Time Perspective in Northern St. Johns Archeology* (New Haven, 1941); William C. Sturtevant, "Spanish-Indian Relations in Southeastern North America," *Ethnohistory*, IX (1962), 41–94.

Royal Sound appeared to offer an extensive anchorage which would be valuable for vessels engaged in raiding the Indies, while the site would also be sufficiently off the beaten track to escape the attentions of Spanish ships reconnoitering the coast. It had probably, in any case, been used by French privateers at an earlier date.

The exact location of the pillar annexing the entry to France and even of the fort which Ribault's men began to build have been subjects of dispute. Parris Island, because the Spaniards later established a fort there, has been the favorite choice: it now appears virtually certain that Charlesfort was established on Battery Creek (named by Ribault the river Chenonceaux) near the present site of Port Royal. In June, La Pierria was left in charge of the small garrison of thirty men which was to create a military outpost on the coast of "Florida," which then comprised the modern shorelines of Georgia and South Carolina as well as Florida itself. He was to get to know the area thoroughly before larger forces came out the following year to create a more effective colony.

Though the Cusabo Indians of the Oristan (Edisto) tribe proved friendly, they had little food to spare; Ribault had not left enough, and there were no obvious signs of minerals which might make the soldiers rich. They eventually revolted during the winter of 1562–3 against privation and military discipline, and overthrew their commander, electing Barré in his place. Under his leadership they constructed, with some aid from the Indians, a small seagoing vessel, but they were not satisfactorily equipped or victualed for an Atlantic voyage. Starvation was ultimately followed by cannibalism. However, some of the men survived long enough to be rescued by an English privateer, and brought back to France to tell of the failure of the first outpost sometime during the first half of 1563. The main legacy of the 1562 expedition was a report prepared by Ribault and a map constructed by Barré.

Meanwhile, though he reported to Coligny on his return to France in July, 1562 Ribault had been unable to obtain supplies for the garrison as Le Havre was in Huguenot hands and besieged by royalist forces. Later in the year English aid was obtained; this provided Ribault with a chance to go to England, which he did early in 1563, hoping to get support from acquaintances there. He used his report to Coligny, when it had been translated into English, to interest persons at court and eventually succeeded in attracting the

attention of the queen—or at least of influential persons close to her. Thomas Stukely—a young English courtier who was interested in both robbery and riches—decided to go to the help of the French in the hope of gaining prizes and possibly finding gold for himself and his men.

After circulating in manuscript, Ribault's report was printed as a pamphlet under the title *The whole and true discoverye of Terra Florida;* in very attractive terms it gave the first description in English of the southeastern part of North America. Stukely prepared an expedition of five ships and set out for Florida in July 1563, but without Ribault.[4] The English had fallen out with their French allies and retired from Le Havre, so that Ribault came under suspicion in England and was imprisoned for a time, during which the fate of the first colony became known. Stukely had decided not to attempt to go to Florida but to set himself up as a pirate off the approaches to the English Channel—this he did with some profit to himself, until eventually he returned to England. In the meantime, peace having been restored to France, Coligny took up the question of a further expedition to Florida. He appointed Laudonnière as commander and received considerable help from the king, who gave Laudonnière the title of lieutenant of New France. The main backing came from Huguenot Normandy, which supplied the ships *Ysabeau,* Jean Lucas, captain, *Petit-Breton,* Michel Le Vasseur captain, and *Faulcon,* Pierre Marchant captain. Several other small vessels accompanied them. A painter, Jacques le Moyne de Morgues, was selected to bring an effective record of the new land back to France.[5] Ribault

4. Public Record Office, London, High Court of Admiralty Examinations, H.C.A. 15/5, nos. 32, 36, 37, 38; and H.C.A. 14/6 no. 4, contain information on the preparations for the English expedition.

5. The basic text is René Goulaine de Laudonnière, *L'histoire notable de la Floride* (Paris, 1586); a facsimile was published in Lyons (1946), and the best French edition is in Suzanne Lussagnet (ed.), *Les Français en Amérique pendant la deuxième moitié du XVIᵉ siècle,* II *(Les Français en Floride)* (Paris, 1958). The first English edition, *A notable historie containing foure voyages made by certayne French unto Florida* (London, 1587), was reprinted in Richard Hakluyt, *Principall navigations* (London, 1589), and *Principal navigations,* III (London, 1600), the best modern reprint being in *The Principal Navigations,* VIII–IX (Glasgow, 1904). A facsimile of the 1587 edition, with an introduction by Thomas R. Adams, appeared in 1964 (Farnham, Surrey, and Larchmont, N.Y.). Réné Laudonniere, *Three Voyages,* edited and translated by Charles E. Bennett (Gainesville, Fla., 1975), is a new translation. Laudonnière is supplemented by Theodor de Bry, *America,* part ii (Frankfurt am Main, 1591), containing the engraved drawings of Jacques le Moyne de Morgues. A full study of these has now appeared.

did not reach France until they had sailed, but was then placed by Coligny in charge of preparing a supply for the colony.

Sailing from Le Havre on April 22, 1564, Laudonnière made a fast passage to Dominica and sailed up through the islands to the Florida Strait. There he made a landfall just south of Cap François, putting in at what is now Matanzas Inlet on June 22. This time the objective of the expedition was the River of May, the St. Johns. The Indian chief, Saturiwa, who had met Ribault, received them with enthusiasm; with his advice a site was selected for a fort and Indian help with the early stages of its construction obtained. The fort was named La Caroline in honor of the king (for convenience it can be referred to as Fort Caroline). It was located on the south bank of the river some way from the mouth and had a deep channel nearby. Laid out on generous lines, it contained extensive quarters inside a strongly defended perimeter. A few words of the Timucuan language enabled Laudonnière to promise to associate himself with Saturiwa in his war with Utina and the tribe of that name (sometimes called simply Timucua) who resided inland, mainly on the west bank of the St. Johns River. A garrison of about two hundred was to occupy the fort and reconnoiter the coast more intensively than Ribault had done and, especially, to explore the interior, since reports that there were precious metals in Indian hands had given considerable support to the belief that rich sources of gold and silver might be found there.

The operation was basically a holding one, to enable a third expedition to found a genuine colony of settlement on a secure basis. It had the disadvantage that its objectives were insufficient to occupy the men fully, or, as it proved, profitably. Yet the fort needed to be of some strength in case a Spanish vessel chanced on it and began hostilities. Indeed, Spain had determined to deny the coast to the French: Manrique de Rojas—though Laudonnière was not aware of this—had scoured the coast earlier in the year and had even

Paul H. Hulton, *The Work of Jacques le Moyne de Morgues* (1977), contains a new translation of Le Moyne, with a critical commentary on his drawings, as well as much information on the French colony. Useful documents, not available elsewhere in English, are included in Charles W. Bennett, *Laudonnière* (Gainesville, Fla., 1965) and *Settlement of Florida* (Gainesville, Fla., 1968), though the appearance of the Le Moyne material in the latter is unsatisfactory. Charles de la Roncière, *La Floride française* (Paris, 1928), also has supplementary material, together with fine reproductions of a contemporary copy of the Le Moyne engravings from Theodor de Bry.

# THE FRENCH IN FLORIDA, 1564-1565

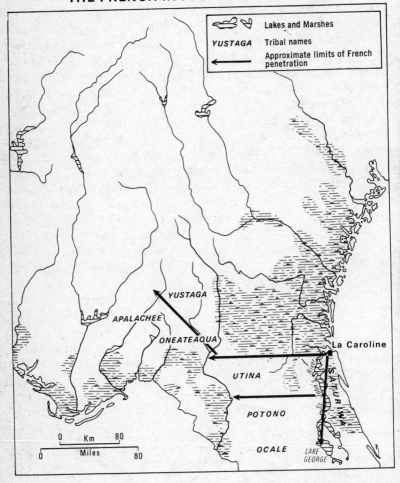

located the site of the deserted fort on Port Royal Sound, while his report was to set in motion a much more formidable Spanish expedition in 1565.[6] As was so often the case in such enterprises, inadequate stores were left with the settlers. This not only created friction in the garrison but forced the French to take on the role of exploiters of the Indian population, whose natural generosity was soon replaced by resentment at being asked for supplies of corn and other commodities of which they had only limited reserves.

Laudonnière saw some gold and silver ornaments in Indian hands and heard from them of further resources in the interior: much could be taken, Saturiwa indicated, from the Utina tribe. The French at this time believed that the metal came from mines in the interior. In fact it was obtained from shipwrecked Spanish vessels, from which it had been taken by the Indians over the previous forty years so that, indeed, substantial quantities were in the possession of various groups in the southern part of the peninsula—the Ais as well as the Utina, the Calusa, and perhaps the Apalachee in the west as well. The St. Johns River seemed to offer access to the sources of gold and silver, which could at first be obtained by trade or war and afterwards, it was hoped, from the mines believed to exist further into the interior. Meanwhile Le Moyne was busy sketching Indian life, which he was to continue to do as the French moved about in Florida, and also, along with other people who were familiar with natural history, examining plants for medicinal and other uses—sassafras in particular was widely used by the Indians for medicinal purposes. Other commodities, skins and furs (the former often highly decorated), feather garments and decorations, dyes, occasional stones thought to be precious, pearls (often charred by cooking) and a few additional items made up a rather meager trade inventory. No preparations were made for agricultural activity and the French did not impress early enough on the Indians that they should grow a special crop of corn for the colony's use in addition to their own harvest. The French may not even have planted gardens to ward off scurvy and provide a little variety in their vegetable diet. The men were either professional soldiers or adventurers, who had come for excitement and gain or both, not artisans or farmers.

6. Lucy L. Wenhold, "The Expedition of Manrique de Rojas to Florida in 1564," *Florida Historical Quarterly*, XXXVIII (1959), 45–62; reprinted in Bennett, *Laudonnière*, pp. 107–124.

To make matters worse, an ideological quarrel was latent in the colony. For some reason no ministers were brought to Florida, though the men were almost entirely Huguenots. The more devout felt bitterly the lack of religious services and inspiration; they also felt that the settlers should play a part in Christianizing the Indians. Left to their own devices, they developed a series of psalm-singing and scripture-reading meetings. But they saw that many of the others, especially the young gentlemen-adventurers, once away from Europe had comparatively little interest in religion, so that the two groups tended to pull further apart from each other. Laudonnière as commander was held responsible for the lack of religious leadership. As for the adventurers, they felt there were only two worthwhile occupations: searching for gold mines, and using the fort as a base for short-term raids on the Spanish Indies.

When Laudonnière learned more about the Indians of the peninsula, he came to consider he had been unwise in promising aid to Saturiwa. There were rumors—quite false ones as it proved—that the gold came from far into the interior. By aligning himself with a coastal tribe, Laudonnière could see himself closing the necessary routes into the interior. As a result he quite soon indicated to Saturiwa that he would not assist him, at least for several months, in his wars. Not unnaturally, this began a period in which relations with the local Indians cooled. Saturiwa made an independent expedition against the Utina, in which he had some success. When he returned, Laudonnière persuaded, or bullied, him into handing over some of his prisoners, who provided new information on the interior.

The change of relationship did not, it appears, lead to any diminution of the supplies of corn which the French got from Saturiwa in August and September, but thereafter the differences between them became more serious. The building and equipping of two shallops (larger than boats and smaller than pinnaces) rendered the settlers more mobile. They made good use of them in making contact and establishing friendly relations with the small tribe of Tacatacuru Indians at the mouth of the St. Marys and Satilla Rivers and, through Captain Thomas Le Vasseur, they renewed their links with the Cusabo group of tribes in the Port Royal Sound area who had not been antagonized during the occupation of the 1562 Charlesfort site. Their relationships with the powerful Guale group

which lay between Tacatacuru and Cusabo are not so evident, but it may well be that these were friendly also. Such contacts ensured that however poor relations with the local Indians might be, some assistance in supplying corn might be had from those along the coast to the north; but we hear nothing of attempts to make contact with the coastal Indians to the south, though Seigneur d'Ottigny, Laudonnière's lieutenant, made a useful reconnaissance southward and westward into the interior of the peninsula.

The first direct contact with the Utina was followed by a second expedition which established good relations with a number of the Utina sub-chiefs. As the territory of this tribe extended westward from the St. Johns to the Suwannee River, the expedition opened up the possibility of access into the interior to the northwest of the peninsula. Their main contacts with the Utina were along the St. Johns, where the Utina had apparently made a bridgehead on the east bank from which the Saturiwa were trying to dislodge them, and were also trying to carry out an offensive against them on the west bank. To make this effective they needed French aid. Toward the south the Utina were in conflict with the Potano, whose territory extended inland from the lower reaches of the Suwannee. The precise relations of the Utina with the Onatheaqua and Yustaga who covered their western border and with the Apalachee whose center was in the vicinity of modern Tallahassee is less clear, but it was not one of unremitting hostility, so that opening up a route for French explorers into this region became possible.

The French tactics were, therefore, to make direct contact with Utina, the chief of the tribe of that name; then to work their way into his good graces, and so get his help in sending individuals or small parties into the territories to the west and northwest of his tribe. This policy they pursued with considerable tenacity and skill, though in the end with little result. It never occupied more than a small number of men; for his own sake, Laudonnière might have been better advised to commit a substantial part of his force to assist Saturiwa as he had originally promised since it would at least have kept them fully occupied. A party who brought back to the Utina chief the prisoners released into French hands by Saturiwa was well received, and went on to assist him in a successful attack on the Potano. Utina, not surprisingly, asked for still more French assistance and Laudonnière sent thirty men under Ottigny.

The victory achieved with their aid opened up a wider area to the southwest in the peninsula to the French. An expedition up the river (that is southward, since below the site of modern Jacksonville the river flows from south to north) made contact with more southerly dependents of the Saturiwa tribe. Laudonnière was now the target for proposals by Saturiwa and his allies for a fresh alliance and an attack on the Utina. He was tempted but eventually refused their overtures. A number of Frenchmen remained with the Utina, several of whom made contact with the next tribe to the northwest, the Yustaga (Oustaca)—it was through these contacts that a misleading impression of the sources of the gold in Indian hands and of the layout of the country in the interior grew up.

The Indians in this area spoke of "Apalatci," but this was the Apalachee tribe in the vicinity of modern Tallahassee; they also described great mountains with which the Yustaga and the adjoining Onatheaqua tribe were alleged to be in contact and which the French considered had the same name, "Apalatci," or something like it. In fact, the Apalachee tribe had been mentioned by Cabeza de Vaca and the name had consequently attached itself either to a mountain range or to a district in the interior, on Spanish maps which the French evidently knew. Actually the range which we know as the Appalachians was some 250 to 300 miles to the north of the Apalachee, Yustaga and Onatheaqua tribes, and there is no evidence that there was any direct contact between them and the highland area. The French are not in the least likely to have penetrated any distance to the north, where even the Piedmont begins some 150 miles away. The fascination with the mountains and the preoccupation with working out a completely erroneous topography, which appears on Le Moyne's map as published in 1591 (and which, because it has some affinities with the real picture of the layout of modern Georgia, has been accepted down to the present day), is explained by the fact that the French believed the mountains were the source of precious metals.

It is, indeed, highly probable that native copper was passed from tribe to tribe from northern Georgia down to the Florida peninsula. There the Mississippian Temple Mound (II) culture was still in being at Etowah and elsewhere and possessed a plentiful supply of copper, both in lump and sheet form. Indians normally had only one word for metal, and the gold and silver that the Indians had in the

peninsula was believed to have come from the mountains, along with the copper which was also used for ornaments and weapons.[7] Several Spanish prisoners released from the Indians could, and probably did, tell Laudonnière of the mistake that had been made (an Englishman learned of it within a few days in 1565); but for propaganda purposes at the time and long afterwards, in Laudonnière's *History* and Le Moyne's map, the legend of the gold of the "Apalatci" mountains was maintained. The fiction that the settlers would—after reinforcements had arrived—march to the mountains and make themselves rich, was therefore cultivated.

Discontent with the poor food and lack of employment fairly rapidly led to intrigues against Laudonnière. These came to a head after a visit to Fort Caroline from a French privateer under a Captain Bordet early in September. Mutineers seized the *Petit-Breton* and one of the shallops and set out to make a raid on the West Indies. After some success, they ran out of supplies and were eventually captured by the Spaniards, some of them proving invaluable guides in the Spanish attack on the French settlement in 1565. After their departure there was quiet for a time; but in November the intrigues revived, this time attracting both gentlemen and the more radical Huguenots who felt they were wasting time which might be better employed in killing Spaniards. A further mutiny led to the seizure of Laudonnière himself and his recently reconciled assistant, La Caille, and their imprisonment, while two shallops (or perhaps a pinnace and shallop) were made ready with guns taken from the fort for a further Caribbean excursion. Nothing more was heard of either party until the following March 25, when a Spanish brigantine and another small craft entered the river. Having lost their own vessels but captured several Spanish ships, the second band of mutineers returned with some spoil. Laudonnière overpowered their ship by a trick, had the four leaders executed for mutiny, and rein-

7. The crucial passage in Laudonnière, *L'histoire notable* (1586), fol. 76 v. (ed. Lussagnet, pp. 137–138); *The notable history* (1587), fol. 40 v. (Hakluyt IX (1904), 55), is where he says that the chief of the Hostaqua (Yustaga) tribe knew the passages to "the mountains of Apalassi," and "sent me a plate of a mynerall that came out of this mountayne, out of the foote whereof there runneth a streame of golde or copper . . . and [they] finde that there are manie small graines of copper and sylver among this sande: which giveth them to understande that some rich myne must needs be in the Mountaine. . . . Not past five or six days journey from our fort lying toward the northwest."

corporated the remainder in the garrison, no doubt also appropriating such stores as they had accumulated.

During the winter of 1564–65, the French demands on the Saturiwa Indians and others within their reach for food intensified and the village granaries were soon exhausted. Saturiwa took his own people away from the villages on their winter hunting excursions rather earlier than usual—they were absent from January until March. They returned to find the French less arrogant than they had been. Now they pleaded for a share of the meat the Indians had brought back and of the fish they could catch: high prices in commodities, especially arms, were asked for by the Indians and paid. Finally, Laudonnière attempted to scour the basin of the St. Johns for food. Ascending the river, he found the Utina equally unwilling or unable to produce corn or beans. In May, he raided their principal village, seized the chief, Utina, and brought him back to Fort Caroline. Most of the corn was, in any case, committed to the spring sowings; only in June, when the first crop was ripening, did the tribe offer to buy their chief back. The party which conveyed him home was given corn indeed, but was ambushed on the way back and lost much of it again. Yet corn was now ripening along the shore as well. Soon boats were being used to work up and down the coast bartering for it—the danger of starvation at least had been averted.

But with Saturiwa maintaining a somewhat reserved attitude, though he was no longer unfriendly, and with the Utina now hostile and able to impede any advance into the interior, it began to seem wise to think of moving the colony. The relief expedition was expected to arrive early in the year, by April at the latest. By June 1565, it was decided to attempt to equip vessels which would be able to bring the settlers back to France if relief should not come. Accordingly, the *Petit-Breton* (apparently a Spanish ship renamed as such) was put in order as far as possible, as well as the Spanish brigantine. Between them there was still not enough room for the garrison. During the winter Laudonnière had had an oar-powered galliot rebuilt to add to his meager shipping resources; she was unsuitable for an ocean crossing, so her sides were raised and she was decked. The fort palisade and a number of buildings inside it were taken down to provide seasoned timber and were not replaced. By early in August the ship of 80 tons and the two pinnaces (as it seems right to call them) of 15 tons each were almost ready, and considerable

stores of corn had been collected to victual them. Shortly before Laudonnière was due to leave, four ships appeared at the mouth of the river, one heavily armed; this aroused first anticipation of relief and then alarm when it was realized they were not French.

In fact, they were not Spanish enemies but English allies. John Hawkins had left England for his second West Indian trading voyage in 1564, having probably decided in advance to make contact with whatever French posts there were in Florida on his return voyage. The Spaniards later claimed that before Jean Ribault left England he had arranged with Hawkins to establish a fort on the Florida Keys in order to intercept Spanish shipping and that he now came to settle this with Ribault, but we have no confirmation of such a specific arrangement. Instead, he found that Ribault had not arrived and that Laudonnière was preparing to leave America. He offered to transport the garrison home safely, but Laudonnière was somewhat suspicious of his intentions and refused. However, he agreed to purchase a ship from Hawkins which would be paid for after he returned to France, though he handed over some guns and, apparently, some Spanish goods brought in the brigantine as an earnest of his good will. Hawkins in turn left, besides the ship, a small quantity of stores—biscuit and dried beans—all he could spare. He sailed off after a brief three-day visit.

Laudonnière had amassed from the Indians, not always by the gentlest means, a substantial quantity of silver and gold of which he did not intend Hawkins to become aware. He might have been expected to sail away with his men now that it was safe for him to do so with the hurricane season under way. Instead, he hung back for another three weeks in a delay that was to prove fatal to almost all his men. On August 28, a further squadron was sighted off the coast: this at last was Jean Ribault with the long-delayed reinforcements.

Meanwhile in Europe decisions were being taken which involved the almost certain downfall of the French experiment in Florida. Philip II was well informed about their activities and was determined to prevent the French from establishing themselves firmly along the track of the homeward fleets. Manrique de Rojas had established the location of the first French fort, and reports from the West Indies made it clear that the second French establishment was being used—by Laudonnière's mutineers—as a base for attacks on

Spanish ports and vessels to the south. The selection of the Asturian nobleman Pedro Menéndez de Avilés to lead the expedition against the French was a good one.[8] He had a fine record as a commander at sea; he had already taken part in 1561 in a reconnaissance of the Florida coast; and he had an implacable hatred of heretics—all qualities which helped to single him out for the task. That he lacked patience and the humbler skills involved in managing a civilian settlement injected into a new land under exceptional circumstances had yet to be discovered. But he was brave, resourceful and implacable. The contract of March 20, 1565, which he signed with the king gave him and his heirs the title of *adelantado* of Florida; for this he was prepared to invest his own large fortune as well as all he could induce the king to contribute.

When Menéndez left Spain on June 29, 1565, he was equipped with full information on Fort Caroline, given to him by three of Laudonnière's mutineers who had been captured in the Caribbean and rushed to Spain as vital links in the intelligence chain. Knowing that the French were already at sea on the way to relieve their colony, he made light of the scattering of his fleet in a storm and set out as soon as possible from Santo Domingo with only five of his ten ships on August 17. Sailing up the Florida Strait, he entered an inlet in the later Anastasia Island and on August 28, St. Augustine's feast day, landed at the site which he therefore named San Agustín. This was the precise day on which Jean Ribault made his appearance at Fort Caroline some 40 miles to the north.

The French preparations in 1565 had been leisurely. Ribault, who had returned to France in 1564, was placed in command of the relief expedition, with instructions to take over as governor from Laudonnière when he arrived and to found a colony of settlement. For this purpose he had men, women and children to found a civilian settlement as well as soldiers. With eight ships he set out on June 14, but took a rapid two months to reach the Florida coast, which was sighted on August 14. Then, although he was four months late, he inexplicably set out to revisit the coast in detail as far north as Port Royal Sound where he had been in 1562 instead of making immediate contact with Fort Caroline. It was a full fortnight before he reached the mouth of the St. Johns River. Laudonnière was to

8. The best account of Menéndez (and indeed of the subsequent events in Florida in 1565) is that of Lowery, *Spanish Settlements, 1562–74*, pp. 120–154.

complain later that this delay proved fatal to the whole enterprise —had he been well established before Menéndez arrived, Fort Caroline would have had a good fighting chance. As it was, the two European forces in North American waters were well enough matched, each with five effective ships, about five hundred trained soldiers, and some three hundred supernumeraries. But Fort Caroline was in ruins, Laudonnière and many of his men ill, and Ribault apparently quite ignorant of the danger which faced him from the Spaniards.

The reunion of the French colonists with the relieving force was an occasion for celebration, continued perhaps too long and too vigorously. It was also one for taking stock. Laudonnière was instructed to hand over his authority to Ribault and to prepare to return to France—though Ribault told him he was ready to waive his instructions and to keep him on as his second in command. The situation at Fort Caroline was not reassuring, the fort being largely demolished, many of the survivors ill (including Laudonnière himself), and little progress made in laying firm foundations for French settlement. Men were set to work to restore the fort entrenchments, but they do not seem to have worked with any sense of urgency as breaches lay still fatally unrepaired some weeks later.

Menéndez, meanwhile, had set to sea to reconnoiter the entrance to the St. Johns River, on which he understood the French settlement to be located.[9] On September 4, at two o'clock in the afternoon, he sighted four French ships anchored off the bar at the entrance. In his own ships he came quite close but sheered off as soon as he had clearly identified them, since a thunderstorm had come up rapidly. He returned at night, anchored close by, and fired some guns to which the French replied. In the darkness he was able to speak to the Frenchmen and taunt them with a promise of death as intruders on Spanish territory. They cut their cables and sailed

9. The principal Spanish authority is the account of Menéndez by Gonzálo Solís de Méras, translated in Jeannette T. Connor, *Pedro Menéndez de Avilés . . . Memorial by Gonzálo Solís de Meras* (Deland, Fla., 1923; reprinted Gainesville, Fla., 1964). The parallel account by Bartolomé Barrientos was translated and edited by Anthony Kerrigan as *Pedro Menéndez de Avilés, Founder of Florida* (Gainesville, Fla., 1965). Francisco López de Mendoza's "Memorial," translated in B. F. French, *Historical Collections of Louisiana and Florida*, 6 vols. (New York, 1846–75), I, 191–234, is also useful. The letters of Pedro Menéndez de Avilés in Eugenio Ruidíaz y Caravia, *La Florida*, 2 vols. (Madrid, 1893), II, 84–125, provide firsthand information.

away, not, it would seem, for fear of being overwhelmed but because the storm had whipped up again and it seemed safer to prepare for action well away from the treacherous bar. Indeed, Menéndez put to sea too soon himself and the vessels lost sight of each other. Later, when it was calmer, Menéndez returned and tried to test the French defenses inside the river. He found that they were now effective, since three ships barred the way and cannon had been mounted on either bank to second them. To invade the St. Johns was clearly impracticable so Menéndez turned southward once more.

He entered the inlet on Anastasia Island and found that the sheltered waters of the inner channel offered him a satisfactory base, though the bar was risky for his largest ship. In the circumstances he considered it wisest to unload and detach the galleon *San Pelayo* and the despatch boat *San Salvador* and send them to Santo Domingo to speed the rest of his expedition on its way while he endeavored to cope with the French by sea and by land. His first fort was built at an Indian village, centering on the large dwelling of the Seloy chief which was soon surrounded by ditch and rampart.[10] He now divided his force into two parts: one, consisting of most of his fighting men, was designed for an attack on Fort Caroline; the rest —largely non-combatants—were to begin the foundation of a Spanish community.

For the moment Jean Ribault held the initiative. He hurriedly reassembled his ships, took on board the greater number of fit men from the old garrison as well as his own men, and on September 10 set out to destroy Menéndez. Both his strategy and tactics were bad. Several of his vessels worked along the coastal islands and located the gap through which the Spanish vessels had gone, indeed just missed catching Menéndez himself. But instead of pushing home his reconnaissance and following it up with an attack on Menéndez before he could consolidate himself, Ribault was distracted by news that two Spanish vessels were on their way south. These were the galleon and dispatch boat. The French ships all sailed off vainly in pursuit, missing the opportunity of defeating the Spanish force at

10. L. A. Vigneras, "Fortificaciones de la Florida," *Anuario de Estudios Americanos*, XVI (1958), 533–552, is the best account of the successive Spanish attempts to fortify themselves in Florida. Verne E. Chatelaine, *Defenses of Spanish Florida* (Washington, D.C., 1941) is also useful.

San Agustín and leaving Fort Caroline tragically vulnerable to Spanish attack. True, Jacques Ribault (Jean's son) had been left with several small vessels and some artillery to defend the fort against attack from the sea, but there was no conception that a land attack might be mounted, and the two large breaches in the defenses still lay unrepaired. About 240 people were in the fort; they comprised the women, children and servants who had come with Ribault, and the sick and convalescent men from the old garrison—including Laudonnière—and the new fleet, with only a handful of fit soldiers. The men on board ship manning the defenses on the seaboard side may have numbered about a hundred, but do not seem to have been kept in a state of high preparedness. And this at a time when a rising storm had caught Ribault's ships and made it impossible for them to return to their base.

Meantime Menéndez had decided on a land attack. With the greater part of his soldiery, he trudged northward from San Agustín between September 16 and 19, and with one of his French prisoners (Jean François) reconnoitered the fort site on the early morning of the 20th. Although the approach was through swampy ground, this enabled him to bring his troops unobserved within striking distance. They were helped rather than hindered by drenching rain and wind which weakened the lookout, poor as it already was, of the garrison. Sentinels outside the fort were either overpowered or chased inside; the wicket was opened to receive them but the Spaniards pressed through it while other assault groups rushed over the breaches. Solís de Méras gave a graphic account of what happened next:[11]

some of the Frenchmen in the houses came out in their shirts and others who were clothed, to find out what was happening: these were killed at once, and others took to flight and threw themselves down from the walls of the fort. Two standards were soon brought in, one belonging to the sergeant-major, which was raised upon a bastion (caballero) by his ensign . . . the other belonged to Diego de Maya, and it was set up on another bastion by his ensign. . . . The trumpeters entered at the same time . . . and placed themselves on those bastions, near the flags, sounding victory. At this the French became terrified. All our men came running through the gate, which was opened wide for them and went through the French quarters without leaving one alive.

11. Ruidíaz, *Florida*, II, 97; Solís de Méras, *Menéndez*, ed. J. T. Connor, pp. 100–101.

The Spaniards killed all the French they could find, Menéndez reaching a score of 132 dead, either with or without resistance and before or after surrender. He did manage to rescue a number of women and boys—afterwards sent to Santo Domingo—and left a few musicians alive.[12] Of those who got away over the defenses, we have accounts from three survivors: Laudonnière, the most authoritative; Jacques Le Moyne, the artist; and Nicolas Le Challeux. From them we can recreate something of the panic, horror and despair of the defeat. Jacques Ribault in *La Perle*, after losing his supply ship when the Spaniards turned the guns of the fort on him, ran downstream and did his best to pick up the little groups of fugitives who were struggling through woods and swamps to the estuary as did the skeleton crew left on *Le Lévrier*. When they had taken on all they could—some twenty strays were later killed by the Spaniards—they set sail across the Atlantic, Ribault still ignorant of what had happened to his father and the major part of the fleet. Ultimately, after great hardships for want of food, the *Lévrier* with Laudonnière in command reached the Bristol Channel and the survivors were rescued and subsequently made their way home to France,[13] where the *Perle* had already arrived.

We lack the full details of the fate of Jean Ribault's fleet. Hit by a hurricane as it turned northward from its fruitless chase of the *Pelayo* and *San Salvador*, one vessel after another was wrecked on the sandy offshore islands south of San Agustín. The first wreck of this sort was followed by the massacre of most of the Frenchmen on board by the local Indians—the Spaniards at San Agustín hearing of it only when a survivor reached the fort some 10 miles to the north; the frigate was afterwards floated off by them and rehabilitated. Then Menéndez himself returned to San Agustín in some trepidation that, despite his success against Fort Caroline, it might have fallen to the French. News soon came of two further wrecks south of Matanzas Inlet, where many Frenchmen had been taken captive by the Indians and others killed; some 140 of them were still

12. Nicolas Le Challeux, *Discours de l'histoire de la Floride* (Dieppe, 1566), reprinted in Paul Gaffarel, *Histoire de la Floride française* (Paris, 1875), p. 465, says "c'estoit lors à qui mieux mieux esgorgeroit hommes, sains et malades, femmes et petits enfants de sorte qu'il n'est possible de songer un massacre qui puisse estre esgalé à ceslui-ci, en cruauté et barbarie."

13. Le Challeux, *loc. cit.*; Laudonnière, *L'histoire notable;* Le Moyne in Theodor de Bry, *America,* part ii (1591).

on the mainland trying to make their way north but had been checked at the inlet. Menéndez made contact with them and reported his victory at Fort Caroline. He would accept surrender only *at mercy,* he said, though implying that it might be granted. Eventually the French, badly off for food, submitted. A few Catholics were segregated; the rest, with their hands tied behind their backs, were hacked to pieces as they passed a predetermined line.

After this slaughter of heretics news followed that Ribault's flagship, *Le Trinité,* had broken up somewhat further south. Ribault and some 240 men had been spared by the Indians but still suffered privation due to lack of food. They too were duly cut off on their northward march by Matanzas Inlet. On October 11, Menéndez induced some Frenchmen to cross in a raft. This time he was able to show the envoys the dead bodies of those previously killed, and the French could have little doubt of the fate in store for them. In spite of this (and there is an allegation from a French survivor that promises were given that mercy would be shown), Ribault and some seventy of his men surrendered. Again, after a few Catholics had been taken out, they were pinioned, attacked with sword and dagger, and exterminated. The remaining French who had refused to surrender made their way to the south; most were eventually rounded up by the Indians. "I had Juan Ribao and all the rest put to the knife," wrote Menéndez to the king on October 15, "considering it to be necessary to the service of God and of Your Majesty."[14] No clearer declaration could have been made of Spain's intention to deny Florida to the French. Menéndez was especially glad that those he had killed were not merely Frenchmen but heretics, so that in addition to praise from his king, he would gain merit from his Church and God for his actions.

The circumstances of the Spanish victory and the three bouts of killing which accompanied it produced a minor diplomatic crisis in Europe. Philip II, taking the initiative on the strength of reports from Menéndez, demanded that responsibility should be placed on Coligny and that he should be punished for planning and committing aggression against the Spanish empire. His special envoy, Fran-

14. "Salvé la vida á dos mozos cavalleros, de hasta diez y ocho años, y á otros tres, que eran pifano, atanhor y tronpeta; y á Juan Ribao, con todos los demás, hize pasar á chuchillo, entendiendo que ansi convenia al servicio de Dios Nuestra Señor y de V.M." (Ruídíaz, *Florida,* II, 103).

cisco de Alava, was bitterly spurned by Catherine de Médicis in March 1566 when he tried to insist on this course of action. The Sieur de Forquevaux, France's ambassador in Spain, carried the offensive back to Philip II[15] by demanding the recall and punishment of Menéndez. But during several interviews the king would give no ground, finally insisting that Menéndez had no option but to kill all the French as he had no means of retaining them as prisoners. When news accumulated, the French took the line that mercy had been promised and the undertaking broken, and national sentiment enabled this to be readily believed. Forquevaux rescued a prisoner brought to Spain—those brought in from Indian hands were not executed after the main body had been killed—but none of the prisoners kept by the Spanish were voluntarily released despite continued pressure. Charles IX and Catherine de Médicis were not willing to fight Spain for Florida: the Spanish *fait accompli* was decisive.

The French achievements in Florida were slight but not insignificant. They helped to build up a picture of European life in contact with the Amerindian population and put some parts of North America in detail on a map (however misleading in certain respects that map has proved to be). This must be qualified by noting that the main evidence of their American activities came out in print only some twenty years or more after they had been driven out, in the form of Laudonnière's *History* and the Le Moyne narrative and engravings, published between 1586 and 1591. It was these which helped to keep alive the misleading impression that in eastern North America there were precious metals to be exploited if access into the interior could be found—an impression which probably operated as a false incentive to later promoters and settlers for an appreciable period.

The Franco-Spanish struggle which developed in Florida in 1565 for the first time exported the power struggles of Europe to North America (if only on a small scale) while it also brought about a

15. Forquevaux rescued Jehan Mennin, who finally reached France after being in Indian and Spanish hands and who gave a firsthand account of the Ribault killing, alleging breach of safe-conduct. See Gaffarel, *Histoire de la Floride française*, pp. 236–261, 408–455; *Dépeches de M. de Forquevaux, 1565–1572*, edited by Célestain Douais, 3 vols., Paris, 1896–1903; Forquevaux despatches and other correspondence in De Coppet Collection, Princeton University Library. These make up (with some overlaps) a remarkable commentary on the diplomatic aftermath of the Spanish conquest.

sanguinary battle between Protestant reformers and Roman Catholics. The Hapsburg-Valois struggle and the contest between the Counter Reformation and the Protestant Reformation had henceforth a small but not perhaps wholly insignificant North American element in them. More decisively, the struggle demonstrated Spain's intention to claim such parts of North America as affected her empire further south and to establish this claim by force. Out of this came the establishment of the first continuous colonial settlement by Europeans on the eastern part of North America. Moreover, the implication was that all future interventions by French, English or Dutch would be marked by Spanish protests and possibly intervention, as well as reiterating the claim that all of eastern North America as far north as Newfoundland (usually conceded to the Portuguese) was Spain's by right of the papal donation, by the Treaty of Tordesillas, and by prior discovery. These claims were to continue, even if they gradually became fainter, into the period marked by the next volume in this series.

# CHAPTER 11

# *The Foundations of Spanish Florida, 1565–1574*

PEDRO Menéndez had proved himself an effective, if brutal, servant of the Spanish crown in destroying the first non-Spanish colony to be planted in North America close to the borders of the viceroyalty of Mexico. It now remained to be seen how he would organize the first permanent Spanish settlements there.[1] This was not, to begin with, merely a question of establishing a few small garrisons along the Atlantic coast in what are now the states of Florida, Georgia and South Carolina, but much else besides. Menéndez considered that his "empire" ranged as far as he might take it up the eastern shores until he met the Portuguese and Basque fishermen whom he was assured dominated the Baccalaos (Newfoundland and adjoining mainland coasts), though his short-term objective in this direction was the Bahía de Santa Maria (Chesapeake Bay) at 37° where he had been in 1561. To the south his reach was wider still: he planned not merely to control peninsular Florida but

1. Lowery, *Spanish Settlements, 1561–1574*, remains the primary narrative. The life of Pedro Menéndez de Avilés is treated in Eugenio Ruidiaz y Caravía, *La Florida*, 2 vols (Madrid, 1893), which also contains many of his letters. Others are printed in Luis Cabreiro Blanco (ed.), *Colección de diarios y relaciones para la historia de los viajes y descobrimientos*, 5 vols. (Madrid, 1943–47), II, 45–90. Gonzálo Solís de Méras, *Pedro Menéndez de Avilés . . . Memorial*, ed. Jeanette T. Connor (1923; 1969); Bartolomé Barrientos, *Pedro Menéndez de Avilés, Founder of Florida*, translated and edited by Anthony Kerrigan (1965); and, from 1570, *Colonial Records of Spanish Florida*, edited and translated by Jeanette T. Connor, 2 vols. (Deland, Fla., 1925–30), are the principal authorities. What follows has been constructed mainly from the letters—a full edition of which in English is much to be desired—and from the narrative in Lowery.

the entire coast of the Gulf of Mexico joining up with Mexico itself. After some heavy-handed diplomacy, he had his southern boundary fixed, as he wished, at the Pánuco River.

Still further, he had read of the expeditions of Hernando de Soto and Francisco Vásquez de Coronado and aspired to explore inland from Florida until he had established a land route to the Pacific. He was thus afflicted with more than a touch of the megalomania which had helped to ruin Hernando de Soto and was to distinguish the later conqueror of New Mexico, Oñate. He intended, too, to convert the Indians to Christianity wherever he penetrated, so that the missionary impulse was joined to his secular ones; in this he was seconded at an early stage by Dominican, Franciscan and Jesuit preachers whose attempts to convert the Indians occupied an appreciable part of the Spanish effort during the years left to him.

Menéndez seems to have had a very full and clear conception of those sites where military outposts were desirable, but not apparently of the economic activities which could make his settlement self-supporting at any stage in its existence. Negro slaves, it is true, were to lay out plantations for the estates he proposed to carve out for himself and his men. Farmers from his native Asturias, he decided in the end, would be needed to cultivate the less extensive holdings and must be given some land of their own to encourage them to do so. But he had little idea of what plants could be grown either to provide subsistence for the settlers or essential cash crops for export. Indeed, he soon came to think that food could be left very largely to be supplied by the Indians under whatever degree of pressure he might think necessary. He was inclined to underestimate the Indians also. They might, for a time, be almost as passive as many of those of Mexico when his soldiers were there in strength; but they were liable to surround and blockade isolated Spanish posts, gradually rendering all but the strongest untenable and the activities of slaves or farmers alike fruitless. Like the French before him, he thought that mines might make him and all his men rich, yet he made no effective mineral surveys. Basically, too, he did not realize that his own fortune would soon be swallowed up and that Philip II, once the French were removed, was not concerned to pour in large subsidies for colonizing experiments which, if they succeeded, would profit only the *adelantado* and not the crown. The crown would pay for and maintain a small basic garrison; but, unless

there was a threat of invasion or attack, that was all.

Because it was an offshoot from an imperial system already existing in the Americas, Florida differed in essentials from the earliest French and English settlements which had no bases nearer than their European homeland. Except in an unusual contingency, it did not need a direct line of contact with Spain herself, but could be financed, fed, supervised and reinforced from the viceroyalty of Mexico, of which it remained a part. It was subject in certain circumstances to orders from the viceroy or from the authorities at Santo Domingo, under the jurisdiction of whose *audiencia* it lay and from which came from time to time the supervisory officials who were an essential part of the bureaucracy of Spanish imperialism. The naval and military authorities at Havana too could play a vital part in providing shipping or soldiers, and in forwarding to Spain correspondence brought from Florida in the advice boat normally based on the colony or taken back to San Agustín. At the same time, the appointment of Menéndez as *adelantado* gave him an appreciable measure of autonomy and a line of communication direct to the king and the Council of the Indies. He had brought out his force straight from Spain and could on occasion plead for direct reinforcements from there. His colonists were recruited by himself, mainly in the Asturias, and had to be reinforced from there or elsewhere in Spain through his own efforts.

The scale of the Spanish effort in Florida in the early years was impressive. Menéndez had brought 1,000 soldiers and a handful of civilian settlers with him when he left Spain in 1565. Although only about half his force was with him when he attacked the French, the remainder came with Esteban de las Alas from Havana later in the year, along with the residue of the five hundred negro slaves he had been assigned. He set the slaves to construct more effective embankments at the Seloy village on Anastasia Island, which became the first San Agustín. It is not clear whether houses for non-combatants were built inside or outside the protecting ditches. Fort Caroline, renamed San Mateo, was burned to the ground on October 10 before the conclusion of the campaign against the French. The building now had to be wholly reconstructed. Below the fort he built two blockhouses, San Gabriel and San Esteban, which would guard the river mouth (it was thought) against a further French incursion.

Early in November, news reached Menéndez that there was still

a French presence in Florida, since a fort had been constructed by survivors from Ribault's fleet well to the south. He set out to capture it, but the French retreated in time to the woods and the fort fell to Menéndez without fighting. The majority of the French were driven by hunger to make contact with the Spaniards and to take the probably fatal risk of surrendering; however, on this occasion they were treated well as prisoners of war. Those who did not surrender fell into Indian hands, and most of them did not survive for long. Menéndez felt he must take precautions against further French incursions in this area also. He marched south to make friendly contact with the chieftain of the Ais Indians, and later left men to establish a small fort, Santa Lucia, on the modern St. Lucie River. He then took some men and prisoners by boat to Havana, a risky journey, in order to find out what had happened to the remainder of his fleet.

In spite of the obstruction of the governor of Havana, García Osorio, Menéndez managed to get some supplies for his men and to send ahead two contingents of reinforcement to Florida under his nephew Pedro Menéndez Marqués and Las Alas respectively. The supplies included livestock, mainly sows, from which a local meat supply could be built up. He himself was anxious to expand both along the west coast of the peninsula, along the coast north of the peninsula, and on that north of the St. Johns River. So he took a force up the west coast, and managed to rescue twelve Spaniards held by the Calusa Indians in the Charlotte Bay region; he also made contact with their principal chief whom the Spaniards called Carlos (Calusa). The discovery that the Indians had much gold and silver (taken from vessels shipwrecked from the Spanish fleets) led them to take extraordinary measures to conciliate the Indians; Menéndez himself accepted Carlos's daughter as his wife (she was sent to Havana to be Christianized but was afterwards returned to her father), and the men, as well as the *adelantado,* gained much bullion. The bay was named San Antonio. Menéndez planned to return later and establish a mission and fort there.

Meanwhile the Santa Lucia fort had been attacked by the Ays Indians and deserters from it were intercepted by Menéndez on his way back from San Antonio. In San Agustín food had gone short before supplies arrived. When the supplies did come, there was a mutiny and the mutineers made off with a store ship; a similar

# SPANISH FORTS AND SETTLEMENTS
## IN FLORIDA

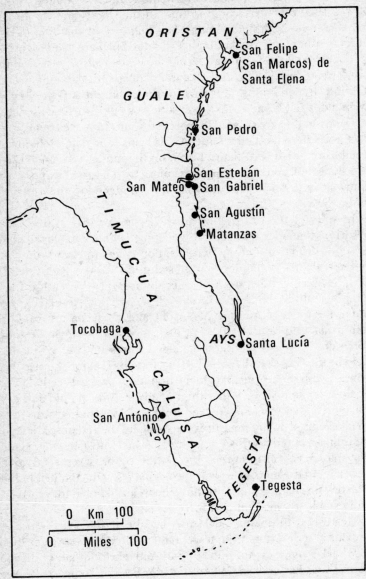

*ORISTAN*

San Felipe
(San Marcos) de
Santa Elena

*GUALE*

San Pedro

San Estebán
San Mateo  San Gabriel

San Agustín

Matanzas

*T I M U C U A*

Tocobaga

*AYS*  Santa Lucía

*C A L U S A*

San António

*TEGESTA*

Tegesta

0  Km  100

0  Miles  100

episode took place again a little later. And the same thing happened at San Mateo, so that between these three episodes some three hundred men had departed. At San Mateo, too, the Saturiwa Indians had turned hostile and were keeping the fort under constant attack, later destroying the two downstream blockhouses. Menéndez did what he could for the remaining soldiers and hurried north with his mobile force, since he had heard there was a French establishment on the Island of Guale (St. Catherine Island). By the time he got there the French survivors had almost all taken off for Newfoundland in a large boat, but there were a few still left among the Guale Indians. By a mixture of force, diplomacy, missionary activity and treachery, he got rid of the remaining Frenchmen and, acquiring two captive Cusabo Indians from Oristan, went north to Port Royal Sound, finally now named by the Spaniards the Bahía de Santa Elena.

There he entered into good relations with the local Indians and was able to establish on Parris Island a small garrison at the fort of San Felipe, where he thought his men would be safe from attack. He then went south again to indicate to the Guale Indians that he had made peace with Oristan and that they should keep with them a small group of Spaniards who would prepare them to receive Christianity. But success and disaster were still intermingled. In mid-May San Agustín, surrounded by hostile Indians, had been set on fire and most of the arms and stores lost, though the major part of the garrison maintained themselves by counterattacks on Indian villages. Hurrying south to Havana for supplies in June, Menéndez learned that, after he left, reinforcements from Spain had come in to San Agustín under Sancho de Arciniega, with no less than 1,500 men and supplies.

The events from October 1565 to June 1566 had (though Menéndez did not realize it) set a pattern which was to be repeated several times: the establishment of outlying posts and the consolidation of the *presidio* at San Agustín, followed by the drying up of supplies and money, pressure on the Indians to provide corn, then Indian attacks which at the least drove the Spaniards behind their defenses and, with starvation threatening, led to mutinies and desertions. The news of this, spreading widely through the Caribbean and ultimately to Spain herself, created the belief that Florida's value was a delusion, her wealth occasional and accidental only, the

country near the coast either swampy and unhealthy or else, as on Anastasia Island around San Agustín, sandy and unfruitful. Florida became a mirage, attractive in the distance, insubstantial on close acquaintance, perhaps deadly as well. And then, when the bureaucratic machine had been got to move with a further effort, reinforcements would come, new advances be made, the optimism revived, and the whole cycle of rise and fall start again. The only constant factor throughout, but increasingly prominent as time went on, was the military presence—the small garrison which would be maintained at all or almost all costs.[2]

Menéndez appreciated that Arciniega had too many soldiers to be kept occupied or fed. Consequently, although he proposed to allocate 250 to each of the three principal forts—Santa Elena, San Mateo and San Agustín—he despatched the rest on a pirate-chasing mission in the Caribbean. San Agustín had to be rebuilt twice as its first rebuilding was too near the water. Its second was on an enlarged scale, and a gun platform, adequate storerooms and some civilian accommodation outside the defenses were provided. The most important new asset was a number of Asturian farmers and their wives. These he proposed to settle on the mainland near San Felipe in the "City of Santa Elena," under the impression that the Santa Elena area provided the most fertile soil available. The Oristan Indians were at this time friendly and the other Cusabo tribes at least acquiescent, while the Spaniards were initially well supplied with food and equipment so that they did not seriously encroach on Indian supplies.

The settlers were quite quickly installed, though we have little impression of what crops, besides corn, they were to grow; they were to breed livestock, both cattle and pigs, since these would be major assets in maintaining the other posts. San Agustín and its organization as the *presidio* of the colony had the next priority. The military ranks were already in existence; the civilian ones had to be created. Menéndez found need of a lieutenant governor to act when he himself was absent, also a treasurer (*tesorero*), a sub-treasurer, an accountant (*contador*), and factor (*veedor*). He was able to fill most

2. C. W. Andrade, "The Failure of Spanish Florida," *International Congress of Americanists, Actas,* II (San José, Costa Rica), 758–766, and Verne E. Chatelaine, *Defenses of Spanish Florida,* passim, contain suggestive generalizations on Florida under Spanish rule.

of these posts from his own relatives, who had by now arrived in strength. The *adelantado* at this time enjoyed a substantial royal subsidy—on paper. The difficulty was that half of it was supposed to come from the profits of the colony, and, apart from the bullion recovered from the Calusa, there was none in sight. But officials had to have salaries and ultimately they might have to be paid by Menéndez himself. This establishment exhibited, like Jamestown later, a good deal of artificiality: offices without much meaning, posts without a location, a skeleton organization without machinery to make it effective. A final stage in construction at this point was to fill the dangerous gap between San Mateo and Santa Elena by an intermediate post. This he established on Cumberland Island, where he had already a small group of Spaniards living; San Pedro therefore became the fourth link in the chain of garrisons.

Menéndez was able to join the cruising squadron in the Caribbean for the latter part of 1566 and to return at the opening of 1567 with his men in good shape so as to give him some scope for opening up new posts. This time he planned to concentrate on the southern and western parts of the peninsula, reinstating Santa Lucia and adding Tegesta on the Miami River somewhat further south. But first he went to the west coast where there should be bullion to be traded in from the Indians. Moreover, by now he had a number of religious, both Franciscans and Jesuits, at his disposal, though their efforts to influence the Indians in the vicinity of the forts had not so far proved very effective, even if a few had picked up something of one or two Indian tongues. The most northerly post on the west coast where he left a garrison was at Tocobaga on Tampa Bay; and a second post, with a Jesuit missionary, Father Rogel, in attendance, at San Antonio on Charlotte Harbor, in the area dominated by the chief Carlos who had most of the bullion. Brother Francis was left at the new post of Tegesta. Menéndez had now an effective-seeming military network, ranging from Santa Elena along with its colony to his western posts with their soldiers and missionaries, seven in all. The theory was that the missionaries would gradually draw the Indians to a more settled life in permanent villages. There they would grow a corn and vegetable surplus, part of which would be taken as a tax levy and part used in trade. Thus revenue in kind and a produce market would provide some of the needs of the garrisons—for clergy and settlers alike. The settlement at San Agus-

tín—consisting of fifty families—might build up with the help of their negro slaves (mostly household slaves by this time) some gardens and orchards, although there is no evidence that anything extensive could be done on Anastasia Island or was attempted on the adjacent mainland. At Santa Elena, it was expected that the civilian settlement would soon be self-supporting and even on the way to providing a surplus. At their most optimistic, then, these arrangements looked forward to a time when the Spaniards would be more or less self-sufficient in basic foodstuffs; but there was still no prospect whatever of substantial trading surpluses for external commerce. It is probable that some dressed deerskins were being exported with samples of sassafras (from which great medical results were expected) and other medicinal herbs, together with gums and choice timbers, though none in any appreciable quantity. The colony was still in need of major injections of capital and some long-term economic planning.

Two further expeditions took place in 1566. When Menéndez was at Santa Elena, he arranged with the Dominican Fray Pablo de San Pedro (who was to go as leader) and Fray Juan de Acuña to take the Indian who had been captured in 1561 back to the Bahía de Santa Maria (Chesapeake Bay). This man, now known as Don Luis de Velasco, had been educated by the Spaniards and had become a Christian. He was the brother of a leading chieftain on the Chesapeake, almost certainly a relative of Powhatan and Opechancanough who were to be so prominent in Virginia forty years later. Captain Pedro de Coronas, with the ship *La Trinidad* and thirty men, was to accompany them, and they were to set up a post and mission station on Chesapeake Bay.[3]

The party missed the entrance to the bay and turned back at 37° 30′ N., working their way back down the coast in bad weather until they came to an entrance in the Carolina Outer Banks and entered at what they reckoned was 36°. They landed, formally annexing the area to Spain as Tierra de San Bartolomé (so that Spain has had a title to North Carolina after 1566), and searched the vicinity for several days without finding any Indians. The precise location of their landing is uncertain and it is impossible to be sure if the latitudes given are correct, but it might seem to have been near the

3. L. A. Vigneras, "A Spanish Discovery of North Carolina in 1566," *North Carolina Historical Review*, XLVI (1969), 398–415.

former Currituck Inlet, since there is little record of Indian occupation there, while there is a great deal for Albemarle Sound and Roanoke Island only a short way to the south. After a brief stay, another attempt was made to work up the coast to the entrance to Chesapeake Bay at the modern Cape Henry; but they were unable to find it and gave up the expedition in very bad weather. On their return they were driven so far out to sea that they set out to cross the Atlantic. They reached Spain late in October 1566, not, apparently, bringing favorable reports of the coast they had explored.

The other expedition was also based on Santa Elena.[4] On November 1 Captain Juan Pardo left Santa Elena with 125 men to attempt the conquest of the interior as far as Mexico. Perhaps it was the very impossibility of the task which spurred him to such efforts. In many ways the two expeditions carried out by Pardo and his lieutenant Boyano in 1566 and 1567 are the closest to that of Hernando de Soto which we have. It is difficult to tell from the surviving, rather laconic narratives how far Pardo was equipped with data on previous expeditions. It seems likely that he had at least some knowledge of, or some men from, the Luna expedition of 1559–60 and that his primary task (whatever might be said about reaching Mexico) was to retrace from Santa Elena, now that it had at last been located and occupied, the route which Luna had followed in vain from the opposite end—or at least to establish where Luna had been. One of Menéndez's objects in sending out the Pardo expedition was to disperse his men. The 125 men who left Santa Elena for the interior were expected to feed themselves off the country. It was, of course, hoped that they would find gold, pearls or other valuable commodities as well as work out the topography of the country. The idea was that once they got into good country, they should establish a chain of small blockhouses (rather as Ralph Lane would propose for the

4. The sources for the Pardo-Boyano expeditions are three laconic narratives in Ruidíaz, *Florida*, II, 465–473, 477–480, 481–486; together with less reliable recollections of the years 1598–1600 in Manuel Serrano y Sanz (ed.), *Documentos históricos de la Florida y la Luisiana* (Madrid, 1913), pp. 142–153. There is a highly concentrated account, with identifications of localities, in J. R. Swanton, *Indians of the Southeastern United States* (1946), pp. 64–70, which is based on much greater detail in his *Early History of the Creek Indians*, Smithsonian Institution, Bureau of American Ethnology, Bulletin 73, 1922. Mary A. Ross, "With Pardo and Moyano on the Fringes of the Georgia Land," *Georgia Historical Quarterly*, XIV (1930), 267–285, is the pioneer narrative ("Moyano" for "Boyano" is a corruption of the 1598–1600 period). Swanton, *Indians of the Southeastern United States*, has usually been followed here.

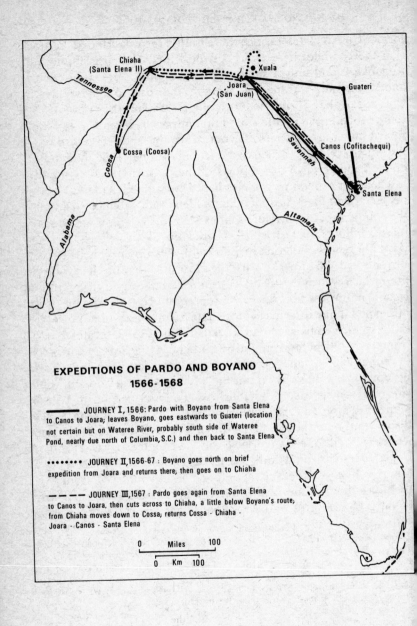

**EXPEDITIONS OF PARDO AND BOYANO**
**1566-1568**

——— JOURNEY I, 1566: Pardo with Boyano from Santa Elena to Canos to Joara; leaves Boyano, goes eastwards to Guateri (location not certain but on Wateree River, probably south side of Wateree Pond, nearly due north of Columbia, S.C.) and then back to Santa Elena

•••••• JOURNEY II, 1566-67 : Boyano goes north on brief expedition from Joara and returns there; then goes on to Chiaha

— — — JOURNEY III, 1567 : Pardo goes again from Santa Elena to Canos to Joara, then cuts across to Chiaha, a little below Boyano's route; from Chiaha moves down to Cossa; returns Cossa - Chiaha - Joara - Canos - Santa Elena

0    Miles    100
0    Km    100

English in Virginia in 1586) in order to keep a line of march open from the coast for successive exploring or settling parties.

Pardo has little to say of trudging through the swamps that lay inland from the mainland behind Parris Island, but it appears that he worked his way to the slightly higher land on the watershed of the Savannah River and eventually came to the Indian town of Canos on the great river, the Savannah. This has been credibly identified with Cofitachequi (in the vicinity of modern Augusta), especially since he makes clear that it was on the Fall Line by saying it was the last place where they encountered swamps and that it was about halfway between Santa Elena and the mountains. From here the going was much easier through the Piedmont. The slope gradually grew steeper and the party entered the highlands. Eventually in the Cheraw country a site was chosen as a staging post, and a small fort, named San Juan, was erected and manned under his sergeant Boyano. This was at Joada or Juora (tentatively identified as near Chattooga Ridge, in the vicinity of Towns Hill, S.C., but possibly over the border into Georgia). Pardo therefore returned, passing somewhat farther to the east and visiting the Guateri Indians and Guatariatiqui, probably on the Wateree River, on his way back to Santa Elena. His report was well received as he could state that mountainous country lay ahead through which he might penetrate first to the west and then southward toward Mexico. Las Alas, in command at Santa Elena, gave him permission to carry his explorations further, so that by September of the following year, 1567, he could set out on his second journey, taking a similar route.

In the meantime, Boyano had been leading an adventurous career. With Indian allies, he had moved north and destroyed a Chiska (Yuchi) town in an area into which Hernando de Soto had earlier penetrated in search of gold. He then marched into and over the Appalachian Mountains in a further campaign against the Yuchi, having left enough men to hold San Juan, and worked down into the Tennessee River Valley.[5] Finally, in the territory of the Chiaha Indians (possibly already part of a loose Creek confederacy), he settled on an island in the river, apparently Burns Island, near the

5. Swanton may not be correct in his location of Chiaha on the Tennessee River, since it is possible that Boyano continued down the Coosa River to the Alabama River and that his Chiaha was nearer modern Montgomery, much further to the south.

modern Tennessee-Alabama border, and established a further fort, named in honor of his base, Santa Elena (II). There he settled down to grow cereals and to build up successfully a sphere of influence amongst neighboring tribes.

Pardo started out again from Santa Elena on his second journey on September 1, 1567, and retraced his previous route to the fort at San Juan, finding its small garrison well established, though temporarily on poor terms with the Cheraw Indians. Learning that Boyano was at Chiaha with the tribe of that name, he followed Boyano's route, making a further journey over the Appalachians and providing some details on villages encountered on his way, until he succeeded in joining Boyano at Santa Elena (II). He was anxious to press on to the southwest, and attempted to do so, reaching as far as Satapo and Cossa—the latter being the Coosa which a detachment of Luna's men had reached in 1560. He heard of Trascaluza, one of the main towns of the Mobile Indians where Hernando de Soto had been, but did not have the resources to march further. The significance of what Pardo had done is clear: he had established the fact that the Luna expedition had gone astray in looking for the Coosa tribe that lived to the west of the mountains instead of the one living to the east, and he had linked up the geographical knowledge gathered by both Hernando de Soto and Luna with the new knowledge of the coastal territories gained since Menéndez's *entrada*. Indeed, the way was now clear, if the existing narratives were read correctly, to reach the Mississippi and the Gulf of Mexico, if not to establish quickly a direct land route to Mexico itself.

Pardo now decided to return to Santa Elena, but to post almost all his men at staging points along his route. Not only did he confirm Boyano's choice of Santa Elena (II) (Chiaha) as a forward base; but as he marched back, he left smaller garrisons at Cauchi (in Cheraw tribal territory); at the already existing San Juan (Juada), also in Cheraw territory; and, having worked his way across the Piedmont, at Guateri (or Guatariatique). He reached Santa Elena by the end of the year. These very promising expeditions were not, however, followed up. Boyano, left over the winter, appears to have been attacked toward the end of the year or at the beginning of 1568 at Chiaha by the local tribe, which had hitherto been helpful. Both the posts in the Cheraw country fell to the local tribe, which had renewed its hostility, while Guateri was also lost. The men were

either killed or absorbed into the Indian tribes.

News of these disasters only slowly trickled through to Santa Elena during 1568 and arrived before Pardo had received permission to make any further journeys. As a result, Boyano and his staging posts disappeared, Pardo was held back, and all advantage from the reconnaissances was lost—except that they had provided a body of evidence about the interior, especially the location of the mountain chain and conditions in the river valleys to the west, which was not wholly forgotten. With time the distances became blurred. At the end of the century, not only Oñate but Florida officials as well considered that a land route westward to New Mexico from Florida was both possible and reasonably short, indeed only a few hundred miles.

By April 1567 Menéndez believed he could regard his rehabilitation of the colony as almost complete. He had ordered the restoration of the two blockhouses at the mouth of the St. Johns. He also took precautions to have the road (little more than a rough trail) between San Mateo and San Agustín patrolled and another post established south of San Mateo to guard it. He set up small stations south of San Agustín to give warning of enemy approaches. Further, he ordered the strengthening of San Pedro on Tacatacuru (Cumberland Island) and the creation of another post on Guale (St. Catherine Island), though it is not clear that this was done. Leaving his forces dangerously extended and with only relatively limited supplies at their disposal, he sailed off to Spain on May 18, arriving there a month later and reaching the court at Madrid on July 25, where he claimed to have brought more than 700 miles of coast under Spanish control and to have begun the penetration of the interior, with the hope of great riches. The six Timucua Indians brought with him duly showed their skill with the bow to the Spanish court.

Philip II rewarded Menéndez with titles and an income, but diverted his attention from Florida to the Caribbean. Menéndez was now needed, he was told, to take charge of a new fleet to scour the West Indies for pirates and to protect the fleets—some ships for which were building in the north and which he had to supervise. Later, he was made governor of Cuba. These appointments partly satisfied his ambition but henceforward limited his direct responsibility for Florida. From the summer of 1567 until his death, Florida

still remained a major commitment for him. But he could not thereafter give it more than intermittent personal attention, and this was to wreck most of his plans for its development. In the short term, he was delayed in Spain well into 1568, and even when he returned to the Caribbean he was able to devote only a limited amount of time and resources to Florida.

During Menéndez's absence in 1567–68 the cycle of decay and disruption was repeated. Over the greater part of peninsular Florida, resistance to Spanish attempts to levy a corn tribute from the Indians led them to withdraw their cooperation and in a number of places provoked active hostility. This was most evident to begin with in the south and southwest. One after another, the small posts there, subjected to increasing pressure, packed up, the soldiers returning by boat to San Agustín. A number were killed and captured. Of them all, only San Antonio survived, though under continued Calusa pressure.

In the north the optimism created by the infusion of settlers and by the expeditions of Pardo and Boyano was soon dissipated. The farmers at Santa Elena maintained themselves for a time, but only at a subsistence level. As the garrison found it more difficult to obtain corn from the Indians, its men too became greedy for the agricultural produce of the farmers. But no one had any money, as wages did not arrive with any regularity, and arrangements for supplies to come by ship appear to have broken down. Inevitably the colony began to decline. Within a year it had shrunk and the soldiers were on very limited rations.

The relations between the Indians and Spaniards in the central coastal sector also deteriorated. The chief of the Tacatacuru Indians surprised the captain and ten men who made up the garrison of San Pedro and killed them, thus adding to the hatred the Spaniards had conceived for him for the killing of the Jesuit, Father Pedro Martínez, in September 1566. Saturiwa also renewed his harassment of the posts on the St. Johns, raiding San Mateo at the end of March and killing and wounding several of the garrison. At San Agustín itself the failure of regular rations and money for salaries to arrive caused discontent and some hardship. Soldiers and civilians were soon at loggerheads, partly over the perquisites of the civilian officials, who were also divided amongst themselves. It was clear that the *presidio* was not becoming a consolidated and stable community.

These accumulated troubles were brought to a crisis point by the long-expected appearance of the French. French privateering interests, composed of Catholics as well as Huguenots, had been exasperated by the Spanish measures to secure their ships and possessions against piratical attacks in the Caribbean and by the failure of the king and queen mother to revenge the destruction of French Florida, from which much had been hoped for as a privateering base. A French Catholic soldier, Dominique de Gourgues, was able to collect a substantial and well-armed force for an attempt at revenge. Setting out from La Rochelle on August 22, 1567, he followed a normal privateering course to West Africa and the Caribbean, successfully taking several valuable prizes there. Early in April he sailed up the coast of Florida, being noticed by the lookouts near San Agustín who exchanged warning shots with him.[6] The acting governor, Las Alas, was probably not unduly alarmed (though he sent warnings northward along the coast), since French vessels were seen from time to time on their way from the Caribbean and in any case San Mateo had recently been reinforced by fifty men under Francisco Nuñez.

Gourgues landed on Cumberland Island and was received with great enthusiasm by the Tacatacuru Indians, who were soon joined by Saturiwa and his subsidiary chiefs. A large force of Indians was assembled, full intelligence of the three Spanish posts obtained, and preparations made for an attack. The northern blockhouse, the ditch of which was still unfinished, was selected for the first attack on April 12.

A frontal assault was combined with a flank attack, using the unfinished works, and with Indian aid the sixty men were soon overrun—a number being killed but the remainder reserved for judicial execution later. Basing himself on this small fort, Gourgues prepared to attack the second blockhouse on the southern bank. He now turned the guns of the northern blockhouse on it, prepared a crossing of the river at two places and, with an impetuous Indian force, frightened the Spaniards into deserting it. A number were caught by his second force, but some escaped to join Las Alas at San Agustín and to alert him as to what was happening further north. In San Mateo itself, Nuñez, who was in command while the com-

6. For a narrative of the French expedition, see C. A. Julien, *Voyages de découverte et les premiers établissements* (1948), pp. 259–263.

mander Castellon was recovering from a wound, had received warning from Las Alas that suspicious vessels were on the coast. But a further warning by messenger failed to arrive in time since, on April 13, a great force of Indians joined Gourgues in an advance on the fort. Once again Gourgues took care to surround the fort at some distance with his reserves, so that when a show of force in front of the main gate tempted part of the garrison to sally out against his men, he managed to catch them between two fires. When they tried to cut their way back to the fort, they were killed off in detail. The remainder of the garrison, terrified by the hordes of Indians and by the French assault which followed the first success, attempted to escape through the woods. Many were killed, more captured and only a few individuals managed to escape entirely. The prisoners were then rounded up, formally told they were to be sacrificed in revenge for the killing of the Fort Caroline garrison and Ribault's men, and hanged *seriatim*.[7] Several hundred men at the least were thus disposed of with the same efficient brutality that Menéndez had shown in 1565.

A number of valuable cannon were found in the fort and taken to be brought back to France (some were French originally), although an explosion in the magazine set the fort on fire and burned it down. Gourgues then got the Indians to assist him, as part of the victory celebrations, in razing fort and blockhouses alike to ground level. During the next two weeks, Gourgues feasted with the Indians and plotted further raids with them. He might have done better to have moved against San Augustín, since the garrison there was weak and soon disheartened by the news brought to them by the few survivors from San Mateo. Gourgues, however, was carrying out a plan of revenge, not a war, and was satisfied he had done enough. He promised the Indians that he would return within a year; leaving

7. Gourgues's action in placarding the trees on which the Spaniards were suspended is related by René de Laudonnière, *L'histoire notable de la Floride* (Paris, 1586), fols. 120v.–121, in the following terms: "Mais au lieu de l'escriteau que Pedro Melandes leur avoit donné, protant ces mots en Espagnol, *Je ne say cecy comme à François, mais comme à Lutheriens,* Gourgues fit escrire en une table de sapin avec un fer chaud, *Je ne fay cecy comme à Espagnols, ny comme à Mariniers, mais comme à traistres, voleurs & meurdriers.*" Paul Gaffarel, *La Floride française*, p. 510, printed a manuscript text of Gourgues's "Reprinse de la Floride," in which "ny comme à Mariniers" was replaced by "n'y comme à marannes." This sounds likely, as a favorite insult of French to Spaniards was to call them *marannes* (*marranos* in Spanish), "the accursed," implying that they were converted Jews or Muslim.

a large number of knives and other weapons with them, he set out for France on May 3, abandoning (as he must well have known) his Indian allies to the vengeance, in their turn, of the Spaniards. He reached La Rochelle on June 6 and was very well received there and in Bordeaux. Catherine de Médicis refused all Spanish requests to have him punished, though the state of her relations with Philip II was such that it was not possible for her to receive him triumphantly at court as so many wished. Internationally, France had revenged herself for the Florida disaster without formal recourse to arms— to that extent Gourgues had salved the national conscience at an easy price. But if France was to retain positive interests in North America, they were not substantially served by the raid since Florida had been left in Spanish hands.

The evangelization of the Florida Indians had now become one of Pedro Menéndez de Avilés's major aims, and he enlisted the support of the Jesuit Order in achieving it. He was himself instructed to act as commander to the outgoing *galeones* fleet in 1568, but he sent ahead the missionaries, fourteen religious in all, under their vice-provincial, Juan Bautista de Segura.[8] They arrived independently of the *adelantado* on June 29 to find San Agustín still reeling from the French attack. The supplies they brought with them proved invaluable, but it remained to be seen what missionary work they could do except among the Indians immediately surrounding the *presidio*. Moreover, Menéndez did not appear with his own supplies and reinforcements. He had in fact been greatly delayed, reached Havana only in November, and was required to go back to Spain without coming to Florida.[9] By the time he arrived in Havana Segura was there too, attempting to set up a training center for the Florida mission. There was little support for the plan, how-

8. The Jesuit mission has been fully documented in Felix Zubillaga (ed.), *Monumenta antiquae Floridae* (Rome, 1946), and is fully discussed in his *La Florida. La misión Jesuítica (1558–1572) y la colonización Española* (Rome, 1941). A Franciscan view is given in Luis Gerónimo de Oré, *Relación histórico de la Florida,* edited by Atanásio López, 2 vols. (Madrid, 1931), I, 63–70, and as *The Martyrs of Florida, 1513–1616,* translated and edited by Maynard Geiger (New York, 1936), pp. 21–32. Menéndez had a letter from Pope Pius V, dated August 18, 1569, encouraging him to go on with the enlargement of the Faith "al acrecentamiento de nuestra Santa Fé" in Florida Ruídíaz, *Florida,* II, 299–300).

9. Lowery, *Spanish Settlements, 1561–1574,* p. 345, could not make up his mind whether Menéndez had or had not called in at Florida as he intended. In fact it is clear he did not have time to do so.

ever, and he eventually had to abandon it. Both Segura and Menéndez also hoped to revive missionary activity on the west and southeast coasts of Florida, but there was no way of expanding Spanish influence among the western Calusa at this time. Shortly afterward the last post, San Antonio, had to be abandoned. What could be done in future depended on whether Spanish control could be re-established over the Indians to the north of San Agustín.

Menéndez appears to have thought the subsidy system (situado) was working properly and that Esteban de Las Alas, whom he left as lieutenant governor, was obtaining regular pay and stores for his men. He realized, however, that it would be necessary to make a further effort to get the colony on its feet by sending out new equipment for the restoration of San Mateo and providing additional settlers for Santa Elena; but these would need to come from Spain and could reach Florida only well into 1570. In the meantime a few Jesuits had gone to Tacatacuru and Guale to begin their mission there, though very tentatively. The support they could expect from the administration at San Agustín was slight. Las Alas was preoccupied with the failure of supplies and money to arrive and by not hearing, apparently, from the governor. It seems likely that to keep his men occupied he had a blockhouse built at Matanzas.[10] As winter advanced, the supplies became really short; and there were complaints about shortages also from Santa Elena and San Pedro. Finally, in early summer, Las Alas made up his mind. The soldiers and such civilians as there were would not remain to starve—he decided to cut down the garrisons to a working minimum which might subsist on local produce, and take all the rest back to Spain. In June he left 50 men each in the three forts, collected the handful of settlers still at Santa Elena and San Agustín, and found enough shipping to take them across the Atlantic, astonishing the adelantado by his appearance at Cadiz in October with 120 men and women. This might, in fact, have brought severe retribution on him. But Las Alas made his case so effectively, and was so well supported by Menéndez, that he was forgiven and arrangements made to send more supplies to the beleaguered colony, while returned settlers

10. Chatelaine, Defenses of Spanish Florida, p. 45.

and others were interrogated to find out just what had gone wrong.[11]

In fact, substantial relief had already arrived there. The *adelantado,* once he had got back to Spain, had prepared his promised reinforcement under his nephew Pedro Menéndez Marqués and sent him out to rebuild San Mateo—he had arrived to find that Las Alas had gone. He also sent some help to the other posts, and new settlers north to Santa Elena, but concentrated on orders for the reconstruction of San Mateo.[12] This he soon found he was unable to complete since the remaining soldiers at San Agustín were deeply discontented. They defied their commander, burned down the fort and were attempting to follow Las Alas's example and leave Florida when Menéndez Marqués at San Mateo heard of it. He went down to the *presidio* and by a mixture of threats and promises induced them to settle down again; nevertheless, their actions indicated that the fate of the colony still remained very much in the balance. Menéndez Marqués took over full control at San Agustín and tried so far as possible to rehabilitate the colony. It is probable that the craftsmen he had at San Mateo enabled him to begin the major task of moving the fort from island to mainland and planting it opposite St. Augustine Inlet. The town was also moved to the mainland and laid out on the waterside some distance from the fort.

Santa Elena seemed to be a key point in the Jesuit mission. To the north of it, Father Rogel was attempting to start a mission at Oristan but was finding the Indians peculiarly resistant to Christian teaching; Fathers Sedeño and Quirós were having little more success at Tacatacuru and Guale.[13] Additional missionaries had come out to Menéndez Marqués, and Father Segura returned from Havana to Florida to regroup his forces. He decided to abandon all three unproductive missions and send most of the Jesuits back to Havana. But Segura would himself make an effort to establish a mission far beyond the borders of Spanish influence at Ajacan—the territory of Don Luis, the Indian captured in 1561 and now a Hispaniolized Christian, willing to conduct and aid missionaries if they came to

11. Connor, *Colonial Records,* I, 293–321; Ruídíaz, *Florida,* II, 568–589; Lowery, *Spanish Settlements,* II, 358.

12. Chatelaine, *Defenses of Spanish Florida,* pp. 46, ⬛–173; L. A. Vigneras, "Fortificaciones de la Florida," *Anuario de Estudios Amer*⬛ XVI (1958), 533–552.

13. Zubillaga, *La misión Jesuítica,* pp. 381–383, ⬛ ⬛ ves details of their pessimistic reports.

Chesapeake Bay.[14] Fathers Segura and Quirós, with five associates, would make up the mission, along with a boy, Alonso de Olmos, the son of a settler at Santa Elena. They would go with Don Luis and found their mission in the wilderness.

A ship came from Havana, and at the beginning of September 1570 they set out. Entering Chesapeake Bay, they found a landing place on September 10. Subsequently they entered a large river, took (on Don Luis's advice) a route up a small stream and, a short way beyond its watershed, found a suitable location near another major river and close to several villages of Don Luis's tribe. The final location has been much in dispute: it has been named as being on the Rappahannock, on the Potomac, and more recently, on the York. Fathers Lewis and Loomie made an elaborate study of the problem and came to the conclusion[15] that the first landing point was at or near Cape Comfort; that the major river they ascended was the James and the small river up which they traveled College Creek (close to modern Williamsburg); while the final mission site was at Chiskiack, close by the York River. This makes a logical reconstruction but cannot be established in detail. It would certainly seem that Cape Comfort was the most probable first landing place; and, since elaborate arrangements were made for signals to be sent from here to guide the ship that would bring supplies to the mission site, it might well follow that the rest of the Lewis-Loomie version is correct also. Certainly the district on the York River where they consider the mission to have been located was the center of the Powhatan tribe's activities at the opening of the seventeenth century.

The ship which brought the equipment for the mission did not go round to its site; materials were transported upstream and over the watershed to be assembled, and the vessel remained until the first assessment of their situation could be made by Segura and Quirós. The report was a somewhat surprising one. The tribe was in very poor condition, since there had been crop failures for several years and many members were seriously ill. They needed seed and extra stores, which should be brought as soon as supplies could be sent to the mission. At the beginning Don Luis had helped the missionar

14. Clifford M. Lewis and Albert J. Loomie, *The Spanish Jesuit Mission in Virginia, 1570–1572* (Chapel Hill, N.C., 1953), give a full account of the mission and translate the principal documents relating to it.

15. *Ibid.*, pp. 36–41.

ies to get established, but they reported that he soon detached himself and began to revert to his native customs, apparently expressing some resentment toward the Spaniards he had guided to his homeland. It seems probable that the Jesuits expected Don Luis to behave as a Spanish Christian and to adopt the moral standards they had set for him, whereas it was more natural for him to prefer his own.

This was the last that was seen of any member of the mission party except one. It appeared that, on February 4, when Segura, Quirós and a third Jesuit were some way from the mission bartering goods for food, of which they had run short, they were set upon and killed. A little later the mission itself was attacked and all the remaining Jesuits killed, the only survivor being the boy, Alonso de Olmos, who was taken into the tribe. Apparently these acts were directed and participated in by Don Luis, though the precise motives are not known. If the Indians were in a bad way economically, even the poor possessions of the missionaries may have seemed worth plundering. There is reason to think, too, that Don Luis came to resent the prohibitions placed on him by his Christian teachers, which he felt would drastically alter the way of life of his people. But the story is so overlaid with hagiographical invention, and the authentic data so scarce, that little more can be said.

Only chance revealed what had happened. A vessel duly appeared in the spring of 1571 from Havana under the command of Vicente González. Near the rendezvous (Cape Comfort?), Indians dressed in Jesuit habits attempted to lure them ashore, thus indicating that the mission had probably been destroyed. As the vessel came close to land, a number of canoes emerged to attack her—some Indians were killed and several taken prisoner. The ship went back to Havana and from one of the prisoners something was gathered about what happened, with an indication that the boy still survived.

By the summer of 1571, a further transformation came over Florida. Pedro Menéndez de Avilés reached Havana in July in command of the *galeones* which were to convoy the homeward-bound fleet.[16] He had several vessels of his own with him, with supplies and some 650 persons, a number of whom, both soldiers and settlers, he proposed to leave in Florida. He put down a substantial number

16. Lowery, *Spanish Settlements*, II, 372–373; Ruídíaz, *Florida*, II, 228–238.

at San Agustín, where they set to work to develop the new town site and fort. His own special concern was Santa Elena where most were to be placed as colonists. The settlers he left there were farming families from northern Spain who had supplied a good deal of their own equipment and had some of their own livestock with them. They had been promised twelve animals each by Menéndez, but all he had was two hundred pigs which he proposed to distribute among them. He required that they should keep them for ten years, not killing any of the increase, and that then the whole herd would be divided equally between him and the farmers. Most of the settlers appear to have rejected these impracticable terms, but it may be that they took over the animals in any case. Then, too, they had been promised extensive farms but were set down, it would seem as an allegedly temporary measure, on the very limited land available on Parris Island outside the fort, a good deal of it swampy. The garrison was considerably enlarged, though Menéndez soon found that his stores did not go as far as he had hoped. A supply ship for the Chesapeake mission put in in September and he appropriated its cargo, no doubt thinking that there was little hope of there being a mission left there to be supplied.

He spent a busy autumn and was in touch with Havana about various problems; in December it was necessary for him to go there. One small vessel arrived safely but Menéndez himself did not appear—he had been shipwrecked near Cape Cañaveral. He and his thirty men got ashore and, surprisingly, were not attacked by the local Indians. He marched his men some 75 miles north to San Agustín; there he learned that the fort had recently been attacked, three well-armed ships having put into the inlet and fired on it. This was replied to and after a time they left. They were apparently under the command of the English naval commander, Sir William Winter, and their reconnaissance had probably been made to test the strength of the Spanish defenses.[17] Menéndez took some precautionary measures but the Indians were quiet and he could at last get to Havana early in July 1572. He had been ordered home to super-

17. Manuel Fernández de Navarrete, *Colección de documentos*, 32 vols. (Nendeln, Lichtenstein, 1971), XIV, fols. 3▮7–338, mentioning "el tres Naos gruesas Inglesas con gran cantidad de gente"; an▮ ▮e I. A. Wright (ed.), *Documents Concerning English Voyages to the Spanish Main, 156▮ ▮0* (London, Hakluyt Society, 1932), pp. xxxvi–xxxvii, 37–39.

vise construction work in the naval yards at Santander, but discussed the position of the mission with Jesuits at Havana and agreed to call in at Chesapeake Bay on his way to Spain.

Menéndez was now able to collect further supplies for the Florida garrisons, and reached Chesapeake Bay safely after he had deposited them there; with him were Father Rogel and two other Jesuits. Anchoring inside the bay, he sent a smaller vessel to explore the rivers and to entice Indians to come on board so that they could be captured. In fact, a considerable body of Indians came to meet them (Lewis and Loomie maintain that this was at the mouth of College Creek on the James).[18] Trading and the exchange of courtesies took place as if there had never been any quarrel with the Spaniards. The chief, Don Luis's uncle, even put in an appearance. At an appropriate moment he and his men were seized, taken away as prisoners, and brought to Menéndez. The Indian captured in 1571 was now able to interpret, so negotiations were begun for the return of Alonso de Olmos. Somehow the Spaniards got the better of the Indians, since they recovered Alonso (and an Indian friend) and kept their prisoners. The latter were formally tried and eight or nine then hanged, including the chief—a clue most probably to the wariness and hostility of Powhatan and Opechancanough toward Europeans a generation later. Alonso was able to give some account of what had happened, and the Chesapeake venture was brought to an end when Menéndez set out the last time for Spain.

Thereafter Florida was left on its own. Pedro Menéndez Marqués stayed in charge of the colony while his uncle was involved for the rest of his life in naval preparations in Spain.[19] But Florida remained very much in the minds of the Council of the Indies. What should be done there? Menéndez suggested several times that the Indians to the south and west of San Agustín should be dealt with once and for all—killed off or sent as slaves to Española. They were "infamous people, sodomites, sacrificers to the devil of many souls in their ancient ceremonies." The Council decided that this kind of action, at the very time when the New Laws of the Indies codifying

18. Lewis and Loomie, *Spanish Jesuit Mission*, pp. 54–55.
19. For Florida in 1573–4, see Andrés Barcia, *Ensayo cronológico para la historia general de la Florida* (Madrid, 1723), pp. 146–149; Connor, *Colonial Records*, II, 322–331; Lowery, *Spanish Settlements*, II, 381.

protective measures for Indians elsewhere in the empire were being promulgated, would be inappropriate, though Menéndez continued to oppose the decision. Colonists who had come back in 1570 were also interrogated in an attempt to find out what had led to the failure at Santa Elena, and severe criticisms were made by them of the *adelantado*'s handling of their welfare. He expected them, they said, to work for his profit and not their own; the rich, fertile land he promised them never materialized; the soldiers in the fort oppressed them. And they could grow so little that "they were driven by hunger to the coast with their wives and children, to eat shellfish, for if they had not done so, they would have perished from hunger."[20] This added up to a sad picture of the complete failure of Pedro Menéndez de Avilés's ambitious plans. Nonetheless, the fact that he sent out other settlers in 1573 at his own cost showed that he was not yet convinced Florida could not be settled by Spaniards.

The remaining Jesuit fathers, Antonio Sedeño and Juan de Salcedo, were withdrawn to Mexico in 1572 when it became clear they could not make converts. Fray Alonso de Reinoso arrived soon after to take up the task on behalf of the Franciscan Order.[21] His first introduction to the field in which he was to work was not a happy one, since the Guale Indians overwhelmed the small Spanish post (and former mission) of San Juan on St. Catherine's Island, killing fifteen of the Spaniards there. The lieutenant governor, Pedro Menéndez Marqués, was quick to intervene to punish and obtain submissions; Alfonso Reinoso, who had been occupied in the villages near San Agustín, was eventually installed there. Menéndez Marqués also decided that he himself should pay a further visit to Chesapeake Bay to see whether there was any possibility of its being useful to Spain. After a careful exploration he decided it could not, and he found no further trace of the Jesuit mission. His was the last Spanish ship to enter the bay for some fifteen years.

Pedro Menéndez de Avilés spent his last days preparing a great armada, designed to dominate the English Channel and the North Sea and to destroy the Dutch Sea Beggars who had asserted their power against Spain on the sea. But he died at Santander on September 7, 1574, before completing his task; the armada never sailed. He had succeeded in giving Spain a lasting foothold on southeast-

20. Connor, *Colonial Records*, I, 85.
21. John T. Lanning, *Spanish Missions of Georgia* (Chapel Hill, N.C., 1935), p. 57.

ern North America, even though most of his more ambitious plans came to nothing.[22] His ruthlessness had overcome the French, yet he had never adapted himself successfully to the planting of colonies. It is clear that he hoped, by the use mainly of slave labor at San Agustín and of free settlers at Santa Elena, to build up large landholdings for himself. But he failed to appoint civilian managers who could bring them effectively into existence. As it was, his efforts to establish something like a Mexican *encomienda* were completely unsuccessful and were abandoned at San Agustín well before his death, even though in 1574 the mirage of a settled estate at Santa Elena still persisted. He was a very able military and naval commander, who displayed a good sense of military priorities in his dealings with Florida. But his plans were not realistic and he allowed himself to be diverted from North America to other tasks precisely when the settlements there needed him most.

The colonization of Florida by Spain had many defects in its execution and did not, at his death, fulfill the role which Pedro Menéndez de Avilés envisaged for it. It would be a mistake, however, to dwell too much on these limitations and to fail to stress the very considerable effect which the establishment of the colony had on the whole political complexion of eastern North America. Before 1565, European intervention had been casual and intermittent: claims to territory had been made but they had never been substantiated. After 1565, there was a Spanish presence in eastern North America and the claim long made by Spain that she had a prior right to conquer and settle the whole of North America for the first time gained some credibility. The presence of permanent garrisons—however limited the territory which they controlled—and the existence of continuing Spanish civilian settlements and missions—however small the total number of people they contained—tended to justify Spanish claims to at least a substantial area in the southeast. Menéndez had attempted to dominate the coastlines of modern Virginia and North Carolina, as well as those of modern South

22. Albert Manucy, *Florida's Menendez* (St. Augustine, Fla., 1962), and Constantino Bayle, *Pedro Menéndez de Avilés* (Madrid, 1928), cover his career fairly adequately. Ruídíaz, *Florida*, I, ccxvii–ccxxv; Jeanette T. Connor, in her introduction to Solís de Méras, *Pedro Menéndez de Avilés;* and Lowery, *Spanish Settlements*, pp. 382–386, sum up the significance of his career in committing Spain to a policy of permanent intervention in North America.

Carolina, Georgia and Florida. Even if he had failed in the more northerly areas, he had retained footholds in the three more southerly ones, though Spanish ambitions need not necessarily remain confined to them. At any time Spain, with great imperial resources at her command, had the means to embark on further large-scale North American expansion. The choice of whether she would give such expansion a high or a low priority remained in her hands; in a real sense, she held the initiative.

This created quite a new situation for the French, English, and even the Portuguese, if and when they considered it desirable to establish North American footholds. The question of whether or not Spain would allow the creation of such beachheads was from this time a much less hypothetical one than it had been before 1565. Any further European colony on the shores of North America ran a considerably greater risk of being attacked and taken over by Spain than had early experiments such as those made by the French in Canada and the southeast.

The events of 1565 in Florida had, moreover, imported European rivalries to the North American sphere. North America now became involved, however peripherally to begin with, in the continuing rivalry between France and Spain, in the growing rivalry between Spain and England, and ultimately too in the situation which was to arise after Portugal became a possession of the Spanish crown in 1580. The establishment of the Florida colony meant that henceforth every major initiative by Europeans in North America had a European dimension. It must be studied within that context, as well as in its own right.

# CHAPTER 12

## The Florida Settlements, 1574–1612

### I

AFTER the failure of the ambitious plans of the *adelantado* Pedro Menéndez de Avilés, it might have been expected that Florida would stabilize as a small frontier garrison, with perhaps a settler element, mainly concerned with maintaining a coastal watch and rescuing shipwrecked Spaniards from Indian hands while safeguarding valuables salvaged from the wrecks.[1] The garrison, it is true, remained the dominating element in Florida's history throughout the subsequent period. The number and condition of the garrison, the effectiveness or otherwise of the forts, the number of places *(plazas)* in the establishment which were to be paid for by the crown, above all the subsidy *(situado)* derived, when it appeared, from a Mexican tax source—these were the topics which filled the administration record. The major excitements were changes in officeholding or the visits of inspectors to audit accounts.

After 1574, the official establishment comprised a governor appointed by the crown, and three royal officials, treasurer, accountant *(contador)* and factor *(veedor)*, together with a number of essen-

1. We lack a detailed, scholarly history of Florida in this period. C. W. Arnade, "The Failure of Spanish Florida," 33rd International Congress of Americanists, *Actas*, II (San José, C.R., 1959), 758–766, and *Florida on Trial, 1593–1602* (Coral Gables, Fla., 1959), give some indication of the problems of the period. Verne E. Chatelaine, *The Defenses of Spanish Florida, 1563–1763* (Washington, D.C., 1941), is valuable for the general history.

tial minor civilian officials such as the scrivener *(escrivano)*, who was effectively the chief clerk, and on the military side the *sargento mayor*, the commander of the infantry in the garrison, usually with several captains at his side who might be posted to command outlying forts or blockhouses. Although both Philip II and Philip III were free to appoint whom they liked as governor, they gave a distinct preference to the family of the *adelantado*, even though Menéndez had no legitimate sons of his own to succeed him. Diego de Velasco, who had married one of the *adelantado*'s daughters, acted as lieutenant governor in 1574–76, while Hernando de Miranda, who had married the older daughter, was governor in 1576–77, but retired in ignominy from the colony after little more than a year. Pedro Menéndez Marqués, son of the founder's sister, had acted as accountant and lieutenant governor to his uncle and had held other offices under the crown elsewhere before he became governor in 1577. The most vigorous of the second generation, he was to continue in office until 1589 and left only to take up more important commands for the crown. Gutierre de Miranda, a relative by marriage, had had a spell as lieutenant governor and then was acting governor in 1589–92. The refusal of a second term of office by Menéndez Marqués in 1593 broke the sequence; but the first outside governor, Domingo Martínez de Avendaño, 1593–95, was confirmed only after the former governor's approval had been given. He died in office in 1595. Gonzalo Méndez de Canzo (more correctly Cancio), 1596–1603, was a naval man but, like the Menéndez family, an Asturian, thus continuing the links between Florida and northern Spain. A six-year term now became usual. Pedro de Ibarra (or Ybarra), 1603–09, was a soldier, as was his successor Juan Fernandez de Olivera, 1609–12, who died in office halfway through his term.[2]

A distinctive feature of the Florida colony is that appointments to it were made direct from Spain and most reinforcements and policy decisions were transmitted directly from there also. This meant that the viceroy in Mexico could more easily wash his hands of it and forget to pay the *situado* on which its day-to-day existence depended; and the governor of Cuba, responsible for overseeing its military effectiveness, whenever there was a gap in communications could

2. Chatelaine, *Defenses*, pp. 27–29, 124–127.

neglect to inquire whether it still survived or not. In fact, successive governors of Florida tried to maintain some continuing contact with Mexico, Cuba, and also with the *audiencia* of Santo Domingo to whose overriding judicial authority they were subject. Some governors may have preferred the wide range of autonomy they enjoyed. Others felt that if the governor of Cuba had more direct responsibility for its government, and the ruler of Florida became one of his subordinates, then Florida might get more regular inspection and assistance, though there is no doubt that inspectors from outside—coming to make a *residencia* or *visita*—contrived to create considerable disruption mingled with reform. The very fact that revenue was irregular and in arrears encouraged peculation. Money put up in advance of revenue by speculating officials was recouped at high profits; what were known in England at the time as "dead pays" were also common, keeping places in the garrison vacant so that the wages assigned to them could go into the pockets of their superiors and the missing men would prove to be discreetly "absent on duty" when inspectors called. Scarcely an administrator got a clean bill of health from the visiting inspectors, who normally returned to their headquarters bearing an official or two to be tried in Santo Domingo for financial irregularities. Needless to say, many aspects of this not very exciting story could be paralleled in other small outlying portions of the vast Spanish imperial network.[3]

Yet Florida's history was far from being without incident. The small garrisons were surrounded by Indians who were reasonably well organized and belligerent at the opening of the period and who remained so for the greater part of it. Indian risings therefore gave color and danger to the record of garrison life, nearly eliminating it on several occasions. The other exceptional feature of the Florida garrison was its continuing duty as policeman, trying to watch French and English activities along the coast and to stop them as soon as possible. French threats in the late 1570s and English actions in the 1580s kept governors and soldiers busy and several times vigorously in action. Franciscan missions also provided an important aspect of the colony's life, and an increasing one. The departure of the Jesuits in 1572 left the colony without effective missionaries for a time, but the first Franciscans arrived in 1573, and

3. Examples can readily be found in Jeanette T. Connor, *Colonial Records of Spanish Florida, 1570–1580*, 2 vols. (1925–27).

from 1587 onward Florida became a major target for Franciscan activity, which had dramatic ups and downs before becoming a principal factor in the continuance and expansion of the Spanish sphere of influence.

All three elements interacted. Foreigners stirred up Indians against the Spaniards; missionaries created rebellions by pressing too hard on Indian mores, or else pacified Indians who had hitherto been hostile.[4] From time to time, governors took up the possibility of expanding the colony and launching it as a major instead of a very minor Spanish enterprise. A main incentive here was the fear, or even the possibility, of French or English settlers establishing themselves on the borders of the colony and ultimately taking it over. But money for experiment and expansion was never readily available during a period when Spain was increasingly involved in European struggles and had to meet much greater threats from the English and French elsewhere. In the end, with little more than a series of alarm bells and no effective counteraction, the English were able to dig in at Jamestown and to block the way permanently to any Spanish expansion over most of the eastern shore of North America. The Spanish assumption that the whole of North America was the inheritance of the Spanish crown continued to be asserted down to the seventeenth century, for example in the *Historia general de las hechos de los Castellanos* of Antonio de Herrera, the first volume of which appeared in 1601, and in the negotiations on the Treaty of London of 1604. It was asserted with equal vigor in the early years of the Jamestown settlement.[5] Florida was the instrument by which the theory could be turned into reality, but this was never attempted.

The smallness of the Spanish population and its sparse distribution along several hundred miles of coastline made the question of Indian relations a peculiarly intractable one. The Calusa and Tequesta in southern Florida, to the south and west of the Spanish settlements, were apparently untameable, and their expulsion and sale into slavery was repeatedly suggested.[6] The Timucua around

4. Arnade, "Failure of Spanish Florida," makes a number of these points.

5. Antonio de Herrera, *Historia general de los hechos de los Castellanos*, I (Madrid, 1934), 50–54; D. B. Quinn, "James I and the Beginnings of Empire," *The Journal of Imperial and Commonwealth History*, II (1973–74), 135–152.

6. See the study by John M. Goggin and William C. Sturtevant, "The Calusa," in W. H. Goodenough (ed.), *Explorations in Cultural Anthropology: Essays in Honor of George Peter Murdock* (New York, 1964), pp. 179–219.

and to the north of the *presidio* had long-continued French sympathies and were liable to break out when their social customs were interfered with or exploitation from San Agustín became too great to bear. The Guale Indians of St. Catherine's Island and the fringe of coast on the mainland were erratic; usually friendly and cooperative, almost uniquely so, they could also be treacherous and violent on occasion. The Cusabo, a branch of the Creek Indians around Santa Elena, not only had French allegiances from time to time but were determined to allow the Spaniards very little chance to operate outside the walls of their fort, if even there. As an Indian tribe came to be dominated by force or diplomacy, Spanish policy was to establish a close nexus by means of a corn tax. This gave an excuse for regular Spanish inspection and supervision, as well as providing badly needed food for garrison and settlers alike. It rose to the height of 1 *arroba,* about 25 pounds, for each married man in the tribe—a heavy burden, which was responsible for several revolts that endangered the survival of the colony.

When an expedition was in progress overland, Indians were conscripted as bearers, as Hernando de Soto had done long before. Attempts were made to get them to provide labor, in effect forced labor, at sowing and harvest times at San Agustín. After the 1597 rising, many were taken as slaves to the *presidio,* until the crown ordered their release. If the Indians rose against the Spaniards, the Indians were killed with the same ruthlessness as if they were French, their villages sometimes burned with the entire population inside. Even in 1597 when milder methods were adopted, we are told, cornfields were burned out and villages smashed or razed to the ground. On the other hand, gifts of clothing, copper and other presents were regularly given to selected chiefs. The missionary objective—whether Jesuit or Franciscan—was to deal with the Indian problem another way: to settle them in villages as Christians and under a screen of Christian morality in place of their own, so that they could live at peace but pay their taxes and do other services to the crown, whose servants, as well as those of the papacy and their God, the friars were. This policy raised basic questions about Indian society and also about the status and purpose of the military garrison.

## I I

The years 1574 to 1576 were quiet under Diego de Velasco as lieutenant governor. Hernando de Miranda, married to Catalina Menéndez de Avilés, was the heir to Florida, provided he could get himself confirmed as governor. He did so after long delays, finally appearing at San Agustín at the opening of 1576.[7] Settling himself and his retinue there with some difficulty, he was soon called on to take decisions of importance at Santa Elena. There the colonists established in 1572 had dwindled to a handful. They had expected large farms on the mainland with, no doubt, willing Indians to work them; instead, they found the Indians both hostile and ever-present. There were not enough soldiers in the small garrison to give them adequate protection on the mainland, so they had to make do with small patches of ground, some fertile, some simply swamp, on the very limited area of modern Parris Island, where the grandly named "City of Santa Elena" became simply a group of households scattered around the fort. By the end of 1575, the settlers had borne all they could and were determined to be taken off from their cramped and perilous location. They demanded that the new governor should listen to them. Miranda duly arrived to do so on February 24, 1576, and settled down to hear their complaints.

It seemed that the settlers had been promised twelve cows by the *adelantado* for each household and had received none. Instead of large farms they had small swampy patches where only maize and squashes would grow, since wheat and barley did not ripen and the few privately owned cattle did not thrive. A number of settlers had been killed or had died; the remainder, in spite of the fact that they had their own *alcalde* and *regidores* and could express themselves through their *cabildo,* felt that these municipal institutions could not shield them from oppression by the soldiers. They stated: "We feel ourselves old and weary and full of sickness," and wished only to be removed to Spain or to other parts of the Indies. Miranda promised to send reports of what they said to Spain and to take action

7. Ray E. Held, "Hernando de Miranda, Governor of Florida, 1575–1577," *Florida Historical Quarterly,* XXVIII (1950), 111–130; Connor, *Colonial Records,* II, 189–191; Manuel Fernández de Navarrete, *Colección de documentos,* 32 vols. (1971), XIV, fols. 345–346v.

as soon as he could. In the short run, he gave them some supplies and instructed Alonso de Solís, in charge of the garrison, to get tough with the Indians, punish them for attacks on Spanish property and persons, and obtain from them supplies of corn for himself and the settlers.

Solís had apparently already distinguished himself by having a number of local chiefs killed. In July this policy produced tragic results. A detachment of troops under a lieutenant, Moyano, entered the village of Oristan and demanded corn. They were refused —there was probably no corn in store at this time of year in any case. As a result, they drove the Indians out and began to plunder. The Indians returned and killed twenty-seven out of twenty-eight of them, the survivor getting back to warn the fort and the settlers, who took refuge there.[8] The adjoining Cusabo tribes came out against the Spaniards and brought out the Guale tribes as well, so that the Spaniards were faced with a major rebellion. The fort was besieged. Soon after this a ship fortunately appeared: Miranda had come back with the supply vessel, which brought food and pay for the troops, and was able to get his men into the fort after the advance party had been wiped out. He succeeded in defending it though it was a poor thing, "propped up, ready to fall," and went on to conduct an orderly evacuation. Behind a military guard he managed to load settlers and soldiers and their cows, 287 persons in all, into two ships.

The colony and fort had come to an end. The handful of settlers were brought to San Agustín, thence to Havana, and were eventually given some compensation for their suffering.[9] The northern link in the Florida chain had been severed; only the southern posts remained. In the longer term, too, this marked the end of a program of systematic colonization. Miranda when he returned to Florida found the garrison at San Agustín very apprehensive for its own safety. He did not provide any considerable help; his experiences at Santa Elena had robbed him of all confidence. At the end of the year he slipped away, taking with him 6,000 ducats from the garrison chest. He arrived in Spain in April 1577 to find a warrant for his arrest awaiting him.

8. Connor, *Colonial Records*, I, 147–193.
9. *Ibid.*, I, 193–202.

## III

When news came of these disasters, Pedro Menéndez Marqués was induced to wind up his duties in the fleets and take on the burden of Florida. He reached San Agustín in July 1577 to find the garrison barely holding its own, though fortunately the Timucua Indians had not attacked either the *presidio* of San Agustín or San Pedro even if their attitude had been hostile. His first task was to assert the king's authority at Santa Elena. He took a force northward and rapidly set up a small new fort on Parris Island, which he named San Marcos, setting the soldiers to work building cottages around it. This he did unmolested by the Indians. He had with him an addition to the colony's garrison of 150 men (actually 139), and with these men he was able to reconnoiter the coast of Guale. But he could do no more without still more reinforcements, which he sent for to Havana. From this time the new establishment was to consist of 300, not 150, men and an addition was made to the annual subsidy if the officials in Mexico could be induced to disgorge it.[10]

What Menéndez did not know when he re-established the fort of San Marcos at Santa Elena was that there was now a French fort a little way to the north of it. The French privateer *Le Prince* (500 tons), with 180 men under Nicolas Strozzi—brother of the more famous Philippe Strozzi and cousin of the queen mother, Marie de Médicis—had worked her way up the coast in December 1576, making some contacts with the Indians and inciting them against the Spaniards. The ship went aground in a storm a little way to the north of Santa Elena and broke up, but her men got ashore. They were apparently attacked by the Cusabo Indians and lost some men before convincing them that they were enemies of Spain, not Spaniards. Then they built themselves a small fort and distributed some men among the Indian villages. Why they did not reveal themselves and try to prevent the rebuilding of the Spanish fort is not known. Menéndez's men stumbled on the wreck of the ship and were able to piece together something of the history of the expedition, though they did not have the forces at hand to search for the French to the north of Santa Elena.

10. Connor, *Colonial Records*, I, 263–277.

During the latter part of 1577 and for most of 1578, Menéndez could take no direct action.[11] He limited himself to pacifying the Indians nearer San Agustín and attempting to divide those of Guale against each other. In the meantime, the Indians had fallen out with their French guests in the north. They rushed the French fort and captured the occupants, who managed to avoid being killed through the good offices of other Frenchmen already quartered in Indian villages. Instead, they settled down as residents scattered amongst the Cusabo tribes. Rather vague news of their doings reached Menéndez from time to time. In 1579, he received reinforcements and with their aid managed to overrun the Guale Indian territory, destroying nineteen villages, killing many Indians, and terrorizing the rest into submission. Interestingly, the Indians admitted to Menéndez that they did not object to submission but did not wish to be subjected to conversion to Christianity.[12] With his full quota of three hundred soldiers, he was now in a stronger position to make a clearance in the north.

In August 1579, he went to Santa Elena and attempted to crush the hostile Cusabo. Aided by some Frenchmen, they retaliated by attacking him but were defeated. Menéndez thereupon burned one of the principal villages, killing many of the forty French it was said to contain and taking some eighteen French prisoners, whom he promptly executed in the traditional way after they had been interrogated. He visited the area again in the spring of 1580. By this time he was able to intimidate the Indians into bringing him a number of Frenchmen, including a Captain Roque of Rouen whom he duly executed also,[13] and he gradually collected others from Indian tribes both far and near. A handful he kept as slaves at San Agustín until he received further orders.[14] In July, however, he had a fresh alarm. A French vessel put into the mouth of the St. Johns, making inquiries about their countrymen. This vessel was under the command of a Catalan in the French service, Gilberto Gil. Menéndez rushed two frigates north and managed to bottle up the French in the estuary. In a confused fight, complicated by a storm, the French ship was destroyed along with one of the frigates, fifty-four out of

11. *Ibid.*, I, 269; II, 27–29, 333.
12. *Ibid.*, II, 79–83, 225–227.
13. *Ibid.*, II, 249–251, 283–285.
14. *Ibid.*, II, 297–303.

fifty-eight French being killed for a loss of eighteen Spaniards. Several other French vessels making their way back from the Caribbean edged into bays along the coast this year, but none made contact with any of their countrymen. Indeed, apart from a few individuals widely scattered in Indian hands, most of whom were eventually purchased for copper by Menéndez and executed when they were handed over, there were none left.[15]

This long epilogue to the struggle of French and Spaniards on the Florida coast ended in complete victory for Menéndez Marqués. He had shown great vigor and ruthlessness whereas the French intervention had been casual, mismanaged, and could be dealt with in detail, as it was, over an extended period. Had the French been better informed of the situation in Florida in 1576 and 1577 they could easily—with a few hundred men well organized and led, and Indian aid—have destroyed the Spanish hold. Menéndez's preoccupation, when he was not engaged in fighting, was to strengthen both San Agustín and Santa Elena. He did all he could to reinforce the garrisons at the *presidio*, at San Pedro and Santa Elena, and he received sufficient extra men and money to do so effectively without undue extravagance. He set the inhabitants of San Agustín to grow more corn so that they would not be so dependent on Indian tributes which were lacking for several years. At Santa Elena he built a village near the fort, making houses of mud and coquina, and lime-washing them so that they looked like stone. But military concerns took precedence over all others. His major achievement was to quieten the Guale Indians, so that they would receive Spanish missionaries in the years following; and also to split up, bribe, and intimidate the formidable Cusabo, so that for the time being they would not offer a further menace to Santa Elena.

In the 1580s, Pedro Menéndez Marqués was still preoccupied by the prospects and realities of foreign intervention. He continued to send home expressions of his opinion that the French would try yet again to destroy the Spanish hold on Florida. In 1584, after having been refused his request to make representations in person, he sent two experienced members of the garrison—Rodrigo de Junco and

15. *Ibid.*, II, 319–323; Navarrete, *Colección*, XIV, fols. 373–378; Mary A. Ross, "French Intrusions and Indian Uprisings in Georgia and South Carolina, 1577–1580," *Georgia Historical Quarterly*, VII (1923), 251–281; Quinn, *England and the Discovery of America*, p. 269.

Juan de Posada—to urge on the Council of the Indies the need for more soldiers and for patrol boats to maintain a full watch on the coast. It is not clear whether any word came to him of the passage of Amadas and Barlowe along the coast in 1584 on their way to the Carolina Outer Banks. But early in 1585, when he was on his way to Spain, he learned at Havana of the presence of Sir Richard Grenville's squadron in the West Indies and of their plans to settle a colony on the North American coast. He hastily returned to San Agustín with what little he could assemble in the way of munitions, and concentrated on partly rebuilding and strengthening the wooden fort there.

Official warnings reached him in May. A vessel to help safeguard Florida was attached to the outgoing *flota,* which arrived during the fall; in December, Menéndez was able to despatch her up the coast to try to track down where the English had settled. Vicente González went far enough north to learn that the English were settled near Chesapeake Bay. Since he sailed back direct to Spain his report was sent back to Florida only in November 1586.[16] At this time the decision was taken in Spain to send two further ships to Florida, along with a substantial military reinforcement, to deal with what was now thought to be a major threat to the settlement.[17] They had not arrived before the threat took concrete form in the shape of a devastating raid by Sir Francis Drake on the colony.

After his shattering attacks on Spanish complaisance, when he sacked and ransomed Santo Domingo and dug another ransom out of Cartagena, Drake had sheered off from his intended attack on Havana and sailed off through the Florida Strait for Florida. Pedro Menéndez Marqués had been given some five weeks warning that Drake might appear. He had further reconstructed the fort (now called San Juan de Ponilla) so as to bring all her guns to bear on St. Augustine Inlet, though he had not completed the new moat when English pinnaces sounded the bar on June 6 after lookout men on the high platform just south of the inlet had signaled Drake's arrival.

The governor had only some 90 effectives and, about a mile away

16. D. B. Quinn (ed.), *The Roanoke Voyages, 1584–1590,* 2 vols. (Cambridge, Eng., 1955), II, 717–720; Irene A. Wright, *Further English Voyages to Spanish America, 1583–1594* (London, Hakluyt Society, 1951), pp. 9–16; A.G.I., Seville, Indiferente General 541, fol. 7v.

17. Quinn, *Roanoke Voyages,* II, 720.

in the town, some 250 non-combatants. He ordered the latter, mainly women and children, to leave the town and take refuge in the forest some little way inland. The same evening, the English began erecting batteries on the island immediately opposite the fort; by the morning they were ready for their attack, which they began with a bombardment from the battery but continued by an assault on the fort. A large force was landed, though the Spaniards sank two pinnaces with some loss, and an attack against the fort began. The English had not, however, surrounded it and Menéndez and all his men were able to escape by the rear. They were clearly so outnumbered that continued resistance would have been foolish, especially as they had learned that the local Indians, presumed to be friendly but by no means to be trusted, had joined the non-combatants in their place of refuge. Menéndez and his men now established contact with them and retreated with such little in the way of supplies as they could muster, remaining in hiding for the next five days.

Drake turned his men toward the almost deserted town, where they were joined by a few negro slaves and three deserters, one of them French. They settled down to rest for a few days, attempting to make friendly contact with the Indians. Then they destroyed the fort and town systematically; the church, the waterside warehouses and dwellings, the six blocks of wooden houses, all were leveled. Then the gardens were destroyed, fruit trees cut down, the maize fields cleared of corn.

Only the household goods, hardware, door locks and so on were collected for the use of the Roanoke colonists and brought away. On June 12 the expedition left, bringing the treasure chest with 6,000 ducats and the flags of the fort, in the expectation that the Indians would deal with Menéndez or that he would starve. On July 17, Drake dropped anchor briefly at the mouth of the Savannah River (Baya de Santa Cruz), searching for Santa Elena. Gutierre de Miranda, in command at San Marcos, had received warning from the governor that Drake might appear and had been told not to respond to any offensive gestures he might make. Drake did indeed fire some guns off the entry to Port Royal Sound but did not get any response and so did not cross the difficult bar as he could not be sure that the Spaniards were there. He entered St. Helena Sound (Oristan) instead, and spent a little time there dealing with Indians, cutting masts, taking firewood and water, and leaving about June 18

for the Carolina Outer Banks. From there he was to take home Ralph Lane and his men, thus removing any threat to Florida from an English colony for the time being.[18]

The Spaniards came back to their ruined fort and town. Somehow Menéndez equipped a tiny vessel and sent it off on June 17 to Havana with an urgent plea for assistance, while he called on Miranda and his men for help also. At Havana the ships which had been sent out earlier were almost ready to come on to Florida when the news arrived there on July 10, so that Juan de Posada was able to reach San Agustín with reinforcements and supplies by July 19. The reconstruction of town and fort was a slow and painful one. The fort was re-established where it had been but rebuilt in a more substantial way.[19] The sites of most of the houses in the town were used for rebuilding, though it would seem that less solid structures —mostly palmetto-covered huts and a rather flimsy wooden church instead of the earlier, heavier buildings—were begun. Yet under the governor's leadership rapid progress was made in reconstructing the *presidio*. In August a squadron, which may have been Sir Richard Grenville's coming from their visit to Roanoke Island, tried to put in at Santa Elena but failed once more to cross the bar. In a reappraisal of his situation, Menéndez advised that Santa Elena should be abandoned for the time being. The evacuation was carried out fairly early in 1587 and Miranda joined the governor at San Agustín. This proved to be a permanent move. Thereafter, the Spanish posts were limited to those at San Pedro and San Agustín; the long coastline to the north, hitherto defended by Santa Elena, was left to missionary enterprise alone.

As ordered by Philip II, Menéndez Marqués himself set out in May 1587 on a reconnaissance, expecting to enter Chesapeake Bay where he believed the English settlement to be. Of this voyage in May and June 1587 we have only brief descriptions.[20] He reached a latitude of 37° but could not enter the bay because of adverse

18. English accounts in Quinn, *Roanoke Voyages*, I, 250–254, 294–399, 303–307; and, especially, in Mary Frear Keeler, *Sir Francis Drake's West Indian Voyage* (London, Hakluyt Society, 1977); Spanish accounts in Wright, *Further English Voyages*, pp. lx–lxiv, 163–165, 180–184, 189–207; Quinn, *Roanoke Voyages*, II, 722–723.

19. Chatelaine, *Defenses*, pp. 50–51; L. A. Vigneras, "Fortificaciones de la Florida," *Annuario de Estudios Americanos*, XVI (1958), 533–552.

20. Wright, *Further English Voyages*, pp. 230–233; Quinn, *Roanoke Voyages*, II, 724–803.

winds. Eventually he was driven southward and reached Havana, reporting that he could see no sign of the English. He returned to San Agustín in July, proposing to make a more effective reconnaissance in May 1588. He was cheered too by news that new and stronger fortifications were contemplated in Spain for Florida. Yet nothing came in the way of shipping or instructions for his 1588 voyage, so he sent a small packet boat in June under Captain Vicente González to carry out the reconnaissance instead of going himself. The vessel had thirty men in all, including Juan Menéndez Marqués, the governor's cousin. She sailed quickly past the Carolina Outer Banks and into Chesapeake Bay without difficulty. A fairly thorough but by no means exhaustive search was made up the estuaries on the western side as far as the end of the bay, when the entry of the Susquehanna River was remarked. Then they worked down the eastern shore. A consultation with some Indians by signs brought no real enlightenment, though there were vague indications of strangers somewhere in the distance. Returning down the coast, González had some rough weather along the Outer Banks and put in for shelter by chance at Port Ferdinando. There at last traces of the English were found: a slipway and some barrels buried in the sand to catch water. He did not attempt to search the sounds and so failed to find the fort site on Roanoke Island, possibly even with some "Lost Colonists" still in it.

González got back to San Agustín in July after a month's voyage[21] to find that the governor had gone to Havana to discover what had happened to his instructions. They had indeed arrived, but merely told him to come to Spain as soon as he could. Returning briefly to San Agustín and receiving González's report, Menendez Marqués set out for Spain but was driven back and put in again to Havana, where he stayed for the winter. Apparently he learned there that the English had settled on Roanoke Island and heard the view expressed that the English had probably by then abandoned their colony or at least that it was in a poor way. Revisiting San Agustín early in 1589 to report this news to Miranda, who was acting as

21. Luis Geronimo de Oré, *Relación histórico de Florida,* edited by Atanasio López, 2 vols. (Madrid, 1931), I, 63–81; Oré, *Martyrs of Florida,* translated by Maynard Geiger (New York, 1936), pp. 44–50; Clifford M. Lewis and Albert J. Loomie, *The Spanish Jesuit Mission in Virginia, 1571–1572* (1953), pp. 185–199; Quinn, *Roanoke Voyages,* II, 772–775, 802–814.

lieutenant governor, he reached Spain at last in July 1589. After discussions, a radical plan was at last decided on. Menéndez Marqués was to be given a substantial force and was to pick up more ships at Havana. He was then to destroy the English settlement and plant a strong garrison of three hundred men on Chesapeake Bay which would mean the permanent exclusion of the English.

But in the year after the Armada, to plan activities at sea was one thing and to have them performed quite another. Menéndez Marqués was first delayed, then his expedition countermanded.[22] Instead, he was given the vital task of organizing and commanding the light sailing vessels (galizabras) which could carry the silver from Havana past the blockading English and French privateers. In this he was wholly successful. As a result, he was fully employed as a naval commander over the following years and was never able to return to his post, though he continued to be associated with the government of the province until 1593. The accountant of Florida, Bartolomé de Arguëlles, came from there in the latter year with a familiar tale of woe—there was no money and supplies were not arriving; all prospects were poor. To this ancient plea Menéndez Marqués, in his report to the king, stressed that Florida was worth maintaining since otherwise no outpost could discern or hold off dangerous enemy activity or rescue shipwrecked men. The colony must, however, be better supplied. Some more women must be sent out, and soldiers with wives and children should get an allowance as the families could not live on their wages. Provision needed to be made too for the regular gifts to Indian chiefs which had kept them friendly. Two vessels must be attached to the colony for reconnaissance purposes, and also to be available to make a run over to the Canary Islands for food when stores ran low early in the year.[23] It was in this practical, matter-of-fact way that he brought his connection with Florida to an end, for he now relinquished his governorship since the king was not prepared to spare him from the fleets. He had done great service to the Spanish crown by his tenacity and resourcefulness.

In Florida itself at the end of his term everything was relatively quiet. Fray Alonso de Reinoso, and his small group of friars, who

22. Quinn, *Roanoke Voyages,* II, 775, 786–795, 812, *England and the Discovery of America,* pp. 278–279.

23. Navarrete, *Colección,* XIV, fols. 347–356; see Lowery, *Spanish Settlements,* II, 465.

had come in 1573, had experimented initially in teaching Indians near the fort. Now, several of them had gone north to Cumberland Island and St. Catherine's Island, and were attempting to establish missions in the field beyond the protection of Spanish arms. This was to prove a vital experiment even if, in the short run, an unsuccessful one.[24]

Domingo Martínez de Avendaño was chosen with the approval of Menéndez Marqués to fill the post of governor. He set out for Florida early in 1594, with Juan Menéndez Marqués as treasurer. His governorship was to be marked by the emergence of the Franciscan mission as a major force in Florida.[25] Thirteen additional friars came out at this time and were urged to scatter themselves among the more amenable villages. To encourage them, Fray Baltasar López staged a mass baptism, which the governor attended. Some eighty Indians were baptized together at Nombre de Dios, just outside San Agustín. Avendaño made a brisk and effective inspection of the coastal areas, being pleased with what he saw in Guale though he did not attempt to revive the Santa Elena outpost. He got a good press from the friars for his assistance to them and appears to have satisfied the soldiers as well. He did not, however, survive long enough to become unpopular, but died of a heart attack at San Agustín in November 1595.[26]

## IV

At about this time the doubts about Florida's prospects were growing. Juan de Posada, in a report on the military value of Florida written in 1595, concluded that it had none, but that a fortified lighthouse and fort should be maintained well to the south to warn

24. On the Franciscans, the primary source is Luis Geronimo de Oré, *Relación de los martires que a avido en las provincias de la Florida* [Madrid, 1617 (?)]; the Spanish edition, edited by Atanasio López, *Relación historico de la Florida escriba en el siglo XVII*, 2 vols. (Madrid, 1931), contains additional documents, translation by Maynard Geiger, *The Martyrs of Florida, 1513–1616* (New York, 1936). M. Geiger, *The Franciscan Conquest of Florida (1573–1618)* (Washington, D.C., 1936), and John T. Lanning, *The Spanish Missions of Georgia* (Chapel Hill, N.C., 1935), cover the ground, though neither definitively.

25. Andrade, *Florida on Trial*, p. 51; Oré, *Relación,* ed. A. López, I, 76, II, 4–8; Oré, *Martyrs,* ed. M. Geiger, pp. 51, 62, 66; Chatelaine, *Defenses,* pp. 142–143, 145–146.

26. Oré, *Martyrs,* ed. M. Geiger, pp. 51, 73, 95.

ships off the coast—all else to be abandoned.[27] The friars by now were very active on St. Catherine's Island and on the mainland coast of Guale, though the first rumblings of discontent at their interference with Indian life were beginning to be heard. However, all was still quiet when the new governor, Gonzalo Mendéz de Canzo, arrived on June 12, 1597,[28] accompanied by a considerable household, his wife and son and numerous servants. He at once began planning the improvement of San Agustín and, especially, the building of a large stone (coquina) house for himself, the first in the colony. At this time, too, reports came of a reconnaissance into the interior up the Altamaha River, which struck Canzo's imagination.

Gaspar de Salas, an experienced member of the garrison, had accompanied two friars to get some impression of the Yamasee Indian territory and had led them inland about 100 miles to a place they called Tama. This area was very fertile. It also had many sparkling stones, especially rock crystal, and possibly diamonds as well. The Indians were apparently friendly. Salas came back with glowing reports and a large block of rock crystal which he afterward peddled in Spain. The possibility of there being diamonds in the interior appealed to Canzo's dramatic sense and to his desire to strike a figure in Florida. Within a few months, however, he had to cope with a severe blow—the overthrow of the mission posts in Guale. The friars had begun to interfere with Indian social customs, especially with the polygamy practiced by the chiefs, and upon meeting with resistance to this and other innovations, they began to tamper with the chiefly system itself. There was one chief who exercised some degree of authority over the others of the group and was known to the Spaniards as the head *mico*. The friars deposed this man, Don Juan, in favor of another, Don Francisco, and also expelled Juanillo, son of Don Juan, who considered himself the heir to the office. The result was a general rising, arranged by the dispossessed pair against the friars, which Francisco also joined. It swept through Guale and affected in turn the Timucua island of Tacatacuru, where the Spaniards had a small military outpost. Five of the Franciscans

27. Navarrete, *Colección*, XIV, fols. 347–356, see Lowery, *Spanish Settlements*, II, 465.

28. On his governorship, Fermin Bouza-Brey, "El almirante D. Gonzalo Méndez de Cancio, governador y capitán general de la Florida," *Boletín del Instituto de Estudios Asturianos*, VI (Oviedo, 1952), 305–331, can be supplemented from Arnade, *Florida on Trial*, and Manuel Serrano y Sanz (ed.), *Documentos históricos de La Florida y Luisiana* (Madrid, 1912), and also from Lanning, *Spanish Missions of Georgia*, pp. 104–126.

were killed mercilessly, but Fray Francisco Dávila was retained as prisoner and survived his experience in hostile Indian hands. The Timucua to the south of Cumberland Island largely resisted the attempts of the insurgents to get them to join them, and even managed to repel an insurgent attack. We gather that those nearer San Agustín were restive, but the check to the southward progress of the Guale Indians enabled Canzo to gain enough time to mount an offensive.

As usual, after gaining their immediate objective, the Indians had little idea how to exploit their victory and simply dispersed to their villages. By using Cumberland Island as a springboard and also by employing a number of small vessels, the Spaniards were able to invade St. Catherine's Island and, later, the mainland Guale villages. Everywhere they went cornfields, granaries and houses were burned. As this was followed by drought, many Indians came close to starvation. A number were killed, but more were rounded up and brought back to San Agustín as slaves. There they were set to work in the fields and on the buildings. Canzo, indeed, wished to enslave the whole population, though the surviving friars strongly disapproved of the idea. Finally, in 1599, Philip III vetoed the proposal and the enslaved prisoners already in Canzo's hands were released and sent home.

In other respects he did not prove severe enough for the friars. Their basic social aim was to tie the Indians down into the villages which they dominated, but those Indians who did not accept the prison-like Christian regulations imposed simply escaped and continued to live as they had always done in the forests of the interior. The friars thought Canzo should have had them caught, brought back and reimprisoned in their own villages. When he did not do so, they blamed him for not supporting them adequately.[29]

In 1598, Canzo began to plan a new expansion of Florida. First there was Tama: it should be explored and occupied. Now that the crown had approved Oñate's New Mexico venture, it was surely necessary for Florida to expand westward to link up with the new colony, since New Mexico was thought to be only some 500 miles

29. Andrés Barcia, *Essayo cronológico* (Madrid, 1723), pp. 133–139; A. Kerrigan (ed.), *Barcia's Chronological History of Florida* (Gainesville, Fla., 1951), pp. 181–182; J. R. Swanton, *Indians of the Southeastern United States* (1946), p. 208; Andrade, *Florida on Trial,* pp. 64, 67; Lanning, *Spanish Missions,* pp. 82–104.

away (Oñate was soon to express similar delusions from his end). No reply had been received in Florida from Philip II when news came that he was dead, and Philip III was duly proclaimed at San Agustín on May 24, 1599. By this time, a cautious reply had come from Spain inquiring whether there was any real basis for supposing Tama would prove to be of value. This gave Canzo a chance to elaborate his views on expansion. He found in the garrison a Hispanicized Irish soldier, Darby Glavin, who had earlier been on several of the English voyages to Roanoke Island and was able to recall and invent various things about the English colony, which he maintained was still in existence on or near Chesapeake Bay. Other officials, like Captain Vicente González and Juan Menéndez Marqués, could tell of the 1588 expedition to this area and indicate that valuable metals were probably to be found there in Indian hands. Canzo's new plan was to wipe out whatever English posts there might be and, after settling three hundred men to guard Chesapeake Bay, to set out on an expedition to link up with New Mexico from there.[30]

These grandiose projects, reminiscent of Hernando de Soto and of Pedro Menéndez de Avilés at their most ambitious, had no chance whatever of being implemented. Reconnaissance had revealed that New Mexico might well provide mineral and agricultural riches (though this also was to prove an illusion), but no one in Spain had any confidence that Florida—and Tama—would do so. There seemed to be no basis or excuse for adventures there at a time when the new administration of Philip III was gravely assessing the salutary effects of the sea war against England and mobilizing all its resources for new blows at England and Ireland, which were shortly to fail and to lead Spain to consider making peace instead.

Canzo's expansion plans, indeed, produced in reaction a series of drastic proposals to cut down or even abandon the colony. The constant nagging by officials about the failure of the *situado* to arrive from Mexico, the poor conditions under which the garrison was maintained, the prospects of further Indian risings—all produced an atmosphere of gloom and despondency. On November 5, 1600, Philip III summed up this disquiet in a letter to Pedro de Valdés, governor of Cuba. Since the Indians of Florida did not appear to

30. Serrano y Sanz, *Documentos historicos*, pp. 136–164; Quinn, *Roanoke Voyages*, II, 776–778, 826–838.

wish to accept Christianity and would not provide corn for the Spaniards, would it not be wise to give up the missionary attempt? Valdés was asked whether Florida could really, if the garrisons were removed, prove a dangerous base for English enemies. Fernando de Valdés was sent by his father to conduct a *visita* in Florida so as to provide the answers to these questions. He arrived to make his inquiry in August 1602, and during September heard evidence which throws much light on conditions in the colony.[31] The case for and against the retention of the military base was put. In the course of this discussion it was urged that since the Spaniards had never found Florida of much value as a military base, their enemies were unlikely to be able to do so either. At the same time all were agreed that the garrison served as a useful rescue service for the ship-wrecked. The Indians were said by some to be improving and by others to be getting worse. The friars, as might be expected, argued strongly that the missions should be kept going and expanded. They had little use for San Agustín and would gladly have had it abandoned and the *presidio* moved to St. Catherine's Island, where they now needed protection for the re-establishment of their mission after Canzo's soldiers had cowed the Indians.

Canzo sent his own recommendations with the deposition. He still favored expansion, at least to Tama and to Coosa (for he had also revived the accounts and objectives of the Pardo-Boyano expedition), though no longer, it appeared, to Chesapeake Bay. On the whole, he had favorable things to say about the Indians; those who had been in rebellion were now both quiet and cooperative, and were handing over known recalcitrants. Their corn levy had been reduced from 25 pounds (an *arroba*) to 6 heads of corn per married man. It was true that some hundreds were brought to labor in the garrison's cornfields at sowing and harvest time, but sufficient corn for the garrison could not otherwise be produced. There was some hope, too, of the hostile Indians to the south becoming more amenable. The Indians were treacherous and did not keep their word; nonetheless, with vigorous punishment for any resistance they could be kept in order, and the mission program could go ahead under military protection.

Valdés sent no recommendation himself. The reports were pro-

31. It is summarized at length in Andrade, *Florida on Trial.*

cessed by the Spanish bureaucracy and little came out of the inquiry, except the negative effect of leaving the colony alone and bringing Canzo's tenure of the governorship to an end. He was recalled in 1603, and afterwards, as was quite usual, criticized for extravagance and corruption. He was certainly ambitious if not especially realistic, but he clearly felt Florida was better fitted to expand than to stagnate.

Pedro de Ibarra (or Ybarra), his successor, who took over in 1603, was an experienced and able soldier. He considered his task to be primarily the military one of maintaining the garrison and keeping a close watch for hostile intruders, while letting the friars proceed with their missionary work. He did not wish to expand, but he had to fight against suggestions that the garrison establishment could be cut without loss of effectiveness. He had to complain, too, that every additional friar who came to Florida was entitled to a place on the payroll and so the number of military effectives was slowly declining. Just then, the effectiveness of the mission was showing an amazing rise. The authority of the friars increased each year as more and more Indians came under their influence and submitted to baptism. The reasons for this sudden expansion of the mission do not appear to be known. It had advantages for the governor in that it created an enlarging screen of passive Indians around the garrisons; but it also meant that more of the resources which passed through his hands were being accumulated by the Church.

Late in 1603, Ibarra sent a reconnaissance vessel by water to the west coast of the peninsula where there were rumors of French activity. She could not provide any definite data, so to follow up, Ibarra induced Pedro de Valdés to send his son Ferdinand with a second, strongly armed vessel to explore the western bays more thoroughly. This he did and was met with the expected resistance and hostility of the Calusa Indians. But he was able to report late in 1604 that there was no need to fear foreign intrusions in this area. In the meantime, the governor had been following up Canzo's preliminary contacts with the Ais Indians to the south of San Agustín. He finally induced the Ais chiefs to come to San Agustín and to promise friendship. They also agreed to admit missionaries, provided they were not compelled to cut off their hair (a revealing sidelight on the interference of the friars with local practice); accordingly, a mission was opened somewhat tentatively, which soon

took hold and began to attract converts. Ibarra followed this with an inspection of the Guale Indians. St. Catherine's Island and the adjoining mainland were quiet and the missions appeared to be effective in controlling and Christianizing the Indians. The Cusabo tribes to the north were not, so far, affected by the new wave of missionary activity. A number of chiefs visited him on St. Catherine's Island and renewed contacts which had by now become very weak. He still regarded Santa Elena as being within the Spanish sphere of influence but had little means of asserting any authority there. At another level, he was busy rebuilding the fort at San Agustín. Plans for a stone fort had been discussed in detail, but the crown was not willing to send in craftsmen, so the original wooden fort was largely dismantled and rebuilt about 100 feet further inland to keep the water from invading its foundations. The parade ground was now enclosed by a stone wall on the landward side. By the beginning of 1605, Florida was in better shape to resist an invader than it had been for some years.[32]

It was in these circumstances that Ibarra had his chance to prove his effectiveness.[33] In 1603 a ship had put in at the St. Johns, and French and English members of her company had gone ashore and made contact, in their own language, with the Timucua Indians. This had caused some alarm, and a very close watch had been kept for shipping thereafter. On February 3, 1605, a small vessel entered St. Augustine's Inlet opposite San Agustín. She was a Spanish *lancha* but was evidently attempting to sound the entry at the southern end of Anastasia Island. Suspicions were aroused, an alarm raised, and she quickly disappeared.

In fact the vessel was part of an Anglo-French partnership, a Spanish ship substituted in the Caribbean for the English *Pollux and Castor* under Captain John Jerome of Plymouth. She had parted company in the Florida Strait with the larger ship, *Castor and Pollux*, under Captain Bertrand Rocque of St. Malo—they had exchanged commands since leaving England. Ibarra sent a patrol to run along

32. Serrano y Sanz, *Documentos historicos,* pp. 164–193; Lanning, *Spanish Missions,* pp. 136–145.

33. Quinn, "James I and the Beginnings of Empire in America," 135–152, "An Anglo-French 'Voyage of Discovery' to North America in 1603," in *Miscellanea Charles Verlinden* (Gent, 1975), 513–534. The older account by Mary A. Ross, "The French on the Savannah, 1605," *Georgia Historical Quarterly,* VIII (1924), 167–194, is still useful, though mistaken in the location of the incident.

the coast to the north, and to keep track of the ship if possible. They were lucky in being able to do so, and to report that she had passed northward following a much larger vessel which had gone ahead. Ibarra was totally without shipping, but a pinnace put into the port on August 8 and was immediately armed and sent north to the St. Johns.

By that time, news had come that the small English vessel had been attacked by the Indians of Cumberland Island, and the captain (Jerome) and pilot killed, though the launch, with four men still in it, had continued to the north. The Spanish pinnace *La Ascunción* relayed this news to San Agustín. Now Ibarra was able to take effective action. The small despatch boat normally attached to San Agustín had been on its way to Havana when it had been intercepted and robbed, at the end of January, by the two privateering ships, then allowed to proceed. On arrival they alerted the Havana authorities, who at once despatched the *San Josephe* and a smaller vessel to Florida. When these reached San Agustín Ibarra immediately diverted them northward, placing command of the expedition in the hands of a veteran member of his garrison, Captain Francisco Fernández de Écija. They later picked up *La Ascunción* at the mouth of the St. Johns and the three vessels made their way northward. Indian intelligence indicated that the ships were in a harbor some 20 miles north of Santa Elena, apparently in modern St. Helena Sound, busily trading with the Indians. Écija found that the smaller vessel was some distance away, near the land. After a demand for surrender, he was able to close in on the *Castor and Pollux,* bombard her, set her on fire and send his men on board, thus forcing her crew to submit and then putting out the fire before much damage was done. The other vessel set out from the shore to discover what was happening and was taken, with the remainder of the personnel of the expedition, on March 5.

This was a most carefully planned and executed piece of military and naval cooperation, very creditable to Ibarra and indeed to the authorities at Havana also. Ibarra had given orders that there was to be no massacre this time, since Spain was officially at peace with both France and England. Instead, prisoners were handed over to Indian tribes who lived in the interior as presents to use as slaves or sacrifices. What happened to them afterwards was not the governor's concern, though none are known to have escaped. A selected

few, including Captain Rocque, were brought to San Agustín and interrogated. From their stories it appeared that this was a joint Anglo-French trading and exploring expedition. It went back to a patent issued to Guillaume de la Mothe and La Rocque by Henry IV in January 1604. The ships were English and some of the financial backing had come from a Channel Island merchant, Pierre Beauvoir, who had settled in London. The ships collected tobacco and maize in the West Indies and were then to go to trade in the Santa Elena area. For this trade with the Indians there they carried many weapons and implements, and they had been busy collecting china root and sassafras and some skins from the Indians when they were captured. Their orders had been to go on to Croatoan to make contact with the "Lost Colonists," and thence to the Penobscot and the Bay of Fundy, searching for minerals and medicinal plants and making a survey of salable resources—for which purpose they had a medical and herbal expert on board, a certain Jean de Bonnesemaine.

Ibarra sent off word of his victory to Havana and Spain, and in May despatched a full report and the depositions he had collected. These apparently reached Spain before the end of the summer, though news of the affair did not leak out until 1606, when it caused some diplomatic activity on the part of both England and France. The incident was used as a diplomatic weapon to warn the English of what their Virginia colonists could expect if the Spaniards caught them, although in fact no record of what did happen to those who had given depositions appears to exist. Ibarra followed up his reports by asking in 1606 for more soldiers, for which he had, it now appeared to him, a very good case. He received a reply which must have seemed like a slap in the face. The king had at last digested the reports of the 1602 inquiry; these had shown that while San Agustín should be retained, it was of no great military significance and that the garrison might be cut down to 150 or less, though the friars should still be supported and encouraged.[34] Ibarra attempted to follow up the news that English colonists were at Croatoan, and sent Écija north in La Ascunción in August. But Écija had no idea where Croatoan was, and after making inquiries between Santa Elena and Cape Roman (or Cape Fear), turned back in September, leaving

34. Chatelaine, Defenses, pp. 76, 119–120.

Ibarra with still another report to send to Spain but no further victories to report. Indeed, he remained in ignorance of the establishment of Jamestown until well after it had become a going concern. In 1606, following up rumors of English activity on the Gulf of Mexico, he had sent Antonio Matheos to make a reconnaissance of the territory of the Apalachee. His report (dated May 19, 1606) threw much important light on the Indians there, especially the Apalachee, and provided an insight into western Florida.[35]

## V

The year 1606 might be regarded as that of the triumph of the friars. Hitherto Florida, though within the diocese of Cuba, had never had a visitation from the bishop. Now, in March 1606, the bishop of Cuba, Juan Cabeza Altamirano, arrived to confirm all and sundry in Florida. He was received as splendidly as possible by Ibarra, by the San Agustín parish priest Father Richard Arthur, an Irishman, and by Fray Francisco de Pareja, the Franciscan guardian, as well as all the rest of the friars. He began by confirming 350 Spanish soldiers, officials, townsmen, their women and their Negro slaves. He then set out on a progress through the missions. Starting at Nombre de Dios nearby, he went on to San Pedro and Guale, and even to Potano in the interior of the peninsula. Everywhere there were confirmations, celebrations of Mass, and dancing (no doubt suitably modified to suit Spanish prejudices); the bishop accepted, it was said, no less than 2,074 Indians into the full membership of the Catholic faith. He left convinced that Florida was now primarily a mission field and that little else mattered.[36]

Thereafter, Ibarra had to work with the missionaries and indeed was prepared to do so, though he grumbled at the number of places on the establishment that now had to be filled by others than soldiers and officials (after the visitation, during which the bishop had ordained some twenty new and old members of the Franciscan Order, the total came to somewhere between thirty and thirty-five).

35. Serrano y Sanz, *Documentos historicos*, pp. 193–198; Oré, *Martyrs of Florida*, pp. 112–120.

36. Oré, *Relación*, I, 37–43; Chatelaine, *Defenses*, p. 121; Maynard Geiger, *The Franciscan Conquest of Florida* (Washington, D.C., 1937), pp. 195–199; Lanning, *Spanish Missions*, pp. 149–160.

He also found the friars arrogant and had to force them to stop searching newly arrived ships for goods coming to them before his officers had been on board and given their clearance. For their part, the friars complained about the continuing food taxes on Indians within the mission belt and the use of the Indians as bearers on long journeys. Ibarra did, however, open up a new area to them. In 1608 he despatched Father Prieto with a guard by sea to Apalachee to follow up Matheo's reconnaissance. Prieto was able, through an interpreter, to speak to an Apalachee assembly and to get a sympathetic hearing for his pleas that they should bring to an end their wars with the Timucua, the interior tribes of which the missions were now reaching. His contact was to open up this part of the Gulf coast to Spanish religious and secular influence a few years later. The friars also appreciated Ibarra's help in opening their bridgehead to the south. By the time Ibarra left in 1609, they had extended this to the tip of the peninsula even though the west coast Indians still remained untouched.[37]

After 1607, the Spanish government was actively concerned with following the known activities of the English in Virginia through diplomatic reports, but could not decide on hostile intervention. Ibarra was told to report all that he could, but in fact he contributed very little and was not given the resources, in the way of additional men and coastal patrol vessels, which would have helped him to do so. Finally, in 1609, he was given orders and the means to send Francisco Fernández de Écija north once more. In June *La Ascunción de Cristo*, under his command, set sail to discover where Jamestown was. Écija spent a considerable time visiting the coastal Indians north of Santa Elena, whose tales of strange visitors were no more specific than they had been in 1605. He then coasted northward in mid-July along the Carolina Outer Banks, seeing many smoke signals, as he thought, but no sign of any Europeans when he reconnoitered an inlet. He came at last to Cape Henry, which was recognized by a man who had been there with González in 1588 as the entrance to the Bay of Jacan, Chesapeake Bay. Before he had time to make any reconnaissance, an English ship hove in view: it was a smallish vessel, commanded by Captain Samuel Argall, which Écija estimated was much more powerful than his own ship. After some

37. Chatelaine, *Defenses*, pp. 76, 119–120.

cautious maneuvers, which Écija calculated were intended to lure him into the James River where he could be set on at a disadvantage, he turned back and made a rapid return southward, entering San Agustín on September 24. Ibarra forwarded his report to Philip III, adding a few footnotes to it in a letter of November 28 before he finally left Florida. All that had been accomplished was to identify precisely where the English colony was located.[38]

Juan Fernández de Olivera—who succeeded Ibarra—did not leave much mark on the colony, which was now coming more and more under the domination of the friars. Florida in 1609 was upgraded in the Franciscan hierarchy and was put under Fray Pedro Ruis as custodian (who was to be responsible for Franciscans in Cuba and the Bahamas as well). Olivera was well thought of by the missionaries since he gave way to them as much as possible. They continued to regard the garrison as being at their disposal, planning, for example, to start a mission in Apalachee territory under the protection of some of Olivera's soldiers. The governor was unable to spare the men, so he said, for this task. Even when friars arrived in Florida specially to undertake the mission he held back. As late as October 1612 he was complaining that to keep more than thirty Franciscans on the establishment cut his resources in soldiers to the bone. His tale, indeed, was very much like that of his predecessors.[39]

Olivera had little to do with the next reconnaissance of Virginia. The vessel to conduct it was engaged at Lisbon and put under the command of Diego de Molina, with some soldiers under Marco Antonio Perez. They put in at San Agustín on May 8, 1611, on their way north and had a rather farcical encounter with the English outpost at Fort Algernon at Kecoughtan. When Molina and Perez went on shore with an English pilot, Francis Lymbrye, they had with them, they were retained as prisoners. This was evidently an afterthought as the English pilot, John Clark had gone out to the Spanish ship from Fort Algernon and was then taken as a hostage in exchange. After failing to get him exchanged for Molina and Perez, the men still on board set off, leaving them behind. They sailed past San

38. Philip L. Barbour, *The Jamestown Voyages*, 2 vols. (Cambridge, Eng., Hakluyt Society, 1969), II, 293–319.

39. Chatelaine, *Defenses*, pp. 5, 119–120, 133, 146; Oré, *Relación*, I, 49–51; Geiger, *Franciscan Conquest*, p. 24.

Agustín without stopping and reached Havana on July 20, after which a long round of diplomatic negotiations about the respective prisoners took place.[40] But Jamestown was left alone and the English intervention tacitly accepted. Before the end of 1612 Olivera was dead, halfway through his term of office.

Florida had by now reached some degree of equilibrium. As a military outpost it was safe, since Spain could not, for diplomatic reasons, give up her only foothold in eastern North America. As a mission field it might grow further or might decline, according to how the hold of the friars over their client Indians rose and fell.

We can form some picture of San Agustín at the end of this period. The wooden fort, set back from the water as it had been, was now serviceable enough to last for some years. Its garrison of about two hundred men were almost all married and carried on some horticulture and agriculture in and around the town. A bridge over a swamp helped to ensure communication with the north. Both the parish church, though built of wood, and the Franciscan house were substantial buildings. So was the governor's mansion. Constructed of stone by Méndez de Canzo for his own use, it had been bought as an official residence for Ibarra. The other houses, rebuilt after the fire of 1599, were mainly palmetto huts, perhaps 150 of them by this time. The streets were dusty and often muddy. There was a plaza with a market, to which Indians came in some numbers from the outlying villages to sell corn, fruit and vegetables. A few civilians were engaged in trade or as craftsmen, but only a handful. As there were a reasonable number of families—those of the married members of the garrison—the population was partly self-perpetuating, producing children of marriages with Indians or more frequently of irregular unions. And there were a good many negro slaves, perhaps about fifty. The rest of the population consisted of officials and their households. Amongst the smaller buildings were a six-bed hospital, two hermitages, and a horse mill. Quite extensive fields of corn surrounded the town, reaching to the Indian village of Nombre de Dios only a short distance away. There were complaints that vessels found it difficult to pass through the channel which faced the

town, and that quite small ships had gone aground at various times; but optimists maintained that it was quite safe for 200-ton vessels to enter. On Anastasia Island a lookout was maintained, and there was a post to the south at Matanzas. Farther north, at the St. Johns, was a subsidiary garrison of probably not more than fifty men. San Juan, on Cumberland Island, usually had a small number of soldiers acting mainly as lookouts.[41] All this was a minor but genuine achievement; yet it seemed a very limited return for nearly fifty years of effort.

The missions made up another story. Aside from pietistic arguments based on the virtue of the Christian message, there is little real explanation of why missions took hold so suddenly after 1600 when they had been in most respects a tragic failure since 1566. The rigorous suppressions after 1597 had probably something to do with it, coupled with assertions by the friars to the Indians that if they accepted baptism no further action would be taken against them, whereas if they did not, repression would be renewed. A great deal must have depended on the development of effective techniques in approaching the Indians. Francisco de Pareja, who headed the mission from 1594 to 1610, clearly saw that they must approach the Indians in their own language and this is the most probable key to the success they had. They gradually established, in the Timucua language, some degree of compromise between native and European ideology which made sense to the Indians. This they coupled with moral and social precepts, many of which altered the Indian ways of living but were enforced by a sanction system of rewards and punishments.

Pareja made each major mission center on a school. The *doutrinas*, the missions where there was teaching, built up a native élite through whom the friars worked. Above all, by excluding the recalcitrant male chiefs from power, they were able to exploit the rules of matrilineal succession in order to secure female chiefs in all the principal coastal tribes—as was shown during the episcopal visitation of 1606. These ladies proved both pliable and influential. Pareja translated a catechism and an instruction book—both of which he would afterwards have printed in Mexico—[42] and so pro-

41. Andrade, *Florida on Trial*, passim; Chatelaine, *Defenses*, pp. 129, 148.
42. Francisco Pareja, *Catechismo* (Mexico, 1612), *Confessionario* (Mexico, 1613), and *Arte y pronunciación de la lengua Timucuana y Castellana* (1614); J. T. Milanich and

vided material which could be taught directly to suitable converts, first orally, and then through reading as the best pupils achieved a degree of literacy. There was some bribery of Indians by both civil authorities and the friars with gifts of copper (greatly prized for ornaments), clothes, and other objects. But the reduction of the corn tax, and the growth of a market in corn as San Agustín expanded, meant that the nearer mission villages were drawn into the orbit of the principal settlement and also of its subsidiary, San Pedro.

The training of interpreters, before venturing into unfamiliar fields, was another development which proved valuable. Certainly, a great deal depended on the personalities of the missionaries. They were able, stern, repressive, but also, in their own terms, generous of time and trouble to keep their flocks enclosed in their villages, purged admittedly of much of the variety and color of their own traditions but scarcely Hispaniolized. The Indians remained largely passive instruments of Spanish frontier policy, brought through the missions into some tangible relationship with European mores. The native policy embodied in the missions had at last brought some degree of substance to the long-aborted Florida enterprise.

In Spanish Florida for the first time in North America a policy toward the Amerindian population had been worked out and applied. Its essence was subordination: military garrisons controlled the tribal groups surrounding them and enforced agreements imposed by military expeditions, which in turn involved the formal submission of the tribes to Spanish instructions, and the payment of taxation in the form of food levies, intermittent porterage and other labor services when required. Experience proved that this policy could have local and temporary successes in which the superiority of Spanish arms and discipline made themselves effective in cowing and subordinating the native groupings, but in itself it had proved in almost all cases impermanent. The Indians tended to melt away from areas within easy reach of the garrisons; they stole from the vicinity of the forts; they kept up an intermittent guerrilla struggle against the Europeans and, from time to time, rose in revolt

---

William C. Sturtevant (eds.), *Francisco Pareja's Confessionario; A Documentary Source for Timucuan Ethnography* (Tallahassee, Fla., 1972).

against them. They were also liable, as had been shown on several occasions, to have their allegiance to Spain subverted by French infiltration of one sort or another. Consequently, the drive to create settled Indian societies under missionary dominance and control became a major preoccupation, especially after the revolt of 1597. If the Indians could be settled into permanent villages and indoctrinated at the same time with Christian ideology and the basic tenets of Spanish civilian social practices, this might bring about a situation in which military repression could be a last rather than a first resort, and in which taxation (if perhaps at a somewhat lower level) could be imposed with some assurance that the income derived from it would be permanent.

The success of the missions tended to be assessed by military and civilian officials not on the strength of how many Indians were baptized but on how well the tribes remained under control under missionary auspices. In practice the missionaries were optimists, always, or almost always, ready to overestimate the scale and effects of the conversions achieved: repeatedly their claims were shown to be exaggerated and their successes evanescent. At the same time, as more missionaries arrived, more resources were devoted to building up the missions themselves, and more effective methods of establishing their influence over the Indians (especially by infiltrating their power structure by nominating their chiefs) worked out, the missions came to appear the salvation of the colony. It has been indicated that the 1606 ceremony marked a turning point, but in fact too many optimistic results were expected to flow from them; a substantial number of Indian groups still remained untouchable by European teachings, while others shook themselves free from time to time, and there were still many revolts ahead. Yet from 1606 onward, the administrators could somewhat relax their employment of the garrisons in police duties over the Indian communities and concentrate on other tasks. A colonial society was being created in which there was a place for the native inhabitants.

Further, by the end of the period Spain had created a nucleus of a white colonial society on an urban basis. San Agustín might still be little more than a large village, whose population was mainly made up of the families of members of the garrison; but it had some sense of itself as a corporate entity and as the representative of the greater cities and towns of New Spain and the other developed

colonial communities in the New World. Missions, town and garrisons together made up a Spanish colonial society which, however small its scale, was still in 1612 the major monument to European colonial enterprise in North America. What potential it had for development remained to be determined. The situation in Spain herself made the possibility of further dramatic, state-inspired expansion a little unlikely, but still not wholly improbable.

From the point of view of the authorities in Mexico and Spain, the Florida settlement's primary function was throughout to act as an outpost guarding the major parts of the Spanish empire from European infiltration or penetration. This was probably the main reason for its continuance. Such a role meant that much of the attention of the garrison and of any ships the governor might have at his disposal was preoccupied with the rumors of French and English interlopers that constantly reached San Agustín, and with action against such traders and privateers as appeared from time to time. The destruction of San Agustín in 1586 by Drake emphasized the colony's protective position on the northern flank of the empire by indicating that Florida was indeed a target worthy of enemy attack. From 1585 also the recurrent news and rumors about English activity further north remained a persistent theme in Florida intercourse with Spain herself. The appearance, in the years 1607–12, of the Virginia settlement as a permanent English threat to the long-maintained Spanish monopoly of the coast provided a possible pretext for renewed Spanish offensives, which was not taken; even so, the English presence continued to provide a new rationale for the traditional defensive role of the Florida garrison.

There was, however, a growing dichotomy between the two aspects of Spanish rule in the southeast. The mission policy required that increasing resources should be used to support the missionaries; that places in the garrison strength should be reserved for the payment of missionaries, not soldiers; and that food taxes should be lowered and labor services reduced or eliminated when missionary pressure indicated that this was necessary if the objectives of the missions were not to be frustrated. This in turn meant that the garrisons were depleted, since it was very difficult to get the *situado* increased, and even harder to get the increase paid after it had been authorized. Thus the two functions of the colony, peacekeeping inside the area which could be reached by the missionaries, and

peacekeeping within the orbit which Spain could protect from interference by other European powers, were in conflict. This inevitably produced an uneasy attitude inside the colony and in the relations between the colonial officials and the authorities at home. It can be argued that this situation helped to limit the effectiveness and growth of the colony, because missionaries and officials tended to frustrate each other's purposes. It may be, however, that the existence of these opposed ends and of the friction generated by their protagonists also kept Florida in the eyes of the home authorities, thus preventing it from being a wholly forgotten outpost, a symbol only of the Spanish empire in eastern North America which might now never come into being.

# CHAPTER 13

## *England's First Virginia, 1584-1590*

$E$NGLAND became involved with the coastline of eastern North America between latitudes 34° and 37° N. as much by accident as design. Englishmen had landed on southeastern North America in 1565, when John Hawkins visited Fort Caroline, and in 1571, when William Winter raided San Agustín. There may have been a few further casual contacts. On the other hand, the French ventures of 1562–68 between 28° and 32° N. rapidly became familiar in England. There was some knowledge of Verrazzano's voyage in 1524 through the Italian version of his letter to Francis I and we know that at least one Verrazzanian map was available in England. Nonetheless, there was no special interest in the coasts north of the area where the Spaniards had installed themselves until after 1583. The Stukely fiasco of 1563 meant that Florida became a bad joke—the name for a bad investment—in England for some years. Gilbert's 1578 patent had given him the right, he contended, to acquire land anywhere in eastern North America either for himself or his associates, even though America was never explicitly mentioned in the patent. Although Gilbert's expedition of 1578 was directed to the West Indies and thence to the North American coast, there is no clear evidence that he intended to concentrate on examining the coastlines of the later English Virginia with the intention of settling there. There is the possibility that his Portuguese pilot, Simão Fernandes, wished Gilbert to interest himself in this region; but all Gilbert's hopes seem to have been set on Norumbega, the later New

England. The notes on colonization in America compiled by the elder Richard Hakluyt in 1578[1] could apply equally to sites in latitudes well up to the 30's or 40's. In practice, Gilbert's efforts of 1580 to 1583 were directed to coastlines north of 40°, and this was true also of the projects which Sir George Peckham and Christopher Carleill had under way at the time Gilbert's loss at sea was reported late in 1583.

On the other hand, the patent which Walter Ralegh, his half brother, obtained in succession to Gilbert's on March 25, 1584,[2] was intended to be used by him only in more southerly latitudes, and the advice he received from both the Richard Hakluyts applied more specifically to lower than to higher latitudes.[3] It is impossible to be more specific than this since there was no knowledge of the differing seasonal climates of North America, which were consequently simply equated by latitude with those of Europe—Mediterranean-type produce was attributed to North American territories well into northern New England.

Ralegh may not have had any clear idea in April 1584 when he sent off Philip Amadas and Arthur Barlowe on a reconnaissance voyage precisely what he wished to do on the basis of his patent. Friction with Spain in European waters and in the Caribbean was increasing, and Gilbert in 1577 had already advocated English occupation of some part of the Spanish territories in the West Indies. It is highly probable that Ralegh included among his objectives from the first the desirability of establishing a forward base from which piratical activities could be maintained against the Spanish Indies. At the other extreme, reports from Newfoundland had indicated in 1583 that, although it was in appreciably lower latitudes than England, it endured an extreme winter climate, which might also, it may have been thought, apply to Norumbega. A site, then, fairly well to the north of Spanish activities in the southeast (though their

1. In Richard Hakluyt, *Divers voyages touching the discouerie of America* (London, 1582), sig.K1–K3*v.;* reprinted in D. B. Quinn, (ed.), *The Voyages and Colonising Enterprises of Sir Humphrey Gilbert,* 2 vols. (London, 1940), I, 181–88.

2. D. B. Quinn (ed.), *The Roanoke Voyages, 1584–1590,* I, 82–89.

3. "Inducements to the lykinge of the viadge intended to that parte of America which lyethe between 34. and 36. degrees of Septentrionall Latytude," in Eva G. R. Taylor (ed.), *The Original Writings and Correspondence of the Two Richard Hakluyts,* 2 vols. (London, Hakluyt Society, 1935), II, 339–343. Professor Taylor (I, 39) considered it to belong to early in 1585; it appears more appropriate to early in 1584 (see Quinn, *Roanoke Voyages,* I, 4, 19).

precise limits were still probably unknown) was probably the most attractive to him. By this time, too, Simão Fernandes had built up the claim that he had a detailed knowledge of the coast north of Florida, so it is probable that in 1584 Amadas and Barlowe were instructed to direct their reconnaissance to this stretch of coast. We cannot exclude the possibility that, after 1565, English pirates had already put in there to refresh themselves on the way home from the Caribbean and reported its attractions on their return, but so far we have no evidence for this.

The movement in England in favor of American colonization at this time could not be called strong, but there were some enthusiasts, including the younger Richard Hakluyt, Edward Hayes, and a few others. One of their major hopes was to find alternative sources for Spanish products—olive oil, wine, leather and suchlike—the continued acquisition of which was becoming uncertain as relations with Spain worsened. It would also be more valuable for the state if such products could be obtained from territory under English control. Sugar, dyes (such as cochineal), medical drugs and spices were some of the other most desirable commodities. Investors had already been mobilized in considerable numbers by Gilbert; if many were disillusioned by losing what they had advanced for his ventures in 1582–3, others may have wished to cast more of their money on the waters. Ralegh, as a rising courtier who was widely said to have the queen's favor, was probably a better investment—though still a risky one—than Gilbert had been. The lure of piratical profit as a sideline may also have been peddled to possible investors. Gold and silver are not likely to have been more than hinted at as North American assets, since the fiasco of Martin Frobisher's northwest gold-mining ventures in 1577–78 had created deep suspicion amongst potential subscribers about such objectives. If there were investors—Ralegh and some gentlemen and merchants, at least—the next question was, would there be settlers? And the answer was probably yes. Some gentlemen could send out tenants as farmers; merchants might encourage young journeymen to go as craftsmen and apprentice merchants; there were nearly always unemployed soldiers available who had served in Ireland (especially at this time after the crushing of the Munster rising there). There were, the Hakluyts believed, craftsmen and farmers alike in various parts of the country who were in depressed eco-

nomic circumstances and would welcome the chance to gain opportunity and some land for themselves in a new colony—doubtless presented to them as being planted in a land full of good things.

But in the spring of 1584, all this was still conjecture. Until some concrete evidence about North America's temperate zone was assembled, little could be done to prepare a settlement. Englishmen had not yet made a success of colonization, but the many plans made for new English settlements in Ireland over the past generation, even if they had achieved no appreciable success, showed that there were both projectors of colonies in plenty and would-be colonists in appreciable numbers. It might be that this source could be tapped by Ralegh, who was well aware of both the advantages and disadvantages of an Irish rather than an American location for new settlements, and could adjust his promises to colonists accordingly.

No attempt was made in 1584–85, so far as is known, to define the limits of Virginia. There was no reason why Englishmen should not attempt to apply the name to any and every part of the coast between Spanish Florida and Cape Breton, though they frequently continued to refer to New England as Norumbega. In practice Ralegh's Virginia extended along the coast roughly from Cape Fear to Cape Henry, that is, it comprised a substantial part of coastal North Carolina and southern Virginia. There was no limitation in its presumed extent to the west: it might be expected to reach as far as Drake's New Albion.

The two small vessels—we do not know their names—which set out in April 1584 for North America by the long transatlantic route, using the Canaries Current, the trade winds, and the Florida Current, represented a private venture by Walter Ralegh, aided perhaps by a group of close friends and relations.[4] If he wished to raise subscriptions from a wider public he had to have some evidence that exploration and settlement in North America were worth while. Philip Amadas, who commanded one vessel, was an experienced seaman; Arthur Barlowe, in charge of the other, was more of a soldier, having served with Ralegh in Ireland. It would seem they had on board the artist John White, who had been at Baffin Island with Frobisher in 1577,[5] and possibly Thomas Harriot, who had

4. Almost all that is known of the voyage is in Quinn, *Roanoke Voyages*, I, 77–118.
5. Paul Hulton and D. B. Quinn, *The American Drawings of John White* (1964), I, 3–14.

been teaching mathematical navigation to pilots in London.[6] More significantly, their pilot was Simão Fernandes, who had been, or claimed to have been, on an earlier Spanish voyage along the coast north of Florida. Fernandes conducted the expedition competently to the coast of the later Carolina Outer Banks, and brought them to land about latitude 36° N. early in July. He claimed that the inlet off which they anchored (soon called Port Ferdinando in his honor, but known by the Indians as Hatarask) was already familiar to him. It corresponded roughly with the modern Oregon Inlet. Formal possession was taken of the country for the English crown on July 13, some eighteen years after a similar ceremony had claimed the coast nearby for Spain.

Contact was soon made with the local Indians, who were of southern Algonkian stock and lived on the Outer Banks, on Roanoke Island inside the sounds, and on the shores of the adjoining mainland. They were friendly and proved willing to trade skins and specimens of other products for English goods, soon taking the Englishmen to see their small village on Roanoke Island. The island proved attractive to the visitors, being detached from the mainland and screened from patrolling Spanish vessels, yet accessible to the roadstead. In spite of the lack of any linguistic bridge, friendly relations were established with Granganimeo, brother of the ruling chief, Wingina. A reasonable amount of information was collected about the topography of the area, its inhabitants and its products, all of which appeared to offer great attractions.

Two Indians—Manteo, from a chiefly family, and Wanchese— were induced to accompany the Englishmen, so that their language could be learned and further information accumulated on their homeland area. Barlowe's ship appears to have left quickly on the homeward voyage bearing the Indian guests, and reached England early in September. There is some question whether, before leaving American waters, she accompanied Amadas's ship further north along the coast. There seems little doubt that one ship at least penetrated into Chesapeake Bay where the Indians gave the Englishmen a hostile reception, perhaps killing or injuring some of them.[7] This was the domain of Powhatan (or, more likely, his prede-

6. J. W. Shirley (ed.), *Thomas Harriot, Renaissance Scientist* (Oxford, 1974), pp. 38–40
7. Compare Quinn, *Roanoke Voyages*, I, 80–81, and D. B. Quinn, *England and the Discovery of America* (1974), pp. 254–256.

cessor), and it made the English aware of the existence of the great bay, Chesapeake Bay, of which Fernandes is likely to have had information from Spanish sources. Amadas's vessel returned by way of the Azores and arrived later than the other—precisely when, we do not know.

The return of Barlowe with the two Indians, and the subsequent return of Amadas, now enabled Ralegh to build up a publicity campaign for launching a major enterprise.[8] When he put his Indians on show in mid-October they were not able to make any intelligible remarks in English, but by mid-December not only had a bill been put before Parliament to confirm Ralegh's patent but it was stated therein[9] that: "some of the people borne in those parties (have been) brought home into this our Realme of England by whose means and direction and by suche of her majesties subjectes as were sent thyther by the said Walter Rawleigh singuler great commodities of that Lande are revealed and made knowen unto us." The Indians were credited with speaking English, perhaps after having been coached by Thomas Harriot, who was to learn some Algonquian from them before he went out in 1585. The reports brought back were carefully edited—Barlowe's were rewritten, it is thought by Ralegh, and all mention of any hostility to the Englishmen omitted—while every effort was made to render country and people alike idyllic and, at the same time, potentially valuable to intending colonists. This was almost certainly circulated to possible subscribers.[10]

The bill passed the Commons on December 18, but failed in the Lords, apparently because the queen did not wish Ralegh to have too much authority in the new lands. On the other hand, he renamed what he gathered to be the "Wyngandacoa" of the Indians (it was actually "Ossomocomuck") Virginia in honor of the queen, was knighted by her on January 25, 1585, and had a seal struck naming him a lord and governor of Virginia. Indeed, the queen was willing to give him practical help in the form of a ship and some supplies. However, she was not prepared to make the enterprise a national one, as Richard Hakluyt had recommended in an elaborate treatise of October 1584. Known as the "Discourse of western

8. On the preparations, see Quinn, *Roanoke Voyages*, I, 118–157.
9. *Ibid.*, 127, and compare 116 n.
10. *Ibid.*, 15–17.

planting" (as its own title is rather lengthy),[11] this mobilized all the evidence on the potential wealth and value North America might provide for England, and was presented to the queen as a confidential document.

More practical plans were also being made. Shipping was assembled. A number of members of parliament—notably the secretary of state Sir Francis Walsingham, and Sir Philip Sidney—assisted in the preparations, while Sir Richard Grenville, Thomas Cavendish, and probably Anthony Rowse all agreed to take a leading part in the expedition, although the queen would not permit Ralegh himself to go. The experienced soldier and fortifications expert, Ralph Lane, was released from his post in Ireland to command the soldiers on the voyage; and another soldier, probably Sir Roger Williams, provided a memorandum on how to establish a fortified settlement and administer it on military lines.[12]

The seven vessels which assembled at Plymouth early in April 1585[13] were to be seconded by a further squadron, under Bernard Drake and Amyas Preston, which was to follow in June. It is probable that the total force was to be about 1,000 strong, some 600 sailing in the first squadron. This was to be commanded by Sir Richard Grenville in the flagship (or "admiral") the *Tiger,* one of the queen's ships, carrying Simão Fernandes as master.[14] The *Roebuck,* John Clark captain, the *Red Lion,* George Raymond captain, the *Elizabeth,* Thomas Cavendish captain, the *Dorothy* probably under Arthur Barlowe and two pinnaces made up the little fleet which sailed on April 9. After transatlantic storms, the *Tiger,* separated from her consorts, sailed alone through the Caribbean from May 7 and landed her men for a rest on the southwest side of Puerto Rico, which was not occupied by the Spaniards and

11. "A particuler discourse concerning the great necessitie and manifolde comodyties that are like to growe to this Realme of England by the Western discoveries lately attempted." Printed in Taylor, *Hakluyts,* II, 211–326.

12. Quinn, *Roanoke Voyages,* I, 130–139. Williams is only one of a number of possible authors suggested (pp. 19–22), but he now seems the least unlikely.

13. The voyages are covered in Quinn, *Roanoke Voyages,* I, 158–253. Our main authority is the journal kept on the *Tiger;* Spanish documents are in Quinn, *Roanoke Voyages,* II, 733–743. A. L. Rowse, *The Elizabethans and America* (Cambridge, Eng., 1959), and his *Sir Richard Grenville* (London, 1937), discuss the expedition in different contexts.

14. Tom Glasgow, "H.M.S. Tiger," *North Carolina Historical Review,* (1966), 115–121.

where temporary entrenchments were set up.

She was joined there by the *Elizabeth* under Cavendish on May 19. Having built a pinnace to replace one which had parted from Grenville on the way out, they sailed on to capture two Spanish prizes and then, insolently, to trade along the north shore of Hispaniola for livestock—cattle, sheep, pigs—and other products needed for the colony, including banana plants and sugar canes. Next, Fernandes brought the *Tiger* to Wococon (now part of the Island of Ocracoke) in the Outer Banks, where on June 29 she ran aground and was damaged, part of her cargo of food being spoilt. During early July, the *Roebuck* and possibly the *Dorothy* came up and joined Grenville. It was later found that Raymond in the *Red Lion* (possibly with another vessel) had landed some men on the next island to the north and then gone ahead to Newfoundland to attempt to take prizes. Some exploring was done and repairs made to the *Tiger*, so that by July 27 the reunited vessels could anchor off Port Ferdinando, having already made friendly contacts with Granganimeo and other members of the Roanoke tribe.

At the beginning of August, the realities of the situation had to be faced. A good deal had been lost. Raymond had clearly left very few men and little stores behind; much of the food in the *Tiger* was spoiled; the harbor at Port Ferdinando was proving very exposed and dangerous for shipping, while only the smallest ships could enter the sounds. To leave behind between three and four hundred men as had probably originally been contemplated was not possible. In the end, agreement was reached with Wingina and his tribe to allow the Englishmen to erect a fort, with cottages outside it for the majority of the men, on Roanoke Island, and to leave Lane there with just over a hundred men; meanwhile Grenville was to go back to organize relief and reinforcements for 1586. Bernard Drake and Amyas Preston with their ships were probably expected in August but did not appear—they had, in fact, been diverted to Newfoundland,[15] where they were told to capture Portuguese and Spanish ships in retaliation for Spanish seizures of English ships in Spanish ports in May. When they arrived in Newfoundland they found Raymond's *Red Lion*, on her way home from Virginia, engaged on a similar mission.

15. Quinn, *Roanoke Voyages*, I, 234–242.

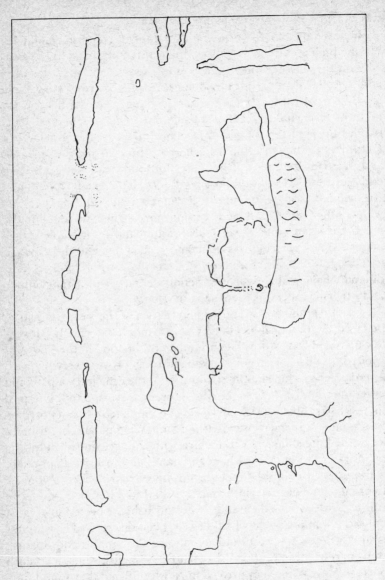

The First Sketchmap of the Carolina Outer Banks, 1585.
(Public Record Office, London, Maps and Plans G. 584)

The scene in Roanoke Island at the beginning of August was one of intense activity. Fort entrenchments were run up, a small headquarters building built inside them, and the cottages erected. The waterways round about were intensively explored, especially the modern Albermarle Sound, on the north shore of which (Weapemeoc) were many Indian villages. Plant specimens were assembled, especially those which the Indians cultivated—maize, beans, squash, sunflowers, tobacco—and timber, particularly cedar, cut in some quantity, while a sketch map of the location of the island was made.[16] The vessels were successively despatched to England, one on August 5, followed by the *Tiger* on August 25 and the *Roebuck* early in September. The *Tiger* took a rich Spanish prize on her way back and thus repaid the entire cost of the expedition, perhaps with some profit.

Lane had been on poor terms with Grenville and there was much rancor in the letters he sent back; but this was balanced by hopes of good economic returns and a boost for the climate and the fertility of the land.[17] The commodities brought by Grenville were also well publicized, though Grenville tempered his optimism with caution,[18] saying: "and as the Countrey of hit selfe, [h]as never bene labored with mannes hande, so I hope that hit being once by our industrie manured will prove moste fertill." Had he known more, he might have realized that the most fertile spots had already been under Indian cultivation and that there were relatively few others unless dense forest was first cleared.

The achievement of the first English settlement in Virginia was primarily a prestige one at a time when unofficial war between England and Spain had begun. The glamour and profits from the privateering aspects of the expeditions—alike in the Caribbean, in Newfoundland and in the Atlantic—rather overshadowed the economic and social aspects of the colony. Nevertheless, they also made it possible to obtain investors for further ventures in 1586, although the shortage of shipping consequent on the release of so many privateers and the launching of a substantial fleet under Drake against the West Indies notably contributed to the delay which took place in actually despatching supplies and reinforcements.

16. It is reprinted in *ibid.*, I, 215–217.
17. *Ibid.*, 197–214.
18. *Ibid.*, I, 219.

Although the Spaniards were alerted very early to the existence of the English settlement, they did not know where it was located. After an abortive reconnaissance in December 1585, which got no further than about 34° N., they were distracted by reports of Drake's progress through the Caribbean from September 1585 until the summer of 1586 when he at last appeared. No attempt was therefore made to destroy the colony before it had established itself firmly.[19]

Meanwhile, Lane and his men (there were 108 in all in the settlement) settled down at Roanoke Island on friendly relations with the local Indians,[20] who were able to supply corn in return for English goods both during and after the harvest, since it was too late to plant cereals. We hear little of the livestock brought from the Caribbean, though they may well have flourished and provided some meat and dairy produce. Otherwise the colonists had to live on their not very substantial stores. Probably they killed some deer, but they proved wholly incompetent in taking fish and got their supplies from Indian fish-weirs. A party was despatched to reconnoiter the Chesapeake. This may have gone by land rather than round Cape Henry, though we have no clear information and it is likely that both land and water routes were tried. On this occasion the experience of the party— apparently with the Chesapeake tribe, which was independent of the dominant Powhatan group of tribes on the James and York rivers —was peaceful, and the men returned in the spring of 1586 with very good reports of the area.

Lane's own activities over that winter do not appear to have been very energetic. It is probable that as the Indian corn surplus disappeared, he put pressure on Wingina (who now called himself Pemisapan) and that this gradually produced first a coolness and later actual hostility between Lane's men and the Indians, so that the settlement had to be placed on the defensive against the possibility of an Indian attack—which may account for his apparent lack of activity. In any case, by March 1586, Lane was ready to explore both the Chowan and Roanoke rivers, at the same time that Wingina was arousing the adjoining tribes against the intruders. Entering the main village of the Chowan tribe, Chawanoac, he met representa-

19. *Ibid.*, II, 720–723, 765–766; Irene A. Wright, *Further English Voyages to Spanish America* (London, Hakluyt Society, 1951), pp. 6–16.

20. Lane's narrative (Quinn, *Roanoke Voyages,* I, 255–1294) and Harriot's later study (I, 317–387) constitute our main sources.

tives of a number of tribes from the interior—including the Iroquoian Tuscarora (Mangoaks)—dominated the assembly by seizing the Chowan chief, Menatonon, and eventually charmed him into friendly association with his men (though retaining his son as a hostage). It was now that he learned for the first time of inland sources of metal, certainly copper and possibly gold too, he thought. He also heard of a land route to a deepwater harbor, clearly Chesapeake Bay, to which he proposed to work out a route from the Chowan.

Next, he rowed up the Roanoke River (which he knew as the Moratuc) in search of the Tuscarora and their metals. But the local Indians made it their business to see that his men got no food, and they were finally forced to return still some distance below the natural copper deposits at modern Virginiola.[21] (These were worked in the nineteenth century and are most probably the ones of which Lane was told.) Making his way back with the men very short of food, he reached Roanoke Island just in time to thwart an attack by Wingina on the colonists. Lane's survival led to a short period of rapprochement during which the Englishmen managed to get sufficient seed corn to plant several fields for themselves. But hostilities developed again in May (precisely why, we do not know), and Wingina prepared a further combined attack on the colonists. This time Lane struck first, entering the village of Dasemunkepeuc where Wingina was and killing the chief; for the time being, all opposition was broken.

We know little directly of what went on inside the colony, but it is clear that shortages produced discontent and that inaction led to boredom and pessimism. There were too many gentlemen in relation to laborers, as was to be the case at Jamestown later; many of the men were soldiers, interested only in the occasional forays Lane made. The failure of supplies to arrive at Easter, as had been firmly promised, led to a growing unease which was intensified as Indian hostility grew. Nevertheless, constructive work was done. Thomas Harriot and John White surveyed the mainland and islands[22] as they

21. Granville County, N.C. See Quinn, *England and the Discovery of America*, p. 474 n.

22. The materials are discussed from various aspects, catalogued and reproduced in Hulton and Quinn, *American Drawings of John White*, I (Commentaries), II (Plates), and see Quinn, *Roanoke Voyages*, I 35–36, 314–461.

moved about, gradually accumulating enough material to map the coastline from Cape Lookout to Cape Henry reasonably well and to carry their survey in outline, at least, some 50 miles inland. Harriot learned the language well enough to speak it and this gave him the entry to Indian villages which might otherwise have been hostile, while John White drew careful Indian scenes which would also have brought him an interested audience.

Harriot investigated the Indian horticulture, their beliefs and customs. Both men also took detailed notes on the topography and surface geology of the area, and endeavored to list, draw and name the fish, mammals, birds and miscellaneous wild life they encountered so as to be able to prepare a full report on the natural resources of the region when they returned. A great deal of this data had been assembled, and it is probable that the two men were some way toward completing their illustrated report by mid-June 1586, in spite of the alarms and excursions which the settlement had survived. The men had been healthy enough, but there was scant future for the colony in its existing form: once the initial exploration had taken place, it could be little more than a holding operation. Nonetheless, by its very survival it had shown that the prospect of maintaining Europeans in this area was not impossible.

Sir Francis Drake had meantime been pursuing his destructive raid through the West Indies. He attacked and forced the surrender of both Santo Domingo and Cartagena, but was unable to attempt his planned crossing of the Isthmus in the hope of intercepting the silver trains, or to attack Havana, the strongest fortress in the Spanish Indies. In the Caribbean he had collected many negro slaves, to whom he promised freedom, and also galley slaves, mainly Moors and Turks, along with a certain number of Central American Indians, both men and women. He next attempted to destroy Spanish Florida. Although he demolished the fort and settlement at San Agustín (as we have seen), the garrison and most of the civilian inhabitants escaped into the woods; but he set off up the coast with much of the equipment and furnishings of the San Agustín houses and some more slaves. He expected a large colony to be developing by now in Virginia—perhaps with three hundred or more from the 1585 voyage and as many again at least from a further reinforcement in 1586. The manpower he brought, black and Indian, was largely intended to provide free labor for the settlers, and the

household equipment he assembled to contribute toward their settlement.

On his way north he missed the entrance to Port Royal Sound and so failed to destroy Santa Elena. Thus, while his blow at Florida was severe, he had not wiped out the only European competitor in North America to the English Virginia.[23] Drake made contact with Lane's outposts on June 9, and arrived at Port Ferdinando on the 10th. He found little to encourage him. Lane had only one hundred men and they were in a poor state since the corn harvest was not yet gathered and morale was low because no relief had come. Lane urged the need for further supplies and suggested that, with suitable vessels, he should explore Chesapeake Bay, pick a site for a later colony, and then return to England to restart the colonizing process from the beginning, since he believed relief would not come this year. Drake offered him a suitable ship and two pinnaces with all the necessary seamen and supplies, but he could not give them enough food to bring them all back to England—corn would have to be found in Indian hands. We do not know what was intended for Drake's negroes and Indian recruits: perhaps it was thought possible to leave them installed on Roanoke Island when Lane had gone.

During the next two days, the transfer of Lane's men from Roanoke Island to the ships got under way: it was about half completed when a storm scattered Drake's fleet and wrecked many of his smaller vessels, the remainder mostly standing out to sea and setting sail for England. Once the storm blew out, all was in disarray. The ship (*Francis*) destined for the colonists had disappeared with some of Lane's men on board; a new vessel was offered but she was too large for exploration, so Lane asked to be taken off and brought directly to England. This was agreed to. The settlers were bundled into boats and in the confusion many of Harriot's and White's precious papers and drawings were tipped into the water and lost. On June 18 (or 19) they sailed away, bringing the first English colony on North American soil to an end. We know nothing of what happened to the negroes and Indians supposed to have been left behind: all are unlikely to have perished in the storm, but too few can have reached England to have left any mark on subsequent news

23. The details are documented in Wright, *Further English Voyages*, pp. 163–165, 180–184, 189–191, 198–205.

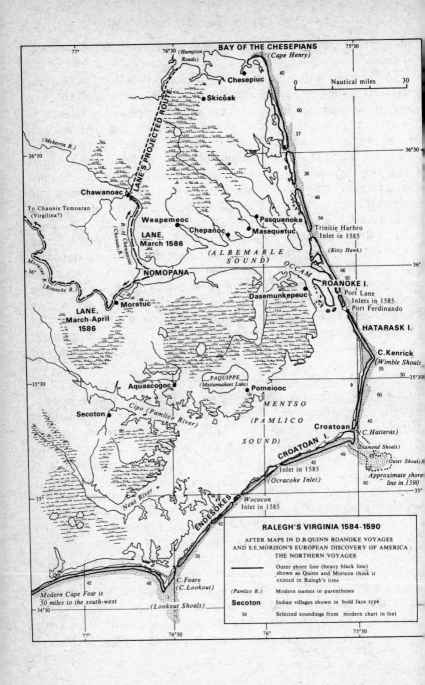

BAY OF THE CHESEPIANS
(Cape Henry)

77°    76°30 (Hampton    75°30
                Roads)

42

0        Nautical miles        30

**Chesepiuc**

60

**Skicóak**

27

(Meherrin R.)          36°30

36°30

36

48

**Chawanoac**

54

To Chaunis Temoatan
(Virgilina?)

**Weapemeoc**        **Pasquenoke**        Trinitie Harbro
            **Chepanoc**   **Masequetuc**        Inlet in 1585

LANE,                                        (Kitty Hawk)
March 1586

(ALBEMARLE
      SOUND)                OCCAM        36°

36°                                        66
                                              60
Moratuc                NOMOPANA                 ROANOKE I.
(R. of Roanoke R.)                              Port Lane
                         **Dasemunkepeuc**        Inlets in 1585
36°                                              Port Ferdinando
LANE,        **Moratuc**
March-April                                  HATARASK I.
1586
                                              C.Kenrick
                                              (Wimble Shoals)
                                              25

                         PAQUIPPE              30   35°30
35°30        **Aquascogoc**   (Mattamuskeet Lake)        60
                              **Pomeiooc**
                                        MENTSO
**Secoton**                            (PAMLICO        42
            Cipo (Pamlico River)        SOUND)        **Croatoan**
                                                    (C.Hatteras)
                                        CROATOAN I.   (Diamond Shoals)
                                              42        (Outer Shoals)
                                              48
35°                                    Inlet in 1585        Approximate shore
        Neus River                    (Ocracoke Inlet)        line in 1590        35°
                                              60

                         Wococon
                         Inlet in 1585
                ENDESOKES
                         42

                         39

                **C.Feare**
Modern Cape Fear is        (C.Lookout)
50 miles to the south-west
                (Lookout Shoals)
42        48
                                        15
77°        76°30        76°        75°30

**RALEGH'S VIRGINIA 1584-1590**

AFTER MAPS IN D.B.QUINN ROANOKE VOYAGES
AND S.E.MORISON'S EUROPEAN DISCOVERY OF AMERICA:
THE NORTHERN VOYAGES

——————    Outer shore line (heavy black line)
          shown as Quinn and Morison think it
          existed in Ralegh's time

(Pamlico R.)    Modern names in parentheses

**Secoton**    Indian villages shown in bold face type

54        Selected soundings from modern chart in feet

reports. Drake arrived back at Portsmouth on July 28, bearing the leaders of the Virginia settlement with him.

In England there had been every intention on Ralegh's part to send out relief early in 1586,[24] although we do not know why it was as late as March before preparations were well advanced. By March 20 it would seem that the supply ship was due to start, but she did not in fact get away until well into April and reached Roanoke Island, nearly three months late, to find the settlers gone. She soon turned back with her supplies to England, arriving some time after Lane himself. Meanwhile Sir Richard Grenville had been preparing the second expedition, which was intended not merely to supply but reinforce the colony. By mid-April 1586, he was ready with six or seven vessels at Bideford, but a mischance held him back until about the beginning of May. He then took up considerable time attacking Spanish and Low Countries' ships in European waters. Eventually, avoiding the Caribbean, he crossed directly from Madeira to the North American coast, though this may have been a rather slow crossing.

We cannot tell precisely when Grenville arrived off the Carolina Outer Banks, perhaps mid-July, perhaps as late as early August. He found no one on Roanoke Island, and the Indians kept well out of his way. He made a series of explorations from the island, though we do not know the details, but did not find three men left behind by Lane because they had gone up-country, probably to Chowanoac, when Drake decided to leave so hurriedly in June. Though he surely intended to supply 150 to 200 men to reinforce Lane, he ended up leaving only 15 or 18 in all. Again, we do not know why, but his men were probably unwilling to stay when so much was to be gained from privateering on the high seas. One Indian was captured and something gleaned from him about the bad relations that had developed with Lane's men. It may have been this which reduced Grenville's interest in a major settlement; or, we may suspect, he did not find the economic potential of the region quite so attractive as it had seemed in 1585. Certainly there was no harbor which could act as a base for attacks on the Spanish fleets or enable privateers to recuperate after a season in the Caribbean. At the same time, he could not do nothing since Ralegh would not forgive total

24. The 1586 voyage is imperfectly documented. See Quinn, *Roanoke Voyages*, I, 60–62, 456–496, 787–792.

neglect. He made the fatal compromise of leaving only a handful of men, then sailed back on a long privateering cruise, reaching home only in December.

The year 1586 had thus been one of mischances. A colony, which started well enough, had returned; supplies had crossed and recrossed the ocean; reinforcements had largely come back also, leaving only a tiny second colony to the mercy of the Indians. The latter —it was learned in 1587—had soon attacked and killed one of the men, set their residence on fire and driven the others out; fourteen were observed on an islet in the Outer Banks preparing their pinnace to leave America, but were not seen again.[25] All the English colonists had gone; however the Spaniards, in the wreck of Florida caused by Drake, had had no time to search out the English base.

Ralegh and his associates now had to rethink their whole position. They were reasonably well aware of the assets and liabilities of the area for settlement. Clearly, Roanoke Island offered too many disadvantages to be adhered to as a continuing center for a colony. Chesapeake Bay would be much better in providing a deepwater port and so enabling a privateering base to be created, while supply ships and others could also come and go without undue danger from the elements. The Indians met with in 1585–6 had been friendly, and so unlike the hostile ones of 1584 that the prospects of good relations with the local people seemed better than they had been at Roanoke Island. The soil had evidently been reported as fertile. At the same time, the possibility of an effective economic base was still slight, since no staple commodities had been exploited earlier and none seemed to be in prospect.

Early in 1587, Thomas Harriot had completed a report out of his imperfect surviving collections, in which he summarized all the advantageous aspects of the Roanoke Island-Chesapeake area he could muster.[26] He could list many small attractions, but apart from pearls nothing of much cash value in itself. He seems to have had some idea that tobacco might eventually make a staple; Harriot, the returned colonists and Ralegh all tried to popularize its use in England, with some success. Clearly agriculture, forestry and perhaps some mineral extraction would have to be the bases; but it was

25. *Ibid.*, II, 528–529.
26. *Ibid.*, I, 317–387; Shirley, *Thomas Harriot*, pp. 41–44.

problematical how much exports would amount to. Indeed, Lane had reported[27] that "the discovery of a good mine, by the goodnesse of God, or a passage to the Southsea, or someway to it, and nothing els can bring this country in request to be inhabited by our nation." Further, the men of Lane's colony had given Virginia a bad name, declaring that there were no riches to be found there and only savage people who were hostile to intruders.

It is probable that Ralegh would have cut his losses and written off Virginia at once had it not been that John White and a few others had conceived a liking, even a passion, for the place. Moreover, they had a plan to live in it—they would bring their families and at least gain a good subsistence there. Some of them were probably uneasy inside the Church of England, not necessarily sectaries but inclining that way; some were apparently tradesmen in the City of London; others had a farming background. It was this group, with limited merchant backing and some help from Ralegh, which took on the task of founding the City of Ralegh in Virginia[28] on the shores of Chesapeake Bay, under the protection, it might seem, of the Chesapeake Indians with whom White had spent some time over the winter of 1585-6. Sir George Carey, captain of the Isle of Wight, gave them encouragement also and arranged some degree of cooperation with his privateering squadron of three ships. White had hoped for 150 people or more. When the *Lion* and two other vessels left on May 8, 1587, he had to be content with 110. White as governor was to rule the colony. With him went nine out of the twelve assistants who shared control of his City of Ralegh syndicate, the other three being presumably left at home to hasten supplies to the colony.

Although White was in command of the *Lion*, the Portuguese master, Simão Fernandes, attempted to dominate the expedition from the beginning. They reached Dominica on June 19 and left the Caribbean only on July 7, after repeated clashes of will between White and Fernandes. Clearly, White wished to spare the women the perils of prizetaking, while Fernandes wished to seize what he could. The Spaniards in the meantime had not been inactive. The governor of Florida, Pedro Menéndez Marqués, had scoured the coast as far as the entrance to Chesapeake Bay without seeing any

27. Quinn, *Roanoke Voyages*, I, 273.
28. *Ibid.*, II, 497-552, White's journal being our principal source.

signs of the English.[29] When the *Lion* and the pinnace reached Port Ferdinando on July 22, the third vessel, a flyboat, had fallen behind. Roanoke Island was found deserted, the fort entrenchments being thrown down and the headquarters building damaged, though some of the earlier houses were still standing. As White left the ship for the island with forty men, Fernandes made it clear that he would not carry out the intended plan, which had been for White to collect Grenville's men off the island, then take the ships to Chesapeake Bay and plant the settlement there. Instead, he specified that they must stay on Roanoke Island.

This policy may have been mainly actuated by malice, but it is obvious that Fernandes considered he had wasted enough time and wanted to get ahead with his privateering business. He may also have felt that the Chesapeake Bay Indians might prove, as in 1584, more dangerous than White thought. In any case, White acquiesced. He made contact with Manteo at his home on the Island of Croatoan, learned of the fate of the second colony, and cooperated with Manteo on a raid on Dasemunkepeuc, which was found recently deserted by the Roanoke Indians. He then installed Manteo as lord of Roanoke and the surrounding area, placing him in the position of Wingina but under English protection and tutelage, and indicating clearly by this that he did not himself intend to stay with his colony on Roanoke Island for long.

His settlers, meanwhile, were busy moving into the old houses and repairing the fort building. The flyboat came up and, when the stores position was examined, the gravest doubts were expressed about whether they would see them through the winter. Finally, the colonists, led by the assistants, insisted that White himself should go back to England to ensure that supplies were sent quickly. He, of all, had the most hostages to leave since his daughter Eleanor, married to one of the assistants, Ananias Dare, had just had a baby girl, christened Virginia, on August 24. White declared later that the settlers intended soon to depart "50 miles into the maine" (presumably overland to Chesapeake Bay), and he arranged for signs to be placed on trees to indicate whether they had left under difficulties or otherwise. He was certain he could find them when he returned. White returned in the *Lion* in November 1587 after a difficult voy-

29. *Ibid.*, II, 724.

age. At this point the third colony was left in isolation.

By the beginning of 1588, the political climate in England had changed again. War with Spain was now official and it was known that Spain hoped to send a great fleet against England. The Virginia colony once more became something of a patriotic symbol. White, too, was convinced that the new settlement would take root and would provide assistance in American waters to English ships. Grenville determined to build up a considerable squadron and to combine colonization and privateering again, evidently receiving much support from Ralegh and from gentlemen and merchants in the southwest.[30] White's aims were more modest: to get a small vessel and set out with supplies for the settlers as soon as possible. He does not appear to have been able to find a suitable vessel or get to sea ahead of Grenville, and seems to have reconciled himself to going with the squadron. Grenville was to command an impressive array of ships: *Galleon Dudley, Virgin God Save Her, Golden Hind, St. Leger,* and several others, perhaps seven or eight in all. But at the end of March 1588, defense of England took priority over aiding and repopulating Virginia. Grenville was told to put his ships under the royal commander at Plymouth.

All that could be done was to give White two small pinnaces, the *Brave* and the *Roe,* in which he set out with about fifteen additional colonists and some stores. But in this Armada year all was confusion and fighting at sea. The pinnaces got no further than Madeira before both were pillaged by French rovers and forced to creep back to England after only a month's absence, April 22–May 22. Their return sealed the fate of the colonists, who were now truly deserted.

By 1588 Virginia was already receding from a live issue in contemporary life into history, as it was later to do into myth. Thomas Harriot's report, entitled *A briefe and true report of the new found land of Virginia,* came out at last early in 1588; it was a fine survey, in a short space, of the English reactions to Virginia, and a clear assessment of both its potentialities and its people, intended for an audience halfway between investors and scholars. The younger Richard Hakluyt came back from an embassy post in Paris later in the year, determined to put English overseas activity on the map and especially to boost settlement in Virginia. His first major collection, the

30. *Ibid.,* II, 533–536, 559–569, again including a White journal.

single-volume *Principall navigations of the English nation*[31] was completed by the end of 1589 and gave a very full documentation including a second edition of Harriot's tract, almost all we have in fact, on the Roanoke voyages of 1584–88. Soon he was negotiating with Theodor de Bry to bring out something like the big complete illustrated Virginia volume that Harriot and White had contemplated if their collections had not been partially destroyed in June 1586. In 1590, part i of De Bry's *America* series[32] was published multi-lingually at Frankfurt. It contained a further reprint of Harriot, notes by him on White's Indian pictures, and a full gallery of the Roanoke Indians and their neighbors. Virginia was leaving a significant record, whatever the failures to exploit it had been.

Although White must have been distracted at his failure to reach his colonists in 1588, once the Armada had been defeated, plans were made to carry on with the search for the colonists and to revive the colony. Ralegh and Hakluyt between them tried to mobilize some backing in the City of London among the more powerful merchants for White's rather weak syndicate.[33] On March 7, 1589, an agreement was reached for the association of both Ralegh and a group of nineteen men, with White and the remaining assistants of the City of Ralegh promoters' syndicate. This was to take over responsibility for finding the colonists and refounding the colony. The strange thing is that, so far as we know, no ships were got to sea in that year. It is impossible to say why, except that all the vessels which could be released from home guard duties in English waters were being purposely directed to privateering, and there may have been none to spare for Virginia.

Eventually one of the 1589 associates, William Sanderson, got things moving early in 1590.[34] He induced John Watts, the privateering entrepreneur, to allow White passage on his *Hopewell* (Captain Abraham Cocke), which was going privateering to the West Indies along with the *John* and the *John Evangelist*. His own ship, the

31. Facsimile, D. B. Quinn and Raleigh A. Skelton (eds.), Richard Hakluyt, *The Principall Navigations (1589)*, 2 vols. (Cambridge, Eng., and Salem, Mass., 1965).

32. In Latin, English, French and German. The English version, under the title of Thomas Harriot, *A Briefe and True Report of the New Found Land of Virginia*, with an introduction by Paul Hulton, has been published in facsimile by Dover Press, New York, 1972.

33. Quinn, *Roanoke Voyages*, II, 557–559, 569–578.

34. *Ibid.*, II, 579–716, including White's final journal.

*Moonlight* (Captain Edward Spicer), was to follow as soon as she was ready. Watts would not hear of White taking any reinforcements or supplies, but the *Moonlight* appears to have carried what stores she could. The *Hopewell* reached Dominica on April 30. During May, June and early July, even after the *Moonlight* had joined the others, White had to endure the dangers and excitements of a privateering campaign, which included the capture of a major Spanish vessel, the *Buen Jesus,* sent home with a prize crew.

Only at the very end of July were the *Hopewell* and *Moonlight* free to go looking for the colonists. It was August 15 before they anchored off Port Ferdinando (or Hatarask, as White now preferred to call it since his break with the Portuguese). The weather was bad and a boat's crew, including Captain Spicer, were drowned making for Roanoke Island. On August 18 they finally reached the fort, which was deserted. A palisaded enclosure now stood round where the houses had been. Inside there was only some discarded heavy gear, some guns, shot and metal bars, until surface indication showed that something had been buried and partly uprooted. There, White found the remains of his armor and of some of his framed pictures, his chests having been buried and partly dug up by prowling Indians. Trees carved with the words "CRO" and "CROATOAN" were found without any sign of distress, a maltese cross, as agreed in 1587. White concluded that the settlers had gone to be near Manteo at Croatoan. He made desperate efforts to get Captain Cocke to wait until he could go south to make contact with them, but the situation of the ships offshore in dangerous weather was so bad and the privateering crews so impatient that he had to desist. After a halfhearted promise to winter in the West Indies, the *Hopewell* turned for home, reaching Plymouth on October 24, and thus bringing the Roanoke ventures to an end.

Indeed, Spain had been rather more active than England in trying to solve the mystery of the English location in 1588.[35] The captain, Vicente González, another Portuguese in the Spanish service, had been sent north in June 1588. With considerable skill and patience he scoured Chesapeake Bay for traces of English occupation but found none. Then, working his way down the Outer Banks, he found at Hatarask a slipway for boats and some barrels buried in the

35. *Ibid.,* II, 772–776, 802–825.

sand to catch water, but no men, English or Indian. He sailed back to Florida in late July, reporting that the English seemed to have disappeared. When Pedro Menéndez Marqués, as Florida governor, reported on these events in Spain, he was instructed to prepare a force in 1589 to establish a Spanish fortress on Chesapeake Bay and deny the coast to the English for all time. However, the sea war was more pressing and he was diverted to running treasure across the Atlantic. Virginia thus escaped Spanish occupation. The power struggle for which both sides were to some extent prepared failed to take place over Virginia at this time; its sovereignty would have to be decided later.[36]

If we look back over the Virginia colonization project from 1584, we may see it as a rather peripheral episode in the Anglo-Spanish struggle. An English settlement on the North American coast could have been valuable as a prestige symbol in the war with the Spanish empire; it might also have fulfilled a useful function as a base and port of call for privateers. From the viewpoint of the queen and her advisers, however, it was not of any major significance. Of course it mattered more to the individuals actually involved in its organization. Ralegh fancied his role as lord of a transatlantic territory; men as varied as Grenville, Lane, Harriot, and, above all, White identified themselves in some degree with its potentialities for white settlement. Even if there were no obvious riches to be found, the novelty of the environment, the relative mildness of the climate, and the characteristics of Indian society, all had some drawing power.

A few people—White clearly among them—saw it as a place where English family and community life could be installed in a new, more spacious environment. From the point of view of historically minded men like Hakluyt, the intrusion of an English colony in temperate America was a significant innovation. Hakluyt also thought of it in economic terms. Virginia could not only grow new products but supply others which England had to import from foreign, possibly hostile, countries. The more astute businessmen saw Virginia as a speculation: one that might produce new trades from which profits could be made, but a marginal gamble in which it might be worth while making a one-time investment

36. Quinn, *England and the Discovery of America*, pp. 264–281.

but not losing money over a long period.

In fact, the prospects for a long-term commercial corporation never developed favorably. White's settlers had evidently invested all their small capital in the search for a new land and a richer social and economic context for themselves and their families. But there were not enough of them, or not enough people with substantial capital to help them on their way, for much to come of such small-scale efforts. The Roanoke voyages were tentative and experimental affairs, which left a considerable residue of knowledge and experience; they were not the kind of ventures, either in scale or power of endurance, which would have been likely to succeed in establishing either permanent settlements or economically viable communities.[37]

By the time the Roanoke colonies were launched, the Englishmen involved in colonizing projects were well aware of the problems which had faced Cartier in the St. Lawrence valley in 1535–36, and they had heard enough of the climate of Newfoundland to make most of them skeptical about the feasibility of colonial settlement there. This was a principal reason—the strategic one in relation to the homecoming Spanish fleets was the other major reason—why the choice of Roanoke Island, relatively so far south, was made. A warm-weather colony had for the first time been attempted by the English, because it was hoped that this would avoid some of the climatic problems of a more northern site; and indeed, so far as Ralph Lane's experience went, the climate had proved favorable and healthy. But the economic results hoped for also required a relatively southern location. Hakluyt and his associates thought in terms of a colony whose products would both supplement and complement English economic resources.

It had been hoped that most of the products received in normal times from Spain and Portugal could be supplied from a colony in this latitude—currants, raisins, wine, citrus fruits, olive oil, and woad—and also that sugar, silk, cotton, rice, bananas, pineapples and various medicinal plants might be produced there. The results of such experiments as we know of were discouraging: the banana, pineapple and sugar plants brought from the West Indies did not

37. *Ibid.,* pp. 282–306.

survive, though this was thought partly to be the result of damage sustained when the *Tiger* went aground; anyway the results were inconclusive. So far as other crops of this sort were concerned, only grapes could be expected to grow satisfactorily. Of the medicinal plants, both sassafras and China root proved to be available in quantity, but these alone were not sufficient to produce much in the way of economic returns. Even Harriot in his *Briefe and true report* could not be very optimistic about major returns from complementary products, though he thought some might prove successful in the longer run.

The other economic objective was to produce materials which would supplement English economic resources, such as timber, pitch, tar, resin, flax, hemp and, of course, minerals and metals of all sorts. Here too, the results were inconclusive. There was plenty of timber, and certain fine timbers for furniture making would clearly be worth exporting; but most of the wood was too bulky in relation to its value to envisage transporting large quantities of it back to England. Timber derivatives like pitch, tar and resin would certainly be possible exports, but the labor cost would be relatively high. Flax and hemp might, it was thought, prove useful crops. Minerals and metals were still largely unlikely speculations. On the whole, the picture was not a very favorable one. Harriot dwelt mostly, as we have seen, on the food plants the Indians grew and a few novel products, grass-silk and so on, which had some possible commercial future.

It cannot be said that the Roanoke colonies were therefore satisfactory as testing grounds for economic enterprise: too little was attempted for any long-term planning as the result of experiments made there to have much value. The descriptive material on what was actually found growing wild or in Indian hands would prove useful to later colonizing attempts. The Roanoke ventures were, then, very much matters of trial and error; they could usefully be looked back to, but the guidelines they provided were in many respects neither complete nor conclusive.

# CHAPTER 14

## *Newfoundland as a Focus for European Activity, 1510–1590*

---

THE chronology of European enterprises at Newfoundland—and in this term we contemporaries often include the southern part of Labrador, the Strait of Belle Isle, Cape Breton Island, Sable Island and, possibly, part of Nova Scotia—is poorly known.[1] The Cabot voyages and those associated with them, 1497–1505, and the Portuguese explorations, 1500–03, had disclosed a great fishing bank well off shore, and also coasts on which there were exceptional quantities of fish—not only cod but such luxuries as salmon, along with seal, walrus and whale if there was any desire to involve the crews in hunting sea mammals. We know very little, too, about the Beothuk Indians of Newfoundland: they do not seem to have been numerous. Probably they conducted timid exchanges of a few furs and skins with the fishermen, and occasionally stole their gear when they left it lying on shore, so that they are more likely to have been treated as wild animals than as men. The Eskimo and the Montagnais-Nascapi Indians of Labrador, on the other hand, are likely to

1. Newfoundland has not found a historian to investigate its early international history in detail. Harold A. Innis, *The Cod Fisheries. The History of an International Economy* (New Haven, 1940), remains the soundest historical outline. Charles de la Morandière, *Histoire de la pêche française de la morue dans l'Amérique septentrionale*, 3 vols. (Paris, 1962–66), is invaluable on the organization and mechanics of the fishery, but disappointing on the early history of European contacts. Henry Harrisse, *Découverte et évolution cartographique de Terre-Neuve* (Paris, 1900), remains invaluable, as, for the area it covers, does E. R. Seary, *Placenames of the Avalon Peninsula of the Island of Newfoundland* (Toronto, 1971). Gillian T. Cell, *English Enterprise in Newfoundland, 1577–1660* (Toronto, 1969), is the only valuable sectional monograph.

have made quite early contact with the Europeans. Eskimo would barter almost anything for iron, and it is likely that trading with them began early though probably in a small way; the Indians of Labrador were few in number and may not have come very frequently in touch with the fishermen.

The main trading partners of the Europeans from the time of the earliest contacts appear to have been Micmac, who frequented the shores of the modern Maritime Provinces during the summer months when the fishermen were present. There was probably some competition between Europeans and Indians for inshore cod and other fish (and possibly sea mammals), but it might appear that small-scale trading for skins and furs was an early feature of Amerindian-European contact, and that it was one reason for the concentration of French (especially Bretons and later French Basques) on Cape Breton Island as a base. This would have provided a useful point from which to direct their fishing operations and to make trading contacts with the Micmac as well. But early fishing contacts were established within Newfoundland itself and with the offshore fishing banks.

It is clear that for most Europeans a spring voyage, a summer fishing season, and an autumn return formed the normal routine. There was no desire to winter and no strong incentive to found a permanent trading base or colony. No one country could easily establish a monopoly since the fishing grounds were so widely dispersed, and there does not seem to have been any great concentration of furs for exchange by the Indians in this early period at any single point which might justify such a base on fur-trading grounds alone.

Fishing was a business enterprise; so was the subsidiary fur trading which accompanied it. Neither left systematic narrative records in any of the countries that engaged in them. The growth of the fishing economy must be traced from such business records as have survived, but these throw very little light on the topography of the fishery or the timing of and reasons for its proliferation. Occasionally, governments became interested in planning to exploit the fishery or the shores which the fishery affected; or some legal case might arise to throw light on the circumstances in American waters and so enable a little knowledge to accumulate about the fishery.

The records of a Bristol fishery now exist for 1502–05, but no

further reference has been found to an English fishing fleet before 1522. We can only guess that the first English fishery was off south-eastern Newfoundland and not elsewhere. Systematic English records of the subsequent growth of the Bristol fishery or of indications as to when other southwestern English and Irish ports began to participate in it are lacking for the period 1506–1573. In particular, there is no evidence that the early charters provided any basis on which an individual, a syndicate, or a company could direct or control any aspect of the fishery. This is certainly true also of France. There the pioneers were apparently the Normans from 1504 or thereabouts, followed very closely by the Bretons, who soon outstripped the Normans and by 1511 were recognized as exceptionally well informed on the Newfoundland area, and the French Basques who are known to have been active from 1512. (Cape Breton early appears on the maps as marking the objective of many European fishermen. It could have been so called from either the Bretons or the Basques, since the first dated Basque voyage was made in 1512 from the French Basque town of Cap-Breton.)[2]

Queen Juana of Castile in 1511 gave a charter to Juan de Agramonte to make a reconnaissance of Tierra Nueva within the Spanish limits, but not touching the parts belonging to Portugal.[3] This is significant as showing that some rough-and-ready line had been agreed which marked off those parts believed to be within the Portuguese sphere from those in the Spanish, even though no clear definition of where the line actually lay would seem to have been possible. He was to take Breton pilots but there was no mention of a fishery; he was to look for gold and objects for trade, and was to report on his return whether a trading post or colony would be desirable. As nothing more is heard of this project, we cannot make further claims for Spanish activity in the area at this time. It is unlikely that the Spanish Basques were appreciably behind their French brothers in the Newfoundland codfishery, though there is also no evidence of their close cooperation at a very early stage. The whale fishery was clearly not extended to American waters until after 1540. The reason for Sebastian Cabot's employment by Spain in 1512 was partly to get the benefit of his knowledge of Newfound-

2. La Morandière, *Histoire de la pêche française*, I, 227.
3. Biggar, *Precursors* (1911), pp. 102–115.

land,[4] but he does not appear to have inspired any Spanish ventures in that direction.

Just as Agramonte's activities did not lead to any implantation of Spanish influence, so the various attempts in England to organize ventures across the Atlantic with more ambitious objectives than commercial fishing are of interest rather for what they projected than what they achieved. When John Rastell set out for America in 1517 (he was the first Englishman to call North America by this name), he had some information on the Newfoundland fishery and French activity there. He believed one hundred vessels went there each year—his own objective was apparently to exploit the fishery from a base nearby, but to go on himself with some merchandise and armed men to trade with Asia. John Cabot in 1498 had proposed to establish some sort of way-station on the other side of the Atlantic which would act as a trading post for commerce with the more southerly parts of Asia. Now that North America was known to be distinct from Asia and Sebastian Cabot had pointed a way to sail round it to the east, Rastell hoped to combine fishing at Newfoundland with trading much further afield in Asia. However, he got no further than Ireland since his sailors would not risk the ocean voyage.[5]

When Sebastian Cabot came back briefly to England in 1521, he acted as consultant on a similar project.[6] This was taken up vigorously by Cardinal Wolsey and Henry VIII's council and was for five ships (two from Bristol and three from London) to sail west or northwest to Asia. There is nothing specific to be found about whether this was simply a Northwest Passage venture—it was certainly mainly such—or one which also had in it the idea of maintaining a foothold on North America. The London merchants refused to accept that any Englishmen had been on this voyage or that Sebastian had been there. If they thought Sebastian was being promoted as someone who had reached Asia by this route they were, of course, correct; if not, they were certainly exceptionally ignorant of the history of the Newfoundland fishery and of Cabot's part in

4. *Ibid.*, pp. 115–116; Williamson, *Voyages of the Cabots* (1929), pp. 83–84.
5. See Quinn, *England and the Discovery of America* (1974), pp. 161–169.
6. Biggar, *Precursors* (1911), pp. 134–142; Williamson, *Voyages of the Cabots* (1929); Laetitia Lyell (ed.), *Acts of Court of the Mercers' Company, 1453–1527* (Cambridge, Eng., 1936), p. 529.

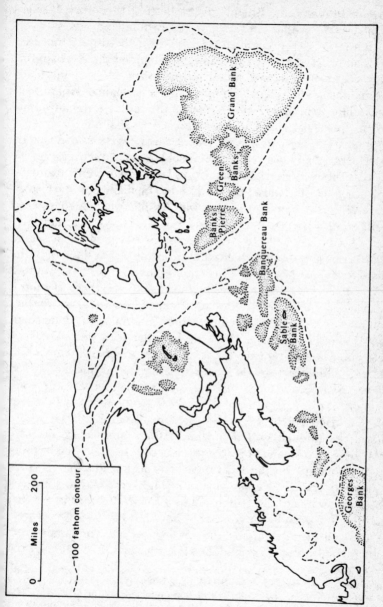

The Newfoundland Fishing Banks

developing it with the Bristol men earlier in the century. It might seem, therefore, that knowledge of Newfoundland was still very much a trade secret, confined to sections of the fishing fraternity and their backers, mainly in Bristol. But it is significant perhaps that the voyage was described simply as one to the "New found land" or "the new found island," no mention being made of Asia. In any case it came to nothing owing to mercantile coolness and unwillingness to speculate, and Sebastian returned to Spain.

About 1519, perhaps before, João Alvares Fagundes of Viana do Castelo, received a charter from Manoel I to make discoveries in the west. In 1520 he returned, claiming to have discovered a mainland and a number of islands: "the land said to be mainland which stretches from the line of demarcation with Castile, which is contiguous in the south with our boundary as far as the land which the Corte Reals discovered, which is to the north," with islands, some along a north-east and south-west coastline and another at the foot of the fishing bank. On March 13, 1521, he was authorized to occupy and govern these lands and to manage the soaphouses there. It cannot be said definitely where these lands and islands were, or whether Fagundes in fact established any colony. The mention of the soaphouses may be significant. Fish oil, together with whale oil later, were important ingredients for soapmaking, which used much timber in the boiling. It might have seemed a worthwhile land-based industrial project to make soap ash and then combine it with train oil in order to create a coarse soap. We may possibly conclude that this was tried out by Fagundes, presumably in 1520. There are indications (though rather late ones) that some Azoreans were brought with mainland Portuguese and a colony attempted by them on or near Cape Breton Island, perhaps also at this time. If so it came to an end quickly, possibly in a single season, though it left traces afterwards found by Basque fishermen. Whether it was that founded by Fagundes or another is not known.[7]

The considerable number of surviving maps containing Portuguese names and ranging in date from about 1504 to about 1525

---

7. Biggar, *Precursors* (1911), pp. 127–131; W. F. Ganong, *Crucial Maps in the Early Cartography . . . of Canada* (Toronto, 1964), pp. 45–72, 478–481, with attempts to fit the islands named into the south coast of Newfoundland and the Gulf of St. Lawrence. Carl Sauer, *Sixteenth Century North America* (Berkeley, Calif., 1971), pp. 49–51, suggests that exploration began on the coast of Maine and ended at Sable Island.

indicate much more Portuguese exploration than we have any other record for. They apparently covered in one way or another the coasts from about the midpoint of Labrador along the east coast of Newfoundland, probably some way into the Gulf of St. Lawrence, and from Cape Breton to some way down the coast of Nova Scotia. But attempts to work out any sequence of events from these maps have led to so many complications and contradictions of one writer by another that it seems unwise to make confident use of them except in very general terms as contributing to evidence of considerable European and especially Portuguese activity in this extensive area.[8]

The voyages of Verrazzano and Gomes are of some importance for Newfoundland in a negative sense. Each of these explorers of the mainland coastline in 1524–25 considered that his task was done when he reached the approximate latitude of Cape Breton. From there northward, at least to some way up the Labrador coast, it was considered that the coastline was well enough defined already: Newfoundland, at least on the south and east, was regarded as *Terra cognita*. John Rut's voyage of 1527[9] was a little different in character and results for Newfoundland, as he was told to go first to the northwest and see whether a passage existed, and only then to explore to the southward. Rut visited Newfoundland on the second stage of his voyage, having already lost touch with the *Samson*, and entered St. John's Harbour on August 3, before making his way to the mainland to the south of the island. There he found a fair sample of the European codfishing fleet—eleven Norman, one Breton and two Portuguese vessels. His own proposed rendezvous was at Cape Spear, and it would appear that the English used the island and bays to the south of the cape, as far as Ferryland Head, as their main center at this time. The inshore fishery at St. John's and elsewhere on the coast was well established. Grounds for stages, flakes and cookhouses were no doubt already being appropriated by men from all four nations, though it is not clear that any definite allocations of shorelines on a national or regional basis had yet been worked out in practice.

8. The fullest study is still Harrisse, *Découverte et évolution*. For some of the problems presented by these maps, see R. A. Skelton, "The Cartography of the Voyages," in Williamson, *The Cabot Voyages* (1962), pp. 295–325.

9. Quinn, *England and the Discovery of America*, pp. 161–169.

If the discourse of "the Great Captain,"[10] which incorporates material on a Sumatra voyage in 1529, is correctly dated, it is possible that its sailing directions for Newfoundland and the adjacent coasts belong to that year or thereabouts also, though they may well be later. The material is important, however, as revealing that the French were penetrating into the Strait of Belle Isle. Indeed, the author maintains that at the Bay of Çastles (*Golfo di Castelli*) on the Labrador side of the Strait there was a large wooden enclosure, which is both unexpected and inexplicable unless whale fishing had already begun and this was a tryworks for rendering whale oil. Although the Spanish and French Basques were to be active in the 1540s and thereafter, there is no indication that they were whaling here so early. Cartier, however, when he penetrated the Strait in 1534, found a Rocheller fishing well beyond it, off the south Labrador coast toward the western end of the Strait of Belle Isle.

This voyage of 1534 is of great importance for Newfoundland since, for the first time, we have a record of the exploration of the west coast of the island. Moreover, Cartier, without making any experiment on this occasion, considered that there was an opening to the southeast of the Gulf of St. Lawrence, and in 1536, returning from his second voyage, sailed through what is now known as Cabot Strait. He is thus the first man known to have circumnavigated the island. The definition of the island in these two voyages, and the exploration of the gulf and river which lay beyond it between 1534 and 1543—especially with the publication of the account of his 1535–36 voyage in 1545—brought the nature of the coastlines in this region to public notice. Moreover, the collection of coastal data on Roberval's 1542–3 expedition by Jean Alfonce de Saintonge, and his publication of a selection of it in 1544 as *Les voyages avantureux*,[11] helped to make available a rutter which could be used by others on later voyages. Nonetheless, most maps continued to show Newfoundland as an archipelago rather than as a single island.

Cartier had, incidentally, shown that Newfoundland's resources

---

10. It comes from J. B. Ramusio, *Navigationi et viaggi*, III (1565), fols. 423*r.*–424*v.*; and is translated and discussed by B. G. Hoffman, "Account of a Voyage Conducted in 1529 to the New World, Africa, Madagascar and Sumatra," *Ethnohistory*, X (1963), 1–79.

11. *Les voyages avantureux*, written circa 1542, was published in Poitiers, apparently in 1544; the extended rutter, *La cosmographie*, edited by Georges Musset (Paris, 1904), contains more detail.

were not confined to fish. He plundered Funk Island (Penguin Island) for birds as stores for his men. The same thing was done by Richard Hore in 1536.[12] It would seem that, in the *Trinity* and *William,* Hore was following Cartier's track of 1534 into the Strait of Belle Island in order to introduce this newly explored area to a number of English gentlemen. The vessels also imitated Cartier in taking great auks, gannets and other seabirds at Funk Island before entering the Strait. The *Trinity* became separated from the *William* and was in sufficient difficulty to have had to put into harbor in south Labrador and been unable to leave until food went short. A French fishing vessel then came up which the English captured and made away with, the French being left to put the English vessel into some sort of shape so that they could get home. Englishmen had thus got a taste of the harsh country (Cartier had already labeled Labrador "the land God gave to Cain"),[13] and had shown that piracy, since this is what their action in the case of the French ship amounted to, could easily arise out of misfortune. The *William* meantime had gone south to rendezvous at Cape Spear and carry on with her fishing there at the "Isles of Spear." Evidently Ferryland Bay and the waters between Ferryland Head and Cape Spear, where these islands were located, were still the center of the English fishery, though we hear of Bretons also using the shores near the cape.

News of Cartier's expedition in 1541 brought the first official Spanish expedition to Newfoundland.[14] In the spring of that year a caravel was sent out, under the command of Ares de Sea, to search for information on what Cartier had been doing. The ship was back in November, but the depositions on what happened have not been discovered. Presumably some fishing crews, Basques and others, were encountered and interrogated. Later, after Cartier came back in 1542, a number of French seamen were induced to tell at Fuenterrabía what they had seen of Cartier in Newfoundland and what they thought he had been doing in the Gulf of St. Lawrence and beyond. The information they gave was somewhat sketchy, but it is of some value on where ships went and what the fishing pattern was.

12. Williamson, *Voyages of the Cabots* (1929), pp. 111–115; Quinn, *England and the Discovery of America,* pp. 182–189.

13. H. P. Biggar, *The Voyages of Jacques Cartier* (1924), p. 22.

14. H. P. Biggar, *Documents Relating to Cartier and Roberval* (1930), pp. 412–422, 447–467; José Toríbio Medina, *Una expedition Española a la Tierra de los Bacallaos en 1541* (Santiago, Chile, 1896).

No subsequent official Spanish expedition is known to have taken place, but Pedro Menéndez de Avilés, as *adelantado* of Florida in 1565–74, considered that Newfoundland came under his jurisdiction and would have liked to assert Spanish authority there.

Glimpses of activities in Newfoundland are scarce after 1542, but we can make a few generalizations which may be relevant to an obscure period. Certainly St. John's had become the great rendezvous. For example, Cartier's returning ships in 1542 there met Roberval's outgoing ones.[15] It might seem that ships engaged in the shore fishery tended to put in at St. John's, either on their first arrival at Newfoundland before going on to other harbors or else before they departed for home. While much fish was caught nearby and dried on its shores, trading between the ships, visiting with each other, drinking, eating and sometimes fighting were the usual occupations of the fishermen and merchants there. Ships, too, came in for supplies or to enable their crews to relax after wet-fishing on the Banks. The practice developed of having a port admiral, who was often (as mentioned earlier) the captain or master of the first ship to enter the harbor in a particular season. His job was to try to settle disputes about drying grounds and boats, as well as personal quarrels. He seems to have been assisted by an informal jury composed of the other captains. When exactly this began, or precisely how it evolved, is not known, but it may have been in operation by or shortly after 1550. Similar precautions were taken in other harbors to which a number of vessels came.

The definition of shorelines on a regional basis seems gradually to have evolved during the years 1540–70. The greatest novelty in this period was the appearance of the Spanish Basques, hitherto cod fishermen, as whalers in the Gulf of St. Lawrence. So far as we can tell, they left the eastern opening of the Strait of Belle Isle to the French, but took over most of the harbors on the Labrador shore of the Strait for their tryworks. There they spent long periods on shore, mainly cutting up whales and boiling down oil for transportation to Spain. Later, their operations extended down the hitherto unexploited west shore of Newfoundland. The Basque cod fisher-

15. Roberval says it was at St. John's (Biggar, *Voyages of Jacques Cartier*, p. 264), but a sailor questioned in Spain in 1542 said it was at the Isle of Spear, just south of Cape Spear, where he might have put in on his way to or from St. John's (Biggar, *Cartier and Roberval*, p. 456).

men concentrated on the south coast; the Spanish Basques mainly toward the west; while the French Basques took over for themselves the remainder of the southern shore of Newfoundland, with their main center at Placentia. The Bretons were most active round Cape Breton, but French Basques apparently divided the shores with them to some extent. The Normans were most active along the eastern shore of Newfoundland, north of St. John's, although there were Bretons there also and probably both used the southeastern harbors of Labrador, possibly not reaching as far north as Hamilton Inlet.

The southeast gradually became the preserve of the English and Portuguese. They worked amicably together, partly perhaps because of old traditions of trading cooperation, but more specifically because the English bought most of their salt from the Portuguese and so friendship was good business for both. They shared St. John's, though other vessels, mainly French, came in and out freely; the other harbors in the south were also apparently shared, even if the English tried to assert the right to appoint port admirals. There were occasional fights where grounds for drying fish were contested by interlopers against the regular users, though these most often arose between members of the same country or region, or when boats were stolen. As the French and Spaniards were at war for considerable periods, their antagonism tended to extend from Europe to Newfoundland in the 1540s; for over a decade, we know that there were raids and counter-raids between French ships and those of the Spanish Basques. But for a long period there is almost no narrative material available.

One episode in the Habsburg–Valois struggle in Europe deserves mention.[16] In 1555 a Spanish Basque privateering squadron of three ships, led by Captain Juan de Erauso and Perez de Hoa, crossed to Newfoundland and found twelve French ships laden with cod in a southern harbor, probably Placentia Bay. Both sides were heavily gunned, showing that the French were prepared for hostilities. The large Basque ships were successful in the ensuing fight and all twelve French vessels were taken, four being assigned to each of the Basque captains. Erauso raised his flag on the *Grande Fantaisie* of Brieuc (Brittany), the largest of the French ships. They moved

16. Edmond Ducéré, *Les corsaires sous l'ancien régime* (Bayonne, 1895), p. 21; Charles de la Roncière, *Historie de la marine française*, III (3rd edition, Paris, 1923), p. 589.

north to the harbor of St. John's, where they found a further eight French vessels full of cod, headed by the well-armed *Grande Française* of Saint Malo. The French erected bastions and forts to command the narrow entrance to the harbor. From these and from the ships they kept up such a strong artillery fire that they prevented the Basques from entering. Erauso then sailed up to Conception Bay, landed and organized a force of men and guns which advanced on St. John's from the north, thus taking the main battery from the rear. They were able not only to capture the fort which dominated the entry to the harbor but also to turn its guns on the French vessels there. By these means they made it possible for the Basque ships to enter and force the French to surrender. In triumph, the Basques renamed St. John's Nuestra Señora de Agosta, the victory having taken place in August. Erauso claimed to have had only nine men killed, and said the French lost seventy-two dead and about one hundred wounded. No less than eighteen French prizes were brought safely to San Sebastian with their cod and some 130 guns. The five hundred prisoners were given a ship in which they could get back to France. Altogether this season the Basques took some forty-eight French Newfoundlanders from Normandy and Brittany and virtually brought the French Newfoundland fishery to a halt for a time. It was revived in 1557 by the aid of heavily armed escorts supplied by Henry II. The Banks fishery remains wholly obscure. Most of the vessels were French and most of them simply came out as early as they could cross the Atlantic, fished steadily until their holds were full of wet fish, then returned to Europe, a few making two voyages a year. Unless they were intercepted by pirates or privateers on their way, as sometimes happened, they left no trace in the political history of the time. Maps of Newfoundland had consistently shown it as a group of islands since early in the century. On the maps and charts drawn from Cartier's voyages these are reduced to two, Avalon Peninsula being shown detached. Other geographic maps continue to show a split into many different segments—the first English map to show it as a single island was that by Edward Wright included in the second volume of Hakluyt's *Principal navigations* in 1599. This fact in itself indicates that the island as a whole was not of consuming interest to any one European nation, since otherwise more effective cartographic measures might well have been taken to ascertain its outlines more precisely.

Portuguese interests did not remain merely concerned with the fishery. The Azorean Portuguese, at least, aspired to colonize either Newfoundland itself or some adjoining islands. Both the descendants of João Vas Corte Real and of Pedro de Barcelos continued to assume that they retained rights to do so. Successive members of the Corte Real and Barcelos families kept the old grants alive. Between 1521 and 1531 Diogo de Barcelos, son of Pedro, and his son Manoel, discovered and began to use lands across the ocean. In 1531 Diogo proposed to bring two ships there. Later voyages were made by Manoel, one in 1563 and another in 1566. On the island called Barcellona de Sam Bardão, apparently Sable Island, they had bred herds of cows, sheep, goats and pigs. In 1568 Manoel bought a ship, *A Vera Cruz,* and with another, proposed to send a colonizing expedition to Sable Island. If he did so, its members did not survive long; but the cattle remained. Sir Humphrey Gilbert heard of them in 1583 and proposed to use some for revictualing, and a French group largely lived on them from 1598 to 1603.

Similarly, Manoel Corte Real, son of Vasco Eannes Corte Real, was recognized in 1538 as "Lord of Terra Nova." How far he played an active part in later years is not known. By 1567, perhaps in competition with Manoel Barcelos, he had prepared three ships at Terceira to go to colonize Newfoundland, even appointing a scrivener to travel to the colony as its clerk. Precisely where this was and how long it survived we do not know.[17] In March 1568, Pedro Menéndez de Avilés picked up news (in the border town of Fuenterrabía) that the Portuguese had begun to colonize *Tierra Nueva,* where there were several large Indian villages on an arm of the sea.[18] Whether this refers to the activities of Barcelos or Corte Real is not clear, but the Spaniards also gathered that from this place the Portuguese hoped to sail round North America to Asia. This makes it more likely to be Corte Real activities which are in question, since the Corte Reals were still actively concerned with the Northwest Passage. Manoel perhaps established or tried to establish a base in northern Newfoundland or southern Labrador from which voyages

17. On Barcelos, see J. A. Vigneras, "The Voyages of Diogo and Manoel Barcelos to Canada in the Sixteenth Century," *Terrae Incognitae,* V (1973), 61–64; on the Corte Reals, see Ernesto do Canto, *Aes Corte Reals* (Punta Delgado, Azores, 1883), pp. 25–26, 31–33; and H. Harrisse, *Les Corte-Reals* (Paris, 1883), pp. 235–236.

18. British Library, Additional MS 33983, fol. 328v.

could be made to the northwest. Information picked up in England in 1582[19] related how Vasco Eannes Corte Real in 1574 worked his way up the Labrador coast to 58° N. and found a passage opening to the west and trending south. He followed it for 20 leagues and then had to turn back for lack of victuals. This may have been the entrance to Hudson Strait. He died in 1581 and the voyage in 1574 is the last Corte Real voyage known.

These movements of the Azorean families indicate that the Portuguese activities in and around Newfoundland included stock-breeding, attempted colonization (how far the various attempts got is not known) and continuing exploration in search of a Northwest Passage, in strict continuity from the expeditions made by their families since before 1500.

As privateering and piracy in the Spanish Indies became an international activity in the 1560s and later, French and English privateers often found it convenient to sail homeward by way of Newfoundland, the extra distance involved being compensated by being able to replenish their victuals from the fishermen. Thus John Hawkins, on his way home from his second voyage in 1565, had his men catch cod on the Banks and later met "a couple of French shippes, and had of them so much fish as would serve us plentifully for the rest of the voyage, the Captain paying for the same both gold and silver, to the joint value thereof, unto the chief owner of the saide shippes, but they not looking for anything at all, were glad in themselves to meete with such good entertainement at sea as they had at our hands." The note of self-congratulation in John Sparke's account[20] indicates that, more often, fish and other things were simply taken without payment from Newfoundlanders. Fish could always be purchased at St. John's and at some other harbors, while wood for fires, and equipment—canvas, ropes and so on—often badly run down after a long privateering cruise, could usually be acquired from fishing vessels also. Such visitors had the power to compel acquiescence to their demands, and it may well be that they did not always pay fair prices for what they got and sometimes took things without paying at all. So far, our information on the development of this practice is very limited, but it paved the way for a

19. Richard Hakluyt, *Divers voyages concerning the discoverie of America* (London, 1582); facsimile edition (Amsterdam, 1967), p. 4.

20. Given in Richard Hakluyt, *Principal Navigations*, X (Glasgow, 1905), p. 63.

greater degree of interference with the fishery as tensions and conflicts in Europe increased in the late 1570s.

Before any interference took place on a substantial scale, we have,
from the merchant Anthony Parkhurst, an English view of Newfoundland. He had been there each year from 1574 and wrote about
the island in 1577 and 1578.[21] He was regarded with some suspicion
by the West Country fishermen, because he went out himself and
did not merely send his ship to Newfoundland: "they also suppose,"
he said, "that I find some secret commodities by reason that I doe
search the harbors, creekes and havens, and also the land much
more then ever Englishman hath done." His observations encompassed the fishery as a whole and the shares in it of English, French,
Portuguese and Spaniards, with some four hundred ships in all,
including twenty to thirty large Basque whalers. This would imply
an annual tonnage in the region of 30,000 and some 12,000 men
at least. It is the first attempt at an overview of the fishery.

The greatest interest of Parkhurst's letters is that they show him
to be a keen observer. He sowed grain, vegetables and herbs to test
how they grew. He listed nut and cherry trees, wild fruits like black-
berries, strawberries, raspberries and dewberries. The thick pine
forests, with some oak and much willow, had, he thought, good
potential. Besides cod, there were many other fish—herring,
salmon, ray, flounders, and what they called a "cat." There were
plenty of shell fish, including mussels containing pearls. He described how the cod chased the caplin and squid ashore, so that
"you may take up with a shove net, as plentifully as you do Wheate
in a shovell." Seabirds were good eating, especially the "Penguins,"
the great auk, that "cannot flie." There was more meat on them than
a goose, and Frenchmen fishing near the Strait of Belle Isle commonly ate them instead of bringing meat with them. There were
deer and elk. Foxes, "black, white and gray," gave promise of good
furs. He had found specimens of iron and copper at St. John's and
"in the Island of Iron"—Bell Island in Conception Bay. He believed
Newfoundland to be fully habitable: "New found land is in a temperate Climate, and not so colde as foolish Mariners doe say, who
find it cold sometimes when plentie of Isles of Ice lie neere the

21. E. G. R. Taylor (ed.), *The Original Writings and Correspondence of the Two Richard
Hakluyts,* I (1935), 122–134. G. T. Cell, *English Enterprise in Newfoundland* (1969),
considers Parkhurst's figures on p. 22, and see p. 526 below.

shore: but up in the land they shall finde it hotter then in England."

Newfoundland begins to come alive under Parkhurst's pen. The English made a practice, he said, of taking control of the harbors when they fished, giving protection to ships of other nations, "which thing they do willingly, so that you take nothing from them more than a boat or twaine of salt, in respect of your protection of them against rovers or other violent intruders, who do often put them from a good harbor." We may, however, suspect that English authority was sometimes enforced over vessels which were not willing to pay this toll. Parkhurst is significant since he is the first to urge that the English should colonize the island, seize control of the Strait of Belle Isle, and dominate the whole fishery in their own interests.

The existence of such a large number of ships and experienced seamen clearly made the Newfoundland fishery of considerable strategic as well as economic importance. In November 1577, Sir Humphrey Gilbert put up a nefarious proposal[22] that an English expedition should attempt to seize the whole fishing fleet, Spanish, Portuguese and French. This would destroy the major fishing assets of these powers, he claimed, though he did not say how he proposed to continue to deny them the seamen who would be captured. If necessary, in order to limit international repercussions, such action need be taken only against the Spaniards. The scheme is not likely to have been seriously considered, and was in fact quite impracticable, but the convergence of Gilbert's and Parkhurst's proposals at this time indicates that the fishery had now become a major European concern, though one of particular interest to the English.

Gilbert's own patent of June 11, 1578, gave him an open authority to seize and colonize for England any lands he might locate. While this could be a cover for Newfoundland activity, it seems that in his first expedition in 1578–9, which did not reach America, he was thinking of a settlement well down the North American mainland coast. Before he finally set out again in 1583, he had assumed that his patent entitled him to dispose of lands in any part of eastern North America to other Englishmen. He had licensed Edward Cotton in 1579 or 1580 to make a voyage into the Gulf of St. Lawrence, which the latter attempted with no success, having probably been

22. D. B. Quinn (ed.), *The Voyages and Colonising Enterprises of Sir Humphrey Gilbert*, I (1940), 170–175.

beaten out by the Basques; and he also relinquished latitudes above 50° N. to Dr. John Dee, though he kept Newfoundland inside his own sphere of influence. When he was prevented from making his reconnaissance to Norumbega (the later New England) in 1582, he determined to take in a visit to Newfoundland on his way there in 1583. His appearance in St. John's Harbour at the beginning of August was a signal for defensive measures against him to be prepared by the English, French and Portuguese vessels in the harbor.

Since the time of Parkhurst's writing in 1577 and 1578, conditions had begun to change. The friction between Spain and England had increased so much that each nation adopted an attitude of hostility toward the other's vessels at sea. In 1580 Portugal was taken over by Spain, and whatever cooperation had existed before this between English and Portuguese at Newfoundland, it now became clear that the Portuguese must be considered to be in the Spanish camp. Moreover, English attacks on non-English shipping in Newfoundland harbors had begun. Two English ships came into Renews Harbour in August 1582—the *Susan Fortune,* under Richard Clarke, and the *Popinjay,* under Henry Taylor—and proceeded to seize three Portuguese ships, stealing the cargoes of two of them and impounding the third to help carry the fish and train oil, then went on to Fermeuse and Bowe (Bois Island?) to do the same thing with two other Portuguese vessels.[23] The English port admiral at Renews was not able to take defensive action, though he and other masters of ships registered their protests and later in England provided the aggrieved Portuguese with evidence against the pirates. The marauding vessels claimed to have letters of marque against Spanish and Portuguese ships, but in fact did not hold any such authority. The subsequent attempt by the fishermen in St. John's in 1583 to oppose Gilbert—though they did not persist in their resistance—can be understood.

Gilbert entered St. John's Harbour after having shown the queen's commission (his patent) and proceeded to act as if he owned Newfoundland.[24] He formally annexed the island on August

23. Public Record Office, London, State Papers, Foreign, Spain, SP94/1, November 9, 1582, Bernardino de Mendoza to Lord Burghley; High Court of Admiralty, Examinations, H.C.A. 13/24, April 25, 1583 (Thomas Peers), April 26, 1583 (William Dill); H.C.A. 13/25, October 15, 1583 (Paulo Dios).

24. A detailed account of Gilbert's actions is given in D. B. Quinn and Neil M. Cheshire, *The New Found Land of Stephen Parmenius* (Toronto, 1972), pp. 50–58.

5, having already levied a toll of fish and other supplies on the sixteen English and twenty French and Portuguese vessels in the harbor. Laws were promulgated to be observed by all ships when in port. Allotments of land on the harbor were made for stages and drying flakes in return for an annual rent: he also issued each non-English vessel with a passport. He enjoyed his sovereignty until August 22, when he left without trying to assert his presumed rights in any other harbor.

Gilbert's gesture of annexing Newfoundland could have had long-term results only if it was followed up by an armed occupation of the principal harbors so that English authority could be asserted. The number of possible harbors and the combined strength of the non-English ships, if they acted in consort (and perhaps under the protection of armed vessels of their own country), made such an assertion of authority quite impracticable. Gilbert was lost at sea on his return voyage, and his heirs do not appear to have attempted to reassert his claims. His half brother Walter Ralegh, when a patent was granted to him in reversion of Gilbert's in 1584, was specifically told not to intervene in Newfoundland.

Edward Hayes, who had captained his own ship, the *Golden Hind*, for Gilbert in 1583, now became for some years a vigorous propagandist for English intervention in Newfoundland. His most elaborate proposals were made to Lord Burghley in 1585 and 1586.[25] He reckoned that by this time four hundred ships in all came to the cod- and whale fisheries, that the Basques used large ships of 300 to 400 tons for the whale fishery, and that the catch of whale and cod was valued at some £200,000. He considered that a corporation should be authorized to assert English control over the whole fishery, but apparently no one else agreed with him.

The seizure of English merchant shipping in Spanish ports in May 1585 brought about a swift reprisal. In view of what had been said about the foreign fishing fleets at Newfoundland in the previous eight years, it is not surprising that it should have been directed against the Portuguese and Spanish vessels in Newfoundland. Bernard Drake and Amyas Preston, who had been intended to reinforce the colony being established on Roanoke Island under Ralegh's auspices, were suddenly diverted in June to go to Newfoundland

25. See below, pp. 419–421.

instead.[26] They were to warn the English fishermen not to bring any catches to Spain and to take such ships in reprisal as they could. Drake's *Golden Riall*, along with Ralegh's *Job* (Captain Andrew Fulford) and one or two other ships, picked up sixteen or seventeen Portuguese fishing vessels—they do not seem to have found any Spanish ones—in the harbors of the Avalon peninsula (Bay Bulls and others) and took them as prizes. Not all of them reached England, several being sunk at sea and one putting into a Breton harbor. Some six hundred fishermen were brought to England, where many died of fever. The result of this act of war, directed at the Portuguese as being subjects of Spain, broke the links between English and Portuguese and must have made it difficult for English fishermen to get their accustomed salt supplies, unless the French were willing to take the place of the Portuguese as suppliers. It might appear that after this the Portuguese confined their activities to the Banks fisheries, though it is said that as late as 1598 as many as sixty ships left Oporto alone for Newfoundland.[27] It was then the turn of the Basques.

From about 1580, Spanish and French Basques tended to collaborate more closely. Huguenot privateers from La Rochelle and others from England preyed on the fishing and whaling vessels of both. The Spanish ports more frequently chartered French Basque ships, and there was rather more cross-capitalization. The Spanish crown made it increasingly difficult for its Basque subjects to carry on either whaling or codfishing on the old scale, since vessels were continually being commandeered for naval purposes and their crews impressed. In these circumstances, a number of Spanish Basque seamen tended to evade royal service by signing on in French Basque ships, though this was risky for them, while the share of the French Basques in the total fishery increased, though we do not know to what extent. Philip II also frequently forbade his Basque subjects to sail to Newfoundland. In Newfoundland itself their ships, especially the codfishing vessels, hung together for mutual protection, and concentrated particularly in Placentia Bay, making Placentia Harbour their rendezvous point. This alignment in-

26. D. B. Quinn, *Roanoke Voyages*, I (1955), 172–173, 234–242.

27. Lucien Cordeiro, "De la part prise par les Portugais dans la découverte de l'Amérique," *Questões Histórico-Coloniaes*, I (Lisbon, 1935), pp. 60–61 (60 being recorded from Aveiro as early as 1550).

volved mutual hostility in Newfoundland waters on the part of Spanish and French Basques toward English ships, which were at war, from 1585, with both Spain and Portugal. When attacked by English vessels, Spanish Basque ships tended to pretend to be French Basque in order to play on the presumed lesser hostility of the English. The French Basques must often have been very divided in their allegiances: they had many reasons to associate themselves with their fellow Basques, but they also had a considerable trade with England, especially as whale oil tended to be available to the English only through French Basque ports.[28]

After 1589 a further European division made itself felt in Newfoundland waters. Civil war in France, following the accession of Henry IV to the throne, tended to throw fishermen from towns aligned with the Catholic League, mainly Bretons, into alliance with the Basques against the English; while the loyalist towns like La Rochelle and those of Normandy, whether Huguenot or not, tended to ally with the English. Many fishermen, especially on the Banks, went on with their trade without being deflected by European divisions, but there was some polarization in the fishery. The English and the ships from the loyalist French towns continued to hold most of the eastern shores of Newfoundland, the Basques and Bretons the rest, so that when one group strayed into the confines of the other there was liable to be conflict. Though still entirely uncolonized, Newfoundland began to be regarded possessively by increasingly divided fishing interests.

Each of the European powers tended to assume that Newfoundland and its dependencies belonged to it in some way, though by the end of the sixteenth century no test of such claims had been made either by force or in law. The Portuguese regarded the Baccalaos or *Terra Nova* as definitively theirs—both by right of discovery by the Corte Reals and by its long-assumed position to the east of the 1494 treaty line with Spain. The repeated renewal of early charters and of colonizing attempts, noted above, indicate that this view was maintained effectively until at least 1580. Even Spain was inclined to admit some Portuguese claim to part of the territories

28. See H. A. Innis, "The Rise and Fall of the Spanish Fishery in Newfoundland," *Proceedings and Transactions of the Royal Society of Canada*, 3rd series, XXV (1931), sect 2, 51–70; Cell, *English Enterprise*, pp. 48–49; and below, p. 523. I am indebted to Mrs Selma Barkham for her help on this still clouded area.

in this area, at least before the development of the Spanish Basque whale fisheries in the 1540s. Both as the "Baccalaos" in Pedro Menéndez de Avilés's commission in 1565 and as "La Provincia de Tierra Nueva"—a term especially though not exclusively used for the parts of southern Labrador frequented by the whalers—Newfoundland was claimed firmly by Spain in the later sixteenth century, possibly at least in part because it had become clear that it was, after all, within the Spanish zone under the 1494 treaty. From the time that the concept of New France was formulated by Verrazzano and consolidated by Cartier's voyages, Terre-Neuve is clearly regarded as French, and as such it is incorporated in grants of authority over French possessions issued from 1577. The English equally clearly regarded Newfoundland as theirs by right of discovery and annexation by the Cabots, even if in late sixteenth-century accounts the identity of the discoverer, John Cabot, tended to get confused with that of his son, and the precise circumstances of the annexation in 1497 to have become obscured by the passage of time. The priority asserted for English port admirals was an expression of this belief. It was consolidated by the formal re-annexation on August 5, 1583, when Gilbert asserted Queen Elizabeth's title before a number of foreign fishermen; and subsequently, early in the seventeenth century, James I on this assumption proceeded to issue grants to colonizing groups to settle on the island. The economic importance of the Newfoundland area is emphasized by all these proceedings, but they did not before 1600 give firm rights of possession in international law to any one European nation.

The primary importance of Newfoundland was economic rather than political. Yet it remained of considerable interest at the political level, since it was the single point on the shores of North America where the interests, the subjects and the ships of all the European powers with any interest in or concern for North America met. Consequently, it is here that we would expect European political rivalries to be most directly represented in the western Atlantic. As has been shown, the changing balance in the relations between European states did have an appreciable effect on relations between fishermen of one country and another in Newfoundland waters. To some extent, after 1580, the balance of relationships in Europe was quite closely reflected in Newfoundland, even affecting the eco-

nomic circumstances of the fishery. At the same time, none of the European powers seriously wished to get involved in an all-out struggle with the others for territory in or near Newfoundland, since none of them had the naval forces to spare for such an operation. The possibility of establishing something of a monopoly in the fishery did crop up from time to time, but its feasibility was thought dubious except by a few enthusiasts. The benefits of such a monopoly appeared remote and insubstantial, while the continuance of the traditional fishing conventions seemed to offer continuing rewards to most of the parties concerned. Thus, although political rivalries in Europe could and did affect Newfoundland, the fishery as a whole continued generally unaffected by them, since its agreed economic basis proved able to withstand political pressures.

# CHAPTER 15

# The Search for a Passage Around North America

SO far as is known, Sebastian Cabot invented the concept of a Northwest Passage around North America though the Corte Reals may possibly have anticipated him. That he set sail in 1508 or thereabouts in search of a route around the newly discovered lands to the west appears unquestionable. Why should he have done so? Either he was armed with the conclusions of the Bristol voyagers of 1497 and later that the landmass facing western Europe was not Asia but an independent intervening entity; or else he had become aware of, and accepted, the views expressed in the world map and globe of Martin Waldeseemüller published at Saint-Dié in 1507, which showed for the first time a continent set in the ocean opposite western Europe which was not Asia. Cabot's voyage took him into high latitudes, but how high cannot be ascertained. They are variously indicated as between 52°, approximating to Hamilton Inlet on the Labrador coast; to 60°, namely, the entrance to Hudson Strait; or even, as he was ultimately to claim, to 67° 30′, well up the east coast of Baffin Island. On his return he made a long coasting voyage down the eastern North American coast, no doubt looking for western passages in lower latitudes as he went. From the time of his return he was a propagandist for the existence of a passage to the northwest.[1]

The Corte Real brothers had been the pioneers of the exploration

1. Quinn, *England and the Discovery of America*, pp. 138–431, and pp. 132–135 above.

of the Labrador coast. It would seem—though we know little of it so far—that once North America was identified as a separate continent the Portuguese, and more specifically the inheritors of the Corte Real family charters, regarded the finding of the passage as a peculiarly Portuguese objective; and that some of the many Portuguese fishing voyages to Newfoundland may well have attempted to probe the approaches to a possible passage, these attempts being continued down to the 1570s. The appearance of a strait extending from the Atlantic to the Pacific, and named the Strait of the Three Brothers in honor of the Corte Real pioneers on the Gemma Frisius globe, usually dated 1537, embodied this tradition.[2] The appearance of a northerly channel on this globe was characteristic of most globes and world maps later in the century, though the name was not necessarily maintained. Further, a passage into western North America also emerges on such maps and globes, continuous with that opposite Europe, which gets the name of the Strait of Anian, and is a prominent feature of such influential maps as Mercator's world map of 1569.

The possible existence of a passage in temperate waters was widely canvassed in the 1520s. The expeditions of Verrazzano for France, Gomes for Spain, and Rut for England were all largely influenced by the discovery by Magellan of a Southwest Passage around South America. The John Rut expedition in 1527 seems to have made an effort to pursue Cabot's old objective, losing a ship in the process, before being directed southward to less arduous climates. Robert Thorne in 1527 endeavored to break away from this stereotype and advised Henry VIII that a voyage over the North Pole was the best way to reach Asia, since he believed the northern seas to be open. This view was revived by Roger Barlow in 1540–1 after he returned from accompanying Sebastian Cabot on his search for a further Southwest Passage through the Río de la Plata, 1526–30. But although we hear of plans to send out ships for this purpose several times, no attempt to verify the theory appears to have been made.[3]

2. Sketch in W. F. Ganong, *Crucial Maps* (1964), p. 200.

3. Richard Hakluyt, in *Divers voyages touching the discovery of America* (1582) (facsimile in D. B. Quinn, *Richard Hakluyt, Editor* [2 vols., Amsterdam, 1967]), first printed Thorne's proposals. They are discussed in J. A. Williamson, *The Voyages of the Cabots*

The Cartier-Roberval voyages between 1534 and 1543 all had the possibilities of access to the western ocean in mind—either by the discovery of a passage from the St. Lawrence Valley, or by the disclosure of a watershed giving access to the Pacific which might serve the same purpose though with less convenience. It was not until the return of Sebastian Cabot to England in 1547 that the question of northern passages was taken up with vigor in England and France. Cabot, from his past record, might be thought to have been committed to a northwest venture. Yet when at last he had attracted sufficient mercantile support, the Willoughby-Chancellor expedition in 1553 was directed to the northeast, not the northwest; and the Muscovy Company which emerged from later ventures devoted itself almost wholly to the trade with Russia, with only occasional attempts—notably in 1556 and 1580—to discover a passage to the northeast.

The next attempt to plan northerly voyages sprang from this secondary consideration of the Muscovy Company. Anthony Jenkinson, their ablest agent in Russia, put forward a proposition for a northerly voyage in 1565, declaring his preference for a northeasterly over a northwesterly venture. At about the same time, Humphrey Gilbert began to urge the queen to sponsor a northwest expedition. The two protagonists were brought together and induced to cooperate, Gilbert converting Jenkinson to his view that a northwest venture offered—though on what appear to us slender grounds—the best prospect. The Muscovy Company was not anxious to get involved in such a venture, but there was enough official interest in the project for Gilbert to draw up an academic treatise on the subject in 1566, and for the project to be continued in 1567. However, Gilbert was distracted by military service in Ireland and Jenkinson by a further Russian venture, so that the matter was left unresolved.

After 1573, Martin Frobisher, as a seagoing soldier, and Michael Lok, a London merchant specializing in Mediterranean trade, took it up independently and in 1575 got some encouragement to launch a venture. Dr. John Dee, the mathematician who was now actively

1929), pp. 255–67. Roger Barlow, *A Briefe Summe of Geographie*, edited by E. G. R. Taylor (Hakluyt Society, London, 1932), sets out (pp. 179–182) the possibilities of a northern venture.

taking up cartographical pursuits, approved, and so did the elder Richard Hakluyt, now a geographical consultant, both of them offering advice. Sir Humphrey Gilbert was induced by the writer George Gascoigne to take out his old discourse and revise it for the benefit of the new venture, and it was then published as *A discourse of a discoverie for a new passage to Cataia* (London, 1576). This gave a slogan for the enterprise: "it were the onely way for our princes, to possesse the welth of all the East partes."[4]

The first northwest venture represented the enthusiastic hopes of a small group of men; Michael Lok and Martin Frobisher enlisted subscriptions from a few eminent merchants and financiers, notably Sir Thomas Gresham, in their highly speculative venture, which was on a modest scale.[5] In June 1576, Frobisher took the *Gabriel*, the *Michael* and also a small pinnace from London to a little north of Cape Farewell. He then sailed westward, losing the *Michael* (she went home), and fetching up at a "strait" which he named Frobisher Strait (now Frobisher Bay, since he did not discover at this time that it was only an inlet) on Baffin Island. At this position (63° 45' N., 68° 30' W.) they considered that American land lay to the south and Asia to the north—no doubt thinking that they had reached the old Horn of Asia and that it overlapped at this point with America. Contacts with Eskimo brought both gain and loss: gain through the first English opportunity to observe their way of life; loss when the Eskimo seized the ship's boat and made off with it and its five men. Hesitating, with only thirteen men and one Eskimo prisoner, to risk a voyage through the supposed strait, Frobisher returned to England in October.

His claim to have discovered the opening to the Northwest Passage was received with interest, even though he had not proved that

4. For the Gilbert-Jenkinson debates, see Quinn, *The Voyages and Colonising Enterprises of Sir Humphrey Gilbert* (1940), I, 4–11, 105–117; and for the *Discourse*, I, 129–168, a facsimile of which (Manston, Yorks., 1972) has also been published.

5. Vilhjalmur Stefansson (ed.), *The Three Voyages of Martin Frobisher*, 2 vols. (London, 1938) has a very good introduction on the Frobisher voyages and prints almost all the existing materials. Of these the most important were George Best, *A true discourse of the late voyages of discoverie, for the finding of a passage to Cathaya, by the Northweast* (London, 1578), covering all three voyages; Dionyse Settle, *A true reporte of the laste voyage into the west and northwest regions & c. 1577* (London, 1577); and Thomas Ellis, *A true report of the third and last voyage into Meta Incognita . . . Anno 1578* (London, 1578). They were all reprinted by Richard Hakluyt in *Principal navigations*, III (London, 1600).

it led any distance to the west. What excited much more interest, however, was a piece of mineral picked up on Halls Island, at the mouth of the "strait," and shown to Lok. After varying reports, several assays asserted that there was gold in the ore. On the strength of this, the Company of Cathay was chartered in March 1577 with Lok as life governor and Frobisher as admiral (of Cathay, amongst other places). The seal of government approval was gained by an investment of £1,000 by Queen Elizabeth. The queen's ship, the *Aid,* was lent to assist the *Gabriel* and *Michael,* and the ships left the Thames late in May. An uneventful voyage brought them into the "strait" on July 17, where they proceeded to forget about the passage, lading some 200 tons of ore which was safely brought back to England in September.

The queen was cautious about identifying the new land as Asia: she gave it the noncommittal name of Meta Incognita, under which it was to appear on maps for a generation. An Eskimo man, woman and child were brought back to Bristol. After being induced to give various demonstrations of their kayak at Bristol, the man died (he had sustained broken ribs on the voyage which presumably pierced his lungs), and was soon followed by the woman and child (the first captive had survived little longer in 1576). Although the assayers were not in agreement, there was soon what seemed to be adequate proof that the ore contained both gold and silver, and preparations were made to smelt it at Deptford. But without waiting for the process to produce more than samples (which were in fact faked), a great new expedition was planned and carried through in 1578. The *Aid,* under Frobisher's command, now headed a fleet of fifteen vessels. It was intended to establish a permanent mining camp, and a large building carried in sections for erection on the spot was brought along for this purpose. One hundred and twenty colonists were to be maintained, after 2,000 tons of ore had been extracted and brought home. They set off on May 27, 1578 from Gravesend. Southern Greenland was duly sighted, and here Frobisher made a landing, annexing the land to the queen under the name of West England. But sailing westward this time involved great difficulties since the weather was very bad. The bark *Dennis* foundered with part of the building and much of the stores for the colony on board, thus putting an effective end to the plan for a mining settlement. The *Aid* sailed too far to the south and continued in open sea well to the

west of the assumed position of the previously located "strait." Frobisher, in fact, had entered Hudson Strait and could have proceeded much further along this "Mistaken Strait," as he called it. But duty called him to mining rather than exploration, so that he robbed himself of the honor of naming what was to be Hudson Strait in order to obtain the necessary ore.

Most of his vessels eventually arrived off Halls Island, where they proceeded to fulfill their quota of ore. Edward Fenton offered to remain with a nominal colony until the next year, and a small building was erected, but it was decided that the risk was too great. Thirteen ships accordingly came home to find that no bullion had been or could be extracted from the previous cargo. There were already financial problems and the Company collapsed almost immediately in an atmosphere of recrimination and debt, much of which settled round the neck of Michael Lok, whose credit had been too heavily pledged. Though attempts were made during the next five years to win some return from the ore, they all proved fruitless.

The failure of this highly prestigious and well-capitalized venture (some £20,000 was lost in the third voyage) was significant. It showed that gold and silver alone could attract high investment in American ventures at this time and that searches for a Northwest Passage or even for places in temperate North America where Englishmen might settle were much less attractive to those court circles, city merchants and landed proprietors willing to gamble in marginal investments. The opening of a possible route to the Northwest Passage and the great publicity which the ventures received somewhat balanced the eventual failure of the Company of Cathay and the continued ill-repute it gave to western speculations.

On the cartographical side, Frobisher and his associates were obsessed with the hypothetical map of the Zeno voyages published in Venice in 1558. This showed a Greenland far to the north, to the southeast of which lay another land of Friesland. This was equated with the southern Greenland coasts sighted and visited by Frobisher. His West England we know was Greenland: to him it was an independent island which was to remain a long time on the maps as did a fictitious island southeast of Friesland "discovered" on the return voyage in 1578, the Island of Buss. At the same time the partial profile of eastern Baffin Island which emerged on the maps represented the first configuration of the American Arctic.

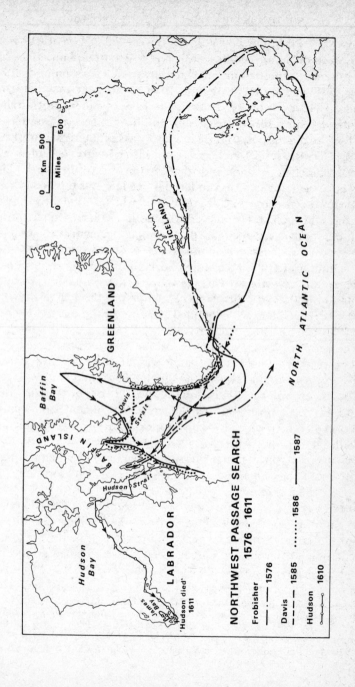

NORTHWEST PASSAGE SEARCH
1576 - 1611

Frobisher ——— 1576

Davis —— 1585  ········ 1586  ——— 1587

Hudson ⊶⊶⊶ 1610

GREENLAND

ICELAND

NORTH ATLANTIC OCEAN

Baffin Bay

BAFFIN ISLAND

Davis Strait

Hudson Strait

LABRADOR

Hudson Bay

James Bay

'Hudson died' 1611

0 Km 500

0 Miles 500

After the Frobisher voyages, Northwest Passage ventures were conducted on a more modest scale and concentrated on discovery, not potential exploitation. Sir Humphrey Gilbert assumed that his generously vague patent of June 1578 to discover new lands included the whole of the North American continent not already occupied. After his unsuccessful colonizing reconnaissance in 1578–9, he did his best to raise money by assigning rights to all and sundry. To Dr. John Dee he assigned his rights to all lands north of 50°, namely, Labrador and what lay beyond to the north. This may have been for services rendered, since Dee was busy constructing maps (he gave one to Gilbert in 1582) which confidently showed passages through and round America both in Arctic and temperate latitudes, and was also engaged in conducting seances to summon up supernatural guidance on the discovery of a passage. Dee joined with Humphrey Gilbert's brother Adrian in 1583 to attempt to get a charter for a Northwest Passage venture, but was distracted by an invitation to Poland which he accepted before the end of the year. It was Adrian Gilbert who obtained a patent for the search in February 1584, after his half brother Walter Ralegh had also dropped out of the project. We know little of Adrian Gilbert's occupations or resources at this time, except that he was interested in silver extraction, and may perhaps have thought of confirming the value or otherwise of Frobisher's mine on the spot. He did not pursue these possibilities, however, but instead enlisted William Sanderson, a London merchant with a weakness for exploration-speculation, and also the navigator John Davis.[6]

Davis was a thoroughly professional seaman and an expert navigator. With the *Sunshine* and the *Moonshine* he left Dartmouth on June 7, 1585, and reached land at Southeast Greenland—"The Land of Desolation," as he called it—before turning Cape Farewell and entering Godthåb Fjord, which he named Gilbert Sound. Setting sail to the northwest, he reached the coast of Baffin Island well to the north of Frobisher's area. At 66° 40′, he named a high cliff Mount Raleigh and eventually entered the wide mouth of Cumber-

6. Richard Hakluyt printed the narratives of the Davis voyages in 1585–87 in *Principall navigations* (London, 1589), and reprinted them in *Principal navigations*, III (London, 1600). They were collected with other material in Albert Hastings Markham (ed.), *The Voyages and Works of John Davis* (London, Hakluyt Society, 1880). Clements R. Markham, *A Life of John Davis* (London, 1891), is a sound narrative. A brief account is in Ernest S. Dodge, *Northwest by Sea* (New York, 1961), pp. 87–102.

land Sound. This he penetrated some way, but was unable to determine how far it extended. Like Frobisher before him, he wanted to find a strait and believed he had done so. His two small vessels returned at the end of September after an expeditious and relatively inexpensive voyage, which at least gave renewed hope of a passage.

In 1586 further monies were raised by Sanderson and the City of Exeter so that a more ambitious expedition could set out. This encountered greater difficulties than had been expected. Two ships, the *Sunshine* and the *North Star,* were assigned to follow the East Greenland coast northward but in fact made little attempt to do so. They went first to the latitude of Iceland and worked round South Greenland, hoping to meet Davis at Gilbert Sound but missing him. Davis had made directly for Gilbert Sound. There he met Eskimo whom he had first encountered the previous year. Close contacts were made with them, and furs and kayaks bought, while a pinnace for coastal survey was constructed and an experiment made in the close survey and charting of a limited stretch of coast. Davis then went north to 63°, but found that ice barred his way, so he crossed to Baffin Island and continued his survey on the way south, having sent the *Mermaid* home with sick men. His object here was evidently to get a general picture of the coast all the way south to Newfoundland rather than to conduct detailed investigation of inlets.

In the *Moonshine* he passed the mouths of both Cumberland Sound and Frobisher Bay, and also, more significantly, failed to explore Frobisher's "Mistaken Strait," Hudson Strait. Davis's observations on the Labrador coast were valuable from the survey aspect but produced no evidence of a passage north of the Strait of Belle Isle. He returned from Newfoundland in October, later discovering that *North Star* had been lost on her homeward voyage. From the geographical viewpoint, the voyage was a fruitful one in confirming the outline of an extensive range of coast; but it had taken the search for a passage no further, since his total failure to enter and survey Cumberland Sound, let alone other inlets, left the quest where it had been. It might appear, that he was becoming skeptical about the chances of finding a passage in the low 60's and was attracted by a voyage in a much more northerly direction as being potentially more promising.

It was not easy to raise money for a third voyage in 1587, since Sanderson's resources were not unlimited. This time Davis in-

tended to penetrate as far north as he could on the west coast of Greenland, though he arranged with two additional ships to come part of the way to fish off Labrador, where he maintained the fishing was very good, and to rendezvous with him on that coast later in the year. In the *Sunshine* he sailed to Gilbert Sound and thence up a relatively ice-free coast of western Greenland. He was at 72° 12′ where he named a high point Sandersons Hope as the limit of his search when he failed to make way against strong northerly winds, though the sea was still clear. Convinced that there was hope of a passage there, he turned to the west and worked his way across to Baffin Island for a third time. He rediscovered Frobisher Bay (naming it Lumley Inlet) and recognized Frobisher's "Mistaken Strait." On this occasion, wind and floating ice prevented him from exploring it, though he named Cape Chidley at its southern limit; he did not find the fishing vessels on the Labrador coast—they had returned already. Davis was home by mid-September, full of optimism about the northerly channel which he had pioneered. But there was no more money and now political exigencies—the feared Armada —curtailed all inessential voyages for several years.

From seeing the Strait of Anian on the maps, it was a short step to making some attempt to find it. Humphrey Gilbert picked up a report that Fray Andrés de Urdaneta, who had sailed across the Pacific and back in the 1560s, had in fact come home around the north of the American continent and incorporated this view in his pamphlet in 1576. Indeed, discussion of the supposed strait had been going on in England for some time before Francis Drake was sent out to the Pacific in 1577, and he was instructed to investigate it. How seriously he took his commission has been debated, yet it is clear that when he left the Spanish-occupied Mexican coast he intended not only to careen his ship and rest his crew well to the north but also to make some search for an entrance to a strait, provided it was to be found in sufficiently low latitudes. He may or may not have reached as far north as 48° before he turned back, having made it clear that no strait opened eastward from California. His formal annexation of New Albion to the English crown in 1579, when he had found a good place to refit and rest, may have been done with the intention of providing an English claim to land from which the supposed strait could be more fully explored at a later stage. Or it may merely have been a gesture of defiance against

Spain, one which he thought might appeal to the queen even if it was of no immediate value or relevance to England.[7]

At the same time, the concept of a strait from Pacific to Atlantic did not fade away. John Davis, after his brave voyages into northern waters of 1585–87, turned his attention to the Pacific. When Thomas Cavendish planned a voyage to China by way of the Straits of Magellan in 1591, Davis determined to accompany him as far as he could and then set out on a lone attempt to find the elusive strait. But his gallant achievement in the *Desire* in passing the straits in 1592 were frustrated by weather and he limped back almost defeated in 1593.[8]

From time to time in the later sixteenth century, the concept of exploring the western coast of North America appears in Spanish plans. It was not however taken very seriously. There is some indication that Sebastian Vizcaino in his voyage of 1602–3 hoped to find such a strait, but he made no attempt to penetrate north of about 43°, and the notion petered out, to be revived occasionally as an object of academic discussion or projector's lore.[9]

In the 1590s, the European interest in northern passages shifted to the Dutch attempts to penetrate a Northeast Passage, particularly the voyages of Willem Barents of 1595–97 which culminated in his death, after his dramatic success in wintering far to the north in Novaya Zemlia in 1596–7. But by the end of this series, Dutch interest had switched to the East Indies and the direct route to Asia round the Cape of Good Hope. The English East India Company also was formed in 1600 and sent out its first conventional expedition to the Indies in 1601. Before it had returned, however, the Company was persuaded, as a second string to its bow, to sponsor a revival of the Northwest Passage ventures in 1602. George Waymouth was commissioned by the Company to go to China via the Passage, bearing letters from Queen Elizabeth to the emperor of

7. See the discussion in K. R. Andrews, "The Aims of Drake's Expedition of 1577–1580," *American Historical Review*, LXXIII (1968), 737–739; Andrews, *Drake's Voyages* (London, 1967), pp. 46–50, 53, 74, 76–178. Documents and further discussion will be found in Zelia Nuttall, *New Light on Drake* (London, Hakluyt Society, 1914), and in Henry R. Wagner, *Sir Francis Drake's Voyage Around the World* (Berkeley, 1926).

8. See D. B. Quinn, *The Last Voyage of Thomas Cavendish* (Chicago, 1975), pp. 7–9.

9. See Henry R. Wagner, *Spanish Voyages to the Northwest Coast of America in the Sixteenth Century* (San Francisco, 1929), pp. 176–178, 273, 376.

China. Under his command, the *Discovery* and the *Godspeed* sailed from London on May 2. The season was bad so that he could not find his way easily along the shores of Baffin Island even in late June and July. He reached 63°, entered Frobisher Bay, explored it fully and found it not to be a strait. He remarked on the current streaming from Hudson Strait, then entered harbors in Labrador. His crew was unsettled, afraid of ice and winds, and eventually they forced him to return. He arrived back in Dartmouth early in August.[10]

It was Henry Hudson who gave a new dimension to the northern explorations.[11] In 1607, in an English ship, Hudson sailed up the east coast of Greenland to the unprecedented latitude of over 80° but could make his way no further north. In 1608 he was frustrated by ice from passing Novaya Zemlia to the northeast, so he then set his sights on passing to the west of Greenland and penetrating the strait from which Frobisher, Davis and Waymouth had recorded the occurrence of an easterly current—the strait that in the end was to bear his own name. Meantime he could get no further employment in England. In the Dutch service he made another unsuccessful voyage in 1609 to Novaya Zemlia, but recrossed the ocean to the western Atlantic toward southern Greenland and then turned south, hoping to link up the hitherto unexplored parts of the North American coast with those recently put on the map by Captain John Smith of which he had seen a copy. It was this voyage which was crowned by success in the rediscovery of the Hudson River, lost sight of since Verrazzano's voyage.

Finally, in 1610, Hudson returned to England, where he found that by this time an enthusiastic group of London supporters for the Northwest Passage concept had appeared. Backed by Sir Thomas Smith and other London magnates, he sailed from the Thames on April 17, 1610. He reached Frobisher Bay on June 9 and worked down the coast to the south of Baffin Island in difficult ice conditions. Between June 15 and August 3 he worked his way carefully into the strait, identifying both its northern and southern shores, until on August 2, as he says, "we were in the mouth of a Streight."

10. Waymouth's narrative was printed by Samuel Purchas, *Hakluytus Posthumus or Purchas his pilgrimes*, 4 vols. (London, 1625), III, 809–814; the narrated voyage is in Dodge, *Northwest by Sea*, pp. 103–107.

11. The principal documents are in Samuel Purchas, *Hakluytus Posthumus or Purchas his pilgrimes*, III, 596–610, edited by G. M. Asher, *Hudson's Voyages* (London, Hakluyt Society, 1860). There is a short narrative in Dodge, *Northwest by Sea*, pp. 120–126.

The next day, his journal continues, "we put through the narrow passage. . . . The head of this entrance on the South side I named Cape Worsenholme [after the merchant John Wolstenholme], and the head on the North-wester shoare, I called Cape Digs [after Sir Dudley Digges]."[12]

The rest of the story we have only from Abacuk Pricket, one of the survivors. They worked their way slowly down the eastern shore of Hudson Strait, not knowing that they were entering the great pocket of James Bay, where on November 1 they hauled the *Discovery* ashore and were soon frozen in. The men had been peculiarly unruly and Hudson had not endeared himself to most of them on the voyage. The winter was not as bad as it might have been since there were birds wintering in the area for several months which supplied them with food. The appearance of Eskimo gave promise of meat, but this was not fulfilled because they did not return; as the ice broke, fishing became possible, though it did not continue to supply enough food for their needs. The men were in poor shape and were already almost ungovernable. The crisis came when the ship cleared from the ice in June and it became clear that Hudson intended to make some further exploration to the west before turning for home.

On June 22 there was a mutiny; Hudson was seized and with his own supporters and the weaker men was placed in the shallop and deserted by the ship. Presumably they all died within a short time. The initial phase of the return voyage was accomplished successfully and the *Discovery* got back through the strait, but dissension and disease so complicated the voyage that only eight men survived to bring her into an Irish port. The mutineers reported that a Northwest Passage had been discovered and this, together with the fact that precise evidence of what had happened during the mutiny was lacking, prevented proceedings against them from being pressed. The impression that the Northwest Passage had been found appeared to justify all the efforts which had been put into the search by English crews since 1576.

The Danes made their reappearance in Greenland waters at the opening of the seventeenth century. The kings of Denmark-Norway

12. Purchas, *Hakluytus Posthumus or Purchas his pilgrimes*, II, 597.

had always maintained in theory a monopoly right to control northern waters, which in turn the English and Dutch refused to recognize. The revelation of the West Greenland coast by English Northwest Passage explorers led to the revival of Danish claims. In 1605 Christian IV employed two English captains, John Cunningham and John Knight, and a pilot, James Hall, to go with a Danish nobleman, Godske Lindenov, to search for the by now somewhat myth-covered medieval settlers in Greenland.[13] Lindenov, in the *Røde Løve,* became detached from the rest and reached the west coast where, near modern Fishenaesset, he met Eskimo and traded with them, then kidnapped two and returned to Copenhagen. Cunningham led the *Trost* and the *Marekatten* well up the west coast, exploring between 66° 35′ and 68° 35′. He traded with Eskimo in Itivdleq Fjord, kidnapped four of them, fought with others and returned safely, having also brought—as Frobisher had done in 1576—some intriguing mineral samples which were declared to contain silver.

This led to a more elaborate expedition under Lindenov in 1606 to exploit the supposed mineral riches, Cunningham and Hall also taking part. The supposed mine at 67° 4′ N. was excavated but, as in 1578, the ore brought back in two of the ships was declared worthless. No signs of earlier European occupation had been found. Scholarly opinion now turned to the view that the early Eastern Settlement had been in Southeast Greenland, but an expedition in 1607 was unable to approach the coast. The Danish initiative in Greenland had proved fruitless; yet it indicated that the region was ceasing to be an English preserve, and in fact both Dutch and Danish ships were to penetrate these Arctic waters within the following ten years.

The English, however, continued in the lead. The discovery of Hudson Bay as told by the survivors of the 1610–11 expedition stimulated large-scale commercial activity in London. Sir Thomas Smith headed a syndicate amongst whom it was commonly believed that the passage had at last been found. A charter was applied for to James I and was granted on July 26, 1612, to the Governor and Company of the Merchants of London, Discoverers of the Northwest Passage. All previous concessions were replaced by a monopoly to the Company of any passage north of 58°, extending to the

13. See Finn Gad, *History of Greenland,* I (London, 1970), 216–226.

north or northwest to China or other parts of Asia.

The first expedition, under William Button, had gone ahead in April so that any chance of rescuing Hudson could be taken and the supposed passage explored at the earliest opportunity. Button in the *Resolution,* with the *Discovery* under John Ingram, entered Hudson Strait without difficulty. Failing to search for Hudson in James Bay, they continued westward to encounter the western shore of Hudson Bay and an apparently unbroken coastline, at 60° 40′. Naming the place Hopes Checked, Button sailed south until he came to the mouth of a river which he named Port Nelson, where he decided to camp for the winter. He lost men through exposure and scurvy and in the spring of 1613 set off in *Discovery* alone. He traced Roes Welcome Sound as far north as 65° but concluded it was a bay, and then turned east along the south coast of Southampton Island and Coats Island, which he thought to be a continuous landmass, thence into Hudson Strait and home in September 1613,[14] to belie most of the hopes of the London Company. William Baffin was to make significant voyages for the Company to the north along the Greenland coast in later years, but Button's voyage was virtually the final stage in northwestern exploration at this time, the expedition of Luke Foxe and Thomas James in 1631–2 being a mere appendix to the earlier efforts.

The search for a Northwest Passage in the sixteenth and early seventeenth centuries was a visionary commercial enterprise—a gamble businessmen were prepared to take on the advice of imperfectly informed geographical experts, which, if it had come off, would have seriously infringed the Iberian monopoly of eastern trade. By the end of our period, both the Dutch and the English had demonstrated that the longer but less hazardous route round the Cape of Good Hope could be used profitably to make that challenge. The lure of a Northwest Passage diminished. In the history of American exploration these episodes are valuable since they did much, if not enough, to define the northern limits of the continent, and produced a substantial amount of information about the eastern fringes of Arctic America. The waste of money, especially on ill-founded mineral ventures, could be balanced to some extent by

14. Dodge, *Northwest by Sea,* pp. 127–134.

the experience the expeditions gave to captains, pilots and seamen. The Frobisher voyages paved the way for more regular, safer voyages across the Atlantic by Englishmen at lower latitudes. It is probable also that the diversion of effort and money in these ventures postponed the application of capital and personnel to the solution of the problems of North American settlement. Though the balancesheet of their influence is hard to draw, the Northwest Passage expeditions are in no way irrelevant to the major story of early North American discovery and settlement.

They demonstrate how eclectic and unsystematic the exploration of North American waters was at this time. North America appeared to many of those interested in commerce rather than colonization to be a more risky speculation even than expeditions to Arctic waters in search of an access route to Asia. The Far East was a first-class overseas objective, since all trade with Asia was believed to fall automatically into the category of a high profit investment. For a long time North America was considered very much a second-class investment where, even if there were profits to be made, they would be relatively modest. This can be seen from the example of privateering; once English vessels began to make really high profits by seizing Spanish ships either in, or coming from, the Caribbean, the money available for colonizing ventures in North America shrank away almost to nothing. At the same time the ebb and flow of interest in Northwest Passage ventures is often difficult to explain precisely. It may be that in the longer run too, some of those who began to interest themselves marginally in America through investment in Northwest Passage voyages were led to become interested also in more prosaic ventures further south, and that the Virginia Company owed some, at least, of its subscriptions to men who had first become aware of North America as a sphere for investment through being involved in Northwest Passage projects.

# CHAPTER 16

## *The Emergence of New England and the Maritimes, 1580–1612*

---

JOHN Smith said—in *A description of New England* (London, 1616) —"That part wee call New England is betwixt the degrees of 41. and 45." This corresponds well enough with the coastline from the mouth of the Hudson (40° 40′ N.) to almost the northern tip of Nova Scotia. In the sixteenth century, after Verrazzano's voyage of 1524, the area from the Hudson to the Penobscot, most of which comprises modern New England, was known as Norumbega, while from the Penobscot north to Cape Breton was known to the French as Acadie (or Acadia). In dealing with the sixteenth and early seventeenth centuries, these names are often appropriate. Economically, Acadia links up closely with the fishing, whaling and fur trading of both the St. Lawrence Basin and the Newfoundland-Labrador complex, and there is much overlap in French activity between these three divisions. Sable Island is really one fragment of Acadia, but it is most conveniently dealt with in connection with the St. Lawrence.

After Verrazzano had sampled the attractions of the Hudson estuary and of Narragansett Bay, and Gomes had mapped in 1525 the coasts of New England, we have little or nothing new on this area in maps or narratives between 1525 and 1580. It is very probable that there were occasional fishing and fur-trading voyages along the coast by Basques and Bretons, and perhaps by Portuguese and English vessels as well; but this is a chapter of history which it is not possible to tell unless new information appears. Acadia appears

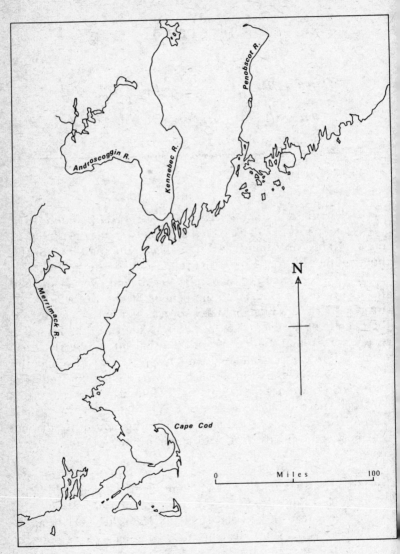

New England

fitfully as part of the approaches to the St. Lawrence and it is clear that French pilots, such as Jean Alfonce de Saintonge, were familiar with most of its coast,[1] from the Penobscot north to Cape Breton. Cape Breton Island itself was essentially part of the fishing and fur-trading zone, but trading with Micmac for furs and ranging the shores of Nova Scotia and possibly Maine was not unusual for Basque and Breton summer traders and fishermen, though again so far we lack detailed maps and narratives.

A change takes place in the late 1570s, which is evident in 1580. In that year the English scholar John Dee made a map of North America for Queen Elizabeth[2] that showed an exaggerated version of Verrazzano's coastline of Norumbega, with several major inlets, one of which was intended to be Verrazzano's "Refugio," Narragansett Bay (which Dee called the Bay of the Five Islands). This was apparently part of a propaganda campaign carried on by Dee and the elder Richard Hakluyt in the interests of Sir Humphrey Gilbert to encourage English exploring and colonizing ventures in this area. As we have seen, Gilbert had obtained a patent from the queen in June 1578 authorizing him to discover and occupy lands hitherto unknown and to attach them to the English crown. He interpreted this, apparently correctly, as giving him a monopoly control of English enterprises to North America outside the area occupied by Spain. We cannot say to what part of the American coast his 1578 expedition was directed, though probably fairly far to the south; after its failure, he had turned by 1580 seriously to consider inhabiting Verrazzano's Norumbega.

A small vessel, the *Squirrel,* under the command of Simão Fernandes, crossed the Atlantic in April 1580 to some part of New England and brought back specimen hides, probably of moose, arriving home again before the end of June. Another English vessel under John Walker, in the same year, penetrated 27 miles up the Penobscot, raided an Abenaki village, and stole three hundred hides (again probably moose) while also bringing specimens of minerals said to show traces of silver. Consequently, in 1582 Gilbert

1. Jean Alfonce, *La cosmographie,* edited by G. Musset (Paris, 1904), pp. 475–503; H. P. Biggar, *Voyages of Jacques Cartier* (1924), pp. 278–303; H. Harrisse, *Découverte et évolution cartographique de Terre-Neuve* (1900), pp. 153–154.

2. Sections of the map are reproduced in E. G. R. Taylor, *The Original Writings and Correspondence of the Two Richard Hakluyts,* II (London, Hakluyt Society, 1935), and D. B. Quinn, *The Voyages and Colonising Enterprises of Sir Humphrey Gilbert,* II (1940).

launched a major colonizing enterprise. He sold off very large quantities of land, sight unseen, around the Dee River and the "Bay of the Five Islands" (which we can only conclude was Narragansett Bay), and one of the rivers at its head—though we have no proof that Fernandes rediscovered this entry in 1580; the dispositions may merely have been made on the strength of Dee's maps. The reconnaissance expeditions planned by his purchasers and Gilbert in 1582 came to nothing. In 1583 he himself set out with five vessels, apparently intending to sail down the North American coast from Newfoundland to some point in New England which he proposed to allocate as a settlement site. But his attempt on the way out to make Newfoundland an English outpost, based on the licensing and taxation of the European fishery, diverted him from further exploration.

Gilbert had three ships only when he sailed from St. John's on August 20, 1583. He lost his largest ship, the *Delight,* on Sable Island and, with the remaining two, one of them the tiny *Squirrel,* turned homeward on August 31, only to be lost himself on the voyage. A single vessel, the *Golden Hind* under Edward Hayes, reached England.[3] By this time both Gilbert and Hayes had turned from their commitment to establish a settlement in Norumbega to the belief that control of Newfoundland by an English colony was likely to be more effective and more immediately profitable. After news of the disaster to Gilbert reached England, some of those who had acquired rights to New England lands, notably the Catholic leader Sir George Peckham, attempted to raise money and men by various propaganda devices to implement the intended settlement in Norumbega. They failed to get an expedition to sea. Christopher Carleill was also at work to bring out a small colony to Acadia (or so it would seem), which would be involved mainly in trading activities, and he appears to have aspired to control some of the approaches to the St. Lawrence. Carleill set out in June or early July 1584 with three ships and a pinnace, but brought his expedition no further west than Ireland. It may well be that his men refused to follow him in an American venture when there was employment for them, which Carleill eventually took, in Ireland. With this, the prac-

3. Documentation of the Gilbert ventures of 1580–83 will be found in Quinn, *Gilbert,* I, 49–100, II, 239–482, and D. B. Quinn and N. M. Cheshire, *The New Found Land of Stephen Parmenius* (1972).

tical attempts by Englishmen to investigate Norumbega and Acadia and to settle colonies in both areas came to an end, although the memory of what had been planned and done remained, and was to be revived later.

The attractions of settlement in these latitudes in North America had been stressed in a number of tracts. In one published in 1582, the elder Richard Hakluyt had argued[4] in favor of colonizing parts of North America in the latitudes of France and Spain. Christopher Carleill in his *A breef and sommarie discourse uppon the entended voyage to the hethermost partes of America* (London, 1583)[5] set out in detail the advantages of settling about 40° or further to the north. Trade, especially in furs, agriculture, and accessibility to England would all help to assure a measure of success to cautious planters. Sir George Peckham's *A true reporte of the late discoveries . . . of the Newfound landes* (London, 1583)[6] spoke generally of settlement between 30° and 60° N., although most of his stress was on the more northern products that might be grown there. Richard Hakluyt the elder wrote another pamphlet of similar tenor,[7] which was said in 1602 to be directed toward planting between 40 and 42 degrees N., but to the effect that "this land that we purpose to direct our course to, lying in part in the 40 degree of latitude, being in like heat as Lisbone in Portugall doth, and in the more Southerly part as the most southerly coast of Spaine doth [36–37° N.]." We can see from this that Norumbega was considered to have a Mediterranean-type climate, and that it was proposed to concentrate on areas which extended southward from 40° as well as northward from it. Yet the lack of detailed and specific knowledge of climate, of natural resources, or even of coastal topography lent to most discussions of this sort an air of unreality.

At the same time, French commercial interests were making contacts with high officials and ecclesiastical leaders in an attempt to gain support for an enterprise in this area which might combine profit with political and missionary advantage. It would appear that

4. Richard Hakluyt, *Divers voyages touching the discoverie of America* (London, 1582), sig. K1–K3v.; facsimile in D. B. Quinn, *Richard Hakluyt, Editor*, 2 vols. (Amsterdam, 1967), II; see also Quinn, *Gilbert*, I, 181–186; Taylor, *Hakluyts*, I, 116–122.

5. Two editions of this tract were published in London in 1583, while manuscript versions also exist (several of which are collated in Quinn, *Gilbert*, II, 351–364).

6. Reprinted Quinn, *Gilbert*, II, 435–480.

7. Taylor, *Hakluyts*, II, 327–338.

reports on the fur-trading possibilities south of Cape Breton had reached France at a time, around 1580, when there was a revived interest in fur trading in the St. Lawrence, but we have no details about this. Étienne Bellenger, a Rouen merchant, was sent out under the auspices of the cardinal of Bourbon and the duc de Joyeuse to investigate the opportunities for combining a fur-trading post and a mission station.[8] His ship, the *Chardon*, examined and charted the coasts from Cape Breton southward into the Bay of Fundy, at the head of which the cardinal of Bourbon's Arms were affixed to a high tree, and the inner shore investigated past Grand Manan Island as far south as the Penobscot. The climate and natural products of the region were described favorably—it was said to lie between 42 and 44 degrees north, when in fact it is 2 degrees higher (44° to 46° N.). The intention was to found a trading post, apparently on the eastern side of modern Nova Scotia; but an Indian attack and the seizing of the ship's pinnace put an end to such plans and Bellenger came home with the furs he had collected. A further expedition was prepared in 1584 but we do not know what success it had. Then the cardinal and the duke turned to other projects. Whether a systematic French fur-trading organization developed to exploit this area in the years which followed is unknown.

The Bellenger enterprise in turn attracted the attention of the younger Richard Hakluyt, attached at the time to the English embassy in Paris. He obtained details early in 1584 from Bellenger himself and later seems to have acquired a map made by Jacques de Vaulx, derived in part from materials assembled on Bellenger's voyage. This he passed on to Edward Hayes, and he, together with Christopher Carleill (before the latter's death in 1593), wrote out a long argument in favor of settling these more northern latitudes in preference to those south of 40°.[9] The latitudes between 40 and 50 degrees were thought to have a climate which would suit Englishmen, as well as natural products which would assist their settlement and soil that might easily be cultivated. They did not, in this document, concentrate solely on the region south of Cape Breton but

8. D. B. Quinn, "The Voyage of Étienne Bellenger to the Maritimes in 1583," *Canadian Historical Review*, XLIII (1962), 328–343; "Étienne Bellenger," in *Dictionary of Canadian Biography*, I (Toronto, 1965).

9. Cambridge University Library, MS Dd.3.85, an extract from which is given in Quinn, *North American Discovery* (1971), pp. 244–247.

included the St. Lawrence Valley within their purview. It relied to some extent on materials Hakluyt had collected on the Bellenger voyage, and was a somewhat more realistic assessment than earlier prospectuses. Indeed, in 1593, the English ship *Marigold*, having missed the entrance to Cabot Strait, had coasted the eastern shores of Cape Breton and Nova Scotia[10] (to an estimated 44° 30′ N.), and made some slight contact with the Micmac, but this does not appear to have been of any seminal importance. The fact that discussion of settlement in these latitudes went on in England during the remainder of the Spanish war, when revival of the southern Virginia colony seemed impracticable, is shown by the arguments in another document of between 1598 and 1600,[11] which stressed that Englishmen going to parts of America compatible in climate and conditions with England must adjust themselves to the slow achievement of prosperity by agricultural pursuits and that even these might need subsidies from England before they could be viable. Utopian sentiment was gradually giving way to a degree of realism, even if the discussion remained too far detached from the objective realities of life in an American environmental context.

Because so much French interest was concentrated on the St. Lawrence after 1599, it became possible for the English to make the first significant voyages of the new century to New England without French interference. The expedition to New England led by Bartholomew Gosnold in 1602[12] stemmed directly from the earlier plans of Gilbert and Edward Hayes. The primary objective in 1602, as in 1582, was to rediscover Verrazzano's "Refugio" (Narragansett Bay). The organizers were equipped with Hayes's treatise of circa 1592–3, and this in turn depended to some extent on the material gathered by Hakluyt on the Bellenger voyage of 1583. Moreover, the immediate intention of the expedition was to establish in or near Verrazzano's Refugio a trading post very like that projected by

10. Richard Hakluyt, *Principal navigations*, III (London, 1600), 191–193.

11. Public Record Office, London, C.O. 1/19 (printed in E. Ballard [ed.], *Memorial Volume of the Popham Celebration* [Portland, Maine, 1863], second pagination, pp. 128–130); see Quinn, *England and the Discovery of America*, pp. 335–356.

12. The sources are Brereton's *Discoverie* (p. 393 below). Gosnold's letter and Archer's narrative are in Purchas, *Pilgrimes*, IV (1625), 164–551, and are conveniently combined in Charles H. Levermore, *Forerunners and Competitors of the Pilgrims and Puritans*, 2 vols. (Brooklyn, N.Y., 1912), I, 25–56. A detailed narrative is in Warner F. Gookin and Philip L. Barbour, *Bartholomew Gosnold* (Hamden, Conn., 1963).

Bellenger earlier, except that it was not intended to have any missionary component. Theoretically, Sir Walter Ralegh still retained all rights under Gilbert's patent of 1578 and his own of 1584; but he was not asked for a licence on this occasion, either because it was forgotten, or because Hayes already had an older licence deriving from either the Gilbert or the Ralegh patent.

Gosnold set out on March 26, 1602 from Falmouth with the *Concord,* effecting a rapid voyage across the Atlantic, making a landfall on the southern coast of Maine, and putting in to shore either at Cape Elizabeth or at Cape Neddick a little to the south. The Indians he met there, rather unexpectedly, were Micmac who had been in the service of the Basques in Newfoundland waters and had stolen a shallop in which they had adventured on a southerly voyage either to trade or to rob. Thereafter Gosnold sailed into Cape Cod Bay, and later rounded Cape Cod (which he was the first to name), before sailing into the maze of sandbanks and islands lying to the south and west of it. His exact route through them has proved impossible to trace, but it seems that after moving erratically around Nantucket Sound he made land at Cape Poge—which was then a separate island and is now part of Chappaquiddick. He named it Martha's Vineyard, but later transferred the name to the larger island as he sailed westward. From the southern shore of Cape Cod Bay he had seen, or thought he saw, a broad sound which he considered must be Verrazzano's bay at last. Rounding Cape Cod, he found it was a channel with only islands to the south; upon entering Vineyard Sound, he was again in a channel bounded by a further string of islands to starboard. Passing Gay Head (Dover Cliff, as he called it), he sailed to the furthest of the islands and landed on Cuttyhunk-Nashawena (then joined), which he named Elizabeths Isle, and designated for his outpost.

While Gosnold set his men to work constructing his post on an islet set in a small lake within the island, he took the *Concord* up Buzzards Bay until it became clear that it was an inlet, not a channel. This could well have seemed to him at first a possible Refugio but did not appear on closer examination to fit: later he was within sight of Sakonnet Point, at the entrance to the real Refugio, Narragansett Bay, but did not penetrate far enough to the west. Gosnold, the Reverend John Brereton, and in particular Gabriel Archer recorded the attractions of the scenery and soil, the plants and the fish, and

the habits of the Indians (mainly Wampanoag), with whom they traded happily for skins and furs (in no great bulk) as well as uprooting sassafras and cutting cedar for their lading. When it came to the point of deciding to leave a party in the outpost, there was not enough food available nor sufficient confidence in a timely supply —nor, indeed, in the continued friendliness of the numerous Indians who were over from the mainland for the summer fishing. In the end, on June 16, they abandoned the project and returned to England.

Gosnold's voyage, if small in scale, had been a seminal one. It revealed a substantial section of the North American coast hitherto not thought to be accessible to Englishmen, and provided a chart of some sort, together with vivid and attractive descriptions. The expedition attracted the attentions of Sir Walter Ralegh, who by accident discovered that Bartholomew Gilbert was bringing ashore sassafras which was in direct competition with that brought by Samuel Mace for him from the North Carolina coast at the same time. After arranging to have it seized, Ralegh compromised with the returned voyagers and allowed them to use his name in the publication on which they embarked, *A briefe and true relation of the discoverie of the north part of Virginia* (London, 1602). This went through two editions in a short time and communicated to its public almost all that was known or said of the region, including a version of Hayes's earlier tract. Ralegh's main interest was in the south, since the fate of the Roanoke colonists was still not established. But he licensed a Bristol syndicate, in which Richard Hakluyt was prominent, to send a further expedition to New England.[13]

Next, Martin Pring, a Bristol seaman, took the *Speedwell* and the *Discoverer* to the Maine coast in June 1603, and the two vessels worked their way south from an estimated 43° 30′ N. down to Cape Cod Bay. There, either near modern Provincetown or on Plymouth Harbor, they built a summer trading enclosure and spent some six weeks trading with the Indians and uprooting sassafras, leaving early in August for a safe voyage home. This was in some ways an unimportant voyage, yet it demonstrated that short, safe and reasonably profitable expeditions could be made in a few months to the

13. Purchas, *Pilgrimes*, IV (1625), 1654–1656, reprinted in Henry S. Burrage, *English and French Voyages, 1534–1608* (New York, 1906), pp. 341–352. See Quinn, *England and the Discovery of America*, pp. 423–427.

coasts explored by Gosnold. New England, if not yet named, was clearly accessible to old England. In summer, too, it had proved agreeable, habitable and fertile.

France had by now declared an interest in the area also.[14] In 1602 Jean Sarcel, sieur de Prévert, trading to Tadoussac, had explored the shores of modern New Brunswick and had received detailed information of a copper mine at approximately 44° N., at what is now Advocate Harbor at the head of the Bay of Fundy, on or near the site from which Bellenger had brought mineral samples in 1583 (some of which had gone to Hakluyt and were mentioned in the Brereton tract). Samuel de Champlain had mentioned this in his *Des sauvages* (Paris, 1603). Consequently, when Pierre du Gua, sieur de Monts, persuaded Henry IV to grant him control over all French intercourse with Acadia on November 8, 1603,[15] he succeeded in obtaining a grant which covered as far south as 40° N. He was content to issue licences for the fur trade but was himself determined to explore and settle in the territory to the south of Cape Breton, where he would be permitted to exercise proprietorial rights.

The publication of *Des sauvages,* which received a royal licence on November 15, 1603, meant that Samuel de Champlain, after his St. Lawrence expedition, had now made his appearance as a writer as well as an actor on the North American scene. His admirably crisp and clear account of his St. Lawrence voyage of 1603 set out firmly to Frenchmen what was and was not to be hoped for from New France. What should be done next, however, rested rather with the sieur de Monts than with Champlain. He wished to find a site where a year-round headquarters could be established. Chauvin's experi-

14. Sources and commentaries on the French experience in this area for 1602–13 are numerous. Samuel de Champlain, *Works,* edited by H. P. Biggar (Toronto, Champlain Society, 1922–36) and Marc Lescarbot, *History of New France,* edited by W. L. Grant, 3 vols. (Toronto, Champlain Society, 1907–14), take precedence. They are supplemented by R. Le Blant and R. Baudry, *Nouveaux documents sur Champlain et son époque (1560–1622)* (Ottawa, 1967), and the massive Lucien Campeau, S.J. (ed.), *La première mission d'Acadie (1602–1616)* (Quebec, 1967). Narratives are in Marcel Trudel, *Histoire de l'Amérique française, 1603–1627* (Montreal, 1967), and *The Beginnings of New France, 1524–1663* (Montreal, 1973). Biographies include articles in *Dictionary of Canadian Biography,* I; W. I. Morse, *Pierre du Gua, Sieur de Monts* (London, 1939); S. E. Morison, *Samuel de Champlain* (Boston, 1972); and Adrien Huguet, *Jean de Poutrincourt* (Paris, 1932).

15. Morse, *Pierre du Gua,* pp. 8, 49.

ences at Tadoussac in 1600–01 had reinforced those of Cartier and Roberval that the winters were hard, perhaps too severe for Frenchmen to survive at all easily. This was the main attraction of Acadia, the coast south of Cape Breton to which the sieur de Monts now turned. But it was not the only reason. French fishermen had extended their efforts to the coasts of modern Nova Scotia and further south still to modern Maine and had found there a promising fur trade with the Indians. Moreover, the French can scarcely have been ignorant of the fact that the English had sent expeditions to New England in the two preceding years, so that the 1603 patent claiming a French monopoly as far south as 40° may be seen as a bid to claim that this was the southern limit of New France, beyond which Englishmen should not venture or at least beyond which English settlements should not be made.

Champlain left Le Havre on April 7, 1604, with de Monts, his lieutenant, François Gravé and Jean de Biencourt, sieur de Poutrincourt, in *La Bonne-Renommée* and another ancillary vessel.[16] The intention was to establish a settlement; much equipment, including materials for buildings, was carried for this purpose. The flagship reached Nova Scotia and de Monts decided to wait for the other vessel, giving Champlain command of a small pinnace with which to locate a suitable site for a colony. Champlain made a close examination of the coast to the southward, then worked round the southern part of the peninsula, through narrow passages between islands and mainland as Bellenger had done, and, passing through the Petit Passage, entered the Bay of Fundy, which he refers to as "la grande baye Françoise." But he had to return to report to his leader and found his ship at Port au Mouton. The sieur de Monts then sailed down the coast, picking up the second vessel on his way. He now wanted to retrace Champlain's course to the Bay of Fundy, which he did in the small pinnace.

Champlain took him through the less perilous entrance by way of Digby Gut. Soon they entered the fine harbor of Port Royal, as he named it, "one of the finest harbours I had seen," the shores as they entered also seeming peculiarly attractive. They worked up to the point at the head of the bay, now Cape Chignecto, where they found traces of copper, though scarcely a rich mine as Prévert had heard.

16. Champlain, *Works*, I, 225–370, covers the period 1604–5.

Sailing down the western side of the Bay of Fundy, the entrance to another harbor and river mouth was found, which was named the St. John, but it did not appear to attract them as a location for a settlement. When they entered Passamaquoddy Bay, with its many islands, they began to look seriously for a site. They penetrated into a further river they called the Sainte-Croix and there found an island (Dochet Island, now renamed St. Croix), where they intended to settle. The choice was governed partly by the desire to have an island site, and a fairly protected one (in midstream), which also had deep water close to it for ease of unlading.[17] Why this one was chosen rather than a coastal island was because (just as in selecting Jamestown later) it was thought an island well into the interior yet not too far from the sea would best serve the interests of the fur traders in making the Indians more accessible to them without putting themselves at their mercy.

A house was built for the sieur de Monts from timber brought from France. Doors and locks, which had also been brought, helped to make the storehouses secure. The quarters for the men were most probably primitive. A garden was laid out and seeds sown, but it was found that the soil was too sandy to be of much value, so further gardens were laid out on the mainland, though it was now late to expect any return from them. The ships were sent home, with Poutrincourt asking if he could return to settle elsewhere the following year. In September, Champlain was sent down the coast of Norumbega—our New England—so that some perspective on the mainland coast could be gained. He was attracted by the island he named Mount Desert, and worked his way round into Penobscot Bay, eventually threading through the islands to the head of the bay.

Indians met them and guided them upstream to meet with their high chief (or Bashabees) until the river suddenly became obstructed at the Fall Line. Champlain was then approximately at the site of modern Bangor. He identified the river as the river of Norumbega (and called it Pentagoët, the Indian name), although he was evidently disappointed that he could bring his vessels no further inland. The Bashabees came down with many Indians (Abenaki of the Penobscot or Etechemin tribe) to meet him. Here Champlain was fortunate in having an interpreter, a Micmac Indian brought to

17. Champlain's chart of the island, showing the layout of the buildings and his detailed plan of the settlement, are in *Works,* I, plates LXX–LXXI.

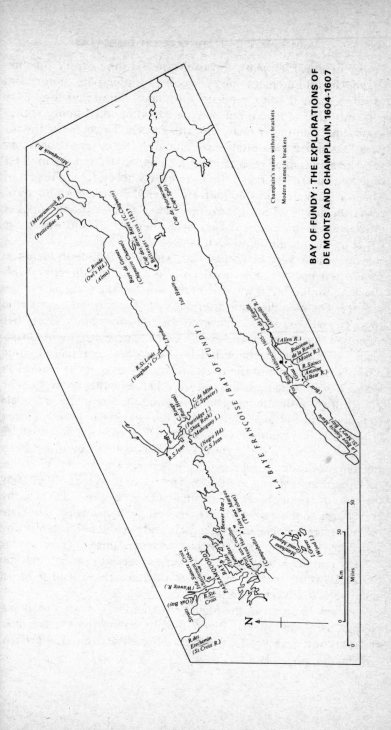

BAY OF FUNDY: THE EXPLORATIONS OF
DE MONTS AND CHAMPLAIN, 1604-1607

Champlain's names without brackets

Modern names in brackets

(Missaguash R.)

(Memramcook R.)

(Petitcodiac R.)

C. Ronde
(Owl's Hd.)
(Alma)

Baye de Gennes
(Chignecto Channel)
(Chignecto Cross 1583?)
Cap des Deux Bayes (C. Chignecto)
Bélanger Cross 1583?
Cap de Poutrincourt
Cap de Cape Split

Isle Haute

R.St. Louis
(Vaughan's Cr.)

I. Perdue

C. de Mine
(C. Spencer)

C. Ronde
(Red Head)

Partridge I.
(Shag Rock)
(Mahogany I.)

R.S. Jean

(Negro Hd.)
C.S. Jean

(Habitation 1605?)
Fort (Moss I.)

R.St. Esprit
(Avon?)

(Allen R.)
Ruisseau
de la Roche
(Moose R.)
R. Sainct
Antoine
(Bear R.)

(Digby Gut)
(St. Mary's Bay)

LA BAYE FRANÇOISE (BAY OF FUNDY)

Beaver Har.

Isles aux Marées
(The Wolves)
(Campobello)

Manchne
(Grand Manan)
I. Grove
(Wood I.)

Strait
Isle Saincte Croix
Sel.1604?
(Oak Bay)
R. Ouexg R.

PASSAMAQUODY
BAY.
(Passamaquoddy Bay)
Les Isles Couillées
(Heta Har.)

R. Ste.
Croix

R. des
Etchemin
(St. Croix R.)

N

0     50
Km

0     50
Miles

France in an earlier year, who could speak to the people for him. Champlain told them that he had come to settle in the country and to teach them how to cultivate their land. They said they were content with it as it was, but they were glad he was coming as they would then hunt more beaver for the French. The ethos of the fur trade was clearly well established already. There were dances and speechmaking and presents, then Champlain set out again. This time he expected to reach the river of Kennebec (Quinibequy) of which the Indians had told him. He entered a number of bays and rivers on the way south, but the weather worsened and supplies were lacking, so he turned back on September 23 and was at Ste Croix by the beginning of October.

Winter came very early that year, with snow falling in October; soon it was up to 3 or 4 feet deep. We learn little directly of this shocking winter, but it was one of the worst of the early part of the century. The men died one after another of scurvy, and those who survived only gradually recovered the following May. Thirty-five men died out of a total of seventy-nine. "There are," said Champlain, "six months of winter in that country."[18] The Indians hunted during the winter, and the fresh meat they brought the settlers in March probably had much to do with their eventual recovery. The French then busied themselves equipping their pinnace and boats to bring them to Gaspé, since relief was late; it was June 15, when Gravé, who had returned to France in 1604, with the first of three ships, finally put into the river. Once Champlain's men had been rehabilitated in some degree, the pinnace was equipped to continue the southernmost exploration.[19] This time they made their way direct to the Kennebec. Champlain was taken by the Indians up the river, through the narrow Back River and the hair-raising Hell Gate to the wide channel near modern Bath and beyond to Merrymeeting Bay. The great complex of rivers here gave promise of considerable trading potential, but perhaps the woods were too menacing and the rock-strewn channel seemed too dangerous to lead them to select this as a place to settle.

They sailed on down the Maine coast and in the Bay of Chouacooit (Casco Bay) at last found Indians cultivating corn, beans, cucurbits and tobacco. This seemed more attractive to the French.

18. *Works*, I, 307.
19. *Ibid.*, I, 367–391.

They explored Cape Ann and the coast nearby, and Indians they met drew them a map with charcoal. Here they also saw "canoes built of a single piece, and very liable to upset unless one is well skilled in managing them"[20] (hitherto they had seen only the birch-bark canoes and not dugouts). First Boston Harbor, then Plymouth Harbor (St. Louis), attracted them—the latter especially. They now realized that they were caught inside a great bay and made their way round Cape Cod (le Cap Blanc) and down its outer coast until they reached the difficult harbor of Nauset (named by Champlain Mallebarre). An Indian village was seen and described. Then some Nauset Indians tried to steal a copper kettle and killed a man in doing so—by this time they had no means of verbal communication since the interpreter could not understand the language. They took a prisoner but let him go, whereupon others came out and made some sort of apology. It was at this point that they decided to sail back again without picking a place to settle. At the Kennebec on July 29 their interpreter learned from the Indians of an English ship which had been only 10 leagues away.[21] (Waymouth's *Archangel* had cleared from the Georges Islands on June 16.)

Other French ships, besides those of the sieur de Monts, were interested in trading along these coasts. In 1603, for example, Villars, admiral of France, had licensed Jean Rossignol in *La Levrette* to trade in Florida. Returning after having apparently wintered in American waters, he was trading at Port au Mouton in Acadia (at an estimated 43° 45') when he was intercepted and his ship captured by de Monts in April 1604 for contravening his monopoly.[22] Another venture, under a royal grant from Henry IV to Guillaume de la Mothe and Bertrand Rocque dated January 10, 1604, authorized them to trade between the Amazon and Cape Breton. But this was an Anglo-French and not just a French venture. When the *Castor and Pollux*, under John Jerome, and the *Pollux and Castor*, under Rocque, left Plymouth in May 1604 under this grant, they were authorized on their return up the American coast to search the River of Gamas (the Penobscot) in order to discover whether there were any mines

20. *Ibid.*, I, 338–339. The story of the voyage continues on pp. 364–565.

21. *Ibid.*, I, 237, 276; Le Blant and Baudry, *Nouveaux documents sur Champlain*, pp. ix, 169–172.

22. See D. B. Quinn, "James I and the Beginnings of Empire in America," *Journal of Imperial and Commonwealth History*, II (1973–4), 141–143.

there and also to locate a copper mine in Acadia at an estimated 44° 15′ N.—apparently Prévert's mine—before returning. They might appear to have had a licence from de Monts, but were intercepted at St. Helena Sound in February 1605 by the Spaniards before they could get so far north.[23]

The English interest in the New England region was more specific than a mere vague search for mines. The movement on the part of certain Catholics who hoped to leave England and found an American colony, combined with the desires of fishing interests in the southwest to discover fresh grounds, converged to produce an expedition under George Waymouth in 1605. The *Archangel*, which left the Thames on March 5, 1605, may have intended to sail to the south of Cape Cod and pick up, where Gosnold left it, the search for Refugio; but in fact she turned north when the shoals and sandhills of Cape Cod became visible and worked her way across the Gulf of Maine to Monhegan on May 17. From there, the Georges Islands and the mainland behind looked so attractive that Waymouth decided to confine his exploration to this area. His major achievement was to explore the St. George River, the banks of which he found open and fertile and the head of which (at modern Thomastown) seemed suitable for settlement. His associate, James Rosier, had the task of collecting information on plants and animals and of making something of the Penobscot and Wawenocke Indians, whom they met in some numbers both on the islands and mainland. Seizing five of the Indians in the hope of using them as guides and interpreters in later voyages, they left the islands on June 15 and arrived at Dartmouth on July 18.

Their return with reports of excellent fishing from secure bases on offshore islands created great interest in southwest England, particularly in Plymouth and on the part of Sir Ferdinando Gorges, governor of the fort there. On the other hand, the attempts to collect English Catholic ex-soldiers from the continent, where they were being discharged from the Spanish army, had met with such opposition on ecclesiastical and Spanish national grounds that Sir

23. Henry S. Burrage (ed.), *Rosier's Relation of Waymouth's Voyage to the Coast of Maine, 1605* (Portland, Maine, Gorges Society, 1887) is the best edition (also his edition in *English and French Voyages, 1534–1608* [1906], pp. 353–394) and his account in *The Beginnings of Colonial Maine* (1914), pp. 27–51, is very useful. For the setting of this venture in its Catholic context, see Quinn, *England and the Discovery of America* (1974), pp. 382–392.

Thomas Arundell, the Catholic gentleman who had been the mainspring of the venture, now lost all interest in it. Then, too, King James created him Lord Arundell of Wardour and chose him to command the auxiliary regiment being raised to serve with the Archdukes in the Spanish Netherlands—an alternative way of employing the soldiers discharged from the regular Spanish regiments. However, Waymouth and Rosier had sufficient support in London to enable them to get a narrative of the voyage into print. James Rosier's *A true relation of the most prosperous voyage made this present year 1605, by Captaine George Waymouth in the discovery of the land of Virginia* (London, 1605) was the first detailed account of a voyage to New England to appear in print (Brereton's contribution to the 1602 publication had been brief and laconic). Moreover, it was well and vividly written, and made out the St. George River to be twice as long and much more imposing than it was. This Thames-like river in fact narrowed to a smallish stream only 10 or 12 miles from the sea, not after the 40 miles indicated by Waymouth. Not only did the land appear attractive for settlement, but the sea was full of cod and other fish and the Indians had furs to trade. Waymouth soon committed himself to leading a fishing voyage to Monhegan for the Plymouth men early in 1606; he also arranged with Sir John Zouche of Codnor to take on the colonizing part of the enterprise under his command.

It might seem that the printed book was not seductive enough to bring in contributors since the venture did not prosper. But it was the Gunpowder Plot of November 5, 1605, which finally killed Catholic participation, since the Catholics came under a cloud of suspected treachery for some little time thereafter. Waymouth, indeed, may have been under some suspicion himself because of his association with the Catholics even though he was very firmly Protestant. In any case, he retired from the venture. Some London fishmongers planned a fishing voyage to follow up Waymouth's finds in a ship, the *Triall,* which should have got off in March, but was delayed and the venture ultimately ruined through the defalcations of her crew. Sir John Zouche did not obtain a permit to leave on the colonizing side of the enterprise until August 1606 and never got his ships to sea.[24] So the Waymouth venture, which had held such promise,

24. See D. B. Quinn, "The Voyage of *Triall,*" *American Neptune,* XXI (1971), 85–103.

faded out. It was replaced and overlaid by the evolution of the Virginia Company, whose charter was granted in April 1606.

The French were not willing to suffer another winter at Ste Croix. As soon as possible in 1605 they had moved to a more favorable site on the eastern side of the Bay of Fundy, located in 1604, and brought everything that was portable from Ste Croix to Port Royal. After Port Royal had been occupied, the sieur de Monts decided to return to France to make sure his privileges were continued, so he left Francois Gravé in command with Champlain and forty-three men. Champlain concentrated on making gardens and fishponds (both for freshwater and sea fish). The *habitacion* thus established was a compact set of dwellings,[25] in the form of a square, with windows looking on to the courtyard, and a ditch round the greater part with two small bastions to protect the single entrance. Champlain then made a brief expedition to the St. John to investigate copper sources there. This year the snow began only on December 20 and the winter was less icy than wet and windy. There were only forty-five men this time but scurvy killed twelve and affected five others. It is clear that they must have had much more fresh food since they suffered less. An attempt to resume the southern exploration in March had to be abandoned on account of bad weather, and on a second attempt in April the pinnace was wrecked, though no lives were lost. Another pinnace which was building was soon completed and thirty-one of the thirty-three men (two remaining to look after the stores) set out for Cape Breton as had been agreed if relief had not come.[26] Going up the coast of Nova Scotia, a French boat was sighted. This brought news that the sieur de Monts had already arrived and was on his way to Port Royal, while two other ships were on their way. Champlain then turned back to discover the ship at Port Royal. There new dispositions were made. Gravé and his men would return to France; Poutrincourt would take over Port Royal with his fifty men; and Champlain would stay with him to complete his survey of the coast and the compilation of his map.

In England after Waymouth's failure to get support for further ventures in 1606, Virginia as a whole became a matter for discussion at a higher level. The lord chief justice, Sir John Popham, and Lord

25. Champlain's chart of Annapolis Basin and his plan of the *habitacion* are in *Works*, I, plates LXVII, LXXVI.

26. *Ibid.*, I, 377–388.

Salisbury, lord treasurer, were in touch with persons like Sir Ferdinando Gorges and William Parker in Plymouth, as well as with a wide range of London intellectual and merchant opinion, including Richard Hakluyt, now prebendary of Westminster, and Sir Thomas Smith, the founding father of the East India Company. The charter which James I granted on April 10, 1606, to the Virginia Company was intended to combine all the interests that were or could be induced to be involved in North America.[27] It is true that "Virginia" to most meant that part of North America between approximately 35° and 37° N. latitude, to which the much-publicized ventures of 1584–90 had been directed; but it now comprised also modern North Virginia, which had, since 1602, attracted more novel interest and which covered latitudes between 41 and 45 degrees. The London interests were primarily engaged with the south; Popham had become interested in the north, as had Gorges, and so too had some of the southwestern fishing interests.

Two divisions in the Company were therefore recognized: one was based on London for South Virginia; the second on Plymouth, but taking in Bristol and Exeter as well, for North Virginia. For most purposes their activities were to be separate ones. The Plymouth division of the Virginia Company was ready with a ship by August 12, 1606, the *Richard*, under the command of Richard Challons, which with twenty-nine men and the Indians Manedo and Sasacomet was to establish a post at "Pama Quidda in Mayaushon" (Pemaquid, within the territory of the Bashabees of the Abenaki group of tribes known as Mawooshen).[28] Challons was captured by the Spaniards in the Florida Strait on November 10, 1606. A vessel under Thomas Hanham and Martin Pring had been despatched to bring supplies to Challons within two months after his departure; failing to find him at Pemaquid, they left one of Waymouth's Indians, Nahanada, there, explored the rivers of the country, particularly the Sagadahoc River (Kennebec), and returned to England late in the year.[29] They

27. See Quinn, *England and the Discovery of America*, pp. 482–488.
28. On Challons, there is a narrative in Purchas, *Pilgrimes*, IV, 183–207; also Public Record Office, London, S.P. 94/13(ii), fol. 148, Feb. 4/14, 1607; H.C. 13/38, Feb. 16, 1607; S.P. 14/28, 35, Aug. 18, 1607; S.P. 14/15, fol. 156, Nov. 10, 1608.
29. A few fragments only on this voyage survive in Purchas, *Pilgrimes*, IV, 1827, 1837, and *Pilgrimage*, 2nd edition (London, 1614), pp. 755–756, while some traces of their explorations survive on the Virginia Chart and Velasco Map (I.N.P. Stokes, *The Iconography of Manhattan Island*, 6 vols. [New York, 1915–28], II, plates 1A, 22).

brought valuable information most of which is now lost.

Poutrincourt, who came out as commander in 1606, laid out new gardens and fields at Port Royal in the summer, then all but one of the ships left for France. It was decided that Champlain and the new commander could pick up the expedition again down the southern coasts.[30] On September 6 they set out. They visited Ste Croix to find that wheat had sown itself and flourished and that garden vegetables "had grown up fair and large," which "gave us the greatest pleasure." They then sailed rapidly down the coast and visited the Indians Champlain had already met at Casco Bay, proceeding to Cape Ann and Beauport (Gloucester Harbor), where they were able to see the Indians completing their harvest. They had some suspicions about the Indian attitudes here but managed to depart on good terms. The harbor seemed good to them and there were "fine meadows for supporting cattle." They sailed almost as far south as Plymouth Harbor, then crossed Cape Cod Bay, to the western shore of the Cape around Wellfleet. Later they rounded the Cape, after which Poutrincourt paid a brief visit to Mallebarre (Nauset) without incident.

At this point they entered new territory, reaching the perilous shoals to the south of Monomoy at the entrance to Nantucket Sound. They sighted the southern tip of Monomoy Point, which they called Cap Batturier (Reef Cape), doubling it not without difficulty and working their way into Stage Harbor with a broken rudder. Here they were able to observe a thick population of Nauset Indians. Poutrincourt was absorbed in refitting his vessel, buying corn, grinding it, making biscuit, and so on, but also became suspicious of Indian preparations for a possible attack. The men engaged on shore refused to come back to the ship when ordered to do so and were caught in an Indian attack, four in all being killed and the fifth wounded. Attempts to take revenge on them were evaded by the Indians. Leaving the place they called Fortuné (Misfortune)—Stage Harbor—the pinnace sailed westward across Nantucket Sound. A small island was sighted (Ganong thinks it was only rocks exposed from the Horseshoe Shoal), and, on approaching the mainland, a river was seen and named Champlain (Mashpee River?). From here the opening of Vineyard Sound further west was observed. The

30. Champlain, *Works*, I, 390–469, covers the years 1606–7.

weather was becoming difficult and the route ahead uncertain, so they decided to return. They made a brief visit to Stage Harbor once again but were unable to catch any Indians alive, though they killed some on shore. Coming back, their rudder broke off the chilly Maine coast and they had to go ashore to put it together. They then left their Indian interpreter ashore not too far from his home in the Ste Croix district (Secoudon). And so they reached Port Royal on November 14, to be greeted by Marc Lescarbot, who for some reason had not accompanied them on this expedition.

Now there was a watermill as well as a forge in operation at Port Royal and various fishponds in being. By this time also the French were in close and friendly contact with the Micmac, whose chief Membertou exercised considerable power in the area—the Micmac were at war with the Penobscot Indians, and were determined to raid them in revenge for killing one of their chiefs. Again the settlers had a mild winter. The snow at the end of December did not continue for long. There were icefloes in the river in February but it did not freeze up completely. Late snow showers came in May and even some frost in June, but in general they found the winter less oppressive than before, though there was still some scurvy and seven men died. The gardens were prepared in March and April and sown in May—the season seemed to be about six weeks later than in France.

A small vessel reached them by May 24 as a herald of the major ships. Under her master Chevalier, she was sent fur trading to the St. John and Ste Croix. Poutrincourt took his shallop to the head of the Bay of Fundy. It was on this occasion that the Bellenger cross was found in the vicinity of Cape Chignecto:[31] the whole northern end was carefully examined and a few specimens of copper found, but no Indians were seen and the heavy forest precluded any decision on the suitability of the area for settlement if a richer lode of copper should be found later on. When he got back, another vessel informed Poutrincourt that he must now bring his men round to Cape Breton. Membertou had led off a war party at the end of June to southern Maine to fight the Saco Indians and returned on August 10 with report of a victory and the killing of several of their chiefs. The majority of the men were sent to Cape Breton, while Poutrincourt, Champlain, and six others waited to complete their corn

31. *Ibid.*, I, 455.

harvest and to chart their way slowly round the Nova Scotia peninsula in mid-August, reaching the ship at Canso and preparing to accompany her back to France. Champlain found the coasts difficult to chart with their many islands, rocks, bars and good and bad harbors; the land appeared only moderately attractive and fertile on the Atlantic side. Cape Breton he described as mountainous but in part pleasant, and he was impressed by the inland waterways of the Gut of Canso. They set sail on September 3 and put into Roscoff on September 28.

The sieur de Monts had had his patent recalled, which now brought this first sequence of settlement voyages to an end. They had clearly been of considerable value. The rigors of the first winter of 1604–05 were an indication of how insecure a small party could be; those of 1605–06 and 1606–07 had been much less severe, and allowed progress to be made in acclimatizing the men. It was established that Europeans could live through the winter at Port Royal if they took sufficient care. Moreover, the Micmac Indians had proved helpful and cooperative, and there seemed no reason to fear their hostility in future. The major difficulty was that not enough furs were obtained to make the settlement pay its way. We have no exact balance sheet, but the time taken up in fur trading was small and the total amount of furs collected must have matched it.

The exploration of the region between Nantucket Sound and the head of the Bay of Fundy had performed a most valuable geographical task which Champlain perfected in an admirable map of the coastal area. Both he and Lescarbot were to write about it in full and graphic detail, and Champlain was to add his characteristic harbor charts, as well as his drawings of the settlements at Ste Croix and Port Royal. Through the materials published by these two men between 1609 and 1612, we can get a full and effective view of the country and, to a lesser extent, of its people. Yet the exploration of the New England coast did not reveal any great economic attractions: there was, for example, no major fur trade in sight in the later New England. No mineral wealth had been located, and the finding of copper in the Minas Basin, though authentic, was too small in quantity to be important. The Indians were at most times friendly, though in the Cape Cod area potentially hostile. Clearly, for the sieur de Monts, neither fortune nor fame were to be gained by further costly experiments. Champlain came back with the five- or

six-month winters strongly in his mind, though he had now, he believed, the knowledge to deal with them even in the St. Lawrence Basin. Poutrincourt alone remained enamored of Port Royal. Whatever happened, he was going to get it assured to him and come back there to live.

On July 17, 1607, the sieur de Monts's monopoly of trading rights was revoked and his men, as we said, left Port Royal. With the founding of Quebec in 1608, France's main efforts in North America were to be diverted to the St. Lawrence. For the remainder of Henry IV's reign, 1607–10, the French, though not abandoning their fishing and fur-trading voyages southward from Cape Breton, did not assert any exclusive claims to settlement or attempt to challenge those assumed by the English, whose Virginia Company charter in April 1606 had claimed as far north as 45 degrees, overlapping with the French claim of 1603 down to 40 degrees. Was this an accident, or was there an element of design? We know that Henry, in these years, was anxious to keep on good terms with James I and may have deliberately eased off French pressure in this area while allowing Champlain to experiment fully with what could be done about the fur trade in the St. Lawrence. No positive evidence for this view can be adduced, but almost as soon as Henry had been assassinated, rivalry and conflict broke out anew between representatives of both nations in eastern American waters.

As the result of the loss of Richard Challons and his ship, the founding expedition of the Plymouth Company had been deferred until 1607.[32] Then the *Gift* (under George Popham) and the *Mary and John* (under Raleigh Gilbert, son of Sir Humphrey) left England on May 30, with about a hundred planters, reaching Pemaquid early in August. They had with them the fourth of Waymouth's Indians, Skicowaros, and soon set sail for the river of Sagadahoc (Kennebec), evidently selected by Hanham and Pring the year before as the most suitable for the establishment of a colony. They picked a site not too far from the mouth, on a spur of land on the west bank of the river,

32. The materials on the 1607–08 settlement are collected in Henry O. Thayer (ed.), *The Sagadahoc Colony* (Portland, Maine, Gorges Society, 1892); there are useful editions of the main narrative (which is incomplete) in Burrage, *English and French Voyages*, pp. 395–419, and Levermore, *Forerunners and Competitors of the Pilgrims*, I, 352–387.

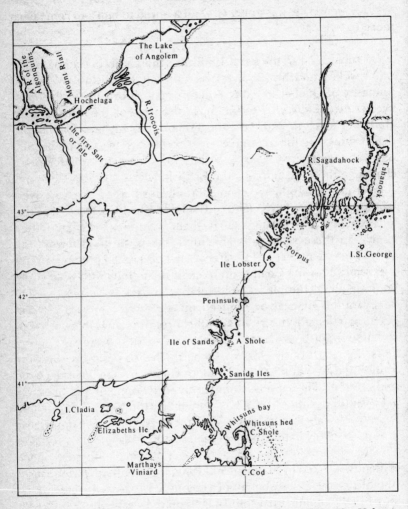

The Lake
of Angolem

A R of the
Algonquins

Mount Riall

Hochelaga

R.Jrocois

the first Salt
or Iale

R.Sagadahock

Tahanock

C.Porpus

I.St.George

Ile Lobster

Peninsule

Ile of Sands

A Shole

Sanidg Iles

I.Cladia

Elizabeths Ile

Whitsuns bay

Whitsuns hed
C.Shole

Marthays
Viniard

C.Cod

The Anglo-French Discovery of New England by 1610: The Velasco
Map Evidence
(Original in the Archivo General de Simancas)

and began actual settlement of Fort St. George (as they named it) on August 20. They fortified the area with a ditch, building a fort and storehouse; during the later months they mounted twelve guns behind a palisade, and built fifteen buildings besides a church and storehouse. Under the supervision of a shipwright named Digby, they also began construction of a serviceable pinnace, the *Virginia*, of 30 tons, as an indication of one use to which such a settlement could be put. They did some exploration, but the returns from fur trading were minimal as it was the wrong season. Moreover, winter set in very early that year, food supplies ran short, and scurvy was evidently rampant. (George Popham died on February 5, 1608, to be replaced by Gilbert, so that, as Purchas said,[33] "that unseasonable winter" was "fit to freeze the heart of a Plantation.")

Robert Davies in the *Mary and John* had been sent back in October and the *Gift*, threatened by ice in the river, followed in December. Davies was sent out again with supplies early in 1608 and reached the settlement with two ships. The fur trade had picked up in the spring, a considerable amount of sassafras had been gathered, and the new pinnace was ready. We know no details of this summer's activity. Later a third vessel arrived, and from her it was learned that Sir John Popham had died on June 10 and that Gilbert's elder brother, Sir John, was also dead, leaving Raleigh Gilbert the head of his family. He determined to go home, and no one else, it appeared, wished to stay to encounter a further long and bitter winter. So Fort St. George was abandoned. The effective phase of the Plymouth Company had come to an end. Fur trading and the exploitation of local timber resources did not prove sufficient to maintain a colony—agriculture on any extensive scale had not proved possible on such a site, though had they moved a little further south along the Maine coast the position might have been rather different. Francis Popham, Sir John's son, continued to send ships to Monhegan in the summer and had a Captain Williams there in the season as a representative of the Company's interests. Other islands were also frequented, but we know little of the next few years. New England had become, we might almost think, an extension of the old Newfoundland summer fishery.

By 1609, the eastern shore from the Gut of Canso to Buzzards Bay

33. Purchas, *Pilgrimes*, IV, 1837.

had been explored and the Indians and natural products of the region sampled; three settlements had given some indications of the conditions under which Europeans could live in these latitudes in America, and the coasts had even (however imperfectly) been placed on the map. Westward from Buzzards Bay and southward there was a gap. It was to be filled, rather fortuitously, by a Dutch rather than an English or French expedition. Henry Hudson, serving the Dutch in another voyage, this year took the *Halve Maen* in search of a Northeast Passage but was checked by ice rather early in the season off Novaya Zemlia. He then made the bold decision, based on correspondence with Captain John Smith and probably a rough map, to investigate the North American shores north of the Chesapeake Bay.[34] He was off Newfoundland early in July and in the middle of the month off the coast of Maine. He entered the Kennebec River to obtain a replacement for a mast (he made his latitude 44° 1' N.), perhaps expecting to find the English colony there, though there is no hint of this in the surviving journal. After making his way with some difficulty past Cape Cod, he sailed away to the southwest as far, he reckoned, as 35° 41' N., well to the south of Cape Henry. Then, turning north, he found the entrance to the Delaware River, but did not enter because of shoals.

Carefully following the coast, Hudson eventually entered the Narrows on September 10. He was welcomed, as Verrazzano had been, by many Indians in canoes, and cautiously entered and followed the river until on September 20 (they were near the site of Albany) prospecting boats found that this river became narrower and shallower and so they decided to return. They had both friendly and hostile contacts with the many Indians on their way downstream. They took especial note of the shore of Manhattan Island and came "out . . . of the great mouth of the great river" on October 4, reaching Dartmouth on November 7 and getting back to Holland a little later. Hudson transferred back to the English service in 1610, yet his discoveries were claimed effectively by the Netherlands. A Dutch ship went out to Manhattan Island in 1610 and a regular

34. Robert Juet's journal is in Purchas, *Pilgrimes*, III, 580–595, and with other materials in G. M. Asher (ed.), *Henry Hudson* (London, Hakluyt Society, 1860). A useful edition is Robert M. Lunny (ed.), *Juet's Journal* (Newark, N.J., New Jersey Historical Society, 1959); also Levermore, *Forerunners and Competitors of the Pilgrims*, II, 389–426, and J. F. Jameson, *Narratives of New Netherlands, 1609–1669* (New York, 1909), pp. 6–28.

trading connection was established, although no settlement was made until 1614. The coast between the mouth of the Hudson and Buzzards Bay still remained obscure and unmapped.

In Acadia in 1608 and 1609 there were only scattered French trading vessels. In 1610 Poutrincourt and his son Charles de Biencourt had managed, with some difficulty, to raise enough money to fit out the *Grâce-de-Dieu* and bring out a party of male colonists to re-establish Port Royal, which the local Indians, under their chief Membertou, had left unmolested.[35] This was to be an agricultural as well as a fur-trading center and some land was distributed to Poutrincourt's men. He had no monopoly and had very little financial backing; he owned only Port Royal, acquired from de Monts, who still retained rights of proprietorship to Acadia as a whole. In France it seemed that missionary activities were about the only thing that would raise cash. Poutrincourt's priest, Jessé Flesché, did his best by baptizing Membertou and his followers (who then considered themselves to be economically dependent on the colonists), and having this extensively publicized in France.

Charles de Biencourt, Poutrincourt's son, sent to France to gain support, found that the news brought in some but not enough money. So, through the queen mother, Marie de Médicis, and the wife of the governor of Paris, the marquise de Guercheville, the Jesuit Order was brought into the enterprise. In return for subsidies, Biencourt entered into a profit-sharing agreement with the Jesuit priests Fathers Pierre Biard and Enemond Massé and finally got back to Port Royal in May 1611, to find Poutrincourt and his men in poor shape after a difficult winter. The latter was not enamored of Jesuits, of the new contract, or of the small supplies brought by the *Grâce-de-Dieu,* and sailed off to France to try to do better for himself. But in attempting to make a new contract with Madame de Guercheville, Biencourt found himself bested when she acquired the sieur de Monts' remaining territorial rights to Acadia, except for Port Royal, from Cape Breton down to 40°. He remained in France attempting to raise support for his enterprise, though a ship sent out under the new arrangement reached Port Royal in January 1612. There Charles de Biencourt and the Jesuits quarreled: Charles attempted to exclude the Jesuits, who replied with a threat

35. Levermore, *Forerunners and Competitors,* II, 438–566, has a balanced selection of materials on the events of 1610–13 in Acadia.

of excommunication; truces followed and both parties suffered together from lack of adequate supplies.

In May 1613, the *Jonas* arrived with startling news—the Jesuits were to leave Port Royal. A new settlement, in which missionary interests would be paramount, was to be planted on the Penobscot by a new commander, René Le Cocq de La Saussaye, who had over eighty men at his disposal to do so. The *Jonas* moved away to make her landing not on Penobscot Bay but at what is now Frenchman Bay, on the eastern side of Mount Desert Island. La Saussaye called the place Saint-Sauveur, where he formally took possession, but as he wanted a more effective means of commanding the coast, no disembarkation took place. The ship moved round to Somes Sound, and there they chose a place for a permanent settlement, also named Saint-Sauveur,[36] where a fort and other buildings were begun, though La Saussaye appeared more interested in exploration than settlement, and scattered his men for this purpose.

Meanwhile the Virginia Company, after 1610, was both stronger and felt a more direct responsibility for the northern area covered by their grant, now that the Plymouth division had ceased to operate a settlement there. In 1611, an English expedition under Edward Harlow was sent out by the earl of Southampton, a leading member of the Company, to prospect sites for other English colonies on the New England shores and to bring home a new selection of Indians who might come up with some fresh clues on useful locations. Harlow carried out his work vigorously, if not tactfully or peaceably. He worked along the Maine coast and seized a French trader, Captain Plastrier, on Matinicus Island, releasing him with a warning not to intrude again on the English area. As it happened, the Frenchman was working closely with Charles de Biencourt (he was to spend the winter of 1611 in the old settlement of Ste Croix), who thereupon went to Matinicus and set up the French Arms there, so that a

36. There is some controversy over the site of the mission. Most American historians place it at Fernalds Point, Somes Sound, Mount Desert. Father Campeau (*Première mission*, pp. 100–101), insists that it is Frenchman Bay, on the Maine coast, northeast of Mount Desert Island. Henry S. Burrage argues that the first landfall was on the east of Mount Desert (he prefers Bar Harbor for this location) and was named Saint-Sauveur. He says that after taking Indian advice, the expedition moved to Somes Sound (*The Beginnings of Colonial Maine, 1602–1658*, pp. 105–109). Having visited both locations in 1964 in Father Campeau's company, I still incline to Burrage's view (accepting Frenchman Bay as likely for the first location), considering that only the Somes Sound site could command the coast as was intended.

confrontation was already in prospect. Harlow then moved south-ward along the coast, calling at various Indian villages where he kidnapped successive "sample" Indians. The last was from Martha's Vineyard—the first visit to the island since 1602 of which we know —and Harlow also seems to have penetrated, like Gosnold, to the head of Buzzards Bay, though no further.

In 1613,[37] Sir Thomas Gates commissioned Samuel Argall to go north in the *Treasurer,* inquire what the French were doing in Acadia, and remove such of them as he found from this sphere of Virginia Company influence. With the help of Indians, Argall discovered the location of Saint-Sauveur; he seized the *Jonas* there on July 2 and intimidated La Saussaye into submission. Sending most of the Frenchmen off to Port Royal, he took Father Pierre Biard and an-other Jesuit, Father Jacques Quentin, with a few civilians, to James-town. There Sir Thomas Dale, who was now in charge of the James-town colony, gave him the task of going at once to destroy all traces of French settlement in the north. The *Treasurer* and the captured *Jonas* took off, with Biard on board, who played into Argall's hands by retailing his quarrels with Biencourt. Argall successively obliterated all signs of French occupation at Saint-Sauveur and Ste Croix, and found Port Royal temporarily vacant as Biencourt was away on an expedition with his men. He destroyed all that he could there, leaving the French behind to suffer virtually an unsheltered winter. The *Jonas* was sent to England with Father Biard on board and was eventually restored to France—not without recriminations from the French government. For the time being, English authority remained unchallenged over a still ungarrisoned New England and influential as well over the Acadian region where the French occu-pation had been effective, in some measure, since 1604.

The obscurities during the period 1580–1602 about the coastline lying between 40° and 45° N. were largely dissipated in the years between 1602 and 1613—Georges Bank especially being identified as such. Now the coastal and insular waters were seen to be good, even very good, fishing ground, if not spectacular in their yields. Furs, it was clear, could bring in some income in the Acadian north but probably little in the more southern region. The winters could

37. The Argall material is in Purchas, *Pilgrimes,* IV, 1758–1762, 1807–1809, 1876–1891. For material on the French side, see Lescarbot, *History of New France,* III, 35–72; Campeau, *Première mission,* pp. 267–637; and note 35 above.

be hard alike on Ste Croix, the Annapolis Basin, and the Kennebec River, if not necessarily deadly; scurvy remained a menace to those who did not grow enough fresh food of their own and preserve it adequately for the winter. The Indians could be cooperative when furs were available in quantities: it was possible they might make good Catholics, though the experiments of 1610, as the Jesuits had been quick to point out, were far from conclusive.

Further south, the problem was what to trade with the Indians, who were well able to look after their own basic needs, although they appreciated copper and trinkets and would give corn, some furs and odds and ends for such luxuries. They were numerous and far from servile so that to maintain good relations with them might prove difficult. True, there might be a future for small posts as bases for furs and fish; but there was as yet no major drive to acquire land in the more favored soil south of Casco Bay or to carry there English communities which for economic or religious reasons could not easily live at home. Neither English Catholics, Puritans, depressed small farmers nor declining gentry had so far been impelled to experiment in making their homes in these parts of North America. Poutrincourt had attached himself to Port Royal and was determined to make an attempt to establish a working estate there for himself and his son. All his efforts from 1607 onward had shown how many frustrations might be encountered in such an enterprise and he was forced by the English to start back from scratch. The future of European enterprise in the region thus still remained entirely open.

So far New England was only on the brink of its existence as a territorial entity—it was to be named as such by Captain John Smith in 1614, replacing the vaguer, more mysterious Norumbega—while Acadia had been more fully explored and was exhibited fully in print to the readers of Champlain's *Les Voyages* (1613). Yet after 1602, the coastline from Buzzards Bay all the way northward to the Penobscot had begun to take on an exceptional degree of reality and familiarity to those Englishmen who visited it. The atmosphere conveyed in the accounts of the Gosnold, Pring and Waymouth expeditions in particular is intimate, homely and familiar. There is much indeed that is novel in detail, but little, apart from the Indians, that is wholly strange: the context is congenial. It would appear to be taking on

already the characteristics that Smith was to emphasize and pull together, the feeling that this was a region which was like England in certain basic ways, and perhaps most fundamentally that it *looked* like England, though a warmer and less rainy England, seen almost wholly in the summer.

If we had detailed narratives of the colony at Fort St. George—the Sagadahoc colony—we should perhaps have more of the other side of the picture: of the effects of the cold inimical winter of 1607–08 which discouraged the settlers and played a part, probably not a major one, in leading to its abandonment in the fall of 1608. Samuel Purchas unfortunately threw away several journals which would have given us a more intimate picture of the exploration of the Maine coast, notably that of the Hanham and Pring expedition of 1606. Perhaps one reason that he did so was that they were too ordinary and too accepting, too empty of exciting novelties, too like accounts of parts of England herself. There may be rather too much speculation in saying this, but from the evidence we have, it would appear that a genuine rapport had been established between Englishmen who had been there and the country they visited—that rapport which was to make it possible to enable a series of enduring settlements to be established during the twenty years after 1612.

New England as seen by Champlain and Lescarbot had a cooler and more clinical look. It did not seem like France to Frenchmen. Champlain could give us valuable pictures of the harbors and coastlines, and the Amerindian inhabitants, but he does not convey much impression of New England as a place where he would like to live and plant colonies. He evokes a far warmer feeling about Acadia: the country beyond the Indian cultivation line appeared to him more sympathetic and it was there, among its native hunting peoples, that he wished Frenchmen to settle. We may perhaps see this as a reflection of the attraction that the St. Lawrence Valley had taken on for him during his expedition of 1603; and it was for the St. Lawrence that he was willing to abandon Acadia in 1608, although Poutrincourt insisted on returning.

The English, for their part, showed little interest in Acadia—perhaps because it seemed, already in the 1590s, very much a French preserve; perhaps because what was known about it did not sound enticing. We can see the French being attracted by the wild hunting country which was yet mild enough for them to plant their

gardens of vegetables and herbs round compact, fortress-like settlements, while the English thought rather of fields to cultivate and graze, of individual farmsteads instead of compact settlements. The switch of the main French effort to the St. Lawrence in 1608 was to make it possible for the tentative probings of the years 1602 to 1608 to be transmuted slowly into a growing determination on the part of the English to occupy the attractive, familiar-looking lands to the south of French Acadia.

# CHAPTER 17

# Newfoundland from Fishing Base to Colony

IN the years between 1590 and 1610, Newfoundland and the adjoining waters passed through a phase of war into one of peace.[1] The war tended to polarize the locations to which the fishing ships of belligerent countries resorted. The English concentrated on the Avalon peninsula and took over where the Portuguese and Spanish Basques had been, so that they became dominant from a little west of Cape Race to Conception Bay. Similarly the French Basques, with Spanish Basques largely under their protection, kept very much to Placentia Bay and the waters to the west of it. The French carried on much as usual. Ships from Leaguer ports, especially those which held out against Henry IV in Brittany, had to keep out of the way of those from royalist ports and from the English. On the other hand, the association between English and French royalist ships became closer. After 1580, if the English wished to buy salt at Newfoundland, they had to do so from the French. So we still find French—and especially Norman and La Rochelle—ships in close contact with English fishing vessels along the southeast coast of Newfoundland. Otherwise the French tried to keep most of the more northerly harbors on the east coast in their own hands, and

1. Daniel W. Prowse, *History of Newfoundland*, 1st edition, with bibliography (London, 1895), 2nd edition without bibliography and some corrections (London, 1896; St. John's, 1971), is still of value; J. D. Rogers, *Newfoundland* (Oxford, 1911), is valuable. Gillian T. Cell, *English Enterprise in Newfoundland 1577–1660* (1969), is essential.

also St. Mary's Bay and to some degree Placentia Bay on the south. The position in southeastern Labrador remains obscure, but it is probable that the French were active there too.

It will be shown[2] that there were clashes between English vessels and those of Brittany and the French Basque country and occasional Spanish Basques when the English attempted to penetrate the Gulf of St. Lawrence between 1593 and 1597. There was a certain amount of violence from time to time in Newfoundland ports also, but, considering the opportunities the circumstances offered, not as much as might, after the episodes of 1582–85, have been anticipated. Most of the damage to the fishery done in the decade from 1590 to 1600—and it was considerable—was done in European waters, when vessels were intercepted by English or French partisans before they reached their home ports. This was, when their cargoes were most desirable to privateers and pirates—the illegal trade in fish stolen from the homecoming vessels was clearly a large and profitable one. There was much subterfuge in the fisheries themselves. The Spanish government was licensing French Basque vessels to leave for Newfoundland when there were no Spanish Basque ships available to do so. At the same time, the English government was giving French Basque captains passes to allow them to get past English privateers on the ground that they were French rather than Spanish. There was much ambiguity in the Newfoundland ports too. While the wars were on, there was no thought of colonizing Newfoundland. But one major change was under way: the apparent disappearance of the Portuguese from the inshore fishery, and the major decline in the Spanish Basque fishery, created opportunities for expansion for both the French and the English. The latter, in particular, were increasing their share of the inshore fishery quite rapidly. This in the end was to lead them to consider whether it might not be worth while consolidating their hold on the fishery, or at least extending the area where they held the major part of the fishing grounds, by colonization.

Colonization was to be for centuries a controversial issue in English politics regarding Newfoundland. The fishermen were to come to regard colonists as intruders on their grounds, unfair competitors because they had a longer fishing season, and unnecessary

2. Pp. 469–472 below.

intruders because they tended to take away trade in articles from vessels which came in at St. John's Harbour almost as much to deal with other ships as to fish. Further, in the maritime policy of the English government a tradition developed that the Newfoundland fishermen were a major reserve of seamen for war and even for the mercantile marine in general. If a colony developed rapidly in Newfoundland, fewer fishermen might be needed to make annual voyages and learn the deep sea seaman's arts, so that to launch a colony might not be desirable. These issues were mostly to remain in the background for some years, but in embryo they probably delayed the decision to attempt year-round occupation of Newfoundland by English colonists.

To Sir Humphrey Gilbert in 1583 it had all seemed very simple. If an English proprietor of Newfoundland, as he regarded himself, could hold the coastline and lease out grounds in the harbors, then he could raise a considerable revenue for himself and give such preference as he felt inclined to English as against non-English fishermen. He did not live to discover how difficult it would be in practice to do anything like this. Any high-handed appropriation or taxation of fishing grounds would lead to many of the foreign vessels finding other harbors where they could carry on their traditional ways. Then they might be tempted to declare stretches of coast where they could concentrate shipping in the summer closed to all English ships, and could perhaps call on their own governments to help them to resist. Further, the fishing interests of southwest England and even of London were not likely to allow themselves to be held to ransom by a colonial overlord if they could avoid it. Indeed, after Gilbert's death, pressure was clearly brought to bear on his heirs against any attempt to follow up his annexation of Newfoundland in 1583—possibly through the lord treasurer, Lord Burghley, who was sympathetic to the shipping interests.

Edward Hayes, who survived the Gilbert voyage and was to have his account of it—along with his boost for Newfoundland—printed by Richard Hakluyt in 1589,[3] attempted in 1585 and 1586 to convince Burghley that the fishing interests were wrong. He believed that a fishery monopoly combined with a colony in Newfoundland

3. *Principall navigations* (1589), pp. 679–699.

would be valuable for England and also for any company or governor acting under authority who might care to establish a permanent
English presence. The abstract which he sent in May 1585 must
have received some encouragement, for he followed it up with a
long discourse in January 1586, which Burghley received in February.

Hayes's plans were not published and the manuscripts are damaged, but they form a complete project for an ambitious takeover
of the fishery by England.[4] He started off by mentioning that there
should be some four hundred ships in the fishery (including the
Banks and whale fishery as well as the inshore fishery), which at a
minimum catch of £500 worth of fish each, taxed at 10 per cent,
would bring in an annual revenue of £20,000. To do this he believed
that a small fleet of galleys, rowed by some two hundred convicts,
would be needed; also the fortification of two or three principal
ports and the occupation during the winter of whaling stations and
fishing harbors where there had been any recalcitrance the previous
summer. The responsibility for this elaborate scheme would be that
of a corporation, with centers in five or six English ports, in which
merchants and shipowners would form one class of shareholder and
small investors, who would back the sending out of a man or go
themselves, another. All ships in the trade would pay a levy to the
corporation and captains would be required to bring out the colonists. They would be entitled to use them to work on the chores of
the inshore fishery in the first summer (like the "green men" who
were carried for this purpose in the following century), then they
would be allowed to settle down as colonists on the island. If they
worked on the guardships or in the forts, they presumably would
remain Company employees. Otherwise, they would be left on their
own.

How were the colonists to make a living? In the summer they
would let out grounds and stages for the fishermen, and charge
them for caring for their boats over the winter. They would build
a number of guesthouses at St. John's Harbour, as these would be
eagerly rented by merchants who came ashore on business during
the fishing. They would trade in fish: salmon, herring and train oil

4. British Library, Lansdowne MS 37, fols. 166–167 (Hayes to Burghley, May 10
1585), with MS 100, fols. 83–87 (apparently 1585) and 88–94 (completed January 11
1586, endorsed as received February 12).

as well as cod. They would provide other trade goods for the fishing vessels who came to "that famous mart" in the summer months. They need not be idle, as the island would produce ships' stores—the naval stores for which England depended largely on imports from the Baltic. These were listed as resin, pitch, tar, soap ash, deal boards, masts, hemp, flax, linen, cables, cordage, hides and furs, not all strictly naval and some needing to be cultivated and processed. The colonists could make iron, which was needed for many purposes on the ships. They could go in for cabinet making and provide chests and tables from fine woods for sale. A man of some distinction should be found to go as "General" or governor, though no governing institutions on the island were prescribed.

Of course, exploitation of the fishery and of the shores on which it depended on this scale was impracticable; yet the possibilities for doing some of the things Hayes listed did exist. It is strange that he does not raise the question of what food the colonists could grow themselves. He thought that the reputation the island had for being very cold in winter was exaggerated; in the north it might be so, but in the south it was hot in the summer and not too cold in winter. He maintained that a corporation of the sort he proposed would not "decaye our Navy," since the development of the island and the taking of a larger share of the fishery from the French would increase the trade so much that it would "norish and trayn up a Multitude of men abell to serve her Majestie by Sea or Land in those partes or elsewhere."

Hayes claimed that the French had planned to make a settlement in Newfoundland in 1585 but that on account of internal strife in the country the attempt had been deferred. There does not appear to be any record of this so far from French sources and it may have only been a rumor which Hayes took up to strengthen his own case. On the other hand when, in 1610, a new proposal for a plantation was made, it was stated[5] that the French had already tried and failed to keep a party there over the winter: "for about the yeare 1580 they enterprised to winter there, but by want of foresight they all perished for want of necessities for plantation." It may be that there was more concern with the possible colonization of Newfoundland in the 1580s than we are aware.

5. Trinity House, London, Transactions, 1609–1625, fol. 1.

In any case, so far as we know, nothing came of these projects. England and France were much too closely involved in wars in Europe. Although privateering and piracy continued to plague the Newfoundland fishermen, it did not get out of hand on the Newfoundland coasts, even if there was probably more of it than we have on record. In the early 1590s, Hayes himself turned to planned settlements on the mainland of what is now New England and the Maritimes instead of Newfoundland, while the English colonization plans generally, when they had developed by 1597, focused on the Gulf of St. Lawrence and, specifically, on the Magdalen Islands.[6] (Had these plans come to anything they would probably have led to some attempt at settlement on Newfoundland also.) The French, after they revived their transatlantic planning in 1597, attempted to settle Sable Island in 1598, just outside the Newfoundland fishing zone, and later concentrated on the St. Lawrence.[7] The Spanish Basques, who spoke of the Strait of Belle Isle in the 1570s and 1580s as if it (and perhaps other parts of the Newfoundland area) was their own "Provincia de Tierra Nueva," might well have done something about establishing permanent whaling stations had it not been for the war and the consequent attrition of their shipping and resources generally. So Newfoundland remained uncolonized, after both the French peace in 1598 and the English peace in 1604. From 1600 on the French were to concentrate on the St. Lawrence, leaving the fishery to look after itself in traditional ways. The Basque whaling industry remained depressed and only began to revive about 1610, so that Spain was not a serious competitor for territory. This left the way open to the English, the rising power in the fishing industry.

A number of Bristol merchant families were becoming interested in the possible development of trade with North America and had, for example, sent out Martin Pring to New England in 1603[8]; some London merchants, too, including members of the Fishmongers Company, were concerned in the expedition to "Virginia" (which was a failure) by the ship *Triall* in 1606–7 outside the Virginia

6. Pp. 469–472 above.
7. See Chapter 19.
8. Pp. 393–394 above.

Company's orbit.[9] Once the Virginia charter had been granted in April 1606, it was risky for merchants to involve themselves in speculative ventures in America inside the Company's monopoly zone, which extended as far north as 45°. But this still left Newfoundland open to speculators. The recent growth of the fishing industry meant there were two hundred English ships by 1609 (with some six thousand seamen). Moreover, those ships which were not fishing vessels but "sack" ships that went out to buy cod from fishermen, mainly at St. John's, were building up a flourishing trade; while a number of the English ships were sailing direct from Newfoundland to the Mediterranean with their catch and bringing commodities from there to England in a triangular trade.

The possibility of combining fishing and planting developed shortly after the Virginia Company had made its initial experiments at Jamestown and at Sagadahoc. John Guy, a Bristol merchant, went to Newfoundland to prospect in 1608 and returned optimistic, although his promotional treatise has not survived. He teamed up with a London merchant, John Slany, a member of the Merchant Taylors' Company and of the East India Company. They gathered round them a miscellaneous group of London and Bristol merchants and, as the project got under way, obtained a certain amount of official patronage in government and court circles. This enabled them to obtain a charter and to make a respectable appeal for financial support among speculating merchants and gentlemen.[10]

The case which Guy and Slany put up in February 1610[11] was based, like that of Hayes more than twenty years before, on the supposed superior climate of Newfoundland which would render settlement easy. Ships going out empty to the fishing could easily carry planters and their gear—a point Hayes had also made. There was the chance that foreign states might occupy Newfoundland and interfere with English fishing if nothing was done. Settlement would secure the English position: it would encourage more, not less,

9. D. B. Quinn "The Voyage of *Triall* 1606–1607: An Abortive Virginia Venture," *American Neptune*, XXXI (1971), 85–103.

10. Cell, *English Enterprise*, pp. 53–70. Professor Cell uses the unpublished Middleton Manuscripts in Nottingham University, as well as better known sources, to give the first authoritative picture of the founding of the colony. Her article "The Newfoundland Company: A Study of Subscribers to a Colonizing Venture," *William and Mary Quarterly*, 3rd series, XXII (1965), 611–625, is also important.

11. Trinity House, London (as n. 5).

shipping to go to Newfoundland—another Hayes point, as was the plea that planters could supply fishermen with many of their needs and could do various services (such as looking after boats in winter) for them. Agriculture, grazing and the exploitation of timber, along with the development of whaling, were incentives to profitable and effective settlement. The same timber products were listed; furs and skins would produce good financial returns; iron and copper mines might be exploited. A new point was that a Newfoundland colony could act as a halfway house between Virginia and England. The promoters claimed that they would not interfere with the existing fishing; they only asked for "a small parte of the saide countrie yet never inhabited by any Christian people." Hayes was still alive but we do not know that he directly influenced this petition.

The charter of the Newfoundland Company when it was sealed on May 2, 1610,[12] was a good deal more elaborate than might have been expected. It contained the names of forty-three persons, headed by the earl of Northampton and including Sir Francis Bacon. Among its members was a Nottinghamshire gentleman, Sir Percival Willoughby, who was to devote himself largely to the Company for some years, and Thomas Aldworth, a member of a Bristol family long interested in America. John Slany, as treasurer, was to have the kind of authority that Sir Thomas Smith had in the Virginia Company under the 1609 charter, along with a nominated council, but there was to be a general assembly of shareholders to exercise some supervision over the administration.

The whole island was not granted to the Company. The northern limit was to start at Cape Bonavista, north of the entrance to Trinity Bay (which had long been French-dominated), run down the east coast and turn westward around the greater part of the Avalon peninsula, which included St. John's Harbour, to the entrance to St. Mary's Bay on the south coast (also formerly a French place of resort) but not to Placentia Bay where the French and Spanish Basque codfishermen mainly concentrated. The Company could send out fishing vessels and sack ships, but its main objective was to establish a colony or colonies. A discreet reticence was observed as to whether or not they could appropriate land along the shore and charge rents to fishermen for its use as drying grounds. The

12. Cecil T. Carr (ed.), *Select Charters of Trading Companies, A.D. 1530–1707* (London, Selden Society, 1913), pp. 51–62.

fishing was to be as free and open as before, but the Company had the right to make ships pay a small customs duty on any goods they brought in or out other than those concerned with the fishery.

John Guy was given instructions by the Company to take out a colony as soon as possible. With thirty-nine colonists he left Bristol in a single ship in July 1610 and had already determined, from his previous visit, on a site "in the bay of Conception . . . in the harbour here called Cupperes cove . . . preferred by me to begin our planta-cion . . . for the goodness of the harbour, the fruitfullnes of the soyle the largeness of the trees, and many other reasons."[13] He had established himself there by early August. Guy had been given abso-lute authority, within the limits of his instructions, to rule the colony (alternates were named in case he was incapacitated); Gillian Cell suggests[14] that this was because the Company knew of the troubles the Virginia Company had had with the divided control set up at Jamestown in 1607. His task was to build a settlement, fortified against possible attack, where agricultural activity to provide crops and grazing was to be combined with making salt, fishing, and exploiting minerals when they were located. Both products for sale and specimens of others which might prove promising were to be sent home by the end of the season. In order to record the variations in temperature over the winter, which could guide future settlers, a weather journal was to be kept. Contacts with the Beothuk were to be made to see if a fur trade with them was possible.

The first stage at Cupids (as Cupers Cove is now called) was to set up temporary houses for the men and concentrate on preparing timber for their ship to take back to England.[15] They also sent specimens of plants and minerals. The second stage was to build a storehouse, a communal dwelling (completed by the beginning of December), a workshed for boatbuilding and a palisade to enclose all, defended by a few pieces of artillery. In this they survived the winter, only four or five men suffering from scurvy, though four died from other causes. The early part of the winter was milder than in England; the first three months of 1611 were wintry but not too

13. Cell, *English Enterprise*, p. 63.
14. *Ibid.*, p. 62.
15. Guy to Slany and the Council, May 11, 1611, Samuel Purchas, *Hakluytus Post-humus or Purchas his pilgrimes*, 20 vols. (Glasgow, 1905–07), XIX, 410–416; excavations in 1973 and 1974 may lead to the tracing of successive occupation stages.

severe—on the whole they were much more fortunate than Champlain had been at Ste Croix in 1604–5 or the Sagadahoc settlers in 1607–08. Guy kept them working throughout the winter. At the end of it, they had built seven boats (including a large one, decked and of 12 tons burden), constructed the framework for a much larger dwelling and cut a considerable amount of timber. They had two sawpits and a forge going, had cleared land for planting and grazing, and had managed to keep goats, pigs, pigeons, rabbits and hens alive and producing. Turnips seem to have been regarded from the beginning as an important crop, but corn (wheat and oats most probably) was planted in the spring. Fishing appears to have continued to some extent through the winter. The first year was probably the best experienced by any colony, English or French, that had hitherto been attempted, and the losses from scurvy were minimal.

A small vessel sent by the Company arrived on May 10, 1611, so that the colonists were not neglected. She was ready to go back with such timber and, probably, fish as had been got ready by May 16, when Guy sent his report to Slany, along with his weather journal from November to April.[16] He stressed one great advantage that the placing of the colony gave the Company: the settlers were on the spot and could claim fishing grounds before any ship came in. They might do well to prepare "a beach, boats and stage," so that the ship using it would have an advantage of perhaps £200 over latecomers. Fishing vessels arrived early from Bristol and Dartmouth, so "nothing could be done to take any of the places desired [presumably at other beaches than their own]: all being possessed here"; but a place had been reserved on their own beach for the Company's fishing vessel, when it came. Gillian Cell comments[17] that the priority which the settlers had did, in fact, infringe upon the freedom of the fishermen to select their own "grounds," and brought out "the inherent contradiction between allowing settlement while insisting on the preservation of an absolutely free unrestricted fishe y." Nonetheless, according to Guy, the Company's request to the fishing vessels "to assist us, and to supply our wants . . . was most willingly accomplished."

No less than three Company ships came out to fish this summer. When the fishing season was over, Guy, who was anxious to report

16. Purchas (XIX, 410) preserved only a brief mention of it.
17. Cell, *English Enterprise*, p. 64.

in person to the Company, was able to bring back charcoal and some furs and skins, as well as products of the shore fishery, on the Company's vessels, along with a few colonists whom he did not wish to retain. Before he left, he issued a series of orders[18] to apply to all the ports inside the Company's orbit, which laid down some fairly elementary ground rules for the conduct of fishermen in port. They were not to obstruct harbors or interfere with the boats of other fishermen, damage buildings, burn the woods and suchlike. These could be interpreted as a means of assisting the port admirals of the fishing fleets to maintain some uniformity of conduct between one harbor and another; if the fishermen chose to disregard them, however, there was nothing that the tiny colony could do to enforce them, nor could it impose any degree of regulation over the long and complex shoreline. Indeed, even to go through the motions of so doing might well raise precisely the kind of antagonism between established fishing interests and the Company which the latter wished to avoid.

According to brief notes from the weather diary, which is all we have,[19] the second winter under John Guy's brother Philip and William Colston, another Bristol man, "was somewhat more intemperate than it had been the yeare before, but not intolerable," and we do not hear of deaths from scurvy. John Guy came out again on June 7, 1612, with some additional settlers, including sixteen women, and a further group arrived a little later. In all, sixty-two persons were left for the third winter, twelve of whom became ill with scurvy and two died, this winter being harsher than either of the first two. The raid carried out on the fishery by Peter Easton, the pirate, in 1612, preoccupied the settlers in defensive measures, and caused them to abandon the second settlement at Renews which they had just begun, though Easton, in the end, did not molest them. The colony had been established moderately firmly over the first three winters, but a series of question marks still lay over its future prospects. Could it, even if the grazing was adequate and root crops grew well (though not corn), become a viable fishing and timber-exploiting concern? Glass and iron-working had been begun, as at Jamestown at a comparable stage, on an experimental basis, but would they develop? How far could a small settlement fish

18. *Ibid.*, pp. 64–65.
19. Purchas, *Pilgrimes*, XIX, 416.

for itself and how far assist the Company's own ships and yet manage to avoid friction with the strongly individualistic fishermen? These questions had not been answered. In the end they were to prove very difficult, almost impossible, to solve. Here no lotteries were held to aid the settlement as there were for the Virginia Company after 1612, when colonies were found to need priming for much longer than had been anticipated. The Newfoundland Company was ultimately to fail, although it established a tradition of permanent settlement which would be maintained in one form or another. However, it was the second English settlement in North America to have endured.

It is now possible to say something about the site at Cupids. Two seasons of excavation, under the direction of Dr. R. A. Barakat, have brought to light a number of features of the early settlement.[20] A series of postholes indicates a palisaded area, within which were two structures, possibly a house and barn or two houses, with a well between them. Another location provided evidence of a sawpit, a smithy and perhaps another structure; associated with these was a filled-in cellar of seventeenth-century date. A third site represents the small fort built in 1612 when Peter Easton threatened the settlement and Guy called back the settlers from Renews. This structure measured some 90 by 60 feet; it is represented by postholes along its western side and a bastion at its northwest corner, and possibly also at its north center, though this cannot now be confirmed owing to earlier disturbance. A substantial quantity of artifacts have been found but they cover a fairly wide chronological range since the site was used into the eighteenth century; however, some clearly belong to the very early phases of settlement. This valuable achievement adds substantially to the small number of early seventeenth-century sites located and examined in Canada and the United States.

20. The excavation report had not yet been published at the time of writing. I am indebted to Dr. R. A. Barakat for the information on the excavation in a personal letter dated July 3, 1975, and for an impressive series of photographs. For a general site view and key, see Plates 24 and 25.

CHAPTER 18

# *The Re-Emergence of Virginia, 1591–1612*

NO detailed account of European contacts with the North American coast beyond the confines of Florida during the decade after 1590 can yet be written. Clearly, French privateers and pirates (technically speaking, privateers until 1598 and pirates thereafter) visited the shore inside the zone of Spanish influence between the St. John's River and Port Royal Sound from time to time; and it is highly probable that in the stretch of coast immediately to the north of it between Port Royal Sound and Cape Romain they had regular trading contacts with the Indians. The pattern was one which we will see established by 1605: a trading and raiding cruise in the Caribbean, then a visit to the mainland coast to get water and firewood for the ships and to sell to and buy from the Indians before setting out for the return to France. Some of the ships may have gone on to trade for furs in the region from the Penobscot to Cape Breton and joined the homebound Newfoundlanders in their autumnal return to Europe. Whether the French regularly visited and traded with the coastal Indians between Cape Romain and Cape Cod in this decade is not yet known, though this may be a measure of our ignorance rather than an accurate reflection of what took place.

The English ships had a similar pattern in their attacks on Spanish shipping in the West Indies, in that most of them came some way up the North American coast before returning across the Atlantic, although they usually turned away from the shore fairly soon in order to return to European waters by way of Bermuda and the

Azores. Others worked their way up the coast as far as Newfoundland, where they bought fish from the fishermen to eke out their failing stores. The English seem to have followed a track which brought them northward somewhat further out to sea than the French, and to have had no tradition of calling regularly at Indian settlements on the mainland to rest, repair and trade. It is very probable, however, that occasional ships put in to careen or make other repairs, or to obtain supplies of fuel and water before crossing the Atlantic. There are occasional suggestions of possible wintering in the country,[1] but nothing more. With so many English ships, up to forty a year, making their privateering voyages through the Florida Strait, the present indications of very occasional English contact doubtless underestimate the actual situation considerably. Yet after John White's last visit to Roanoke Island in 1590, the English were preoccupied with the war with Spain in European waters and the West Indies, and pickings were so good from the Spaniards that it is unlikely trade with the Amerindians of this region offered substantial attractions to most English privateering captains.

The Lost Colonists too were not forgotten—even if John White, writing in 1593, indicated that they had been.[2] Sir Walter Ralegh maintained in 1596 that he had intended to call in to look for them on his way back from Guiana in 1595, but in the event was unable to do so;[3] and it was the continued presumption of their existence which provided a basis for regarding his patent of 1584 (giving him exclusive control of English enterprises on the North American coast) as still valid. Had the Lost Colony been proved to have been wiped out, it would probably have been argued that his rights had lapsed. If he could find strong indications that any appreciable number of them were still alive, then it would be worth while putting together a large expedition to replace them or bring those who wished to return to England. If there was no news, it was in his own best interests to hang on, on the assumption that they were still living, until he was ready to take up American colonization at a new level or at least to license others to do so. Opinions were freely expressed during the decade 1590–1600 on the chances of the

1. K. R. Andrews, *Elizabethan Privateering* (Cambridge, Eng., 1964), p. 195.
2. Quinn, *Roanoke Voyages*, II, 715–716.
3. Sir Walter Ralegh, *The discoverie of Guiana* (London, 1596), p. 5.

colonists being still alive in America; these appear to have been fairly evenly divided between those who thought them dead and those who considered them to be alive.[4] The indications are that toward the end of the decade Ralegh was sending out small trading expeditions, as secretly as possible, in order to try to obtain positive news one way or the other about the fate of the colonists of 1587.

It is clear from their later actions that a number of those who had been concerned with the Roanoke voyages kept very much in mind the desirability of reviving English colonizing enterprises when an opportunity should arise. The desire to emulate Spain in possessing territories across the Atlantic was enhanced by the war: to settle in North America could be a symbol of victory over Spain.

The problems of raising capital, which had seemed so great in the 1580s, appeared less formidable as large-scale privateering and other ventures emerged during the war and capital resources were built up from the spoil taken at sea. Further, the number of persons who wished to find alternative places to live outside England, whether for religious, social, or economic reasons, had multiplied. The competing claims of the Irish Munster plantation, which had been substantial between 1585 and 1590, became less considerable when internal war developed in Ireland in 1595 and thereafter (it was to engulf the Munster settlement in 1598). Moreover, men like Richard Hakluyt, who had left on record such a full account of the Roanoke voyages in his *Principall navigations* of 1589, were still at work maintaining their propaganda for continued English attempts to settle North America. Hakluyt was to express his views forcibly on the need for American colonization in the new edition of his great work, *The principal navigations,* as successive volumes appeared between 1598 and 1600.

We have a statement that an expedition under Samuel Mace in 1602 was the fifth made under Sir Walter Ralegh's auspices to search for the Lost Colonists. If we take the expeditions of John White in 1588 and 1590 as the first two and Mace's in 1602 as the last, there are still two voyages unaccounted for. While there is no precise evidence on this point so far, there is a suggestion in Hakluyt's *Principal navigations* of 1600 that colonists were to be sent out at about the time of publication. Then, too, the presence of Sir

4. Quinn, *England and the Discovery of America* (1974), pp. 442–445.

Walter Ralegh at Weymouth in August 1601, almost exactly a year before he met Mace there, indicates that he may well have revived his searches in 1600 and continued them during 1601.[5] It is possible that the two untraced searches were made earlier, between 1593 and 1600, though this is less likely. We know a little, if not much, about Mace's voyage. Made in a small bark, it left Weymouth in March 1602 and was directed to the coast north of Cape Fear; the men went ashore somewhere north of Cape Fear and well south of Roanoke Island. During a month's stay they collected a quantity of sassafras and smilax roots, as well as "Benzoin," "Cassia lignea" and a very strong-smelling bark, none of which can be certainly identified. Mace was carrying a substantial quantity of sheet copper, much of it cut into ornamental plaques (gorgets), hatchets, and knives for trade with the Indians. We cannot be certain that he had any trading contacts with the Neuse and Coree Indians of this part of the coast, but it is quite likely. It was Thomas Harriot, from his earlier Virginia experience, who advised Mace about making the copper gorgets and suggested the other trade goods they should take with them. An Indian phrase on his notes may indicate that he also compiled for them from his Roanoke Island materials a short phrasebook on the Indian languages, which could have been some help to them in America or at least have taught one member of the expedition a few key words in Algonquian.

Mace returned to Weymouth in August 1602, and handed over his cargo to Ralegh for sale without indicating that any contact had been made with the Lost Colonists or that any information of any sort had been collected about them.[6] Ralegh, after his contest with the *Concord,* returning (as we saw) from an unlicensed visit to New England also laden with sassafras, hired Bartholomew Gilbert to conduct a further expedition for him to search for the Lost Colonists in 1603, in which Mace was also to take part. A brief note on Mace's voyage of 1602—the only one we have—was included in John Brereton's account of Gosnold's 1602 voyage to New England in the *Concord, A briefe and true relation of the north part of Virginia,* which was published before the end of 1602.[7]

In 1603 we have our first indications of Anglo-French coopera-

5. *Ibid.,* pp. 410, 443.
6. *Ibid.,* pp. 405–413.
7. (London, 1602), p. 14.

tion in trade and exploration in the southeast. During that year a ship with both Englishmen and Frenchmen among the crew put into land in Florida in the vicinity of the St. Johns River. There at least one of the men showed some familiarity with the Timucua language (we would assume him to have been French rather than English).[8] They probably did some trade north of the St. Johns and then disappeared from view as they worked their way up the coast. It is likely that they represented an Anglo-French syndicate, organized by Peter Beauvoir, a merchant settled in London who had strong connections both with the Channel Islands and with St. Malo, though we have no certain evidence on this point. It seems likely that the main focus of their trading activities was the coast in the vicinity of the Port Royal and St. Helena sounds; whether they called in further north along the coast or made any inquiries for the Lost Colonists we cannot tell.

We do have an account, in this year also, of the unfortunate voyage of Bartholomew Gilbert. Our narrative of the voyage of the *Elizabeth*[9] deals with the experience of a single ship under Gilbert's command, no mention being made of any consort. She left London on April 17 and had instructions to buy tobacco and cut *lignum vitae* in the West Indies before making for Chesapeake Bay and a search for the Lost Colonists there. She spent most of June in the Caribbean, mainly at Nevis, and early in July sailed through the Florida Strait. Gilbert seems to have had little idea of how to control his ship (or his sailing master) and reached a latitude of something over 40 degrees, so that the *Elizabeth* was sailing, perhaps, in the vicinity of Long Island. Land was seen but no harbor; she turned southward in a strong northeasterly wind on July 23, and on July 25 came, so the narrator thought, "neere the mouth of the Bay," but was driven off by contrary winds. Finally, on the 29th, land was seen, well wooded and with some indication of a river mouth. Anchoring about a mile off shore, Gilbert took a boat's crew ashore, and with four of his men marched inland, only to be ambushed and killed by Indians. Some of his companions reached the boat and after a tussle for it with the Indians got back to the ship, having lost three men besides their captain. The remaining eleven men, under the master, Henry Sute, took the ship back to London by the end of September.

8. See p. 310 above.
9. Purchas, *Pilgrimes*, IV (1625), 1657–1658.

There is no clear indication at all where the landfall was made, but it is likely that it was a little to the north rather than the south of the entrance to Chesapeake Bay—perhaps well up the eastern shore where the forest would come fairly close to the coast.

Samuel Mace was to have gone also. We have no direct evidence that he did so, but he would in any case have sailed from one of the southern ports, Weymouth most likely, not London. There is clear information that Indians from some part of North America were brought to London at dates earlier than the arrival of either Martin Pring's ships at Bristol, which had been to New England, or of the *Elizabeth* at London. On September 2, and on successive days after that, rewards were given by members of Lord Cecil's household to "Virginians," culminating with a reward to some Thames boatmen "that waited on the Virginians when they rowed with ther Cannow."[10] These men could have been brought from Chesapeake Bay by a ship under Mace's command, though they could also have come from the Anglo-French vessel which was earlier in the vicinity of the St. Johns River at Florida, or, indeed, from some other expedition of which we know nothing. We do know, however, that the Powhatan Indians in 1607 claimed to have lost some Indians taken by force by a vessel operating some way north of the York River inside Chesapeake Bay. This was apparently an English ship and two or three years before 1607 (which in the vague terms we have could as well be 1603 as 1604 or 1605). If we put these hints together we may, or may not, see confirmation of the opinion that these were the Indians who were on the Thames in September 1603 and that they may have been brought by Mace. Further evidence is needed. But if this hypothesis is correct, they could also have brought indications that some white men were known to be still living somewhere to the south of Powhatan's sphere of influence, possibly with the Chesapeake tribe just south of the bay, as is indicated below.

The reason for thinking that some rumors of their continued survival were known and were being very skeptically received in London lies in the appearance of jibes about what are clearly intended to be the Lost Colonists in the comedy *Eastward Hoe*. This was produced in the earlier part of 1605 and was published in September, being reprinted twice before the end of the year.[11] The

10. Quinn, *England and the Discovery of America*, pp. 419–431.
11. *Eastward Hoe*, 3 editions (London, 1605); ed. J. H. Harris (New Haven, 1926).

author was George Chapman, with contributions by John Marston and Ben Jonson. The play assumes that the audience is familiar with the story of the Lost Colony and with its alleged "rediscovery," which may point to the recent circulation of broadsheet ballads or news tracts on the subject that have since been lost. We are told: "Virginia longs till we share the rest of her maidenhood," which picks up an earlier statement of Ralegh about Guiana[12]—"A whole country of English is there, man, bred of those that were left in 79. They have married with the Indians, and make 'hem bring forth as beautiful faces as any we have in England." Virginia is also boosted in mock promotional terms: it is the most pleasant country "as ever the sun shined on; temperate and full of all sorts of excellent viands; wild boar is as common there as our tamest bacon is here; venison as mutton." The Indians love the English settlers so much that "all the treasure they have they lay at their feet," gold (easily acquired in exchange for copper), rubies and diamonds without limit. Certainly, Virginia was news in London in 1605.

The sea war against Spain was scaled down from 1602—drastically so after James I came to the throne in 1603. As this occurred, the incentives to build up trade with parts of the Spanish territories with which contacts had been made during the war, or even earlier, was considerable. Privateers who came to be labeled pirates and penalized in English courts increasingly tried to transform themselves (at least partly) into traders. Consequently, the voyages to the Caribbean which continued throughout the years before and after 1603 were becoming commercial rather than purely predatory, though many operators combined both types of activity. This change of objective is a principal reason why English expeditions to North America—both to the more northerly shores of the later New England and to those north of Spanish Florida—took on a new lease of life and why attention turned toward a renewal of the colonizing objectives. Such a transition had already been made by the French after the Peace of Vervins in 1598 in regard to Canada. The peace negotiations of 1604 and the Treaty of London which ensued accelerated the movement. While Spain made no formal concessions to the English demands for access to parts of the Americas where there was no substantial Spanish presence, the treaty gave English-

12. *The discoverie of Guiana*, p. 96 ("Guiana is a Countrye that hath yet her Maydenhead").

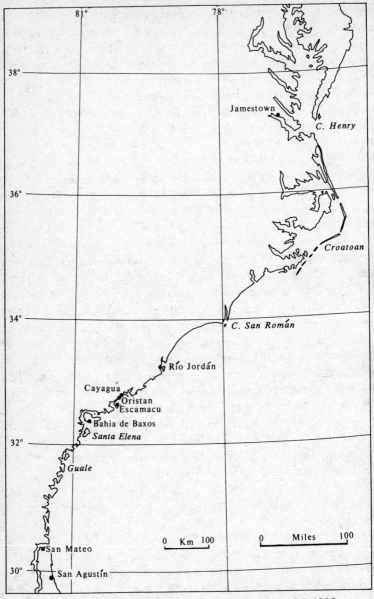

**ÉCIJA'S VOYAGES OF RECONNAISSANCE, 1605 AND 1609**

men such liberty to trade and settle as they had already taken before the Spanish war.[13] Moreover, many seamen were now released from the royal ships and privateers, and soldiers from the royal armies, so that men anxious for adventure, who were looking for new outlets for their energies and economic support for their livelihoods, were available in quantity. The London entrepreneurs were obliged also to find further means of investing their capital now that war industry and privateering had ceased to call for its full employment.

The Anglo-French expedition which came to an abrupt end in St. Helena Sound in modern South Carolina in February 1605 was also intended to call at the Carolina Outer Banks. The fate of the *Castor and Pollux* and *Pollux and Castor* at the hand of the Spaniards has already been indicated.[14] The instructions they received from the Anglo-French syndicate headed by Guillaume de la Mothe and Peter Beauvoir, which were related in turn by prisoners in Spanish hands, were that when they left Florida, they were to go in search of the herb "Oysan" or "Byssanque." This had been found where Sir Walter Ralegh had left his colonists in 35° 30′ at "Crotuan" (Croatoan, to which White in 1590 believed that the Lost Colonists had gone), called by the English "La Verginia," and where the English were settled. The plant was the "Wisakon" or milkweed, whose seed pod contained silklike fibers thought to be a valuable new textile material. Nothing was said to the Spaniards of any new information about the Lost Colonists, but the prisoners were quite confident that they survived, their instructions at least having said so. If they left England in May 1604, new information about the Lost Colonists (supposing there was any) must have reached England as a result of the 1603 voyages to which we have referred.

Further, Christopher Newport,[15] an old associate of John White's and one of the most experienced English privateer commanders, had an interview with James I late in 1605 when he presented him

13. Chapter 13 above. An expedition under Captain Francisco Fernández de Écija left Florida in August 1605 to track down the colonists in Croatoan, but in a month had gone no farther than Cape Romain, a long way from the Carolina Outer Banks, before turning back.

14. D. B. Quinn, "An Anglo-French Voyage of Discovery and Its Sequel," in *Miscellanea Charles Verlinden* (Gent, 1975), 513–534; see pp. 310–312.

15. See K. R. Andrews, "Christopher Newport of Limehouse, Mariner," *William and Mary Quarterly*, 3rd series, XI (1954), 28–41.

with a crocodile (or alligator). If any English privateering captain ever watered at a North American landing place after 1590 it is likely to have been Newport: he had been intending to go with White to Roanoke Island in 1590 but was diverted by an engagement with the Spaniards and sustained a wound which led him to return direct to England. That he may have called in at Chesapeake Bay or elsewhere on the Virginia coast in casual search for the Lost Colonists is not unlikely, since it was assumed in 1606 that he knew the entrance to Chesapeake Bay, and he conducted the first Virginia Company there impeccably in 1607. He could therefore have made a reconnaissance of the bay in 1605 to follow up rumors circulating in England. There is only a web of speculation and very few firm facts about English activities on the coast northward from the Spanish zone in the years 1600 to 1605. It is enough, however, to indicate that the Lost Colonists were being looked for in two separate places —one south of Roanoke Island at Croatan, near the modern Cape Hatteras; the other inside Chesapeake Bay, the ultimate objective of the colonists in 1587—and that this second location had in some measure come to be regarded as the correct one.

It has always been hard to believe that the 1607 colony was founded without a more recent reconnaissance than that of 1585–6. It is now highly probable that the bay was examined at least once between 1603 and 1605, even if we cannot be precise about details. What is also clear is that there is solid evidence (dating from the years 1609–12) that some of the Lost Colonists survived until at least 1606, and possibly to early in 1607, within easy reach of the James River, and that the members of the Chesapeake tribe living on and near the southern shore of Chesapeake Bay were massacred by Powhatan possibly as late as May 1607.[16] The two events may be one and the same. Thus Lost Colonists living with the Chesapeake Indians since 1587 or thereabouts, perhaps also married to them, and dimly heard of in London in 1603 or 1604, may have been finally liquidated along with the Indians on the very eve of English resettlement. All such reconstructions of imperfectly documented sequences must by their nature remain fallible, but it now appears likely that there was much more continuity between the Roanoke voyages and the Jamestown settlement than has hitherto seemed possible.

16. For a detailed discussion, see Quinn, *England and the Discovery of America*, pp 452–458.

Up to the summer of 1603, Sir Walter Ralegh had been the guiding and controlling figure in English voyages to North America northward up the coast from Florida or southward down the coast from Newfoundland. In July he was arrested, and by the end of the year he had been convicted of treason, though, with the sentence of execution suspended, he was kept a prisoner in the Tower. This meant that he was stripped of all rights under the patent of 1584, which reverted to King James. Ralegh was henceforth only an occasional adviser on Virginia from his place of imprisonment.[17] James did not decide on a policy toward Virginia until 1606, and even then he remained subject to Spanish pressure to withdraw from colonizing activities for several years before finally deciding, in 1609, to go ahead and defy the Spanish threats. Consequently, North American activity on the part of Englishmen up to 1606—whether in the later New England or in the Virginia which the Roanoke voyages had pioneered—remained the work of small groups and was quite uncoordinated. At the end of 1605 or early in 1606, a movement for a more coherent approach toward North America, with the idea of exploiting it both by trade and settlement under the auspices of a single body, took shape. The Virginia Company emerged with its charter on April 10, 1606.

By 1606 it was much easier to contemplate a major trading and colonizing venture in Virginia than it had been either in 1584 or at any time after 1590. Peace with Spain had not settled whether Englishmen could or could not be permitted to settle within the lines of the old papal donation of 1493 (though this remained very much the canon of classical Spanish thinking on the subject) and the issue was left open. A certain amount of trade seemed possible on the fringes of the Spanish empire in the Caribbean, even if the acquisition of permanent trading bases there did not seem likely to be practicable in the face of Spanish opposition, unless perhaps through plantations in Guiana. More was known about North America; much of the coast from Cape Cod northward had been explored and some experience gained of fur trading and fishing prospects there, as well as a little more about trade with the Indians between Florida and Cape Fear.

The East India Company, formed in 1600, had had its first profit-

17. See D. B. Quinn, *Raleigh and the British Empire* (New York, 1962), pp. 172–176.

able cargoes home in 1603 and was set on a course which should supply England with many tropical products, particularly spices. The Levant trade had opened up after the war, and the Spanish and Portuguese trades when peace had been ratified in 1605, yet neither looked like being very profitable—the one being beset by pirates, the other by the hostility and bureaucracy of Spanish officials. Could not England attempt to emulate some of the less spectacular trading gains of Spain's western empire by settling in latitudes similar to those of Spain and her dependencies in America in the temperate zone, and so gain a similar lead on the French and Dutch by installing herself where she could exploit the timber, furs and fish of the more northerly mainland coasts, though still within latitudes lower than those of home? Clearly by the beginning of 1606 a growing number of people were coming to think so. And it had already been demonstrated that investments for such speculative but potentially profitable overseas ventures could attract merchants, gentry and aristocrats, many of whom had already responded to earlier appeals for capital for comparable enterprises.[18]

There were survivors of the old Roanoke ventures who were still interested and concerned in North American ventures: Ralegh in the Tower, if he still had much influence, which was somewhat doubtful; Thomas Harriot, living quietly at Syon House, but recently involved through his new employer the ninth earl of Northumberland on the outer margins of the Gunpowder Plot; Richard Hakluyt, who was still an active and influential propagandist for colonization. Much more significant was Sir Thomas Smith, who had been involved in the Roanoke ventures also and was by now head of the East India and Levant Companies and much besides. By 1606 he had become convinced that Virginia settlement was potentially profitable and was willing to throw his great influence and wealth behind the venture, which virtually assured it of major support amongst the London merchants in general. Edward Hayes, along with Hakluyt, was in touch with Robert Cecil, now earl of Salisbury and lord treasurer, who had the requisite political power to get government authorization at the highest level. Lesser men, like George Waymouth and Christopher Newport, had been interesting the king personally in certain aspects of American venturing,

18. See Theodore K. Rabb, *Enterprise and Empire* (Cambridge, Mass., 1967), pp. 19–101.

so that he was at least not wholly unfamiliar with the issues involved, and was ready to be flattered by the prospect of extending his dominions into transatlantic areas if this could be done without danger to his European aspirations or activities.

It might seem that Sir Walter Cope, who had long been interested in American curiosities and was almost certainly a spectator of the Indian canoe trial in the Thames in 1603, acted, with Sir Thomas Roe, as an intermediary between City interests and Lord Salisbury. Merchants in Plymouth, Bristol and Exeter—many of them involved in a booming trade in Newfoundland cod—were increasingly interested in the commercial prospects of Norumbega, or North Virginia as it was now being called. Waymouth's voyage had gained considerable publicity in 1605 and had drawn attention to fertile agricultural and wooded land, as well as to fish and furs in a still fairly novel area. Waymouth's supporters in Plymouth included a number of influential merchants and sea captains, men like William Parker, while the governor of the fort, Sir Ferdinando Gorges, had suddenly become enthusiastic through contact with Waymouth's Indian captives. The sons of Sir Humphrey Gilbert, Sir John and Raleigh Gilbert, had revived their interest in their father's old North American objectives; and the dean of Exeter, Dr. Matthew Sutcliffe, had become an enthusiast also.

Richard Hakluyt was influential with eminent Bristol merchants like Richard Aldworth. A very important recruit was Sir John Popham, the lord chief justice. He had influence in Bristol where he had been recorder, and his grandson, Thomas Hanham, recorder of Plymouth, was to lead one of the early enterprises from there. Popham seems to have become interested largely because he thought colonies might be a way of diverting able-bodied men to labor outside England—there were many such unemployed once war had ended—who might otherwise become involved in crime. He may well have been the instrument that brought the Westerners into corporate association with the Londoners in the April 1606 charter. At the center of the picture Lord Salisbury remains the most important figure. Both Ralegh and Hakluyt had for some years been pressing him to take up seriously the question of English colonization in North America. In 1606 he did so with results that produced the charter of April 10. This united in a sophisticated, perhaps ultra-sophisticated, way the economic and political inter-

ests which wished to make an international imperialistic gesture and at the same time to engender corporate profits by the commercial fruits of settling Englishmen in a climatic zone between 36° and 45° N. latitude, appreciably south of England and so capable of producing commodities that would profitably complement those of northern Europe.[19]

The charter set up a tripartite structure. In England the apex was to be a royal council. This would be composed of royal nominees, both officials and leading merchants, and would have broad duties in defining the structure of government inside the colonies, and laying down the framework at home and in America within which they operated. It was to be an embryonic Council of the Indies, perhaps, if there was ever an English Indies to justify its existence. Two bodies were to be charged with regional development, whose directors were named in the charter. The one, whose orbit lay between 38° and 45° N., was to cover North Virginia and to be based on Plymouth, although it would comprise the Westerners as a whole. The other was the mainstay of the enterprise, the London Company, limited to the area from 34° to 41° N., which would raise the major capital for the South Virginia settlement. Each of these companies was headed by nominated councils. The shareholders were to have no rights in the actual running of them, except to invest, by installments, a certain sum and to get returns in profits or land (or both) after seven years.

The royal council was to define the organization to be followed in each colony. It was decided to have a president and a council nominated for each, with the latter exercising some control over the former. Regulations would be laid down for the administration and the rule of law in the colony, but in general the law of England was to prevail. This was an extensive yet fairly flexible arrangement. It committed the crown to some direct responsibility internationally for the enterprises in relation both to France and Spain, while leaving the main commercial and colonizing responsibility in the hands of a small group of the principal investors in each of the

19. On the background of the Virginia Company, see Pomfret and Shumway, *Founding the American Colonies* pp. 1–24; D. B. Quinn, "The Road to Jamestown," *Shakespeare Celebrated,* edited by Louis B. Wright (Ithaca, N.Y., 1966), pp. 50–66; and, for the social background in England, Carl Bridenbaugh, *Vexed and Troubled Englishmen, 1590–1642* (New York, 1968).

Company's divisions. But it was to be the performance of the Company and its agents, not its structure, which would determine the success or failure of both enterprises.[20]

In the case of the Westerners, they were already in a position to have access to most of the potential benefits, if not all, of the new areas. If furs and fish were to be the staples of New England and Acadia, much of the benefit from them could be obtained by summer voyages—as had long been shown in the Newfoundland fisheries. So that even though a settlement would have the advantages of enhancing national prestige and preventing the French from occupying certain areas, it might have been enough simply to develop the fish and fur trade of North Virginia without attempting any intensive settlement.

For the Londoners, the situation was wholly different. True, they could in theory use a Virginia colony to mount a major piratical and trading onslaught on the Caribbean. But King James would not agree to this. He wanted peace, not war; friendship, though not perhaps at any price, with Spain. The returns from South Virginia (as it should have been called after the charter was granted) must come from the country itself. Summer voyages, trading for skins and dyestuffs, perhaps inducing the Indians to supply roots of sassafras and smilax, might or might not pay their way; but the journey was too long, the chances of profit relatively too small, for any large capital investment in such enterprises to be possible. What the Londoners wanted was another Mexico. They might hope for a "good mine" (which Ralph Lane said could have made the fortune of the Roanoke ventures), but they could not reasonably count on this. Rather, they wanted the other economic benefits which Spain derived from Mexico and which were contributed to the European economy by Spain herself, as well as some of those unique, it was thought, to North America. These were hides, sugar, dyewoods and

20. For the Company's charter, see Philip L. Barbour (ed.), *The Jamestown Voyages, 1607–1609,* 2 vols. (Cambridge, Eng., 1969), I, 24–34, and also Samuel M. Bemiss (ed.), *The Three Charters of the Virginia Company* (Williamsburg, Va., 1957), pp. 1–12. For the early history of the Company, see Pomfret and Shumway, *Founding the American Colonies;* C. M. Andrews, *The Colonial Period of American History,* 4 vols. (New Haven, 1934–39), I, 98–150; Wesley F. Craven, *The Southern Colonies in the Seventeenth Century* (Baton Rouge, La., 1949), pp. 60–137, and his brief *The Virginia Company of London* (Williamsburg, Va., 1957). Alexander Brown, *The Genesis of the United States,* 2 vols. (Boston, 1890; New York, 1964), remains invaluable for reference.

other dyestuffs, medicinal substances derived from trees and plants, wines, olives, citrus fruits and perhaps other exotics, fine timber, utility timber for masts, shingles, clapboard and barrelstaves (which could be roughly processed on the spot), iron, glass, potash, pitch and tar, all of which used timber for their processing, together with useful minerals of every sort. All these would be produced in latitudes more southerly than England and yet in climates in which Englishmen might live and work without being riddled with tropical and equatorial fevers. Indians might supply a little labor, though it was not felt they could be relied on to add appreciably to the labor force. Criminals might provide servants who could be coerced into doing hard manual labor. Men and women could also be hired on contract, repaying their passage money in return for an eventual grant of land, while in the meantime filling essential places in the growing agricultural economy. Above all, there had to be settlers who would manage affairs and eventually take a leading role in the running of the colonial economy, within the limits of the Company's authority.

In the early stage there were to be managers and sub-managers; otherwise, a president and councillors, with sub-officials of various sorts, all Company men, administering the rank and file as if they were primarily laborers, artisans in the Company's service. In the circumstances of the time, many would be former soldiers, now unemployed at home, who would be given a semi-military role in the colony. If the Indians yielded land and commodities to the settlers, a protective and educative attitude would be adopted toward them, rather than a repressive one. Eventually, most of the settlers would become entitled in their own right to holdings of land. The Company demanded seven years to organize the colony on the lines it desired; throughout that period, all the colonists would work only for the Company. The bait would be landed proprietorship, perhaps even landed wealth, when their investment (if they made any), plus the land due to them under their indentures, would repay them for their period in the Company's service. Some men, mostly soldiers and minor officials, served for wages only and might return to England after a year or so. But all, while in Virginia, were theoretically secure against starvation or want, since they would be serviced from the Company's stock of provisions or from corn and other supplies bought from the Indians. For anything more than necessi-

ties, however, money had to be paid out. Orders dispatched for clothes and books and other such luxuries must be sent out to England usually with a year's delay and at a high level of charges.[21]

The Company's calculations were not very precise at the beginning, nor could they be. Many of the backers hoped that a small measure of social improvement in England would be a result of exporting men, women and children to America. Artisans would either gain by the fostering of decaying English industries or else could apply their skills (or suitable variations of them) to production in the colony. Unemployed ex-soldiers would be taken off the roads and their aggression diverted to pioneering in Virginia. Landless laborers could aspire to become independent farmers while helping the Company in the short run to build up and maintain plantations and other enterprises. Debtors and minor offenders might be released from their unnecessary prison sentences if they went to Virginia. More serious offenders might be sent out under licence to work out sentences there, thus probably escaping execution, since long prison sentences were reserved for state prisoners of some rank. Women of poor character and less desirable occupations might be sent to gain husbands who would oblige them to live a more regular life. Orphan boys and girls might be sent to become servants in colonial households, with promise of a future on the land when they grew up.

If there was little hope that the Indians would work for the English systematically, there was more for their eventual conversion to Protestant Christianity. Harvesting the pagan Indians for the Church of England was a much-publicized and half-believed-in objective, but in the early stages it was a propaganda point only, though one which constantly recurred in various guises. More serious thought was given to the spiritual welfare of the colonists themselves. In the new atmosphere of James's reign, there was no intention of sending out anyone who was severely discontented with the Church of England. But the inculcation of solemn Anglican observances would do much, it was hoped, to enforce social discipline and uniformity of religious practice. In providing an active clergy, the Company could

21. This point is usefully brought out in the lists of goods sent by his family to George Percy during the early years at Jamestown. John W. Shirley, "George Percy at Jamestown, 1607–1612," *Virginia Magazine of History and Biography*, LVII (1949), 227–243.

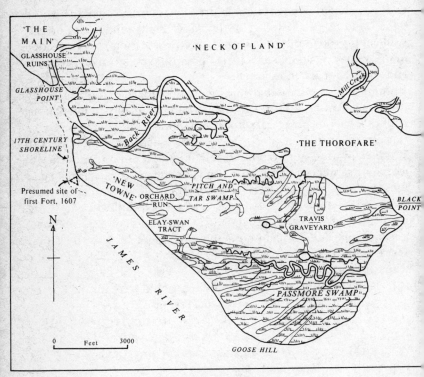

Jamestown 1607–1612
After John L. Cotter, *Archeological Excavations at Jamestown*, Washington,
D.C., 1958

serve God as well as Mammon, to which the grace of Indian conversions might perhaps be added.

The expedition which left the Thames on December 20, 1606, was under the overall command of Christopher Newport, in the *Susan Constant,* with Captain Bartholomew Gosnold in the *Godspeed* and Captain John Ratcliffe (*alias* Sicklemore) in the pinnace *Discovery.* They sailed on Newport's accustomed route through the Caribbean, with little delay and no opposition from the Spaniards. On April 26 (old style), 1607, they sailed directly into Chesapeake Bay, as if they had a pilot who had been there before. They landed a little to the west of Cape Henry (named as such three days later) and were attacked before going back on board by some Indians. But a few wounding arrows were all they experienced, and the Indians had disappeared the following day. On the 29th, they entered the James River (again rapidly so called); a party sailed upstream making friendly contact with successive Indian villages while assessing the value of sites for settlement. When they had decided on one which appeared suitable about 60 miles inland from Cape Henry, they went back to the ships and then piloted them upstream to moor in deep water alongside a peninsula almost detached from the land. Here they laid out the site of a settlement, "Jamesfort"—a name soon changed to Jamestown.

They settled down to establish themselves,[22] and here the first president, Captain Edward Maria Wingfield, an old soldier, took up office, having been named with his councillors in the sealed orders which were opened after they landed. The friendly contacts with the Indians, at least those of the Paspahegh tribe into whose land they had entered, quickly altered for the worse. As Sir Walter Cope put it:[23] "The people used our men well untill they found they began to plant & fortefye, Then they fell to skyrmishing & killed 3 of our people." After that the Englishmen had always to remember they were intruders in an at least potentially hostile territory, although the Virginia Company claimed in 1610 that "Paspehe, one of their kings, sold vnto vs for copper, land to inherite and inhabite."[24]

22. Barbour, *Jamestown Voyages,* I, 133–139.
23. *Ibid.,* 110.
24. *A true declaration of the estate of the colony in Virginia* (London, 1610), reprinted in Peter Force, *Tracts,* 4 vols. (Washington, D.C., 1836–47; Gloucester, Mass., 1963), I, no. 1, 17.

Then, later in May, they followed the river to the Fall Line below modern Richmond, and set up a cross "at the head of this River, naming it the Kings River, where we proclaimed James King of England to have the most right to it."[25] If they were opposed by its Amerindian occupants thereafter they had asked for, even invited, opposition. A triangular fort at Jamestown was completed on June 15 and the colonists considered themselves well protected by it.[26] Corn was sown; the prospects looked good.

Newport set sail with the larger vessels on June 22 and reached Plymouth on July 29, an exceptionally good voyage. He had on board a wide range of specimens of local produce; and he had stones which might be precious, including one which might contain gold. The stones proved simply to be stones, but alchemists reported there was gold in plenty in the ore samples. The first result of this was great enthusiasm in the official group backing the enterprise, Lord Salisbury amongst them, followed by extreme dejection when a second assay established that there was nothing of value there.[27] Gabriel Archer had sent with Newport[28] details of what he considered Virginia offered: sturgeon, "Clapboard and waynscott (if shipps will but fetch it)," "terra Sigillata" (a medicinal earth), sassafras, tobacco (after they had learned to cultivate it), dyes, pitch, resin, turpentine, maple syrup, perhaps apothecary drugs, pearls; and, if they could learn to cultivate grapes and olive trees, wine and olive oil, perhaps soap ash and wood ash, as well as iron and copper from ores when industry got going. Newport set out again from England on October 8. He arrived with the first supply on January 2, 1608, his pinnace taking until April 20, so perhaps Newport was peculiarly expert in making Atlantic crossings.[29]

We hear more of divisions and intrigues than anything else for the time he was away. Wingfield was self-important and indiscreet, Archer ambitious and unscrupulous; the man of best character in the council was Gosnold and he died on August 22. There appears to have been a pro-Spanish and Catholic group and also an ultra-Protestant one, but we cannot distinguish too sharply who was in

25. Barbour, *Jamestown Voyages*, I, 141.
26. *Ibid.*, I, 142–143.
27. *Ibid.*, I, 108–113.
28. *Ibid.*, I, 101–102.
29. *Ibid.*, I, 189–190, 227–228; II, 389–390.

what. The deaths in August chronicled by George Percy were the first of a long tragic sequence. It is possible the settlers were already infected by typhoid and most probably there was scurvy as well. In September, after an agitation by Captain George Kendall, who was expelled from the council, there was an outbreak against Wingfield, who was himself deposed and expelled for a time from the council, Ratcliffe (Sicklemore) being elected in his place. Not long after, Kendall was arrested, tried and executed for treason.[30]

Food was short, men were sick, and the Indians varied in their attitudes between threatening force against the settlers and bringing in corn to help out their dwindling supplies. Captain John Smith's task, and also Captain John Martin's, was to try to trade corn from the Indians. Smith made gradually extending journeys from the fort along the river to do this, and met with some but no outstanding successes. Finally, penetrating up the Chickahominy River in December, he was ambushed and captured by the local tribe. His ability by this time to speak some Algonquian led him to be retained as prisoner by the chief Opechancanough, elder brother of the high chief Powhatan. He conversed easily with his captor. The Indian, in turn, took Smith to the Rappahannock River to see whether he could be identified as the European explorer who, a few years ago, had turned on the Indians, killed several and taken others away with him. Finally, he was brought to Powhatan's lodging at Weromacomaco on the York River. Again, after a mock-sacrifice ritual admitting him to the tribe, he was well received and was eventually released and conducted back over the mere 12 miles across the peninsula to Jamestown. Newport arrived there a few hours later on January 2, 1608. The total number of settlers remaining was not more than half the 104 Newport had left the previous June. Then, on January 7, Jamestown caught fire and burned to the ground. The settlers lost their shelter and equipment in midwinter and what Newport had brought (even though he had new men with him) could not make up the loss. Smith blamed the fire for further deaths of both new and old settlers by exposure.[31]

Smith spoke so much of Powhatan and the power he exercised over all the adjacent Indian tribes that Newport insisted on visiting

30. *Ibid.*, I, 178, 225; II, 386.
31. *Ibid.*, I, 190.

him. The visit was carried out with caution, ceremony and success. It also involved the acquisition of additional corn from Indian sources, Powhatan proving a tough and skillful negotiator. Newport evidently considered that his friendship was worth acquiring, though Smith, he tells us, distrusted him.[32] Both were right. Powhatan was valuable to the tiny settlement if he could be kept on any reasonable terms with the colonists, since in effect he had them in his power. Smith was correct in that Powhatan might, at any time, decide to eliminate the foreign intruders. As it was, except for some mild harassment by the Paspaheghs on whose land they had settled, the colonists were left alone. They took a few prisoners, but ostentatiously returned the spies who came from Powhatan's and Opechancanough's camps to observe their activities at Jamestown.

Newport's pinnace, the *Phoenix*, after her slow voyage, appeared on April 20, bringing supplies and some further reinforcements; but Nelson, her captain, would not allow her to be used for further exploration. Cedar wood was laden in the pinnace; corn was planted; fish-weirs were constructed with some Indian help, but no decisive steps were taken to establish control over a wider area of land.[33] They were still a tolerated, not entirely beleaguered, garrison in territory which might prove wholly hostile. The sometimes malicious and often ridiculous behavior of Martin, Ratcliffe, Archer, Kendall and Smith, and of Wingfield before Newport shipped him back to England in April 1608, had endangered the continuance of the colony. But it is possible to sympathize to some degree with Wingfield when he said: "If it be objected as my oversight to put my self amongst such men, I can saie for my self there wear not any other for our consort."[34]

John Smith emerges as the man who carried the colony through from early in 1608 to the spring of 1609. That he does so largely on the evidence of his own narratives is to some extent a disadvantage for the historian since it is difficult to know precisely how to apportion the responsibilities of others. Still it is clear that he was pre-eminently the man of action, able to push ahead the rebuilding of Jamestown,[35] competent in finding out and trading for the sup-

32. *Ibid.*, I, 201–202; II, 394–395.
33. *Ibid.*, I, 208; II, 445–446.
34. *Ibid.*, I, 234.
35. *Ibid.*, II, 394–395.

plies of corn without which the settlement was at the mercy of its evidently not very successful corn patches and the exiguous rations retained from successive supplies. Above all, he was the man who professed to understand the Indians and how to deal with them. Newport had insisted on pacific relations being maintained, though Smith tempered this with firmness and reprisals if he thought them necessary. He would not tolerate any attempt by the Indians to withhold supplies from the intruders.

Where Smith was most in his element was exploration. In June 1608 he set out to explore Chesapeake Bay, making contacts with the Indians of the Eastern Shore, and discovering and penetrating some little way into the Potomac, where the Indians were found to be suspicious and potentially dangerous. Arriving back on July 21, Smith and his men found much sickness at Jamestown, and a resulting unwillingness to tolerate any longer the rule of the governor, John Ratcliffe.[36] A palace revolution substituted Matthew Scrivener, who at least was exempt from reproaches by the older settlers since he had come out only this year. Smith was anxious to get away once more and set out as soon as possible on a further excursion. This time he made for the head of the bay and there made one of the most interesting contacts so far with the Iroquois tribe, the Susquehanna, on the river of the same name. With these tall and powerful men, there was no linguistic bridge; but they were traders and were already peddling French goods as far south as Chesapeake Bay, indicating how European artifacts were already permeating the Indian economy in the east. There were exchanges of presents since the Iroquois had skins with them for trade. Smith got back to Jamestown on September 7.[37]

Smith tells us that under Ratcliffe little had been done to rehabilitate Jamestown, but that Scrivener got the colonists moving, while he himself replaced Scrivener as governor by a friendly exchange of responsibilities in September. Boats were prepared to go out to purchase corn. At this point Newport appeared with the second supply and altered Smith's whole perspective. His preoccupations were to find gold, to penetrate the upper reaches of the James, and perhaps advance over the watershed so as to discover "a certainty

36. *Ibid.*, I, 218–227, 231–232; II, 399, 405, 409.
37. *Ibid.*, II, 407–409.

of the south sea,"[38] while Powhatan was to be crowned as a sub-king under James I. More important, he had brought out technicians to start up the industrial production of pitch and tar, glass, iron and soap ash (potash): they were mainly Poles and Germans. Smith thought this was a good thing if it could be achieved, but he considered the ceremonial vesting of Powhatan a waste of time and bad in itself since it would enhance his already high opinion of his own status.

Smith did not make the subsequent expedition to the falls of the James. This time Newport marched 50 to 60 miles inland and caught sight of the Quirauk Mountains some 30 miles further on. Peter Wynne reported: "this land is very high ground and fertill," but there was no sign of a watershed. Although several Monacan Indian towns were examined with interest, Newport did not think there was any hope of exploiting the Piedmont at this time. Of the many specimens of minerals brought back, none proved to be of more than passing interest.[39] Smith and the council—now reinforced and according to Smith giving him little freedom of action—did their best to assimilate the 70 new settlers (including 2 women, mistress and maid) to the 130 survivors, by giving an example to the gentlemen in going out to cut trees for clapboard. Smith complained that settlers and Newport's men alike squandered the new supply by selling tools and other metal objects to the Indians for furs and skins, baskets and specimens of animals to be brought back to England. Newport was sent off with samples of pitch, tar, glass, "frankincense" (from *Magnolia virginiana*?), potash, clapboard, wainscot and also a red dye (apparently poccoon).[40]

The search for corn then went ahead. The Indians were now reluctant to trade, Smith saying it was Powhatan's policy to starve them out. Nonetheless on the Chickahominy and the York rivers a certain amount was obtained. Late in December Smith set out for Pamunkey, meeting and being entertained by Powhatan on the way, and duly reaching Opechancanough, from whom he had a somewhat hostile reception. Although they reached some sort of agreement, he did not get much corn. Other searches brought in only a little more. Smith lamented that the time to have gathered in corn

38. *Ibid.*, II, 410.
39. *Ibid.*, I, 245–246; II, 468–469.
40. *Ibid.*, II, 418.

was during the period when Newport was on his expedition up-stream. An expedition to the York River showed that Powhatan had now moved away from Weromacomaco. Smith said this was due to the advice of two Germans whom he had taken under his wing when they fled from Jamestown; in fact it was more likely to be due to the onset of the winter hunting season during which many Indians left their settlements. This visit did in the end produce valuable additions to the store since some Indian villages were found still to have reserves of corn. Defending their own lack of positive achievement, Smith and his associates urged that Virginia had to be exploited *ab initio,* either by slowly building up experience in growing crops, or by teaching the Indians the arts of agriculture and commerce. He thought that they could have done little more with their current resources than explore and accumulate a store of information; nonetheless, the failure to produce a sufficient amount of corn and other basic foods to keep two hundred people over the winter of 1608–9 was not very creditable. The survival of the English over the second winter, however, convinced Powhatan and his subordinate chiefs of the Englishmen's strength; so too, Smith claimed, did his own firmness with thieves and would-be intruders, so that soon better relations between settlers and Indians were established.[41]

The end of winter and spring were busy. Jamestown was repaired and a guarded entrance to the peninsula established so that thieving could be stopped. A sizable amount of pitch, tar and potash was made, and a sample of glass (all there was to be achieved at this time) prepared. With the aid of advice from Indians whom they "tamed," some 30 to 40 acres of land were tilled,[42] and fish-weirs and nets were got ready so that when the sturgeon ran they were able to make a considerable haul; the pigs were increasing and a pig farm on an island was developed under a guard, while domestic fowl were being bred. On the other hand, rats ate much of their reserve of corn and the men had to be dispersed to fish and get oysters, gather roots and so on, while the Indians gave them what they had at this season—deer meat and wildfowl. The food thus provided did not please everyone, and those who were lazy were dragooned into searching for sustenance. Samuel Argall came in to fish for sturgeon

in July and sold them enough wine and biscuit to keep them going. As a result, Smith says that not more than seven or eight out of the two hundred died of disease over the season.[43] This is the best testimony to his capacity as a commander and organizer, and might suggest that the process of acclimatization was developing rapidly.

Leaving England on May 15, 1609, the ships *Blessing, Lion, Falcon,* and *Unity* entered the James River on August 11, being later joined by *Diamond* and *Swallow.* Mostly they were in a bad way, having been damaged and losing men at sea during a hurricane, while two had serious sickness on board. But the *Sea Adventure,* with a new lieutenant governor, Sir Thomas Gates, and the headquarters staff of the new establishment, failed to appear. Strangely, no emergency provisions had been made for a deputy or for the installation of a temporary régime. Lord De La Warr, appointed governor, was to follow the next year. The colonists were found in good shape having been relieved by Argall, who was still there, but they had come home to Jamestown again after being "dispersed in the Savages townes, living one their almes for an ounce of Copper a day."[44] Accompanying the 350 or so new colonists were Captains John Ratcliffe, John Martin and Gabriel Archer, with Francis West, Lord De La Warr's brother.

The assimilation of so many men and women presented the colony with its first major challenge: the chance to transform itself from a garrison into a community. It failed to meet it. There broke out what a Company pamphlet in 1610 called "the tempest of dissention: euery man ouervaluing his own worth would be a Commander: euery man underprising an others value, denied to be commanded."[45] Smith was in a quandary—the old authority was his, the new uncertain. The seamen appear to have backed Smith in an attempt to maintain his authority; the planters, or at least many of them, opposed him and supported Francis West for the presidency as the highest-ranking gentleman in the colony. "Insomuch," said Archer, "as the President, to strengthen his authority, accorded with the mariners, and gave not any due respect to many worthy Gentlemen . . . the Kings Patent we ratified, but refused to be governed by the President that now is, after his time was expired

43. *Ibid.,* II, 448.
44. S. Purchas, *Pilgrimes* IV (1625), 1734.
45. *A true declaration* (1610), in Force, *Tracts,* II, no. 1, 14–15.

and onely subjected our selves to Master West whom we labour to have next President."[46]

West took 120 men to plant at the falls and so removed himself from Jamestown and its immediate difficulties. We know little about this settlement—only the second in Virginia—except that Smith went up, he tells us, to sort out some difficulties with the Indians,[47] but when he had done so the settlers again got into trouble (although after this it seems to have been healthy and prosperous for a time). John Martin was put in charge of another one hundred men in a settlement on the south side of the river, which again, after initial troubles with the Indians, was successful enough.[48] The outpost at Cape Comfort was maintained and developed under Ratcliffe.[49] Smith attempted to get the succession to the presidency for Martin on the expiry of his year of office, but Martin insisted on Smith remaining. Later Smith burned himself severely in a powder explosion and handed over authority to George Percy, who had at least the advantage of birth. Virtually incapacitated for the time being, Smith induced the returning ships to take him with them.[50] With his departure it seemed as if the pioneering days of the colony were over.

The confusion which followed when the fleet had left for England was considerable. Once the corn-buying season began, Ratcliffe went with one pinnace to the York River, was set on by Indians, and he and his men apparently killed.[51] West's pinnace seems to have been more successful. A third vessel, the Swallow, collected so much corn that her men made off with her on a piratical cruise, a number of them getting back to England after various misfortunes.[52] West eventually evacuated the upstream colony (our information on its collapse at this stage is not complete) and set out himself in a small vessel for England in despair at being unable to keep the settlement going. Percy was ill and the council divided. The men died fast at Jamestown. A conservative report admits that one hundred colonists fell ill and fifty died, while Smith says: "within 6 monthes after

46. Purchas, *Pilgrimes*, IV, 1734.
47. Barbour, *Jamestown Voyages*, II, 453.
48. *A true declaration* (1610), in Force, *Tracts*, III, no. 1, 14.
49. Barbour, *Jamestown Voyages*, I, 284; II, 460.
50. *Ibid.*, II, 456-457.
51. *Ibid.*, II, 460.
52. *A true declaration* (1610), in Force, *Tracts*, III, no. 1, 15-16.

there remained not many more than 60. most miserable and poore creatures."[53] The Indians boycotted the colony, chased the deer far into the interior, killed the colony pigs, and managed to trade secretly with men who smuggled out weapons and other artifacts from the store. Jamestown went to rack and ruin—morale declined so that few if any did their work.[54] Was this only because the quality of the settlers was low? Or were the circumstances so grim, with threats from the Indians so real and disease so prevalent that, in the absence of morale-raising activity, hope and effort seemed scarcely worth while? By late May no corn had been planted, no good nets were available to catch the sturgeon when they ran, the Indians had no corn to sell, and food stores were within a few days of being empty. The "Starving Time" almost brought the colony to an end.

The *Sea Adventure* had gone aground on Bermuda in May 1609, but the circumstances of the grounding and the intelligence and skill of Sir Thomas Gates, Sir George Somers and, not least, Captain Newport, enabled the 150 men from her to live well on their own stores and the many pigs which had run wild on the island. The salvage of most of the equipment made it possible to build two pinnaces over the winter and to stock them well. They duly appeared in the James on May 21, 1610, to be greeted by Captain James Davies who was in charge of a garrison of forty men at Fort Algernon, Cape Comfort.[55] At Jamestown, George Percy was found acting as governor over what was left of the colony. The dilapidated settlement and its almost foodless men were a shock to Gates. After a hasty calculation of his stores, he decided that his only chance of rescuing the colonists from starvation was to load the whole colony onto the four small vessels now available. He would take them, crowded as they were, to Newfoundland in the hope of getting fresh food there as well as transport home for those who could not be accommodated for the Atlantic voyage. By June 7 all were on board, leaving Jamestown intact. The little fleet set out to sail down the river. The day before, June 6, Lord De La Warr had at last appeared at the mouth of the river, having left England on April 1, 1610. He encountered them on their way downstream and they all turned

53. Barbour, *Jamestown Voyages*, II, 461.
54. Purchas, *Pilgrimes*, IV, 1749.
55. *Ibid.*, 1748–1749.

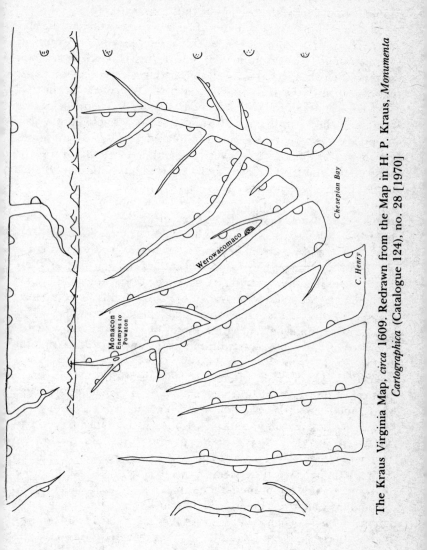

The Kraus Virginia Map, *circa* 1609. Redrawn from the Map in H. P. Kraus, *Monumenta Cartographica* (Catalogue 124), no. 28 [1970]

back. The colony was re-established on June 8, 1610.[56]

Archer had remarked on the small amount of produce which could be sent back with the ships in 1609 because, as he pointed out, food and self-maintenance came first and production for export only second. This state of affairs almost led the Virginia Company to abandon the whole venture, since the return from the colony was so much below expectations. But they had prepared a further large expedition under De La Warr early in 1610, which was to be the final test. He was asked to send Sir Thomas Gates back to England to report on the potentialities of the colony as a viable commercial proposition. As soon as he could be spared, Gates was sent home, arriving in September 1610. We have only a partial report of the consultations of the Company's officers with him. This made much of timber and timber products, which were evidently considered the major items the colony had to offer, in the form of clapboard, wainscots and masts, with derivatives in the form of soap ashes, potash, and gum. Mulberry would make food for silkworms: iron, a silk-grass, and furs from beaver, otter, foxes and squirrels could be obtained. Oranges had tested well and fruited in winter, so there was hope of lemons, sugar, almonds, rice, aniseed and so on. Much sturgeon and other fish were available. Natural products would have to do for a start: "a few yeares labour by planting and husbandry, will furnish all our defects with honour and security." This edited summary of the report was still optimistic, and proved acceptable to the Company for a time at least.[57]

Lord De La Warr threatened the colonists with "the sword of Justice" if they did not proceed to work, and managed to get the ships laden with cedar, clapboard, walnuts and iron ore, with which they and Gates set off in mid-July. Roots, such as turnips and carrots, were planted extensively and produced food for winter. An attempt by Argall and Somers to get to Bermuda for a supply of pigs failed, although Argall brought back some fish and seal meat. He then successfully established trade with the Indians on the Potomac, beyond Powhatan's régime, from whom he got plenty of corn as harvest came in. Their relations with Powhatan remained bad, with minor attacks and reprisals on both sides, but there was no major war. Powhatan is said to have told the English to "depart the Coun-

56. *A true declaration* (1610), in Force, *Tracts*, III, no. 1, 21.
57. *Ibid.*, 21–23.

try, or confine ourselves to James Towne only, without searching into his Land or Rivers."[58] We hear little of the winter but it was evidently not too severe, although in the spring conditions, as usual, were none too good. Cattle, we are told, did well. De La Warr suffered successively from ague, dysentery, and scurvy, which certainly indicates that the food was inadequate even for the leaders. He proposed to take himself with his doctor to Nevis to recover, but his ship got carried out to sea and he turned up in England in May, having left Percy in charge. He met Gates going out again at Cowes, and reported he had left two hundred men well established in Virginia. Gates had Sir Thomas Dale with him, to take over from Percy as De La Warr's deputy. Three new forts had now been planned— Fort Henry and Fort Charles at the entrance to the bay, with another above the falls.[59]

Dale had three ships and three hundred men ready to leave in May, with much in the way of cattle and provisions; he planned to man the new forts and to move the center of the colony further inland (this was not in fact done). Gates followed in August with a similar number and much essential livestock, so that the total reinforcements now amounted to some 550 men and fifty women. When he had taken over at Jamestown, Gates put his plans for diversifying the colony into action as swiftly as possible. Dale was sent in September 1611 to build a second town at the falls, an important piece of diversification; "Henrico" (as it was called) was "strongly impaled" inside seven acres of ground, with watchtowers at each corner, "a faire and handsome Church, and storehouses . . . convenient houses and lodgings for himself and men."[60] The colony had at last begun to expand physically.

By the end of 1611 also De La Warr, Gates and Dale had worked out between them a draconic code of laws for handling the colonists. They were to be prevented from doing anything against the interests of the Company, were to submit to severe, army-style discipline and avoid any suspicion of social or ideological deviance (such as failing to attend church services) under threat of severe penalties, frequently the death penalty itself. The terms for those

58. Purchas, *Pilgrimes*, IV, 1756.
59. *Ibid.*, 1763.
60. Ralph Hamor, *A true discourse of the present state of Virginia* (London, 1615), pp. 29–30.

settlers designated to act as soldiers inside the colony were especially severe. The code was basically one of martial law, to which the new rulers were well accustomed. William Strachey, who had arrived as secretary of the colony with Gates in 1610, brought back a set of these laws and published them in London in 1612 so that later settlers were able to know on what terms they would be governed in Virginia.[61] The development can be seen as a counsel of desperation; it was also realistic, perhaps even necessary. The colony was to be kept in a straitjacket. All the energies of its members were to be devoted to working for the Company, its profits and welfare; individual initiative was a luxury which had to be dispensed with, for the time being at least, since it had almost brought the colony to an end several times since 1607. The new situation of 1611-12 was that the Company's exploitation of the settlement was to be fully developed so as to give it for the first time a potentially profitable investment and the English state its first effective colony in America.

The Virginia Company had started off in a blaze of publicity in 1606, and early reports from Jamestown in 1607 and 1608 had given hope of speedy success in rooting Englishmen effectively, for the first time, in the New World. Yet there were problems even during these enticing years, since King James and his secretary of state, Lord Salisbury, were soon under severe Spanish pressure to disavow the Company and relinquish all claim to settle the North American mainland. He was expected to submit, leaving the settlers to their fate with Jamestown wiped out by Spanish forces from Florida, without any serious protest, Spanish envoys alternated between offering James an attractive marriage alliance for his eldest son with a Spanish princess, and cruder pressure by killing, imprisoning and proceeding against English seamen and merchants taken at sea in American waters, many of whom were used as hostages and subjected to a cat and mouse policy in order to win concessions from the king. For a time in 1607, it seemed as if James might well submit to such pressures and surrender the Virginia Company. Then, late in the year, he saw some prospect of influencing the peace negotiations between Spain and the United Netherlands, and switched his

61. William Strachey, *For the colony in Virginea Britannia. Lawes divine, morall and martiall, etc.* (London, 1612); reprinted, ed. D. H. Flaherty (Charlottesville, Va., 1969).

own policy to a measure of cooperation with Spain in Europe combined with a stiffer line on Virginia. The Company and its colony, Spain was told, would not now be repudiated; the Spaniards would have to submit to a continued English presence there. This attitude was maintained thereafter in the face of repeated Spanish threats and pressures.[62]

It was notable that in the period of stress with Spain over Virginia the royal council, which in 1606 had been given supervisory power over Jamestown and any other colonies which might be established, remained entirely inactive. It certainly did not fulfill the function originally designed for it as an English counterpart to the Spanish Council of the Indies. Perhaps James came to feel that it identified the crown too directly in colonizing activities which still created international complications and could best be dealt with by more flexible diplomatic means. This was one factor leading to the modification of the Company's charter. During 1608, the prospects for investors appeared to be declining when good reports of Jamestown were replaced by bad in spite of Company attempts to prevent the publication of any pamphlets on Virginia except its own. The return of the colonists from Fort St. George on the Sagadahoc River before the end of the year brought the Plymouth division of the Company to an effective end as a colonizing body and is likely to have alarmed the Londoners as well.[63]

Yet on Newport's return in January 1609, there seemed to be some good prospects left. The main point was that Virginia had now become a matter of national prestige, and therefore had court backing such as it had not boasted before. The preparations for the 1609 venture were on a wholly new scale. Gates was to establish the colony in 1609 at a new, higher level. His fleet had not yet left Plymouth when a new charter granted on May 23[64] placed the Company on a stronger basis. Ministers of the crown, courtiers, members of both houses of Parliament, gentlemen, London companies, many merchants and professional men had been assembled as subscribers and were named

62. Quinn, "James I and the Beginnings of Empire in America," *Journal of Imperial and Commonwealth History*, II (1973–4), 135–152.
63. See especially Craven, *Virginia Company of London* (1957).
64. Bemiss (ed.), *Three Charters of the Virginia Company* (1957), pp. 27–54.

in the charter.[65] The council of the Company was now to be termed the Royal Council for Virginia, and the old separate royal council abolished: henceforth James was not to imitate Spain by having a version of the Council of the Indies but was to treat each overseas project and company in isolation. The Company was to have an extended coastline for its colony, 200 miles north and south of Jamestown and inland to the Pacific, thus presenting an uncompromising challenge to Spain. The first councillors were to be nominated, but as they fell out new ones were to be elected by the members at large (though they had to take a special oath to the crown); it was accepted that the adventurers should in time control the Company for their own profit. Firm regulations were to be made to control government inside the colony. Under the 1609 charter, the Virginia Company became a national venture.

The events of the following years—the disappearance of the *Sea Venture* in 1609; the departure of Lord De La Warr to bring the formality of royal government under the Company to the colony early in 1610, and then the return of Gates in September 1610—presented new challenges to Sir Thomas Smith and his core of advisers in London. By playing up the drama of these events and playing down the sufferings and deaths of the winter of 1609–10 at Jamestown, a new wave of enthusiasm was built up and some £18,000, a large sum in the circumstances, raised to send out more colonists. The Company kept up the wave of patriotic enthusiasm, not unmixed with promises of riches from Bermuda and elsewhere if the subscribers persevered. In due course a third charter was granted to the Company on March 12, 1612.[66] This now granted it rights extending some 900 miles out to sea between 30° and 41° N. so as to include Bermuda and to warn Spain off from a still larger area; moreover, the adventurers were given a wider interest in the Company. Henceforth, the quarterly courts, consisting of all subscribers, were to be able to elect officials and councillors, to admit (or refuse admittance to) new adventurers, and to legislate for the government of the colony or colonies, as well as to plan the business

65. An analysis and lists of subscribers under the second (and so far as is known the first) charter is given in Theodore K. Rabb, *Enterprise and Empire* (1967), especially pp. 89–94; biographies in Brown, *Genesis*, II.

66. Bemiss (ed.), *Three Charters of the Virginia Company*, pp. 76–94.

organization of the Company. With the third charter, the Virginia Company had grown into a major corporation with public responsibilities and a colony which it could now be felt would survive and proliferate. In spite of all the difficulties that still lay ahead, this assumption proved in the end to be justified.

The Virginia enterprise had seen from 1607 to 1612 the first attempts on any considerable scale to create a colony whose economic activity would be complementary to that of England. The emphasis on Mediterranean-type products, from grapes to silkworms, had been continuous, but almost wholly useless so far as exports were concerned. Yet these efforts were continued well after 1612, indeed down to the ending of the Company's rule, and it was in the period 1612–24 that a complementary product, tobacco, at last provided an effective export crop. In effect the colonists expended more of their effort, apart from trying to feed themselves on products taken over from the Amerindian population, on products that were complementary to those of England. The cedar wood, the barrelstaves and clapboards, the tar and pitch and resin, the sturgeon, were all intended to demonstrate that the new colony could help out the English economy, especially in timber which was running short there. More particularly, there was a systematic attempt to substitute Virginia timber for English oak in the manufacture of industrial products which in England were consuming increasing quantities of scarce timber. The effort put into the production of iron, glass and potash was substantial but produced very little result. Only samples of iron and glass ever left Virginia, with perhaps some cargoes of potash.

The attempt then to develop what we can call the complementary colony met with only qualified success. The efforts to grow English grains appear to have been unsuccessful, although gardens with English fruits and vegetables were established and English livestock in considerable variety successfully acclimatized in the end. The colony gradually made itself to some extent self-sufficient in food by growing corn and beans in the Indian manner, although some of its tribulations derived from its tardiness in doing so. Mainly it was parasitic on the Indians, depending for corn basically on levies and purchases from them. Thus the lines of possible advance were visible in 1612, but firm economic bases had yet to be established: much of the subsistence of the settlers had still to come from the

Company's English resources. Virginia was an object lesson in the making of colonies. The theoretical plans for producing saleable surpluses proved very different from the realities of so doing. In 1612, the long period of trial and error before Englishmen learned to live on what they could grow in Virginia and on what they could export from there was still far from over.[67]

67. See "The Jamestown Fiasco," in Edmund S. Morgan, *American Slavery, American Freedom* (New York, 1975), pp. 71–91.

# CHAPTER 19

# *The Reopening*
# *and Settlement of the St. Lawrence*

---

AFTER the return of the Roberval expedition from New France in 1543, a veil of silence falls over most of the Gulf of St. Lawrence and the river valley for over thirty years. No narratives record exploring expeditions over the greater part of the area; we have no record of the extent of competition for furs in Indian hands, or for skins and fat from seal and walrus and oil from whale, let alone the extent to which cod fishermen penetrated beyond Cape Breton into the Gulf. The one exception to our ignorance is the emergence of valuable information on the whaling activities of the Spanish Basques. From very soon after Roberval's return, they were developing their whaling activities in the northeastern entry to the Gulf, which came to be known as the Grand Bay, or to the Basques as the central area in their "Provincia de Tierra Nueva." This extended from St. Peters Bay and Chateau Bay at the mouth of the Strait of Belle Isle, all along the Labrador coast westward as far, ultimately, as Grande Coste, part of Jacques Cartier Passage between Anticosti and the mainland. It would appear that from the mid-1540s, the Basques concentrated very much on the eastern harbors of the Strait itself, but gradually extended their range to the west. So far as we know, they remained in the waters quite close to the rocky bays where their ships lay at anchor, while their boats followed and killed the whales which were afterwards brought into the harbors for processing. Some of the bays probably saw men working on shore rendering down the whale oil between June and November in most

years, often with substantial tryworks in operation. It is to be hoped that archeology may in due course provide a map of the sites where these activities were carried on.[1]

What was happening elsewhere in the Gulf we do not at present know. French Basques were active along with the Spanish Basques in the whale fishery, sometimes cooperating with them, sometimes hostile, but operating on a smaller scale. Initially, they seem to have been active mostly at the eastern end of the Strait of Belle Isle. But they may have extended their activities westward and southward into the Gulf, that is, beyond the range of the Spanish Basques, as early as the 1560s and 1570s, since they were later to be found on the western shores of Newfoundland, the Magdalen Islands, and eventually in the St. Lawrence River itself, mainly taking the small white whale (beluga) and walrus. It may be also that the Bretons and French Basques who used the harbors on the northeast of Cape Breton Island for cod fishing and fur trading were also penetrating into the Gulf from the south. Apart from what is coming to light on the Spanish Basques, so far we can only speculate on these problems.

A change, however, comes over the scene in the late 1570s, at the time when Anthony Parkhurst was first calling attention to the "20. or 30. more [ships] that come from Biskaie, to kill Whale for train [oil]," and himself offered to prospect the St. Lawrence River in the English interest.[2] When, in 1580, an English voyage to the Gulf under Edward Cotton of Southampton apparently failed owing to bad organization and probably also effective Basque hostility,[3] French interest in the fishery had already been re-aroused. Troilus de La Roche de Mesgouëz, marquis de La Roche Mesgouëz, obtained in March 1577 a grant from Henry III which entitled him to appropriate such territories of the "Terres-Neuves" as he could make himself master of and exploit for his own benefit. In January 1578 he was made first viceroy in the "Terres-Neuves," though his expedition in that year failed to leave European waters.[4] It seems

1. The material is mainly in the Archivo General de Protocolos de Guipúzcoa, Oñate, and a calendar is being compiled by Mrs. Selma Barkham for the Public Archives of Canada, part of which I have been privileged to see. I am indebted to the P.A.C. and to Mrs. Barkham for their help. See also pp. 518–524 below.

2. Taylor, Hakluyts, I, 126, 128, 134.

3. John Parker (ed.), Merchants and Scholars (Minneapolis, 1965), pp. 120–121.

4. Marcel Trudel, Histoire de la Nouvelle-France, I, Les vaines tentatives, 1524–1603 (1963), 217–218.

clear that he was intending to act as the spearhead of a new Breton drive not only to Newfoundland but to the Gulf and River of St. Lawrence. What we cannot tell, so far, is whether this was on his own initiative or an attempt to follow where Breton fishermen and fur traders had already led—into the zone which the Basques had hitherto kept for themselves. On our present evidence, it would seem that it was the former rather than the latter, since we are told that a small Breton ship in 1581 was the first to make a profitable fur-trading voyage into the St. Lawrence Valley (the evidence is almost wholly from English rather than French sources).[5] The syndicate which owned her took the precaution in 1582 of hiring a Jersey ship, but with a Breton crew, in order to keep the trade secret; but their success was such that they were no longer able to keep their destination quiet when they made a profit of 1400 to 1500 percent by selling furs to a Paris skinner.[6] At least three ships were ready early in 1583 to take up the enterprise from St. Malo. They were back in August after making the first recorded voyage since Roberval into the Gulf of St. Lawrence, "Canada" from Gaspé southwestward, Saguenay, Hochelaga (the vicinity of Montreal), the Lachine Rapids, and beyond, so that they "discovered the sea to the backside of Hochelaga."[7] Moreover, the Indians encountered, including the "Esquimawes" of the Gulf, proved willing to exchange furs of sable, beaver, otter, and moose hides for woolen caps, coarse woolen cloth, iron, copper and trinkets.[8] Again, these furs were sold in Paris and the hides in the Netherlands, bringing in a very high return (20,000 crowns for the furs).[9] We know nothing from French sources of the organizers of these seminal expeditions, but it might appear that one of the leaders of the 1583 venture was Jacques Noël, a nephew of Jacques Cartier, and the heir, so he claimed only a little later, to his patents from Francis I.

The 1583 voyage of Étienne Bellenger to the Bay of Fundy and the Maine coast also enlarged the fur-trading area. The result was something of a boom in 1584. La Roche re-emerged in 1583 as the potential leader of an attempt to combine Norman, Breton and

5. Quinn, *Gilbert*, II, 362, 467.
6. *Ibid.*, II, 362–363; Taylor, *Hakluyts*, I, 205–206.
7. Taylor, *Hakluyts*, I, 206; II, 235, 269, 288.
8. *Ibid.*, I, 205–206; II, 233, 269–270.
9. *Ibid.*, I, 205–206.

French Basque initiatives (the Basques having petitioned Henry III
to plant the recently explored land),[10] in an expedition which would
establish a permanent French colony in New France, apparently on
the St. Lawrence rather than in Acadia. He was again frustrated and
retired from the attempt when his principal vessel went aground
after leaving Brouage.[11] It might seem that Christopher Carleill,
when he sailed for North America in May or June 1584, may have
planned to enter the St. Lawrence instead of attempting to establish
a settlement in New England or Acadia as had originally been intended,[12] but, like that of La Roche, his venture was checked at
birth, since he got no further west than Ireland. The five St. Malo
ships which made the fur-trading voyage to Canada in 1584 brought
two Indians back with them to Brittany in August.[13] No less than ten
vessels were projected for 1585, though we do not know how many
actually sailed, while some of the Norman vessels prepared to follow
Bellenger to Acadia in 1584 may have gone in fact to the St. Lawrence.[14]

The Noël family continued actively in the fur trade during the
1580s. From Jacques Noël's letters in 1587,[15] it is difficult to know
whether it was in 1583 or later (Trudel thought 1585)[16] that he had
gone up the St. Lawrence to Hochelaga, climbed Montreal and saw
the river beyond the rapids, hearing from the Indians of the great
lake (Lake Ontario) which lay beyond the rapids. His sons Michel
and Jean were out in 1587 and seem to have expected to penetrate
at least as far inland, but instead they met competition. This may
have been from rival Breton and Norman vessels or from Spanish
Basques: in the event, three of the small vessels of the Noël firm
were destroyed.[17] As a result Noël tried to revive Cartier's monopoly rights, and on February 12, 1588, obtained (with his partner,
Étienne Chaton de la Jannaye) a twelve-year monopoly of mines and
the trade of furs in Canada. They were to send out colonists, re-

10. *Ibid.*, II, 278, 232.
11. *Ibid.*, II, 227, 278.
12. *Ibid.*, I, 209; Quinn, *Gilbert*, I, 94–95; Quinn, "The Voyage of Étienne Bellenger
to the Maritimes in 1583," *Canadian Historical Review*, XLIII (1962), 342.
13. Taylor, *Hakluyts*, II, 278.
14. Quinn, "The Voyage of Étienne Bellenger," 342–343.
15. Richard Hakluyt, *Principal Navigations*, VIII (1904), 272–274.
16. Trudel, *Histoire de la Nouvelle-France*, I, 221–232.
17. Trudel, *The Beginnings of New France*, p. 59.

prieved prisoners and others, and also to begin missionary work. This led to an uproar in Brittany and the revocation of the grant by Henry III, first leaving free fishing and trade except in lands to be discovered by the partners, and later confining the monopoly to minerals only.[18] This would have left only the territory beyond the rapids to the syndicate, so it withdrew altogether from the Canada trade. The fleet which went from St. Malo annually to the St. Lawrence probably centered its operations at Tadoussac, though individual vessels are likely to have gone further up the river. Norman ships may have participated also, and almost certainly the Spanish Basques continued their traditional combination of whaling and fur trading, though by this time the demands of Philip II's navy for men and the privateering activities of English ships may have begun to take their toll of Basque shipping. We find the emergence of a new pattern in this area: the shipping tended to be owned by French Basques (to save it from being impressed by Philip), while the men came from the Spanish Basque country; financing appears to have been shared, the greater part coming from the French side.

In 1591 the attention of the English was dramatically drawn to the riches of the Gulf of St. Lawrence[19] when a French Basque ship, the *Catherine de St. Vincent*, was captured with a cargo of cod, salmon and oil and also rich furs (beaver, marten, otter, etc.). She was restored after some diplomatic pressure from France. Another French ship, the Breton *Bonaventure*, was also taken in the same year. From the latter it appeared that the Breton ships going to Tadoussac in 1590 had found Basques busily catching walrus on the Isle of Ramea, in the core of the Magdalen Islands. In 1591 a special expedition had been made to the island by two ships, the *Bonaventure* being one of them, and they laded a valuable cargo of walrus ivory, oil and skins. The result was that Lord Burghley, the lord treasurer, inspired a program to obtain a Basque pilot from the French Basque country who would guide English ships to the island, and Bristol merchants began to prepare an expedition to catch walrus. The Basque pilot,

18. *Ibid.*, p. 60.
19. The events of 1591–97 are dealt with in detail between Parker, *Merchants and Scholars*, pp. 119–143; Quinn, "The First Pilgrims," *William and Mary Quarterly*, 3rd Series, XXIII (1966), 368–382; and, more briefly, in *England and the Discovery of America*, pp. 316–333.

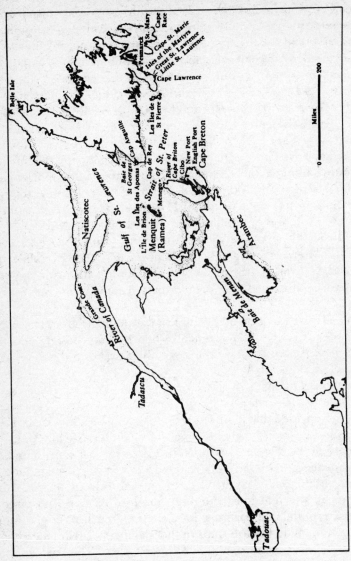

The English in the St. Lawrence, 1591–1597

a Huguenot named Steven de Bocall, duly arrived in 1593, and one ship from London and one financed from Bristol put to sea. The first vessel, under George Drake, with the pilot on board, reached the Magdalens and chased away a Breton ship, taking over the part of her walrus cargo left on land and capturing some more walrus; the second ship had missed her consort at Cabot Strait and merely fished desultorily off the coast of Cape Breton Island and the later Nova Scotia. Bocall was employed to go out again in 1594 with a Bristol ship, the *Grace,* to loot a cargo of whalebone from a wrecked Basque whaler on the west coast of Newfoundland. This again was accomplished, yet neither venture proved very profitable. Whether a further project to capture a Basque whaler which had wintered in the Gulf was carried through or not in 1595 we cannot tell. But at least English interest in the area had been aroused.

From the correspondence surrounding these episodes it is clear that Bocall as a pilot was familiar with whaling, walrus hunting, codfishing, the fur trade, and also, it was said, with the location of copper mines; but the Englishmen were rather narrowly concerned to occupy a base in the Gulf which would give them some security against competitors, Breton or Basque. A London Separatist congregation, most of whose members had been in prison for some years, was given permission to prospect Ramea as a site for a colony. A commercial venture to take walrus and cod, under Captain Charles Leigh, was combined with a reconnaissance by four Separatists, led by the distinguished minister Francis Johnson. The *Hopewell* and the *Chancewell* set out from the Thames on April 28, 1597. Unfortunately, the ships missed each other when making for Cabot Strait. The *Chancewell* ran aground on Cape Breton, and was plundered by Basque cod fishermen. The *Hopewell* reached a harbor in the Magdalens on June 18. Two Breton ships appeared friendly, two Basque vessels unresponsive. When the English attempted to disarm the Basques and seized one vessel, the Bretons collaborated with the remaining Basques, and a number of Micmac Indians as well, to force the *Hopewell* out of the harbor and away from the islands. After some discussion of the possibility of going on to Anticosti, she turned for home, fortunately picking up the *Chancewell*'s crew at Cape Breton on her way back. The would-be pilgrims had to go to the Netherlands instead. Clearly, the Basques had come to accept the Bretons as legitimate associates in the walrus fishery and

would cooperate with them against non-French intruders. Although Leigh put forward a further plan after his return for the seizure of the islands and the installation of a garrison to protect a cod and walrus fishery there, nothing came of it, but these episodes throw some light on an otherwise obscure period. The French interests were clearly so pervasive that only a major effort by another power could have enabled it to penetrate into the Gulf and establish commercial bases there.

Islands were, however, in fashion at this time with the French as well as the English as forward bases in the attempt to acquire oil and skins. In 1597, the marquis de La Roche got the approval of Henry IV to revive his old claims to a monopoly in New France, and sent out a reconnaissance in that year to prospect Sable Island as such a base.[20] There the livestock placed on the island had multiplied, so providing some basic supplies for the colonists, while it had been found that it was a great resort for seal and walrus, and could also possibly be made into a whaling base. The *Catherine* (Thomas Chefdhostel captain) evidently reported favorably. On January 12, 1598, La Roche received a new commission as lieutenant general under the crown in the lands from Canada to Norumbega (New England) to which France was held to have claims. He was to have control and licensing rights over all trade, though not over the fisheries. It was intended that he should plant colonies, but his first objective was a more limited one: to establish a penal settlement on Sable Island which could be made to produce short-term profits for him.

La Roche collected some two hundred men and fifty women, either minor criminals or beggars, though he is not believed to have had more than fifty with him, as well as a number of soldiers, when the expedition set sail with the *Catherine* and the *Françoise* in March 1598. The unwilling colonists were established on Sable Island (named by him Île de Bourbon) in a settlement constructed on a little stream called Boncoeur. The core of the settlement was a large warehouse under a Captain Coussez; we have no details about other buildings. The overall commander was named Querbonyer and we have the names of four other guards. The operations of the settlers

20. The Sable Island story appears in Gustave Lanctot, *Réalisations françaises de Cartier à Montcalm* (Montreal, 1951), pp. 29–50; Trudel, *Beginnings of New France*, pp. 63–65.

were evidently profitable, and La Roche is believed to have had a good cargo when he was picked up by the vessels on their way back from the codfishery and brought back in October. Henry IV made him a present of money for his efforts.

This little settlement was the first French colony in New France to endure for more than a single year. Captain Chefdhostel brought out wine, clothing and hardware in 1599, and carried another cargo back, presumably of sealskins and oil. By this time gardens had been established on the island and the settlers appear to have been self-sufficient in food. In 1600 and 1601, the same pattern was repeated. For some reason—perhaps difficulties in making a landing in bad weather—no aid came to the colonists in 1602. When he reached Sable Island in the late spring of 1603, Chefdhostel found that the colony had disintegrated. In fury at the non-arrival of supplies and frustrated by what must have seemed an endless exile, the settlers had turned on their guards, killed them all, and ransacked the storehouse. They had then begun to kill each other—though it is possible that some escaped from the island. Chefdhostel assembled the many skins which were by then available, and took the eleven survivors under guard to France. Threatened with execution, they were finally pardoned by Henry IV and received part of the profits of their prison labor. This curious episode showed that it was possible to exploit white labor profitably in exceptional circumstances in North America, but that the creation of a stable commerce on such a basis was a risky and uncertain affair.

La Roche had not gone to North America himself after 1598; indeed, he was said to have done little but impede the efforts of the traditional fur traders. In 1599, Pierre Chauvin of Dieppe, a Protestant, with the aid of François Gravé, a Breton Catholic living in Normandy, went behind La Roche's back at court; on November 22, 1599, Chauvin received a grant as the king's lieutenant in Canada and Acadia.[21] This brought immediate complaints from La Roche that he had been cheated. In the end, the king recognized Chauvin as one of La Roche's lieutenants on January 15, 1600, and gave him authority under La Roche to hold part of the St. Lawrence between its mouth and Tadoussac, provided he colonized it.

Chauvin's resources were limited, but he had some experience of

21. On the events of 1599–1603, see Trudel, pp. 65–70.

the fur trade and fishery. In 1600 he went to Tadoussac and set up a small post there, a single building (said to have been only 24 feet long by 18 feet wide) with a palisade and ditch, in which he left, with adequate stores, sixteen men. This was the first French settlement on the mainland since 1543. It proved quite inadequate to withstand the Canadian winter. A number of the men died, and a handful took refuge with the Montagnais, who sheltered them until Chauvin's ship, *L'Espérance,* reached them in the spring. The colonizing gesture, however, had been made, and Chauvin went on repeating his trading pattern in 1602. By the second half of 1602, the Bretons had mobilized their resources against this sectional Norman monopoly. Henry IV attempted first to widen Chauvin's syndicate by including the Rouen merchants in it and then tried to get the Bretons to join the Normans in combining a joint trading monopoly with colonization. They refused and were still holding out against a monopoly of any sort when Chauvin died early in 1603.

It was left to Aymar de Chaste to integrate the Norman effort in 1603, although the Bretons still held out for free trade, and it was his initiatives which bring us fresh light at last on the St. Lawrence Valley. The French hitherto had been successful inside the narrow range of a summer trade in furs. But this did not fully serve the French national ends which were—especially after the Treaty of Vervins with Spain in 1598—directed toward establishing some permanent footholds for France on the North American mainland. King Henry, however, was not going to commit himself to regular and substantial royal expenditure to achieve this. He was determined that the merchants should pay for colonization, if it did not pay its own way, out of the profits they could make in the Indian trade. Eventually this provided a French colony on the St. Lawrence, but a nominal one rather than an effective transfer of a French community to Canada. Even this might not have happened within the short span of Henry IV's lifetime if Samuel de Champlain had not emerged as a personality with an exceptional capacity for adjusting himself to the borderland between France and America, between Indians at one cultural level and Frenchmen at another, and so rendering both commercial and cultural exchanges possible.

Our first clear view of the St. Lawrence Valley comes in 1603. In that year a further agonizing reappraisal of the longer-term prospects of exploiting the fur trade, by a colony if this was essential, but

by other means if it was not, was embarked on. Pierre Chauvin died and Aymar de Chaste took over the headship of the little Norman-Breton oligarchy which still held the monopoly. He selected François Gravé to command the latest expedition, along with Samuel de Champlain, who after some experience in the West Indies and Mexico could, it was thought, give a balanced report on the prospects of New France. Two small vessels were to accompany them to engage in the business side of the enterprise, one of them under the command of Captain Prévert. Gravé's ship, *La Bonne Renommée*, carried a knocked down pinnace for exploration work. She left Honfleur on March 13 and on May 24 anchored at Tadoussac.[22] They had two Indians with them, who had earlier been brought to France; with their aid they made friendly contact with the nearby Montagnais chief, Anadabijou, who was holding a feast (*tabagie*) to celebrate a victory that the Algonquin Indians from high up the St. Lawrence Valley combined with the Etchemins from what would now be the interior of the Maritimes had won over the Iroquois of the Richelieu River. Champlain was thus plunged at once into the problems of Indian politics, in the midst of roughly a thousand Indians who had all moved in to Tadoussac for the trading season.[23]

A few days later, Champlain did his first piece of exploration by sailing up the broad fjord of the Saguenay River, which greatly impressed him by its scale and its possibilities as an entry into the country.[24] When the pinnace was ready, they set out on June 18 to retrace Cartier's old route upstream. They anchored in the narrows named Quebec. Rivers were examined as they explored and landed from time to time, but no mention is made of Indians until they came to the mouth of the Iroquois (the Richelieu) River. There they saw a fortified camp of the Montagnais and other Indians who were about to set off up the river to attack their enemies. Champlain made a short reconnaissance into its channel, but found the current adverse and so returned. From the Indians he learned something of the course of the river from Lake George northward, and also of the further river, the Hudson, "which leads down to the coast of Florida."[25] They had a few Montagnais Indian guides with them as

they approached Montreal. From its vantage point they were able to glean something of the Ottawa Valley from which the Algonquins came, of the chain of rapids on the St. Lawrence, and also of Lake Erie, where their Indian guides had been—and even more vaguely of other great lakes beyond. A huge salt sea lay some distance away, which Champlain thought might possibly be the Pacific.

In all this, Champlain, usefully recorded the topography of the land and water he saw, but also reached out for all the information the Indians could give him about the territories that lay beyond his reach. His appreciation of natural scenery is more specific than that of the Cartier narratives but less wondering and excited. However, he conveys a very different picture of Indian distribution from that of Cartier for the 1530s. The peoples with whom Cartier had lived on the St. Charles River had gone, as had those of Montreal. The Montagnais had emerged from the small roving bands of southern Labrador as a powerful, though still largely nomadic people, occupying lands on the north bank of the St. Lawrence well beyond Quebec. They were closely linked with Algonquins from the Ottawa River valley, even, as was to be found later, with Hurons from still more distant Georgian Bay on Lake Huron, who came down the river from time to time in summer. All these Indians, collectively—with Etchemin bands coming up from the southeast to aid them—were embattled against the Iroquois tribes of the Richelieu River. The old tribal groupings in "Canada" in its original meaning as the region upstream from Tadoussac, and of "Hochelaga," the Montreal region, had disappeared. Montagnais had taken their place in the former; no one in the latter. Was there a St. Lawrence Iroquois culture which died out by natural causes or was snuffed out by southern Iroquois aggression after 1543? Or was there a smaller mixed Iroquois-Algonkian grouping which disappeared from "Canada" and a Huron grouping in "Hochelaga" which retreated to the Huron homeland on Georgian Bay? These problems still excite ethnographers. The theory of a distinctive St. Lawrence Iroquois culture appears to be on the defensive, but no final solution is in sight.[26]

Champlain's account of his return voyage is largely concerned with geographical speculation. The Montagnais, if not at any ad-

26. See Bruce G. Trigger, "Trade and Tribal Warfare in the St. Lawrence in the Sixteenth Century," *Ethnohistory*, IX (1962), 240–256.

vanced stage of culture, were shown to be widely conversant with the country through which they roamed or where they had contacts, and were able to hand out much information which was valuable in enlarging the picture the French could draw. In particular, they were able to tell Champlain about "le bon Irocois," the Hurons, who came far down the river to barter with the Algonquins, who had bartered with the Montagnais, who had bartered with the French.[27] The chain of French commerce had thus already extended as far west as Lake Huron and as far south as Chesapeake Bay. Much of the new-found influence of the Montagnais had come through the fur trade.

Back at Tadoussac in July, La Bonne Renommée worked her way along the southern shore of the river to Île Percée at its mouth. There she made contact with Prévert, who had traded nearby and had heard of a copper mine which had led him to make an expedition into modern New Brunswick. From Indian stories, he gathered that at the head of the Bay of Fundy there was a major source of copper and, he thought, silver also. Champlain then gave a description of Chaleur Bay, gathered from Prévert, and of the outlines of the western part of the Gulf of St. Lawrence—the first we have since that of Cartier in 1534. The information gathered about the land which lay to the south in Acadia, which we know as the Maritimes, was attractive. The ships set out on their return on August 24 and reached Le Havre on September 20.[28] The most immediate result of the voyage was the publication of Champlain's little book, Des sauvages,[29] which was based on his journal and stressed both the geographical and the ethnographical results of his review of what was already, to many French seamen and traders, familiar ground, but had not been described since Cartier's day for the expanding public in France which was interested in the New World.

Aymar de Chaste died in 1603. Pierre du Gua, sieur de Monts, took his place at the head of the syndicate.[30] His appeal to Henry IV produced, as has been indicated above, a very wide-ranging

27. Champlain, Works, I, 145–165.
28. Ibid., I, 166–189.
29. Des sauvages, ou Voyage de Samuel Champlain, de Brouage, fait en la France nouvelle l'an mil six cens trois (Paris, 1603).
30. See William I. Morse, Pierre du Gua, Sieur de Monts (London, 1939); Trudel, Beginnings of New France, pp. 74–81; "Pierre du Gua, Sieur de Monts," and "François Gravé du Pont," in Dictionary of Canadian Biography, I, (1965).

grant which included all the territories north of 40° N., and so comprised the whole of the Gulf of St. Lawrence and the river beyond. The broadening of the base on which the monopoly was based, by the admission of new shareholders, did not satisfy all the Frenchmen with interests in the fur trade, particularly the French Basques and some Bretons; and it could not, of course, affect the Spanish Basques whose preserve the Gulf still largely was. From 1604 onward, however, all fur traders in the Gulf and river were supposed to bear licences from the sieur de Monts, and severe penalties might be enforced on them if they were found guilty of interloping. However, the monopoly was charged with the duty of settling sixty colonists a year in New France. The reports brought by Champlain suggested that little profit was to be gained by a settlement on the St. Lawrence, since, if the monopoly was maintained, the fur trade would produce as much without as with a colony, the costs of which would eat into profits. The decision was therefore taken not to colonize the St. Lawrence but Acadia, where climatic conditions were believed to be better and where Prévert's mines were an attraction, as well as holding out the prospect of being able to grow crops which would sustain the settlement.

The colonizing ventures of 1604–7 thus belong to the eastern seaboard and are treated as such.[31] The monopoly sent out its own vessels to the St. Lawrence each year to take as large a share as it could of the Tadoussac fur trade, but was unable either to police the main exchange point or to patrol the immensely long coastlines covered by the grant in the Gulf and river. The Basques, both Spanish and French, ignored the monopoly and traded as a side activity to their whaling program as they had done in the past. Other anti-monopoly groups also sent vessels from France on interloping missions. In 1605, the Dutch seriously contemplated entering the fur trade and acquired most of the beaver skins collected in 1606. Though seizures were made, and proceedings against eight men taken in 1604 were brought the following year,[32] policing operations interfered with the codfishery which the monopoly did not cover, and gradually the profits of the fur trade to the monopoly

31. See above, pp. 395–406.
32. H. P. Biggar, *The Early Trading Companies of New France* (Toronto, 1901), p. 57; Trudel, *Beginnings of New France*, p. 91, where he says that "It had been an illusory monopoly."

group fell. By the summer of 1607 it was agreed to withdraw the monopoly and the colony from Acadia. When this was done, the sieur de Monts was left with considerable losses; on Champlain's advice he decided to try to recoup them by getting a short-term monopoly of the St. Lawrence River only. The argument for this was that, in view of the competitive position which had developed at Tadoussac, the profitable thing to do was to establish a post well upstream where the flow of furs down the river could be intercepted. This the sieur de Monts accepted, and he was empowered to make the attempt in 1608.

On January 7, 1608, Henry IV granted the sieur de Monts a one-year monopoly of the St. Lawrence fur trade, since "We have resolved to continue the settlement which had already been begun in those parts."[33] While it was true that this was a continuation of the policy of settlement embarked on in 1604, and that Poutrincourt was to return to Port Royal to maintain some degree of continuity there, this grant was the starting point for almost all later French colonization in North America. On this occasion Champlain and Gravé were empowered, under the sieur de Monts's patent, to establish a permanent settlement on the great river—the fifth in point of time, but the first to endure.

Gravé left France for Tadoussac on April 5, arriving there in late May. He found Basque whalers already lying off the mouth of the Saguenay trading for furs. Gravé tried to stop them by asserting the monopoly rights granted by the king, but they fired on him, wounded him, killed one of his men and disarmed his ship, while continuing with their trade. Champlain, arriving with a second vessel on June 3, resisted the temptation to begin an armed struggle with the Basques, and eventually made an agreement between them and Gravé. They would cease fur trading—they had probably got their lading already—and Gravé for his part would not interfere with their whaling.[34]

In and round the harbor inside the entry to the Saguenay were many Indian birchbark canoes, up to 25 feet in length and about 4 feet in breadth. These had come from great distances, many of them down the great fjord of the Saguenay itself. Leaving his men to load

33. Champlain, *Works*, II, 5.
34. *Ibid.*, II, 8–16.

the equipment he would need to make a settlement further up-stream, Champlain set out to explore the Saguenay. He does not give any details of how far he went, but it was probably further than he had gone in 1603. He would have seen the great fall at the head of the fjord at Chicoutimi which marked the terminus of the broad waterway. He would know henceforth that this was no channel into northern seas, even though it was a vitally important portage route for the fur trade of the more northern regions—the Indians told him of the salt sea (Hudson Bay)—and this route extended westward as well as northward from the head of the fjord, linking up eventually by portage with Georgian Bay itself.[35] It was on the mouth of the Saguenay that Indian routes converged, bringing furs of beaver, marten, lynx and otter to be exchanged at Tadoussac.

On June 30 Champlain set out for the site of his intended settlement, Quebec. As always, the Île d'Orléans excited admiration for its low shores, its trees, its meadows, its game. On July 3, he selected his site for his *habitacion* on the mainland on level ground, at the extreme tip of the great bluff which faces the Île d'Orléans and which towered up behind the site. He cleared the nut trees, dug out cellars and ditches, and, getting his sawmill going, built first of all a storehouse in which the essential provisions for the winter could be stored. He then sent the pinnace back to Tadoussac to obtain the rest of the equipment left on Gravé's ship.

Not all Champlain's men were willing to stay over the winter in Canada. A conspiracy to kill him was discovered—inspired, he alleged, by Spanish Basques—and one conspirator was hanged. The rest of the doubtful men were shipped back to France when Gravé left on September 18. The *habitacion* was now completed as rapidly as possible. It consisted of three two-story buildings and a large storehouse. A gallery ran round the outside of the upper story, linking building to building. The whole was surrounded by a deep ditch, outside which bastions for artillery were constructed, and a palisade enclosed the entire complex. This represented a substantial and well-equipped center of operations—fortress, residence, and trading post all in one. Just outside the palisade, gardens were laid out and planted, and a landing stage constructed on the river.[36]

The rhythm of Montagnais Indian life established itself around

35. *Ibid.,* II, 16–19.
36. *Ibid.,* 24–25, 29, 35–36: see Plate 17.

him. Many canoes were fishing for eels and bringing them to be dried on shore from mid-September to mid-October. The Indians left their eels and gear with Champlain, trusting him to protect them, while they went off to hunt beaver—not very fruitfully—until mid-December. For another month they remained nearby, living largely on the dried eels. On January 20 they set out on a moose hunt, and in search of other larger animals like bear. They came back in the spring with the meat they had saved and the skins they had assembled, but had to be helped out with supplies by Champlain until summer came round again. The French found the Montagnais improvident, gorging themselves one month, starving the next, with only limited patience and foresight in preserving food, and neither skill in growing crops nor the will to do so.[37]

The winter wheat and rye had been sown in October and came up in the spring—evidently the winter was not a very hard one. There were gales and snow in November but they did not last; snow was on the ground from January onward and ice on the river. In February there was heavy snow, and floating ice. It was at this time that a band of Indians crossed the river at great peril to themselves to get food from Champlain to keep them alive. He had much difficulty in keeping them from eating all he had, and they ate the carrion and other organic debris thrown out by the French as well as what they were given. The snow had gone by the end of April, a month earlier than from Tadoussac to the eastward.[38] Scurvy had struck Champlain's little colony of twenty-eight men; ten died of it, five later of dysentery, and then the surgeon of an unspecified complaint. This left twelve men alive, five of whom had recovered from scurvy. Champlain reckoned that from April to mid-December Canada was healthy, but that winter was dangerous; he himself blamed the salt food for most of the winter deaths.[39] The result of the experience of the year 1608–9 was to show that settlement on a permanent basis was feasible, although there were to be worse winters than that first experienced. The careful construction of warm quarters, skill in administering the *habitacion,* above all confidence in their leader and his ability to deal with emergencies as they arose, had brought the French colony through its first critical

37. *Ibid.,* II, 44–46, 52–57.
38. *Ibid.,* II, 56–58.
39. *Ibid.,* II, 58–63; Trudel, *Beginnings of New France,* p. 94.

winter with some real degree of success.

Gravé arrived at Tadoussac on May 28, 1609, and sent a boat upstream to make contact with Champlain, who came down to meet him there. It was arranged that Gravé should make the experiment of wintering at Tadoussac, while Champlain first took an expedition upstream from Quebec and then returned to France, where the sieur de Monts had had his monopoly extended for a further year.[40]

Champlain was determined to make contact with both the Algonquins and the Hurons who came down the river each summer before they reached Tadoussac, since the whole purpose of the Quebec settlement was to gain control of the furs which were brought down the St. Lawrence. He expected to meet parties descending the river in the vicinity of Montreal before the end of June. He set out from Quebec on June 18, and had gone only some 60 miles when he encountered a mixed war band of Algonquins and Hurons on their way to attack Iroquois territory south of the river. They were determined that Champlain should accompany them to seal their earlier compact, but first of all they wished to inspect Quebec. Once they had returned there, a vigorous trade in furs followed, accompanied by feasts and dances. Gravé came up from Tadoussac for the occasion. Champlain fitted out a shallop to accompany the expedition, which now included some Montagnais, to the junction of the Richelieu River with the St. Lawrence. The French boats were able to work up the river as far as the St. Louis Rapids, then Champlain and his men had to join the Indians in their canoes. The borders of the Iroquois country proved totally uninhabited. Champlain had only nine of his own men with him, and some sixty Indians. He accompanied the Indians on hunting trips as they proceeded and came to know a good deal about their behavior and their complex war maneuvers. The most significant geographical information he obtained confirmed what he had been told in 1603, that beyond the lake in which the river was said to rise (Lake George), another river lay not far away to which a portage was possible (the Hudson), that this flowed to the south, and that from it, he understood, it would be possible to get to Florida.

On June 29 they at last encountered an Iroquois war party of some two hundred men. A battle was arranged, with considerable

40. Champlain, *Works*, II, 63.

formality, for the following morning. Champlain was posted so that he could shoot at the three Iroquois chiefs at the head of their men as the affray began. He killed two and wounded one. This so disconcerted the Iroquois that they broke under the attack of their enemies, even though they were so much superior in numbers, leaving about a dozen prisoners behind.[41] This Battle of Lake Champlain —for so he named the lake—was the first assertion of European firepower in an area where the gun was soon to be a regular weapon of war. Otherwise it was of interest for its revelation that even one Frenchman could be a valuable fighting asset to an Indian raiding party, even if the encounter was war only on a minuscule scale.

The Indians and French made their way back to the St. Lawrence, where Champlain observed the way the victors tortured their prisoners. Then they separated, Algonquins and Hurons returning to their homes, while the Montagnais, with their share of the prisoners, went back with Champlain to Quebec and on to Tadoussac where the victory was duly celebrated. At Quebec, Champlain found that Gravé had, after all, decided to go back to France and that he was to accompany him. The man who was left in charge was Pierre Chavin (possibly a relative of the dead Pierre Chauvin). With fifteen men he was to see the *habitacion* through its second winter. In October, Champlain had an audience with Henry IV who expressed his interest in what was being done in his name in Canada. It was decided that Champlain would return to complete the exploration of the St. Lawrence Basin, which the Hurons had promised to facilitate if he would aid them in their wars in return. The sieur de Monts hoped to extend his monopoly to cover the upper part of the St. Lawrence Valley, but this was not permitted. However, the Quebec base was to be retained—a significant move toward its being regarded as permanent.[42]

Champlain finally left France for Canada on April 8 and reached Tadoussac on the 26th, having had a quite exceptionally fast passage. He found that other vessels had already reached there on the 18th, and there was very little ice. An unusually mild winter had helped Chavin to survive at Quebec with little except minor illnesses amongst the men. Champlain put it on record that if fresh meat was

41. *Ibid.,* II, 82–101.
42. *Ibid.,* II, 107–112.

available instead of salt, wintering in Canada might be as easy as it was in France.

The Montagnais had promised to conduct Champlain on an expedition up the St. Maurice River as far as Hudson Bay and back by way of the Saguenay River, but they decided against this, putting it off for another year (and even then it did not take place). He was, however, engaged to go up the river to meet Algonquins and Hurons, he hoped in their own country, later in 1610. Finding Quebec safe and the men there well, he continued upstream with a war party of sixty Montagnais, taking four pinnaces of merchandise to trade for furs with the more than four hundred Algonquins and Hurons who were expected at the mouth of the Richelieu River. There it was assumed that they would repeat the pattern of their activities in 1609: trading, followed by a raid to the south. Champlain was met by an Algonquin chief bearing him a present of a fine, large piece of pure copper, which he explained had been found at a great lake, melted into sheets and hammered flat with stones. Except for the melting, this described what happened at Lake Superior where there were extensive beds of natural copper. Champlain was also disconcerted to find that Basque shallops were coming up to prevent the sieur de Monts from enjoying a monopoly of the fur traffic above Quebec.[43]

Arriving at the mouth of the Richelieu, the situation was found to be quite different from what it had been in 1609. The Iroquois had built a strongly entrenched fort a little way up from the confluence of the Richelieu and St. Lawrence. Champlain went ahead with four of his men and the Montagnais party to assist in an attack which had already begun on the fort by an Algonquin war party. He swiftly took command, firing through the barricade with considerable effect. Other Frenchmen came up from the boats and a combined assault enabled them to overrun the fort. A number of Iroquois were killed or taken prisoner, and the rest forced to flee. While this was going on, a busy fur market was being held on the St. Lawrence, the interlopers forcing Champlain's men to pay rather more than they would otherwise have done for their furs. Champlain saw further scenes of torture as the prisoners were divided—his own share was one man, who later escaped. A Huron party of eighty men

43. *Ibid.*, II, 118–125.

arrived too late for the fighting, though not for trade.[44]

One Huron chief, named Iroquet, who had been with him in 1609, now arranged with Champlain that a French boy (apparently the later celebrated Étienne Brulé, though he is not named) should accompany the Hurons to learn their language and their customs, while a young Huron, Savignon, would remain with the French and be sent to France. This opened up the way for further contacts with the Hurons and perhaps a visit to Huronia on Georgian Bay. It was not, however, a wholly satisfactory summer. The total number of urs brought down the river was not large, and competition from the Basque free traders had reduced the number which Champlain was able to secure. Moreover, news had come of the king's assassination on May 14, which upset both Champlain and Gravé and made the future for them and for the sieur de Monts most uncertain, as the last two were Huguenots and it might well be that a Catholic reaction would destroy any influence they had at court. At Quebec, a young man, Du Parc, who had been there in 1609–10, was left in charge with only sixteen men to see the third winter through. The garden was now well stocked with vegetables; both European grains and Indian corn had been grown successfully, so that the basic supply problem appeared to have been overcome. Champlain was back in France on September 27, 1610.[45]

Setting out once more for Canada on March 1, 1611, he met icebergs off the Newfoundland Banks and was in some danger from them, then, at Cape Breton, he encountered pack ice at the mouth of the Gulf of St. Lawrence. By working his way along the southwestern shore of Newfoundland he found enough open water to get to Tadoussac, which was still wrapped in snow, on May 13. He hurried upstream past Quebec to meet the Hurons as arranged in 1610, but they were not at the rendezvous near the Richelieu River. So he made his way to Montreal, where he laid out a possible trading base on a site which he called Place Royale (the later Callières, near the St. Pierre River), though he could build nothing there for the present. Gravé had followed him with additional trade goods; so did other French traders and some Spanish Basques, thirteen pinnaces in all.

On June 13 two hundred Hurons, including Iroquet and the

44. *Ibid.*, II, 125–134.
45. *Ibid.*, II, 137–148.

French boy left with him, appeared, and the Indian taken to France, Savignon, was returned safely. Champlain received from them a present of one hundred beaver skins and gave presents in return. He found that the Hurons wished to have serious discussions with him. They were prepared to accept Champlain as their friend and ally, but they were suspicious of the other traders and did not want to become involved with them. (This story may be correctly reported, but it may be that Champlain loads it somewhat against his competitors.) Now, with adequate interpreters, Champlain could learn a great deal about the interior so far as it was known to the Hurons. Their range was considerable since they were not themselves so much hunters, though they did hunt, as entrepreneurs for furs obtained by more distant tribes. There was a sea very far distant and difficult of access on which he could get no precise bearings. Further, an Indian had come to them from a far country, to the south of the Iroquois country—Florida, he thought—and told them of "our" ocean (the Atlantic). John Smith had already met Susquehanna Iroquois in 1608 on Chesapeake Bay who were trading in French axes and other goods, so that reciprocal information on regions on or near the eastern coastline was now possible. The Hurons had comparatively few skins to barter, and what there was had to be shared with the competing pinnaces; but they declared that they wished to trade exclusively with the group of Frenchmen under his leadership. Presents of "4 carquans de leur porcelaines," wampum belts of great value in their eyes, were given to Champlain and Gravé. They told Champlain that he could winter with them with forty-six to fifty men, and they would set up trading post (habitacions) for him if he wished; but we cannot be sure that they understood what inviting Frenchmen to live among them might imply in the longer run.

For the first time, Champlain was conducted to the head of the rapids for further conferences and then shot the Lachine Rapids on the way back, along with a young Indian in a canoe. At last he had proof they were not impassable. Another exchange of French lad for a Huron was arranged. The first Algonquin group appeared on July 12 and July 15 only. There were not many of them and they had few furs. They complained that many of them had been sick—had they caught some European disease from the French? Others had gone on the warpath instead of coming to

trade, but they exchanged what they had amicably.[46]

The picture we get of French commerce with the Indians in these exchanges is an interesting one. The Indians are willing to bring to their rendezvous substantial presents and to accept gifts in return. They have little idea of systematic and priced exchange, and are more concerned with questions of prestige and ceremony than commerce. They accept Champlain as a friend and an ally in war on his own merits—or so he says, and he carries conviction. They do not wish to become involved in haggling with numerous Frenchmen, who may, they fear, prove too formidable for them if they should turn hostile. Champlain, on his side, exhibits a massive confidence. He appears to have had no thought of treachery but accepted the Indians on their own merits, so long as their exchanges with him were conducted with due ceremony. He acted not so much like a trader as a soldier and diplomat. This, at the early stage, was his great strength. But it remained difficult to see how an expanding market could be raised on the system of mutual esteem which he was so successful in establishing.

The knowledge which Champlain had now gained covered a wide expanse of territory, ranging from the Hudson River Valley to Hudson Bay in the north, and from the mouth of the St. Lawrence to, in outline at least, Lake Superior. He knew something too of the long and complex series of portages from Georgian Bay to the Ottawa, to the St. John and eventually to Saguenay. There was even in the west the mysterious sea which lay, so far as he could tell, beyond all the known lakes. This was either a confused reference to one of the Upper Great Lakes or to Lake Winnipeg, but at the stage at which he heard of it, it sounded at last like news of the Pacific Ocean.

The French now knew that, from season to season, the conditions of the fur trade varied very much. The more commercially indoctrinated Indians came all the way to Tadoussac; those less interested in trade than in warfare or social intercourse would come only as far as Quebec or Montreal to exchange furs. The latter could not be expected to attempt to maximize their output of pelts. Indeed, they were inclined to regard collecting beaver as a sport of which they might, in some seasons, easily tire. As the Hurons depended for

46. *Ibid.*, II, 173–213.

some of the furs and skins they used themselves on distant tribes, they were tied into a widening circle of uncertainties. Champlain felt that if he himself went to their homelands and assessed the trade situation, he might be able to come up with novel solutions for his demanding masters in France, whose only desire was for more beaver. He understood very well that he must wait upon events, live up to the Indians' expectations of him if he could, and avoid pressing trade on the Algonquins and Hurons beyond the point at which they would freely accept it, at least for the time being.

With this knowledge and understanding he got back to France on September 10. The sieur de Monts had at last been pushed out of his commanding position in the Canada trade, which he had held since 1603, and for which he had done a great deal. Merchant rivals, playing on anti-Huguenot feeling, had at last succeeded in getting rid of him. Champlain set to work to get what he considered essential, a stable organization with some degree of permanence, behind him. He also felt that he must put his experiences on record while they were fresh in his mind and, perhaps, when they could still be influential in promoting his future plans. The reorganization of 1612–13, after Quebec had survived five winters, and the publication of *Les voyages* in 1613,[47] fitly mark the completion of one major stage in the installation of European influence in a significant part of North America. The French presence was in the form of a trading post only and a summer trade at that; but even in a few years it had established roots in North American soil and had cast its influence hundreds of miles from the *habitacion* at Quebec. Although its circle of influence went on expanding after 1612 reasonably rapidly, it was to be a long time before the French began to colonize in earnest.

In perspective, the French achievement in the few years from 1608 to 1612 is more impressive than that of the Spaniards in Florida or of the English in Virginia. This is partly because by the time they seriously began to establish a year-round trading center in the St. Lawrence Valley they had accumulated sufficient experience on how it could be done effectively without too much elaboration in manpower and costs. The concentration on the fur trade and the subordination of all other economic effort to this proved suc-

47. *Les voyages faits au grand fleuve Sainct Laurens . . . depuis l'année 1608, jusques en 1612* (Paris, 1613).

cessful. This limitation of ends and consequent economy in means was basic to the success of the venture. That this might not have been possible without the exceptional qualities of leadership and organization which Champlain brought to his task we have seen; but beyond this, there is the point that had it not appeared to the Indians that their interests would be served by its continuance, the French post at Quebec could not have survived. Well before 1608, the French had conditioned the Indians of the St. Lawrence Valley to accept and to count on the duties and benefits which the fur trade brought to them. Consequently, the alliance of the French with the tribes whose interests were best served by the continuance of the trade enabled the trading post to be established and maintained with very little use of force. Otherwise it would have been wiped out. In a peculiar degree, therefore, the French established themselves in the St. Lawrence Valley on sufferance. In no other case in the early settlements which had been attempted so far by Europeans was the self-interest, or presumed self-interest, of a substantial indigenous population so directly served by a continuing European presence. The aid that the French gave to the Indians in war was a consideration in assuring the safety of their trading post. But it was the French beads and copper, axes and knives, and the economic power and prestige which these conveyed, which provided essentially for the continuance of the French settlement. This argues, perhaps, a degree of sophistication among the Indians of this region which was not equaled elsewhere in their early relations with Europeans. Elsewhere the Amerindians were almost invariably exploited to their disadvantage by the Europeans: here the exploitation was mutual, with the balance of advantage, if anything, on the side of the native peoples. This situation was to change gradually with the growth of French efforts to indoctrinate the Indians with European ideology and religion, and the ultimate appearance of French settlers; but it was in large measure the key to the peculiar and successful establishment of the French in North America on a permanent basis.

# CHAPTER 20

## The Revival
## of Spanish Interest in the West, 1580–1612

THE failure of the great expeditions of Coronado and Hernando de Soto to discover either men or metals which could be profitably exploited turned the attention of the viceregal government in Mexico away from any further northern adventures, whether toward the Atlantic or the Pacific shores of North America.[1] No attempt was made to follow up the littoral discoveries of Cabrilho, and neither miners nor missionaries penetrated into the Gulf of California, much less along the outer coast. There was much to do in the meantime to extend the Mexican mining frontier in detail, though this still remained well to the south of the area traversed by Coronado. Admittedly, the discovery of the northern Pacific return route from the Philippines by Arellano and Urdaneta in 1565 revived interest in the Pacific coast, and the institution of the Manila Galleon as an annual trading link between the Philippines and Mexico in 1572 and thereafter made the outer coastline of potential concern to the viceregal government, since galleons might conceiv-

1. There is a good summary of Spanish policy and activity in the west in Warren L. Cook, *Flood Tide of Empire, Spain and the Pacific Northwest, 1543–1819* (New Haven, 1973), pp. 1–17; and a fuller general treatment in Charles E. Chapman, *A History of California, Spanish period* (New York, 1921). Henry R. Wagner, *Spanish Voyages to the Northwest Coast of America in the Sixteenth Century* (San Francisco, 1929; reprinted Amsterdam, 1966) has many documents, and is supported by the rich but unannotated collection, W. Michael Mathes (ed.), *Documentos para la historia de la demarcación comercial de California, 1580–1630*, 2 vols. (Madrid, 1965).

ably be cast away there.[2] The theory became current that the galleons sometimes sighted a hazily known Cape Mendocino at about 44° and came down the coast to pick up Cape Lucas at the tip of the California peninsula as the guide to their destination in Acapulco. But it is very doubtful if such vessels, except under unusual stress of weather, sighted land north of Lower California. Nonetheless, California was the equivalent on the west to what Florida had been on the east in the early part of the century: a place which might be worth investigation, possibly even settlement, if ships were wrecked far beyond the limits of authority in this area.

Not even this slight impetus existed for a long time toward land exploration northward from Mexico to the pueblo country.[3] The northern limit became and remained Santa Bárbara, many hundreds of miles to the north. Moreover, in 1573 the New Laws of the Indies laid down restrictions calculated to curb adventurous pioneers, since no new territorial conquests were to be permitted in future without very formal royal sanction, which it was not proposed to give except in unusual circumstances. If new discoveries were entirely concerned with the conversion of Indians, they might hope for rather lighter treatment. In later expansion toward Pueblo North America, the question was whether expeditions there might be regarded as new discoveries, or whether Coronado's visit had conferred some legitimacy on further ventures since these would not, perhaps, be entirely novel. This did not arise until 1581. In that year, as the result of vague rumors of wealthy populations in the north reaching Santa Bárbara, the Franciscan Agustín Rodríguez, and two other friars, determined to make an expedition to the north with a soldier, Francisco Chamuscado, who had obtained some sort

2. See Philip W. Powell, *Soldiers, Indians and Silver. The Northward Advance of New Spain, 1550–1600* (Berkeley, 1953), for the expansion of Mexico in the later sixteenth century. See William L. Schurz, *The Manila Galleon* (New York, 1939; reprinted 1959), for the background on trans-Pacific navigation.

3. On the exploration of the interior, the older collections have been largely superseded by George P. Hammond and Agapito Rey (eds.), *The Rediscovery of New Mexico, 1580–1594* (Albuquerque, N.M., 1966), and *Oñate, Colonizer of New Mexico*, 2 vols. (Albuquerque, N.M., 1953), though H. E. Bolton, *Spanish Exploration in the Southwest, 1546–1706* (N.Y., 1908), is still useful. Albert H. Schroder and Dan S. Matson (eds.), *A Colony on the Move. Gaspar Castaña de Sosa's Journal, 1590–1591* (Santa Fe, N.M., 1965), has useful notes. Gaspar Perez de Villagra, *A History of New Mexico*, translated by Gilberto Espinosa (Los Angeles, 1933; reprinted Chicago, 1962), which was first published at Alcala in 1610, has some colorful passages.

of licence to make discoveries.[4] Nine soldiers, three friars and their servants set out on June 5, 1581, made a long journey through barren country, and eventually reached the valley of the Río Grande del Norte, on the southern fringes of the Pueblo country. They took possession of it for the king as San Felipe del Nuevo Mexico on August 21, though whether such action had any legal force in Mexico itself was somewhat doubtful.[5] Two of the friars, Rodríguez and López, remained at Puarey to lay foundations for a mission, while the remainder returned to Santa Bárbara in April 1582, though Chamuscado died on the return journey.

The return of the remnants of the Chamuscado mission brought exaggerated reports of the riches and novelty of the pueblos, and preparations were made to follow up the discovery. After some confusion, an adventurer, Antonio de Espejo, emerged as the leader of a small party of soldier-volunteers, with a single friar, Bernardino de Beltrán. This set out on November 10, 1582, to go to the aid of the missionaries of Puarey and to prospect the alleged wealth of the region. After surviving an Indian attack, they reached the Pueblos in December and soon ascertained that the friars had been killed by the Tigua tribe, which had deserted the pueblo (in the modern Sandia-Bernalillo area) on the news of the arrival of the Spaniards: they found no traces of the missionaries there in February 1583. When they reached the Zuñi territory, they were well received and were impressed by the three- and four-story pueblo villages. They ranged widely from there without interference from the Indians, locating a mineral outcrop which showed that copper and a little silver (later exaggerated by Espejo) were present. Fray Bernardino and Espejo's lieutenant, Gregorio Hernández, insisted on setting out for the return journey since they had seen enough; but Espejo himself, with the remainder of his party, ranged widely, in extended forays, looking for minerals until mid-July, when they turned back,

4. On the emergence of New Mexico, D. W. Meinig, *Southwest* (New York, 1971) has a succinct account. Jack D. Forbes, *Apache, Navajo and Spaniard* (Norman, Okla. 1960) throws much light on Spanish-Indian relations, as does Oakah L. Jones, Jr. *Pueblo Warriors and Spanish Conquest* (Norman, Okla., 1966). W. A. Beck, *New Mexico A History* (Norman, Okla., 1962), and W. A. Beck and Ynez D. Haase, *Historical Atlas of New Mexico* (Norman, Okla., 1969), are standard works. Edward H. Spicer, *Cycle of Conquest* (Tucson, Ariz., 1962), and Elizabeth A. H. John, *Storms Brewed in Other Men's Worlds* (College Station, Tex., 1975) are valuable for the broader perspective on the southwest.

5. Hammond and Rey, *Rediscovery*, pp. 6–15, 67–150.

reaching Santa Bárbara by September 10, 1583. The variety of the country, the interest of the people seen and the prospects of successful agriculture along the Rio Grande, combined with the hope of minerals, aroused still further ambitions in Mexico of a rich country open for conquest and exploitation. The optimistic reports which reached Europe were shortly to have wide publicity there also. The king had already instructed the viceroy on April 19, 1583 (before the return of the Espejo expedition) to select a suitable person to carry through the conquest in the king's name; but it was to be fifteen years before this instruction was effectively acted upon, though in the meantime the fame of New Mexico grew by report, and exaggeration, until it was widely, if inaccurately, known in Spanish America and in Europe.[6]

The valley of the Río Grande offered a feasible extension of Spanish influence northward from Mexico. The pueblos were strung out along the river for some 200 miles from Senacu at the south, on the edge of the desert, to Taos near the foot of the high mountain barrier at the head of the valley. The area extended westward into the valleys of the tributaries of the Río Grande as far as the modern Gran Quivira. On the east they crossed the mountain chain to the Upper Pecos Valley, which was to become an outpost for the exploration of the Great Plains. Modern estimates of Indian population put it at about 40,000, dispersed into perhaps 60 villages. Each pueblo was a compact series of structures, sometimes consolidated into a single communal building, and with an area of irrigated corn land around it; each was reasonably self-contained and virtually independent of its neighbors, though the different language groups had certain broad tribal loyalties. They totally lacked any overriding political structure or institutions. The area gained some of its unity from its isolation in a wider sea of roving Apache tribes, which tended to raid into the settled area though they also traded with it. The relatively advanced social organization of the pueblos, together with their lack of any common organs of defense and the generally pacific character of the people (though

6. *Ibid.*, pp. 213-1231. J. González de Mendoza, *Historia . . . de la China* (Madrid, 1586), contained a reasonably full account of the Espejo expedition. Richard Hakluyt extracted and reprinted it as *El viaje que hizo Antonio de Espejo* (Paris, 1586), a French translation following, *Historie des terres nouvellement descouvertes* (Paris, 1586), and an English one, *New Mexico* (London, 1587), being finally reprinted in Richard Hakluyt, *Principal navigations*, 3 vols (London, 1598-1600), III, 383-406.

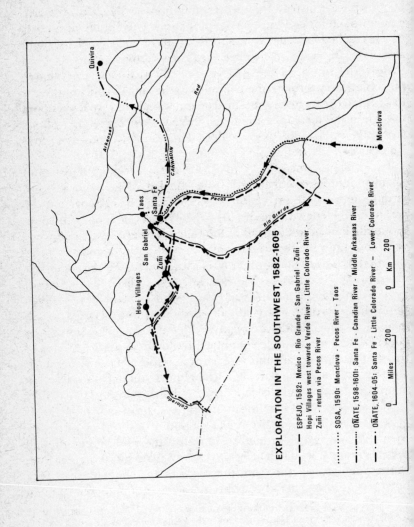

**EXPLORATION IN THE SOUTHWEST, 1582-1605**

- - - ESPEJO, 1582: Mexico - Rio Grande - San Gabriel - Zuñi -
Hopi Villages west towards Verde River - Little Colorado River -
Zuñi - return via Pecos River

············· SOSA, 1590: Monclova - Pecos River - Taos

············· OÑATE, 1598-1601: Santa Fe - Canadian River - Middle Arkansas River

—·—·— OÑATE, 1604-05: Santa Fe - Little Colorado River - Lower Colorado River

they could fight fiercely when driven to it), appeared to make the Río Grande Basin an ideal area for combined Spanish missionary activity and mine-based settlement.

Drake's appearance on the Pacific coast of Mexico in 1579 and his activities in the north—though how rapidly his annexation of New Albion became known is not clear—was a further element in calling Spanish attention to the potential value of the Pacific coast, if not for Spaniards, then for their enemies.[7] The first move came at the initiative of Francisco Gualle (or Gali), who made the passage from Manila to Acapulco in 1584 and who came within sight of land at about 37° N. He planned an exploring voyage down the coast on his next return from the Philippines and was given permission by the viceroy to make it, but died before his ship was ready.[8] The command devolved on Pedro de Unamuno, who set out with a small vessel on July 12, 1587. He examined a bay at what he estimated to be 35° 30′, possibly Morro Bay, which he named Puerto de San Lucas, and made a short excursion inland, but his discovery was soon forgotten. However, the capture of the Manila galleon *Santa Ana* by Thomas Cavendish off Cape San Lucas in November 1587 emphasized the continued danger from foreign interlopers on the coast. This produced two contradictory reactions from the authorities: some advocated that the Pacific coast should be explored as far north as possible, so that defensive measures should be taken if they were required; while others held that the coast was best left unexplored, since if it was charted and described foreigners would get to know of it and be more likely to intervene there. The question of the Strait of Anian—the myth created by the cartographers of a strait running from the Pacific to the Atlantic—brought similar arguments. If Spain found it, it would be wise, said some, to make it impassable to other Europeans; alternatively, if it was not brought to light, the danger of other Europeans attempting to find it could be held to be less. Exploration of the coast was, therefore, left to lie in the limbo of unrealized projects.

The next *entrada* was by a Portuguese, Gaspar Castanha de Sousa,

7. H. R. Wagner, *Sir Francis Drake's Voyage Round the World* (San Francisco, 1926; reprinted Amsterdam, 1969), pp. 135–153. The Spaniards certainly learned in 1584 and 1587 something of Drake's activities in naming New Albion as an English possession—Zelia Nuttall (ed.), *New Light on Drake* (London, 1914), pp. 31–32, 50–51—though it is not known how widely this information had been disseminated.

8. Wagner, *Spanish Voyages*, pp. 132–153.

best known by his Spanish name, Castaña de Sosa.[9] In 1589, he was lieutenant governor of the Mexican frontier province of Nueva León. Excited by the pueblo discoveries of the earlier years of the decade, and disappointed at the relatively low silver yield of his own province, he hoped to do much better in New Mexico. Consequently, he mobilized the mining population of Almadén, men, women and children, and, though no permission to make an expedition had arrived, set out with his caravan to colonize New Mexico on July 27, 1590, with wagons, cattle and some 150 persons. He pioneered a very difficult, and now it would seem untraceable, route northward to the Pecos River, which he ascended. In December, Indians attacked one of his scouting parties which was stealing corn at Pecos. Sosa thereupon attacked and occupied the pueblo at the end of December. He crossed the mountains to the Río Grande in the vicinity of the later Santa Fé, moving northward through the pueblos in cold, winter weather, but was generously supplied with food by the frequent pueblos he encountered. He did not find it easy to determine on a site for his colony but settled for the time being at the pueblo he named Santo Domingo, in a north-central position in the valley.

In June 1590, Juan Morlete, a captain stationed at Mazapilin in Nueva León, had been sent by the viceroy to Almadén to warn Sosa that he was not to make his expedition to New Mexico, and was also to cease the slavetrading in which he had apparently been engaged. But Sosa insisted on going, so Morlete was in due course commissioned to follow him and bring him back. Following the route pioneered by Chamuscado and Espejo to the Río Grande, Morlete reached Santo Domingo with forty men on March 29, 1591. Sosa was on a short expedition at this time. He returned to find that his companions had submitted to Morlete and that he was isolated. He made the best of his situation, submitting to being treated as prisoner and to the order to return to Mexico. Morlete undertook a brief survey of the surrounding area, then rounded up the colonists and convoyed them all back to Mexico in August. The process against Sosa was, as usual, protracted, but he was found guilty of disobedience in 1593 and sentenced to exile in the Philippines. (He was afterwards rehabilitated by the Council of the Indies—but too

9. Hammond and Rey, *Rediscovery*, pp. 245–295; Schroeder and Matson, *Colony on the Move*, passim.

late, as he had by then been killed in the Moluccas.) These proceedings against Sosa did not prevent a further expedition into the northern lands.[10] Francisco Leyva de Bonilla took a party from Nueva Vizcaya up the Arkansas River to the Buffalo Plains in modern Kansas, but there a servant killed Leyva, the Indians accounted for the remaining Spaniards, and only a half-Hispanicized Indian survived to tell the tale. Thus it was clear that official policy was skeptical about New Mexico and would certainly not countenance any half-baked colonizing or prospecting ventures there.

The repeated suggestions to Philip II that an exploration of the Pacific coast should be carried out in the interest of the Manila Galleons seemed to have had some effect at last when the viceroy of Mexico, Luis de Velasco the younger, reported that on April 6, 1594, a Portuguese pilot, known in Spanish as Sebastian Rodríguez Cermeño, had left in command of the *San Agustín* on this long-deferred mission. Cermeño examined the coast in the vicinity of 41° 46′ N. and named a cape which he found Cape Mendoçino.[11] He then took possession of a bay—the modern Drake's Bay—and explored the adjoining coast in his pinnace, being the first to do so since Drake's visit. Unfortunately his ship was wrecked off the shore through negligence and, with twenty-two men, he had to work his way down the coast in the *lancha*, making some slight examination of the harbors and islands, and reaching Mexico in January 1596. The information he brought was well received and it was intended to follow up his discoveries by a more intensive examination of the coast. However, just as Espejo's discoveries were followed by a considerable gap while the official discussions about what to do next went on, so in Cermeño's case it was six years before a successor to carry on his task was got to sea. Clearly there was no sense of urgency about coastal exploration. In the interval, the old discussions of whether to carry on with discovery or to leave the coast unexplored were revived, during which the official expedition to colonize New Mexico at last got under way.

The commissioning of Juan de Oñate as governor and captain general of New Mexico on September 21, 1595, seemed to mark the

10. Hammond and Rey, *Rediscovery*, pp. 48–50, 323–326.

11. Wagner, *Spanish Voyages*, pp. 154–167; Donald C. Cutter, *The California Coast: Documents from the Sutro Collection* (Norman, Okla., 1969), pp. 27–40.

end of a period of indecision.[12] The governor was a man of considerable influence in Mexico. As the son of the discoverer of the rich silver mine of Zacatecas, he was regarded as being wealthy enough to bear the major part of the cost of the conquest; he was promised the office of *adelantado,* with the nomination of his heir as his successor, should he be successful in his enterprise. He was to raise two hundred men, and equip them and their wives and families with supplies, horses, cattle and transport. Toward his costs he received some arms only and a loan from the crown. Oñate had some grandiose ideas. He wanted the authority to establish ports on both the Atlantic and Pacific shores of his dominion, since the great distances between the oceans (revealed by Coronado and Hernando de Soto) had been totally forgotten. He also aspired to act directly under the Council of the Indies, independently of the viceroy of Mexico—to be a viceroy of North America indeed. He did himself no good by these extravagances since the new viceroy of Mexico cut down his powers further, denying him the authority to appoint the first royal officials in New Mexico, who were to remain under the control of the viceroy. In fact, during the delays there were reports that a rival candidate, Pedro Ponce de León, was being favored in Spain to replace him. At length in 1597 Oñate was able to complete his preparations, and on January 8, 1598, his force was officially inspected on leaving Mexico.[13] He was somewhat undermanned: with him were only 129 men, accompanied by their wives, children and servants, making perhaps some 500 souls in all. There were also eight Franciscan friars under the commissary, Alonzo Martínes, and two lay brothers, since this official expedition set great store on the task of converting the Pueblo Indians to Christianity. Oñate had been instructed to regard assistance to the friars as one of his highest priorities.

The expedition was designed to reach out 700 miles beyond Santa Bárbara and to take under its control the whole of the pueblo area. To envisage the permanent conquest of a population of some 40,000 with such a small force was a sign of almost Cortésan confidence. Oñate, in the early stages of his march, showed himself very

12. Hammond and Rey, *Oñate,* I, 42–69.
13. Paul Horgan, *Conquistadors in North America* (London, 1963), pp. 215–289, has a useful general account. The documentation in Hammond and Rey, *Oñate,* is exhaustive.

much the resourceful pioneer, marking out and following a new and somewhat shorter route from Santa Bárbara to the Río Grande. Upon reaching it on April 20, all the kingdoms and provinces of New Mexico were solemnly incorporated into the Spanish empire, to be placed under military control, their ecclesiastical organization to be created and the governor to allot lands at will to those who were to settle there—without regard, it would seem, for any prior rights of Indian occupation.[14] These grandiose pronouncements and plans indicated that the air of unreality which had surrounded the enterprise since its inception was to be continued.

A 200-mile march up the valley to the confluence of the Chama River with the Río Grande and a little beyond showed off the cavalcade to the majority of the pueblos. The Indians were, we are told, submissive and anxious to supply gifts of food and other things. Indeed they were even willing, with what degree of pressure we do not know, to vacate certain pueblos in favor of the newcomers. From the first, the friars made Santo Domingo their center, and dispersed themselves fairly quickly over the major pueblos, hoping to learn enough of the local languages to begin their effective mission rapidly. Two pueblos well to the north, Ohke, renamed San Juan de los Caballeros, and Yanque, renamed San Gabriel, at the confluence of the Chama and Río Grande, were taken over for the settlers, who found in them adequate accommodation. San Juan, on the west side, north of the Chama, was named the capital. As always a church was built as the primary foundation, and wheat and chilis planted to supplement the corn and cucurbits received from the Indians. A number of families settled down to raise stock, to irrigate and cultivate, in circumstances rather better than those to be found in the rough mining areas of the Mexican frontier. Most of the men however, being soldiers, resented the lack of opportunities open to them for wealth and domination. As Indian hospitality declined, so pressure on the neighboring pueblos to provide additional food, blankets, and so on, increased. When enough was not forthcoming the soldiers forced their way into the peaceful pueblos and subjected the inhabitants to violence. The Indians on the whole submitted to insult, rape and robbery with stoicism, while the friars attempted to protect their charges as they could see little chance of

14. Villagra, *History of New Mexico* (1962), pp. 129-137.

success in their mission if the inhabitants were antagonized and ill-treated.

Oñate's solution for unrest amongst his men was exploration, which they gladly embarked on. Juan de Zaldívar was sent to the east over the mountains to the buffalo country where meat and skins should be obtained, though catching and killing the prairie cattle did not prove as easy as they expected while they worked their way along the Canadian River. They left Fray Francisco de San Miguel to found a new mission at Pecos just over the divide between the valleys of the Rio Grande and the Pecos River. Oñate himself struck out westward in October, reaching in turn Ácoma, Zuñi, and the Hopi pueblos, and being well received at each. A party under Marcos Farfán went on a long prospecting trip into what is now central Arizona, finding fairly extensive mineral deposits which appeared to be worth revisiting and, possibly, working. Moreover, Farfán was able to inform Oñate to his great delight that he had found evidence that the Pacific was not too far away, since the tribesmen he met had seashells which they claimed had been traded eastward from the ocean.[15] After waiting in vain for reinforcements, which failed to arrive, Oñate at last decided to return to San Juan to spend Christmas there. When he arrived he was met with bad news. His reinforcing party had indeed set out. But the men had made too free use of their hands and weapons in Ácoma, and the inhabitants had turned violently on them, killing their leader, Juan de Zaldívar, and twelve of his men, the remainder making their way back in defeat to San Juan.

Oñate, after consulting the Spanish colony, determined to destroy Ácoma in reprisal. He took seventy men for the attack on the pueblo. Climbing up to a position commanding the village, he mounted several cannon which pulverized the adobe structure. His men then swept down, killing great numbers of Indians and taking seventy men and some five hundred women and children captive to San Juan. The victory was followed by the mutilation of all the men and the enforced servitude of the entire population for a twenty-year term, which none are known to have survived. Early in 1599 it was thus demonstrated that in New Mexico, as elsewhere, brutal exploitation went hand in hand with benevolent missionary inten-

15. Hammond and Rey, *Oñate*, I, 408–415.

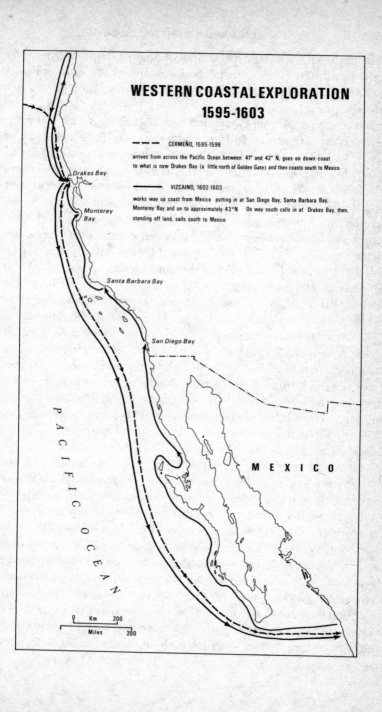

# WESTERN COASTAL EXPLORATION
## 1595-1603

– – – – CERMEÑO, 1595-1596

arrives from across the Pacific Ocean between 41° and 42° N, goes on down coast
to what is now Drakes Bay (a little north of Golden Gate) and then coasts south to Mexico

———— VIZCAINO, 1602-1603

works way up coast from Mexico putting in at San Diego Bay, Santa Barbara Bay,
Monterey Bay and on to approximately 43°N   On way south calls in at Drakes Bay, then,
standing off land, sails south to Mexico

*Drakes Bay*

*Monterey Bay*

*Santa Barbara Bay*

*San Diego Bay*

P A C I F I C   O C E A N

M E X I C O

0        Km        200
Miles       200

tions in the characteristic dichotomy of Spanish imperial rule. The majority of the pueblo dwellers were cowed by this episode; thereafter, the amount of resistance was limited, though still not entirely absent.

By the spring of 1599 Oñate had established a basis for a permanent settlement, with agriculture and a system of food levies on the pueblos as its key elements. But he was still without any capacity to enrich his men or to justify the importation of additional settlers who alone could create a strong Spanish community. He had sent Vicente de Zaldívar to take up his interrupted march to the South Sea, but he, after wandering some hundreds of miles westward, returned without finding either the ocean or any other desirable incentives. Nonetheless, the reports that Oñate was now sending to Philip III, who had succeeded to the Spanish throne, were far from pessimistic. He could offer him "a new world, greater than New Spain,"[16] and his agents were busy rounding up additional settlers in Mexico by rosy promises of wealth. He was so successful that on December 24, 1599, seventy-three male recruits with their families reached the capital. This had by now been moved to the second of the Chama pueblos, San Gabriel. Seven more friars came to join those scattered through the pueblos and were soon making some minimal progress in their task of conversion, though Oñate's tactics, not unknown earlier in Mexico, were to resort to mass baptisms and then intimidate the Indians into some show of conformity with the ruling religion.

The new settlers were spread out along the Río Grande to form new settlements; but the prospects for such additional members were not good unless more profitable resources could be discovered. Indeed, the reinforcements threatened the whole basis of the continuance of the colony in its present form. The tales of the rich country of Quivira, which had led Coronado astray, were still current, so in June 1601 Oñate took about one-third of his men on an expedition to the east. He got his wagons over the mountains to Pecos and eventually onto the open plains. The party encountered many buffalo on the hoof and did not go short of meat. Some of the Indians they met were only semi-nomadic and could supply them with some corn; others were wholly nomadic, though mostly

16. *Ibid,* I, 23–24.

friendly. Oñate, like Coronado before him, found the plains endless and, since no Quivira appeared, he eventually turned back. He returned safely in November after one savage brush with the Indians en route, with his men in good condition after their long march.

The inevitable growing pains of colonial settlement had by this time become evident. The Indian pueblos had grown sullen in their response to demands for continued supplies of food and blankets. The friars were discouraged—the exploitation of the Indians had ruined the chances of winning them over by kindness to any effective acceptance of Christianity. The settlers could make only a living (some of them scarcely that) on their holdings, while the soldiers, in the absence of mineral wealth, were becoming mutinous. Thus the picture which Oñate continued to draw of a prosperous colony in the midst of a docile Indian population, 40,000 of whom had accepted baptism and were cheerfully supplying the Spaniards with corn, cucurbits, chickens and meat, had become ridiculously false.[17] Moreover, highly critical reports were also being sent to Mexico at the same time since the friars continued to hold some independent lines of communication. On September 7, 1601, the lieutenant governor Francisco de Sosa Penalosa presided at a mass meeting of settlers in which the great majority decided to abandon the colony completely. Friars like Francisco de San Miguel approved of this as the only answer if a just way of life was to be restored to the Indians. Most of the leading soldiers declared that their families were not making a reasonable living and there was no hope at all of wealth. Only a minority held out, calling a rival meeting under Sosa and Géronimo Márquez to support Oñate's policy. But by then a majority of the settlers had packed up and were already on their way home to Mexico, accompanied by a number of the friars. During October and November their wagons made their way back along the long trail to Santa Bárbara. There they denounced Oñate for his deceptions, and even called in question his loyalty to the crown.

Oñate, returning to San Gabriel on November 24, 1601, found that his empire had crumbled; only a handful of faithful followers, and the men he had brought back with him, remained. He sent off messages to Mexico and to Spain to denounce the traitors, who had, he said, deserted their posts; meanwhile, he managed to pull the

17. Horgan, *Conquistadors*, p. 244.

remaining settlers together, much as they had been before the reinforcements arrived in 1600.

For several years the reduced colony went through a period of obscurity and consolidation; it had found something of a level, and the few remaining friars at last began to make some genuine progress in conversion. The high hopes with which the colony began had been stultified; there remained only a small Spanish salient at the end of a 700-hundred-mile trail from Santa Bárbara. Had the wheels of Spanish bureaucracy ground even a little faster, Oñate would almost certainly have been rooted out and the colony finally abandoned; as it was, the semi-oblivion that descended on New Mexico in the end meant that something was salvaged.

Some leisurely progress in exploring the Gulf of California alone had been made in the interval. Sebastian Vizcaino had made detailed though inaccurate observations there in 1596 when prospecting for a pearl fishery. By 1598 the viceroy was anxious to have the outer coast explored, since to do so might throw light on Oñate's plans to link New Mexico with the Pacific. Such was the difficulty of reaching a final decision that it was 1602 before Vizcaino was eventually ready to go.[18] He left Acapulco on May 5 with two ships, the *San Diego* and the *Santo Tomás*, and the pinnace *Tres Reyes*. He was to sail at least as far as 44° N. and to bring back a full account of the coast, with indications of places which might be worth occupying and perhaps employing as ports of call for the Manila Galleons. He was to take possession of "the Kingdom of California" for the king, while the three Carmelite friars who accompanied him were to estimate the prospects for missionary work along the coast. It is not quite certain whether he also had specific instructions to look for the supposed Strait of Anian.[19]

Although Vizcaino encountered contrary winds on his way up the coast, he made quite reasonable progress after rounding Cape Lucas. His first port of call was at the Bay of San Bernabé in Lower California, where the Indians proved to be well disposed. The ships were unable to keep together, the *Santo Tomás* losing contact for a

18. The Viscaino voyages are the subject of a monograph by W. Michael Mathes, *Vizcaíno and Spanish Expansion in the Pacific Ocean, 1580–1630* (San Francisco, 1968). There is extensive documentation in Wagner, *Spanish Voyages*, pp. 168–282, 435–449; Cutter, *The California Coast*, pp. 45–118.

19. Wagner, *Spanish Voyages*, pp. 168–185.

time, but they were reunited at the Isla de Cedros at the beginning of September. After sailing for some distance up a good coast, the vessels again met contrary winds and separated when a mountain range, the "Mesas de San Cypriano,"[20] became visible after they had passed modern Punta Antonio. Near this point the *San Diego*'s men met Indians who had some exciting news to impart by signs. According to what was understood by Vizcaino's men, they knew of men in the interior who carried firearms. This appeared to be information that Oñate's men were making their way, as planned, to the Pacific. At the Bay of San Simon y Juda the Indians were less accommodating, and thieving by them was replied to by gunfire, though afterwards trading relations were established.[21] On November 10 they entered San Diego Bay, where contacts with Indians were again friendly. They moved up the coast on December 14 and sighted the mountain "Sierra de Santa Lucia," which "is the one which ships from the Philippines ordinarily sight" (evidently the range culminating in Mount Carmel, 4,000 ft). Two days later they entered Monterey Bay, named in honor of the viceroy.[22] This appeared to Vizcaino a suitable place in which to take stock of what they had done and could still do.

The expedition was now threatened by severe outbreaks of scurvy on all three vessels. Men were becoming incapacitated very rapidly and a number had died. It was decided, before worse befell, to send home the badly sick in the *Santo Tomás,* which could also carry back interim reports for the viceroy and the king. Vizcaino reported optimistically on the results of his mission so far, and recommended Monterey highly: "besides the fact that the port is in such a favorable latitude to fulfill the intentions of His Majesty for the relief and security of the ships which come from the Philippines, any needs which they have can be filled because it has a great quantity of pine trees for masts and yards, even for a ship of a thousand tons . . . and a plentiful supply of sweet water . . . the country is well settled with Indians and is very fertile. The climate and soil are like those of Castile, and whatever seed may be sown will produce crops."[23] The depleted vessels sailed on, the men perhaps a little recovered after

20. *Ibid.,* pp. 222, 298.
21. *Ibid.,* pp. 226, 230.
22. *Ibid.,* pp. 242–245.
23. *Ibid.,* p. 405.

a rest at Monterey. Francisco Bolaños, who had been with Cermeño earlier, could now act as an effective pilot. He took the *San Diego* and the pinnace to within sight of Point Reyes, and a search was made along the shores of "San Francisco Bay," that is, Drake's Bay, for signs of the wrecked *San Agustín*, though without success.

Setting out again, they sighted what they reckoned to be the mysterious Cape Mendocino at a latitude of 41° 30′ N. This was not the modern cape of this name but probably a headland ending in Trinidad Head at 41° 3′ (their latitude reckonings being anything from 20 to 60 minutes out). The men on board the *San Diego* were again suffering most severely from scurvy, so it was decided to turn back at about 42° instead of carrying on to 44° as their instructions required. The *Tres Reyes* had gone ahead and reached about 43° N. before she too turned back on her course, since "no news or signs of the City of Quivira could be had during the whole course of the exploration." The *San Diego* reached Acapulco on March 21, 1603; the *Tres Reyes* had a worse time, and most of her men had died before she reached Navidad. Carrying detailed sketches of the coastline, logs and narratives, Vizcaino and the survivors made their way to Chapultepec, to be duly congratulated on their persistence and on the discoveries they had made.

At last a reasonably full record of the California coast to well beyond the limit reached by the *San Agustín* was in the hands of the authorities in Mexico and in Spain. No sign of the fabled Strait of Anian had been seen. The authorities in Mexico believed that publicity about the coast would be more likely to attract English interlopers than to aid Spanish enterprises. It was not accepted that the Manila Galleons needed a way-station anything like as far north as Monterey. Though Vizcaino praised the coast, other members of his expedition considered much of it to be of little value for settlement. True, the possibilities for missions looked favorable. But on the whole, the verdict was negative. Unless and until the New Mexico settlement made contact with the ocean, there seemed little point in burdening the viceroyalty of Mexico with a further long line of coast whose protection would employ resources already fully stretched. Vizcaino's expedition thus served the cause of geographical knowledge—when the news became known—but not the further expansion of the Spanish dominions.

Meantime, Oñate had remained in New Mexico, hearing nothing

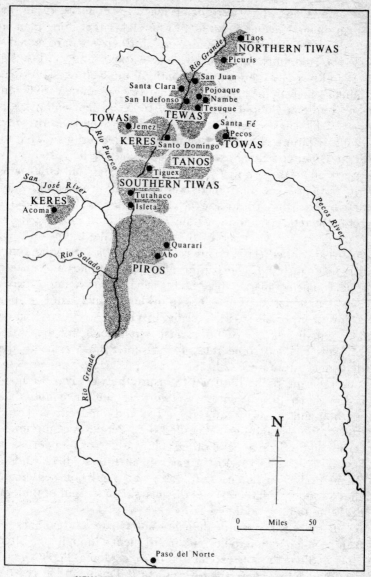

**NEW MEXICO: EASTERN PUEBLOS ABOUT 1612**
This includes from 50 to 79 pueblos in 9 language groups
(After Spicer, Cycles of Conquest [1962])

of the many plans which were being made to reinforce, recall, or reprimand him. Leaving about fifty of his eighty remaining men at San Gabriel, he took the remainder on a further westward expedition to the Hopi pueblos. From there he worked southward to the Colorado River and thence to its mouth on the Gulf of California, thus linking up with the earlier exploration by Vizcaino in 1596. On returning to San Gabriel on April 25, 1605, he sent enthusiastic reports of his latest discovery to Mexico.[24] The new viceroy, the marqués de Montesclaro, had begun to consider seriously what to do about Oñate and New Mexico. His report of March 31, 1605, was lukewarm about the colony;[25] there were no riches, and little trade was to be done since the Indians were poor. But since there were some converts, they could scarcely be abandoned. Oñate should therefore be replaced and the colony maintained on a limited scale. This program was endorsed by the Council of the Indies on June 17 that year. Nonetheless, Oñate remained in office for some time. Finally in August 1607, despairing of further supplies and unable to collect sufficient marketable goods to enable him to import what was needed, he resigned his office to his lieutenant, Juan Martínez de Montoya (who was later succeeded by Oñate's son Cristóbal de Oñate), and divested himself of formal responsibility for the settlement. This enabled some relief to be sent from Mexico to the settlement in the interest of the missions. Fray Lázaro Ximénez, who led the relieving party, returned to assure the viceroy, now again Luis de Velasco, that the colony was worth rescue, since more than seven thousand converts required spiritual and some temporal care. In 1609, after yet another delay, Pedro de Peralta was appointed governor and captain general of the colony, the crown undertaking to pay his salary, to support a garrison of fifty soldiers, and to maintain twelve missionaries. It was to be a mission settlement confined to the pueblo area—all dreams of empire and of mineral riches were to be abandoned.

Peralta took over with little difficulty, and Oñate was sent back for trial and condemnation to fine and banishment—though long after, in 1624 in Spain, he was exonerated of wrongdoing. Peralta's task was to found a new center of government.[26] This he did in 1610 in

24. Hammond and Rey, *Oñate*, I, 31; II, 1012–1031.
25. *Ibid.*, I, 30–31; II, 1001–1005.
26. *Ibid.*, I, 32–33; II, 1040–1049.

La Villa Real de la Santa Fé de San Francisco (the second capital of a Spanish province in North America), some 30 miles to the south of San Gabriel and in a more central position, from which the missions could be supervised. A church and convent were soon established and the military and civil organs of Spanish power displayed. Though the first church fell down shortly after its erection, the new settlement took root: there were thirty households in it by 1620, and sixteen friars were at work. The colony was now a permanent part of the empire. It remained poor, but its Spanish population gradually expanded; sheep, wool, blankets, hides, and pinenuts were found to carry down the long trail to Santa Bárbara in exchange for the modest luxuries which the colonists required.[27]

The Spanish salient in New Mexico was to be enduring, but it was of little economic or strategic importance at any time, though it had some prestige value for its missionary basis. Like Florida, it served some small purpose in the imperial structure; but, again like Florida, it did not, indeed was not, allowed to develop any inner dynamic of expansion. North America at the end of our period, as it had been throughout the sixteenth century, remained only marginal in relation to the greater empire to the south.

New Mexico is the sole example of a permanent settlement within North America (admittedly, rather arbitrarily defined) which was a direct extension from the older Spanish imperial territory of New Spain. It was not a normal extension of what had been since Cortés's arrival the moving frontier of Spanish dominion, because it was an exception to the rule of 1573 that there should be no new expansion outward from the Mexican frontier. As it had temporarily housed Coronado and his men, it was—or so it could be argued—in Spanish hands before the restrictions were imposed. New Mexico was a curious salient into the north, given its special character, because of the fertile nature of the Upper Río Grande Valley and the compact and developed society of the Pueblo Indians who lived there. Oñate had dreamed of making this salient the nucleus of a new northern empire; but, like Coronado before him, he was forced to concede that its unique character as a fertile oasis between the Great Plains and wide deserts did not lend itself to expansion. Nor indeed did

27. *Ibid.*, I, 34–35; II, 1076–1105; Meinig, *Southwest*, pp. 9–12; Forbes, *Apache, Navaho and Spaniards*, pp. 112–113.

it prove adequate to sustain any substantial number of Spanish settlers, in addition to its own people, at more than subsistence level. If it had not been for the missionary friars, who saw in it an opportunity to create a small, closed Christian community, dominated by themselves, but with a tiny Spanish administration and colony to prevent them from being massacred by their sometimes unwilling converts, New Mexico would have soon disappeared as a Spanish possession. As it was, it survived for the next century or more as a curious link with the pioneering past, rather than as a forward base for Spanish imperial progress into North America.

# CHAPTER 21

## European Exploitation
## of North America During the Period
## of Discovery and Early Settlement

### I

THE Europeans who went to North America in the period from its first discovery down to the establishment of the first permanent settlements did so, in the main, to profit themselves or their employers. But exploitation for profit might take many different forms.[1] The largest single area of exploitation—the Banks fishery off Newfoundland—was entirely external to the mainland of North America. The shore fishery with which it was associated, did however bring Europeans into close contact with the land and some few of its peoples. Similarly, the searches for gold by Frobisher's men in 1577 and 1578 had little effect on anyone except the miners, although they brought about incidentally the first contacts, not wholly happy ones, between Eskimo and Englishmen. Other commercial contacts, such as the fur trade, involved very close contacts between Europeans and Amerindians, in which the latter not only became the agents of the Europeans in catching or trading in the furs but even associated themselves in their production, since the early stages of preparing the furs were done before they came into European hands.

The exchange of European commodities for American ones

1. No modern treatment of the economic implications of the initial discovery and attempted settlement has yet been carried out. A few general indications are given in the introduction to D. B. Quinn, *North American Discovery* (1971).

brought into play the productive capacity of western Europe. Objects had to be found which would attract Amerindian cupidity, or would appear to be valuable additions to hunting or military equipment. Almost all metal objects might at first prove disposable, but later objects might have to be made to suit the Amerindian requirements, for example, copper cut into holed gorgets for hanging round Indian necks and beads searched for from Italy or specially manufactured in the Netherlands to fit demand. All such operations involved the application of capital—a small amount in the case of the short-term casual trading contacts, but a large one in the case of repeated fishing or whaling commitments, which became significant as the scale of investment in shipping, ships' stores, and seamen grew.

There was a major investment, too, by those governments and speculating syndicates which were occupied in preparing and conducting expeditions to explore and allocate territories between one state and another. Such exploration involved shipping, arms, food, and all kinds of equipment to be gathered up at the European end (or perhaps, in the Spanish case, at the colonial end), as well as mustering men who must be paid or promised benefits in lieu of payment. Sometimes when the expenditure was intended to deny to another power access or territory, the repayment of such investments was not an immediate objective; but in most cases recoupment was at least implicit in making the original investment. The return might take the form of mineral exploitation, although in fact all attempts at this down to the early seventeenth century were to come to nothing; or it might be the exploitation of land or labor and the payment of rents and taxes as settlements became viable. Large expeditions like that of Hernando de Soto might attempt to live chiefly off the country, and leave the burden of transporting food and equipment to native labor recruited along the way. More usually, their aim was to plant men on land which would produce food crops for subsistence and also cash crops for export. To do this with the aid of indigenous labor was the ideal, but it was one which was rarely achieved for long in North America. There, the usual experience was that the newcomers would have to rely on themselves, their wives and children (when they had got them settled), their servants brought along for the purpose of laboring, and such negro slaves as they had been able to afford to bring with them. The end

result aimed at in such cases was appropriation of the land from its occupiers, its exploitation for European purposes, and the wiping out, removal or (at least) taxation of the Amerindian population.

In all this the twentieth-century historian would like to have the effects of European action quantified. By establishing unit costs in different countries at various points along the time scale, it might be possible approximately to cost the scale of the European states' investments in exploration and attempted settlement in the early period. But it is doubtful how much light would emerge from such an attempt, since the data is broken and discontinuous. The fishing industry can probably in the end be quantified in at least some aspects, but a great deal of documentary analysis still remains to be done before it becomes clear what can be worked out in this area. The prospects for the fur trade are less optimistic, though not perhaps entirely nonexistent. In other areas of more casual and intermittent trade, we can hope for very little unless additional data emerge on a quite unexpected scale. Then, too, we shall probably be able to strike some balance of costs and results in relation to the various attempts to establish settlers, particularly for those settlements which by the end of the initial period had become sufficiently rooted to have some real chance of survival. But at present, we can only illustrate what was happening, without giving any precise indications of how much, at whose expense and to whose benefit. Clearly, this whole area is still at the preliminary stage of knowledge.

## II

North America rapidly became the focus for a major development in European capital investment. Long-distance fishing and whaling had probably attracted substantial amounts of capital over a period of time—whether in the Iceland codfisheries of King's Lynn and Bristol (for example) or in the whaling along the eastern Atlantic seaboard of northern Spain. But Newfoundland rapidly attracted substantial investments in the exploitation of the codfisheries. The first two decades of the sixteenth century saw the earliest experiments by English, Portuguese and French. During the years 1520–40, the industry became a substantial one all the way from Lisbon to Dieppe and Bristol, with northern Spain joining the rest; and in the decades 1540–60, it became and thereafter remained big busi-

ness for French, Portuguese, English and Spaniards alike. Shortly after mid-century it was already amongst the largest European business enterprises. A full analysis of the economic development of the fishery and its ramifications throughout Europe remains to be done. Only then will it be possible to assess its relative importance.[2]

A quantity of fish was made available to Europe at relatively cheap rates by the Newfoundland fisheries. In a period when meat was scarce and dear, fish protein provided a vital element in the European diet, which in its salted and dried forms could be kept and utilized over the winter. Religious observances also ensured that those in the interior of all western European countries, as well as the coastal inhabitants, provided a constant market for fish which apparently expanded continuously throughout the sixteenth century. Moreover, as the victualing of overseas maritime enterprises and of armies in action in Europe became more systematic, the use of Newfoundland cod for such purposes meant that fish became increasingly a strategic national asset. We do not know to what extent the European fisheries along the continental shelf were affected by the development of the North American fisheries, but it is probable that they continued to grow also, if only because the sixteenth century was a period of rising population when local needs pressed on the exploitation of all available maritime resources.

There is very little information extant about the organization of the earliest fishing voyages to Newfoundland. The English syndicate of 1502, the Company of Adventurers into the Newfound Islands, was probably a very small one, consisting of Robert and William Thorne, Hugh Elyot, Sebastian Cabot, Thomas Assehurst, the two Azorean Portuguese Francisco Fernandes and João Gonsalves, together with the London goldsmith, Bartholomew Rede, and a handful of others. The association was almost certainly in the form of a

2. Harold A. Innis, *The Cod Fisheries* (1940), is still the only general treatise: it pays some appreciable attention to the economic aspects of the fishery. Charles de la Morandiére, *Histoire de la pêche française de la morue* 3 vols. (1962–66), gives an admirable account of the topography and techniques of the French fishery (mainly illustrated from the eighteenth century), but does not pay much attention to the growth of the fishery as a business enterprise. Charles Bernard, *Navires et gens de mer de Bordeaux,* 3 vols. (Paris, 1968), II, 805–826, has an excellent case study of the Newfoundland activities of one French port down to 1550, Georges Musset, *Les Rochelais à Terre-Neuve, 1500–1550* (Paris, 1893) and *Les Rochelais à Terre-Neuve, 1500–1789* (La Rochelle, 1899), providing comparable data on another French port.

partnership, voyage for voyage, with fixed shares agreed for returns, and either wages or more probably shares for the crews. The only thing we know about the business arrangements is that they broke down after four seasons at Newfoundland and may not have been resumed.[3] We do not know whether the later voyages, which were well established by 1522, were those of individual shipowner-captains, who financed their own ventures, or whether the more usual type of organization was that of the 1502–05 syndicate; most probably a mixture of both. Bristol and Plymouth merchants are likely to have been involved throughout, but with probably a continued infiltration of London capital.

In the case of the Azorean enterprises, we can be reasonably sure that the Corte Real and Barcelos businesses remained family ones and did not draw on mainland capital. We do not know whether the Corte Reals were able to draw in revenues from licences in view of their priority, in Portuguese eyes, in discovering the fishery. On the organization of the mainland fishing industry, we have so far no clear evidence. It is most probable that, like the English industry, it consisted of both individual and semi-corporate enterprises, in the form of syndicates.

From the beginning the initiative in France, certainly in Normandy and probably elsewhere, came from the greater merchants. The Newfoundland fishery was simply another investment, speculative at first but routine later, in which they placed part of their capital. This consisted primarily in ships. The *armateur* (merchant-shipowner in English, perhaps, but with no exact equivalent) set one of his ships to sea under a captain of his choice, fitting the ships out with gear and arms; he, or another merchant or group of merchants, would also arrange to victual the vessel. She would then go out in shares of thirds, one-third of the proceeds going to the shipowner (or *bourgeois*), one-third to the victualer, and one-third to the captain to be divided on an agreed basis between him and the rest of the crew.[4] This was the normal method in France of financing ventures

3. We have no more than the materials in J. A. Williamson, *The Cabot Voyages* (1962), D. B. Quinn, *England and the Discovery of America* (1974) and A. A. Ruddock, "The Reputation of Sebastian Cabot," *Bulletin of the Institute of Historical Research*, XLVII (1974), 95–99, to go on.

4. The system of shares as used for privateering, fishing in distant waters and other speculative enterprises is set out in Eugène Guénin, *Ango et ses pilotes* (Paris, 1901), pp. 17–30 (*armateur* is later used interchangeably as shipowner and victualer in some contexts).

in which there was a speculative element. It also enabled syndicates to own ships or to participate as victualers, while the captain might not be precluded from having a share in either ship or victualing if he had money to invest. Such risk-spreading was not the only method employed. A captain who owned his own ship might be chartered by a merchant to sail on a specific voyage and would then have his crew on wages, with victuals supplied by the charterer or his associates. This was the normal method of proceeding in the case of settled trades, but it cannot clearly be established that it was used, at least in the early stages, in the fishery. In the case of an experienced captain and a small ship, the whole venture might be financed and victualed by him, with appropriate terms, part shares and part wages[5] perhaps, with his men. It was probably on third-sharing terms that Jean Ango the elder began his family's New-foundland activities with the *Pensée*, Thomas Aubert captain, in 1508[6]; these continued as one branch of the many enterprises of his son, Jean Ango, down to his death in 1551. It is clear also that from early in the century, Dieppe—on which the extensive Ango family business was based—had a well-organized market for Newfoundland fish.

The same would probably be true, with local variations, of other Norman, Breton, Rochelais, Bordelais and French Basque ports. Nor is there any reason to consider that arrangements for codfishing at Newfoundland varied in the Spanish Basque ports from Pasajes to Bilbao. The growth of the industry in all these areas tended to produce specialization. A few great *armateurs*, who owned ships and might victual them themselves (the *armadores* on the Spanish side were victualers only) held a key position in marketing the product as well. More usually the investment was spread, with ships owned in shares, the victualing being done by syndicates and the marketing kept separate from production.[7] This enabled the investment to be spread over an appreciable number of individuals, and it also allowed inland towns and country landowners to participate.

The numbers of vessels engaged in the trade remain obscure. It

5. H. A. Innis, *Cod Fisheries*, p. 15, indicates that in a Breton voyage to Newfoundland in 1510, the crew were in wages.

6. See C. A. Julien, *Les voyages de découverte et les premiers établissements* (1948), pp. 24–26; Guénin, *Ango et ses pilotes*, pp. 2–3.

7. Innis, *Cod Fisheries*, pp. 16–23, gives examples of charter parties with varying sharing arrangements in the years 1523–55.

might seem that the Norman and Breton ports were well ahead of the others in exploiting the fisheries, but the figure of one hundred French and other vessels given by John Rastell in 1519[8] might seem to be something of an overestimate. Normandy was well ahead; for the decade 1520–30, an estimate of eighty to ninety vessels in all is given for Dieppe and Rouen.[9] Western France was slower to get going, and while there are examples of 1512 and 1517 for Cap-Breton and Bordeaux, those for La Rochelle begin only in 1523. Up to 1530, with very full documentation available, there are only seven voyages from Bordeaux known; after 1530 the number rises sharply, and increases further after 1540, so that for 1530–49 we have a total of ninety-seven, approximately five a year.[10] The figures for La Rochelle are sixty-eight voyages in all for 1523–50, an average of almost four a year; but of these thirteen are French Basque ships coming to be victualed at La Rochelle.[11] From 1546 onward, at least four Spanish Basque vessels were sailing each year and eight are recorded for 1549.[12] We have no comparable figures for Portuguese and English participation in the first half of the sixteenth century.

From quite an early stage the Newfoundland fishery ceased to be a purely localized activity. Breton pilots were in demand as early as 1511, and are found thereafter on ships from other French ports, and on Spanish and English vessels. A ship owned in one port was liable to be victualed in another—as early as 1523, La Rochelle merchants were victualing a ship owned and manned in Brittany, while by 1537 French Basque ships were regularly being victualed by merchants in both La Rochelle and Bordeaux. The ship *Jacques* in 1530 was owned by two Bordeaux merchants; one-third of her victualing was supplied by an investor from the inland town of Toulouse; her master was a French Basque and her pilot a Breton.[13] Soon money was being raised at interest by the *armateurs* for invest-

8.          "Now frenchemen & other haue founde the trade
             That yerely of fyshe there they lad
             Aboue an. C. sayle."
—John Rastell, *A new interlude . . . of the .iiij. elementes* (London, [1519]), sig. C2v.
9. Innis, *Cod Fisheries*, p. 16.
10. Bernard, *Navires et gens de mer*, II, 807.
11. Musset, *Les Rochelais à Terre-Neuve, 1500–1789*, p. 30; La Morandière, *Histoire de la pêche française de la morue*, I, 246–253.
12. Public Archives of Canada. List of documents from Archivo General de Protocolos de Guipúzcoa, Oñate: personal information from Mrs. Selma Barkham.
13. Bernard, *Navires et gens de mer*, II, 810, 814–815, 818, 820, 823.

ment in voyages to Newfoundland and insurances being effected for the dangerous voyage there.

Investments by merchants of one port in voyages from another were common, and might cross state boundaries. Certainly marketing was international at this early stage. A shipmaster from one port might be told to dispose of his catch in another—even though it might be in a foreign country. Newfoundlanders sailing from Bordeaux delivered their catch as far afield as Rouen and Bilbao.[14] In 1547, a Spanish Basque master was told to dispose of his catch (whether of train oil or cod) in England, at Bristol or Southampton, before returning to Spain; while after 1546, when whaling developed in American waters, a Spanish Basque whaler in 1550 was instructed to bring the oil directly to London.[15]

It is still not clear precisely when and how whaling extended from the coast of Galicia—where it had long been pursued inshore by Spaniards and by French Basques in small vessels—to American waters, where it came to be dominated by Basques from the Spanish provinces of Guipúzcoa and Vizcaya. It appears probable that the transition took place gradually and that, to begin with, whaling was an offshoot of the codfishery. The import into Bordeaux in 1544 of a combined cargo of blubber and cod (gresse de ballene et moullue) indicates that some ships were engaged in both whaling and fishing for cod. Moreover, during the years 1546 to 1556 the appearance (alongside cargoes of whale oil) of cauldrons for rendering oil on a scale unsuited to cod-liver-oil production, with harpoons and their lines, and also "lances" and axes for whale disposal, demonstrates clearly the development of American whaling.[16] It was first illustrated on the Desceliers map of 1546,[17] where a large, three-masted vessel standing off the eastern shore of Labrador is shown sending

14. *Ibid.*, II, 221–222.

15. A.G.P., Oñate, Partido de Vergara, legajo 2574 (Motrico), fols. 42–43*v.* (1547); legajo 1779 (Orio), fols. 124–124*v.* (1550), with acknowledgments to Mrs. Selma Barkham.

16. The footnotes in Bernard, *Navires et gens de mer,* II, 806, 812, 815, 819–821, provide some basic information, but the sparsity of local records in the French Basque country makes firm conclusions almost impossible to establish. Blubber (French: *graisse de baleine;* Spanish: *grasa de ballena*) and whale (or train) oil (*huile de baleine*) were not always sharply distinguished in records of imports.

17. The map is in the John Rylands University Library, Manchester. Reproductions such as that in H. P. Biggar, *The Voyages of Jacques Cartier* (1924), p. 192, do not give adequate detail on this sketch.

off a boat in which are five men engaged in harpooning a somewhat unlikely-looking whale. This could apply to any location between modern Hamilton Inlet and the Strait of Belle Isle, though more probably the latter. It might appear that the whaling pioneers in this were the French Basques, but they were closely followed and soon surpassed by the Spanish Basques, whose greater experience of the older coastal whaling techniques on the Spanish coast no doubt stood them in good stead. Well before 1554 they had established themselves on the southern shore of Labrador at Butus (now Red Bay) and possibly other posts along the Strait of Belle Isle. Both groups concentrated from the beginning on the Strait of Belle Isle, and set up tryworks for the preparation of whale oil in a limited number of harbors. These ranged from Grande Coste on the west (behind Anticosti) eastward, and included at various times Blanc Sablon, Puerto de los Hornos (East St. Modeste), Chateo (Chateau Bay), Gradun, Sembrero, Brest, Puerto Breton, Butus (Red Bay) and Puerto Novo (possibly St. Peters). In 1554 French Basques were located in strength at Butus, from which they mounted an attack on the Spaniards at Puerto de los Hornos.[18] Earlier, they may have shared this and other harbors, and French ships continued to be chartered by the Spaniards. Later, the Spanish Basques appear to have monopolized most or all of these harbors, possibly leaving to the French Basques the more easterly and westerly ends of the whaling coast, where whales coming through the relatively narrow straits could be taken most easily by boats based on ships in safe harbors. How early shore stations were established is not known. Puerto de los Hornos ("Port Furnace") was operating early in the 1550s. The basic requirement for rendering blubber into oil was a boiler on which a container could be placed.[19] The furnace was constructed of stone (or possibly brick) and fireclay, on which would be placed a great copper cauldron, in which the cut up blubber

18. The basic paper on this subject is Selma Barkham, "The Spanish Province of Terra Nova," *Canadian Archivist*, (November 1974), and I am also indebted to her for personal communications and for the privilege of seeing the Public Archives of Canada file of Basque material which she prepared. René Belanger, *Les Basques dans l'Estuaire du Saint Laurant* (Quebec, 1971), though mainly concerned with a somewhat later period, has also interesting information. Martin de Hoyarzabal, *Les voyages vantureux* (Bordeaux, 1579), has some valuable information which has not been reprinted.

19. The classical account of early whaling technology is in William Scoresby, *An Account of the Arctic Regions*, 2 vols. (Edinburgh, 1820), II, 172–177.

would be rendered into oil. Cooling vats, which could also be used for storage, were needed for settling the oil, and were probably clay-lined receptacles, from which the barrels, knocked up by the coopers, were filled. Huts were also needed for the stowage of gear and possibly for men to sleep ashore, if they did not continue to live on shipboard. Tiles (and possibly bricks) and clay were brought on shore, and in 1563 we hear of tiles and other building materials being used to repair cabins.[20] The ship lay in harbor near the try-works, while the whaling was done from the numerous boats brought out, and the dead whales dragged in shore to be flensed. Whalebone, spermaceti and hard bone were valuable by-products of some species.

The burden of the codfishing vessels using Bordeaux as a base in the first half of the sixteenth century probably gives an adequate sample of the early Newfoundlanders as they were drawn from the coast between Brittany and the Spanish border. They ranged from very small vessels of 30 tons (with a crew of nine) to 80 tons, through a medium range of 100 to 130 tons (with twenty to thirty men), representing most of the ships listed, to an occasional vessel of 200 tons or over—though the 270-ton *Françoise* of St. Vincent in 1550 was most probably intended for whaling rather than the codfishery. The value of the ships between 70 and 130 tons would range between 900 and about 1,500 livres tournois. We have no precise estimates for costing the setting out of such a ship, but it would not have been very high.[21] Capital represented by the ship and her victualing could be composed of a few large shares and a considerable number of smaller ones, but investors tended to spread their investments over a considerable number of ships.

The position of the whalers was very different. The vessels were much larger. The 1550 French Basque ship at Bordeaux of 270 tons could probably have brought home a cargo equivalent to that of the *Marie* of St. Jean de Luz in 1549 of 500 barrels of whale oil, worth 5,000 livres tournois. The continuance and development of the French Basque whaling industry has not yet been chronicled, but there appears to be no evidence of a great expansion after 1554. It was very different in the Basque provinces of Guipúzcoa and Vizcaya. The earliest reference to a whaling voyage from there is in

20. Barkham, "The Spanish Province of Terra Nova."
21. Bernard, *Navires et gens de mer*, II, 815–818.

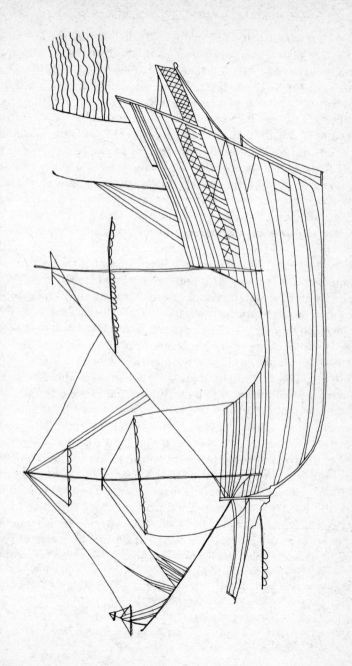

A Basque Newfoundlander (After a document in Archivo de Protocolos, Oñate, Spain. Courtesy of Mrs. Selma Barkham)

1546, but the whaling trade developed steadily thereafter. The majority of the vessels employed in it were ships of over 200 tons, carrying as many as 10 shallops, and with a crew of anything up to 120 men. At the peak of the trade between 1560 and 1580, they numbered up to twenty vessels a year. Such a vessel would bring something like 1,000 barrels of oil, selling normally for 6,000 to 10,000 ducats at least in Spain. Insurances were high for the double voyage, out and back, from 10 to 15 percent on the hull of a whaler with about 1 percent less for the codfishing vessels. The result was to build up a highly capitalized industry, offering good returns. Money was drawn in from landowners and professional men like notaries and priests, as well as from the Spanish Basque merchants, while inland towns also invested and an appreciable amount of capital came from French Basque sources. Insurances were effected mainly in the inland city of Burgos.[22] The rapidity of capital formation in this case is striking. This industry declined slowly after 1575 and rapidly after 1580, as a result of the demands on Basque ships and seamen by the Spanish crown and the privateering losses at sea to French Huguenots and English men-of-war. But at its peak, it represented one of the major concentrations of commercial capital in the early exploitation of North American resources.

While the main whaling industry was carried on in the comparatively narrow channel making up the Strait of Belle Isle (the "Grand Bay" in very many documents), some whalers may have ranged farther afield; certainly the search for seal and walrus, valuable supplements in the search for animal fats (and for "ivory" in the case of the walrus) did so, but we have little indication of the scale of these pursuits, or whether they were subsidiary to whaling or to codfishing ventures. It may well be that they were engaged in mainly by French Basques. Anthony Parkhurst in 1578 reckoned that twenty to thirty vessels were sent by Basques to the Strait of Belle Isle, but some may well have been French Basques.[23] Certainly by the 1590s, if not before, the French Basques were ranging over the western coasts of Newfoundland, the islands in the Gulf of St. Lawrence and the mouth of the river, and were associated in some

22. S. Barkham, "Mercantile Community in Inland Burgos," *Geographical Magazine* (November 1973), 106–113.

23. Quinn, *North American Discovery* (1971), pp. 233–235; Hakluyt, *Principal Navigations*, VIII (1904), 9–16.

degree with the pursuit of the white whale *(beluga)* which frequented the river. Tryworks were established on some islands in the St. Lawrence, where remains of furnaces (known as "ovens") have been located.[24] Moreover, it appears probable that the vessels engaged in such activities were those most active in the casual fur trade. They were concerned with skins of seal and walrus, and picked up from Montagnais and Micmac Indians much miscellaneous peltry.[25] They emerged as competitors of the Bretons and Normans in the main center of the inland fur trade in the 1590s—Tadoussac—which lay well up the St. Lawrence River. It is even likely that they had been combining whaling and fur trading there before the Bretons appeared about 1580. It is probable that ton for ton, this mixed trade in oil, furs and skins was by far the most valuable section of the trade but also the most speculative one, so that it is impossible to estimate investments or profits.

In 1577, plans were made for English participation in the whaling industry. On February 12, 1577, the Muscovy Company received a monopoly of whale fishing for twenty years and was authorized to hire "certain Biscayans, men expert and skilful, to instruct our subjects therein."[26] But it is not known whether the Company attempted to operate a whale fishery in American waters within the period of this grant (1577–99).

The precise extent of French Basque activity in this industry between 1555 and 1585—beyond supplying some ships on charter for the Spanish industry—is not clear. As the position of the Spanish Basque shipowners and seamen became more difficult after 1585, on account of government intervention, substantial French Basque vessels were built to take over at least part of the Spanish Basque whale fishery, even though these continued to use some Spanish Basque crews. It might appear that they ceased to rely so much on a limited range of harbors on the Strait of Belle Isle, and began to range widely along the west coast of Newfoundland, Anticosti, the St. Lawrence River up to Tadoussac, and possibly up the east coast of Labrador as well. Apart from Isle aux Basques, opposite Sague-

24. Belanger, *Les Basques dans l'estuaire du Saint-Laurant* (1971).
25. See, incidentally, Quinn, *England and the Discovery of America*, pp. 314, 317–319, 325–326, 350–354.
26. Cecil T. Carr (ed.), *Select Charters of the Trading Companies, 1530–1707* (London, 1913), pp. 28–30.

nay, their shore stations have not been identified. We know also that walrus at the Magdalen Islands and Anticosti occupied them to some extent and may even have led some shipmasters to concentrate on them rather than on whale.

The techniques of codfishing varied widely and governed to some extent the organization of this industry. The simplest and, in some respects, easiest was the Banks fishing. There the vessel made her way as early as possible (Norman vessels leaving in January and February) to the fog-covered fishing banks to the south and southeast of Newfoundland, and anchored. Her men fished from her sides and also from the boats she carried with her, at least two shallops and two others, not going too far away in case they should get lost in the fog. The fish were gutted and trimmed and immediately heavily salted in the hold. When this was full, it was sealed, and the ship returned home as rapidly as possible to dispose of her "green" or wet-salted cod. The turn round was rapid, the financial return relatively low. If she could get back across the Atlantic before the end of June, it was desirable for her to make a second voyage, though how often this was practical is not known. Some of the cod she brought back, especially in Portugal, was sun-dried to preserve it and sold as "dried" cod. Barreled livers for oil and, in some cases, salted roe, were also brought back. The Banks fishing was monotonous; it could be dangerous when icebergs were moving and fog was dense, and it was not as profitable as inshore fishing, where the cod was normally dried and of higher value when brought back to Europe. Nonetheless, the wet fishery formed the mainstay of the large Portuguese fishery and included many French—especially Norman—vessels. Its main attraction was that it was relatively cheap to mount and had a more rapid turnover than the other branch of the fishery.[27]

The inshore fishery was the most pervasive and significant European investment in North America in its period.[28] It centered especially on the Avalon peninsula in Newfoundland, more particularly at St. John's Harbour on the east and at Placentia Harbour on vast

27. La Morandière, *Histoire de la pêche française de la morue*, I, 150–157.
28. *Ibid.*, I, 161–184 (most of the information derives from the eighteenth century); F. N. L. Poynter (ed.), *The Journal of James Yonge* (London, 1963), pp. 55–60 and plate 4 (evidence from 1663); G. T. Cell, *English Enterprise in Newfoundland*, pp. 4–5 (a succinct and expert summary).

lacentia Bay on the west, though it was scattered throughout many
naller harbors also. But it was not limited to this one area—Con-
eption Bay and other centers in eastern and northeastern New-
oundland were significant, and so was the southwest. And Cape
reton was an important independent center. There was also an
opreciable amount of fishing along the southeastern coast of Lab-
ador, about which little is known. Though the inshore fishing was
sually dominated by the French—Normans, Bretons, vessels from
ordeaux and La Rochelle and those from French Basque ports all
naring in it with some degree of equality between the four main
gions—the Portuguese probably maintained the second place up
about 1580, with the Spanish Basques not very inferior in num-
rs. Until the late 1570s the English were fewest in number of
ips, though their vessels may have been somewhat larger than
erage. No very significant differences between the various Euro-
an countries in planning and organizing the industry have been
scerned so far, but with additional research it may become possi-
e to establish local variations and, in particular, to discover on
nat scale the *armateurs* operated.

Robert Hitchcock, who published his *Politique platt for the honour of*
*e Prince* in 1580,[29] urging the building of four hundred substantial
hing vessels (busses) for the English North Sea and Newfound-
nd fisheries, gives us a glimpse of the industry as it appeared from
ngland:

ere goeth out of Fraunce commonly five hundreth saile of shippes
arely in March to Newefoundlande, to fishe for Newlande fishe, and
mes home againe in August. Amongst many of theim this is the order,
ine or twelve Marryners doeth conferre with a Money man, who fur-
heth them with money to buy Shippes, Victualls, Salte, Lines and Hookes
be paied his money at the shippes returne, either in fishe or in money,
h five and thirty pounde upon the hundrethe pounde in money lent.
ewise here in Englande, in the West countrey the like order is used, the
nerman conferres with the money man, who furnisheth them with money
provide victualls, salte and all other needefull thinges to be paied twentie
e pounde at the shippes returne upon the hundreth pound in money lent.
d some of the same money men dothe borowe money upon ten pounde
the hundreth pounde and puts it forthe in this order to the Fishermen.

9. (London, 1580), sig. F₁ v. Reprinted in R. H. Tawney and E. Power, *Tudor*
*nomic Documents*, 3 vols (London, 1924), III, 253.

And for to be assured of the money ventered, they will have it assured
gevyng sixe pounde for the assuring of every hundreth pound to hym tha
abides the venture of the Shippes returne.

Hitchcock takes no note of Portuguese and Spanish participants in
the fishery, and his figure of five hundred French ships could well
be too high. His information on the financing of ventures may
indicate that the vital factor in the organization of the industry was
the entrepreneur, whose role was primarily financial and who could
raise money at 10 percent, and lend it out at 25 percent in England
(35 percent in France), with 6 percent insurance to cover the ship
and her victualing. The whole operation would be arranged, he
said, in England by a group of fishermen who took collective responsibility for the voyage and who satisfied the lender on their
return. In France he thought this fishermens' syndicate numbered
some ten or twelve. This would seem to mean that money might be
raised both to hire or buy the ship and to victual her, and that once
the remainder (when loan and interest were paid) would be divided
in shares, the fishermen who made the bargain being presumably
entitled to a somewhat higher proportion.[30]

Ships usually left Europe for the inshore fishery between March
and early May. The cod did not normally come inshore in considerable numbers until June, when they followed shoals of caplin,
small fish which was their favorite food, to the beaches. A ship
picked her harbor and, if she was the first there, her captain was
installed as port admiral to take a lead in settling disputes. The
vessel then remained at anchor while the men caught fish by line
from boats which they either carried with them or had left on shore
since the previous season. A shore base was essential. Stages close
to the water enabled boats to land and provided a place for the
cutting tables on which the fish were cleaned and opened, the liver
being barreled as the fish were gutted. From the stage, the fish was
taken to the "flakes." These were large drying platforms, with a low
frame covered with green twigs. There the opened fish was laid flat,
salted, and turned when necessary so as to be dried in the sun. It
had to be watched to see that it did not get too much heat or
moisture; if either threatened, it might be stored under cover for

30. Cell, *English Enterprise in Newfoundland*, pp. 5–18, develops the details of Engli
practice, notably on shares.

time. Eventually the dried fish, carefully stacked, was brought on board the ship and, protected from further moisture, sealed in the hold. The cod-liver oil might need heat, applied to cauldrons, to extract it fully, though much of it was expressed in the barrels as the livers deteriorated. It is clear that teamwork of a high order was essential to obtain effective results, and that the production of dried cod was labor-intensive. Ships' masters, or the pursers they carried, had to be effective organizers as well as good seamen.

As the industry grew, the obtaining of places—"grounds"—on shore became more difficult. Competition often led to violence and stealing. The shore installations were expected to survive the winter, at least in basic essentials, though some degree of restoration and rebuilding was necessary each year. Boats, spare barrels, huts, stages and flakes constituted property which might be interfered with by Indians during the winter or by greedy skippers who arrived before the owners. But the port admiral, acting often as chairman of an informal council of shipmasters, managed to keep some degree of order in most ports. There was some piracy, and in time of war between any two countries involved, some privateering. Before 1580, however, this rarely got out of hand.

The masters found it valuable to have a central rendezvous where they might call on arrival at Newfoundland or which they might visit before they returned to Europe. St. John's Harbour and Placentia Harbour became the main rendezvous points, each being an important drying ground in its own right. At St. John's, ships arriving would sell salt and other goods like wine, especially to English vessels, before moving to their chosen harbor; returning vessels would purchase stores needed to fill gaps in their supplies for the return voyage, or they might offer surplus fish for sale to vessels which had not done too well—or, later in the century, had come solely to buy fish ("sack" ships). All the ships hoped to return with full cargoes in late August or September, with some latecomers appearing in October and a few arriving home later still. Fish might be disposed of at the ship's own port, and probably usually was; or it might be taken for sale by previous arrangement to another port. In the case of England, West Country ships might bring their catches to London, or the cargo might be exported directly to another country. Some English ships, well before 1580, were bringing their catches to Spain, selling their fish and taking on a cargo

of Spanish and American products for England. Later, they were to go as far as Italy to do this. The dispersal of dry fish over continental Europe was a matter for coastal and inland commerce, but Newfoundland fish reached a great part of Europe, as well as victualing ships bound for many other parts of the world.

By and large, the codfishery appears to have expanded continuously in all the main fishing centers from 1550 to 1580 with little break. The statistics for the total number of ships engaged in the codfishery after the middle of the century are both incomplete and unreliable; at the same time, some indications of the scale of the enterprise can be given. For the Norman ports, figures of annual sailings might range, it would appear, between 57 and 151, so that 100 would not be an unduly high average number. The Breton figures are very incomplete. The maximum obtainable from them would be thirty-one in one year, but Parkhurst estimated them as the most numerous French contingent in 1578, and they must be credited with at least fifty (and conceivably up to one hundred). La Rochelle would have a minimum of 54 a year after 1559 and reached, it is claimed, 100 within a decade; while Bordeaux, with 231 contracts for 1563 alone, representing a much smaller number of voyages, must be credited with at least 50, and substantial numbers have also been claimed for Olonne. Parkhurst put the total French figure at 150 in 1578, but he was not in close touch with the Banks and Cape Breton fisheries. The correct total would appear, on a conservative estimate, to be about three hundred. Parkhurst thought that there were one hundred "Spaniards" in the codfishery, yet he almost certainly includes in this both French and Spanish Basques and Spaniards from other North Spanish ports. French Basque figures of seventy or more are met with late in the century, while a maximum of fifty from the Spanish side is likely. A combined figure of one hundred for both for the period 1560–80 would appear likely. In Portugal, Aveiro's sixty vessels in 1550 would point to at least one hundred Portuguese ships at that time, but Parkhurst credited them with having declined to fifty in 1578 and this is the probable figure. The English had crept up only in 1578 to fifty, but thereafter were to go on increasing in number.[31] We can therefore

31. Parkhurst says there were only four English ships in the fishery in 1572 (though this must have been quite exceptional), with thirty when he came out in 1574, forty in 1577, and fifty in 1578 (Taylor, *Hakluyts*, I, 123, 128). Other estimates are from

say, with reasonable probability but no certainty, that there were some five hundred vessels engaged in the fishery in 1580, which is Hitchcock's contemporary figure for France alone.[32] At a modest average of 70 tons per ship, this would represent a total tonnage of 35,000, and might well have been higher. With crews averaged at 30, some 15,000 men would be employed. If we add 5,000 tons of shipping for whalers, with 2,000 men, we can see what a major industry the North American fishery had become.

The English trade in Newfoundland fish was affected by disturbed international circumstances after 1580. Gradually, Spain, Portugal and Leaguer France were closed to English exports of fish, so that only the royalist French ports and, occasionally, the Mediterranean remained open to them. This loss was partly balanced by the increased demands for navy and army victualing, and by the exemption of the fishery from many of the embargoes and restrictions which impeded other trades. The rise of prices during the war proved beneficial, and trade with France redeveloped rapidly in the 1590s, while the naval and military demands on the industry for victuals—especially during the Nine Years' War in Ireland—continued to be very high. The result was that capital flowed into the industry and it expanded rapidly, so that, when peace came between 1598 and 1604, the English fishing industry was in a good condition to meet European competition. The years after 1604, especially, were ones of increasing prosperity.[33]

The rather scattered information on French ports for this period does not suggest that the French Newfoundland fleet declined substantially. The French Basques frequently complained of interception by privateers from England and from La Rochelle, but the French Basque fishing fleet sailed with the consent of and sometimes under the protection of the Spanish government, since both

La Morandière, *Histoire*, I, 234–242 (Normandy), 242–247 (Brittany), 247–252 (Olonne, La Rochelle, Bordeaux), 252–253 (French Basque ports); Bernard, *Navires et gens de mer*, II, 807; Innis, *Cod Fisheries*, pp. 39–45.

32. Edward Hayes (British Library, Lansdowne MS 100, fols. 83–94) considered that in 1585 there were some four hundred vessels (including whalers) in all, most of them being from 100 to 120 tons, the remainder usually between 60 and 80 tons, with none under 60; the whalers ran from 300 to 400 tons.

33. Cell, *English Enterprise*, pp. 6–16; J. D. Rogers, *Newfoundland* (1911); Innis, *Cod Fisheries*, pp. 45–51.

fish and oil were badly needed in Spain. Some Spanish vessels sailed with them from time to time. (Spanish Basque vessels were usually kept at home or used for other purposes.) With the French Basque fleet of seventy ships of some 12,000 tons burden that was held up in the spring of 1589 at Pasajes, there were probably only a small number of Spanish vessels; while of sixty Basque ships in Placentia Bay in 1594, only eight were Spanish, even though many more of the crews were from the Spanish Basque country.[34] We can say with some confidence that the French Basque fishing fleet did not fall below fifty and crept upwards to considerably higher levels. In Brittany the ports were divided in their allegiance between Leaguer and Royalist, and so we find Leaguer St. Malo seizing Royalist Granvelle vessels laden inwards from Newfoundland, but the aggregate of Breton vessels does not appear to have declined by much. Norman shipping to Newfoundland was maintained and even appears to have shown something of a rise.

We know almost nothing of Portuguese vessels: they disappeared from the inshore fishery, and presumably still carried on the Banks green fishing only. It was otherwise with the English, who prospered. We have estimates of 60 ships for 1583, 100 for 1594, 150 for 1604 and 200 for 1610, which appear to be reasonably realistic, and the numbers were to go on increasing after 1612. If we regard the earlier French figure of 300 as being maintained, though it could well have increased to 400 or thereabouts, we can say that, allowing the Portuguese and Spaniards only 50 between them (since the Spanish Basque revival was delayed until about 1610), we have a total of between 550 and 650 vessels on the Banks and in the inshore fishery by 1612, together with a whaling fleet whose precise number is unknown,[35] but probably contained only 2 to 4 Spanish Basque vessels.

Ships were getting larger. An average English Newfoundlander in 1580 was 70 tons, with twenty-four men; well before 1620, the

34. See *Calendar of State Papers, Foreign, January–July 1589* (London, 1950), pp. 151, 231–232, and *C.S.P.F. July 1590–May 1591* (London 1969), p. 387; R. Hakluyt, *The Principal Navigations* VIII (1904), 165 ("three-score and odde sayles").

35. La Morandière, *Histoire de la pêche française de la morue*, I, 238, 240–242, 250, 253; Cell, *English Enterprise*, pp. 3, 22–25, 33; H. A. Innis, "The Rise and Fall of the Spanish Fishery at Newfoundland," *Transactions of the Royal Society of Canada*, 3rd series, XXV (1931), Sect. 2, 51–70.

average size had gone up to 100 tons, with forty men. These larger vessels would use some five to eight boats, some of them substantial shallops of 3–5 tons or larger. The same process was going on in France. The La Rochelle ships by the end of the sixteenth century were of between 100 and 150 tons, and we hear of many French Basque ships of over 200 tons which are not apparently whalers. This meant that more fish could be brought back ship for ship, and that the total product of the fishery was increasing in the early seventeenth century at a faster rate than the number of ships alone would indicate.[36]

The technique of wet (or "green") fishing and storage remained unaltered. For the dry fishing industry, we have seventeenth-century descriptions from English sources which suggest that techniques had been elaborated and the division of labor developed so as to produce fish of higher quality,[37] though it is impossible to say whether or not these refinements had developed earlier. The French evidence for this century indicates similar refinements.

What we do not yet know is precisely when the Dutch began to take part in the fishery. Sir Walter Ralegh alleged they were doing so as early as 1593.[38] Dutch documents indicate that fishing voyages were being made in 1601 and between 1609 and 1611.[39] Later, the Dutch were to concentrate on sending "sack" ships—vessels which bought fish at St. John's or elsewhere from the fishermen, but they had not appeared in significant numbers by 1612.

During the period from about 1580 to about 1612, the organization of the fishing industry remained basically unchanged, though it became more complex. The details of the financing of ships in England grow clearer and they have become quite elaborate. Though the great merchant could control a considerable number of ships, there were still many opportunities for small investors. The ship might be owned by many different people, each holding a

36. Cell, *English Enterprise,* pp. 3–4; La Morandière, *Histoire,* I, 38.
37. Cell, *English Enterprise,* p. 4, give details of refinements in the drying process, as does La Morandière, *Histoire,* I, 168–182, though again he draws mainly from the eighteenth century.
38. Simonds d'Ewes, *The Journals of all the Parliaments During the Reign of Queen Elizabeth* (London, 1682), p. 509.
39. Public Archives of Canada, *Kupp Collection. Finding Aid no. 740* (1974), nos. 69, 13–15, 9–11 (for which I am indebted to Mrs. Selma Barkham).

number of sixty-fourth parts in the vessel, even though one or two people might have a majority holding. Risk-sharing meant that contracts spread the risk over backers, owners, victualers, shipmasters and even crew. A significant number of ships continued to be chartered, and a number of different forms of charter were developed to meet particular types of risk. Marine insurance was slow to develop in England—though Hitchcock recorded its existence in 1580—and the earliest surviving contract for the fishery dates only from 1604, while it rarely covered the whole of the capital risked in a fishing venture. The crew continued to be paid from shares in thirds, but these were supplemented in the seventeenth century by small lump sum payments. London capitalists continued to invest substantially in fishing; the West Country too had grown in prosperity as the fishery developed, and so its townsmen were able to enlarge their share in a capital-intensive industry, though the precise methods of capital formation in the outports have not yet been investigated. After 1600 the fish market became much better organized, and the disposal of fish at the port of disembarkation and at foreign ports to which it was directed was marked by specialization in marketing arrangements—a factor often being sent with the ship to supervise this aspect of the enterprise. It would appear that the English industry was catching up with the more sophisticated business methods practiced earlier in France and Spain.[40]

The advanced character of its business arrangements and the large number of ships engaged in it meant that by 1612 the Newfoundland fishery had become a major European industry which was expanding into New England waters also and still growing. But the Dutch and English enterprise in other spheres—the East Indies, for example—was such that the relative position of the industry was declining as it became overshadowed by other yet more profitable overseas trades. The importance of the fishery as a "nursery of seamen" was to be constantly urged from the sixteenth century onwards; and in numbers of ships and men employed, the North American fishery remained outstanding.

40. Cell, *English Enterprise*, pp. 6–21.

# III

One of the primary purposes of contact at the economic level between Europeans and Amerindians was to trade furs and skins.[41] We have almost no details about the development of this trade from Chesapeake Bay southward. Yet dressed deerskins are mentioned incidentally often enough to indicate that these were one attractive object of commerce from early in the sixteenth century, and that those decorated by the Indians had a special interest and value, though we have little evidence that the many Spanish expeditions to the southeast in the first half of the sixteenth century developed any systematic trading in skins and furs. If a French vessel was trading with Indians in Chesapeake Bay and elsewhere in 1546,[42] then it is probable that the French had already established a regular trade in deerskins and possibly furs by this time. Though we hear little about furs and skins in connection with either the French or Spanish activities in Florida from 1560, it seems probable that a certain amount was collected both by the Spaniards in their settlements and by the French ships which continued to put in to get water and wood to the north of the Spanish settlements both before and after 1600. Again, in the Roanoke colony of 1585–6 there was some trade of this sort. That it was considered of potential significance is shown by Thomas Harriot in his 1588 tract,[43] where he spoke of furs as being a potential trade product if the settlers would take otters for themselves, indicating that the Indians had not been conditioned to hunt them and use their skins. Deerskins were clearly available in quantity from the Indians: "Deere skinnes dressed after the maner of Chamoes or undressed, are to be had of the naturalls thousands yearely by way of traffique for trifles." It would thus seem that trading relationships for deerskins had been established on a fairly substantial scale during 1585–6 with the Carolina Algonkian tribes.

In Virginia, too, in the early years of the Jamestown colony, it is

41. Harold A. Innis, *The Fur Trade in Canada*, revised edition (Toronto, 1956), pp. 1–26; H. P. Biggar, *The Early Trading Companies of New France* (1901), pp. 1–93, contains useful outlines, but a comprehensive treatment is still needed.

42. See Quinn, *England and the Discovery of North America*, pp. 189–191.

43. *A Briefe and true report of the new found land of Virginia* (London, 1588); *Virginia Voyages from Hakluyt*, ed. D. B. and A. M. Quinn (1973), p. 52.

clear that the Powhatan and Potomac Indians were prepared to trade both furs and skins with the English. We have indications that when a supply ship came in, the sailors would try to trade for individual furs or skins with the Indians, though we do not know what was the scale of the trade which passed through the Company's own warehouse. John Smith indicated his hope of an extensive trade in both furs and skins when he made his first contacts with the Potomac Indians in 1608, and these contacts were later developed by Samuel Argall and others. It cannot, however, be said that any significant trading nexus with the Indians southward from Chesapeake Bay had been established before 1612. Trading in furs and skins seems to have been incidental to commercial contacts in this region.

The position was very different farther north. It is true that we do not know how much or how little exchange of furs and skins there was between Europeans and either the Beothuk of Newfoundland or the Eskimo of Labrador. But between the Micmac along the shores of the later Maritime Provinces and the Montagnais of the southern Labrador and Quebec shores, an early, expanding commerce had developed. Bretons, Normans, French Basques and probably Spanish Basques as well were all trading in furs and skins from an early stage, but for much of the sixteenth century the trade was an offshoot of the shore codfishery rather than an independent branch of commerce. In 1534, Cartier found that the Indians who had come down to Gaspé were willing to exchange furs for European commodities,[44] but we do not gather from his experiences in the St. Lawrence between 1535 and 1542 whether he engaged extensively in the trade or regarded it as a major potential of the region. It was probably during the period between 1543 and 1580, of which we know very little indeed, that the St. Lawrence became the main focus for a major trade in furs. Fox, especially the "black" Arctic fox, marten, muskrat, lynx and bear were all attractive, and the beaver became increasingly so. Beaver fur was sought for itself, but after the middle of the century especially it was in demand for felt, to make the beaver hats which gradually but inevitably swept over Europe for male and female wear until by 1600 they had become almost universal amongst the wealthier social groups. It

44. See pp. 173–174 above.

was found that if the Indians sewed up the cured beaver skins into robes and wore them for the winter, the coarse guard hairs were loosened or lost, leaving the resulting short fur ideal for felting and so particularly desirable to the French. By 1580 the Basques (probably mainly French rather than Spanish) had come up the river after the white whale *(beluga)* and remained to collect furs off the mouth of the Saguenay—an old Indian summer rallying point where Hurons, Montagnais, Micmac and others had originally come to do their own exchanges in the summer and now came to do so increasingly for the Europeans, who in their turn competed to offer tools, weapons, beads and trinkets for beaver skins and other furs.

The St. Malo men (and some from Jersey also for a while) were active after 1581 each summer. We suspect that the Basques resented their appearance but they do not seem to have violently opposed them. The most energetic fur traders were the nephews of Jacques Cartier, the Noëls, who, as we saw, reopened the exploration of the Upper St. Lawrence. Their attempt to gain a French monopoly in 1588 was resisted in Brittany since the trade was too profitable, and in 1589 it was thrown open, by which time Normans were also active in it. The Normans had pioneered the trade in furs along the inner shores of the later Maritimes, Étienne Bellenger bringing from the Bay of Fundy in 1583 "Bever skynes verie fayre as many as made 600 bever hattes,"[45] as well as lynx, otter, marten (fisher rather than Canadian sable?) and other pelts, while profits were high. Fur trading along these shores and those of Maine developed from this time on, independent of the codfishery. The English voyages to New England of 1602–1605 attempted in a desultory way to tap the trade, but the Sagadahoc colony's attempt to exploit it fully showed (as Champlain found in 1604–07) that there were not enough furs in the coastal parts of Maine to keep it going profitably.

The fur trade had early effects on the economy and relations between the interior tribes. Montagnais, Algonquin, Micmac, and Etchemin joined to keep the rivers open for the collection and distribution of furs; the Hurons far inland had good relations with them and added their furs from time to time to the common pool. The settled Iroquois, south of the river, who had long dominated internal trade in eastern North America, were pushed out of the

45. Quinn, *North American Discovery,* p. 243.

profitable new nexus unless they were prepared to act in a secondary capacity to supply the Indians who held the key to the French riches. Consequently, they were prepared to fight against the fur traders for a share of the French goods. Champlain observed the results of their defeat in 1603, and in 1608–9 aligned himself with the victors. The Iroquois were strong enough to keep up the struggle and intensify it in the years after 1612. The monopoly of the sieur de Monts, and the subsequent monopolies of 1603 to 1611 (with a few intermissions), were recognitions of the fact that Bretons and Normans had enough in common to combine, and even to admit the Rochelais, rather than let the trade become a free-for-all. The Spanish Basques obligingly faded out shortly after 1600. The French Basques who remained in the trade could be challenged or compromised with, so long as they combined whaling with a little fur trading and did not move wholesale into the latter.

From its casual beginnings, the fur trade in the latter years of the sixteenth and early years of the seventeenth centuries became a major reason for permanent European participation in North America. The various tentative efforts of 1600 onward produced in the end the *comptoir*, the business center of the fur trade—which is all Quebec was and remained for many years—where the collective interests of the French in the trade could be focused.[46] The fur trade was not like the fishery. Fishing could be carried on without the direct participation of the Amerindians; not so the fur trading. Indians caught the animals, employed their women to cure the skins, and then had to exchange them with the Europeans in the summer. So the trade was fitted into the traditional pattern of life and modified it in many ways. For the first time, American society became geared into a branch of the European economy.

IV

Any account of the initial exploitation of North America must give some consideration to the nature of the settlements attempted by Europeans. The building of forts, residential towns and villages,

46. Marcel Trudel, *Histoire de la Nouvelle France*, vol II, *Le Comptoir, 1604–1627* (Montreal, 1966), demonstrates this fully. The distribution of European artifacts testifies to its success (see John Witthoft, "Archaeology as a key to the Colonial Fur Trade," *Minnesota History*, XL [1966], 204–207).

trading posts and individual farmhouses, represented the creation of social capital on which the foundations of economic life could be laid. The specific installations made in the early period proved to be transitory and superficial; not being designed to last, they did not do so. Nor indeed did any of them survive in the form in which they had been originally designed for even a generation after the end of the initial period. Thus we have today no surviving structures and few archeological remnants from early settlement sites. They did, however, provide bases on which some temporary and other permanent settlements could be established; and the social capital represented by them survived in the form of pioneered and cleared sites on which modified structures, to suit new and more intensive occupation, could be erected.

The form of colony which was either manned by convicts or assisted by their efforts appears in early discussions and figures in later experiments. When John Cabot thought in 1497 that he had found the scarcely inhabited northern fringe of Asia, he proposed to set up an entrepôt on it, so that a halfway house to the trade of Cipango and Cathay could be prepared. And the inhabitants for this purpose were to be convicts. So, too, it is likely were a number of the workers in Frobisher's proposed mining settlement on Baffin Island in 1578, which, like Cabot's, was not in the end established. The Cartier-Roberval settlement of 1541–43 included amongst its members a number of convicts. The Brownist settlement on the Magdalen Islands in 1597 may not have been envisaged as a place where the settlers would be unfree; but as they would be bound firmly to exile from England, they would be virtual prisoners of their environment as they had earlier been prisoners of the state. The first convict settlement to be brought into effect was that on Sable Island in 1598. Little detail on its internal history—that of a group of condemned men under a group of guards engaged in sea and walrus hunting in a natural prison—is known. Supplied annually by the ship which took away the results of their labor, they revolted when the vessel did not arrive in 1602. They overpowered their guards and set up on their own. But it seems likely that they then turned against each other, since there was only a handful left to be rescued in 1603.

Gradually, these convict settlements shade into those formed by men who left Europe for religious or other ideological reasons. The

Pilgrims of 1620 are the most famous—their solution was an English village, though lightly protected by a palisade and fort. The open, mainly civilian, character of the settlement may indicate the sort of community which the Brownists would have planned for their congregation, comparable in size to the Pilgrim community of 1620, if they had in 1598 followed up their reconnaissance of the Magdalen Islands by the intended settlement of their gathered church. Though Roman Catholics were to envisage settlements in southern New England in 1582-3 and again in northern New England in 1605, we cannot say that their plans were in any way peculiarly influenced or dominated by the preconceived ideas on settlement patterns in contradistinction to those of Protestant landowners of conservative leanings. The latter were exemplified in the plan developed by Sir Humphrey Gilbert in 1582, for a network of great estates, with a major town which would become the capital city of a seigneurial colony; but it remained wholly on paper.

The Spaniards had, from the beginning, a strong sense of the central nature of the town in colonial society. The primacy of the urban settlement in the colonization of the Caribbean Islands, the Spanish Main, Mexico, Peru and elsewhere was bound to have repercussions on North America. Unfortunately, we do not know what sort of nucleus Ponce de León envisaged in Florida in 1521, and we have only the sketchiest idea of the town which Ayllón laid out in his colony in 1526. Official views on towns gradually crystallized: we can see this in Tristan da Luna's projected urban settlement on a Spanish model in 1559.

San Agustín did not precisely conform to other Spanish patterns. Once the site had been moved to the mainland, the location of the fort town established there was dictated by the need to command the gap in the coastal island chain which fronted the mainland. The forts which were wooden ones, had to be frequently renewed as the result of decay or destruction, and were intended mainly to accommodate a garrison which could oppose any English or French intervention. Since a church, a monastic house, and quarters for civil government were designated, the town itself was planned separately from the fort and to the south of it, on open and more favorable ground. This meant that the settlers had room to lay out fields and orchards; after an interval, the orchards in particular flourished. But the settlement itself did not. Pedro Menéndez de Avilés had poured

men and women into it in 1566-7, but they did not stay. What remained was only a nucleus of civilian officials and their families, the households of a few married members of the garrison, a tiny group of craftsmen and traders, some with families, and an assorted group of regular and secular clergy. The church was the focal point of the civilian settlement. But the administration was centered on the fort, and it was there that the governor lived until almost the end of the century, when Méndez de Canzo erected a large dwelling in the town for himself. Certainly Indians came to trade, but none lived there, though there was an Indian village, Nombre de Dios, close by. A novel factor was the presence of the black household and field slaves who served the small civilian population.

The town was very vulnerable. It was damaged in the English raid in 1571, and Drake in 1586 destroyed the fort completely and leveled the town itself, even cutting down the orchards. When the soldiers and civilians re-emerged from hiding, they had to start from scratch. The fort was re-established much more firmly, but the town was only slowly rebuilt on its earlier scale. The Franciscan mission, on the other hand, was well established after 1584, with its own house in the town; doubtless there was much coming and going of friars and probably of some of their Indian charges too. A clearly planned Spanish town had been created by 1610, which was growing and diversifying round its central *plaza* by 1612. The pattern of this Spanish town survived to stamp its character on later Saint Augustine, even if its buildings were transient.

The French attempts at settlement in the sixteenth century have a special character of their own. They were intended to be almost wholly masculine in their personnel but not primarily military, though capable of defense. Their main function was to demonstrate whether or not survival was possible for western Europeans in the exceptionally severe winter conditions of the St. Lawrence Valley. This was the pattern of Cartier's holding in 1535-6 and 1541-2, though Roberval in 1542-3 had at least a token female element in his contingent of settlers, and, apparently, a more pronounced military element also. This climatic defensiveness carried over into the seventeenth century. Its nature was well illustrated both by the form of the Ste Croix settlement of 1604-5 and by its experience during the winter; it appears in Port Royal from 1605 and is a basis for the Quebec settlement from 1608.

We can, however, see a degree of specialization setting in. The proposed Bellenger settlement on the Bay of Fundy in 1583 is the earliest we know of to have the twin objectives of trading post for furs and missionary center that were to be peculiarly French combinations in the centuries following. The concept of the trading post inspired Tadoussac in 1599–1600, Port Royal, and later Quebec. The form of the *habitacion,* first adopted at Port Royal in 1605 and developed at Quebec from 1608, gave expression to this objective. It was a protected unit, primarily a place where a handful of men (perhaps with one or two families among them) could live and carry on trade. It became the symbol of Maurice Trudel's *comptoir* economy which he sees to be characteristic of Champlain's Canada. The *habitacion* also proved physically durable: Port Royal, abandoned from 1607 to 1610, was found to have suffered only minor disrepair in three years.[47]

Some English and French settlements had a certain amount in common, namely, their military aspect and their defensive function. Thus Ribault in 1562, Laudonnière in 1564, and Lane in 1585 thought in terms primarily of a garrison, though one with specialists attached, and with duties to explore as well as to guard a base. Fort Caroline had, it is true, some accommodation which could be used for civilians; but it was primarily a military fort and barracks, which could overawe the Indians if necessary, and might be used defensively if Spaniards attacked, though when they did so it was in fact neither adequately defended nor equipped.

The plan which some military-minded man, perhaps Roger Williams, put forward for the English Roanoke Island settlement in 1585[48] was for a strongly defended town. Military considerations were to govern its layout and to dominate it in detail. Yet it is clear that the greater part of its population was envisaged as civilian. In the event, the fortification at Roanoke Island was large enough only to accommodate a small guardhouse, and the cottages where most of the soldiers and all of the civilians lived were some little way from it and undefended. The colonists of 1587 were a more representative civilian nucleus. They represented the view that a balanced group of men, women and children could best establish roots in the new land, and it is clear that they were not dominated by military

47. Trudel, pp. 68–72, 86, 90–91.
48. D. B. Quinn, *The Roanoke Voyages,* I, 130–139.

men or military considerations. Their "City of Ralegh" on Chesapeake Bay was probably never begun. We cannot know exactly how
or for what length of time they lived on Roanoke Island, but evidently they took down the old fort defenses and built themselves a
stout defensive outer work, with flanking outshots of a military
character within which a party might then remain protected while
the main body removed to a new, permanent, and most probably
purely civilian settlement.

Jamestown was, from the beginning, something of a prestige symbol. It had to represent at least a token royal colonial capital, even
if it was occupied only by a very small permanent population. We
have very little indication of precisely what the original 1607 settlement looked like, though we have more detail on that of 1608. This
was halfway between the French *habitacion* and the defended village.
Manned exclusively by company servants, dependent largely on the
central magazine for food and stores, it had its triangular defensive
works around but inside was more of a village than a fort, with the
church and magazine as its effective public buildings. The theory
was that the agricultural land needed by the settlers was to be
farmed immediately outside its gates. The settlements at Henrico
and elsewhere were thought of primarily as military outposts,
though the settlement established briefly at the falls in 1609 was a
mixed military and civilian one. At the same time, as Jamestown
expanded, the new settlement became rather an undefended village
spreading outward from the defended village. The Jamestown that
grew up thereafter was a rather loosely planned town, mainly consisting of small holdings with considerable distances between the
individual dwellings or groups of houses, and conveying little impression of a beleaguered pioneer settlement. From Jamestown it
proved possible to expand individual holdings of land and
households.

Was there any appreciable degree of planning ahead in colonial
community life? Certainly the Spaniards, with their early experience
behind them, believed in preparing for the municipal administration of their settlements from the earliest moment. Thus Ayllón had
officials already appointed as *alcalde,* and probably *regidores,* before
the expedition landed so that his town of Gualdape could be immediately manned by municipal officials. The same was done in
Luna's expedition. Similar officials were provided for his intended

settlement near Santa Elena and were apparently employed in the successive settlements of Ochuse and Nanipacana in 1559–60. Moreover, he was equipped with a standard formula for a town layout,[49] though we do not know if he followed it in either of the two sites his men actually occupied. This provided for a *plaza,* round which church and official buildings would be erected, and a rectangular layout, with defined districts *(barrios)* indicated in each quarter of the extended quadrilateral, the whole surrounded by a ditch and fence.

We do not know whether the French prescribed any very specific form for their 1564 Florida settlement, but it was clearly in the French tradition to enclose barracks and residences inside a defensive ditch, and in the form in which we see Fort Caroline in Le Moyne's pictures. This was followed by Champlain at Ste Croix in 1604. But at Port Royal and Quebec, he made his settlement in the more compact form of the *habitacion,* combining storehouses, barracks and private quarters in a single complex of buildings, defensible in themselves, though surrounded by an outer ditch and defensive palisades.

The Spaniards in Florida showed little consistency in their settlement arrangements. A square fortress, inside which was some division into stores and quarters, was the pattern of all their early wooden forts at San Agustín. But until the 1590s there seems to have been little systematic planning of the town, when the central *plaza* with surrounding rectangular *barrios* was laid out. The fort continued to be rebuilt frequently, whether to move it to a slightly better position, to strengthen it or to replace rotting timbers. In Santa Elena, likewise, the fort was separate from the town; but it would seem that the civilian settlement, though it was governed by an *alcalde* and *regidores,* was never much more than a cluster of farm dwellings assembled loosely in the fields around the fort on the cramped site on Parris Island, which was all that could be developed. The plan for a town or a group of villages on the mainland was never brought into effect on account of Indian resistance. As the settlers were moved away, all semblance of a town withered—the

49. H. I. Priestley *The Luna Papers, 1559–1561,* 2 vols. (Deland, Fla., 1928), I, 21, 19–33; II, 225. A *plaza* with a church, monastery, and governor's palace, adding up to forty *solares* (houselots), and one hundred *solares* for residents, plus defenses and four gates, were to make up the town.

fort alone remained. In San Agustín most of the early settlers left too, but the households of the married soldiers took their place, together with a very few non-official traders and craftsmen. Santa Fé was barely taking shape by 1612, but it was planned from the beginning on the standard Spanish pattern.

The English plans for the 1585 colony (as has been indicated) envisaged a fairly elaborate defended town, with walls and gates with a central blockhouse. The actual Roanoke settlement comprised a defended enclosure with a headquarters building and store, while the settlers were distributed in undefended cottages nearby. The revised form of settlement created by the 1587 colony—but not planned in advance—produced a strongly palisaded center inside which apparently only temporary dwellings in place of the old headquarters building were erected. For Jamestown we have no surviving plans. There the triangular fort was intended only as a headquarters enclosure, though it could probably shelter the majority of the settlers in a crisis. When it was reconstructed in 1608, it was more like a small defended town, with the principal buildings near the center and a reinforced ditch and palisade enclosing the whole.[50] Fort St. George at Sagadahoc in 1607 was planned as a more elaborate version of this type of settlement, but may never have been completed before the settlement was abandoned.

Settlement in North America as a whole was nominal rather than effective by 1612. The Quebec *habitacion* was proving a good fur-trading station, but was not capable, in its existing layout, of being transformed into a colonial town. Port Royal was a similar but still more limited outpost. Fort St. George (Sagadahoc) had been abandoned in 1608 and was not revived. Jamestown was a small English town with a predominantly civilian layout, but a military type of government. Henrico had been planned on similar lines. The Paspahegh blockhouse was no more than that. In Newfoundland, there was something like a *habitacion*, with living quarters and stores, inside a palisade, with perhaps a few cottages parallel with the shore at Cupids Cove. The Spanish town and fort at Santa Elena had been abandoned. There was a fort and probably a handful of civilians in

50. The problems of identifying and assessing the early materials found at Jamestown and collating them with the literary evidence can be seen by comparing Henry C. Forman, *Jamestown and St. Mary's* (Baltimore, 1938), and John L. Cotter, *Archaeological Excavations at Jamestown* (Washington, D. C. 1958).

houses round San Mateo on the St. Johns River and one or two blockhouses at the mouth of the river. San Agustín was a small Spanish town, best rooted of all, if not yet firmly, alongside its enlarged fort. Santa Fé was newly begun. Otherwise Europeans had only a few scattered mission stations in modern Florida and Georgia, some with churches, and a few missions in Pueblo villages in New Mexico. The total European population can be estimated at between 1,000 and 1,500, of which some 600 were English, some 500 Spanish, and the remainder French. The influence and orbit of each of them was extremely limited, yet most provided a growing point for rapid transformations in the near future, especially on the part of the English settlement in Virginia. The economic significance of towns, villages, forts, trading posts and missions was thus far almost wholly potential.

Farms around the fort at Santa Elena; gardens and orchards at San Agustín, with a few cornfields nearby; cornfields around the cottages on Roanoke Island in 1586; gardens inside the settlement perimeter at Ste Croix and outside it in Port Royal and Quebec; Company cornfields and experimental garden patches outside Jamestown, together with glass and iron furnaces and potash, tar, and pitch workings nearby—these made up almost the whole range of exploitation of the land, apart from the actual sites for dwellings, barracks and defensive works. Such horticulture, agriculture and industrial workings did almost nothing to store up permanent social capital for the settlers of the post-1612 period. At best they provided trial ventures, upon which more effective and larger experiments could be based, and gave some information on what it was and was not possible to grow in or extract from the American soil. In 1612, then, the only material signs of white occupation which had any durable qualities were the coquina house built by Méndez de Canzo which was used as the governor's official residence at San Agustín, and the *habitacions* at Port Royal and Quebec which had shown themselves to be reasonably durable and adaptable. White settlement had made virtually no economic impact on North America. The main areas of economic activity—the fisheries and the fur trade—remained totally peripheral.

If the effects of settlement were still minimal, trade as a means of opening up North America was still limited also in its effects by

1612. There had of course been a considerable amount of casual bartering with Indians for·bows and arrows, feathers and feather garments, and other specimens of their clothing and gear of one sort or another, and these had no doubt introduced an appreciable quantity of minor European artifacts into Amerindian hands. Part of the European exploitation of the coastal territories was the direct removal of American plants; sassafras and china root, for example, were grubbed up by shore parties of seamen, as were cedar and other desirable trees, though these usually needed the use of a sawpit before they could be comfortably stowed on board. It is likely too that Indians who were encountered along the shores were induced by promises of gaudy or useful artifacts to assist in these activities. The Indians in most areas were prepared to surrender almost anything they had—though mostly they did not have very much that was attractive to Europeans—for metal of any sort, especially knives and axes, but copper also for ceremonial wear, brass, and, most usually and in greatest quantities, beads. As scientific archeology gradually investigates the sites of the early contact period, the number and variety of European artifacts found in graves and village sites for the period before permanent European settlement developed is proving to be larger than might be expected. So far our knowledge of European trade is, except in the case of the fishery, impossible to quantify, and our information on it derives from scattered references. The archeological evidence might suggest that the bulk and variety of European trade with Amerindian populations has been underestimated in the past. Whether a careful assembly and analysis of such data as there is will provide any more satisfactory answers has yet to be determined. The total commercial impact of the Europeans was clearly not negligible, though it is only in the case of the fur trade that we have any inkling of its major effects on Indian society.

# CHAPTER 22

## *For the Record*

---

THERE could be no real discovery of North America unless, and until, there was a record of that discovery; on this all the authorities are agreed.[1] America would not have existed, argues Edmundo O'Gorman, unless it had been invented.[2] We need to take note of how that record developed.

It is clear that word-of-mouth description of discovery and exploration must have played an important part in the development of both the myth and knowledge of America, but we have very little chance of evaluating either its nature or its precise effects. Only when oral tradition was written down did it become part of the sustaining record. In the case of the sagas, this tradition of oral transmission has conveyed to us essential information—though in a form which is often difficult to interpret—without which we would have scarcely any knowledge whatever of the Norse discoveries in North America. Unfortunately, some at least of the problems in interpreting such evidence appear to be insoluble. We have also hearsay elements written down as part of the record throughout the sixteenth century, but though these are often suggestive they are rarely explicit.

Most of the record is contained in manuscripts which have been

1. See Wilcomb E. Washburn, "The Meaning of 'Discovery,' in the Fifteenth and Sixteenth Centuries," *American Historical Review*, LXVIII (1962), 1–21.

2. Edmundo O'Gorman, *La idea del descubrimiento de América* (Mexico, 1951), and his shorter book on the same topic, *The Invention of America* (Bloomington, Ind., 1961).

preserved down to our own day. A number are known to have circulated by means of copies made fairly close to the time of their composition; others were handed down and then published some considerable time after their composition. For the most part, such materials were in narrative form, and were circulated in manuscript or printed either for their geographical and human interest or as examples for others to emulate the achievements of early voyages or take warning from the fate of exploring parties. But many other documents arose in the course of the administration of expeditions and the formal recording of their results, and these usually did not come to light or see publication until the archives of states and institutions were opened during the past century and a half. Most such documents, unless they were circulated for official purposes, were scarcely part of the effective record with which we are here concerned.

Maps are in a somewhat different category. We have comparatively few of the rough sketches from which explorers' maps were compiled.[3] What we have in most cases is the result of the circulation of copies of such sketches in a semi-compiled form amongst the mapmaking fraternity. Its members were mostly Italians, in the early part of our period at least, and they handed on from one to another in various parts of Europe the data from which more general maps could be put together. Many of these Italianate maps were composed in Italy, but others were made by Italians working in Spain or Portugal, often under some difficulty since Portugal and Spain usually regarded maps of the New World as something to be kept confidential. Later, groups of French mapmakers who exchanged cartographical data amongst themselves appeared; and, later still, there were similar groups in England and the Netherlands. Toward the end of the sixteenth century, the compilation of maps covering wide areas—some of them assembled in world atlases—became professionalized. The map publishers copied each other in stereotyped ways, though also trying to steal a march on one another by acquiring new information which would put them ahead of their business rivals. In the case of maps, we cannot rigidly separate what

3. The sketch which Columbus made on the coast of Española in 1492–3 (see R. A. Skelton, *Explorers' Maps* [London, 1951], p. 53), and a sketch of the Roanoke Island area made in 1585 (D. B. Quinn, *The Roanoke Voyages*, I [1955], 215) are exceptions.

has survived in manuscript from what was put in print because many of the maps we have clearly circulated in manuscript form in or near their own time. Maps are often important records of what is not always preserved in the printed sources, but they are very fallible records also. Often, their material is much less reliable on some areas than others; a certain amount was almost always based on tradition rather than direct observation, and the problems of scale, in circumstances when latitude could not usually be calculated with any exactness and longitude was normally unobtainable, were formidable. Maps were often difficult for contemporaries to interpret and have remained so for their successors.

The graphic record was not confined to maps alone. From earliest times, sketches of fauna and flora and especially of foreign peoples seen on voyages were made. Only a tiny proportion of these have survived. Of those which have, many were copied onto maps for decorative purposes ("to garnish the plot," as was said in Elizabethan times). We have recognizable Brazilian parrots on the Cantino map only two years after "the land of Parrots,"[4] Brazil, was discovered. But a good many of the figures on North American maps are imagined ones. Sometimes such sketches were preserved in the form of engravings, though they suffered modifications in being transferred to wood or copper. Our earliest representations of the bison (buffalo) show this very well, since one engraver copied from another and the modifications he made could produce rather bizarre results.[5] It is sometimes difficult in such illustrations to separate fact from invention in figures and artifacts. Thus in André Thevet's illustrations of North American Indians, the houses and the snowshoes may have an authentic origin while the figures of Indians are quite fanciful.[6] Moreover, engravers tended to develop stereotypes of native peoples based on the earliest groups of engravings which happened to circulate. Thus figures of Tupi-Guaraní Indians of Brazil, which by accident became the type-figures for the peoples of America, are often found representing North American

4. R. A. Skelton, W. P. Cumming and D. B. Quinn, *The Discovery of North America* (London and New York, 1971), fig. 53 (p. 57).

5. The successive versions given by Gómera (1554), Thevet (1558), and Theodor de Bry (1595) are shown in George Parker Winship, *The Coronado Expedition* (Smithsonian Institution, Bureau of American Ethnology, *Fourteenth Annual Report* [1897], pp. 512, 516, 520.

6. André Thevet, *Cosmographie universelle* (Paris, 1575).

Indians. Only for the latter part of the sixteenth century have we original drawings as well as engravings of certain North American subjects, which enable us to judge how far the engravers followed the sketches they had before them. Though the depictions of such natural objects and peoples as survive are relatively few in number, they are important in that they reflect mental attitudes as well as knowledge and representational techniques amongst the Europeans. The pictures of the savage, which were circulated amongst Europeans, were perhaps as important as the maps showing the layout and shape of North American lands in forming European impressions of America.

Although the Caribbean, Central and South American discoveries, because of their dramatic nature, soon led to an outpouring of printed material after 1493, North America remained for a long time of very marginal interest to Europeans, and consequently published material was slow to appear. The earliest circulated materials on North America were, clearly, maps which moved around from Italian mapmaker to mapmaker, modified according to such new information as came to light. From before 1500 almost to the middle of the sixteenth century, much of the more important evidence we have is contained in maps which, though they may not have been published, gathered up information on voyages through the mapmakers' network spread over most of western Europe. After 1507 there were cartographic representations of North America, or parts of it, in print and the published cartographic record becomes significant.

The map of Juan de la Cosa, begun in 1500,[7] is the first significant record of North American exploration, and includes material on the 1497 voyage of John Cabot. The question of the scale of the English coast, on the Cosa map, and of the representation of what we know to be North America as part of Asia, remain matters of scholarly debate. The Oliveriana map of a year or two later[8] is significant as showing the emergence of some degree of scientific skepticism about the location and definition of discoveries across the Atlantic,

7. Full-size facsimile, Juan de la Cosa, *Carta geográfica*, with *Ensayo biográfica* by Antonio Vascáno (Madrid, 1892); J. A. Williamson, *Cabot Voyages* (1962), plate 9; details in J. A. Williamson, *Voyages of the Cabots* (1929), p. 191, and Henry Harrisse, *Découverte et évolution cartographique de Terre-Neuve* (1900), plate II.

8. Harrisse, *Decouverte*, plate IV; Williamson, *Cabot Voyages* (1962), plate IX.

since alternative, unfinished coastlines give us indications, not alleged certainties, of what had been discovered. The Cantino map of 1502[9] is an important political document: under Portuguese influence, it placed the western discoveries of Gaspar Corte Real in 1501 on the Portuguese side of the demarcation line of 1494. The land which lay beyond this island discovery on the map is clearly intended as part of Asia, but as it terminates in a Horn of Asia which is very like the Florida peninsula it also has aroused academic debate which has not been wholly resolved. The Pedro Reinel map (known as Kunstmann I) of about 1504[10] adds a further degree of sophistication since it indicates by a scale the latitude of what was to become the Newfoundland-Labrador-Greenland area; while a later map, probably by the same hand (Kunstmann III),[11] repeats the latitude scale but also indicates the compass variation first noted by John Cabot in 1497. The map and globe published by Martin Waldseemüller at Saint-Dié in 1507[12] were, however, of crucial importance. Although it is hard to trace the precise influences from earlier maps embodied in its profile of the coasts so far discovered, this did for the first time put them into revolutionary geographical perspective by showing them to be part of a new continent, separated by an ocean from Asia. The name "America" on it was also original, though it was applied only to South America, the northern landmass being labeled "Terra ulterius incognita." However, unlike the manuscript maps previously referred to, which remained unknown to all but a limited group of mapmakers and certain officials, the Waldseemüller map was widely influential in presenting an outline of some authority for subsequent makers of world maps. Soon their work began to show the northernmost of the new continents carrying the name America also. At the same time a rival profile was current for some years. The Contarini-Roselli manuscript map of 1506[13] had given a clue to this by depicting South America as a new

9. As note 3 above; the North American part in Harrisse, *Découverte*, plate III.

10. Williamson, *Cabot Voyages* (1962), plate XII.

11. Harrisse, *Découverte*, plate V; Williamson, *Cabot Voyages* (1962), plate XIII.

12. Map, Emerson D. Fite and Archibald Freeman, *A Book of Maps* (Cambridge, Mass., 1925; New York, 1969); detail, W. P. Cumming, *The Southeast in Early Maps* (Princeton, N. J., 1958), plate 1; gores, *Antilia and America* (James Ford Bell Library, Minneapolis, 1955). The whole map on a large scale is in Josef Fischer and Franz von Weiser, *Die älteste karte mit dem Namen Amerika aus dem Jahre 1507* (Innsbruck, 1907).

13. Fite and Freeman, *Book of Maps*, plate 6; Williamson, *Cabot Voyages*, plate VIII.

continent, but attributing the North American discoveries to a great outshot from eastern Asia. The Ruysch map, printed in 1508[14] and reprinted a number of times subsequently, presented this view in a sophisticated form. It was not until after 1520 that the Wald-seemüller profile finally prevailed, as subsequent exploration rounded out the shores of the Caribbean and showed them to be continuous with those of eastern North America.

The first inhabitants of North America brought back to Europe, so far as is known, were those brought as slaves to Portugal by one of Gaspar Corte Real's ships in 1501.[15] It is likely that they were Micmac or other Algonkian Indians, but nothing seems to have been recorded of their ultimate fate. We know that two Indians were brought to London in 1501 or 1502 and were seen at court dressed in English clothes, though not speaking any language which could be interpreted. They were duly mentioned in a London City chronicle, but it was not published at the time.[16] The seven Indians, either Micmac or Beothuk, brought to Rouen with their canoe and weapons in 1509 were the first to be celebrated in print in an appendix to a chronicle published in Paris in 1512.[17] Moreover, it would appear that they inspired the first representation by a European artist of an American Indian in a sculpture made about the time of publication.[18] They may indeed have been brought back to North America by the French, as they did this with other American Indian visitors later. The Portuguese map of eastern North America of about 1519 in the Miller Atlas[19] shows a considerable amount of detail for Newfoundland and adjacent coasts, and has also a woodland scene with deer drinking at a stream, though whether this derived from sketches or from imagination cannot be ascertained. These slight indications give some impression of the gradual nature of the impact of North America on Europe.

The expeditions of Giovanni da Verrazzano, Estevão Gomes and John Rut along the coasts of North America between 1525 and

14. Fite and Freeman, *Book of Maps*, plate 9.

15. H. P. Biggar, *The Precursors of Jacques Cartier* (1911), pp. 65–67.

16. Williamson, *Cabot Voyages*, pp. 220–222.

17. *Eusebii Caesarienis Episcopi Chronicon*, edited by Henri Estienne (Paris, 1512), fol. 172; Harrisse, *Découverte*, pp. xxx–xxxi, 162–163.

18. This was in the church of St. Jacques at Dieppe (Louis Vitet, *Histoire de Dieppe* [Paris, 1844], p. 119).

19. Harrisse, *Découverte*, plate VII (p. 84).

1527, and the resulting maps and narratives, enabled something of a synthetic picture of the eastern shores of North America to emerge for Europeans, even if most of the evidence remained confined to official archives or the limited circle of the mapmakers. The letter reporting on his voyage which Verrazzano wrote to Francis I on his return is known to have been circulated by him to friends in Italy. Moreover, his brother Gerolamo recorded his voyages on a map of which copies circulated not only in Italy but in England. This came to constitute for Frenchmen and many Italian cartographers an outline of the coast which continued to be influential in England and France until early in the seventeenth century.[20] The voyage of the Portuguese Estavão Gomes, in the Spanish service in 1525,[21] added an alternative profile of eastern North America, rather more misleading in certain respects than Verrazzano's, to European knowledge. Incorporated in the *padron real*—the official sailing directions and atlas of the Spanish administration—it became the standard Spanish outline for the coast throughout the remainder of the sixteenth century. Diogo Ribeiro assimilated it to earlier information on the voyages of the Corte Reals and of Ayllón to create an influential profile of the coast in his atlas of 1529.[22] The Spanish cartographer Alonso de Santa Cruz, somewhat later, drew a number of maps based on Gomes's discoveries which came to influence published maps also.[23] An example is the printed map of Diego Gutiérrez of 1562.[24]

Publications in the Iberian peninsula on North America were very slow to appear. Most of the publicity focused on the discoveries in the Caribbean, Mexico and Peru, so that North America, which was always marginal to Spanish activities, appears late and lightly in Iberian literature. Álvar Núñez Cabeza de Vaca had, however, a story to tell which found readers for his *Relación* in 1555[25] on his

20. The maps of the Verrazzano expedition are in Lawrence C. Wroth, *The Voyages of Giovanni da Verrazzano, 1524–1528* (1970), plates 18–22. Gerolamo Verrazzano's map is Fite and Freeman, *Book of Maps*, plate 15, Maggiolo's plate 12.

21. Castiglione, 1525, Harrisse, *Découverte*, plate X.

22. Detail, Cumming, *Southeast in Early Maps*, plate 4; world map, Fite and Freeman, *Book of Maps*, plate 14.

23. Franz R. von Wieser, *Karten von Amerika in dem Islario General des Alonso de Santa Cruz* (Innsbruck, 1908); W. F. Ganong, *Crucial Maps in the Early Cartography . . . of Canada* (1964), pp. 138–141, 153–159.

24. Skelton, Cumming and Quinn, *Discovery of North America*, fig. 156, pp. 141–143.

25. *La relacion y comentarios del governador Alvar Nuñez Cabeça de Vaca* (Valladolid, 1555; reprinted, in 2 vols., Madrid 1906).

famous excursion across the greater part of North America. This was followed by the appearance at Évora, Portugal, of the experiences of a companion of Hernando de Soto whom we know only as the Gentleman of Elvas. His *Relaçãm verdadeira* (1557) created no great impression at first but later in the century became a well-known authority.[26] The Spanish map of the Soto expedition remained in manuscript, but a version of it was used by Alonzo de Chaves and later influenced the map of this area published by Ortelius in 1584.[27]

The Cartier-Roberval voyages of 1534–43 stimulated the cartographers of the Norman school to place on the map the exploits surrounding the discovery of the St. Lawrence. A series of maps, which had a wide influence on the subsequent cartography of North America, was made. That of Nicholas Desliens (1541) is probably the earliest of the surviving series to show the results of the Cartier voyages of 1534–36.[28] That of Jean Rotz formed part of an atlas presented to Henry VIII of England in 1542.[29] The so-called Harleian map also probably belonged to 1542,[30] as did one of two by Pierre Desceliers (the second being of 1546),[31] while the printed world map with which Sebastian Cabot had some connection put the discoveries on public record in 1544.[32] It now became possible to draw with some conviction the profile of eastern North America from the tip of the Florida peninsula to Labrador, whether the Verrazzano or Gomes view of the coastline north of Spanish Florida was adopted. The first French published work of value on North America was *Brief récit de la navigation faicte és isles de Canada,* which appeared in Paris in 1545 and gave a detailed journal of the second Cartier expedition. The sailing directions for Canada in Jean Alfonce, *Les voyages avantureux* (Poitiers, 1559), who had been with

26. James Alexander Robertson (ed.), *The Expedition of Hernando de Soto in Florida* 2 vols. (Deland, Fla., 1925).

27. Cumming, *Southeast in Early Maps*, plates 8 and 9.

28. On the maps derived from Cartier's voyages, see T. Layng, *Sixteenth Century Maps Relating to Canada* (Ottawa, 1956), nos. 235 (Rotz, 1542), 240 (Desliens, 1541), 240 (Desceliers, 1542), 241 (Harleian, 1542–3), 259 (Cabot, 1544), 293 (Desceliers, 1546), 306 (Vallard, 1547). There is a section of the Desliens map in Harrisse, *Découverte,* plate XI.

29. Biggar, *Voyages of Jacques Cartier* (1924), plate V.

30. *Ibid.,* plate X.

31. *Ibid.,* plates XII, XIV.

32. Fite and Freeman, *Book of Maps,* plate 18.

Roberval in 1542–3, added something further.

A new phase in the published documentation of North America begins with the publication of the third volume of Giambattista Ramusio's great collection, *Navigationi et viaggi*, at Venice in 1556. This contained materials on the Cabots, Verrazzano's letter, narratives of the first two Cartier voyages, and material on the expedition of Vásques de Coronado, 1540–42, as well as other incidental evidence.[33] Thereafter, Ramusio was extensively used by secondary works and his documents became the basis for published translations in languages other than Italian.

The French intervention in Florida of 1562 to 1565, and the Franco-Spanish conflict which ensued, produced a substantial body of literature on the French side. Jean Ribault's *The whole and true discoverye of Terra Florida* appeared in English in London in 1563. This was on the first French expedition. The second French venture of 1564–5 was recounted along with its tragic end in Nicolas le Challeux, *Discours de l'histoire de Floride* (Dieppe, 1566), which was translated and published in London in the same year. Other accounts had to wait until passion was replaced by history. Voisin de la Popellinière, *Les trois mondes* (Paris, 1582), has some interesting material, but the full narrative by René de Laudonnière, *L'histoire notable de la Floride,* came out in Paris only in 1586 and in English in London in 1587. The Spanish accounts of the victory over the French were composed in eloquent and eulogistic terms but were not published at the time though they may well have circulated, the two most outstanding being Gonzalo Solís de Mérás's *Pedro Menéndez de Avilés: Memorial* and Bartolomé Barrientos's *Vida y hechos de Pero Menéndez de Valdés.*[34]

The Frobisher voyages in search of a Northwest Passage were the first English ventures to attract publishers in any number. Sir Humphrey Gilbert's *A discourse of a discovery for a new passage to Cataia* (London, 1576) acted as a curtain raiser, but it was not until

33. Giovanni Battista Ramusio, *Navigationi et Viaggi,* facsimile edition, 3 vols. (Amsterdam, 1967–70), with an analysis of contents and sources, by G. B. Parks, I, 1–39.
34. Eugenio Ruidíaz y Caravia, *La Florida: su conquista y colonización,* 2 vols. (Madrid, 1893), first printed Solís de Merás; Jeannette Thurber Connor, *Pedro de Menéndez y Avilés: Memorial by Gonzalo Solís de Merás,* (1923), published a translation (reissued Gainesville, Fla., 1964). Barrientos first appeared in Genaro Garcia, *Dos antiquos relaciones de Florida* (Mexico, 1902), and was translated by Anthony Kerrigan as *Pedro Menéndez de Avilés, founder of Florida, written by Bartolomé Barrientos* (1965).

Dionyse Settle's *A true reporte of the last voyage into the west and north-west regions* (London, 1577) appeared that sufficient interest was aroused to lead to translations, which came in the years following in French, German, Italian and Latin. Richard Willes, *History of travel* (1577), also helped to publicize the voyages. Thomas Ellis's *A true report of the third and last voyage into Meta Incognita* (London, 1578) attracted interest only in England, but George Best's *A true discourse of the late voyages of discoverie for the finding of a passage to Cathaya* (London, 1578) became a standard work of reference and was reprinted several times.[35] Dr. John Dee had made a notable map of North America for Queen Elizabeth, which was widely referred to in England, and a more private map to illustrate the proposed voyage of Sir Humphrey Gilbert in 1582, neither of which was published.

Publication in England in the early 1580s was largely a popularization of earlier known materials. Richard Hakluyt the younger began the process by getting John Florio to publish his translation of Cartier from Ramusio in *A shorte and briefe narration of the two navigations . . . to . . . Newe Fraunce* (London, 1580), while he himself edited *Divers voyages touching the discoverie of America* (London, 1582)[36] to make available Ribault and other texts to subscribers to Gilbert's expedition and also maps of circa 1527 and 1582 showing different aspects of North America. In these years, too, propaganda pamphlets in favor of English colonial ventures began to appear. The earliest was Christopher Carleill's *A discourse upon the intended voyage to the hethermost partes of America* (London, 1583), and the next Sir George Peckham's *A true reporte of the late discoveries* (London, 1583), though these did not have an international currency.

Information also began to trickle out on North America in publications devoted to other areas. The most notable example was connected with the expedition of Antonio de Espejo in 1582–3. A fairly full account of this was contained in the Madrid edition in 1586 of Juan González de Mendoza's *Historia . . . de la China*. This was extracted and published in Paris in the same year by Richard Hakluyt as *El viaje que hizo Antonio de Espejo* (Paris, 1586), and was

35. The narratives are conveniently collected in Vilhjalmur Stefansson (ed.), *The Three Voyages of Martin Frobisher*, 2 vols. (1938).

36. Facsimiles of both are included in D. B. Quinn, *Richard Hakluyt Editor*, 2 vols. 1967).

subsequently translated into French and English.[37] Similarly, Walter Bigges (and others), *A summarie and true discourse of Sir Francis Drakes West Indian voyage* (London, 1589), which contained incidental material on Florida and Roanoke Island, also had a European circulation.[38]

Two publishing ventures between 1589 and 1591 did much to bring North America before the English public and into European consciousness. The first was Richard Hakluyt's *The principall navigations . . . of the English nation* (London, 1589), which not only reprinted what had been printed already about English activity in North America, but added especially full accounts of the Roanoke voyages, 1584–88, and the expeditions of John Davis, 1585–87, in search of a northerly passage, as well as other incidental information.[39] The second was the multilingual series of illustrated volumes planned by Theodor de Bry at Frankfurt am Main. The first volume of his *America* series appeared in 1590, containing both a reprint of Thomas Harriot's *A briefe and true report of the new found land of Virginia* (already published in London in 1588, and, in Hakluyt's collection, again in 1589) with annotated engravings from drawings of Indians made in Virginia (that is, the area round Roanoke Island) between 1585 and 1587. This appeared in Latin, English, French and German, and gave North America a unique currency in Europe. It was followed by *America*, part ii, in 1591, with engravings of Florida Indians from drawings made by Jacques le Moyne de Morgues in 1564–5, together with accounts of the French Florida colony by him and others. This was in Latin and German only.[40] Both volumes were illustrated with maps, which gave considerable detail on southeastern North America as far north as Chesapeake Bay, and the information in which was soon incorporated into general maps of North America. The Indians as shown in these volumes became, and remained, type-figures for illustrations of North American Indians down until well after 1700. The Hakluyt volumes thus set the tradi-

37. See p. 493, note 6, above.
38. For the editions, see D. B. Quinn, *The Roanoke Voyages*, I, 294.
39. Facsimile, ed. D. B. Quinn and R. A. Skelton, 2 vols. (1965).
40. Facsimile, with introduction by P. H. Hulton, as Thomas Harriot, *A Briefe and True Reporte of the New Found Land of Virginia* (1972). The original drawings on which the engravings are based appear in P. H. Hulton and D. B. Quinn, *The American Drawings of John White*, 2 vols. (1964). P. H. Hulton, *The Work of Jacques Le Moyne de Morgues* (1977), is a comparable volume on Jacques Le Moyne de Morgues.

tion of systematically documenting North America, while those of De Bry, which continued to be reprinted, peopled North America with credible figures who could be visualized in relation to the Europeans who went to explore or settle there.

The second edition of Hakluyt's work, expanded to three volumes (*The principal navigations*, [1598–1600]), contained much material on French and Spanish as well as English activities in North America, some of it not hitherto published.[41] Valuable indications were given, for example, on the Cartier-Roberval voyages of 1541–43, and on some post-Cartier activity in the St. Lawrence; there was also further information on the Roanoke Island area and new material on English activity in the Gulf of St. Lawrence. This meant that the third volume, devoted to the Americas and published in 1600, became the major European documentary collection on North America for some considerable time. Hakluyt had supplied Ortelius in the 1580s with North American material to bring his atlas maps of North America up to date. He also got Felips Galle to construct a map which contained a good synthesis of existing materials for his edition of Peter Martyr, *De novo orbe . . . decades octo* (Paris, 1587); and finally, he supplied Edward Wright with valuable new materials on North America and elsewhere for the world map which was published in the second volume of *The principal navigations* in 1599 and which represented an excellent summary of what was known of the topography of North America at the end of a century of exploration, though much still remained obscure.[42]

The revival of French activity in North America from 1598 onwards, and the appearance on the scene of Samuel de Champlain, who was as indefatigable a writer and cartographer as he was to be as an explorer, led to the appearance of a new wave of narrative accounts of the St. Lawrence Basin and of the coast from Cape Cod northward. Champlain's *Des sauvages* (Paris, 1603) represented a graphic narrative of his recent expedition as far as Montreal. His companion for part of the next series of explorations, Marc Lescarbot, examined the earlier history of France in North America and

41. The North American items are contained in vol. III of *The principal navigations*, 3 vols. (1598–1600), reprinted in *The Principal Navigations*, 12 vols. (1903–05), VIII–XI, and analyzed in D. B. Quinn (ed.), *The Hakluyt Handbook*, 2 vols. (London, 1974), II, 430–60.

42. See Helen Wallis, "Edward Wright and the 1599 World Map," in Quinn, *Hakluyt Handbook*, I, 69–73.

continued it to 1607 in his *Histoire de la Nouvelle France* (Paris, 1609), part of which was rapidly translated into English.[43] The next Champlain volume, *Les voyages* (Paris, 1613), contained his account of the foundation of New France from 1608 to 1611, so that a systematic description, almost up to date, was by then available to readers. Champlain had composed a fine map of his discoveries on the shore from Cape Cod northward in 1607, but he had not published it; he had also sent over in 1605 and probably at other times illustrations of Indians and of fauna and flora—but all have unfortunately been lost. His engraved map of 1612, however, gave a very full picture of New France; this was decorated with pictures of Indians and of natural products which indicate by their fidelity what a loss his original drawings constitute.

Spain continued to maintain an attitude of considerable reserve on her activities in North America. Antonio de Herrera's massive *Historia general* in eight volumes, published in Madrid in 1601–15, gradually built up an outline of Spanish activity there, but indicated how small a share of Spanish energies North America absorbed in relation to her total imperial effort. Garcilaso de la Vega, the Inca, produced the first full-length book in Spanish on North America in *La Florida del Inca* (Lisbon, 1605). Spanish missionary activity in North America remained only slightly covered until the publication of Luis Gerónimo de Oré, *Relacion de los martires que a avido en las provincias de la Florida,* appeared obscurely, probably in Madrid and possibly in 1617;[44] this contained much useful material on the area from the Florida peninsula up to Chesapeake Bay. Many major Spanish narratives were to remain in manuscript until the nineteenth century.

After 1600 much of the published material on North America, of which there was a good deal, appeared as small pamphlets which made little or no impact outside England. Such were those which revealed the coast later known as New England, John Brereton's *A brief and true relation of the discoverie of the north part of Virginia* (London, 1602) and James Rosier's *A true relation of the most prosperous voyage*

43. The English version, *Nova Francia* (London, 1609), was edited by H. P. Biggar (London, 1928).

44. Reprinted by Atanásio Lopez, *Relación histórica de la Florida,* 2 vols. (Madrid, 1931–33), and translated by Maynard Geiger as *Relation of the Martyrs of Florida* (1936).

. . . by Captaine George Waymouth (London, 1605). Once Jamestown had been founded in 1607, the Virginia Company and its agents kept up a thin stream of publications. Some of them were sermons which contained much exhortation but little information. John Smith's *A true relation of such occurrences and accidents of noate as hath hapned in Virginia* (London, 1608), Robert Gray's *A good speed to Virginia* (London, 1609), and Robert Johnson's *Nova Britannia* (London, 1609), provide some narrative and analytical materials. More substantial were the Company's pamphlets in 1610, *A true and summarie declaration of the purpose and end of the plantation begun in Virginia* (London, 1610) and *A true declaration of the estate of the colonie in Virginia* (London, 1610), which because of the similarities in their titles are often confused. These were followed by *The relation of the right honourable the Lord De-La-Warre . . . of the colonie planted in Virginia* (London, 1611), and Robert Johnson, *The new life of Virginia* (London, 1611). John Smith's *Map of Virginia* (Oxford, 1612) set a new, higher standard both in description and narrative.[45] Moreover, Smith's map of the Chesapeake Bay area contained much new significant detail and it, too, like those of Le Moyne and White earlier, was soon absorbed into more generalized maps of North America. Much of the additional material which survived on English activities in North America down to 1612 had to await publication until the appearance of Samuel Purchas's *Hakluytus posthumus or Purchas his pilgrimes* in four volumes (London, 1625).[46] A number of printed maps have already been mentioned (e.g., those of Cabot, 1544; Gutiérrez, 1562; and Wright, 1599). Cartography had become a considerable industry in the 1560s and thereafter. Gerard Mercator's world map of 1569 reached an unsurpassed standard of completeness and accuracy, and the representation of North America[47] it contained long remained influential. Abraham Ortelius, who published his *Theatrum orbis terrarum* at Antwerp in 1570, was responsible for another generalized version of North America, which he attempted to revise in subsequent editions of his atlas. Mercator's separate map of North America (1584) was also significant. Drake's

45. A modern edition is available in Philip L. Barbour, *The Jamestown Voyages Under the First Charter*, 2 vols. (1969), II, 327–464.

46. Listed by Colin L. Steele, in Quinn, *Hakluyt Handbook*, I, 74–96.

47. Facsimile, ed. B. Van't Hoff. (Amsterdam, 1965); Northeastern North America, in Skelton, Cumming and Quinn, *Discovery of North America*, fig. 98 (p. 93).

voyage of 1577–80 drew attention to western North America—hitherto somewhat neglected. Jodocus Hondius's map entitled *Vera totius expeditionis nauticae descriptio D.Franc. Draci* (London, 1595),[48] was an elaboration of the map already engraved by his son Michael in London (1589) on the medallion known as the "Silver Map."[49] Gerard and Cornelis de Jode, in their *Speculum orbis terrae* (Antwerp, 1593), Cornelis Wytfliet's *Descriptionis Ptolemaicae augmentum* (Louvain, 1597) and Jodocus Hondius's edition of Mercator's *Atlas* (Amsterdam, 1606) all continued to assimilate materials on North America, though Wytfliet was the first to put out a separate atlas on North America.

Two maps which remained in manuscript assimilated much new English and French material. One is the so-called Virginia chart of about 1610,[50] and the other the map known as the Velasco map of 1610–11 (though it is of English origin).[51] Both managed to put together material from unpublished French sources; both attempted to bring up to date earlier synthetic views of the eastern seaboard. The success of the Velasco map in assimilating the results of Hudson's voyage of 1609 as well as those of Champlain of 1604–09 and of various English expeditions, made it almost complete from Cape Fear to Labrador. Unlike the cartographers, the artists of these years have left us little. We have, for example, almost nothing that is original down to 1612 in drawings of Indians seen in Virginia. Such illustrations as there are derive from those of De Bry, embellished with additional clothing or decorations.[52]

Contemporaries had usually to wait for some considerable time before they could see in print, on maps or in pictures, the results of the activities of the earlier discoverers and the subsequent explorers. North America did not, for most of the sixteenth century, have the glamour or the popular appeal that the discoveries of Columbus or Cortés or Pizarro had, and which brought accounts of

48. See F. P. Sprent, *Sir Francis Drake's Voyage Round the World: Two contemporary Maps*, 2nd ed. (London, 1931).

49. Hans P. Kraus, *Sir Francis Drake: A Pictorial Biography* (Amsterdam, 1970), pp. 104–105, 218–221.

50. I. N. Phelps Stokes, *The Iconography of Manhatten Island*, 6 vols. (New York, 1919–28), IV, plate 21A.

51. *Ibid.*, IV, plate 21B.

52. See Christian Feest, "The Virginia Indian in Pictures," *The Smithsonian Journal of History*, II (1967), 1–28.

their exploits readily into print. The first half of the sixteenth century, in relation to what was actually being accomplished in North America, had very little to offer the reader. From the time of Ramusio's publication onwards the publication of materials, though far from systematic, became gradually more frequent, though it remained often a matter of chance whether some particular expedition was or was not given publicity. Ramusio, Hakluyt and Theodor de Bry between them contributed most to the documentation of the period for contemporaries or near-contemporaries. Had Hakluyt completed the third edition of the collection on which he was engaged by 1612, we might have been able to claim that documentation had reached some significant terminus in that year. As it was, though Purchas published later much of what Hakluyt had collected, he lacked his wide European contacts and range of vision. The *Pilgrimes* of 1625 gave a good deal less than Hakluyt would have provided.

Yet, as we survey the additions which modern scholarship has made to the documentation of European activity in North America in this period, we must admit that the outline had been well enough drawn and sufficient detail filled in for students of the early seventeenth century to gain a reasonably full and accurate picture of how the process of discovery and exploration had progressed, and also to grasp roughly what still remained to be discovered. The great advances by both English and French in their knowledge of North America in the years which followed 1612 had been well prepared for.

# CHAPTER 23

# *A Conclusion*

---

IF we look over the broader perspectives of European contacts with America, we can see emerging certain broad divisions. The medieval period—in spite of the light, flickering still but at least visible, that we have of the Norse presence—is so far a blank, filled, if at all, with untenable speculation and vague inferences. Once we move into the period of discovery, the start of which may possibly be placed as far back as about 1480, we gradually leave speculation for the realms of positive knowledge, slight though it may continue to be for some appreciable time. Slowly an outline of land emerges across the North Atlantic, which at first appears to be Asia but by degrees takes on an independent character of its own. Between 1507, when the concept and the name of America first appear, and about 1520, the continent takes some shape, even though no one yet knew how far it extended in any direction, or whether it was a single landmass or was divided into two or more major insular masses. By about 1526 we can say definitely that it can be fairly sharply distinguished, at least by Portuguese, French and English explorers, from the rest of the Americas—though the Spaniards might well insist, and go on insisting, on the indivisibility of the Americas as a whole. Discovery gradually shades into exploration of the parts which make up the whole.

Between 1520 and 1550, or thereabouts, most of the important physical elements making up the North American landmass had been identified and it became possible to put together credible

maps of the continent as a whole. Verrazzano, Gomes and Rut had explored the east coast; Cartier and Soto had penetrated far into its interior from the east; Coronado had made a comparable penetration from the west, while Cabrilho had shown at least the major trends of the western coast. There was continuing debate on precisely how these discoveries interrelated with each other, and the maps reveal continuing conflict and alternative solutions. Some major continuing mistakes—the perpetuation of the idea of the Verrazzanian sea, for example—appear in numerous quite late cartographical representations of North America. The problem of defining and formulating acceptable hypotheses about the northern limits of continental America was to defy solution not only before but long after 1612. Yet we can say that by about 1560 the preliminary phase of understanding the major characteristics of North America had been passed, though perhaps it is easier for us, with our command of many materials that were not uncovered until much later, to appreciate this than it was for contemporaries.

The third phase, from about 1560, represents continuing exploration. This was largely concerned with filling in the details on selected areas, mainly on the eastern coastal belt, but also, most significantly, with attempts to exploit North America by European settlement. Such attempts might be represented by garrisons or missions, communities on American soil or merely small-scale shore bases for fur trading or fishing. Spain, France and England were all involved in them. The Luna expeditions centering on 1559 may be taken as the first of their type—a colonial settlement venture on the part of the Spanish state. The three major French expeditions of the years 1562 to 1565 would have created a zone of French occupation on the southeast coast between the St. Johns River and Port Royal Sound, but instead, in reaction, they led to permanent Spanish occupation of approximately the same coastal strip (with occasional extensions to north and south) and so produced the first enduring European colony in North America.

The Spanish settlement demonstrated many of the problems later European colonies would have to face: the great difficulty of getting a civilian European community to put down firm roots in North America; the limitations, expense and recurrent risks (through Indian risings) of a military occupation; the gamble which a mission program represented when it might flourish for one or two years

and then be almost totally liquidated. The end result was to establish a garrison, assured of permanence only because a watch had to be kept (or Spain felt it had to be kept) on the English presence further to the north, although a screen of mission stations was just beginning, by 1612, to offer the prospect of some wider territorial domination.

The English attempts at settlement on Roanoke Island from 1585 represented, first, an important scientific experiment to work out what kind of settlement it might be possible to insert into a particular ecological setting; and second, the testing of certain conclusions formed in 1586 by the despatch the following year of a balanced group of families who could perhaps adapt to the conditions they would expect to find on the southern shores of Chesapeake Bay. The experiment of 1587 was wholly inconclusive, since it did not prove possible to reinforce and supply the colony; it disappeared, though the survey work of 1585–86 had some enduring influence. The French again began thinking of colonies from about 1580 onward, but no major experiments are known to have been made by them until after 1597. Those that were made in the period 1598 to 1607 (Sable Island, Tadoussac, Ste Croix and Port Royal) were inconclusive. English projects for commercial settlements in the northeast (Magdalen Islands, Elizabeth Islands, Georges River) also came to nothing before 1607. The crucial period began in 1607 with the creation of both Jamestown and Sagadahoc (the second of them failing to endure), under the auspices of the first large-scale colonizing company, the Virginia Company. This was closely followed by the permanent French trading post on the St. Lawrence, Quebec, in 1608. And these, in turn, led the Spaniards to reinforce and stabilize their base in Florida from which, a few years before, they were thinking of withdrawing.

Thus each of the three nations was left between 1608 and 1612 with at least one center of occupation on the east coast and were busy working out their own longer-term settlement plans. The English gave up their first New England settlement but created another colony at Cupids in Newfoundland. The French kept Port Royal alive after an interval but concentrated on Quebec as a fur-trading post. All were small, and their social and economic impact very limited. Only Virginia—with repeated injections of capital and of colonists to replace the heavy losses in manpower and to expand the

settlement's potential—was obtaining the degree of support from Europe which was to give it, after 1616, the capacity for substantial expansion, even if this was by no means certain in 1612. The Spaniards also had moved back into the area first explored by Coronado. When Oñate took over the Pueblo area in 1598–9, his ambitions were only bounded by the two oceans. Though his grandiose schemes went for nothing, the founding of Santa Fé in 1610 meant that a Spanish military and ecclesiastical presence was established in a salient well to the north of Mexico in the southwest, even if the coastal explorations of Viscaino produced no attempt to occupy Alta California. The total range of European experience of North America by 1612 was thus still very limited but by no means negligible.

Neither the application of theory or the practice of exploration had solved the problem of the north. But there was a prevailing determination among Europeans to believe that, whether to the west, to the northwest, to the north, or to the northeast, there was some direct access by sea from Europe to Asia. The gradual uncovering of the eastern shores of North America put an end to the easy optimism of Behaim's globe of 1492, but not to the belief in some direct passage to the Far East. World maps and globes and the growth of discussion in northern Europe, stimulated by the works of Gemma Frisius, Sebastian Münster and others, perpetuated into the second half of the century the idea of possible openings in the polar zones that were ice-free. Circular currents round the seas of the north were thought to keep them free of ice, as Humphrey Gilbert argued in the 1560s in England. The failure of all attempts to find a western passage in latitudes south of 50° between 1524 and 1543 enabled these northerly speculations to grow and take new directions. Robert Thorne's theory of the open Polar Sea put forward in 1527 was still believed by some until the 1580s or even later. And the series of world maps put out by Gerard Mercator—especially the world maps of 1538 and 1569—gave the idea of an open passage wide and lasting currency.

The Open North had also a basis in experiment. Sebastian Cabot and some of the Portuguese voyagers of his time had tried it out, and Cabot, at least, believed in a northerly passage from 1509 until his death nearly fifty years later. In the early 1550s he was toying with voyages to the northwest, north and northeast, and it was by

chance almost that the northeast was chosen and the route to Russia (if not to Cathay) opened up for the English in 1553. At the same time, the Open North was primarily a theory until the 1570s. Under the influence of men like John Dee, Humphrey Gilbert and Michael Lok, it became a matter of practical experiment during the decade 1576–86, when first Martin Frobisher and then John Davis sailed far into northern waters. They found enough indication of channels to the northwest and north to lead to further voyages from 1602 to 1611 which brought the knowledge, at last, that appreciable progress by water could be made to the northwest. In 1612 the hope that Henry Hudson had at last discovered the Northwest Passage was high. It did not take long thereafter to learn that, like the passage to Russia of 1553, this was only the first step on a long and painful process of investigation, the end of which would not in fact be in sight for more than another two centuries.

Historians have been accustomed to think of the events and problems presented in this volume in two distinct ways, or rather, from two distinct angles, the American and the European. For Americans, they were the first steps in a transforming experience which was in the end to be total, and which brought to an end the process of human adaptation to and compromise with the natural environment which had been under way for at least 20,000 years. In its place a new European—if a transformed European—character was to be given to the whole range of human life on the continent. From such a standpoint, for Americans, the period is the start of a long, continuing and not-yet-ended process. For the original inhabitants it was precisely the opposite, the beginning of a relatively short period when their old relationships with, and domination of, the environment were challenged, first in one area and then in another, and finally completely, with the Eskimo coming to experience the final European impact latest of all.

But there is another perspective: that of Europe. From the aspect of the Europeans, North America during the period with which we have been concerned was only one, relatively unimportant area of those which had been opened up by the great discoveries and explorations at the end of the fifteenth century. Its attractions lay mainly in the fact that it was not very firmly hedged around by papal bulls, by treaties, or by armed Iberian ships and fortresses. It was a free field open to enterprise. Yet it was, and remained to the end

of the period, a risky field for investment. Cod and whale—and marginally beaver—were alone providing appreciable profits for European enterprise as the seventeenth century entered its second decade. All attempts to colonize North America so far had involved appreciable losses of effort, money and people. At the same time, it offered a continuing challenge to determinedly speculating individuals, companies and government officials. By 1612, Spain, England and France had each two tender-plant settlements in North America. In 1612 no one in Europe—and none of the inhabitants of those tiny settlements—could tell whether they would fade away, fail spectacularly, survive or grow.

The two viewpoints, American and European, now need to be brought into closer relationship than hitherto, and to be looked at clearly in dual harness, probed and analyzed. A general introduction such as this book has aimed to provide can only hope to lay some reasonably solid foundations on which such a synthesis may be created.

# Bibliographical Essay

THE degree of selectivity in any bibliography that deals with such an extended branch of the European reconnaissance overseas must necessarily be high. I have had to use a certain arbitrary standard of academic respectability and relevance in setting the criteria for the titles chosen; where there were a number of good books and papers on the same subject, some have had, for reasons of space, to be eliminated. In the case of biographies, a somewhat lower standard has been applied, as they can often form useful elementary introductions to an unfamiliar field. Again, I have tried to keep a reasonable balance between materials in English and those in other western European languages, though some preference has been given, when weighing one item against another, to matter in the English language. Only major libraries will contain all the items included; those in English should be in most reasonably good collections. No attempt has been made to emulate the detail of John E. Pomfret and Floyd M. Shumway, *Founding the American Colonies, 1583–1660* (1970), the succeeding volume in the series, for the wealth of reference material it includes for the period, 1583–1612, where there is an overlap with this volume. The bibliographies in other volumes in the series—Charles Gibson, *Spain in America* (1966), W. J. Eccles, *France in America* (1972), Wallace Notestein, *The English People on the Eve of Colonization* (1954), and Wilcomb E. Washburn, *The Indian in America* (1975) —are also relevant.

The most extensive bibliographical listing is *Harvard Guide to American History.* The version edited by Oscar Handlin (and others) in 1954 is still of use, but it has been largely superseded by that edited by Frank Freidel and Richard K. Showman (Cambridge, Mass., 1974), whose listings go

down to June 1970. John Roach (ed.), *A Bibliography of Modern History* (Cambridge, Eng., 1968), is useful for the broader context. Conyers Read, *Bibliography of British History, Tudor Period*, 2nd edition (Oxford, 1959), and Godfrey Davies and Mary Frear Keeler, *Bibliography of British History, Stuart Period*, 2nd edition (Oxford, 1972), cover much of the published materials on England. A comparable coverage of continental materials (with a much wider range than North America) is given in Pierre Chaunu, *Conquête et exploitation des nouveaux mondes* (Paris, 1969). On Spain in America, a supplementary bibliography down to 1960 was added by Benjamin Keen to the reissue of Edward G. Bourne, *Spain in America, 1450–1580* (New York, 1962); while Robin A. Humphreys, *Latin American History: A Guide to the Literature in English* (London, 1958), and Benito Sanchez Alonso, *Fuentes de la historia española e hispanoamericana*, 3rd edition, 3 vols. (Madrid, 1952), may be found useful. H. R. Wagner, *The Spanish Southwest 1542–1794*, 2 vols (Albuquerque, N.M., 1937) remains valuable. C. A. Julien, *Voyages de découverte et les premiers établissements* (Paris, 1948), has a very helpful list on France. For contemporary published material, there are full listings for France in Geoffroy Atkinson, *La littérature géographique française de la Renaissance* (Paris, 1927) and *Supplément* (1936); and in English, with a valuable introduction, in John Parker, *Books to Build an Empire* (Amsterdam, 1965). For materials in Spanish and Portuguese, it is probably still advisable to go to Joseph Sabin (and others), *Bibliotheca Americana, A Dictionary of Books Relating to America*, 29 vols. (New York, 1868–1936).

For annual listings likely to be of value, see *Bibliographie Internationale de la Renaissance* (Geneva, 1965– ); *Bibliographie Géographique Internationale* (Paris, 1947– ); *Writings on American History* (Washington, D.C., 1904– ); followed by *Cumulative Register 1962–1973* (1974) and *Annual Register 1973–1974* (Millwood, N.Y., 1975– ); *International Bibliography of the Historical Sciences* (Washington-Zurich-Paris, 1930– ); *Indice Histórico Español* (Barcelona, 1953– ); and *Bibliographie Annuelle de l'Histoire de France* (Paris, 1956– ).

Manuscript sources for North America as a whole in this period are so far not covered systematically. Library of Congress, *National Union Catalog of Manuscript Collections in the United States* (Washington, D.C., 1961– ), Seymour de Ricci and W. J. Wilson, *Census of Medieval and Renaissance Manuscripts in the United States*, 2 vols. (New York, 1937), and the *Supplement*, by C. V. Fage and W. H. Bond (1962), with Philip M. Hamer, *Guide to Archives and Manuscripts in the United States* (New Haven, 1961), cover this broad area thoroughly. Bernard R. Crick and Miriam Alman, *Manuscripts Relating to America in Great Britain* (London, 1961), is useful but requires updating; the same is less true of Henry P. Beers, *The French in North America: Bibliographical Guide to French Archives, Reproductions and Research Missions* (Baton Rouge, La., 1957), as its scope is wider. Dirección General de Archivos y Bibliotecas,

*Guía de fuentes para la historia de Ibero-América Conservadas en España,* 2 vols. (Madrid, 1966–69), is essential for all research on Spanish activities in North America. The older listings of American material, W. R. Shepherd, *Guide to the Materials for the History of the United States in Spanish Archives* (Washington, D.C., 1907); Charles E. Chapman, *Catalogue of Materials in the Archivo de Indias for the History of the Pacific Coast and the American Southwest* (Washington, D.C., 1919); and James A. Robertson, *List of Documents in the Spanish Archives Relating to the United States* (Washington, D.C., 1910), can still prove of some value.

*Periodicals:* For this field the range is very wide and could include almost all the main historical, geographical and maritime journals of western Europe and North America. *Imago Mundi* (London) is especially valuable for cartography; *Terrae Incognitae* (Amsterdam) for discovery; *Mariner's Mirror* (London) and *American Neptune* (Salem, Mass.) for voyages; *William and Mary Quarterly* (Williamsburg, Va.) for colonization; *Hispanic American Historical Review* (Durham, N.C.) and *Revista de Indias* (Seville) for Spanish concern with North America; *Revue d'Histoire de l'Amérique française* (Montreal) and *Canadian Historical Review* for Canada. The Hakluyt Society publishes several volumes of texts each year, a reasonably high proportion being on American discovery and exploration; The Society for the History of Discoveries (in association with the Newberry Library, Chicago) publishes monographs and texts on exploration. The Champlain Society (Toronto) is the leading publishing society in this field in Canada.

## General

Only a few indications of the general context inside which the earliest European contacts with North America take place can be given here. John H. Parry, *The Age of Reconnaissance* (London, 1963); Pierre Chaunu, *L'expansion européenne du XIII<sup>e</sup> au XV<sup>e</sup> siècles* (Paris, 1960), and *Conquête et exploitation des Nouveaux Mondes* (Paris, 1969); Charles Verlinden, *Les origines de la civilisation Atlantique* (Neuchâtel, 1966); Boies Penrose, *Travel and Discovery in the Renaissance* (Cambridge, Mass., 1955); *New Cambridge Modern History,* vols. I–III (1957–68); Ralph Davis, *The Rise of the Atlantic Economies* (London, 1973); Gerald S. Graham, *Empire in the North Atlantic* (Toronto, 1950); Carlo M. Cipolla, *Guns and Sails in the Early Period of European Expansion, 1400–1700* (London, 1963); and Michel Mollat and Paul Adam (eds.), *Les aspects internationaux de la découverte océanique* (Paris, 1966) are probably the most helpful starting points.

General works on North America of some interest are Herbert E. Bolton, and Thomas M. Marshall, *Colonization of North America, 1492–1783* (New

York, 1920); and Herbert I. Priestley, *The Coming of the White Man* (New York, 1938). J. B. Brebner, *The Explorers of North America* (London, 1933; new ed., New York, 1956), is valuable as an outline; so is W. P. Cumming, R. A. Skelton and D. B. Quinn, *The Discovery of North America* (London, 1971). Carl O. Sauer, *Sixteenth Century North America* (Berkeley, 1971), and S. E. Morison, *The European Discovery of America*, I, *The Northern Voyages*, II, *The Southern Voyages* (New York, 1971–74), are essential general reading. D. B. Quinn, (ed.), *North American Discovery, circa 1000–1612* (New York and Columbia, S.C., 1971), provides a selection of documents for the whole period.

The context of international law and relations can be traced in Demetrios Ramos (ed.), *El tratado de Tordesillas*, 2 vols. (Valladolid, 1973); Adolf Rein, *Der Kampf westeuropas um Nordamerika im 15. und 16. Jahrhundert* (Stuttgart, 1925), Henry Folmer, *Franco-Spanish Rivalry in North America, 1524–1763* (Glendale, Calif., 1952), and Charles de la Roncière, *Histoire de marine française*, 6 vols. (Paris, 1909–32), III and IV (3rd ed., 1923).

On France, the best survey is Charles-André Julien, *Les voyages de découverte et les premiers établissements* (Paris, 1948); on England, Walter Oakeshott, *Founded Upon the Seas* (Cambridge, Eng., 1946), James A. Williamson, *Age of Drake* (London, 1933), and Alfred L. Rowse, *The Expansion of Elizabethan England* (London, 1951), are of some use. For Spain, Herbert E. Bolton, *The Spanish Borderlands* (New Haven, 1921 and John F. Bannon, *The Spanish Borderland Frontier* (N.Y., 1970) are outline introductions, W. J. Eccles, *The Canadian Frontier, 1534–1760* (New York, 1969), is helpful.

The cultural context is well covered in Fredi Chiapelli (ed.), *First Images of America. The Impact of the New World on the Old*, 2 vols. (Los Angeles, 1976). For France it is sketched in Julien, *Voyages de découverte . . . ,* and covered in some detail in Gilbert Chinard, *L'exotisme americain dans la littérature française au XVIᵉ siécle* (Paris, 1911), and Geoffroy Atkinson, *Les nouveaux horizons de la Renaissance française au XVIᵉ siècle* (Paris, 1935). Manuel Ballesteros-Gaibrois (and others), *La découverte de l'Amérique* (Paris, 1968), has some useful contributions. For England, Gustav H. Blanke, *Amerika in Englischen Schrifttum des 16. und 17. Jahrhunderts* (Bochum-Langendreer, 1962), is the most general treatment: Robert B. Cawley, *The Voyagers and Elizabethan Drama* (Boston, 1938), and *Unpathed Waters* (Princeton, N.J., 1940), provide more specialized views. Rosario Romeo, *Le scoperte Americane nella cosienza Italiana del Cinquecento* (Milan, 1954), offers comparable material on Italy.

The use of maps is essential for the study of this subject and period. A start may be made with Carlo Sanz Lopez, *Mapas antiquos del mundo* (Madrid, 1962); Adolf Erik Nordenskiold, *Facsimile Atlas* (Stockholm, 1889; New York, 1973); Emerson D. Fite and Archibald Freeman, *A Book of Old Maps Delineating American History* (Cambridge, Mass., 1926; new ed., New York,

1969); and Egon Klemp (ed.), *America in Maps from 1500 to 1856* (New York, 1976). W. P. Cumming, R. A. Skelton, and D. B. Quinn, *The Discovery of America* (London, 1971), has the best single-volume selection. William P. Cumming, *The Southeast in Early Maps* (Princeton, N.J., 1954; 2nd ed. Chapel Hill, N.C., 1962); Henry R. Wagner, *The Cartography of the Northwest Coast of America*, 2 vols. (Berkeley, 1937), and Marcel Trudel, *Atlas historique du Canada française* (Quebec, 1961), provide broadly based selections of contemporary maps. *The United States National Atlas* (Washington, D.C., 1970) contains the best map (no. 134) of the early explorations. More specialized publications are Armando Cortesão and A. Teixera da Mota, *Portugaliae monumenta cartographica*, 6 vols. (Lisbon, 1960–62); Edward L. Stevenson, *Atlas of Portolan Charts* (New York, 1911); Ministerio de Fomento, *Cartas de Indias* (Madrid, 1877); Duque de Alba, *Mapas de América* (Madrid, 1955); T. Gasparrini-Leporace (ed.), *Il mappomondo di Fra Mauro* (Venice, 1956); Juan de la Cosa, *Carta geográfica*, with *Ensayo biográfica* by Antonio Vascáno (Madrid, 1892); Josef Fischer and Franz von Weiser, *Die älteste Karte mit Namen Amerika aus dem Jahre 1507* (Innsbruck, 1907; Amsterdam, 1968); B. Van'T Hoff (ed.), *Gerard Mercator's Map of the World (1569)* (Rotterdam, 1961).

Introductions to cartography include G. R. Crone, *Maps and Their Makers* (London, 1953), L. Bagrow and R. A. Skelton, *A History of Cartography* (London, 1964) and Carlos Sanz Lopez, *La géographia de Ptolemeo ampliado* (Madrid, 1959). More specialized books include William F. Ganong, *Crucial Maps in the Early Cartography and Place-name Nomenclature of the Atlantic Coast of Canada* (Toronto, 1968); Theodore Layng, *Sixteenth Century Maps of Canada* (Ottawa, 1959); Henry Harrisse, *Découverte et évolution cartographique de Terre-Neuve* (Paris, 1900); R. A. Skelton, *Explorers' Maps* (London, 1958); and Armando Cortesão, *History of Portuguese Cartography* (Lisbon, 1969–71).

Navigation can be studied from David W. Waters, *The Rutters of the Sea* (New Haven, 1967), and *The Art of Navigation in Elizabethan and Early Stuart England* (London, 1958); Eva G. R. Taylor, *The Haven-finding Art* (London, 1956), is also valuable.

## Aboriginal Peoples and European Contacts

The most up-to-date bibliography is in Wilcomb E. Washburn, *The Indian in America* (1975). The general reference book on tribal locations is John R. Swanton, *The Indian Tribes of North America*, Smithsonian Institution, Bureau of American Ethnology, Bulletin no. 145, 1952. Gordon R. Willey, *An Introduction to American Archaeology*, I, *North and Middle America* (Englewood Cliffs, N.J., 1966), is the most useful introduction to the material culture, and Harold E. Driver, *Indians of North America*, 2nd edition (Chicago, 1969), to cultural analysis; while Washburn, *The Indian in America*

(1975), is the fullest consideration of the Indian in his historical setting. Francis Jennings, *The Invasion of America* (Chapel Hill, N.C. 1975), is a highly critical account of the methods of white penetration.

On the western Indians, A. L. Kroeber, *Handbook of the Indians of California*, Smithsonian Institution, Bureau of American Ethnology, Bulletin no. 78, 1925; Robert F. Heizer and M. A. Whipple, *The California Indians*, 2nd edition (Berkeley and Los Angeles, 1971); and Robert F. Heizer, *Elizabethan California* (San Francisco, 1974), cover adequately the coastal Indians with whom the Spaniards were in contact. On the Pueblo Indians and their neighbors, Oakah L. Jones, Jr., *Pueblo Warriors and Spanish Conquest* (Norman, Okla., 1966), Jack D. Forbes, *Apache, Navajo and Spaniard* (Norman, Okla., 1960), Edward H. Spicer, *Cycles of Conquest* (Tucson, Ariz., 1962), and Elizabeth A. H. John, *Storms Brewed in Other Men's Worlds* (College Station, Texas, 1975) are all of value.

On the Indians of the southeast from the Mississippi to Florida and Virginia, John R. Swanton, *The Indians of the Southeastern United States* Smithsonian Institution, Bureau of American Ethnology, Bulletin no. 137, 1946, is the fullest compendium of information. William C. Sturtevant, *The Significance of Ethnological Similarities Between Southeastern North America and the Antilles*, Yale University Publications in Anthropology, 54 (New Haven, 1960), and "Spanish-Indian Relations in Southeastern North America," *Ethnohistory*, IX (1962); with J. T. Milanich and W. C. Sturtevant (eds.), *Francisco Pareja's 1613 Confessionario: A Documentary Source for Timacuan Ethnography* (Tallahassee, Fla., 1972), are valuable. John W. Griffin (ed.), *The Florida Indian and His Neighbors* (Winter Park, Fla., 1949); Gordon R. Willey, *Archeology of the Florida Gulf Coast*, Smithsonian Institution, Miscellaneous Collections 113 (Washington, D.C., 1949); John M. Goggin, *Space and Time Perspective in North St. Johns Archeology*, Yale University Publications in Anthropology, 47 (New Haven, 1953), and his *Indian and Spanish Selected Writings* (Coral Gables, Fla., 1964) cover Florida and adjacent areas.

For Algonkian Indians from North Carolina northward, Regina Flannery, *An Analysis of Coastal Algonquian Culture*, Catholic University Anthropology Series 7 (Washington, D.C., 1939), is useful to the historian. Maurice A. Mook, "Algonkian Ethno-history of the Carolina Sound," *Journal of the Washington Academy of Sciences*, XXXIV (1941), 182–197, 213–228; and William G. Haag, *The Archeology of Coastal North Carolina*, Coastal Studies Institute, Technical Report no. 8, part B (Baton Rouge, La., 1956), offer some help on North Carolina Indians of the Roanoke Island area. Roy G. Pearce, Ben C. McCary and Norman Barka, *Bibliography of the Virginia Indians*, Archaeological Society of Virginia, Special Publication no. 1 (Richmond, Va., 1969), is a comprehensive guide. Maurice A. Mook, "The Anthropological Position of the Indian Tribes of Tidewater Virginia," *William and Mary*

*Quarterly*, 2nd series, XXII (1943), 27–40; Christian F. Feest, "Powhatan: A Study in Political Organization," *Sonderdruck aus Wiener völkerkundliche Mitteilüngen*, XIII, Band VIII (1966), 69–83, and "Seventeenth Century Virginia Algonquian Population Estimates," *Quarterly Bulletin of the Archaeological Society of Virginia*, XXVII (1973), 66–79, deal with significant aspects of Virginia Indian society. Bernard G. Hoffman, "Ancient Tribes Revisited: A Summary of Indian Distribution and Movement in the Northeastern United States from 1534 to 1799," *Ethnohistory*, XIV (1967), 1–45; Charles C. Willoughby, *Antiquities of the New England Indians* (Cambridge, Mass., 1935); Gordon M. Day, "English-Indian Contacts in New England," *Ethnohistory*, IX (1962), 24–40; and Alfred G. Bailey, *The Conflict of European and Eastern Algonkian Cultures, 1504–1700*, 2nd edition (Toronto, 1969), throw some light on the northeast. Frank G. Speck, *The Iroquois*, Cranbrook Institute of Science, Bulletin 23 (1945); Elizabeth Tooker (ed.), *The Ethnography of the Huron Indians* (Smithsonian Institution, Bureau of American Ethnology, *Bulletin*, no. 190, Washington, D.C., 1964), Charles F. Wray and Harry L. Schoff, "A Preliminary Report on the Seneca Sequence in Western New York, 1550–1687," *Pennsylvania Archaeologist*, XXXIII (1953), 56–63, and, especially, Bruce G. Trigger, *The Hurons: Farmers of the North* (N.Y. 1969) indicate the nature of Iroquois culture.

The St. Lawrence Indians present considerable problems. Bruce G. Trigger, "Archeological and Other Evidence; A Fresh Look at the Laurentian 'Iroquois,' " *American Antiquity*, XXXIII (1968), 429–440, examines the evidence. His "Trade and Tribal Warfare in the St. Lawrence in the Sixteenth Century," *Ethnohistory*, IX (1962), 240–256, and *The Hurons: Farmers of the North* (New York, 1969); and John Witthoft, "Archaeology as a Key to the Colonial Fur Trade," *Minnesota History*, XL (1966), 204–207, illustrate the problems. On the northern peoples, Frederick Johnson (ed.), *Man in Northeastern North America*, Papers of the Robert S. Peabody Foundation for Archaeology 3 (Andover, Mass., 1946); Edward M. Weyer, *The Eskimos* (New Haven, 1932, Hamden, Conn., 1962); and H. G. Bandi, *Eskimo Prehistory* (London, 1969), are useful.

## Norse Voyages to America

Halldór Hermansson, *The Vinland Sagas* (Ithaca, N.Y., 1944), and Gustav Stern, *Islandske Annaler indtill 1578* (Christiana, 1888), provide texts of the original materials. Gwyn Jones, *The Norse Atlantic Saga* (London, 1965), gives both translations and a historical commentary. Magnus Magnusson and Hermann Pálsson, *The Vinland Sagas* (Harmondsworth, Middx., and Baltimore, 1965), provides another valuable translation. Ari Thorgilsson, "The Book of the Icelanders," edited and translated by H. Herman Her-

mannsson, *Icelandica*, XX (1930), and Adam of Bremen, *History of the Arch-bishops of Bremen*, translated by Francis T. Tschan (New York, 1959), almost complete the translated documentation of the Norse period.

Gwyn Jones, *A History of the Vikings* (London, 1968), is valuable for background; Fridtjof Nansen, *In Northern Mists*, 2 vols. (London, 1911), is still one of the most expansive treatments of the northern scene. Hans-Georg Bandi, *Eskimo Prehistory* (London, 1969); Finn Gad, *A History of Greenland*, I, *To 1700* (London, 1970); and Knud J. Krogh, *Viking Greenland* (Copenhagen, 1967), provide additional background on Greenland. Einar Haugen, *Voyages to Greenland* (New York, 1942), and Magnus Thordarsson, *The Vinland Voyages* (New York, 1930), are still helpful, as is Helge Ingstad, *Land Under the Pole Star* (London, 1966).

On the archeological discoveries, Helge Ingstad, *Westward to Vinland* (London, 1969), and Anne Stine Ingstad, "The Norse Settlement at L'Anse aux Meadows: A Preliminary Report from the Excavations, 1961–1968," *Acta Archaeologica*, XLI (Copenhagen, 1970), 109–154, are significant.

The real or alleged later developments have filled many volumes. Erik Wahlgren, *The Kensington Stone* (Madison, Wis., 1958), disposed of one of them; Raleigh A. Skelton, Thomas E. Marston and George Painter, *The Vinland Map and the Tartar Relation* (New Haven, 1965), brought a voluminous literature into existence, including Wilcomb E. Washburn, *Proceedings of the Vinland Map Conference* (Edison, 1971). The evidence for the map's authenticity has now been undermined, as Helen Wallis (and others), "The Strange Case of the Vinland Map," *Geographical Journal*, CXL (1974), 183–214, show. Tryggvi J. Oleson, *Early Voyages and Northern Approaches, 1000–1632* (Toronto, 1963), tries to show that Norse settlers, assimilated with Eskimo, spread across northern North America.

## The Prediscovery Period to 1492

The period is somewhat amorphous and so is much of the literature. The most useful outline, with the best bibliography, is Pierre Chaunu, *L'expansion Européenne du XIIIe au XVe siècle* (Paris, 1969). The older work by C. Raymond Beazley, *The Dawn of Modern Geography*, 3 vols (Oxford, 1904–06), goes to 1420 and is still valuable. W. H. Babcock, *Legendary Islands in the Atlantic* (New York, 1928), and Richard Hennig, *Terrae Incognitae*, 2nd edition, 4 vols. (Leiden, 1944–56), contain much information, sometimes uncritically adopted; T. J. Westropp, "Brasil and the Legendary Islands of the North Atlantic," *Proceedings of the Royal Irish Academy*, XXX (1912), sect. C, no. 8, is authoritative on Irish legends and the appearance of the name on the map. Charles Verlinden, *The Beginnings of Modern Colonization* (Ithaca, N.Y., 1970), deals with the westward migration of colonial techniques,

mainly in the fifteenth century. The more influential texts in Atlantic history in this period were Claudius Ptolemy, *The Geography*, translated by E. L. Stevenson (New York, 1932), and Carlos Sanz, *La géographia de Ptolemeo ampliado* (Madrid, 1959); *Navigatio Sancti Brandani*, edited by Carl Selmer (Notre Dame, Ind., 1959); Pierre d'Ailly, *Ymago Mundi*, edited and translated by Edmond Buron, 3 vols. (Paris, 1930); and Marco Polo, *Travels*, edited by Sir Henry Yule and Henri Cordier, 3rd edition, 3 vols. (London, 1903–20). Fridtjof Nansen, *In Northern Mists*, 2 vols. (London, 1911), reflects both knowledge and good judgment. Carl O. Sauer, *Northern Mists* (Berkeley, 1968), moves backward and forward on the same territory. Alfred P. Newton (ed.), *The Great Age of Discovery* (London, 1932), is still useful as an introduction.

Most of the works of the period cover the activities of a single country. Florentino Perez Embid, *Los descubrimientos en el Atlantico hasta el Tradado de Tordesillas* (Seville, 1948), is useful on the Spanish involvement. J. Ramos-Coelho (ed.), *Alguns documentos da Torre do Tombo* (Lisbon, 1891), contains the early Portuguese charters. Armando Cortesão, *The Nautical Chart of 1424* (Coimbra, 1954), links the earliest Portuguese voyages with an important chart. Samuel E. Morison, *Portuguese Voyages to America in the Fifteenth Century* (Cambridge, Mass., 1940), reflects his view, reiterated in *The European Discovery of America*, 2 vols. (New York, 1971–74), that the Portuguese did not reach America in the fifteenth century. Sofus Larsen, *The Discovery of America Twenty Years Before Columbus* (Copenhagen, 1925), proposes a Portuguese-Danish discovery in 1472. Damião Peres, *História dos descobrimentos Portugueses*, 2nd edition (Coimbra, 1960), Jaime Cortesão, *Os descobrimentos portugueses*, 2 vols. (Lisbon, 1959–60), Duarte Leite, *História dos descobrimentos*, 2 vols. (Lisbon, 1959–60) and Eduardo Brazão, *A descoberta da Terra Nova* (Lisbon, 1964), all favor early Portuguese crossings.

The case for an English discovery prior to Columbus is made in Louis-André Vigneras, "New Light on the 1497 Cabot Voyage to America," *Hispanic American Historical Review*, XXXVI (1956), 503–509, "The Cape Breton Landfall," *Canadian Historical Review*, XXXVIII (1957), 219–228, "État present des études sur Jean Cabot," Congresso Internacional de História dos Descobrimentos, *Actas*, III (Lisbon, 1961), 655–688. It is adopted by D. B. Quinn, *England and the Discovery of America, 1481–1620* (New York, 1974), and, in a very different form, by Alwyn A. Ruddock, "John Day of Bristol and the English Voyages Across the Atlantic Before 1497," *Geographical Journal*, CXXXII (1966), 225–233, and rejected by S. E. Morison, *European Discovery of America*, I. Marianne Mahn-Lot, *La découverte de l'Amérique* (Paris, 1970) (see her "Colomb, Bristol et l'Atlantique Nord," *Annales*, XIX [1964], 522–530); Francisco Morales Padron, "Los descubrimientos en los siglos XIV y XV y los archipielagos Atlanticos," *Anuario*

*de Estudios Atlanticos,* XVII (Seville, 1971), 429–465, and Demetrios Ramos, "Los contactos trasatlanticos decisivos como precedentes del viaje de Colón," *Cuadernos colombinos,* 2 (Valladolid, 1972), are general reviews of the situation at the opening of the 1570s. Wilcomb E. Washburn, "The Meaning of 'Discovery' in the Fifteenth and Sixteenth Centuries," *American Historical Review,* LXVIII (1962), 1–21, raises an important question.

R. A. Skelton, Thomas E. Marston and George D. Painter, *The Vinland Map and the Tartar Relation* (New Haven, 1965), produced valuable material on Atlantic navigation in the fifteenth century, even though the map must now be rejected (see Helen Wallis [and others], "The Strange Case of the Vinland Map," *Geographical Journal,* CXL [1974], 183–214). R. A. Skelton, "English Knowledge of the Portuguese Discoveries in the Fifteenth Century," *Congresso Internacional de História dos Descobrimentos, Actas,* II (1961), 365–374; Eleanora M. Carus-Wilson, *Medieval Merchant Venturers* (London, 1954), and *The Overseas Trade of Bristol in the Later Middle Ages* (Bristol, 1937); William Worcestre, *Itineraries,* edited by John H. Harvey (Oxford, 1969); E. G. Ravenstein, *Martin Behaim, His Life and His Globe* (London, 1907), are useful as background.

## Discovery from 1492 to 1543

On Columbus, the most elegant selection of materials is S. E. Morison (ed.), *Journals and Other Documents on the Life and Voyages of Columbus* (New York, 1965). Cecil Jane (ed.), *Select Documents Illustrating the Four Voyages of Columbus,* 2 vols. (London, Hakluyt Society, 1930–33), contains texts as well as translations. Cesare de Lollis, *Scritti di Colombo,* 2 vols (Rome, 1892), contains all the texts. Cecil Jane and L. A. Vigneras (ed. and trans.), *The Journal of Christopher Columbus* (London, 1960), is the best edition in English, Carlos Sanz (ed.), *Diario de Colón* (Madrid, 1962), and J. Ibañez Cerdá (ed.), *Diario de Colón,* 2d edition (Madrid, 1972), the most useful in Spanish. Fernando Colón, *The Life of the Admiral Christopher Columbus,* edited and translated by Benjamin Keen (New Brunswick, N.J., 1959), is the only good English version; Rinaldo Caddeo, *Le Historie della vita e dei fatti di Cristoforo Colombo,* 2 vols. (Milan, 1930), the most useful edition of the original.

S. E. Morison's long string of works, *Admiral of the Ocean Sea; Christopher Columbus,* 2 vols. (Boston, 1942), and the single-volume unannotated edition of the foregoing (Boston, 1942); *Christopher Columbus, Mariner* (Boston, 1956), and S. E. Morison and Mauricio Obregón, *The Caribbean as Columbus Saw It* (Boston, 1964), illustrate varying facets of his career. Antonio Ballesteros Beretta, *Cristobal Colón,* 2 vols. (Madrid, 1945), is important. Charles Verlinden and Florentino Perez-Embid, *Cristobal Colón* (Madrid, 1962), represents a summary of what is now generally acceptable: Armando Ál-

varez Pedroso, *Cristobal Colón* (Madrid, 1944), is useful. Gerald R. Crone, *The Discovery of America* (London, 1969), is a useful short synthesis.

John Cabot's contribution is best documented in James A. Williamson, *The Cabot Voyages and Bristol Discovery under Henry VII* (Cambridge, Eng., Hakluyt Society, 1962), and *Cabot Voyages and English Exploration in the Reigns of Henry VII and Henry VIII* (London, 1929), the latter being now mainly valuable for the period 1508–1536. Alwyn A. Ruddock, "The Reputation of Sebastian Cabot," *Bulletin of the Institute of Historical Research*, XLVII (1974), 95–99, is important.

Papers already noted, L. A. Vigneras, "New Light on the 1497 Cabot Voyage," "The Cape Breton Landfall," "État present des études sur Jean Cabot," and A.A. Ruddock, "John Day of Bristol", are important in this context. Quinn, *England and the Discovery of America*, prints a little new material, and treats English voyages 1497–1505 in detail. S. E. Morison, *European Discovery of America*, I, has a valuable contribution to the argument. Roberto Almagiá, "Sulle Navigazioni di Giovanni Caboto," *Revista Geografica Italiana*, LXVII (1960), 1–12, and *Commemorazione di Sebastiano Caboto* (Venice, 1958), are significant. Melvin H. Jackson, "The Labrador Landfall of John Cabot: The 1497 Voyage Reconsidered," *Canadian Historical Review*, XLIV (1963), 122–141, John T. Juricek, "John Cabot's First Voyage," *Smithsonian Journal of History*, II (1967–8), 1–22, and Lucien Campeau, "Jean Cabot et la découverte de l'Amérique du Nord," *Revue de l'Histoire de L'Amérique Française*, XIX (1965), 398–408, and Arthur Davies, "João Fernandes and the Cabot Voyages," C.I.H.D., *Actas*, II (1961), 135–150, are also of interest. L. A. Vigneras, *The Discovery of South America and the Andalusia Voyages* (Chicago, 1976), is important.

On the early Portuguese voyages, H. P. Biggar (ed.), *The Precursors of Jacques Cartier* (Ottawa, 1911), remains the main source collection. S. E. Morison, *Portuguese Voyages* (1940), remains important. Eduardo Brazão, *A Descoberta da Terra Nova* (Lisbon, 1964), and Lucien Campeau, "Découvertes Portugais en Amérique du Nord," *Revue Historique de l'Amérique Française*, XXL (1967), 171–227, and A. Texeira da Mota, *Portuguese Navigation in the North Atlantic in the Fifteenth and Sixteenth Centuries* (St. John's, 1965), are recent surveys.

The English voyages of 1517–1536 are covered in Biggar, *Precursors*, Williamson, *Cabot Voyages* (1929), Irene A. Wright (ed.), *Spanish Documents Concerning English Voyages to the Caribbean, 1527–1568* (London, Hakluyt Society, 1929) and Laetitia Lyell (ed.), *The Acts of Court of the Mercers' Company, 1453–1527* (Cambridge, Eng., 1936). For discussions, Morison, *European Discovery of America*, I, and Quinn, *England and the Discovery of America*, can be supplemented by Peter J. Piveronus, "John Rastell's Proposed Voyages to North America from Ireland, 1517–1519," *Terrae Incognitae*, III

(1971), 59–65; H. P. Biggar, "An English Expedition to America in 1527," *Mélanges d'histoire offerts a M. Charles Bémont* (Paris, 1913). Bernard H. Hoffman, *Cabot to Cartier* (Toronto, 1959), has a useful review of the materials for both English and Portuguese voyages, and Franklin T. McCann, *English Discovery of America to 1585* (New York, 1951), is a study of the emergence of English interest in America as a whole. Gordon Connell-Smith, *Forerunners of Drake* (London, 1954), throws some light on early Anglo-Spanish relations in the New World.

On the French side, the documentation of the Verrazzano voyage as well as the narrative is now well covered in Lawrence C. Wroth, *The Voyages of Giovanni da Verrazzano* (New Haven, 1970). Charles-André Julien (ed.), *Les Français en Amérique pendant la première moitié du XVI^e siècle* (Paris, 1946), has valuable notes. Biggar, *Precursors;* Henry Harrisse, *Découverte et évolution cartographique de Terre-Neuve* (Paris, 1900), and Bernard G. Hoffman, "Account of a Voyage Conducted in 1529 to the New World," *Ethnohistory*, X, (1963), 1–79, have minor documentation.

The beginnings of French activity are best studied in C. A. Julien, *Les voyages de découverte et les premiers établissements* (Paris, 1948); Marcel Trudel, *Histoire de la Nouvelle-France, I, Les vaines tentatives, 1524–1603* (Montreal, 1963), and, more briefly, *The Beginnings of New France, 1524–1663* (Toronto, 1973), and also Gustave Lanctot, *A History of Canada*, I (Toronto, 1963). J. Habert, "J. de Verazzane: État de la question," M. Ballesteros-Gaibrois (and others), *La découverte de l'Amérique* (Paris, 1968), pp. 51–60, and Instituto e Museo di Storia della Scienza, *Giovanni da Verrazzano* (Florence, 1970), are significant.

The Cartier-Roberval voyages, 1534–43, are best studied in H. P. Biggar (ed.), *The Voyages of Jacques Cartier* (Ottawa, 1924), and *A Collection of Documents Relating to Jacques Cartier and the Sieur de Roberval* (Ottawa, 1930), though the notes to C. A. Julien, *Les Français en Amérique pendant la première moitié de XVI^e siècle*, are also important. Jean Alfonce de Saintonge, *La Cosmographie*, edited by Georges Musset (Paris, 1904), is of some interest. James F. Pendergast and Bruce G. Trigger, *Cartier's Hochelaga and the Dawson Site* (Montreal, 1971), represents an attempt to locate the 1535 site and to re-examine the problem of the Laurentian Iroquois. A good recent biography of Cartier in English is lacking. James P. Baxter, *Jacques Cartier* (New York, 1906), Gustave Lanctot, *Jacques Cartier* (Montreal, 1947), Charles de la Roncière, *Jacques Cartier* (Paris, 1931) and Gaston Martin, *Jacques Cartier* (Paris, 1938), are of some value.

## Spanish Expeditions, 1511–1561

Henry R. Wagner, *The Spanish Southwest, 1542–1794,* 2nd edition, 2 vols. (Albuquerque, N.M., 1937) is invaluable. F. W. Hodge and T. H. Lewis (eds.), *Spanish Explorers in the Southern United States, 1528–1543* (New York, 1907; reprinted 1963), covers Narváez, Cabeza de Vaca, and Hernando de Soto in useful translations. Individual voyages have to be traced through the Spanish texts, or translations of them, the most important of which will be found in Peter Martyr, *Decades of the New World,* edited and translated by F. A. MacNutt, 2 vols. (New York, 1912); Bernal Díaz del Castillo, *The true History of the Conquest of New Spain,* edited and translated by A. P. Maudsley (London, Hakluyt Society, 1908–16); Gonzalo Fernández de Oviedo, *Historia general y natural de las Indias,* 5 vols. (Madrid, 1959), IV; Francisco López de Gómera, *Historia general de las Indias,* 2 vols. (Madrid, 1932); Antonio de Herrera y Tordesillas, *Historia de los hechos de los Castellanos,* 17 vols (Madrid, 1934–57), II; Manuel Fernández de Navarrete, *Obras,* 3 vols. (Madrid, 1964), II. For Antonio Galvão, *Tradado* (Lisbon, 1563), modern edition *Tratado dos descobrimentos,* ed. Visconde de Lagoa (Oporto, [1945] ), we have Richard Hakluyt's early translation, *The Discoveries of the World,* edited by C. R. D. Bethune (London, Hakluyt Society, 1862). Alonzo de Santa Cruz, *Islario general de todos las islas del mundo,* edited by Antonio Blasques (Madrid, 1922), is useful on Gomes. H. P. Biggar, *Precursors of Jacques Cartier* (1911), documents the 1511 initiative. Extracts relating to Ponce de León are translated in J. F. Davis, "History of Juan Ponce de Léon's Voyages to Florida," *Florida Historical Quarterly,* XIV (1935), no. 1. There is no such alternative for Ayllón. The basic text for Álvar Núñez Cabeza de Vaca is his *Relación* (Zamora, 1542), edited, with introduction, by Manuel Serrano y Sanz, 2 vols. (Madrid, 1906), a translation of which is in Hodge and Lewis, *Spanish Explorers. The Journey of Alvar Núñez Cabeza de Vaca,* translated and edited by Fanny and Adolph Bandelier (New York, 1905), has been re-edited as *The Narrative of Alvar Núñez Cabeza de Vaca,* with Oviedo's version of the official report, translated by G. Theisen, and with an introduction by J. F. Bannon (Barre, Mass., 1972); a racy modern version is *Cabeza de Vaca's Adventures in the Unknown Interior of America,* edited and translated by Cyclone Covey (New York, 1961).

The narrative of the Gentleman of Elvas, *Relaçam verdadeira* (Evora, 1557), is basic for Hernando de Soto. There is a translation in Hodge and Lewis, *Spanish Explorers.* The best edition is *True Relation of the Hardships Suffered by Governor Fernando de Soto,* edited by James A. Robertson, 2 vols. (Deland, Fla., 1933). *Narratives of Hernando de Soto,* edited by Edward G. Bourne, 2 vols. (New York, 1904), usefully contains translations of accounts

by Ranjel and Biedma. Additional material is in "Source Records" (translations by James A. Robertson and others), *Florida Historical Quarterly*, XIV (1935), 174–187, 221–223. Richard Hakluyt's translation, *Virginia richly valued* (London, 1609), is in *The Discovery and Conquest of Terra Florida*, ed. Walter B. Rye (London, Hakluyt Society, 1851).

Woodbury Lowery, *The Spanish Settlements Within the Present Limits of the United States, 1513–1561* (New York, 1901), is still the basic narrative. Herbert E. Bolton, *The Spanish Borderlands* (New Haven, 1021), remains a useful introduction, developed in John F. Bannon, *The Spanish Borderlands Frontier, 1513–1821* (N.Y., 1970). Vicente Murga Sans, *Juan Ponce de Léon* (San Juan, P.R., 1959) is the standard biography. For Estavão Gomes, papers by Louis-André Vigneras appear definitive: "El viaje de Esteban Gomez a Norte América," *Revista de Indias*, XVII (1957), 1–19 (and Supplement), "The Voyage of Esteban Gomez from Florida to the Baccalaos," *Terrae Incognitae*, II (1970), 25–27, "The Cartographer Diogo Ribero," *Imago Mundi*, XVI (1962), 76–83. Paul Quattlebaum, *The Land Called Chicora* (Gainesville, Fla., 1956), is useful, though somewhat amateurish, on Ayllón. Cleve Hallenback, *Journey and Route of Cabeza de Vaca* (Glendale, Calif., 1940), and Carl O. Sauer, *The Road to Cíbola* (Berkeley, 1932), are careful studies. Morris Bishop, *The Odyssey of Cabeza de Vaca* (New York, 1933) and John U. Terrell, *Journey into Darkness* (New York, 1962), are readable popular biographies. Study of Hernando de Soto must start with United States De Soto Expedition Commission, *Final Report* (Washington, D.C., 1939). Its chairman summarized its findings in J. R. Swanton, *Indians of the Southeastern United States* (Washington, D.C., 1946). R. B. Cunninghame Graham, *Hernando de Soto* (London, 1903), and Theodore Maynard, *De Soto and the Conquistadores* (New York, 1930), are readable, but somewhat out of date. Vincent F. O'Daniel, *The Dominicans in Spanish Florida* (New York, 1930), is useful. Herbert I. Priestley, *Tristán de Luna* (Glendale, Calif., 1936), is a standard biography. Herbert E. Bolton, *Coronado on the Turquoise Trail* (Albuquerque, N.M., 1940), republished as *Coronado, Knight of the Pueblos and Plains* (New York, 1940; Albuquerque, N.M., 1964), and A. Grove Day, *Coronado's Quest* (Berkeley, 1940), are standard biographical accounts. Paul Horgan, *Great River*, 2 vols (New York, 1954), and *Conquistadors in North American History* (New York, 1963), with Stephen Clissold, *The Seven Cities of Cíbola* (London, 1961) provide useful supplementary materials. A. F. Bandelier and E. L. Hewitt, *Indians of the Rio Grande Valley* (Albuquerque, N.M., 1937), and Frederick W. Hodge, *Hawíkuh* (Los Angeles, 1937), are important for the background of the western expeditions. Garcilaso de la Vega, el Inca, *The Florida del Inca* (Lisbon, 1605), is in *Obras completas*, 3 vols. (Madrid, 1962), I–II, and translated by John G. and Jeanette Varner (Austin, 1951), is the most colorful, if often unreliable, narrative. Herbert I. Priestley (ed.), *The*

*Luna Papers, 1559–1561,* 2 vols. (Deland, Fla., 1928); contains a generous selection of translated documents.

On the western expeditions, George P. Hammond and Agapito Rey (eds.) *Narratives of the Coronado Expedition, 1540–1542* (Albuquerque, N.M., 1940), is the best selection of materials on Marcos de Niza and Coronado. Cleve Hallenback (ed.), *The Journey of Fray Marcos de Niza* (Dallas, Tex., 1949), is useful. The classical account of Coronado is by Pedro de Castañeda, first published by G. P. Winship, "The Coronado Expedition," Smithsonian Institution, Bureau of American Ethnology, Bulletin no. 14, 1896, 329–637, with a revised translation as *The Journey of Coronado, 1540–1542* (New York, 1904); it was reprinted in Hodge and Lewis, *Spanish Explorers,* and retranslated in Hammond and Rey. The Cabrilho and other coastal voyages are documented fully in Henry R. Wagner, *Spanish Voyages to the Northwest Coast in the Sixteenth Century* (San Francisco, 1929; reprinted, Amsterdam, 1966); the Cabrilho document is also in Herbert E. Bolton (ed.), *Spanish Exploration in the Southwest, 1542–1706* (New York, 1908; reprinted 1963).

## French and Spanish Florida and the Southeast, 1562–1612

The basic French documents are Jean Ribault, *The whole & true discoverye of Terra Florida* (London, 1563), reproduced with another text, edited by Jeanette T. Connor (Deland, Fla., 1927; Gainesville, Fla., 1964), and René de Laudonnière, *L'histoire notable de la Floride* (Paris, 1586), reprinted in translation by Richard Hakluyt, *Principal navigations,* III (London, 1600), and VIII, IX (Glasgow, 1904): *A notable history containing four voyages made by certain French captains unto Florida* (London, 1587), the first edition of the English translation, is printed in facsimile, with an introduction by Thomas R. Adams, Jr. (Farnham, Surrey, and Larchmont, N.Y., 1964). The best edition of both texts is Suzanne Lussagnet (ed.), *Les Français en Amérique pendant la deuxième moitié du XVIᵉ siècle. Les Français en Floride* (Paris, 1958). René Laudonnière, *Three Voyages,* trans. and ed. Charles E. Bennett (Gainesville, Fla., 1975), is a new translation. The text and illustrations in Jacques le Moyne de Morgues, *America,* part ii (Frankfurt am Main, 1591), are reproduced in contemporary color in Charles de la Roncière, *La Floride française. Scènes de la vie indienne peintes en 1564* (Paris, 1928). Paul H. Hulton, *The Work of Jacques Le Moyne de Morgues* (London, 1977), provides a new annotated edition and study. Paul Gaffarel, *Histoire de la Floride française* (Paris, 1875), and Charles E. Bennett, *Laudonnière and Fort Caroline* (Gainesville, Fla., 1964), and his *Settlement of Florida* (Gainesville, 1968) contain additional documentation.

Manuel Fernández de Navarrete, *Colección de documentos,* 32 vols. (Nen-

deln, Lichtenstein, 1971), reproduces the material in the Navarrete Collection in the Museo Naval, Madrid, including much on Spanish Florida (notably in vol. XIV); letters of Pedro Menéndez de Avilés from this collection are in Luis Cabrero Blanco (ed.), *Colección de diarios y relaciones para la historia des los viajes y descubrimientos*, 5 vols. (Madrid, 1943–47), II, 47–90. Other correspondence of Menéndez is in Eugenio Ruídiaz y Caravia, *La Florida*, 2 vols. (Madrid, 1893), II. Gonzalo Solís de Merás, *Pedro Menéndez de Avilés*, edited and translated by Jeanette T. Connor (Deland, Fla., 1923), reissued with introduction by A. N. McAlister (Gainesville, Fla., 1969), and Bartolomé Barrientos, *Pedro Menéndez de Avilés, Founder of Florida*, translated by Anthony Kerrigan (Gainesville, Fla., 1965) (this, with a Spanish document on an episode in 1593, first appeared in Genaro Garcia, *Dos antiquos relaciones de la Florida* [Mexico City, 1902] ). Together they comprise on impressive narrative of the Spanish conquest. Andrés Barcia, *Ensayo cronológico* (Madrid, 1723), translated by Anthony Kerrigan, *Barcia's Chronological History of the Continent of Florida* (Gainesville, Fla., 1951), has some documentary value. Alonso Escobeda's poem "La Florida" is roughly translated by James W. Covington and A. F. Falconer, *Pirates, Indians and Spaniards* (St. Petersburg, Fla., 1963). Irene A. Wright (ed.), *Documents Concerning English Voyages to the Spanish Main, 1569–1580* (London, Hakluyt Society, 1932), and *Further English Voyages to Spanish America, 1583–1594* (London, Hakluyt Society, 1951), contain significant material on Florida, as do D. B. Quinn, *The Roanoke Voyages*, 2 vols. (Cambridge, Eng., Hakluyt Society, 1955), and Mary Frear Keeler (ed.), *Sir Francis Drake's West Indian Voyage* (London, Hakluyt Society, 1977). Two compendia, Juan López de Velasco, *Geografía y descripción universal de las Indias* (Madrid, 1971), and Antonio Vásquez de Espinosa, *Compendio y descripción de las Indias Occidentales* (Washington, D.C., 1948), translated by Charles U. Clark, *Compendium and Description of the West Indies* (Washington, D.C., 1942; reprinted 1968), have material on Florida. Jeanette T. Connor (ed. and trans.), *Colonial Records of Spanish Florida, 1570–1580*, 2 vols. (Deland, Fla., 1925–30), is most important. Luis Gerónimo de Oré, *Relación historica de La Florida*, edited by Atanásio López, 2 vols. (Madrid, 1931–33), translated by Maynard Geiger, *The Martyrs of Florida* (New York, 1936) is a significant contemporary history of missions. Félix Zubillaga (ed.), *Monumenta Antiquae Floridae (1566–1572)* (Rome, 1946), prints all the documents on the Jesuit mission, while Clifford M. Lewis and Albert J. Loomie, *The Spanish Jesuit Mission in Virginia, 1570–1572* (Chapel Hill, N.C., 1953), translate and comment on those concerned with the Chesapeake mission of 1570. Manuel Serrano y Sanz (ed.), *Documentos historicos de La Florida y Luisiana* (Madrid, 1912), contains some documentation from 1598 onward.

C. W. Arnade, "Spanish Florida Source Material," *Florida Historical Quar-*

*terly,* XXXV (1957), 320–25, and Lawrence C. Wroth, "Some Materials of Florida History in the John Carter Brown Library," *ibid.,* XX (1941), 3–46, give useful bibliographical assistance.

Woodbury Lowery, *Spanish Settlements Within the Present Limits of the United States, 1562–1574* (New York, 1905) is still the best narrative. Henry Folmer, *Franco-Spanish Rivalry in North America* (1963), and Albert Manucy *Florida's Menéndez* (St. Augustine, Fla., 1962) are of some value. Modern histories of Florida are of limited use. C. W. Tabeau, *A History of Florida* (Coral Gables, Fla., 1971), may be consulted. William R. Jackson, *Early Florida Through Spanish Eyes* (Coral Gables, Fla., 1954), and Charles W. Arnade, *Florida on Trial, 1593–1602* (Coral Gables, Fla., 1959), C. W. Arnade, "The Failure of Spanish Florida," 33rd International Congress of Americanists, *Actas,* II (San José, C.R., 1959), 758–766, are valuable. Constantino Bayle, *Pedro Menéndez de Avilés* (Madrid, 1928) is a useful biography. Mary A. Ross, "With Pardo and Moyano on the Fringes of the Georgia Land," *Georgia Historical Quarterly,* XV (1930), 267–285, "The Spanish Settlement of Santa Elena," *Georgia Historical Quarterly,* IX (1925), 352–379, Ray E. Held, "Hernando de Miranda, Governor of Florida, 1575–1577," *Florida Historical Quarterly,* XXVIII (1949–50), 111–130, Fermin Bouza-Brey, "El almirante D. Gonzalo Méndez de Cancio, governador y capitán general de La Florida," *Boletín del Instituto de Estudios Asturianos,* VI (Oviedo, 1952), 305–331, are valuable for internal history. James Leitch Wright, *Anglo-Spanish Rivalry in North America* (Athens, Ga., 1971), 265–279, Mary A. Ross, "French Intrusions and Indian Uprisings in Georgia and South Carolina, 1577–1580," *Georgia Historical Quarterly,* VII (1923), 251–281, and "The French on the Savannah, 1605," *ibid.,* VIII (1924), 167–194, D. B. Quinn, "An Anglo-French 'Voyage of Discovery' to North America in 1604–1605 and Its Sequel," *Miscellanea Charles Verlinden* (Gent, 1975), 513–534, and D. B. Quinn, *England and the Discovery of America* (1974), deal with external relations. St. Julian R. Childs, *Malaria and Colonization in the Carolina Low Country, 1526–1696* (Baltimore, 1940), throws light on settlement at Santa Elena.

Missions are extensively covered. On the Jesuits, Félix Zubillaga, *La Florida. La Misión Jesuitica (1566–1572) y la colonizacion Española* (Rome, 1941), is authoritative. On the Franciscans, John Tate Lanning, *Spanish Missions of Georgia* (Chapel Hill, N.C., 1935), Maynard Geiger, *The Franciscan Conquest of Florida (1573–1611)* (Washington, D.C., 1937), and *Biographical Dictionary of the Franciscans in Florida (1573–1616)* (Patterson, N.J., 1940), Gregory J. Keegan and L. Tormo Sans, *Experiencia misionera en La Florida* (Madrid, 1957), Ignacio Omaecheverría, *Sangre viscaina en los pantonos de La Florida: Fr. Francisco de Beráscola, O.F.M. (1564–1597)* (Vitoria, 1948), and *Mártires franciscanos de Georgia* (Madrid, 1955), are exhaustive, but some-

times mainly hagiographical. Verne E. Chatelaine, *The Defenses of Spanish Florida, 1563–1763* (Washington, D.C., 1941), and L. A. Vigneras, "Fortificaciones de La Florida," *Anuario de Estudios Americanos*, XVI (1958), 533–552, and "A Spanish Discovery of North Carolina in 1566," *North Carolina Historical Review*, XLVI (1969), 398–415, are important.

## Discovery and Attempted Settlement of Eastern North America, 1544–1608

Documentation of English activities between 1578 and 1590 is reasonably complete in D. B. Quinn (ed.), *The Voyages and Colonising Enterprises of Sir Humphrey Gilbert*, 2 vols. (London, Hakluyt Society, 1940) and *The Roanoke Voyages, 1584–1590*, 2 vols. (Cambridge, Eng., Hakluyt Society, 1955); Paul H. Hulton and D. B. Quinn, *The American Drawings of John White*, 2 vols. (London and Chapel Hill, N.C., 1964), adding the visual records. Richard Hakluyt, *The Principall navigations* (London, 1589), was the earliest publication of most of the documents: with an introduction by D. B. Quinn and R. A. Skelton and an index by Alison Quinn, it was published in facsimile, 2 vols. (Cambridge, Eng., and Salem, Mass., 1965). The documents on the Roanoke ventures from it were edited by D. B. and Alison M. Quinn, *Virginia Voyages from Hakluyt* (London, 1972). Hakluyt, *Principal navigations*, 3 vols. (London, 1598–1600), was reprinted, 12 vols. (Glasgow, 1903–05).

Additional documentation is to be found in Richard Hakluyt, "Discourse of Western Planting," and other documents, in Eva G. R. Taylor (ed.), *The Original Writings and Correspondence of the Two Richard Hakluyts*, 2 vols. (London, Hakluyt Society, 1935); Richard Hakluyt, *Divers voyages touching the discoverie of America* (London, 1582), issued in facsimile, with accompanying text by D. B. Quinn, as *Richard Hakluyt, Editor*, 2 vols. (Amsterdam, 1967); John White and Edward Topsell, *The First Water Colors of North American Birds*, edited by Thomas P. Harrison (Austin, Tex., 1964); E. G. R. Taylor, "Instructions to a Colonial Surveyor in 1582," *Mariner's Mirror*, XXXVII (1951), 48–62; and Edward Edwards, *The Life of Sir Walter Ralegh Together with His Letters*, 2 vols. (London, 1868).

Among the general works which are useful in this area, Wesley Frank Craven, *Southern Colonies in the Seventeenth Century* (Baton Rouge, La., 1949); Alfred L. Rowse, *The Expansion of Elizabethan England* (London, 1955), and *Elizabethans and America* (Cambridge, Eng., 1959); Quinn, *England and the Discovery of America*, and Kenneth R. Andrews, *Elizabethan Privateering* (Cambridge, Eng., 1964), are important. George B. Parks, *Richard Hakluyt and the English Voyagers* (New York, 1928), and D. B. Quinn (ed.), *The Hakluyt Handbook*, 2 vols. (London, Hakluyt Society, 1974), are helpful on the background. Biographies are numerous, but rarely of exceptional value. D.

B. Quinn, *Raleigh and the British Empire* (latest editions, New York, 1962; Harmondsworth, Middx., 1973), is directed to this area. W. G. Gosling, *Sir Humphrey Gilbert* (London, 1911), William Stebbing, *Sir Walter Ralegh,* 2nd edition (Oxford, 1899), Edward Thompson, *Sir Walter Raleigh* (London, 1935), Willard M. Wallace, *Sir Walter Raleigh* (Princeton, N.J., 1959), A. L. Rowse, *Ralegh and the Throckmortons* (London, 1962), and *Sir Richard Grenville* (London, 1937), J. H. Adamson and H. F. Folland, *The Shepherd of the Ocean* [Ralegh] (New York, 1969), George H. Bushnell, *Sir Richard Grenville* (London, 1936), and Rachel Lloyd, *Elizabethan Adventurer, a Life of Captain Christopher Carleill* (1974), are all of some limited value. William S. Powell, "Roanoke Colonists and Explorers: An Attempt at Identification," *North Carolina Historical Review,* XXXIV (1957), 202–226; Edmund S. Morgan, "John White and the Sarsaparilla," *William and Mary Quarterly,* 3rd series, XIV (1957), 414–417; Tom Glasgow, Jr., "H.M.S. Tiger," *North Carolina Historical Review,* XLIII (1966), 115–121; Paul Hulton, "John White, Artist," *North Carolina Museum of Arts, Bulletin,* V (1965), 3–43, and *The Watercolor Drawings of John White* (Washington, D.C., 1965), are useful.

Jean C. Harrington, *Search for the Cittie of Ralegh. Archaeological Excavations at Fort Raleigh National Historic Site, North Carolina* (Washington, D.C., 1962), *An Outwork at Fort Raleigh* (Washington, D.C., 1966), and "The Manufacture and Use of Brick at the Raleigh Settlement on Roanoke Island," *North Carolina Historical Review,* XLIV (1967), 1–17, are comprehensive on the physical remains on Roanoke Island.

On the earliest French activities in the New England-Maritimes area, D. B. Quinn, "The Voyage of Étienne Bellenger to the Maritimes in 1583: A New Document," *Canadian Historical Review,* XLIII (1962), 328–343, and William I. Morse, *Acadiensia Nova (1598–1779),* 2 vols. (London, 1931), provide a little documentation. On the English in the Gulf of St. Lawrence, the documents are mainly in Hakluyt, *Principal Navigations,* VIII (1904), and George Johnson, *A discourse of some troubles and excommunications in the banished English church at Amsterdam* (Amsterdam, 1603). N. E. Dionne, *La Nouvelle France de Cartier à Champlain, 1540–1603* (Quebec, 1891); Gustave Lancot, *Réalisations françaises de Cartier à Montcalm* (Montreal, 1951); and René Bélanger, *Les Basques dans l'estuaire du Saint Laurent* (Quebec, 1971), are helpful. Apart from Quinn, *England and the Discovery of America,* there is little on the English side.

The English and French were active in New England after 1600. On the French, the major sources are in Champlain, *Works,* and Lescarbot, *History of New France* (for which see the section on New France, 1608–1612). John Brereton, *A briefe and true relation of the discoverie of the north part of Virginia* (London, 1602), the first edition having been reproduced in facsimile, with an introduction by L. S. Livingston (New York, 1903), but the enlarged

second edition has to be consulted in the original; James Rosier, *A true relation of the most prosperous voyage made in this present yeare 1605, by Captain George Waymouth* (London, 1605), the best edition of which is edited by Henry S. Burrage as *Rosier's Relation of Waymouth's Voyage to the Coast of Maine in 1605* (Portland, Maine, 1887). Henry O. Thayer, *The Sagadahoc Colony* (Portland, Maine, 1892), is the best edition of "The Relation of a Voyage to New England," on the colony at Fort St. George on the Sagadahoc (Kennebec) River. James P. Baxter, *Sir Ferdinando Gorges and His Province of Maine*, 3 vols. (Boston, 1890), is comprehensive. Charles H. Levermore (ed.), *Forerunners and Competitors of the Pilgrims and Puritans*, 2 vols. (Brooklyn, N.Y., 1912), is the best collection of English and French materials; and Henry S. Burrage (ed.), *English and French Voyages, 1534–1608* (New York, 1906), the best selection of English materials, 1602–08. Douglas R. McManis, *European Impressions of the New England Coast, 1497–1620* (University of Chicago, Department of Geography, Research Paper 139, Chicago, 1972), is a useful survey of the European impact.

Warner F. Gookin and Philip L. Barbour, *Bartholomew Gosnold* (Hamden, Conn. 1963); Richard A. Preston, *Gorges of Plymouth Fort* (Toronto, 1953); Quinn, *England and the Discovery of America*; and, an attempt at reinterpreting Gosnold's objective, Harold C. Wilson and William C. Carr, "Gosnold's Elizabeth's Isle: Cuttyhunk or Nuashon?", *American Neptune*, XXXIII (1973), 131–145, cover parts of the ground. Henry C. Burrage, *The Beginnings of Colonial Maine, 1602–1658* (Augusta, Maine, 1914), is essential. Charles K. Bolton, *The Real Founders of New England* (Boston, 1929), and Henry F. Howe, *Prologue to New England* (New York, 1943), are useful for placing the early expeditions in their setting.

On the Dutch beginnings in North America, J. Franklin Jameson (ed.), *Narratives of New Netherlands, 1609–1663* (New York, 1909), is standard. Ronart M. Lunny (ed.), *Juet's Journal* (Newark, N.J., 1959), is useful. Simon Hart, *The Prehistory of the New Netherlands Company* (Amsterdam, 1959), prints new material. Henry C. Murphy, *Henry Hudson in Holland*, 2nd edition (The Hague, 1909), prints material from Jean de Laet, *Niewe Wereldt* (Leiden, 1625), and other sources.

## The Northwest Passage

Major texts were first printed in Richard Hakluyt, *Principall navigations* (London, 1589), and elaborated in scale in *Principal navigations*, 3 vols. (London, 1598–1600), and also Samuel Purchas, *Hakluytus Posthumus or Purchas his pilgrimes*, 4 vols. (London, 1625), of which the modern editions are indicated above. The materials on the Frobisher voyages, 1576–78, were first collected in Richard Collinson (ed.), *The Three Voyages of Martin*

*Frobisher* (London, Hakluyt Society, 1867), and this was extended in Vilhjal-mur Stefansson (ed.), *The Three Voyages of Martin Frobisher,* 2 vols. (London, 1938), which forms the best source collection. G. B. Parks, "New Material on the Third Voyage of Martin Frobisher from the Huntington Library," *Huntington Library Bulletin,* 7 (1935), 181–190. Sir Humphrey Gilbert, *A discourse of a discoverie of a New Passage to Cataia* (London, 1576) was issued in facsimile (Manston, Yorks., 1972), and, with other material on his north-west interests, is reprinted in D. B. Quinn (ed.), *The Voyages and Colonising Enterprises of Sir Humphrey Gilbert,* 2 vols. (London, Hakluyt Society, 1940). Albert H. Markham (ed.), *The Voyages and Works of John Davis* (London, Hakluyt Society, 1878); G. N. Bugge (ed.), *Trerejser til Grønlønd i Aarene* (Copenhagen, 1930); and George M. Asher (ed.), *Henry Hudson, the Naviga-tor* (London, Hakluyt Society, 1860), have not been replaced.

Probably the most useful outline is Ernest S. Dodge, *Northwest by Sea* (New York, 1961). Sir Laurence P. Kirwan, *The White Road* (London, 1959); Leslie H. Neatby, *In Quest of the North-West Passage* (Toronto, 1958); Nellis M. Crouse, *In Quest of the Western Ocean* (London, 1928), and *The Search for the Northwest Passage* (New York, 1934); V. Stefansson, *Northwest to Fortune* (New York, 1958); and Laurence J. Burpee, *The Search for the Western Sea,* 2 vols. (New York, 1908), all have all something to offer, though some of them not a great deal. Biographies, as often, have lagged behind: we have Sir Cle-ments R. Markham, *Life of John Davis* (London, 1891); William MacFee, *Sir Martin Frobisher* (London, 1928); Llewelyn Powys, *Henry Hudson* (London, 1926); and L. J. Burpee, "The Fate of Henry Hudson," *Canadian Historical Review,* XXI (1940), 401–406.

## Later Western Expeditions, 1580–1612

H. R. Wagner, *The Spanish Southwest* (1937) is the basic bibliography. The basic documentary series is G. P. Hammond and Agapito Rey (eds.), *The Rediscovery of New Mexico, 1580–1594* (Albuquerque, N.M., 1966) and *Oñate, Colonizer of New Mexico,* 2 vols. (Albuquerque, N.M., 1953). H. E. Bolton, *Spanish Exploration in the Southwest, 1546–1706* (1908), is still useful. An English translation of J. González de Mendoza's account of Antonio de Espejo's voyage appeared as *New Mexico,* translated by A. F. (London, 1587) and, with other western material, notably on Drake, in Richard Hakluyt, *Principal navigations,* III (London, 1600). Albert H. Schroder and Dan S. Matson (eds.), *A Colony on the Move. Gaspar Castaña de Sosa's Journal, 1590–1591* (Santa Fé, 1965), is useful. Gaspar Perez de Villagra, *A History of New Mexico,* translated by Gilberto Espinosa (Los Angeles, 1933; Chicago, 1962), is a poem on Oñate, with colorful passages, first published in 1610. C. W. Hackett (ed.) *Historical Documents Relating to New Mexico,* 2 vols. (Wash-

ington, D.C., 1923–37), is also of value. H. R. Wagner, *Spanish Voyages to the Northwest Coast of America* (1929), remains essential. W. Michael Mathes (ed.), *Documentos para la historia de la demarcación comercial de California, 1580–1630*, 2 vols. (Madrid, 1965), has significant new material. Miscellaneous documents are translated in George B. Griffin, and Donald C. Cutter (eds.), *The California Coast. Documents from the Sutro Collection* (Norman, Okla., 1969), and G. P. Hammond and A. Rey, *New Mexico in 1602* (Albuquerque, N.M., 1928). Drake material appears in [Philip Nicholls and others], *Sir Francis Drake revived* (London, 1628); and [Sir Francis Drake, the Younger], *The world encompassed* (London, 1628). The latter was edited by W. S. W. Vaux (London, Hakluyt Society, 1853) and by N. M. Penzer and Sir Richard Carnac Temple (London, 1926); the former is in Irene A. Wright (ed.), *Documents Concerning English Voyages to the Spanish Main, 1569–1580* (London, Hakluyt Society, 1932). A useful general collection is John Hampden (ed.), *Francis Drake, Privateer* (London, 1972).

Warren L. Cook, *Flood Tide of Empire. Spain and the Pacific Northwest 1543–1819* (New Haven, 1973), has a good summary of west coast history. Charles E. Chapman, *A History of California: The Spanish Period* (New York, 1921), and Maurice G. Holmes, *From New Spain to the Californias, 1519–1668* (Glendale, Calif., 1963) are standard works, as are D. W. Meinig, *Southwest* (New York, 1971) and W. A. Beck, *New Mexico; A History* (Norman, Okla., 1962). Ynez D. Haase, *Historical Atlas of New Mexico* (Norman, Okla., 1969) has useful material. Edward H. Spicer, *Cycles of Conquest* (Tucson, Ariz., 1962) and Elizabeth A. H. John, *Storms Brewed in Other Men's Worlds* (College Station, Tex. 1975) cover a wide sweep of Indian-white relations. Henry R. Wagner, *The Cartography of the Northwest Coast*, 2 vols. (San Francisco, 1937; Amsterdam, 1968), is important. John F. Bannon (ed.), *Bolton and the Spanish Borderlands* (Norman, Okla., 1964) is helpful. John V. Terrell, *Pueblos, Gods and Spaniards* (N.Y., 1973) is a popular introduction. Philip W. Powell, *Soldiers, Indians and Silver. The Northward Advance of New Spain, 1550–1600* (Berkeley, 1953), and William L. Schurz, *The Manila Galleon* (New York, 1939; reprinted 1959), are useful on the Spanish background. W. M. Mathes, *Vizcaino and Spanish Expansion in the Pacific Ocean, 1580–1630* (Los Angeles, 1972) is a valuable monograph. Oakah L. Jones, Jr., *Pueblo Warriors and Spanish Conquest* (Norman, 1966), and Jack D. Forbes, *Apache, Navajo and Spaniard* (Norman, Okla., 1960), are helpful on the New Mexico background and Max L. Moorhead, *New Mexico's Royal Road* (Norman, Okla., 1958) on Oñate's route. For Drake, Henry R. Wagner, *Sir Francis Drake's Voyage Round the World* (San Francisco, 1926; Amsterdam, 1969), remains the fullest treatment; while Kenneth R. Andrews, "The Aims of Drake's Expedition of 1577–1580," *American Historical Review*, LXXIII (1968), 724–744, and *Drake's Voyages* (London, 1967), provide a more recent context.

*Sir Francis Drake's Voyage Round the World, 1577–1580: Two Contemporary Maps,* edited by F. P. Sprent 2nd ed. (London, 1930), is valuable. Marilyn Ziebarth (ed.), "The Francis Drake Controversy: His California Anchorage, June 17–July 23, 1579," *California Historical Quarterly,* LIII (1974), 197–292, provides an exhaustive but inconclusive debate. The "Plate of Brass," discovered in the 1930s, continues to excite controversy. Herbert E. Bolton (and others), *Drake's Plate of Brass* (San Francisco, 1937), Colin G. Fink and E. P. Polushkin, *Drake's Plate of Brass Authenticated* (San Francisco, 1938), with papers in *California Historical Quarterly* by Allen L. Chickering, "Some Notes with Regard to Drake's Plate of Brass," XVI (1937), 275–281, "Further Notes on the Drake Plate," XVIII (1939), 251–253; Walter A. Starr, "Drake Landed in San Francisco Bay in 1579. The Testimony of the Plate of Brass," XLI (1962), 1–29, are all favorable. There have been doubters, including R. B. Haselden, "Is the Drake Plate Genuine?", *California Historical Quarterly,* XVI (1937), 271–274; W. Hume-Rothery, reviewing Fink and Polushkin, *Geographical Journal,* CXIV (1939), 54–55; and S. E. Morison, *European Discovery of America,* II, *The Southern Voyages* (1974).

## Virginia to 1612

The bibliography in Pomfret and Shumway, *Founding the American Colonies,* is excellent. E. G. Swem and John M. Jennings, *A Selected Bibliography of Virginia, 1607–1699* (Williamsburg, Va., 1957), is useful.

For sources, Samuel Purchas, *Hakluytus Posthumus or Purchas his pilgrimes* (abbreviated to *Pilgrimes*), 4 vols. (London, 1625); 20 vols. (Glasgow, 1905–6) is valuable. For 1606 to 1609, Philip L. Barbour (ed.), *The Jamestown Voyages, 1606–1609,* 2 vols. (Cambridge, Eng., Hakluyt Society, 1969), is authoritative; from 1609, John Smith, *Works,* edited by Edward Arber, 1 vol. (Birmingham, Eng., 1886); 2 vols. (London, 1907 and 1910) should be used (a new edition under the auspices of the Institute of Early American History and Culture is in active preparation). Lyon G. Tyler (ed.), *Narratives of Early Virginia* (New York 1907 and 1953) is a useful selection. Peter Force, *Tracts,* 4 vols. (Washington, D.C., 1836–47; Gloucester, Mass., 1963), contains a number of Virginia tracts, notably the important *A true declaration of the estate of the colony* (London, 1610). Susan M. Kingsbury, *Records of the Virginia Company of London,* 4 vols. (Washington, D.C., 1906–35), has some material in vol. III. William Strachey, *The Historie of Travaile into Virginia Britannia,* edited by R. H. Major (London, Hakluyt Society, 1849), and *The Historie of Travell into Virginia Britania,* edited by Louis B. Wright and Virginia Freund (London, Hakluyt Society, 1953) are editions of two copies of the same document: with them John P. Harrington, "The Original Strachey Vocabulary of the Virginian Indian Language," Smithsonian Institution, Bureau of

American Ethnology, Bulletin 157 (Washington, D.C., 1955), 189–202, should be used. Norman F. MacClure (ed.), *Letters of John Chamberlain*, 2 vols. (Philadelphia, 1939), is valuable. Alexander Brown, *The Genesis of the United States*, 2 vols. (Boston, 1890); New York, 1964) is now more valuable for its biographical material than for the documents it contains. Irene A. Wright, "Spanish Policy Toward Virginia, 1606–1612," *American Historical Review*, XXV (1919–20), 448–479, is valuable. Samuel M. Bemiss (ed.), *The Three Charters of the Virginia Company* (Williamsburg, Va., 1957) is a convenient reprint, as is William Strachey, *For the Colony in Virginea Britannia Lawes*, edited by David H. Flaherty (Charlottesville, Va., 1969). Other convenient republications are Louis B. Wright (ed.), *Newes from the New-World* (San Marino, Calif., 1946); George Percy, *Observations*, edited by D. B. Quinn (Charlottesville, Va., 1967); Louis B. Wright (ed.), *A Voyage to Virginia in 1609* (Charlottesville, Va., 1964); *A Good Speed to Virginia* (Edinburgh, 1970); Ralph Hamor, *A True Discourse of the Present State of Virginia*, with an introduction by A. L. Rowse (Richmond, Va., 1957). For the period 1590 to 1606, insofar as we have any information on Virginia, see Quinn, *England and the Discovery of America*, "The Road to Jamestown," in Louis B. Wright (ed.), *Shakespeare Celebrated* (Ithaca, N.Y., 1966), 31–60, "An Anglo-French 'Voyage of Discovery' to North America in 1604–5 and Its Sequel," *Miscellanea Charles Verlinden* (Gent, 1975), "The Voyage of *Triall* 1606–1607: An Abortive Virginia Venture," *American Neptune*, XXXI (1971), 85–103, and "James I and the Beginnings of Empire in America," *Journal of Imperial and Commonwealth History*, II (1973–74), 135–141.

Of the major narratives, Charles M. Andrews, *The Colonial Period in American History*, 4 vols. (New Haven, 1934–49), W. F. Craven, *The Southern Colonies in the Seventeenth Century* (Baton Rouge, La., 1949) and E. S. Morgan, *American Freedom, American Slavery* (New York, 1975) are the best. Herbert L. Osgood, *The American Colonies in the Seventeenth Century*, 3 vols (New York, 1904–07; Gloucester, Mass., 1957) and Richard L. Morton, *Colonial Virginia*, 2 vols. (Chapel Hill, N.C., 1960), are also useful. Short treatments by W. L. Craven, *The Virginia Company of London;* Charles E. Hatch, Jr., *The First Seventeen Years: Virginia, 1607–1624,* and William W. Abbot, *A Virginia Chronology* (all Williamsburg, Va., 1957), are helpful. Biographical material is extensive, but not in general of high quality: Philip L. Barbour, *The Three Worlds of Captain John Smith* (Boston, 1964), is the best there is. K. R. Andrews, "Christopher Newport of Limehouse, Mariner," *William and Mary Quarterly*, 3rd series, XI (1954), 28–41; John W. Shirley, "George Percy at Jamestown," *The Virginia Magazine*, LVII (1949), 227–243; P. L. Barbour, "Captain George Kendall," *Virginia Magazine*, LXX (1962), 297–313, and S. G. Culliford, *William Strachey* (Charlottesville, Va., 1965), are useful. P. L. Barbour, "The Earliest Reconnaissance of Chesapeake Bay Area: Captain

John Smith's Map and Indian Vocabulary," *Virginia Magazine*, LXXIX (1971), 280–302, LXXX (1972), 21–51, is important. Wyndham B. Blanton, *Medicine in Virginia in the Seventeenth Century* (Richmond, Va., 1930), and Gordon W. Jones, "The First Epidemic in Colonial America," *Virginia Magazine*, LXXI (1963), 3–10, are illuminating. J. C. Harrington, *Glassmaking at Jamestown* (Richmond, Va., 1952), John L. Cotter, *Archeological Excavations at Jamestown, Virginia* (Washington, D.C., 1958); and J. L. Cotter and J. Paul Hudson, *New Discoveries at Jamestown* (Washington, D.C., 1957), throw light on the physical setting of the colony. Edward D. Morgan, "The Labor Problem at Jamestown 1607–1618," *American Historical Review*, LXXVI (1971), 595–611, and Charles E. Hatch, Jr., "Mulberry Trees and Silkworms," *Virginia Magazine*, LXV (1967), 3–61, are helpful on economic conditions. For the economic background in England, Theodore K. Rabb, *Enterprise and Empire* (Cambridge, Mass., 1967) is important, and for the social setting, Carl Bridenbaugh, *Vexed and Troubled Englishmen, 1590–1642* (New York, 1968).

## New France, 1603–1612

This is very well documented in Samuel de Champlain, *Works*, edited by H. P. Biggar, 7 vols. (Toronto, Champlain Society, 1922–36; reissued, 1971); Marc Lescarbot, *History of New France*, edited by W. L. Grant and H. P. Biggar, 3 vols. (Toronto, 1907–14); Robert Le Blant and René Baudry (eds.), *Nouveaux documents sur Champlain et son époque, 1560–1622* (Ottawa, 1967); Lucien Campeau (ed.), *La première mission d'Acadie (1602–1616)* (Quebec, 1967); and Francis W. Gravit, "Un document inédit sur le Canada. Raretés rapportées du Nouveaux-Monde par M. de Monts," *Revue de l'Université Laval*, I (1946–47), 282–288. H. P. Biggar edited Marc Lescarbot, *Nova Francia*, translated by Pierre Erondelle (London, 1928). W. I. Morse, *Pierre du Gua, Sieur de Monts* (London, 1939), has a few documents. W. L. Grant (ed.), *Voyages of Samuel de Champlain* (New York, 1907), and Hubert Deschamps (ed.), *Les voyages de Samuel de Champlain* (Paris, 1951), are useful selections.

Marcel Trudel, *Histoire de la Nouvelle France, 1603–1627. Le comptoir* (Montreal, 1966), is the fullest history. His *Beginnings of New France* (1973), and G. Lanctot, *History of Canada*, I (1963), are also valuable, as is Claude de Bonnault, *Histoire de Canada française, 1534–1763* (Paris, 1950).

Biographies of Champlain in descending order of usefulness are S. E. Morison, *Samuel de Champlain, Father of New France* (Boston, 1972), Morris Bishop, *Champlain, the Life of Fortitude* (New York, 1949), and Narcisse-Eutrope Dionne, *Samuel de Champlain* (Quebec, 1891–1906). Adrien Huguet, *Jean de Poutraincourt, fondateur de Port-Royal*, Mémoires de la Societé

des Antiquaires de Picardie, XLIV (Amiens and Paris, 1932), is also valuable.

## Newfoundland

There is no up-to-date general bibliography of early Newfoundland history. Primary sources dealing with English activity are better represented than most. Richard Hakluyt, *Principall navigations* (London, 1589), of which the facsimile edited by D. B. Quinn and R. A. Skelton, 2 vols. (Cambridge, Eng. and Salem, Mass., Hakluyt Society, 1965), has a modern index by A. M. Quinn, and *Principal navigations*, 3 vols. (London, 1598–1600), modern edition, 12 vols. (Glasgow, 1903–05); with Samuel Purchas, *Hakluytus Posthumus or Purchas his pilgrimes*, 4 vols. (London, 1625), modern edition, 20 vols. (Glasgow, 1905–07), contain many valuable documents, as does E. G. R. Taylor (ed.), *The Original Writings and Correspondence of the Two Richard Hakluyts*, 2 vols. (London, Hakluyt Society, 1935). J. A. Williamson, *The Cabot Voyages* (Cambridge, Eng., Hakluyt Society, 1962) and *The Voyages of the Cabots* (London, 1929), and also H. P. Biggar, *Precursors of Jacques Cartier* (Ottawa, 1911), contain important documents. D. B. Quinn, *North American Discovery* (New York, 1971), contains a smaller selection. D. B. Quinn, *The Voyages and Colonising Enterprises of Sir Humphrey Gilbert*, 2 vols. (London, Hakluyt Society, 1940), and D. B. Quinn and Neil M. Cheshire, *The New Found Land of Stephen Parmenius* (Toronto, 1972), continue the documentation. A few additional French documents will be found in H. P. Biggar, *A Collection of Documents Relating to Jacques Cartier and the Sieur de Roberval* (Ottawa, 1930), and in Jean Alfonce, *La cosmographie*, edited by Georges Musset (Paris, 1904), but later French materials and almost all Spanish and Portuguese materials remain in manuscript. Simon Hart, *The Prehistory of the New Netherlands Company* (Amsterdam, 1959), has some Dutch material.

Daniel W. Prowse, *History of Newfoundland* (London, 1885), with bibliography, 2nd edition (London, 1896; St. John's, 1971) without bibliography, remains the only large-scale history, but it is out of date in many respects. J. D. Rogers, *Newfoundland* (*Historical Geography of the British Colonies*, edited by Sir Charles Lucas, V, part iv [Oxford, 1911]), is an effective short summary. Gillian T. Cell, *English Enterprise in Newfoundland, 1577–1660* (Toronto, 1969), is an excellent short monograph and the only one, so far, in its field.

Harold A. Innis, *The Cod Fisheries* (New Haven, 1940; revised edition, Toronto, 1954), is the best introduction to its subject. Charles de la Morandière, *Histoire de la pêche française et de la morue dans l'Amérique septentrionale*, 3 vols. (Paris, 1962–66), relied mainly on eighteenth-century sources, but summarizes all that is known of earlier ones so far as France is concerned.

Jacques Bernard, *Navires et gens de mer à Bordeaux,* 3 vols (Paris, 1968), has excellent illustrative material down to 1550. Georges Musset, *Les Rochelais à Terre-Neuve, 1500–1550* (La Rochelle, 1897), *Les Rochelais a Terre-Neuve, 1500–1789* (La Rochelle, 1899), and E. Trocmé and M. Delafosse, *Le commerce rochelais du début du XVᵉ au XVIIᵉ siècle* provide other illustrations. Eugène Guénin, *Ango et ses pilotes* (Paris, 1901), illustrates the beginnings of Norman participation. Ralph G. Lounsbury, *The British Fishery at Newfoundland, 1634–1763* (New Haven, 1934; reprinted 1969), has an introduction on the earlier period. Harold A. Innis, "The Rise and Fall of the Spanish Fishery at Newfoundland," *Proceedings and Transactions of the Royal Society of Canada,* 3rd series, XXV (1931), sect. 2, 51–70, Selma Barkham, "The Spanish Province of Terra Nova," *Canadian Archivist,* November 1974, and "Mercantile Community in Inland Burgos," *Geographical Magazine,* November 1973, 106–113, with René Belenger, *Les Basques dans l'estuaire du St Laurent* (Quebec, 1971), throw light on the Spanish cod- and whale fisheries. We lack a modern edition of Martin de Hoyarzabal, *Les voyages avantureux* (Bordeaux, 1579). G. T. Cell, "The Newfoundland Company," *William and Mary Quarterly,* 3rd series, XXII (1965), 611–625, is valuable.

Henry Harrisse, *Découverte et évolution cartographique de Terre-Neuve* (Paris, 1900), is valuable for much besides the mapping of the island; as is William E. Ganong, *Crucial Maps in the Early Cartography and Place-Nomenclature of the Atlantic Coast of Canada* (Toronto, 1964). E. R. Seary, G. M. Story, and W. J. Kirwin, *The Avalon Peninsula of Newfoundland; an Ethnolinguistic Study* (Ottawa, 1968), and E. R. Seary, *Place Names of the Avalon Peninsula of the Island of Newfoundland* (Toronto, 1971), use place names as historical evidence.

# Index

Abenaki Indians, 158, 387, 396, 403
Acadia, 411, 413–15, 467;
    commodities, 443; French plans
    for, 394–5, 415–16, 472, 477–8
Acapulco, 222, 495, 504, 506
Achelay, St. Lawrence river, 179, 186
Achuse, Fla., 210, 214
Ácoma pueblo, 200–1, 500
Acosta, Joseph de, 20
Acuña, Fray Juan de, expedition
    (1566), 270–1
Acuna, Pedro de, with Luna, 237
Adam of Bremen, "History," 23
Adventurers into the Newfound
    Islands, Company of, 127, 130,
    514–15
Advocate Harbour, B. of Fundy, 394
Afonso V, king of Portugal, 58, 59–60
Africa, west coast of, 43, 44, 50, 84,
    123; on maps, 48; as route to
    Asia, 55
Agona, Indian chief, 190
Agramonte, Juan de, charter (1511),
    349
Ailly, Pierre d', "Ymago mundi," 46,
    66
Ais (Ays) Indians, 247, 265, 309
Ajacan (Chesapeake Bay), 281
Alabama, 213; Indians, 215
Alabama River, 214, 215, 234, 273n
Alaminos, Pedro de, with Ponce de
    Leon, 142
Alarcón, Hernando de, voyage (1540),
    197, 199–200, 222–3
Alas, Esteban de las, in Florida (1565),
    264, 265, 273; lieut-gov. San
    Agustín, 277–8, 280
Alaska Indians, 8
Alava, Francisco de, envoy to France
    (1566), 259–60

Albany, N.Y., 410
Albemarle Sound, 155, 271, 331
Alcaráz, Diego de, with Coronado, 203
Aldworth, Richard, Bristol merchant,
    411
Aldworth, Thomas, of Bristol, 424
Alfonce, Jean, Les voyages avantureux,
    553
Algarve, Portugal, 53
Algonkian Indians, 7, 10, 11, 13, 15,
    239; of Carolina, 9, 326–38;
    language, 327, 334, 432, 449
    drawings of, see White, John
Algonquin Indians, 11, 475–7; with
    Champlain, 482–3, 484; trading,
    486–8, 535
Allegheny Mts., 8, 14, 16
Almadén, Mexico, 496
Aloysia (Block I.), 156
Altamaha River, 305
Alvarado, Hernando de, with
    Coronado, 200–1
Alvarado, Pedro de, 223
Alvarez de Pineda, Alonso, expedition
    (1519), 138, 142
Amadas, Philip, 299, 323, 324; voyage
    (1584), 325–7
Amaye Indians, 220
Amayne, Thomas, voyage (1502), 125
Amazon River, 399
Amichel, Gulf of Mexico, 147
Aminoya, Miss. river, 221
Anadabijou, Indian chief, 475
Añasco, Juan de, with Soto, 210
Anastasia I., Fla., 242, 254, 255, 264,
    270, 310, 317
Andalusia, 84
Ango, Jean, of Le Havre, 516
    Jean (son), 153, 516
Angoulême (Manhattan), 156, 165

597